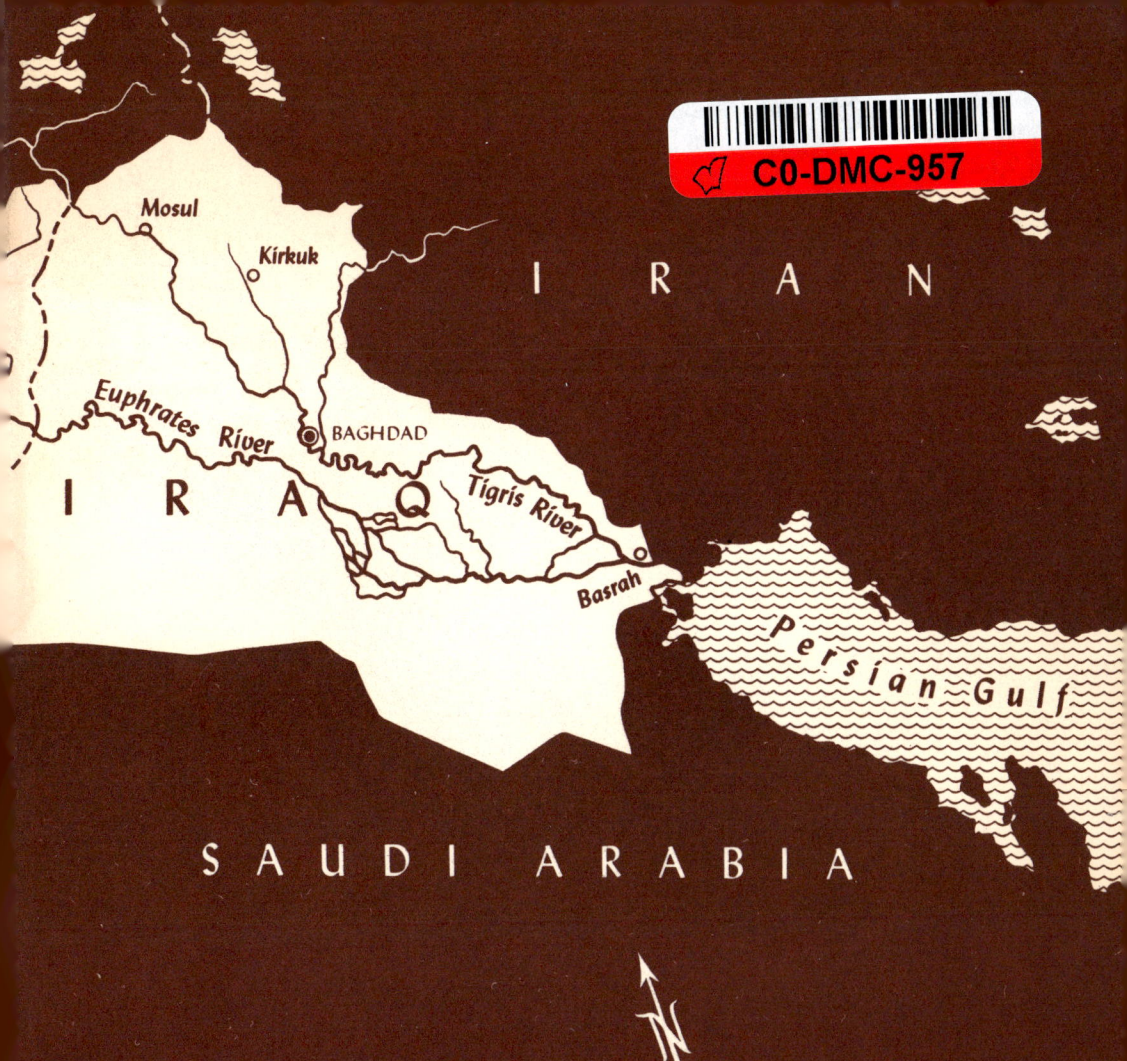

Mosul
Kirkuk
Euphrates River
BAGHDAD
IRAQ
Tigris River
Basrah
IRAN
Persian Gulf
SAUDI ARABIA
N

Arab Countries of the Near East 1946

0   100   200 Miles
Scale of Miles

EDUCATION
IN ARAB COUNTRIES
OF THE NEAR EAST

SHAYKH SAYID NAWWAR AND TWO OF HIS AMERICAN STUDENTS IN THE SCHOOL OF ORIENTAL STUDIES, AMERICAN UNIVERSITY AT CAIRO, EGYPT

EDUCATION
IN ARAB COUNTRIES
OF THE NEAR EAST

By Roderic D. Matthews
Professor of Education, University of Pennsylvania

and Matta Akrawi
Director General of Higher Education, Iraq

EGYPT

IRAQ

PALESTINE

TRANSJORDAN

SYRIA

LEBANON

التربية في الشرق الأوسط العربي

AMERICAN COUNCIL ON EDUCATION • Washington, D.C.

COPYRIGHT 1949 BY THE AMERICAN COUNCIL ON EDUCATION
744 JACKSON PLACE, WASHINGTON 6, D.C.

PRINTED IN THE UNITED STATES OF AMERICA
BY GEORGE BANTA PUBLISHING COMPANY
MENASHA, WISCONSIN

FOREWORD

*E*DUCATION makes the person, and persons make the nation. Therefore, the kind of education that is being offered to the youth of the Arab world today suggests the kind of world they will have tomorrow. What the leaders of the Arab countries think, what they aspire to, especially as expressed in their laws and regulations governing education, throws a searching light upon the future that we may expect. These laws and regulations show a profound concern with both the quantity and quality of education. It must be admitted, however, that the translation of aspirations into taxes is a slow process in lands where the great masses of population live by subsistence agriculture. Notwithstanding the obvious economic difficulties and the political unrest in the Near East in the last twenty-five years, the study reported here shows a most gratifying expansion in numbers of schools and students, and a modernization of curriculum. This factual document—the descriptive report of personal visits to 471 schools in six countries—Egypt, Iraq, Lebanon, Syria, Transjordan, and Palestine—is evidence that the social awakening in the Arab world is more than a phrase.

The Council was fortunate in securing Dr. Roderic D. Matthews, Dr. Matta Akrawi, and Mr. Emam Abdel Meguid to make this long and complicated study. Dr. Matthews, professor of education at the University of Pennsylvania, taught at the American University at Cairo some years ago and has always retained a considerable knowledge of, and interest in, the educational institutions and the people of that area. Dr. Akrawi, Director General of Higher Eduction of Iraq, now on leave of absence to serve in the Education Department of UNESCO at Paris, has an exceptional knowledge of comparative education from study and extensive travels in the Arab world, Europe, and the United States; he took his bachelor's degree at the American University of Beirut, and his master's and doctor's at Teachers College, Columbia University. Mr. Meguid, a graduate of the Higher Training College in Cairo, has had many years of teaching experience both in Egypt and in Iraq. He is at present on the staff of the Arab League.

Dr. Matthews, Dr. Akrawi, and Mr. Meguid traveled many thousands of miles. They talked to government officials and obtained from them statistical information about schools, students, educational expenditures, and copies of laws regulating education; they talked to teachers, observed their methods, laboratories and physical equipment in general, and obtained courses of study; they studied the pupils, their backgrounds, their attitudes, and their response to learning. The significance of their report in its broadest sense—its significance for international cooperation—is plain to thoughtful men both in and out of governments. It will also have concrete value to American educators and registrars of universities and colleges in clarifying the records of educational attainments of students and teachers from the Near East who are coming to the United States, and other Western countries, in numbers that are greatly increasing every year. Indeed, one of the reasons for undertaking this study was to encourage the more extensive exchange of students and teachers. What do these people need? How can we cooperate better with them?

Educators in the Arab countries will find the comparison of systems suggestive, and will be able to use the best features of the divergent systems—influenced as they have been by different European nations—for the improvement of their own national system. To that end the Department of State is making a wide distribution of this English edition to the educational authorities of the Arab countries. An edition in Arabic, translated by Dr. Amir Boktor, of the American University at Cairo, is also in preparation.

The American Council on Education takes great pleasure in presenting this study of education in six countries of the Arab world to the Department of State of the United States, at whose request the study was made, to the governments and peoples of the countries studied, to American educators, and to all people in all the countries of the world who are concerned that diverse peoples should know and understand each other.

GEORGE F. ZOOK, *President*
American Council on Education

January 1949

PREFACE

THE COMMISSION to study education in Arabic-speaking countries was established in the early months of 1945 by the American Council on Education at the request of the United States Department of State. Many requests for assistance had been received by the division responsible for cultural cooperation, and it was felt that insufficient information was available upon which to make sound decisions relative to these requests. It was thought that a description of the provisions for education in certain countries of the Near East would be helpful not only to the Department of State but also to educators and laymen who are interested in education in the Near East. Representatives of the United States were requested to secure approval for such a study from the governments of countries in the Near East. Such approval was obtained from Egypt, Iraq, Palestine, Transjordan, Syria, and Lebanon.

Since the initiative did not come from the countries to be studied, it was thought that the survey should be descriptive rather than evaluative or critical. Care has been taken, therefore, to avoid evaluations of any of the schools and systems studied, and recommendations have not been included. An attempt is made in the final chapter to give some interpretation of the situation relative to education.

The members of the Commission—Matta Akrawi of Iraq, Emam Abdel Meguid of Egypt, and Roderic D. Matthews of the United States—met in Shimlan, near Beirut, Lebanon, in July 1945 to lay plans for the study and to examine background materials relating to each of the countries to be visited. The itinerary and schedule agreed upon provided that Iraq was to be visited from September 15 to November 14, 1945; followed by Egypt from November 15, 1945, to February 15, 1946; Palestine from February 15 to April 1, 1946; Transjordan from April 1 to April 8; Syria and Lebanon from April 8 to May 30, 1946. In the course of the travels in six countries a total of 471 schools (240 elementary, 128 secondary, 66 vocational and teacher-training institutions, and 37 institutions of higher learning) were visited, distributed as follows: Egypt, 106; Iraq, 100; Lebanon, 89; Syria, 78; Palestine, 77; and Transjordan, 21. Most (297) of the schools visited were public or government schools, but 71 private schools and 69 foreign schools, as well as 34 Hebrew schools in Palestine, were also visited. The summer of 1946 was spent in Shimlan, Lebanon, where the writing of the report was begun. The report was completed in the United States during 1946 and 1947.

An effort has been made to approximate the international system of transliteration used by most orientalists as far as it is possible to do so without resorting to diacritical marks. Only one such mark is used—the inverted apostrophe (') for the *ayn* to distinguish it from the *hamzah* or to show its presence in the middle or at the end of a word. The *hamzah* itself has not been indicated, partly to avoid confusion with the inverted apostrophe and partly because it occurs usually at the beginning of a word and is sufficiently indicated by the presence of a vowel, in which case there is little chance of mispronunciation.

"Q" is used for the hard "qaf" except in the words "Koran" and "Latakia" where the current English spelling is maintained.

Arabic words and names with a familiar English spelling are used in the English form, for example, "Koran," "Effendi," "Beirut," "Latakia," "Cairo."

A final "h" is added after an "a" to all names ending in a silent "ha" or *"ta marbutah,"* thus, "Amarah," "Hulah," "Buhayrah," except for "Hama" which has been written as pronounced without an "h."

The diphthong "ay" has been used consistently in words such as "Husayn," "Faysal," "Bani Suayf," thus eliminating entirely the diphthongs "ai" and "ei" of popular writing. In cases where the double "y" comes after an "i," one of the y's has been eliminated, thus "Khayriyah," "Ahliyah."

The article *"al"* has been kept constant, whatever the inflection and without regard to *shamsi* or *qamari* letters. Exceptions are " 'Abdullah" and " 'Abdul-Hamid."

In any activity as extensive as the work of this Commission many individuals have rendered invaluable assistance and have given unsparingly of their time. The list would be long if an attempt were made to include all who were helpful. In all the countries the Commission was cordially welcomed by government officials, heads of schools, and laymen interested in education. All requests for information and assistance were promptly fulfilled, and frequently needs were anticipated and provided for. To the many persons who were helpful, the appreciation of the Commission is gratefully extended. The Iraq government was very generous in loaning the services of Matta Akrawi to the Commission for a period of two years. We are especially appreciative of the enthusiastic cooperation of Dr. Ibrahim 'Akif al-Alusi, Minister of Education in Iraq in 1945; Abd al-Razzaq al-Sanhuri Pasha, Minister of Education, and Shafiq Ghurbal Bey, Isma'il Qabbani Bey and Sadiq Gawhar Bey of the Ministry of Education in Egypt; Jerome Farrell, Director of Education for the Government of Palestine,

PREFACE

and Jibrail Katul, Ahmad Sami al-Khalidi, and Ahmad Qasim of the Department of Education of Palestine; M. Soloveitchik, Director of Education, and Joseph Meyouhas, Inspector, of the Hebrew system in Palestine; Shaykh Fahmi Hashim Pasha, Minister of Education, and Sayyah Bey al-Rawsan, Director General of Education in Transjordan; Sati' Bey al-Husri, Adviser, Tawfiq Bey al-Jabiri, Director General of Education, Jalal Zurayq and Jamil Saliba of the Ministry of Education, Syria; Phillippe Bey Taqla, Minister of Education, and Alfred Sham'un, Secretary of the Ministry of Education, Lebanon. The assistance of Amir Boktor of the American University at Cairo and Majid Khadduri of the Higher Teachers College of Baghdad in the preparation of background material for the information of the Commission is gratefully acknowledged. Frances E. Roberds, of the U. S. Department of State, played an important part in the initial planning of the study and has given much help and encouragement in all stages of the work. Dr. George F. Zook, president of the American Council on Education, has contributed much to the completion of this report by his enthusiastic support of the project and by his counsel in times of difficult decisions. To these and many others who remain unnamed, the Commission is deeply indebted. In any joint undertaking there is always a distribution of duties, but it is only fair to say that the greatest burden in the writing of this report has fallen upon the capable shoulders of Matta Akrawi, and if credit is due, he deserves the greater share.

RODERIC D. MATTHEWS
Director

September 1948

CONTENTS

	PAGE
FOREWORD BY GEORGE F. ZOOK	v
PREFACE	vii
LIST OF ILLUSTRATIONS	xvii
LIST OF CHARTS	xix
LIST OF TABLES	xxi

PART ONE: EGYPT

1. ORGANIZATION AND ADMINISTRATION OF THE EDUCATIONAL SYSTEM	3
The Ministry of Education	4
Provincial Educational Administration	13
Educational Finance	15
Educational Legislation	21
The Educational Ladder	23
Recent Trends	27
Growth and Status of Education in Egypt	33
2. PUBLIC EDUCATION FOR CHILDREN BELOW SECONDARY-SCHOOL AGE	40
Kuttabs	40
Compulsory Half-Day Schools	40
Elementary Schools	41
Schools for the Memorization of the Koran	45
Rural Elementary Schools	45
Nursery Schools	46
Kindergartens	46
Primary Schools	49
3. SECONDARY AND VOCATIONAL EDUCATION	57
The Program of Studies in Secondary Schools	58
The Girls Colleges	63
Secondary-School Examinations	64
Vocational and Technical Education	66
4. HIGHER EDUCATION AND EDUCATIONAL MISSIONS	71
Fuad I University	72
Faruq I University	85
Progress in Higher Education	87
Higher Institute of Agriculture	88
Higher School of Finance and Commerce	89
Higher School of Fine Arts	89
Educational Missions	89
5. INSTITUTIONS FOR TEACHER TRAINING	95
Training School for Elementary Teachers	95

Training Colleges for Primary Teachers	96
Higher Institute for Women Teachers	96
Dar al-'Ulum	97
The Institutes of Education	98
6. AL-AZHAR AND ITS INSTITUTIONS OF MUHAMMADAN LEARNING	103
Programs of Study	107
7. PRIVATE AND FOREIGN SCHOOLS	111
American United Presbyterian Mission Schools	113
The American University at Cairo	115
Other Foreign Schools	116
Informal Educational Agencies	117

PART TWO: IRAQ

8. ORGANIZATION AND ADMINISTRATION OF THE EDUCATIONAL SYSTEM	121
The Ministry of Education	121
Educational Finance	127
Educational Legislation	128
The Educational Ladder	131
Public Examinations	135
Educational Statistics for Iraq	139
Expansion of the Public Primary-School System	139
9. PUBLIC PRIMARY EDUCATION	146
The Primary Course of Study	148
Description of the Iraqi Public Primary School	152
10. SECONDARY AND VOCATIONAL EDUCATION	162
Secondary Education	163
Description of the Public Secondary Schools	168
Vocational Education	175
11. THE EDUCATION OF TEACHERS	181
Primary Teachers	181
Rural- and Elementary-Teachers Colleges	184
The Education of Secondary-School Teachers	188
12. HIGHER EDUCATION AND EDUCATIONAL MISSIONS	199
The Royal College of Medicine and Associated Schools	199
The Law College	204
The College of Engineering	205
Educational Missions	206
13. PRIVATE AND FOREIGN SCHOOLS	209

PART THREE: PALESTINE

14. ORGANIZATION AND ADMINISTRATION OF THE GOVERNMENT (ARAB) EDUCATIONAL SYSTEM	217
Administration	220
Educational Finance	221

CONTENTS

Educational Legislation	226
The Arab Educational Ladder	228
Government Examinations	231
Expansion of the Arab Educational System	236

15. Public and Private Schools for Arabs 239

Public Elementary Schools	239
Public Secondary Schools	246
Postmatriculation Study	249
Nursing Education	250
Vocational Training for Boys	250
Law Classes	252
Private and Foreign Schools	253

16. The Hebrew Educational System 256

Administration	257
Educational Finance	263
The Hebrew Educational Ladder	270
Vaad Leumi Examinations	272
Expansion of Jewish Education	274

17. The Jewish Schools and Their Programs 278

Kindergartens	279
Elementary Schools	279
Secondary Schools	284
Vocational Schools	286
Nursing Education	290
Teacher-Training Colleges	290
Higher Education	291
Other Hebrew Schools and Cultural Associations	296

PART FOUR: TRANSJORDAN

18. Organization and Administration of the Educational System — 299

Administration	299
Educational Finance	300
Educational Legislation	302
The Educational Ladder	304
The Development of the System	306
Public Examinations	308

19. The Schools of Transjordan 310

The Primary Course of Study	310
Secondary Education	315
Vocational Education	318
Nongovernment Schools	319

PART FIVE: SYRIA

20. Organization and Administration of the Educational System — 325

Administration	327

Educational Finance	332
Educational Legislation	340
The Educational Ladder	342
Public Examinations	347
Development and Extent of the Educational System	350

21. PUBLIC ELEMENTARY, SECONDARY, AND VOCATIONAL SCHOOLS 356

The Kindergarten	356
Primary Education	356
Secondary Education	364
Vocational Schools	373

22. HIGHER EDUCATION AND THE EDUCATION OF TEACHERS 379

The Syrian University	379
Educational Missions	384
The Education of Teachers	384

23. PRIVATE AND FOREIGN SCHOOLS 388

Grants-in-Aid	392
Private Schools	393
Foreign Schools	399

PART SIX: LEBANON

24. ORGANIZATION AND ADMINISTRATION OF THE EDUCATIONAL SYSTEM 407

The Administration of Public Education	408
Educational Finance	411
Educational Legislation	413
The Educational Ladder	415
The Growth of Education	421

25. PUBLIC EDUCATION 426

Kindergartens	427
Primary Education	427
Description of Primary Schools	438
Public Primary-School Examinations	440
Secondary Education	443
Public Secondary-School or *Baccalauréat* Examinations	451
The Education of Primary Teachers	454
The School of Arts and Crafts	455

26. FRENCH SCHOOLS 458

Program of Studies	461
Examinations	467
Description of Some French Schools	467

27. AMERICAN AND BRITISH SCHOOLS 479

American Institutions	479
Description of American Schools	484

CONTENTS

British Schools	499
Other Foreign Schools	501
28. Private Lebanese Schools	503
Denominational Schools	506
Nondenominational Schools	515

PART SEVEN: INTERPRETATION

29. Education and Cultural Change in the Arab World	521
Background of Arab and Near Eastern Life	522
Chief Aspects of Modern Arab Life	525
Educational Problems and Prospects in the Arab States	539
Centralized Systems	542
Index	579

LIST OF ILLUSTRATIONS

Shaykh Sayid Nawwar and Two of His American Students in the School of Oriental Studies, American University at Cairo, Egypt	*Frontispiece*
Main Building of the School of Applied Engineering, Cairo ..... *facing*	40
The Elementary School for the Village of Manayil, Egypt ...... *facing*	40
A Kindergarten Band Practicing Out-of-Doors, Heliopolis, Egypt .. *facing*	41
Upperclassmen on the Steps of the Entrance to the Assembly Hall of the American College for Girls, Cairo .... *facing*	41
Basketmaking in a School for the Blind, Cairo .... *facing*	72
Extracurricular Activity Group Making Perfumes in a Primary School, Cairo ....*facing*	72
A Boy Scout Outing in the Gardens of the Barrage, Egypt .... *facing*	73
Girl Guides Playing Basketball, Primary School, Cairo .... *facing*	73
Recess at the Rural School Used as a Practice School by the Students of the Rural Teachers College, Rustumiyah, Iraq .... *facing*	168
Secondary School for Girls, Baghdad .... *facing*	168
A Laboratory Class in Chemistry, Higher Teachers College, Baghdad *facing*	169
A Reading Class in the First Grade of the Mamuniyah School, Baghdad ....*facing*	169
A First Grade in a Village Primary School, Za'faraniyah, Iraq ... *facing*	200
The Sixth Grade in the Same School .... *facing*	200
The Circulation Desk of the Library of Baghdad College .... *facing*	201
Snack-time at the Kindergarten of the Demonstration School of the Elementary Teachers College for Women, Baghdad .... *facing*	201
The Arab College, Jerusalem .... *facing*	248
The Kadoorie Agricultural School (Arab), Tulkarm, Palestine .... *facing*	248
Arab Boy at Blackboard in a Primary School, Palestine .... *following*	248
A Government Village School (Arab), Showing Part of the School Garden, Palestine ....*following*	248
Between Classes at a Government Village School (Arab), Palestine ....*following*	248
A Class in Industrial Arts, Government Secondary School for Boys (Arab), Jaffa .... *facing*	249
Recess at the Government Primary School for Girls (Arab), Jaffa ... *facing*	249
Jewish School Children Planting Trees during Arbor Day Celebration, Beisan, Palestine .... *facing*	280
A Class Out-of-Doors in a Jewish Colony, Tel Joseph, Palestine .... *facing*	280

xvii

The Playground of a Primary School in a Jewish Colony, Palestine *following*	280
The Seminary for the Training of Jewish Teachers for Schools of the General Trend, Tel-Aviv, Palestine .... *following*	280
The Library of the Hebrew University, Jerusalem .... *following*	280
The Jewish Technical Institute (Technion), Haifa, Palestine ... *following*	280
A Class in Farm Machinery Repair, School of Agriculture, Mikveh Israel, Palestine .... *facing*	281
A Demonstration in Bee-keeping in a Jewish School, Palestine .... *facing*	281
The New Secondary School for Boys, Irbid, Transjordan .... *facing*	312
Recess at the Secondary School for Boys, Irbid .... *facing*	312
Class in Arabic at Damascus College, Damascus, Syria .... *facing*	360
Teacher and Part of Top Class in Primary School for Girls, Suwayda, Syria .... *facing*	361
Former French Army Barracks Now Used for a Government School for Boys, Suwayda .... *facing*	361
Aleppo College, Aleppo, Syria .... *facing*	392
One of the Classroom Buildings of the Secondary School for Boys, Homs, Syria .... *facing*	393
A Village Primary School with a School Garden, near Homs ..... *facing*	393
Some of the Students in the Preparatory Department of the American University of Beirut, Lebanon .... *facing*	456
Students Approaching Rockefeller Hall of the American University of Beirut .... *facing*	456
View of the Campus of the American University of Beirut ...... *facing*	457
American School for Boys, Tripoli, Lebanon. Tennis Match ..... *facing*	457
A Reading Class in a Village Primary School, Bishmizzin, Lebanon *facing*	488
A Village Primary School, Bishmizzin .... *facing*	488
Laboratory of the American Junior College for Women, Beirut ..... *facing*	489
Undergraduates of the American Junior College for Women Relax between Classes in the Rock Garden .... *facing*	489

LIST OF CHARTS

		PAGE
I.	Egypt: Administrative Organization of the Public School System, 1945–46 ....*facing*	4
II.	Egypt: The Public School System, 1945–46 ....*facing*	24
III.	Iraq: Administrative Organization of the Ministry of Education, 1945–46 ....*facing*	122
IV.	Iraq: Public School System, 1945–46	132
V.	Palestine: Administrative Organization of the Government (Arab) Department of Education, 1946	218
VI.	Palestine: The Government (Arab) School System, 1946	229
VII.	Palestine: Administrative Organization of the Hebrew Public School System, 1946	259
VIII.	Palestine: Hebrew School System, 1946	271
IX.	Transjordan: Administrative Organization of the Ministry of Education, 1946	300
X.	Transjordan: Public School System, 1945–46	304
XI.	Syria: Administrative Organization of the Ministry of Education, 1946	328
XII.	Syria: Public School System, 1946	343
XIII.	Lebanon: Administrative Organization of the Ministry of National Education and Fine Arts, 1946	409
XIV.	Lebanon: Educational System, 1946 ....*facing*	416

LIST OF TABLES

		PAGE
1.	Expenditures on Public Education in Egypt, 1882–1946	16
2.	Budget of Ministry of Education, Egypt, 1945–46	17
3.	Number of and Enrollment in Public, Private, and Foreign Schools in Egypt, 1913–14 and 1944–45	34
4.	Distribution of Pupils by Grade in Public (Compulsory, Primary, Secondary) Schools in Egypt, 1940–41 and 1942–43	35
5.	Teachers in Egyptian Schools, 1942–43	38
6.	Program of Studies for Elementary Schools, Egypt, 1945–46	42
7.	Program of Studies for Public Kindergartens, Egypt, 1945–46	47
8.	Program of Studies for Primary Schools, Egypt, 1945–46	50
9.	Public Primary Examination Results, Egypt, 1939–40, 1941–42, 1943–44	55
10.	Public Primary Examination Results, Egypt, 1910–40	55
11.	Program of Studies, General-Culture Stage, of Secondary Schools, Egypt, 1945–46	58
12.	Program of Studies for Orientation Year of Secondary Schools, Egypt, 1945–46	61
13.	Public Secondary-School Examination Results, Egypt, 1939–40, 1941–42, 1943–44	65
14.	Distribution of Students by Faculties, Fuad I University, Egypt, 1945–46	75
15.	Enrollment in Institute of Education for Men, Cairo, 1945–46	101
16.	Enrollment in Egyptian Schools under Public, Private, and Foreign Control, 1942–43	112
17.	Activities and Attendance of the Division of Extension of the American University at Cairo, 1944–45	116
18.	Public Examination Results, Iraq, 1944–45	137
19.	Number of Schools, Teachers, and Pupils in Iraq, 1920–45, According to Level and Type of School	140
20.	The Growth of Primary Education, Iraq, 1920–45	142
21.	Enrollment of Pupils by Grades in Public Primary Schools, Iraq, 1920–45	142
22.	Enrollment in Secondary Schools, Iraq, 1944–45	143
23.	Enrollment of Secondary-School Students by Years, Iraq, 1924–45	144
24.	Public Primary-School Program of Studies, Iraq, 1945–46	149
25.	Public Primary Teachers Classified According to Qualifications, Iraq, 1945–46	161

26. The Secondary-School Program of Studies, 1943 Revision, Iraq 167
27. Secondary-School Teachers Classified According to Qualifications, Iraq, 1946 172
28. Program of Studies for the Commercial Secondary School, Baghdad, 1945–46 178
29. Program of Studies for Primary Teachers, Queen 'Aliyah Institute, Iraq, 1945–46 183
30. Rural-Teachers College Enrollment, Iraq, 1944–45 185
31. Enrollment in Higher Teachers College, Baghdad, 1945–46 189
32. Program of Study of the Higher Teachers College for Arabic, English, and Social Studies Sections, Iraq, 1945 190
33. Program of Study of the Higher Teachers College for Chemistry-Biology and Physics-Mathematics Sections, 1945 191
34. Program of Studies, Queen 'Aliyah Institute for Women Teachers, Iraq, 1945–46 197
35. Enrollment in Primary and Secondary Schools in Iraq, Classified According to Control, 1945–46 210
36. Relation of Educational Budget to Total Budget, Palestine, 1920–21 to 1945–46 222
37. Results of Secondary-School Certificate Examination According to Language Medium, Palestine, 1945 233
38. Results of Secondary-School Certificate Examination According to Type of School, Palestine, 1944 233
39. Development of the Arab Public-School System, Palestine, 1920–46 . 236
40. Distribution of Pupils by Grades, Arab Public Schools, Palestine, 1944 and 1945 238
41. Elementary-School Program of Studies for Arabs, Palestine, 1945–46 . 242
42. Program of Studies for Arab Secondary Schools, Palestine, 1945–46 .. 247
43. Sources of Income for the Maintenance of the Jewish Public-School System, Palestine, 1918–45 264
44. Number of Jewish Schools, Teachers, and Pupils, Palestine, 1920–45, According to Type of Control 275
45. Number of Teachers and Pupils in Jewish Public Schools, Palestine, 1920–45, According to Level of School 275
46. Jewish Private-School Enrollment, Palestine, 1943–44 276
47. Program of Studies in Hebrew Boys Elementary Schools, General Trend, Palestine, 1945–46 281
48. Program of Studies in Elementary Schools of the Labor Trend, Palestine, 1945–46 281
49. Program of Studies of Hertzliah Secondary School, Tel-Aviv, 1945–46 287

LIST OF TABLES

50. Total Budget and Estimates for Education, Transjordan, 1924–46 .. 301
51. Number of Public Schools, Teachers, and Pupils, in Transjordan, 1922–46 306
52. Enrollment by Grades in Public Schools, Transjordan, 1945–46 307
53. Results of Public Secondary-School Examinations, Transjordan, 1940–45 309
54. Program of Studies in Primary Schools for Boys, Transjordan, 1945–46 311
55. Program of Studies for Secondary Schools for Boys, Transjordan, 1945–46 315
56. Growth of the Educational Budget, Syria, 1923–46 333
57. Budget of the Ministry of Education, Syria, 1945 334
58. Results of Public Examinations, Syria, 1943 and 1945 350
59. Growth of Syrian Education, 1923–45 351
60. Syrian Schools Classified According to Type of School and Type of Control, 1944–45 353
61. Enrollment by Grades in Public Primary Schools, Syria, 1944–45 358
62. Primary Course of Study for Syrian Public Schools, 1945–46 359
63. The New Program of Studies for Secondary Schools, Syria, 1945–46 .. 367
64. Distribution of Pupils in Classes in Secondary and Vocational Schools, Syria, 1944–45 371
65. Program of Studies of the Three-Year Course for the Education of Teachers, Syria, 1946 386
66. Public, Private, and Foreign Schools and Their Enrollments on Various Levels, Syria, 1944–45 390
67. Foreign Schools and Enrollment Classified According to Nationality of Governing Body, Syria, 1944–45 390
68. Comparison of Enrollment in Public, Private, and Foreign Schools, Syria, 1944–45 and 1945–46 391
69. Distribution of Private Primary Schools According to Religious Control, Syria, 1944–45 394
70. Program of Studies, High-School Section, Aleppo College, Syria, 1945–46 403
71. Growth of the Education Budget, Lebanon, 1921–45 412
72. Number of Schools and Pupils Classified According to Control, Lebanon, 1924–46 422
73. Distribution of Schools and Pupils by Type of School, Lebanon, 1941–42 423
74. Distribution and Size of Foreign Schools by Nationality, Lebanon, 1942–43 424
75. Sectarian Composition of the School Enrollment of Lebanon as Com-

pared with the Composition of the General Population, 1941–42 ... 424
76. Program of Studies for Primary and Higher Primary Schools, Lebanon, 1946 429
77. Subjects for the Primary-Certificate Examination, Lebanon 441
78. Subjects for Higher Primary Certificate Examination, Lebanon 442
79. New Program of Studies for Secondary Schools, Lebanon, 1946 445
80. Subjects for Lebanese *Baccalauréat* Examinations, Parts I and II ... 452
81. Program of Studies for Preparation of Primary-School Teachers, Lebanon, 1946 454
82. Distribution of Periods in Two Grades of the Lycée Français of the Mission Laïque, Beirut, 1946 462
83. Program of Studies for the Commercial Section, Lycée Français, Tripoli, 1946 463
84. Number of Students and of Faculty Members, Université Saint-Joseph, 1945–46 472
85. Elementary- and High-School Programs of Studies, American Presbyterian Mission Schools, 1945–46 482
86. Enrollment in the American University of Beirut, 1945–46 487
87. Program of Studies for the *Section Secondaire*, Regular Course, American University of Beirut, 1946 490
88. Program of Studies for *Section Secondaire*, Commercial Course, American University of Beirut, 1946 491
89. The Two-Year Course for Teachers at the British-Syrian Training College, 1945–46 500
90. Distribution of Private Schools and Pupils According to Denomination, Lebanon, 1941–42 504
91. Program of Studies of al-Hikmah College 508
92. Proportion of Children in School in Six Arab Countries, 1942–45 ... 544

Part One

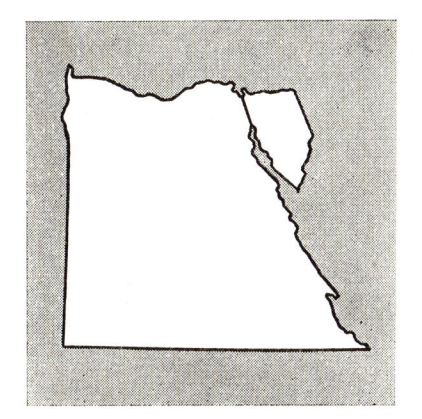

EGYPT

EGYPT

Population: *19,092,104 (a preliminary estimate issued in August 1948).*

Area: *About 386,100 square miles.*

Form of government: *Constitutional monarchy, with a Parliament consisting of a Senate and a Chamber of Deputies.*

Principal occupations: *Agriculture, mining, industry, commerce, finance, services, public service, religion, law, medicine, education, transport.*

Principal exports: *Cotton, cotton-seed, cottonseed oil, cigarettes, onions, rice, mineral oils, phosphates, skins and hides.*

Principal imports: *Textiles, machinery and vehicles, fertilizers, minerals and fuels, metals, wood, paper manufactures.*

Monetary unit: *Egyptian pound (£E), equivalent to approximately $4.15.*

Chapter 1

ORGANIZATION AND ADMINISTRATION OF THE EDUCATIONAL SYSTEM

*E*GYPT's educational system has a considerably longer history than that of any other country studied in this survey. Whereas the other Arab countries of the Near East made a fairly complete break with the educational policies of the Ottoman Turks and started afresh after World War I, the Egyptian educational system in general dates back more than a century, while the religious system represented by the University of al-Azhar and its associated schools goes back a thousand or more years.

The complexity which its long history has given the Egyptian system makes the systems of the other countries appear comparatively simple. In Egypt in the course of the last century, new circumstances, ideas, and needs intermittently produced new types of schools, educational legislation, and ever-newer experiments with educational organization. While some of these innovations were ephemeral, many left a permanent impress on the educational system, with the result that Egypt today has a multiplicity of types of schools—some having their roots in ancient and medieval times, some being modern and westernized—a multiplicity of laws affecting schools, and an exceedingly complex administrative organization.

There are seven principal agencies concerned with education in Egypt:

1. Most important is the Ministry of Education, which administers and finances a major portion of the public educational program of the country, aids and exercises technical control over another significant part, and supervises all private and foreign schools.

2. The Ministry of Interior, operating through the provincial councils, conducts the councils' elementary schools of the provinces.

3. The ancient Muslim system of education is administered by the time-honored University of al-Azhar, with its colleges in Cairo and its secondary and primary schools in Cairo and other cities.

4. The Ministry of Waqf (the department of the national government which supervises religious endowments) maintains a number of elementary schools, which are administered and supervised by the Ministry of Education.

5. The Directorate of Railways supports a number of elementary schools under the professional supervision of the Ministry of Education.

6. More recently the Ministry of Social Affairs began a large anti-illiteracy campaign in the cities and the provinces. It maintains schools and asylums for poor or orphan children and institutions for the training of social workers.

The six agencies mentioned above are public agencies, departments of the Egyptian government.

7. A group of agencies which supports "free" education—a term used in Egypt to designate private and foreign schools. Private schools are those maintained by Egyptian charitable, sectarian, or private groups, or individuals. Foreign schools are those maintained by either lay or religious bodies of French, American, British, Greek, Italian, or other nationalities.

The Ministry of Education

The Ministry of Education, the arm of the government responsible for the conduct of the major portion of all educational enterprise in Egypt, was founded in 1836–37 by Muhammad 'Ali, first viceroy of Egypt, and except for a short interval when it was abolished during the reign of Sa'id Pasha, the fourth viceroy, it has carried on its functions ever since.

Starting with French influence, though under Egyptian control, the Ministry naturally derived inspiration from French methods of education, and the French language had a favored place in the curriculum. Later, in the course of the British occupation, the Ministry gradually came under British influence. Although the English language was introduced, neither the French language nor the French cultural influence was eliminated. Finally, after the adoption of the constitution in 1923, the Ministry of Education passed into purely Egyptian hands.

Education in Egypt, as in the other Arabic-speaking countries, is highly centralized. The Ministry, as the central office, reserves the powers of appointment, promotion, distribution, transfer, and discipline of teachers, and dispensation of fiscal matters. It devises the curriculum for each type of school (except the universities and higher institutions), determines what textbooks shall be used, administers the public examinations for primary, secondary, and certain other types of education, and regulates school examinations and grading. In addition to regulating almost all phases of public-school education, the Ministry exercises considerable control over private and foreign schools.

Some attempts at decentralization have been made in recent years. In

Chart I
EGYPT: ADMINISTRATIVE ORGANIZATION OF THE PUBLIC SCHOOL SYSTEM, 1945-46

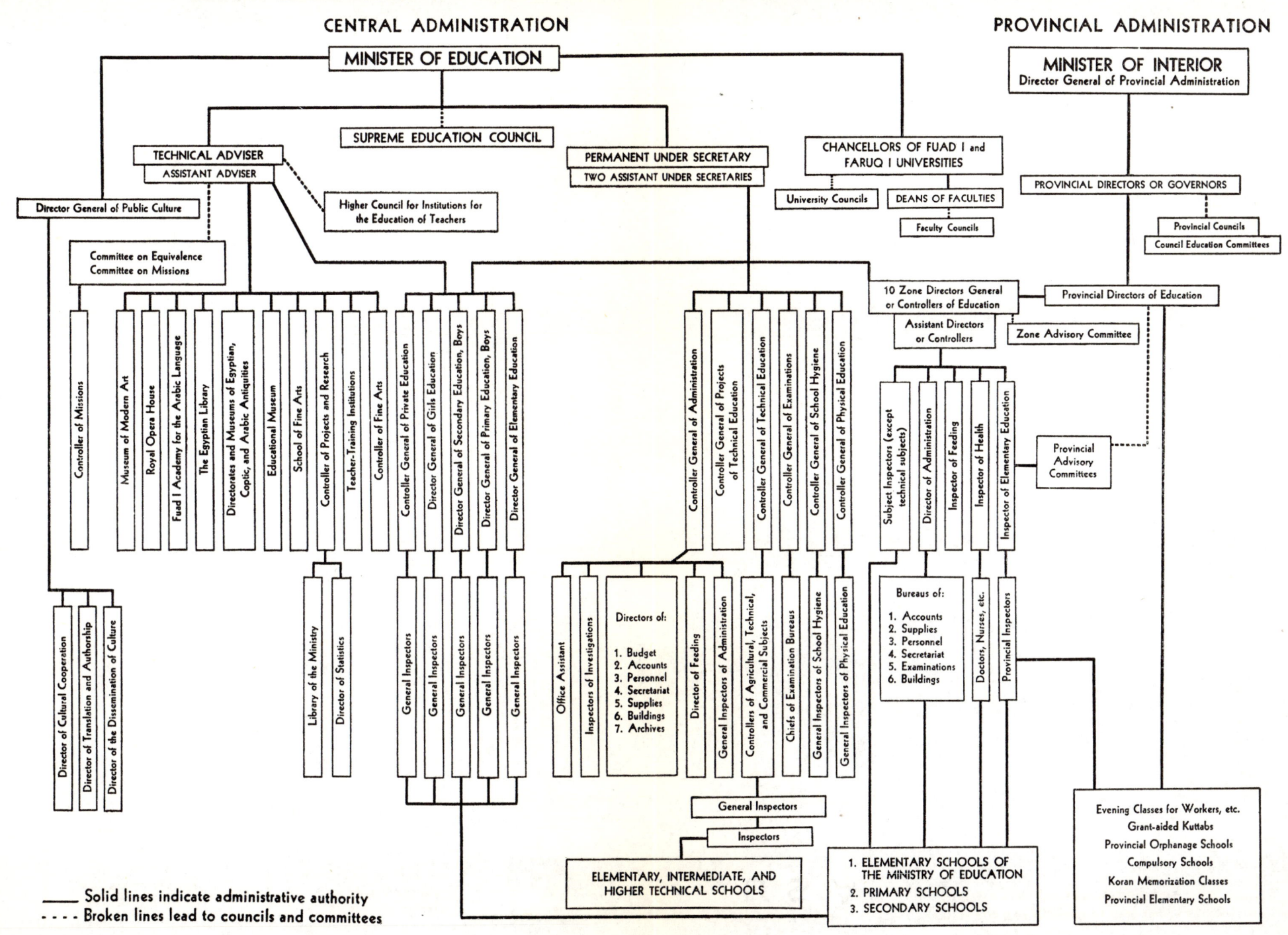

ORGANIZATION AND ADMINISTRATION

1938 Egypt was divided into educational zones. Originally there were ten zones—this division was still in effect at the time of the visit of the American Council's Commission in 1946, but subsequently the number of zones was reduced to nine, the two zones for Cairo being merged into one. Each zone is under the direction of a "controller" or "director" appointed by the Ministry. The zone controllers have limited powers to make expenditures and to appoint and promote elementary-school teachers.[1] Although the central office still tends to take matters into its own hands, it seems likely that as time goes on increasing responsibility will be placed with the zone controllers.

Chart I shows the organization of educational administration in the Ministry of Education and in the provinces. The Minister, who stands at the head of the system, is a cabinet member and thus responsible to Parliament. His sanction is required for all major decisions, policies, and expenditures, and for new appointments and promotions of personnel above elementary-school level.

THE SUPREME EDUCATION COUNCIL

Some form of a higher education council has existed off and on since 1836. Its form, powers, constitution, and performance have varied from time to time. The present Supreme Education Council held its first meeting on December 22, 1945, having been established by special decree after a lapse of more than three years during which no higher council existed. With the Minister of Education as its chairman, the council consists of all former ministers of education, the Permanent Under Secretary of Education, the Technical Adviser and his assistants, the chancellors of the two government universities (Fuad I and Faruq I Universities), the Secretaries of the Ministries of Commerce and Industry and of Public Health and Social Affairs, the chairmen of the Finance and Education Committees in both houses of Parliament, and four members of Parliament who are interested in education and are appointed by the King acting upon the nomination of the Minister of Education. Directors of educational sections in the Ministry and the heads of higher institutions not included in the universities may attend the council meetings upon the invitation of the chairman when matters pertaining to their offices are under discussion.

The council holds two sessions a year at the invitation of the Minister, who may call it for an extraordinary session at his discretion. Its advice is sought on matters of general educational policy, on courses of study and basic rules for examinations, on the founding, transferring, or abolishing

[1] For further description of the responsibilities of the zone controllers, see pp. 8–9.

of an educational institution, and on any educational matter which the Minister sees fit to present.

THE ADVISORY COMMITTEE

In addition to the Supreme Education Council, an Advisory Committee exists to assist the Minister. It consists of the Permanent Under Secretary, the two assistant under secretaries, the Technical Adviser and the assistant adviser, and is under the chairmanship of the Minister. Directors or controllers of the various types of education are invited to attend meetings when matters concerning their departments are under consideration. The Minister lays before this committee important projects, laws, regulations, and plans, as well as the draft budget and recommendations for appointments and promotions to important posts.

THE BUREAUS

Two bureaus also assist the Minister. The Private Bureau is headed by a director who performs the functions of private secretary to the Minister. The Technical Bureau is headed by a director of long experience in the Ministry. He controls all correspondence and handles official queries and complaints that are submitted to the Ministry.

THE DEPARTMENTS

The Ministry is divided into five departments, the heads of which are directly responsible to the Minister. The universities of Fuad I in Cairo and Faruq I in Alexandria constitute two of these departments. They enjoy a considerable measure of independence. The chancellors represent their universities to the Minister. The other three departments are those of the Permanent Under Secretary of Education (Wakil), the Technical Adviser (Mustashar), and the Director General of Public Culture.

OFFICES UNDER THE PERMANENT UNDER SECRETARY

The Permanent Under Secretary of Education is the administrative head of the public educational system. He is responsible for the execution of laws and regulations in the departments and schools under his jurisdiction and for the application of regulations in the educational zones. He superintends all financial and administrative activities of both the central office and the educational zones and the preparation of the Ministry's budget. In addition, he has charge of appointments, transfers, and promotions of officials. Two assistant under secretaries relieve him of a share of his burden.

ORGANIZATION AND ADMINISTRATION

Responsible to the Under Secretary or to one or the other of the two assistant under secretaries are the following officials: the Controller General of Administration, the Controller General of Examinations, the Controller General of School Hygiene, the directors general or controllers of the educational zones, and three controllers of specialized instruction—the Controller General of Physical Education, the Controller General of Technical Education, and the Controller General of the Projects of Technical Education.

The Controller General of Administration has charge of all administrative matters in the central office, the zone offices, and the school system. Under his jurisdiction a director of feeding is responsible for the extensive feeding program conducted in schools of the Ministry and provincial schools. Seven bureaus headed by directors operate under the guidance of the Controller General of Administration: budget, accounts, personnel, secretariat (in charge of all files and papers at the Ministry), supplies (school furniture, equipment, and books), buildings, and archives (charged with registering all incoming and outgoing correspondence).

There are two controllers general for technical education. The Controller General of the Projects of Technical Education supervises the planning of the vocational-education program and the drawing-up of curriculums for the various kinds of technical schools. The Controller General of Technical Education has charge of supervising and inspecting technical education in these schools, preparing the budget, and appointing, transferring, and promoting teachers and officials in this field. Under this controller general are a controller for technical (trade) education proper, a second for commercial education, and a third for agricultural education. These three are assisted by general inspectors and inspectors of each field of enterprise, who visit the various types of technical schools. Inspection of technical schools alone has remained independent of zone authority. These technical inspectors operate under orders from their department in Cairo. When it is considered that the zones are qualified to take charge of technical education, the technical inspectors will be distributed among the zones and the office of the Controller General of Technical Education in the central office will be abolished, leaving only the Controller General of the Projects of Technical Education.

The Controller General of Physical Education is responsible for the planning and development of physical-education and military-training programs in the schools. He personally visits schools to keep in direct touch with their programs and to develop his plans and recommendations. He acts as a liaison officer between the Ministry and the sports clubs of the country, organizes athletic competitions and Scout camps, and makes recommendations for the appointment, promotion, and transfer of physical-education teachers. He is assisted by a staff of general inspectors.

The Controller General of School Hygiene is responsible for the sanitary conditions of the schools and is in charge of the school medical service. He recommends the appointment, transfer, and promotion of doctors in the service.

The Controller General of Examinations issues, through the Ministry, detailed instructions for the conduct and content of the yearly examinations for each type of school. His department reviews the results of examinations held for schools above the primary level, and it organizes, issues questions for, and supervises correction of the public examinations conducted by the Ministry. It tabulates the results of the public examinations and issues detailed annual reports about them. Finally, it is responsible for issuing certificates and diplomas and for determining the equivalence of the various Egyptian certificates.

In 1946 the ten educational zones were apportioned as follows: two for the city of Cairo, five for the provinces and governorates of the Delta, and three for those of Upper Egypt lying between Cairo and the Sudan. Subsequently the two Cairo zones were merged into one, reducing the number of zones to nine. The Cairo zones were headed by two directors general; the other zones have controllers. The difference between the positions is in grade and seniority rather than function. Aside from Cairo and the large province of Gharbiyah, each of which constitutes a single zone, a zone includes two or more provinces.

The zone controller has charge of all professional and administrative matters pertaining to all schools except vocational in his zone; of vocational schools he has administrative, but not professional charge. He is the representative of the Ministry and its liaison officer within the zone. He is responsible to the Under Secretary, to whom he makes two reports yearly, describing the educational situation in his zone, making recommendations, and summarizing the reports of inspectors. He supervises the application of programs of study for all types of schools except the vocational and is expected to encourage new methods and experiments suggested by local needs. He organizes inspection, assigns teachers and officials, and supervises professionally and administratively the free schools and recommends grants-in-aid to them. He reviews results of school examinations and keeps informed about the list of free places (scholarships) in schools. He can appoint personnel for elementary schools of the Ministry, grant salary increments, and make recommendations for re-

ORGANIZATION AND ADMINISTRATION

appointment, transfer, or promotion in other schools. He has limited disciplinary power over teachers and officials. With students he has authority to impose two punishments, exclusion from school and exclusion from final examinations. He prepares the budget for his zone, approves the monthly payroll, tenders, and other specified expenditures, decides on buildings to be rented for educational purposes, and can sanction rents not in excess of nine Egyptian pounds ($36) a month.

The zone controller is assisted by one or more assistant controllers who act for him in his absence and review all matters submitted for his decisions. In addition, there is a director of administration who has jurisdiction over the various administrative bureaus of the zone office and over the administrative and financial affairs of the schools, to see that expenditure takes place in accordance with prescribed procedures.

Each zone has an advisory committee composed of the controller as chairman, the assistant controllers, principals of senior secondary and senior primary schools, senior zone inspectors of social sciences, natural sciences, mathematics, and Arabic, and—when matters relating to elementary education are under discussion—the chief inspector of elementary education. All these officials are appointed by the Permanent Under Secretary. The zone director of administration serves the committee as secretary. The zone controller must submit the following matters to the committee before taking action upon them: (1) the zone budget; (2) assignment of teachers and officials, recommendations for their promotion, confirmation, contract renewal, salary increases, and their transfer to points outside the zone; (3) recommendations concerning appointment of teachers and head teachers of elementary schools belonging to the Ministry and also of zone clerks; (4) recommendations regarding the qualifications and the appointment of teachers of free (private and foreign) schools and the fixing of the grants to these schools.

Inspectors within the zones are of four types: health inspectors, feeding inspectors, elementary-school inspectors, and subject inspectors for primary and secondary schools. The inspector of health is a doctor and is responsible for the hygienic condition of the schools and for the performances of doctors, nurses, and other health workers in the schools. The inspector of feeding has charge of the program under which midday meals are provided gratis for pupils in all government primary schools and in many government and provincial elementary and compulsory schools. Even in the provincial schools the cost of feeding is borne by the Ministry of Education. In the secondary schools midday meals are paid for on a yearly basis by all students except those exempted from tuition fees.

This is an extensive program; the annual budget for 1945–46 allocated £E1,470,000[2] for it, £E870,000 of that total being assigned to the feeding program in elementary and technical schools.

The inspector of elementary education assists the controller in the professional supervision of elementary education and of the work of provincial inspectors. He also represents the Ministry in certain provincial bodies and makes recommendations for the appointment, promotion, and transfer of elementary-school teachers. Subject inspectors operate in primary, secondary, and other schools, excepting the elementary and technical. They are specialists in the various academic subjects and present their reports to the assistant zone controllers, who take such action as is considered necessary.

Departments under the Technical Adviser[3]

The regulations assign to the Technical Adviser responsibility for the professional obligations of the Ministry, especially those relating to educational policies, laws, plans, courses of study, and methods. It is his duty to recommend reforms and to suggest projects for the extension and modernization of education throughout the country. He is charged with the professional inspection of schools and with the supervision of teacher training. He has an assistant adviser who performs the functions assigned to him by the Adviser, but who is especially concerned with organizing and directing inspection, supervising the training of teachers, and overseeing the work of the Controller of Projects and Research and the Controller of Missions.

Some departments within the province of the Technical Adviser are subject to a dual control, being administratively under the Permanent Under Secretary and professionally under the Technical Adviser. These are the five departments of general education. Four of them—the Directors General of Elementary Education, of Primary Education for Boys, of Secondary Education for Boys, and of Girls Education—are responsible to the Under Secretary for assignment, transfer, and promotion of the teachers and inspectors of their systems, while the fifth, the Controller General of Private (free, that is) Education, is charged with presenting his opinions regarding zone recommendations concerning qualifications of teachers for

---

[2] £E is the symbol used for Egyptian pound. It is equivalent to approximately four United States dollars.
[3] The title of the Technical Adviser has since been changed to Under Secretary. The Ministry thus now has two under secretaries. The responsibilities of the different men, however, remain as here described.

ORGANIZATION AND ADMINISTRATION

private schools and regarding the apportionment of grants-in-aid to these schools. Each of these officials makes semiannual reports to the Technical Adviser concerning personal visits to the schools, with recommendations and suggestions involving general plans, courses of study, and textbooks. Each has a staff of inspectors to visit and appraise school performance.

Three other officers in the central office of the Ministry work under the general direction of the Technical Adviser. The Controller of Missions has charge of students studying abroad at government expense and of such students as study abroad at their own expense but who put themselves under government supervision. He prepares the missions budget, has charge of the equivalence of foreign degrees, and serves as secretary of the Committee on Missions and the Committee on the Equivalence of Degrees. The Controller of Fine Arts is concerned with the encouragement of fine-arts activities in the country and serves as liaison officer between the Ministry of Education and artistic organizations. The Controller of Projects and Research has charge of studies and research required for new plans, policies, and courses of study considered by the Ministry. He supervises the preparation of all necessary information, documents, and statistics for this purpose. He is in charge of the bureau of statistics and the library of the Ministry. The library is composed of about 50,000 volumes, principally in Arabic, English, and French, and lends material to officials of the Ministry and to teachers in all parts of the country.

In addition, a number of schools and institutions are at least formally under the jurisdiction of the Technical Adviser, though some have their own boards, which often meet under the chairmanship of the Adviser, and others have their own independent organizations. Teacher-training establishments of all levels and the Higher School of Fine Arts belong to this category. The other cultural institutions include the Educational Museum in Cairo; the Royal Opera House built by Isma'il Pasha at the time of the opening of the Suez Canal; the Fuad I Academy of the Arabic Language—a self-perpetuating body of twenty scholars from Egypt and the other Arabic countries and of Orientalists which holds a yearly session of conferences on linguistic matters and publishes its own journal; the Egyptian Library of 300,000 or more books, and valuable manuscripts and illuminated Korans; and various museums. The Department of Egyptian Antiquities, which maintains the famous museum in Cairo and smaller museums in other parts of the country, employs many experts, archeologists, a large staff of inspectors, and other officials, and carries on its own excavations and a ceaseless work of reconstruction and preservation of

Egyptian monuments. The Department for the Preservation of Arab Antiquities performs the same functions for Arab and Islamic remains in the country. A Museum of Arab Antiquities is independently maintained in a building adjacent to the Public Library, and a fine Coptic Museum is kept in the old part of Cairo. Finally there is the Museum of Modern Art. Though nominally attached to the Technical Adviser, these institutions are to a large measure independent.

THE DIRECTORATE GENERAL OF PUBLIC CULTURE

Originally attached to the Technical Adviser, the Directorate General of Public Culture was in recent years made a separate department directly under the Minister. It now consists of three principal directorates: the Directorate of the Dissemination of Culture, the Directorate of Translation and Authorship, and the Directorate of Cultural Cooperation.

The director of the first of these departments has perhaps the most varied activities, as he is concerned with adult education and popular culture. One of his most interesting responsibilities is the projected Peoples University at Cairo. The only requirements for admission of anyone over sixteen years of age are ability to read and write and willingness to pay a nominal registration fee. At the time of the visit of the American Council Commission in early 1946, applications for admission were being studied to discover the range of knowledge and interest among prospective students, so that the program could be shaped accordingly. The Peoples University[4] has been constituted a body with its own governing board by three ministerial decrees. It aims at raising the level of general culture without preliminary academic requirements. Courses will be both theoretical and practical and will include trips for study and cultural purposes. Political, national, international, historical, literary, scientific, commercial, agricultural, and industrial subjects will be offered. In addition, there will be courses in the social sciences, religion, medicine and hygiene, home arts, and fine arts. Lecturers will be recruited from university circles and among specialists in various fields of learning. Certificates of attendance at various courses, but no degrees, will be given.

Aside from organizing the impressive project of a popular university, the Directorate of the Dissemination of Culture is opening cultural centers in the larger towns and initiating a movement for archeological culture in cooperation with museums. The latter enterprise includes an evening school of archeological education, independent of the Directorate of Public Cul-

[4] The university has been in operation since the spring of 1946. It is now called the Cultural Foundation.

ORGANIZATION AND ADMINISTRATION

ture, which offers a three-year course above the secondary certificate, and also a simplified course of the same length for sons of dragomans and guides but not requiring the secondary certificate for admission. Cultural weeks are projected for the capitals of the provinces. In January 1946 school radio broadcasts (daily, except on Friday) were inaugurated, the programs consisting of music and talks on timely topics. Educational films are projected, and an expansion of the public-library service to reach various quarters of the main cities is underway.

The title of the Directorate of Translation and Authorship is self-explanatory. It is planned to stimulate the writing and translation of books of specialized, technical value and also of books of popular interest. A long list of recognized books in various languages has been drawn up, translators have been selected, and, to insure a high standard of excellence in the translations, reviewers have been chosen to pass on the work. Rates of remuneration for translators and reviewers have been fixed, and the work is in progress.

The Directorate of Cultural Cooperation seeks to develop cultural relations with other Arabic-speaking countries and foreign countries in general. It assists in the placement of students from other Islamic countries in the various Egyptian institutions of learning, helps to select teachers for schools outside Egypt as requests come in from other countries, encourages group travel of Egyptian students abroad, and develops programs for the visits of students from other Arabic-speaking countries. The new cultural treaty, drafted by the Cultural Committee of the Arab League in 1944–45 and approved by the Council of the League, makes provision for the forms of cultural cooperation just mentioned and also recommends exchange of publications, copyright measures, concerted effort to publish Arabic classics as well as translations of world classics, coordination of research, mutual recognition of educational certificates and degrees, and consultation regarding school curriculums. Much of the Egyptian participation in this broad program comes under the jurisdiction of the Director of Cultural Cooperation, whose work extends beyond Arabic countries to the European states. Since 1942–43 an Egyptian Cultural Center has been maintained in London.

Provincial Educational Administration

For purposes of internal administration, Egypt is divided into governorates (*muhafazat*) and provinces (*mudiriyat*). The eight governorates comprise the larger cities of Cairo and Alexandria, the Canal Zone, Damietta, and Suez, and three desert or frontier areas bordering the Red

Sea—the southern desert, the western desert, and the Sinai Peninsula. The provinces are fourteen in number; six in the delta north of Cairo—Sharqiyah, Daqahliyah, Qalyubiyah, Gharbiyah, Manufiyah, and Buhayrah—and eight in Upper Egypt, extending along the Nile from Cairo to the frontiers of the Sudan—Gizah, Bani Suayf, Fayyum, Minyah, Asyut, Girga, Qina, and Aswan.

Education in the governorates is administered directly by the Ministry of Education through the zone controllers and directors general described previously. The governorates interfere little in the administration and pay little or nothing for the upkeep of the schools. The provinces, however, have had special powers in the educational system since 1909, when a law permitted them to levy an additional tax not to exceed 5 percent of the total land tax in the province for purposes of education and other local public services. The provincial council may, if it sees fit, spend the entire additional tax on education. It was stipulated that 70 percent of the expenditure should go for elementary, agricultural, and industrial education, and 30 percent for primary and postprimary education. Thus, a system for varied types of schools that were almost parallel with those conducted by the Ministry of Education grew up within the provinces, and by 1934 the provincial councils had expanded their systems to include 10 secondary schools, 18 industrial and agricultural schools, and 27 orphanages. In that year, however, a new law restricted the educational activities of the provincial councils to providing only elementary education in the towns and villages of the provinces and to establishing and administering orphanages, while schools of other types were transferred to the Ministry of Education. At the same time compulsory schools, previously conducted by the Ministry in the provinces, were transferred to the provincial councils.

The administration of provincial education emanates from the Ministry of Interior through the Director General of Provincial Administration, who is in charge of all activities of the provincial councils. The Director General functions under the authority of the Permanent Under Secretary of Interior. At the regional level, the administration of each province is headed by a *mudir* (governor) who is appointed by the Minister of Interior and is responsible to him. Each province has its council, consisting of elected members and ex officio members who represent some ministries of the national government. The Ministry of Education is represented by a director of education, an official of the Ministry delegated by the Minister upon the request of the council to serve as executive officer for education in the province. He receives his salary from the council with an additional stipend for his administrative services. The provincial council, which has its own education committee, determines major lines of policy within the province, such as establishment of new schools, transference of old ones, approval of the annual budget, supervision of the appropriate expenditure of the budget, and so forth.

The provincial education director, an assistant zone controller, and the zone inspector of elementary education make up a provincial advisory committee, which usually meets in the summer to recommend appointments, transfers, and promotions of elementary-school teachers. New teachers are selected from graduates of the elementary-teacher training schools on the basis of scholastic standing. The Ministry of Education does not interfere in the matters of appointment or of the actual administrative running of the schools, but it has exclusive responsibility for the technical supervision of elementary education in the provinces, the formulation of syllabuses, selection of textbooks, training teachers, and inspection of the schools.

Jurisdiction over public elementary education within the province is the specific prerogative of the provincial councils. The commonest types of elementary school are the five-year compulsory half-day schools, which are gradually being converted to full-day session, and the four-year full-day elementary schools of the towns and larger centers. In many elementary schools there are special classes for memorizing the Koran. Additional responsibilities of the provincial council include the operation of evening classes for workers, which are becoming common in larger centers, and the supervision of orphanages or orphanage schools for boys and girls with workshops to prepare pupils for employment. Finally, provincial councils give grants-in-aid to approved *kuttabs* (elementary religious schools), approval being largely dependent on enrollment, but also upon sanitary conditions.

Educational Finance

Because of financial stringency during the early part of the British occupation of Egypt, financial provision for education was extremely scanty for more than twenty years. To increase its revenues, the Ministry of Education introduced fees for attendance in primary and secondary schools so that only a very small proportion of children were admitted into these schools without charge.[5] In the first decade of this century the Ministry of Education began to receive greater financial support. By 1910

---

[5] Jacoub Artin Pasha, *Considerations sur l'Instruction Publique en Égypte* (Cairo: 1894), pp. 77-89.

provincial councils began to supplement provisions for education. Financial provisions for education, which had rarely exceeded 1 percent of the national budget in the early years, rose in 1910 to 3.4 percent and in 1920 to 3.9 percent. However, the real turning point in Egyptian educational policy came after the termination of British occupation and the adoption of the Egyptian Constitution in 1923 when actual control of education passed into Egyptian hands. Spurred on by a desire for universal compulsory elementary education, the government authorities mapped out an expanded program and made budgetary provisions to permit its accomplishment. Thus, by 1945–46 the expenditure for education amounted to 11.7 percent of the annual national budget.

TABLE 1
Expenditures on Public Education in Egypt, 1882–1946

Year	Total State Budget	Expenditure for Education	Percentage of Total Budget
1882..........	£E 8,763,968*	£E 89,464	1.02
1890..........	9,500,000	82,337	0.87
1900..........	10,380,000	106,483	1.03
1910..........	15,130,000	515,063	3.40
1920–21.......	40,271,000	1,584,161	3.93
1930–31.......	44,915,000	4,894,614	10.90
1940–41.......	47,718,000	5,614,848	11.77
1945–46.......	89,968,000†	10,496,768†	11.67

* £E1 (Egyptian pound) is equivalent to slightly more than $4.00.
† Estimated.

Table 1 indicates the steady increase in expenditure for education in Egypt since 1882. However, it must be pointed out that these figures understate the actual expenditure, for they do not include expenses of al-Azhar and educational projects of ministries other than Education, nor do they include expenditures on antiquities, museums, the public library, and various institutions listed separately. Beginning with 1910, expenditure by provincial councils on education is included.

Taking into consideration the expenditures for education not included in these figures, the actual percentage of the general budget devoted to educational matters in 1945–46 was closer to 12.7 than to the 11.67 shown above.

More than 90 percent of the expenditure for education comes from the budget of the central government. Provincial councils contributed £E357,398 collected from their local taxes in 1945-46. The universities of Fuad I and Faruq I received revenues estimated at £E367,000 from tuition fees and other sources in addition to the large grant from the central government of £E914,590. Al-Azhar receives little more than one-

ORGANIZATION AND ADMINISTRATION

sixth of its revenue from its own endowment, the rest being grants from the Ministry of Waqf and the Ministry of Finance.[6]

The estimated budget for 1945–46 was distributed among the various types of education as shown in Table 2.

These figures show that elementary education, which is intended to be available to all children, receives 39.4 percent of the budgetary provisions, while nonelementary education (in Egypt available to the somewhat privileged classes) receives 48.4 percent, virtually half. In 1944–45 more than a million children attended elementary schools, but only about 328,000 attended other types of schools. Thus, about 24 percent of the

TABLE 2
Budget of Ministry of Education, Egypt, 1945–46

Division	£E*	Percent
Administration and educational missions	£E 1,293,763	12.0
Higher education (including universities)	1,469,461	13.7
Secondary education (boys)	1,122,344	10.5
Primary education (boys)	1,167,739	10.9
Vocational education	661,050	6.2
Kindergarten and other girls schools, except elementary	759,458	7.1
Elementary education (boys and girls)	4,232,703	39.4
Fine arts	25,882	0.2
Total	£E10,732,400	100.0
Expected economy not included in items	235,632	
Net total	£E10,496,768	

* £E1 (Egyptian pound) is equivalent to slightly more than $4.00.

Egyptian school children were receiving approximately 50 percent of the educational expenditure.

Although all fees in elementary schools were abolished in 1925 when compulsory elementary education was launched, primary aand secondary schools continued to charge fees. In 1943 the Ministry of Education, to promote "equality of opportunity," abolished fees in primary schools altogether and increased the number of free places in secondary schools, agreeing to compensate private schools for the loss of revenues derived from fees.

In return for agreeing not to charge fees, private primary schools are compensated by the government in three ways: (1) If the school occupies rented premises, the government pays the rent. (2) The government pays the teachers according to the salary scale of government teachers, reserving the right to transfer any of the teachers to its own schools. (3)

[6] Muhammad Khalid Hassanein Bey, *Reform at Al-Azhar University* (Cairo: 1940), p. 22.

The government pays in addition a lump sum to cover operating expenses of the school; the payment varies from £E45 to £E65 per class section in the large cities and is slightly lower in the provinces. Schools are classified into three grades depending on the number of qualified teachers, quality of buildings, and other considerations.

Private secondary schools are compensated for free places provided for better students in two ways: (1) The government makes payment per teacher, varying from £E2 a month for noncertified teachers to £E10 a month for the best-qualified teachers loaned by the Ministry of Education. (2) A lump sum is paid by the government to assist with operating expenses on the basis of the rating of the school, the amount varying from £E200 to £E500 per year.

In this way the Ministry of Education assumes most of the financial burden of private primary schools; or, to put it a different way, most private primary schools are now supported by the taxpayers. The effect has been to bring the private primary schools within the framework of the national system and into line with the public-school program. The influence upon secondary schools is less pronounced.

PROVINCIAL FINANCE

Provincial councils are empowered to levy an additional tax of 8 percent on agricultural land and if necessary to appropriate 11 percent of the total land tax for educational purposes. By Article 19 of the Law on Elementary Education (Law No. 46, 1933), 66 percent of the additional tax and 1 percent of all revenues of the municipal councils are to be spent on elementary education. Although the provincial councils have applied the maximum sum of 11 percent on education, their total revenue of 11 percent plus the municipal 1 percent was estimated at only £E357,398 in 1945–46. Nevertheless, the councils were spending an estimated £E3,455,172 in that year on elementary education and the orphanages, the balance being contributed in a lump sum by the central government. In addition, the feeding program is controlled and paid for by the Ministry of Education. Altogether £E1,470,000 was provided by the budget of 1945–46 for feeding purposes.

SALARIES, PROMOTIONS, AND PENSIONS

Procedures of appointment and promotion of teachers (who are considered government officials) are basically governed by a decree of the Ministry of Finance issued in 1939. However, many supplementary decrees, regulations, and instructions issued since have resulted in an ex-

ORGANIZATION AND ADMINISTRATION

tremely intricate system. The following attempt at a simplified statement of this system is based on study of some of the documents involved and on talks with persons in charge of personnel work.

The cadre of government officials is divided into nine grades, each having a lower and an upper limit. The ninth, or lowest, grade carries a monthly salary of from £E3 to £E6. The first, or highest, grade has a monthly salary range of from £E75 to £E90. In addition to the nine regular grades there are four upper grades: director general, Grade B, with a salary of £E1,200 per annum; director general, Grade A, at £E1,300; assistant under secretary of state at £E1,400; and under secretary of state at £E1,500. The under secretary of state in any ministry is the highest civil servant in the ministry. The lowest three grades of the cadre, the maximum of which rates £E15, are usually for clerical posts and elementary-school teachers—though the latter rarely exceed £E10. The other grades, commonly known as the technical cadre, are made up of the more responsible executive posts and include teachers in primary, secondary, and other nonelementary schools, as well as instructors and professors of higher institutions. A person classified in one grade may receive a salary lower than the minimum specified for that grade. For instance, recent university graduates are appointed in grade six, for which the scheduled minimum salary is £E15, but may receive salaries as low as £E10, according to their qualifications and the available vacancies.

Within each grade, increments varying from £E1.5 in the lower grades to £E5 in the highest grade are granted periodically. At one time the interval was two years; later it was lengthened to four. If an increment is proposed for any shorter period, the case is referred to the Council of Ministers. In practice a large number of teachers went so long without promotion or increment that in 1943 what was known as the "law of the officials forgotten in their grades" was passed, stipulating that any officials who had not been promoted for fifteen years prior to 1943 should be promoted to the next grade. Personnel receiving a salary lower than that of their grade were to receive automatic increments every two years until they reached the minimum salary of their grade and proceed from that point at the normal rate.

In government service salaries are definitely linked with degrees and diplomas. Equal initial pay is given for equal qualifications whatever the department in which the official is appointed, and a single salary schedule prevails for men and women. Although lower salaries are paid when no vacancies at the appropriate level exist, the usual initial grades and salaries according to diplomas and degrees are as follows: bearers of the secondary-school certificate and of diplomas from intermediate vocational schools, eighth grade, £E7.5; diplomas from higher technical and other higher schools, sixth grade, £E10.5; B.A. or equivalent, sixth grade, £E12; M.A., sixth grade, £E13.5; diplomas from institutes of education, two years above B.A., sixth grade, £E15; doctorates, varying according to source, sixth grade, £E14–£E17.

In actual practice qualified primary-school teachers and headmasters occupy the sixth grade (£E15–£E25) and the fifth (£E25–£E35). Some have recently been promoted to the fourth grade or occupy this grade nominally while their salaries lag behind. Secondary-school teachers occupy the fourth, fifth, and sixth grades, and some headmasters of secondary schools have reached the third grade (£E45–£E60). Staff members of higher institutions and universities begin at the sixth-grade level, but if, during service, they receive higher academic degrees and rise to the posts of lecturers, assistant professors, and professors, they may hope to reach the first grade (£E75–£E90). Deans of faculties and chancellors of universities receive higher pay. Usually a dean may reach the rank equivalent to that of a director general at £E1,200–£E1,300 a year, and a chancellor, that of an under secretary of state at £E1,500.

Salaries of elementary-school teachers are lower. Previously an elementary-school teacher's pay ranged from £E3–£E6 a month; but in 1943, under a policy known as *insaf* (redress) all elementary teachers were supposed to have started at £E6 and were given retroactive compensation in a lump sum equal to the difference in pay for the whole period of their service. Head teachers of elementary schools may rise to £E10 a month. At present graduates of elementary training schools begin teaching at £E4.

Until 1930 government service of twenty-five years produced a pension equal to half the average salary of the last two years of service. With longer service an official could have a larger percentage of his salary up to a maximum of 75 percent. Since 1930 new appointments have been on the basis of a contract with the government; and on leaving government service, the official receives compensation of half a month's salary for each year of service. New appointees, therefore, with some exceptions, are no longer included in the pension scheme. The exceptions are admitted to it by special decision of the Council of Ministers, or are graduates of government missions abroad, or officials on the permanent staff of a provincial council who are transferred to government service. Elementary-school teachers contribute 5 percent of their monthly salaries to a provident fund to which the provincial councils or other employing authorities contribute an equal sum. The accumulated fund is given to teachers receiving honorable discharge from the service.

Educational Legislation

Three articles of the Egyptian Constitution adopted in 1923 deal directly with education: Article 17 guarantees the freedom of education within the limits of public security and morals; Article 18 specifies that educational affairs shall be regulated by law; and Article 19 stipulates that elementary education shall be compulsory for Egyptian boys and girls and shall be free in all public elementary schools (*maktabs*).

Elementary education is regulated by Law No. 46 of 1933, which defines "compulsory" education. All boys and girls of seven to twelve years of age must attend school. Six-year-old children may be admitted in preparation for primary schools or religious institutes. Exemptions are made for sick, disabled, and imbecile children, and for those who live farther than two kilometers (a mile and a quarter) from the nearest school. Parents are held responsible for the school attendance of their children and may be fined or imprisoned for evasion of this law.

The law of 1933 names the subjects of the elementary-school curriculum, including the memorization of the Koran, sets the weekly schedule at twenty-four periods of forty minutes each, and divides the day into two sessions, one for boys and one for girls. The school year is ten months. Teachers may be graduates of teacher-training schools for elementary-school teachers, al-Azhar colleges, and secondary schools. The law made provincial councils responsible for elementary education, subject to the instructions and hygienic inspection of the Ministry of Education, and laid down the terms of financial operations as previously described.[7] It stipulated that all elementary schools should be made public *maktabs* (compulsory half-day schools). Under the same law, nonelementary schools were removed from the control of the provincial councils.

The Law of Primary Education for Boys was enacted in 1928, with various subsequent amendments. Primary studies occupy four years. First-year pupils must not be less than seven or more than ten years of age at the time of admission; the age limit for second-year admissions is twelve; for third year, fourteen; and for fourth year, sixteen. Admission to the first year is granted on completion of the kindergarten course or by examinations in arithmetic and reading and writing of Arabic; admission to the other grades is by examination in the work of the previous year. The

[7] See pp. 14, 18.

law sets the number of weekly periods at thirty-eight and lists the subjects of instruction. Details of the curriculum are left to the Ministry of Education. The length of the school year and the distribution of hours among the subjects taught are decided by royal decree. Punishments are specified, corporal punishment being expressly forbidden. No pupil is allowed to repeat a year more than once. The Certificate of Completion of Primary Studies is awarded to pupils who pass the public primary examination.

Secondary education for boys is regulated by the frequently amended law of 1928. The five-year course consists of a general stage of four years and a final year of orientation during which the student elects work in one of three sections—the literary, the scientific, or the mathematical. No student above seventeen years of age is admitted to the first year of the secondary school, and no one above twenty-two years of age is permitted to stay in the fifth year. Admission to the first year is by Certificate of Completion of Primary Studies, and to the fifth year, by Secondary-School Certificate, General Section. Rules for exemption from fees are laid down, linking the exemption with the scholastic record of the student, on the one hand, and with his economic disability, on the other. Subjects to be taught are listed and permissible punishments specified. Rules of examinations for promotion from year to year and also for public examinations conducted at the conclusion of the fourth and fifth years are laid down. The public examination at the end of the fourth year leads to the Secondary-School Certificate, General Section, and that of the fifth year to the Secondary-School Certificate, Special Section. The latter mentions the particular section in which the student studied and his scholastic standing if his general average is 75 or above.

Free or private schools operate under a special law passed in 1934. This law defines free schools as private schools, complete or incomplete, which have as a basic aim the preparation of pupils for public examinations conducted by the Ministry of Education, and which give the Ministry the right to inspect and supervise them. The Ministry requires that sites and buildings be sanitary and prohibits the opening of schools in localities that might menace the morals of the pupils. It sets the qualifications of the teachers. Anyone wishing to open a private school must file an application with the Ministry three months before the proposed opening date. On the basis of information supplied, the Ministry may within a month object to the opening of the school. The school must follow a syllabus identical with that approved by the Ministry of Education for such studies as the syllabus covers, but the school may add other subjects to its program. The Ministry has power to impose three kinds of penalty upon teachers and officers of private schools: warning, partial disqualification,

ORGANIZATION AND ADMINISTRATION

and complete disqualification. The first is imposed by the Minister, the others being decided by a special disciplinary board formed for the purpose. The right of appeal is allowed. The law authorizes the Ministry to make grants-in-aid to free schools and to allow them to buy schoolbooks from the Ministry's stores. Grants-in-aid are subject to special ministerial decrees, one of which reserves for the Ministry the right to transfer a free-school teacher to another free school or to a government school.

These are the most important laws governing education in Egypt. Other laws regulate kindergarten education, commercial education in intermediate schools, and studies in the Higher Institute of Fine Arts. Dar al-'Ulum, the Institutes of Education for Men and Women, and certain other institutions are governed by ministerial decrees. Fuad I and Faruq I Universities operate under their own laws, which will be described in chapter 4.

The Educational Ladder

Chart II attempts to depict the public-school system in Egypt in such a way as to show the paths open to a student and the relationship between the various parts of the school system.

The Egyptian educational system is a two-ladder system with each ladder pursuing its own separate course. They may be referred to as the "elementary ladder" and the "primary-school ladder." At the bottom of the first are the elementary schools of various types, attended by the great majority of the children. This side of the national ladder does not prepare pupils for higher schools except for the comparatively small number going on to the religious schools of al-Azhar, a larger number who transfer to primary schools, and a few who go to vocational and elementary-teacher training schools. The other ladder, however, beginning with the primary schools and their attendant kindergartens, leads not only into various types of vocational and cultural schools, but also into the secondary schools, universities, and other higher institutions.

The elementary schools, being free of tuition, are attended by the children of the great masses of the Egyptian people. The primary schools have until recently been fee schools, as have the higher schools and colleges to which they lead, so that only the minority capable of paying fees could send their children to the primary schools. Thus the distribution of pupils between the two types of public schools has been on a class basis. It was in an effort to alleviate this situation that the Ministry of Education in 1943 abolished fees in primary schools and increased the number of free places in secondary schools with a view to ultimate abolition of fees at this level.

THE ELEMENTARY LADDER

The original elementary school in Egypt, shown in the middle of Chart II, evolved from the *kuttab,* the age-old Muslim ungraded school in which children learned the Koran and the rudiments of the "three R's." Only Egypt, of the six countries included in this report, has attempted to adapt this indigenous school to modern requirements. The other Arab countries, considering it inadequate for modern purposes, paid little attention to it and started new types of schools on the Western model. Since 1869, when the Ministry of Education began inspecting the *kuttabs,* many changes have been introduced until now the course of four years includes not only the study and memorization of the Koran, religion, and the fundamentals of reading, writing, and arithmetic, but also the study of object lessons (general science), hygiene, geography, drawing, history, elements of geometry, ethics and civics, physical education, and "children's activities," and needlework for girls. The schools are graded and have better physical facilities and teachers than was true in the old *kuttabs.* This type of school (*maktab*) is now the standard elementary school in Egypt.

A second type of elementary school was devised in 1925 in order to meet the constitutional requirement of compulsory free elementary education. This was a half-day school of six, and later five, years which reduced the costs of education by using the same physical facilities and teachers in a session in the mornings for boys and in the afternoons for girls, or the reverse. It was thought that parental support of the program would be greater if the children were available for work in the fields for one-half of each day. A great deal of enthusiasm, energy, and money was spent in opening a large number of these schools between 1925 and 1940. More than 3,000 such schools were opened, involving about 900,000 children. However, the plan has not worked well, and this school is being replaced by full-time schools.

A third type of elementary school, offering a six-year course, was established in 1943. This is the rural elementary school designed to provide rural children with a type of education suited to their environment and future needs. In the period 1943–45, 78 of these schools were opened, but no new ones were established in 1945–46.

Thus, it is seen that elementary education, in contrast to primary education, is offered in three types of schools providing programs of four-, five-, and six-year length. All are free of tuition charges and are attended by children of the masses. Their common points are two: the stress on religion and the "three R's," and the omission of a foreign language from their programs.

Chart II

EGYPT: THE PUBLIC SCHOOL SYSTEM, 1945–46

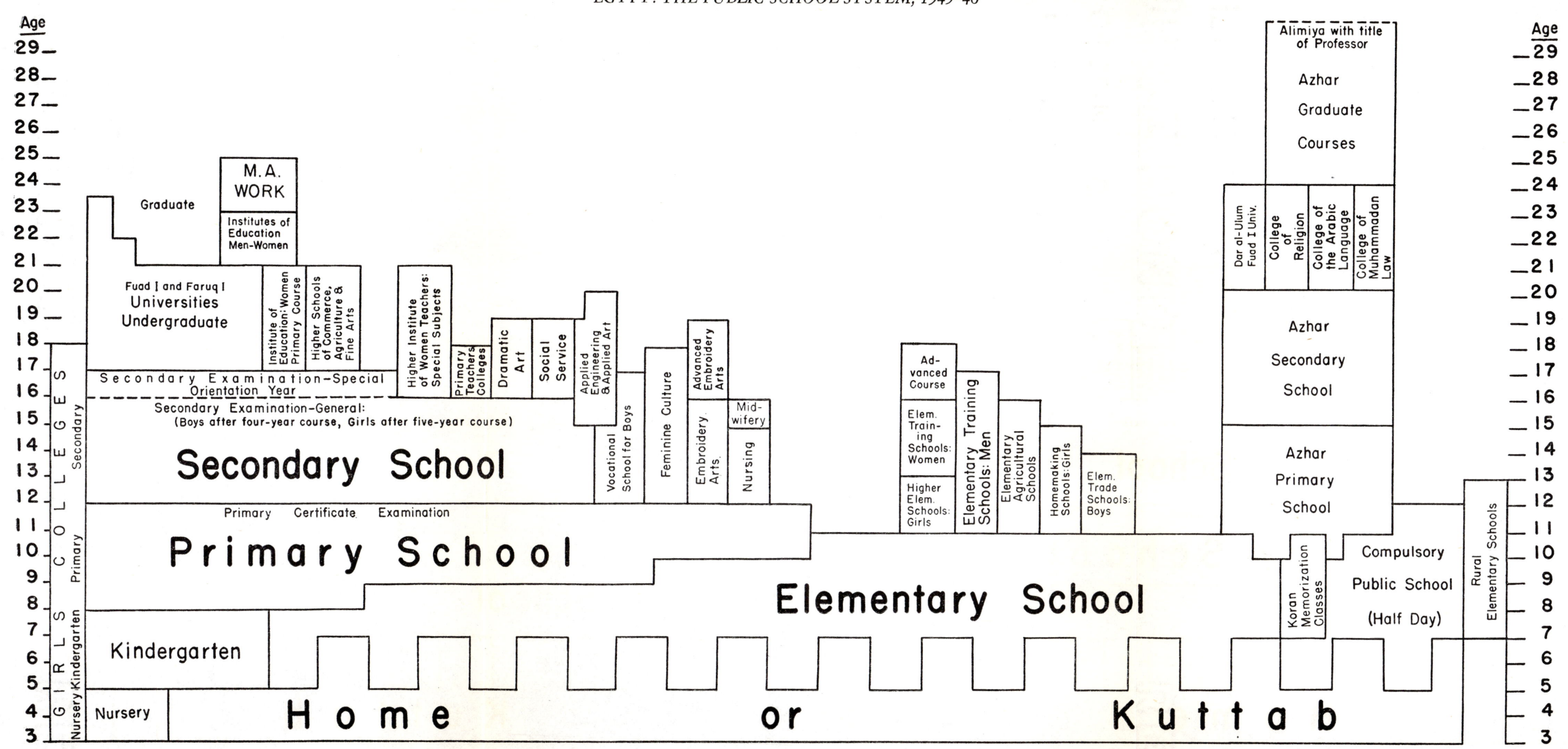

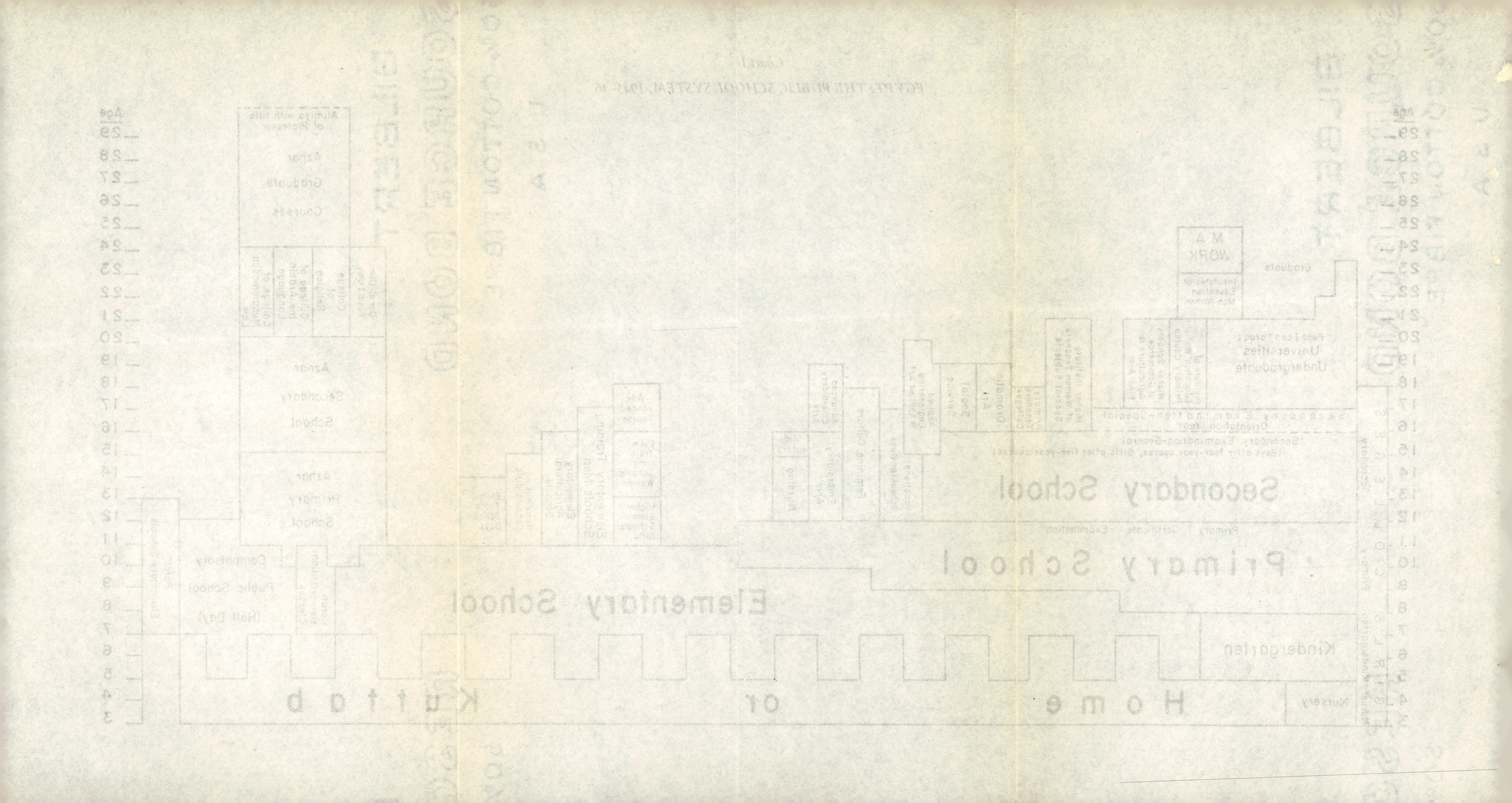

The opportunities of further education for those who attend elementary schools are limited. Some pupils after two or more years in elementary schools may transfer to primary schools if successful in entrance examinations administered by the primary school. Graduates of elementary schools may enter an elementary vocational school (either an agricultural or a trade school for the boys, a homemaking school for the girls), or many enter a teacher-training school for elementary-school teachers. Others may be admitted to the religious institutions affiliated with or preparing for the University of al-Azhar—a possibility if they can read and write and have memorized the entire Koran. The combined primary and secondary courses in the al-Azhar system are nine years in length, after which successful students may enter the University to specialize in Arabic, Muslim religion or law, or enter Dar al-'Ulum, where teachers of Arabic for primary and secondary schools are prepared. The great majority of pupils, however, either drop out before completing the elementary school or seek no further education after its completion.

Certain other activities are included in the elementary-school system. There are evening classes for workers conducted on school premises. The Ministry of Education conducts 81 of these with 2,544 pupils, while 87 with 3,137 students are operated by provincial councils. There are 1,066 classes with 28,000 pupils in which memorization of the Koran is the important activity. Of these, only 18 with 654 pupils are conducted by the Ministry, the rest being under the direction of the provincial councils. Finally, there are 7 institutions for the blind, caring for 207 pupils—5 institutions with 161 pupils are maintained by the Ministry and the other 2, by private associations.

The primary-school ladder

The primary-school ladder, beginning with the kindergarten and ending with the university, has developed through foreign influences, principally French. It was created during the reign of Muhammad 'Ali, in the 1830's, in order to meet the needs of his expanding army and navy as well as the needs of civil administration.

The steps in the ladder are a kindergarten, usually of three years, a primary school of four years, a secondary school of five years, and higher institutions, including the universities, of four to six and a half years.

The kindergartens, existing mainly in the large cities, accept boys and girls of five years of age and prepare them for entrance to the primary school at the age of eight. Since there are too few kindergartens to provide for all who wish to enter the primary schools, village and town elementary schools serve as kindergartens or preparatory schools for primary schools. The last two years of kindergarten in Egypt are similar to the first two years of primary schools in most countries. Fees are charged in kindergartens.

The primary school in Egypt is not a school for beginners. Pupils who enter the first grade are expected to be able to read and write and to solve elementary problems in arithmetic. Two or three years of study in a kindergarten or elementary school are necessary to meet the standard set for admission to the primary school. The four-year primary school program lays emphasis on language (both Arabic and foreign), mathematics, and science. Postponement of the beginning of a foreign language from the first to the second year, which was promulgated in 1939, and then to the third year, as revised in 1945, has made transfer possible from the upper years of the elementary school to advanced standing in the primary school. Since 1943 tuition fees have not been charged in any public primary schools or in many private schools. Success in the public examination given at the end of the fourth year is a requirement for entrance to the secondary school.

The secondary school, the next step in the ladder for primary-school graduates, is divided into two parts: the first part, or general course, continues for four years for boys and five years for girls and ends with a public examination (*thaqafah*). The second part, or orientation course, one year for both boys and girls, provides for a choice of specialization in literary, scientific, or mathematical studies, and ends with a second examination (*khas*). The programs for boys and girls are essentially the same except that home economics and child care are added for the girls, thus requiring an additional year in the first, or general, course. Not only must candidates pass the examinations to continue their education, but also choice of the specialization in the last year of a secondary school or admission to a particular part of the university is dependent upon rank in the examinations. Fees are charged in secondary schools, but approximately one-third of the pupils are exempt either because they do superior work or because they are in need of financial assistance to continue their study.

If a boy graduating from a primary school wishes a more practical type of training than the secondary school provides, he may be admitted to an intermediate vocational school. Separate schools are provided, each with a five-year course, to prepare pupils for trades, commercial employment, or agricultural work. The first two years in all these schools parallel the corresponding years of the secondary school. This enables pupils to transfer from a vocational school to a secondary school, or vice versa, during the first two years.

ORGANIZATION AND ADMINISTRATION

Girls may enter a three-year nursing course, or a four-year vocational school of embroidery arts followed by an advanced course of three years, or go to a six-year feminine culture school which combines cultural and academic subjects with home economics and child care.

It is possible to leave the secondary school one or two years before graduation to enter some other type of school. After three years a boy may enter the School of Applied Engineering or the School of Applied Art, in either of which he takes a five-year course. Both boys and girls may change at the end of the general stage (next-to-the-last year) of the secondary school to enter the School of Dramatic Art or the School of Social Service, both three-year courses. In addition, boys may enter the new primary-teacher training colleges, opened in the fall of 1945, to prepare in two years to be teachers in the new program of expansion of primary education. Girls may enter the Higher Institute for Women Teachers in Cairo and, after four years of study, graduate as teachers of art, music, home economics, or physical education for primary or secondary schools.

For the graduate of the full secondary course there is a wide range of opportunity for further training. He may enter the one-year course of the school of telegraphy or the three-year course of the police or military colleges. Four-year higher institutions admitting holders of the secondary-school certificate are the Higher School of Agriculture, the Higher School of Finance and Commerce, the Higher School of Fine Arts, and the Institutes of Education for Men or for Women (which prepare teachers for primary schools). Finally, graduates may enter one of the two universities—Fuad I, in Cairo, and Faruq I, in Alexandria, where they may specialize in arts, sciences, agriculture, commerce, law, engineering, veterinary medicine, medicine, pharmacy, or dentistry. Courses in these specializations vary in length from four to six and one-half years. Opportunity is provided for postgraduate work in the professional fields or in preparing to teach in one of the Institutes of Education.

The brief description given above furnishes a picture of the variety of opportunities available for boys and girls in the public-school system of Egypt and the pathways by which they can be reached. Some special provisions involving relatively few pupils have been omitted. More details of these provisions will be given in the chapters which follow.

Recent Trends

The enthusiastic pursuit of the compulsory-education plan and the opening of thousands of schools between 1925 and 1935 to provide free education for the masses constitute ample evidence of the growing awareness among the ruling and educated classes of Egypt that a modern state cannot afford to let the great majority of its people remain illiterate. However, by 1940 it had become apparent that the plan was not working too well. Not only was the Ministry of Education having to compensate for the inability of the provincial councils to support their share of the expense, but the teaching results were generally unsatisfactory. It was realized that children were too tired to concentrate on lessons after a half-day of hard work in the fields, teachers working a double shift were too tired to be thoroughly competent, and the schooling offered in half-day sessions for a five-year period of erratic attendance was too meager to be effective.

Accordingly in 1940 a ministerial committee under the chairmanship of the Under Secretary of State for Education was formed to study the problem. The existing dual system of education, maintaining, on the one hand, a high standard and leading to the highest stages of culture for the privileged few, and, on the other hand, a minimum-essentials program just barely above illiteracy for the great masses of the people, was recognized to be neither just to the individual nor to the best interests of the nation, since it deprived the nation of utilization of the abilities inherent in its economically handicapped but intelligent youth. The committee reported that the aim of compulsory education should be, not the mere elimination of illiteracy, but the preparation of the masses for a good national life; that effort must be made to unify within a reasonable period the programs of elementary and primary education so that a common foundation of a national culture can be established and a gateway to higher stages of education opened to all children who have ability; that the compulsory-elementary education course should be lengthened within a reasonable period—say, fifteen years—from five to six years; and that the compulsory half-day school should become a full-day school. The committee recommended further that the curriculum of the elementary school be adapted to the needs of the local environment in the last two grades, and that a midday meal be provided gratis.

Unification of the primary and elementary ladders did not materialize, but steps were taken to carry out three of the committee's recommendations: The first, the decision to make full-day schools out of half-day schools, is well on its way to completion. The second, the provision of free midday meals to pupils of the compulsory schools, has not only improved the health of the children but also increased attendance. Together these steps have effected improved teaching and better pupil response to teaching. The third step was the establishment of the six-year rural schools.

In 1943 a fourth step was taken toward the goal of a unified school

ORGANIZATION AND ADMINISTRATION

system. The Minister of Education, al-Hilali Pasha, influenced by current reports from England and America on postwar educational reconstruction, decided to abolish fees in primary schools and to make more free places available in the secondary schools. He ordered schools to admit pupils on the basis of their achievement in their examinations in numbers that would fill all vacant places without regard to fees. After admitting pupils on a basis of academic standing, the school authorities should look into requests for exemption from fees and thus find out empirically what the proportion of free places would be. In this way no school refused a poor student because he was poor or admitted a rich one because he was rich; the principle of equality of opportunity was established, and a way for the brighter pupil, rich or poor, to reach the top of the educational ladder was facilitated.

This decision had two very important outcomes. In the first place it brought most of the private schools within the orbit of the public-school system. Since the private schools owed their existence to fees paid by their pupils, they could not hope to compete with government schools once the latter had abolished all fees from the primary schools and increased free attendance at the secondary level. The Ministry, however, agreed to compensate private schools for loss of fees if the private schools abolished fees entirely from primary schools, increased the number of free places in secondary schools and granted the Ministry of Education the right to move teachers from one private school to another or from a private school to a public school. The private schools were in no position to refuse, and, as most of them had been following the government program of study for some time past, they became, with the abolition of fees, virtually a part of the national system of education.

The other outcome—which in the long run may be the more far-reaching—was the great influx of pupils into the government primary and secondary schools. Once the financial barrier to primary schools was eliminated, it was only natural that parents who had previously sent their children to elementary schools should send them to the primary schools where instruction was better and opportunities for advancement up the educational ladder were unlimited. In fact, the demand made on the primary schools was so great that despite the opening of many new classes and new schools and filling classes beyond their capacity, it was estimated that about 10,000 eligible children could not be admitted because of lack of space. One writer, in discussing this congestion, points out that the abolition of fees changed the primary school from its status of school for the few to that of school for the people as a whole, and prophesies that the demand for its benefits will increase to such a degree that the logical outcome will be the ultimate extinction of the elementary ladder. He therefore argues that the abolition of fees makes the unification of the primary and elementary ladders a necessity.[8] He is probably right. Certainly, with the abolition of fees an accomplished fact, it would be impossible for the Ministry to go back on this popular move and attempt to reinstate primary-school fees. The only apparent solution to the problem of primary-school congestion seems to be some means of unifying the primary and elementary schools.

Since 1943 the Ministry of Education and Egyptian educators in general have been wrestling with this problem. It is a triple problem: the financial burden involved, the length of the compulsory common school—closely connected with the question of finance—and the teaching of a foreign language.

It was estimated that there were in 1945 approximately 2,500,000 boys and girls in the six-to-twelve age group in Egypt and that this number would increase to 3,700,000 by 1970, the year set for realization of the goal of having all children in this age group in school. However, the estimated cost per annum of primary education would at that time be £E37,000,000, about 40 percent of the present total budget of the Egyptian government. It was in an effort to reduce this heavy burden that one authority proposed dividing primary and secondary education into three stages of four years each for children of six to eighteen years of age. The first stage, for children of ages six to ten, would be compulsory; two higher grades would be added in as many rural schools as possible. This scheme would reduce the 1970 cost of the compulsory stage to about £E26,000,000,[9] a sum that is more conceivable since it is only double the educational budget forecast for 1946–47.

Two other virtues are claimed for the scheme. It would postpone the necessity of choosing a career until the age of fourteen—after the completion of the middle school. It also would make it possible to start the first foreign language at the age of eleven, instead of thirteen—as would be the case if the primary school were lengthened to six years—and the second foreign language could be started at fifteen, that is, at the commencement of the third stage (fifteen-to-eighteen age group). Furthermore, the scheme provides that rural children who finish the higher years—at about the age of twelve—may enter either vocational or other schools offering two- or three-year courses or the third year of the middle school.

---

[8] Isma'il Qabbani, *Memorandum on the General Policy for the Expansion of Education in Egypt* (Mimeographed; Cairo: 1945), pp. 19–24. (In Arabic.)
[9] *Ibid.*, p. 25.

ORGANIZATION AND ADMINISTRATION

Children finishing the middle school at about fourteen might then enter an academic secondary school, a vocational secondary school, or a teacher-training school.

This scheme has not found favor in educational circles or in the Ministry, however. A committee of the Conference on Educational Policy held by the Teachers Association in November 1945 offered the following criticism of the scheme: four years of compulsory schooling do not prepare the child to lead a better modern life; such schooling is hardly sufficient to teach the "three R's," and some of the children would doubtless revert to illiteracy within a few years. Furthermore, the committee feared that the plan would result in a lowering of the present standard of education.[10]

In the opinion of the committee the principal defect of the present system of education lies in the fact that compulsory and elementary schools cut off the education of the children at a very rudimentary stage, whereas the kindergarten and primary schools lead the children on to higher stages of education. The committee found the following essential differences between these two types of schools: (1) the primary school teaches a foreign language and the compulsory and elementary schools do not; (2) the primary schools are better equipped; and (3) the primary school benefits by better-trained teachers and more effective supervision. The following recommendations were made: (1) the first stage of education should accommodate children from six to twelve years of age; (2) all education in this stage should be unified, due allowance being made for environmental differences; (3) foreign-language teaching should be abolished or at least made elective, so that it could not be made a condition of entry into the next stage; and (4) equipment, standard of training of teachers, and supervision in the compulsory and elementary schools should be improved.[11]

A second committee of the conference studied the general organization of the educational scheme. Beginning with the six-year compulsory school, it considered that about 65 percent of the children graduating from this school would want to go to work and that these should be provided with popular means of education through clubs, evening classes, radio educational programs, and public libraries. Of the remaining 35 percent, it was estimated that about half would enter religious, vocational, homemaking, or teacher-training schools for elementary-school teachers; the other half would enter the middle school of two years with a flexible program de-

---

[10] Teachers Association, *Report of the New Education Fellowship on the First Stage of Education:* Presented to the General Conference on the Consideration of Educational Policy (Cairo: the Association, 1945), pp. 7–9. (In Arabic.)
[11] *Ibid.*, pp. 10–11.

signed to discover their aptitudes. At the end of this phase, the pupils with practical bent might proceed at the age of fourteen to vocational schools; from these, the better students might proceed, after four years, to higher vocational and technical schools. The other pupils leaving the middle school might continue their secondary education till graduation at about seventeen and proceed to higher technical schools, the university, or primary and higher teacher-training institutions, from which they could go on to graduate study or to institutes of professional education.[12]

The recommendation submitted by the Ministry of Education to the Higher Education Council in December 1945 showed the influence of the Teachers Association. They endorsed the idea of the compulsory six-year school for children of six to twelve years of age and the omission of a foreign language from the program of this school. It was recommended that the present primary schools be maintained, with a foreign language taught from the third year, on the grounds that alteration would deprive the country of a good type of schooling and omission of the foreign language at this level would lower the standard of secondary education. The Ministry recommended that teachers for the compulsory schools should be trained in schools giving a five-year course above the six-year elementary school; that control of elementary schools should be taken from the provincial councils and transferred to a special committee in each province or governorate, headed by the director of education and composed of prominent education officers, some parliamentary representatives of the province, and other individuals interested in education. The recommendations included a proposal for reorganizing the secondary school, the first two years of which should be general, ending in a public examination, and the remaining years would be divided into an academic course of literary and scientific sections, leading to the university, and a modern or practical—though nonvocational—course. Students in the literary section would work in a language group which included Arabic and two foreign languages, a social-studies group, and a philosophy group; scientific-section students would have a language group, a science group, and a mathematics group. Advanced classes in some subjects would be given for elective specialization. Studies in the modern section would consist of a language group, a technical group (with courses in manual arts, mechanics, commerce, gardening, music, and art), and a choice of two out of three of the following groups: social studies, mathematics, and science. Public examina-

[12] Teachers Association, *Report of the Second Study Committee:* Presented to the General Conference on the Consideration of Educational Policy (Cairo: the Association, 1945), p. 13. (In Arabic.)

ORGANIZATION AND ADMINISTRATION

tions would conclude the courses of all sections. Students in the modern section who passed the public examination would qualify for admission to the higher technical institutes and, if they obtained high marks in the subjects connected with the "Faculty"[13] they wish to enter, they could enter the university. The length of the course in both sections in this proposed secondary school would be the same for boys and for girls.

The Higher Education Council referred the proposals to a special committee of its members under the chairmanship of a former Prime Minister and Minister of Education.

After a century of a dual ladder in education, Egypt is now working toward a single ladder rising from a free common school.

Growth and Status of Education in Egypt

Table 3 gives information relative to the status of education in Egypt in 1944–45. Data for the year 1913–14 are included for purposes of comparison. It will be seen that the total number in all types of schools has nearly trebled in the thirty-one years. Most of the gain in absolute numbers has occurred in elementary and compulsory schools, as is to be expected since compulsory elementary education was introduced in this period. The relative increases in secondary schools (nearly seven times) and in higher schools (more than seven times) are more conspicuous and probably more significant. An analysis of detailed statistics for 1942–43 (Table 4) shows that nearly half of the total number of pupils in compulsory half-day schools were in the first year, while 77 percent were in the first two years. In 1942–43 there were 410,856 boys and girls in the first year, although at the same time there were only 9,663 in the fifth, or last, year. This would indicate that a considerable number of the total pupils enrolled in compulsory schools are receiving only one or two years of half-day schooling.

Analysis of data for the same year, 1942–43, reveals that a different situation existed in primary schools. The numbers enrolled in the second and third years were slightly greater than in the first year, showing the effect of transfer of pupils from elementary schools to primary schools. In general, in both primary and secondary schools pupils apparently continue in school till the end of the course. An analysis of the progress of individuals would be necessary to be sure of this point, and records were not available to make such an analysis.

---

[13] As in French education, a term used to designate a part of a university. Equivalent to the term "college" in American education.

TABLE 3
Number of and Enrollment in Public, Private, and Foreign Schools in Egypt, 1913–14 and 1944–45*

Schools	1913–14 Number of Schools	1913–14 Boys	1913–14 Girls	1913–14 Total	1944–45 Number of Schools	1944–45 Boys	1944–45 Girls	1944–45 Total
Elementary and compulsory:								
Public	3,669	205,944	26,514	232,458	3,985	476,835	418,254	895,089
Private	3,577	87,250	4,666	91,916	737	79,525	31,800	111,325
Foreign	...	...	...	...	...†	2,777	1,252	4,029
Total	7,246	293,194	31,180	324,374	4,722	559,137	451,306	1,010,443
Kindergarten and primary:								
Public	94	11,810	2,168	13,978	216	48,319	11,620	59,939
Private	615	52,358	13,735	66,093	400	56,978	31,353	88,331
Foreign	302	21,615	19,896	41,511	...†	33,627‡	12,678	46,305
Total	1,011	85,783	35,799	121,582	616	138,924‡	55,651	194,575
Secondary:								
Public	6	2,532	...	2,532	53	33,322	3,332	36,654
Private	5	2,238	14	2,252	74	13,513	893	14,406
Foreign	10	2,859	1,467	4,326	...†	6,298	5,032	11,330
Total	21	7,629	1,481	9,110	127	53,133	9,257	62,390
Vocational, special, and teacher training:								
Public	45	5,124	594	5,718	136	16,940	8,762	25,702
Private	12	878	220	1,098	22	184	1,875	2,059
Foreign	11	1,820	125	1,945	...†	1,582	789	2,371
Total	68	7,822	939	8,761	158	18,706	11,426	30,132
Higher schools:								
Public	8	1,554	...	1,554	11	14,035	1,040	15,075
Private	1	70	...	70	...	...	...	...
Foreign	1	410	...	410	...†	14	...	14
Total	10	2,034	...	2,034	11	14,049	1,040	15,089
Religious: primary, secondary, higher:								
Public	354	21,608	...	21,608	1§	14,023	...	14,023
Private	...	...	...	...	...	...	...	...
Foreign	1	12	...	12	...	...	...	...
Total	355	21,620	...	21,620	1§	14,023	...	14,023
Total:								
Public	4,176	248,572	29,276	277,848	4,402	603,474	443,008	1,046,482
Private	4,210	142,794	18,635	161,429	1,233	150,200	65,921	216,121
Foreign	325	26,716	21,488	48,204	289†	44,298‡	19,751	64,049
Grand Total	8,711	418,082	69,399	487,481	5,924	797,972‡	528,680	1,326,652

* Data for 1913–14 summarized from Amin Sami Pasha, *Education in Egypt*, pp. 113 and 115. For 1944–45 data supplied by the Ministry of Education, Cairo, but not including police and military colleges and the School of Calligraphy and Archeological Culture enrolling 1,365 students; 168 evening classes attended by 5,681 workers; 1,048 classes for the memorization of the Koran, with 28,000 pupils; and 7 schools for the blind, with 207 boys and 56 girls.
† The total number of foreign schools was not distributed as to type.
‡ Includes 20,768 kindergarten children in foreign schools unclassified as to sex.
§ The University of al-Azhar, which administers a number of units.

TABLE 4

DISTRIBUTION OF PUPILS BY GRADE IN PUBLIC SCHOOLS (COMPULSORY, PRIMARY, SECONDARY) IN EGYPT, 1940–41 AND 1942–43*

| GRADES | ENROLLMENT IN 1940–41 |||| | ENROLLMENT IN 1942–43 ||||
| | Boys || Girls || | Boys || Girls ||
	Number	Percent†	Number	Percent†		Number	Percent†	Number	Percent†
Compulsory elementary schools:									
1st grade	216,177	40.8	211,631	47.8		211,442	44.5	199,414	48.5
2nd grade	151,819	28.5	136,282	26.7		128,461	26.9	115,716	28.0
3rd grade	103,716	19.5	81,167	17.6		88,916	18.6	69,972	16.9
4th grade	49,632	9.3	29,334	6.4		41,421	8.6	24,037	5.8
5th grade	9,557	1.8	4,801	1.0		6,743	1.4	2,920	0.7
Total	530,901	...	463,215	...		476,983	...	412,059	...
Primary schools:									
1st year	4,027	16.8	622	17.6		6,306	22.0	1,029	22.7
2nd year	6,068	25.7	1,058	30.7		6,910	24.6	1,339	29.9
3rd year	7,844	33.2	1,094	31.1		7,563	26.9	1,226	27.0
4th year	5,651	23.9	744	21.1		7,339	26.1	939	20.7
Total	23,590	...	3,518	...		28,118	...	4,533	...
Secondary schools:									
1st year	5,301	25.9	426	25.3		6,775	28.9	650	29.9
2nd year	4,017	19.6	309	18.3		4,581	19.2	427	19.6
3rd year	4,002	19.6	318	18.7		4,215	17.6	336	15.5
4th year	3,564	17.4	243	14.4		3,734	15.6	293	13.5
5th year	3,562	17.4	250	14.7		4,538	19.0	246	11.3
6th year‡	...	...	137	7.1		...	...	220	10.1
Total	20,446	...	1,683	...		23,843	...	2,172	...

* Figures compiled from Ministry of Education, *Statistics of the Number of Classes and Pupils in Schools of the Various Types of Education* (Cairo: Government Press, 1941 and 1944) for 1940–41, pp. 4, 46–49, and for 1942–43, pp. 4, 62–65.
Distribution of enrollment by grades for elementary (full-time) schools was not available.
† Percent is found by dividing the number of boys or girls in each grade or year by the total enrollment of boys or girls in each school.
‡ The secondary school for boys requires five years; for girls, six years.

The reduction in the total number of schools (Table 3) is explained partly by a difference in method of tabulation, and partly by the consolidation of the schools. In its tabulation, the Ministry of Education does not seem to include certain types of schools, notably some schools that are of the nature of *kuttabs,* which figure prominently in the 1913-14 statistics, or such a higher school as the French School of Law in Cairo. On the other hand, schools with more than one unit are counted as one school each, while formerly each unit was counted as one.

However, the policy was followed of consolidating elementary schools. The opening of compulsory schools by the Ministry of Education and the local councils resulted in the elimination of a large number of *kuttabs,* which were so numerous in 1913-14. Thus, a great increase in elementary-school enrollment took place in spite of the decrease in the number of schools. In 1913 the average elementary-school enrollment was 62 for public and 25 for private schools—the latter being old-style *kuttabs,* and the former, *kuttabs* improved by government control, supervision, and aid. By 1945 average attendance in public elementary schools had risen to 222, and in private elementary schools to 151 pupils.

Table 3 clearly shows the increase in the number of girls attending school in 1944-45 as compared to 1913-14. The number in elementary schools was nearly fifteen times greater in 1944-45 than in the earlier year; the girls in kindergartens and primary schools more than one-half greater; the girls in secondary schools more than six times greater; and the number in vocational, special, and teacher-training schools was more than ten times greater. There were no women in higher institutions in 1913-14, while in 1944-45 there were 1,040. It will be noticed that there were no public secondary schools for girls at the earlier date, while in 1944-45 there were 3,332 girls enrolled.

The number of pupils in foreign primary and secondary schools has increased, but the change has been relatively less than in either the public or private schools. This is particularly noticeable in the primary and secondary schools. It is not clear as yet what effect the abolition of fees in public and many private schools will have upon the enrollment in foreign primary schools.

The apparent reduction in number of students in religious institutions requires some explanation. Inspection of detailed tables shows that the enrollment in higher sections of al-Azhar had more than doubled from 1913 to 1943 (1,876 to 3,935), and secondary-school pupils had increased about 50 percent (6,249 to 9,469) in the same period. The reorganization of al-Azhar University during this interval has resulted in graded sections

ORGANIZATION AND ADMINISTRATION

and an increase in enrollments in the secondary and higher years. The reduction in numbers is entirely in the earlier stage. Public elementary schools and classes for the memorization of the Koran (enrollment, 27,381 in 1942–43) have taken over much of the elementary religious education formerly carried on by al-Azhar.

TEACHERS

In 1942–43 there was a total of 49,170 teachers in all the schools of Egypt, of whom 27,953, or 56.8 percent, were in elementary schools and 21,127, or 43.2 percent, were in schools and educational institutions other than elementary. Table 5 gives the distribution of teachers in schools of all types according to qualifications in the year 1942–43. In the same year there was a total of 1,479,649 pupils in Egypt of whom 1,178,913, or 79.6 percent, were in elementary schools and 300,736, or 20.4 percent, in schools other than elementary. Thus, in the elementary schools about 57 percent of the teachers teach about 80 percent of all the pupils of all the country, while in the nonelementary schools 43 percent of the teachers teach only 20 percent of all the pupils of the country. While the elementary-school teacher teaches an average of 42 pupils, the nonelementary teacher teaches only 14, showing an uneven distribution of the teachers in favor of what was termed the primary ladder. This situation is further accentuated by the much higher standard of education for the teachers of this ladder as compared with that of the teachers of elementary schools.

The total of 49,170 teachers in all types of schools in 1942–43 was two and one-quarter times the number in 1913–14. In the later year 19 percent were women as compared to 9 percent in 1913–14. In 1942–43 only 1,524 out of 24,549 public elementary-school teachers were teaching without diplomas, and 1,912 had diplomas but did not have professional training. Private elementary-school teachers were not as well prepared, since 60 percent were teaching without diplomas of any kind.

Of the total of 21,217 teachers of schools other than elementary, only 1,628, or 7.6 percent, are teaching without any form of diploma. The public schools have a better standing, with only 3.5 percent of the teachers without diplomas. Foreign schools are next, with 8.2 percent lacking diplomas; and private schools are lowest, with 14 percent without diplomas.

The following data, supplied by the personnel department of the Ministry of Education, show the training of public primary-school teachers in 1945–46. Of 2,414 teachers in public primary schools 1,402, or 58 percent, were graduates of higher institutions. Not included among these is a

TABLE 5
Teachers in Egyptian Schools, 1942–43*

Type of School	Holding Diploma Male	Holding Diploma Female	Holding Diploma Total	No Diploma Male	No Diploma Female	No Diploma Total	Total Male	Total Female	Total Total
Teachers in Nonelementary Schools									
Public schools									
Ministry of Education	5,775	1,736	7,511	198	78	276	5,973	1,814	7,787
Fuad and Faruq Universities	944	8	952	...	...	...	944	8	952
Religious institutions	897	...	897	8	...	8	905	...	905
Other government institutions	486	121	607	61	9	70	547	130	677
Total, public schools	8,102	1,865	9,967	267	87	354	8,369	1,952	10,321
Private schools	4,295	1,201	5,496	640	264	904	4,935	1,465	6,400
Foreign schools									
French	942	1,102	2,044	27	93	120	969	1,195	2,164
British	188	332	520	34	39	73	222	371	593
Greek	264	195	459	28	59	87	292	254	546
American	148	284	432	35	39	74	183	323	506
Italian	324	234	558	3	8	11	327	242	569
Other nationalities	56	57	113	2	3	5	58	60	118
Total, foreign schools	1,922	2,204	4,126	129	241	370	2,051	2,445	4,496
Total, nonelementary schools	14,319	5,270	19,589	1,036	592	1,628	15,355	5,862	21,217
Teachers in Elementary Schools									
Government, Council-aided	19,967	3,058	23,025	1,046	478	1,524	21,013	3,536	24,549
Private unaided schools	1,282	123	1,405	1,890	109	1,999	3,172	232	3,404
Total, elementary teachers	21,249	3,181	24,430	2,936	587	3,523	24,185	3,768	27,953
Grand total, all teachers	35,568	8,451	44,019	3,972	1,179	5,151	39,540	9,630	49,170

* From *Statistique Scolaire, 1942–43* (Cairo: Imprimerie Nationale, Egyptian Government, Ministry of Finance, Statistical Dept., 1945), pp. 182–221 and 266–69.

ORGANIZATION AND ADMINISTRATION

large number of graduates of quasi-higher institutions such as the School of Applied Engineering and the Khedivial Training College. Among the 2,414 there were 1,328, or 55 percent, who had professional training in education. Teachers having only a secondary-school certificate or less constitute a minority among primary-school teachers. The Egyptian educational authorities have for some time approved the principle of higher education for primary-school teachers. Graduates of the old Higher Training College and of its successor, the Institute of Education, ordinarily had their first appointments in primary schools. After some years of experience at that level the better teachers were transferred to the secondary schools. Graduates in science and mathematics, being fewer relatively, were usually appointed directly to the secondary schools. This plan of providing experience in the primary school before they were assigned to the secondary school worked well as long as primary and secondary schools were on a restricted basis, but with the rapid expansion of primary schools in the last few years and with the plans for further expansion of primary education to include all types of education in the elementary or "first stage," the plan became inadequate. Therefore, in 1945–46 a new program for training primary-school teachers was begun which allowed students who passed the public secondary-school examination in general culture (end of the fourth year for boys) to receive two years of professional and academic training in a special teacher-training school. Three of these institutions were opened in 1945–46, and more are being planned.

Chapter 2

PUBLIC EDUCATION FOR CHILDREN BELOW SECONDARY-SCHOOL AGE

A VARIETY of institutions which are partially or completely supported and controlled by national or provincial governmental agencies provide education at all levels below the secondary school. The elementary ladder includes the following very different types: *kuttabs,* compulsory half-day schools, elementary schools, schools for the memorization of the Koran, and rural elementary schools. The primary ladder is made up of nursery schools, kindergartens, and primary schools.

Kuttabs

The *kuttab* represents early attempts to provide beginning education for Arab boys who were destined to receive training as religious leaders. It is administered by a *shaykh* who collects fees from pupils, receives grants from religious endowments and subsidies from public funds. Boys are admitted at the age of four or younger and continue for two to four years before being transferred to one of the other types of elementary school, either religious or secular. The *kuttab* is usually a one-room school in which boys of all levels of progress are grouped together. Emphasis is placed on memorizing the Koran, and each individual progresses at his own rate. Some elementary arithmetic may be taught. Pupils study aloud and at intervals are called before the teacher to recite portions of the Koran. Boys sit on benches or at desks and study with the accompaniment of a rocking motion of the body. It is a noisy school although this apparently does not disturb the pupils. The school is not considered a satisfactory type of school for beginners and is being replaced by compulsory elementary schools, kindergartens, and modern schools for the memorization of the Koran, which offer a wider curriculum than the *kuttab.*

Compulsory Half-Day Schools

Compulsory elementary schools were established in 1925–26 to eliminate illiteracy quickly and at low cost to the government. They are free

Above: Main building of the School of Applied Engineering, Cairo, Egypt
Below: The elementary school for the village of Manayil, Egypt. (Photo by Zareh Tashjian, USIS, Cairo.)

Above: A kindergarten band practicing out-of-doors, Heliopolis, Egypt
Below: Upper classmen on the steps of the entrance to the assembly hall of the American College for Girls, Cairo

PUBLIC EDUCATION BELOW THE SECONDARY SCHOOL

half-day schools of five years for children from seven to twelve years of age, with the same staff and building serving boys in the morning and girls in the afternoon, or vice versa. The curriculum includes reading, writing, arithmetic, hygiene, religion, and drawing. Little instructional material is provided, teachers are poorly trained for their work, and the product of the school is admittedly of low standard. The school is usually housed in a rented building consisting of a series of rooms opening upon a porch or a small play area. Pupils sit on benches which are generally attached to desks; three to six pupils commonly use a desk designed for two. The door is usually left open to allow more light than is provided by the one or two small windows. Teachers are generally assigned by grade or year—with the possible exception of special teachers for drawing. This type of school is not considered successful and is rapidly being replaced by the full-day elementary school. In 1944–45 there were 2,698 public compulsory schools with 639,391 pupils—333,321 boys and 306,070 girls.

Elementary Schools

The elementary school of full-day session is expected to carry the major burden of education for boys and girls between six and twelve years of age. Nominally, it offers a four-year course, but the course is prolonged to five or six years for the slower pupils. Brighter children from families of better-than-average social and economic status who expect to continue their education in secondary schools may transfer after the first, second, or third year of study to an appropriate level of the primary school, on the basis of examinations administered by the primary school. No fees are charged for instruction in the full-day elementary school, and in 1944–45 more than 500,000 free lunches were provided. The practice of providing lunch for elementary- and primary-school children has resulted in more regular attendance and improved health. As compulsory half-day schools are converted to full-time elementary schools, the trend is toward coeducation wherever physical facilities can accommodate the numbers involved.

Children in the elementary schools are in most instances from families of low economic status. While careful and systematic attention to physical condition has improved health, endemic diseases, such as trachoma, bilharziasis, malaria, and ancylostomiasis, as well as rickets and skin diseases, continue to reduce the efficiency of the pupils. The schools are commonly housed—especially in cities—in buildings formerly used as dwellings. Play areas are limited to a court which is occasionally large enough for a small basketball field, but often permits only limited calisthenics for one class at a time. Classrooms are frequently so crowded that writing is difficult and movement of pupils during class is next to impossible. In some of the most recently established village schools, land has been available to permit the inclusion of elementary work in agriculture in the program.

THE ELEMENTARY PROGRAM OF STUDIES

The program of studies and the distribution of periods is shown in Table 6.

Effort is made throughout the school program to relate subject matter to the immediate environment of the child and to select materials and activities which are common to Egyptian village or city life.

TABLE 6

PROGRAM OF STUDIES FOR ELEMENTARY SCHOOLS, EGYPT, 1945-46

SUBJECT	1st Year		2nd Year		3rd Year		4th Year	
	Boys	Girls	Boys	Girls	Boys	Girls	Boys	Girls
Koran and religion	3	4	6	6	7	6	7	5
Arabic	13	12	11	10	11	10	11	10
Arabic writing	...	...	3	2	3	2	3	3
Geography and history	...	...	2	2	3	2	3	2
Needlework	...	...	...	5	...	6	...	6
Arithmetic	6	6	6	6	6	6	6	6
Civics and ethics	...	...	...	...	1	1	1	1
Nature study	...	1	...	1	...	1	...	1
General science and hygiene	2	1	2	1	2	2	2	2
Drawing	3	2	3	2	2	2	2	2
Physical training	3	2	3	1	2	1	2	1
Handwork	4	6	3	3	2	...	2	...
Total	34	34	39	39	39	39	39	39

In *religion* classes, aside from memorizing the Koran, the children read or hear stories designed to develop better relationships between family members and to foster desirable habits and attitudes concerning personal cleanliness, manners, neighborliness, and ethical concepts. Requirements of the Muhammadan religion relative to prayer, fasting, pilgrimages, and feasts are included in the religion classes. Non-Muslim children are excused from these courses and, when practicable, receive instruction in their own religion. In drawing and handwork pupils use pencil, colored paper, clay, plasticine, native palm fiber, and cotton stems to make drawings and models of vegetables, fruit, furniture, farm implements, pyramids, villages, animals, and illustrations for stories bearing on their own environment.

Geography is introduced in the second year with conversations involving

PUBLIC EDUCATION BELOW THE SECONDARY SCHOOL

the children's observations of sun, moon, and stars, physical features of the locality, methods of determining directions by day and by night, occupations within the villages and elementary facts of irrigation. In the third year study is devoted to the home province and neighboring provinces, together with simple facts about Egypt's location in relation to neighboring countries. The continents and oceans, factors in climate and weather, and variations in animal and plant life caused by difference in climate are included in this year's work. In the fourth year the geography of Egypt and the importance of the Nile River are studied in detail, and considerable attention is given to the elementary facts of Egypt's foreign trade, the geography of the Sudan, and the relations of Egypt with the other countries bordering on the Mediterranean Sea.

The study of *history* begins in the second year with short stories of Egypt's ancient period. Achievements of great leaders and the social life, customs, and civilization of that early age are emphasized. Excursions are made to ancient sites and monuments in the vicinity of the school. History in the third year includes study of Islamic leaders and their achievements, the Turkish conquest, and life in Egypt under the Mamluks. Emphasis in the final year is on events of the past two centuries: the period immediately preceding the Napoleonic conquest, the military activities of the French, Turks, and British, the achievements of Muhammad 'Ali and his successors, the opening of the Suez Canal, the British occupation, the development under Fuad I, the revolt of 1919, the biography of Sa'id Zaghlul Pasha, the declaration of independence of 1922, and the events following upon that important act.

Civics and ethics are studied in the third and fourth years. In the third year pupils consider character traits that are desirable in the home, in school, and in public life, as well as in social and political organizations. In the fourth year character-building continues to be stressed, and the organization of the national government is studied in some detail to give the pupil knowledge of the constitution and of the functions of the various branches of government and their different departments. The rights and obligations of citizens are taught in this final year.

General science—commonly called "object lessons"—begins in the first year with observation of common vegetables and familiar animals and poultry. Second-year pupils learn to classify and identify parts of the plants and animals studied in the first year and, in addition, study trees, wild animals, and some of the less common animals and insects. The third-year syllabus includes the characteristics, varieties, and uses of water and methods of insuring a pure supply; air and its physical characteristics; functions of characteristic parts of birds and water animals; further study of common vegetables and cereals; agricultural industries, especially dairying; and the nature and uses of such common commodities as sugar, salt, and glass. In the final year birds and insects are studied in relation to agriculture, and methods of destroying harmful insects are taught. Advanced study of common plants and animals previously considered is included, and attention is given to cotton, tea, coffee, oil, coal, iron, copper, gold, and silver.

Hygiene is studied in all four years of the elementary school, the first-year course stressing personal cleanliness and the development of fundamental health habits relating to eating, drinking, exercise, and proper care of eyes, ears, nose, and mouth. Topics included in the second year are healthful sleeping arrangements; balanced diet; the importance of using individual plates, knives, forks, and spoons; appropriate clothing and care of clothing; and the digestion and assimilation of food. In the third year attention is directed toward the dangers of common insects of the home and how these insects can be eliminated or controlled; proper care of house animals is stressed; descriptions of suitable and unsuitable housing are formulated, and model villages are constructed. The fourth year stresses diseases common in Egypt, methods of prevention and control of disease, fundamental principles of care of the ill and elementary first aid. This study is supplemented by lectures, discussions, and treatment by visiting health officials.

A third or more of the pupils' total time spent in elementary school is devoted to the study of the *Arabic language and literature.* Classical Arabic differs considerably from colloquial Arabic and, therefore, presents more problems than the study of a mother tongue usually does. The alphabet method of teaching reading is commonly used, though some teachers are experimenting with the word and sentence approach. Flash cards, reading, conversation, and dictation are employed to varying degrees during the four years of instruction. Study of formal grammar begins in the third year, when elementary composition is introduced, pupils having learned the different styles of Arabic script in the writing classes of the second year.

First-year *arithmetic* includes counting, reading and writing of numbers from 1 to 9, simple addition and subtraction of these numbers, and identification of common coins. Multiplication and division are added in the second year along with a study of simple measurement and more difficult currency problems. The third-year course includes long division, problems in buying and selling, fundamental operations with common fractions, written problems and knowledge of the multiplication tables through 12x12. Fourth-year students study decimals and measurement of length, area, volume, and weight.

The major adaptation of the curriculum to meet special needs of girls is the addition of *needlework* in the second, third, and fourth years. In the second year small articles are made, such as napkins, collars, bags, and embroidered pillow covers; knitting and crocheting are introduced. Third-year pupils make a cotton-flannel dress decorated with ornamental stitches. In the fourth year the girls take up advanced knitting and make either a blouse or a simple dress for special occasions. At the end of the course a girl is expected to be capable of doing household mending, of making simple clothing, and of selecting materials for durability, economy, and ease in laundering or cleaning.

Schools for the Memorization of the Koran

Schools for the memorization of the Koran provide a program, usually of four years, which parallels the elementary school. These schools are sponsored by organizations of Muslims who think that insufficient attention is given to the study of the Koran and the religion of Islam in the public elementary schools. No tuition fee is charged. The schools receive their support from societies organized to preserve the Koran, from gifts of individuals, from the government department which administers religious foundations (Waqf), and from local and central departments of education and social welfare. The contributions from public funds are relatively small.

The program of studies provides twenty-two periods per week for the study of the Koran and religion with twelve periods allotted to arithmetic and history. The pupils are expected to memorize the entire Koran by the end of the fourth year. Pupils who finish the program usually continue in one of the institutes of al-Azhar to prepare for religious work or in an elementary training school to prepare to teach in elementary schools. Some pupils transfer to public primary schools after one or two years in a school for the memorization of the Koran.

Rural Elementary Schools

In 1943 a variant of the elementary school was developed to provide elementary technical training for village children in agriculture and other subjects appropriate in a rural area. In 1944–45, 78 of these schools were opened, but no new ones were established in 1946. The six-year course includes instruction in religion, Arabic, arithmetic, drawing, hygiene, physical training, cooperatives, crafts, and agriculture. About one-half of the total number of school hours is assigned to physical training, crafts, and agriculture. All subjects taught in the school are directed toward agriculture. Local materials are used in the crafts, and skills are developed in rug-making, pottery, mat-making, and such activities as can be practiced in leisure time or at periods when field work is slack.

One of the most promising schools of this type is being developed at Kom Ombo near Aswan in southern Egypt. A specially designed building, which will be used as a community center as well as school, is being constructed of inexpensive materials. Completed, it will include a hall for the use of school and community, a medical center, a community kitchen, a library, and the usual classrooms and shops. One feature is an exhibit hall so arranged that pupils passing from class to shop or to the farm will pass exhibits set up to illustrate improved farm practice, better health habits, and better housing conditions. A large tract of land adjacent to the school has been acquired for practical agriculture, poultry-raising and dairy-farming, and experimental purposes.

Nursery Schools

Public nursery schools, the lowest step in the primary-school ladder, were introduced in Cairo in 1944 to provide daytime supervision for boys and girls of two and one-half to four and one-half years of age who have no mothers or whose mothers are employed. In 1945–46 there were seven such schools, all in Cairo. In addition to fees for activities, health insurance, and transportation, if provided by school bus, an annual tuition fee of £E9 ($36) is charged. The nursery school aims at developing cooperation and respect for the rights of others, improved physical development, and a more gradual introduction to formal education than is provided by the typical kindergarten. Supervised play and rest, storytelling, encouragement of self-dependence and self-control, and the development of manipulative skill by games, handwork, and drawing are the principal features of this type of education.

Kindergartens

Publicly supported and controlled kindergartens are provided for boys and girls of the five-to-eight age group. They are preparatory schools for primary schools—to which they may be attached. Their upper classes are parallel to the early years of elementary schools, but the fees limit attendance to children of higher social and economic background. Major emphasis is placed upon teaching reading, writing, and the fundamental processes of arithmetic. In schools where physical facilities permit, some attention is given to developing character and personality by means of a

PUBLIC EDUCATION BELOW THE SECONDARY SCHOOL

freer type of activity program. However, most kindergartens are conducted in rented buildings with rooms too small to allow much activity.

THE KINDERGARTEN COURSE OF STUDY

Table 7 suggests the range of the kindergarten program.

Stories used for *character-building* in the first year deal with personifications of animals and plants and with children in relationship to interesting aspects of the local environment; they stress kindness to animals,

TABLE 7
PROGRAM OF STUDIES FOR PUBLIC KINDERGARTENS, EGYPT, 1945–46

SUBJECTS	PERIODS PER WEEK		
	1st Year	2nd Year	3rd Year
Character-building	2	2	2
Arabic (conversation, reading, writing, and songs)	8	10	12
Arithmetic	6	6	6
Nature study and hygiene	2	2	2
Handwork	8	8	6
Drawing	4	3	3
Games and music	4	3	3
Total	34	34	34

helping the poor, and polite social behavior. Stories used in the second year are selected with a view to developing a sense of humor and appreciation of fairy tales, and to encourage love of family and companions, charity, hospitality, truth, helpfulness, and good manners. In the third year some stories are correlated with nature study, others are selected to increase knowledge of people of other nations, and others are chosen to develop ideas of conservation, self-dependence, self-control, cooperation, and honor; stories of national heroes and religious prophets are also used.

Study of *Arabic* begins in the first year with conversation about objects and events of the children's everyday life. Shape and sound of letters are associated in introducing the written language, and attractive pictures are used to illustrate the teaching. Joining letters to make words is carried out with plasticine and other materials, and gradually words and simple sentences from reading materials are learned by the children. In the second year reading books are provided by the Ministry of Education, and materials from these books are used in the teaching of writing. Dictation from unfamiliar books or sources is given to test proficiency. Third-year conversation is largely description of what the pupils observe in pictures or on excursions, and exposition of their activities, the object being to develop a simple Arabic style of expression in complete sentences and a larger vocabulary. Reading is from books provided by the Ministry and other available books of appropriate difficulty. In the third year pupils are encouraged to write, illustrate, and bind small books and magazines, and by the end of the year they are expected to write with pen and ink from dictation.

In *arithmetic* first-year pupils learn to count up to 50 and to do simple exercises with objects involving classification and counting. Subtraction from numbers up to 20 is taught, and simple oral problems dealing with familiar objects and situations of daily life are solved. In the second year the pupils use numbers up to 100, learn operation signs for addition, subtraction, and equality, study the multiplication table as far as 5x5, and continue with oral and written problems involving simple processes. Third-year pupils study numbers up to 999, learn the borrowing principle in subtraction, advance to 10x10 in the multiplication tables, and learn to multiply three-digit numbers by one-digit numbers. They are made familiar with Egyptian coins in common use. Quick and accurate solutions of oral problems and written problems to be solved in exercise books are part of the final year's work.

Handwork in all three years is designed to develop skill in using such materials as clay, sand, paper, cane, wool, raffia, palm fiber, and plant stalks to illustrate stories and real happenings both in and out of school. Drawing begins with free expression in white and colored chalk on the blackboard, the children being encouraged to depict common scenes from their environment, to illustrate stories they have heard, and to sketch familiar toys. In the second year pupils draw both from memory and from models of a simple sort. Third-year pupils study simple designs for decoration, correlate drawing with the course in nature study, begin to use the compass and to paint with water colors.

Nature study is taught in the first year by stories that deal with familiar animals, milk and its products, and common fruits, and observation of the development of pigeons, chickens, rabbits, and some plants is carried on by raising birds and animals in the school and keeping a school garden. In the second year pupils study common flowers and grow common vegetables, go into more detail on the breeding and raising of animals and the growing of plants, and study the life and habits of common birds. The third-year course includes more detailed study of germination of seeds, parts of plants and trees, and characteristics and habits of wild animals. The children raise silkworms and frogs for practical work and are encouraged to collect leaves, shells, and other objects to form a small museum of natural science for the school.

Games are selected for *physical development* as well as for their recreational value and are designed to develop coordination, a sense of rhythm, and mental alertness. Piano or phonograph music is used in instruction. Simple musical instruments, such as cymbals, triangles, and drums, are introduced in the third year.

In 1944-45 there were 7,101 boys and girls (including those in 5 nursery schools) in public kindergartens and 44,300 in private and foreign schools.

Primary Schools

Primary schools with a four-year course prepare pupils for entrance to the secondary school. Fees were abolished in 1943, but admission is still selective on the basis of entrance examinations in reading, writing, and arithmetic, and a physical examination. Boys and girls attend separate schools, and some modifications in the program are made to suit special needs of girls. In general, primary-school pupils are from families of higher social and economic status than the families of elementary-school children, but this condition will be less marked now that fees have been abolished and free lunches are provided.

Buildings constructed for primary schools are well planned and equipped. Equipment—particularly maps, charts, models, and handwork materials—is extensive. The spectacular growth in these schools since the abolition of fees has caused serious crowding in some schools, and a shortage of qualified teachers has necessitated increasing the size of classes. In schools which are housed in rented buildings—frequently former residences—the crowding is even worse.

The timetable varies with local conditions, some schools having a long morning session, a late lunch, and no classes afterward, while others have lunch at 12:30 and one or two classes after lunch. Class periods are usually 45 minutes in length separated by 5-minute intervals except for a 15-minute break between periods in midmorning. Most schools do not serve lunch on Thursday as no classes are held on that afternoon. Friday, being the Muslim holy day, is a holiday in all government schools. Monday afternoon is usually reserved for club meetings and free activity. The organizations and activities include societies associated with the different subjects of the curriculum; they may meet on afternoons other than Monday in some schools. In most schools these societies hold annual exhibits of their work to which the public is invited.

Qualified teachers in the primary schools are expected to have completed a four-year course beyond the secondary school and two years in the

Institute of Education. In the case of girls schools, graduation from the four-year course of the Institute of Education for Women is required (see chapter 5 on the education of teachers). However, the severe shortage of teachers has necessitated the temporary appointment of teachers just out of secondary school or from staffs of private or foreign schools.

The public Primary-School Certificate examination is held yearly in June for pupils who have completed the four-year primary-school course. Pupils who fail to pass all subjects or fail to make the required average in the June examination are permitted to try again in September in the subjects in which they failed or had low marks. Those who fail at the second attempt are required to repeat the fourth year. Only one repetition is permitted in government schools.

THE PRIMARY PROGRAM OF STUDIES

The subjects studied and the distribution of periods through the four years of primary school are shown in Table 8.

The course in the *Koran and religion* stresses memorization of parts of the Koran each year. The first-year children read or hear stories about

TABLE 8
PROGRAM OF STUDIES FOR PRIMARY SCHOOLS, EGYPT, 1945–46

Subjects	1st Year	2nd Year	3rd Year	4th Year
Koran and religion	3	2	2	2
Stories	2	2	...	...
Songs	1	1	...	...
Arabic language and writing	12	12	9	9
Foreign language	...	...	8	8
Arithmetic and intuitive geometry	6	6	6	6
History	...	...	1	1
Geography	...	1	1	1
Nature study and general science	3	3	2	2
Hygiene	...	...	1	1
Drawing	3	3	2	2
Handwork*	3	3	2	2
Physical training and games	3	3	2	2
Total	36	36	36	36

* Needlework and domestic science in girls schools; gardening, if possible, for boys.

Noah, Abraham, Moses, and Muhammad, all emphasizing good character traits, and attention is paid to attitudes and habits relating to cleanliness, helping the weak and the poor, obedience to parents, respect for elders, and good manners in school, in public, and at home. At the end of the first year pupils are expected to know procedures of ablution and prayer. Second-year pupils acquire further knowledge of good manners, kindness to animals, obedience, honesty, perseverance, and good sportsmanship, and the life of Muhammad is treated in some detail. The third-year course includes explanations of some selections of the Koran which are of particular ethical significance, and study of the life of Muhammad and the religious teachings of Islam is continued. In the final year pupils read or hear stories about 'Abu Bakr, 'Umar, 'Uthman, 'Ali, and other caliphs and study and memorize sayings of the Prophet; in addition, harmful superstitions are discussed, and ways of combating them are indicated.

History, in the year of its introduction—the third—is studied through stories and discussion and deals with ancient Egypt, the Greco-Roman period, and the early period of Islam. In the fourth year, the pupils study the period dating from the time of the Mamluks to the present. Study in history is confined to Egypt and such countries as are directly involved in Egyptian history.

Geography begins in the second year with study of the four directions, sketches of the classroom and school, and discussions of the topography and commercial and productive features of the district. Third-year pupils study the geography of the earth, including its composition of land and water, latitude and longitude and rotation, learn map-reading and -making, and begin the study of the Nile Valley including the Sudan. Fourth-year pupils consider the Nile Valley in more detail and study the climate, physical features, systems of irrigation and drainage, agricultural industries, and natural resources of Egypt; they learn the administrative divisions of the country with their capitals and spend some time studying about the Sudan. Finally they study geographical features of other Arabic countries and the Mediterranean basin.

In first-year *arithmetic* pupils learn to read and write numbers up to six digits, add equal numbers, add orally two numbers whose sum does not exceed 100, subtract from numbers not exceeding 100, and solve oral and written problems involving addition and subtraction. They learn multiplication of numbers whose product does not exceed six figures, multiplication by 10, 100, and 1,000, division by numbers not larger than nine, and, finally, units of time, currency, weight, and distance commonly used in Egypt. Second-year work includes reading and writing numbers up to nine digits, multiplication by 11 and 12, exercises in the four fundamental processes, and units of measurement of length in the metric system. Decimals and compound fractions are introduced in the third year, along with conversion of English to Egyptian units of measurement, and the reverse. Topics of the second year are continued, and problems become more difficult. Fourth-year topics are ratio and simple proportion, conversion of English and French money into Egyptian money and vice versa, simple interest, profit and loss, problems involving measurement of areas and volumes in metric and Egyptian units, and review of the entire four-year course.

Currently, *intuitive geometry* is taught with arithmetic in each of the four years. Pupils are taught to identify geometrical figures such as spheres, cylinders, spirals, circles, and cubes and to study their incidence in nature. Cutting and measuring activities convey understanding of terms such as diameter, radius, circumference, angles, parallel lines, triangles, and quadrilaterals. Methods of bisecting angles, reproduction of angles, and erecting perpendiculars are learned through practice. The equality of base angles of an isosceles triangle is discovered by experiment. Pupils learn how to construct regular polygons.

Drawing is studied in each of the four years, the media being pencil, pastel, and water color. Common objects in the child's environment are used as models: vegetables, fruits, and flowers, flowerpots, books, matchboxes, jugs, and pans. In addition, pupils are asked to reproduce scenes, objects, and activities from memory or imagination. Decorative designs are developed by repetition of objects of nature, geometrical figures, or Arabic script. Horizontal and vertical projections are made without resort to instruments. In the upper years the theory of color is presented.

Systematic study of *hygiene* is begun in the third year, when pupils study the importance of proper diet, dangers attached to eating food that has not been carefully cleaned or cooked, the necessity of following the doctor's directions in case of illness, untreated Nile water as a source of disease, the digestive and respiratory systems and good habits to be developed in relation to them. Fourth-year pupils study the circulatory system, simple first aid, protection against infection and contagious disease, insects which carry disease and how to combat them.

The course in *handwork* for boys utilizes clay, plasticine, and colored paper. First-year work emphasizes the development of skills in relation to such material. Necklaces, models of fruits and vegetables, simple baskets, and trays are made. Making of original models is encouraged. In the second, third, and fourth years more complicated objects are made, and simple carpentry is introduced, plywood and cardboard being the most common materials. Small boxes, towel racks, inkwell stands, and baskets are made in the fourth year; in some schools leather-work is taught.

Handwork for girls takes the form of needlework and domestic science. Using loosely woven cloth and colored thread, first-year pupils make handkerchiefs, napkins, bags for personal belongings, and sewing kits. In the

PUBLIC EDUCATION BELOW THE SECONDARY SCHOOL 53

second year they make pillowcases, aprons, tray covers, tea-table covers, scarfs, and tea napkins. Third-year girls learn to knit, and each girl is expected to make herself a pullover sweater. A simple blouse or skirt is the major project of fourth-year sewing. In addition, girls in the third year of domestic science are taught to clean brushes, combs, shoes, and common objects of the home, and to set the table, wash dishes and utensils in a sanitary fashion, and do laundry-work. In the fourth year they learn to prepare simple foods, such as milk pudding, jelly, custards, biscuits, omelets, ice cream, coffee, tea, lemonade, cocoa, and salads.

Nature study and general science begin in the first year with observation of such familiar animals as chickens, pigeons, rabbits, rats, and fish. Silkworms are bred and raised, and the different stages of their development noted. Wild animals are studied through books and pictures. Common vegetables and flowers are raised in the school garden and observed at different stages. The children make monthly lists of flowers, fruits, and vegetables they have seen. Similar activity is pursued through the other three years, with lists of animals, birds, and plants increased and the study becoming more detailed and advanced. Fourth-year students are introduced to elementary principles of physics, including conduction of heat, expansion of solids and liquids with changes of temperature, and the simpler industrial processes are explained. Visits to factories are made to permit the students to see the processes carried out.

Study of the *Arabic language and literature* consumes a third of the pupil's time in the first two years and a fourth of the time in the third and fourth years. Children are required to be able to read simple material before they are admitted to the first year. Oral and written exercises, dictation, formal study of grammar, handwriting drills, recitation, and conversation are all used to develop skill in oral and written expression in Arabic, and materials appropriate to the stage of development of the pupils are used. Correlation with other courses is emphasized by selection of reading materials that deal with geography, history, government, science, good health habits, good character traits, and situations common to the life of the children. Topics of current interest are used as a basis for conversation and discussion.

Prior to 1945–46 study of a foreign language, usually English (though French was taught in some government schools), was begun in the second year. In 1945–46, partly to permit transfer from the elementary school at the third year instead of the second—elementary-school children are taught no foreign language and so cannot pass primary examinations above the year when foreign language is begun—it was decided to postpone study of a foreign language to the third year. The aim of foreign-language study is competence in speaking, reading, and writing. The direct method is used in the beginning, and much practice in oral and written composition, as well as in reading, is provided. Dictation plays an important part in developing knowledge of the language. Subjects of oral and written composition are derived from the immediate environment of the pupils and deal with situations known to them.

The physical-training course includes simple games which are expected to develop respect for rules and team spirit. Where playground space is limited, more time is devoted to formal calisthenics, performance of which provides the basis of annual field or sports days. Relay races, jumping, and team games are the major activities of the upper years.

The primary school, being the only type of school that leads to the secondary school and hence to the universities, is an important part of the Egyptian education system. In 1944–45 there were 183 primary schools for boys or girls supported and controlled by the Ministry of Education, with an enrollment of 44,122 boys and 8,716 girls. In addition, there were 56,978 boys and 17,821 girls attending private primary schools and 12,859 boys and 12,678 girls attending primary schools established by foreign agencies.

EXAMINATIONS IN PRIMARY SCHOOLS

Previously school examinations were held at the end of the first, second, and third primary years as the basis for the pupil's promotion to the next higher grade. In 1942, however, promotion from these classes began to be based on the general average of the year's work. Pupils were required to obtain at least 50 percent in Arabic and arithmetic, 40 in the foreign language and general information, and 20 in drawing. If they fail to obtain these averages, they are obliged to pass an examination in these subjects at the end of the year before they may be promoted to the next grade, and the results have to be reviewed and approved by the Ministry of Education.

A public examination conducted at the end of the fourth primary year by the Ministry is open to pupils from public primary schools and from nongovernment schools which are inspected by the Ministry. Pupils who have had private instruction are also entitled to sit for this examination. It is held at the close of the school year with a repetition at the beginning of the next school year for those who failed in the earlier session or who were prevented from attending by reasons beyond their control. The examination is both written and oral. The written part covers the following subjects

—the passing mark for each is indicated in parentheses: Arabic, including penmanship (25/50);[1] English or French, including penmanship (20/50); arithmetic (25/50); general information (9/30); and drawing (4/20). The pupil must not fall below the minimum in any subject and must have a total of 45 percent. The oral examination is in Arabic, with

TABLE 9

Public Primary Examination Results, Egypt, 1939–40, 1941–42, 1943–44*

YEAR	Boys			Girls		
	Entered	Passed	Percent Passed	Entered	Passed	Percent Passed
1939–40	6,194	5,398	87.0	797	749	94.0
1941–42	6,833	5,773	86.0	897	819	91.0
1943–44	7,215	5,470	75.6	1,028	848	82.5

* Figures for the first two years are from *Statistique Scolaire, 1942–43* (Cairo: Imprimerie Nationale, Egyptian Government, Ministry of Finance, Statistical Dept., 1945), p. 273. For the third, they are compiled from tables of examination results supplied by the Ministry of Education.

TABLE 10

Public Primary Examination Results, Egypt, 1910–40*

YEAR	Percent Passing	Average Age	
		Years	Months
1910	43.4	15	8
1915	37.9	15	...
1920	43.4	14	10
1925	53.0	14	6
1930	51.0	13	10
1935	79.0	12	11
1940	87.0	...	...

* Ministry of Education, *Memorandum on the Examination for the Completion of Primary Studies* (Cairo: 1939), pp. 2–3. (In Arabic.)

the minimum passing mark 25/50, and in the foreign language, with the minimum 20/50.

Questions for the written examination are prepared by the Ministry of Education and sent sealed to the examination centers. All examination papers are confidential and anonymous, each student receiving a number which he uses in lieu of his name on the examination book. The papers are corrected by committees appointed by the Ministry. Thus, the schools have nothing to do with the examination, which is intended primarily as a ministerial check on the performance of the schools. The pupil who passes

[1] *Read* 25 out of 50, which means that the passing mark is 25 out of a maximum grade of 50 allotted to the subject. The denominators show the weighting of the subjects: the larger the denominator is the more important the subject.

is granted the Certificate of Completion of Primary Studies, without which he cannot enter a secondary school.

Table 9 contains the results of three public primary examinations for public-school children.

Despite the drop in percentage passed between 1940 and 1944, children had actually been passing in greater proportion and at an increasingly early age since the institution of the public examinations, as shown in Table 10.

Chapter 3

SECONDARY AND VOCATIONAL EDUCATION

*S*ECONDARY SCHOOLS provide in separate institutions a five-year course for boys and a six-year course for girls above the primary school. Boys for four years and girls for five years follow a general course, alike in content for both boys and girls, except that courses in the domestic arts are added for girls. In the final year (fifth for boys and sixth for girls) students may specialize in one of the three sections provided: the literary, the scientific, or the mathematical. Such is the theory. In actuality some secondary schools do not have all three sections in the final, or orientation, year, while in others the science section cannot accommodate all applicants. In the latter case acceptance is based solely on the standing in the first part of the public secondary-school examination. The science section is in demand mainly because specialization in it is a prerequisite for admission to the schools of medicine.

Public secondary schools are usually housed in buildings that were designed for the purpose. However, some—particularly the ones for girls—use rented houses which have been remodeled or enlarged to meet the increasing demand for secondary education. Schools for either sex provide ground space for basketball, volleyball, and tennis; boys schools that lack space for football obtain access to a nearby field. Adequate equipment is provided in the secondary schools, especially for the teaching of the sciences. Interest in developing libraries is increasing, but thus far few schools have adequate library service. Many of the schools have facilities for boarding students to accommodate out-of-town pupils. About 5 percent of the students are boarders.

Day pupils pay fees amounting to £E20 ($80) and boarders, £E40 ($160) per annum. The fee for day pupils includes the cost of lunch, which is served five days a week. From 25 to 30 percent of the pupils are exempt from part or full payment of fees, the exemption being determined on the basis of academic standing in relation to age.

Most secondary-school teachers are graduates of Egyptian or foreign universities or of four-year institutions above the secondary-school level which train teachers in special subjects such as drawing, Arabic, and physical training. On the whole the teachers are well prepared in their fields, and many of them have had professional training taken at the Higher Training College,[1] at the Institutes of Education, or at a foreign university.

Program of Studies in Secondary Schools

Table 11 shows the program of studies for boys and girls in the general course of the secondary schools.

Distribution of time in the courses described in the following paragraphs applies to the schools for boys. Essentially the same material is studied by

TABLE 11
PROGRAM OF STUDIES, GENERAL-CULTURE STAGE, OF SECONDARY SCHOOLS, EGYPT, 1945–46

SUBJECTS	1st Year Boys	1st Year Girls	2nd Year Boys	2nd Year Girls	3rd Year Boys	3rd Year Girls	4th Year Boys	4th Year Girls	5th Year Girls
Religion	2	2	1	1	1	1	1	1	1
Arabic	8	8	8	6	6	6	6	6	6
First foreign language	8	7	8	7	7	7	7	6	7
Translation	...	...	...	...	1	...	1	1	1
Second foreign language	...	...	4	4	4	4	4	4	4
History and civics	2	2	2	2	2	2	2	2	2
Geography	2	2	2	2	2	2	2	2	2
Mathematics	4	4	4	4	5	4	5	4*	5*
General science	4	4	3	3	...	...	...	...	...
Physics	...	...	...	...	2	2	2	2*	2*
Chemistry	...	...	...	...	3	2	...	2	...
Biology	...	...	...	...	...	...	3	1†	3†
Drawing	2	2	1	2	1	2	1	1	1
Handwork	2	...	1	...	...	...	...	...	...
Physical training	2	2	2	2	2	1	2	1	1
Needlework and domestic science	...	2	...	2	...	2	...	2	...
Music	...	1	...	1	...	1	...	1	1
Total	36	36	36	36	36	36	36	36	36

* Girls not intending to enter the university or higher schools may substitute drawing (including interior decoration and history of art), child care and psychology, or needlework and domestic science for physics and mathematics.
† Includes child care.

the girls, but their course extends over five years instead of four in those subjects which are studied each year.

Religion is included in the secondary-school program to provide spiritual guidance to young people, to extend knowledge of the Koran, and to prepare students for independent study of religion. Certain aspects of Muhammadan beliefs regarding prophecy, the Prophet Muhammad, the hegira, and the Koran in relation to everyday life and personal status are

---
[1] Closed in 1934; succeeded by the Institutes of Education.

SECONDARY AND VOCATIONAL EDUCATION

studied. The influence of Islam on spiritual life and the effect it had on early Arabian life, details of devotional life in Islam, and, to a slight degree, characteristics of the various Muhammadan sects and the development of jurisprudence are considered.

The study of *Arabic* includes reading, history of literature, composition, and grammar. There is much oral reading from books prescribed by the Ministry of Education, and attention is given to correlating the history of literature and texts studied during a given period. In the first year, students study the modern period dating from Muhammad 'Ali, and thereafter work back till the final year covers the pre-Islamic period. Prose and poetry up to sixty lines of each are memorized each year. Topics for composition are selected appropriate to the stage of development of the students, with fourth-year composition centering about current problems of economic and social significance. Class discussion of topics precedes the writing, which is usually done in the classroom. Oral composition is stressed each year to develop good diction and expressive speech.

Grammar, previously studied in the primary school, is continued throughout the secondary school to increase understanding of the technical structure of Arabic, to perfect usage, and to develop in the student an appreciation of the beauty of the language. Figures of speech are studied intensively in the final year.

Facility in the use of one or more *foreign languages* is essential both for cultural and vocational activities in Egypt and for advanced study at home and abroad. It is not surprising, therefore, that more than a fourth of the total secondary-school schedule is devoted to the study of foreign languages. In government schools English is commonly the principal language and French the secondary. Effort is made to develop competence in both oral and written expression, and class time is apportioned to reading, recitation, composition, and translation. Books studied are textbooks in grammar and simplifications of standard classics which have been written especially for Egyptian students. Much attention is given to dictation from good models and to compositions written by the students. In the advanced years attention is given to developing vocabulary by use of material dealing with current affairs and scientific subjects.

History is studied chronologically. The students progress from study of ancient Egypt, Greece, and Rome, in the first year, to Islamic history through the Mamluk period in the second year; to the Renaissance in Europe, the rise of the Ottoman Empire, and the events of the latter part of the eighteenth century in Europe and America in the third year; to modern Egypt in the fourth. Civics is concentrated in the third year, and the emphasis is upon developing an understanding of the nature and functions of national and local government.

In the first three years, *geography* consists of study of general facts about the earth and the moon, discussions of time, seasons, climate, distribution of vegetation, and regional study of the continents. The fourth year is devoted to intensive study of the Nile Valley, including the Sudan and the adjoining deserts.

The *mathematics* course includes arithmetic, algebra, and intuitive geometry in the first year; arithmetic, algebra, and demonstrative geometry in the second and third years; and algebra and geometry in the fourth. Arithmetic stresses square and cube root, areas and volumes, simple and compound interest, commercial discount, and graphs. At the end of the fourth year of algebra, students are expected to be able to solve problems involving quadratic equations, simultaneous quadratic equations, ratio and proportion, logarithms, and elementary surds. Geometry goes as far as elementary trigonometry in the final year.

Physics includes the elementary principles of mechanics, heat, light, sound, electricity, and magnetism, with emphasis upon their qualitative, rather than quantitative, aspects. Experiments are carried out by individual students, small groups, or by the teacher. Visits to industrial plants and factories where principles are applied are encouraged, as are informal organizations of students interested in extending the formal study of physics beyond the classroom.

The course in *chemistry* is elementary in scope, with emphasis upon applications to everyday life. Half of the time is spent in laboratory work. Topics studied are solutions, rusting, nitrogen, oxygen, acids and bases, hydrogen and water, carbon and its compounds, sulphur, sodium chloride and hydrogen chloride, nitric acid, silicon, starches, fats, and proteins.

Biology in the secondary school is an extension of nature study. Study of plant and animal life is based on observation in the school garden and on excursions. The processes of germination and growth, nutrition, respiration, and reproduction in plants and animals are studied. Microscopic study is included, but is not stressed. Many excellent large-scale models and charts are available in most of the schools.

Drawing is studied to develop aesthetic appreciation and good taste as much as to develop skill, and is designed to improve habits of observation, memory, and imagination. What is learned in the classroom is expected to carry over to interior decoration, selection of apparel, and choice of pictures. The work in drawing is correlated as far as possible with other activities of the school. The course includes drawing natural objects such as

SECONDARY AND VOCATIONAL EDUCATION

animals, birds, twigs, and plants, imaginary and memory drawing, and design based on Arabic or Egyptian ornamentation.

Handwork receives scant attention in the formal program of the secondary school for boys, but the boys are encouraged to join an organization which provides activities of construction and repair. The formal course offers work in wood, leather, clay, metals, weaving, bookbinding, linoleum-cutting, and stenciling. It is expected that boys will make use of the acquired skills in their leisure hours.

Physical training is largely a matter of calisthenics and marching. Soccer, basketball, volleyball, and tennis are popular with the students but are played informally in out-of-school hours as part of the sports-club program.

ORIENTATION YEAR PROGRAM OF STUDIES

The final year of the secondary school, fifth year for boys and sixth for girls, in which the students specialize in one of the three sections—literary,

TABLE 12

PROGRAM OF STUDIES FOR ORIENTATION YEAR OF SECONDARY SCHOOLS, EGYPT, 1945-46

	PERIODS PER WEEK		
SUBJECTS	Literary Section	Science Section	Mathematics Section
Arabic language	6	6	6
First European language	7*	6*	6*
Second European language	7*	3	3
History	5	...	...
Geography	4	...	...
Philosophy or mathematics	3	...	...
Library	2	...	...
Biology	...	9	...
Chemistry	...	6	3
Physics	...	4	4
Pure and applied mathematics	...	...	10
Drawing or additional physics or biology	...	...	2
Total	34	34	34

* One period a week is devoted to translation into Arabic.

scientific, or mathematical—had, in 1945–46, the program of studies shown in Table 12. The curriculum of the orientation year is the same for both sexes.

The approach to *Arabic literature* in the orientation year is analytic. Influences perceptible in the rise and decline of that literature are investigated. Relationships of foreign literatures to Arabic are studied, and the influence of Greek philosophy and thought upon the literary life and expression of the Arabs is traced. The place of oratory in the development of literature is stressed. Students participate in debates on current issues and, according to their fields of specialization, write articles on literary or scientific subjects. Reading, too, is assigned with a view to the student's field of specialization. The intensive study of figures of speech is continued, and the more complicated types of sentence structure are analyzed in order that the students may develop a more polished writing style.

The study of *foreign languages* in this final year is similarly influenced by the academic field of the student. Prose, poetry, and drama by standard authors are studied in complete, rather than condensed or simplified, editions. Students from the mathematics and science sections read biographies of men of science or general treatments of the history of scientific progress. Effective and accurate oral and written expression is stressed, and practice in reading is given in unstudied selections from current publications.

History is confined to the literary section in the orientation year. Modern and contemporary periods are studied more intensively than in the preceding year, the following topics receiving major emphasis: the Napoleonic era, the constitutional movement, national movements and the Eastern question in the nineteenth century, modern economic organization, international relations since the Congress of Berlin, and Greek, Roman, and Islamic institutions.

Geography for the literary section includes detailed study of lithosphere, hydrosphere, and atmosphere. Attention is given to the effects of land forms, climate, and vegetation upon the life of man. The students learn to make and read maps, meteorological charts, and weather reports, and to construct graphs of geographical phenomena.

Literary-section students have a choice between *philosophy* and *mathematics*. The philosophy course combines psychology and logic, and its purpose is to give the student a better understanding of the thinking and the behavior of man. The mathematics course ranges from simple study of foreign exchange to the fringe of speculative mathematics.

The *library course* is designed to familiarize the student with library materials, resources, and the arrangement and classification of collections and to give him training in the techniques of elementary research.

Biology, including systematic study of botany and zoology, is taken as an elective by students of the mathematics section and as a required subject by the students of the science section. Laboratory work is provided for both groups, although the course for the science section is more detailed and technically more advanced, with more time devoted to laboratory work. Similarly, chemistry, required in both mathematics and science sections, absorbs more of the time of the scientific students and is studied by them

SECONDARY AND VOCATIONAL EDUCATION

in greater detail. Laboratory work for the mathematics section averages one and one-half hours weekly and for the science section, three hours. The advanced course in physics, however, is the same for both mathematics and science sections, with emphasis on the quantitative aspects of physics. Theoretical and practical study of heat, light, magnetism, and static and current electricity is carried out. A second course, offered as an elective in the mathematics section, permits more intensive study of specific physical phenomena.

The course in *mathematics* for the mathematics section includes algebra, geometry, trigonometry, and mechanics. Work in algebra covers arithmetic, geometric, and harmonic progressions and means, theory of quadratic equations, imaginary quantities, permutations and combinations, binomial theorem for positive integral indices, and elementary ideas of the theory of error. Geometry includes similar figures, theorems showing relationship between chords and segments of intersecting chords drawn in a circle, loci, construction of circles under given conditions, simple cases of maxima and minima, special theorems, and an introduction to solid geometry. The trigonometry course progresses from elementary matters to an introduction to analytical geometry and the study of rectangular coordinates. Topics dealt with in mechanics are equilibrium of forces acting on one plane, equilibrium of two couples, determination of centers of gravity of objects of uniform thickness, mechanical advantage of simple machines, fundamental properties of the forces of friction and the determination of the coefficient of friction, uniformly accelerated motion, resolution of forces, Newton's laws of motion, and preliminary notions of impulse, work, energy, and power.

The Girls Colleges

A special type of school for girls from families of higher social and economic status overlaps to some extent the program of the regular secondary school. Two schools of this type exist, one in Cairo and one in Alexandria. Although supported and controlled by the Ministry of Education, these colleges for girls charge higher fees than other public schools. They maintain facilities for boarding girls from the provinces. The complete course requires thirteen years—three for kindergarten, four for primary, four for secondary, and two for postsecondary study. Through the primary school the courses are standard; girls who obtain the Certificate of Completion of Primary Studies are accepted in the regular secondary school. However, the program of the secondary years of the college for girls is directed toward a social and domestic life of a rather high level. Time is taken from mathematics and science and given to foreign languages, art, needlework, cookery, hygiene, and child care. The postsecondary years offer seven subjects: Arabic, English, French, cooking, needlework, art, and social studies. The student chooses six subjects and spends six hours weekly on each. The total enrollment in the school in Cairo for 1945–46 was 371, with 156 in the kindergarten, 97 in the primary school, 95 in the secondary school, and 23 in the postsecondary course.

Secondary-School Examinations

In secondary schools written examinations are held for promotion at the end of the first, second, and third years (also fourth for girls). Passing marks in these examinations are as follows: Arabic, 50 percent; first foreign language, 40; second foreign language, 30; drawing, 20; social-studies group, 40; mathematics, 40; science group, 40. The student must receive at least 20 percent in the individual subjects of the groups. These school examinations, as well as the public examinations, are held in two sessions to accommodate students who fail in or are unable to attend the first.

The public examination for the secondary-school certificate is held in two sections, the general section at the end of the fourth year for boys and fifth year for girls, and the special section at the end of the orientation year. Both sections are open to students from private schools and to students who have had private instruction as well as to public-school students although public-school students and private-school students who have taken yearly promotion examinations are examined only in studies of the year in which the examination is held. Others are examined in the general-section examinations in the subjects of the four-year course for boys and of the five-year course for girls.

General written-examination subjects and passing marks are as follows: Arabic, 25/50;[2] first foreign language, 20/50; second foreign language, 9/30; drawing, 4/20; social-studies group, 16/40; mathematics, 16/40; science group, 16/40. In individual subjects of the groups the student must have 4/20. Oral examinations in the languages require the same passing marks as the written examinations in these subjects. At the end of the orientation year the student takes the examination in the subjects of the division of his specialization. All students are examined in Arabic and the two foreign languages. Arabic is allotted 50 marks, with 20 for

---

[2] *Read* 25 out of 50, which means that the passing mark is 25 out of a maximum grade of 50 allotted to the subject. The denominators show the weighting of the subjects, the larger a denominator is, the more important the subject.

SECONDARY AND VOCATIONAL EDUCATION

composition, 15 for literature, and 15 for grammar. The passing mark is 20/50. The first foreign language is allotted 50 marks, with 20 for composition, 25 for literature, and 5 for translation; passing is 20/50. The second foreign language has 50 marks; 20 for composition, 25 for grammar and dictation, and 5 for translation; the passing mark is 20/50 for the literary division and 12/50 for the science and mathematics divisions. In addition, students of the literary division have to take examinations in

TABLE 13
Public Secondary-School Examination Results, Egypt, 1939–40, 1941–42, 1943–44*

Section	Boys			Girls		
	Entered	Passed	Percent Passing	Entered	Passed	Percent Passing
General section:						
1939–40	3,145	2,162	68.7	195	168	86.1
1941–42	3,823	2,962	77.5	208	185	88.9
1943–44	3,912	2,759	70.3	350	302	86.3
Special section:						
Science						
1939–40	2,135	1,277	59.8	51	31	60.8
1941–42	2,629	1,646	62.6	144	114	79.2
1943–44	3,138	1,713	54.6	131	86	65.6
Literature						
1939–40	483	255	52.7	28	12	42.9
1941–42	529	310	58.6	69	57	82.6
1943–44	805	447	55.5	187	131	70.0
Mathematics						
1939–40	905	598	66.0	...	...	...
1941–42	835	558	66.8	...	...	...
1943–44	972	526	54.1	12	8	66.6
Total, special section						
1939–40	3,523	2,130	60.2	79	43	54.4
1941–42	3,993	2,514	62.9	213	171	80.2
1943–44	4,915	2,686	54.6	330	225	68.1

* Data for the first two years from *Statistique Scolaire, 1942–43* (Cairo: Imprimerie Nationale, Egyptian Government, Ministry of Finance, Statistical Dept., 1945), p. 273; for the third year, from the Ministry of Education.

history (20/50), geography (20/50), and mathematics or principles of philosophy (12/40). Science-division students take examinations in biology (20/50), chemistry (20/50), and physics (16/40). Mathematics students are examined in chemistry and physics (20/50 each), drawing or additional physics (8/20), and mathematics (100 marks, with 30 for mechanics, 20 each for algebra and geometry, and 15 each for trigonometry and analytical geometry; passing, 40/100). To pass, the student must receive a general average of 50 percent for the entire examination. Again, the oral examinations in the languages follow the marks of the written examinations in those subjects.

These public secondary-school examinations are conducted in much the same way as the public primary-school examinations, with questions set and correction done by committees of the Ministry of Education and the identity of the student shielded by a number. However, the universities contribute to the conducting of the secondary-school examinations—staff members assist in formulating questions and in marking the papers.

Table 13 shows the results of the public secondary-school examination for three years.

The table indicates that the number of students taking the secondary-school examinations is increasing, that the percentage of students passing is considerably lower than that for the public primary-school examination, and that on the whole a greater proportion of girls than boys pass. Formerly no public girls school presented students for the mathematics examination, but recently Saniyah, in Cairo, the oldest girls secondary school, opened a division of mathematics and began presenting students for the examination.

Vocational and Technical Education

Vocational and technical education is provided for boys in schools of trade, commerce, agriculture, applied arts, and applied engineering. For girls there are schools of homemaking, embroidery and dressmaking, feminine culture, and workshops.

Trade schools

The trade schools admit boys who hold the primary-school certificate. The course is free and five years in length. Those who do exceptionally good work may transfer at the end of the third year to the School of Applied Engineering. The schools provide training in fitting, turning, forging, sheet metal work, furniture-making, carpentry, automobile repair, painting, and decoration. Additional fields of specialization, preparation for which is offered in one or more schools, include electricity, radio, dyeing, spinning, watchmaking, pattern-making, tailoring, plumbing, musical-instrument making, and processing of granite. Some kinds of specialization, for instance watchmaking and plumbing, begin in the first year, but ordinarily specialization begins in the second or third year.

Practical work in the shops occupies nearly 75 percent of the total time spent in these schools. The remainder of the time is spent on Arabic, English, arithmetic, algebra, science, geometry, mechanical drawing, and shop administration. Activities in these subjects are correlated closely with the shopwork. The normal school week consists of forty-four periods. Shops are well equipped with tools and machinery, and the work produced is of excellent quality. At annual exhibits each school offers the products of its work for sale to the public. The income thus obtained reduces materially the cost of this type of education. These schools produce skillful technicians, many of whom become foremen or managers or owners of shops.

Elementary trade schools exist, some as sections of regular trade schools, others as separate institutions, which accept elementary-school graduates and give them three years of training in carpet-making, weaving, carpentry, decoration, and shoemaking.

INTERMEDIATE SCHOOLS OF COMMERCE

The intermediate schools of commerce, admitting boys who hold the primary-school certificate to a five-year course, were established to prepare clerks for both governmental and private employment. The program of the first two years approximates that of the first two years of the secondary school. Specialized work begins in the third year and includes bookkeeping, business methods taught in Arabic and in either English or French, commercial geography and arithmetic, and Arabic and English typewriting. Since most business enterprises in Egypt which employ clerks operate on a bi- or trilingual basis and follow about equally European and Egyptian business practices, it is necessary to prepare pupils in at least two languages and two systems. A tuition fee of £E12 ($48) a year is charged in these schools, but approximately half of the boys are exempt from the fee, the exemptions being based on standing in the primary-school examinations and age. The government schools do not provide commercial training for girls.

INTERMEDIATE SCHOOLS OF AGRICULTURE

Intermediate schools of agriculture provide, in a five-year course above the primary school, vocational training in agriculture. Recently the program of the first two years has become identical with that of the same years in secondary schools, except that horticulture and agriculture are substituted for the handwork of the secondary school. At the close of the second year those considered unsuited to the agricultural course are allowed to transfer to a secondary school or to some other type of vocational training. Those who remain study agriculture, botany, zoology, elementary veterinary medicine, chemistry, poultry- and cattle-breeding, agricultural trades, and agricultural bookkeeping. The aim of the school is to train practical agriculturalists who will be competent in crop-raising, agricultural industries, and dairying. Here, as in the commercial schools, the tuition fee of £E12 ($48) a year is not collected from the brighter boys. The schools have facilities for extensive practical work in cultivation of the soil and in animal husbandry.

SCHOOL OF APPLIED ENGINEERING

The School of Applied Engineering, of higher standard than the trade schools, trains boys to be junior officials in government departments that are responsible for technical work and to be foremen, supervisors, or contractors in private employment. One course of five years is for boys coming from the third year of trade or secondary schools. In the first year of this course, trade-school boys are given more theoretical studies, and the secondary-school boys are given more shop training to equalize the different backgrounds. Specialization is offered in mechanical, electrical, and transportation engineering. The second course is of three years' duration and is for boys who have passed the public examination given at the close of the fourth year in the secondary schools. This course offers specialization in building construction and civil engineering, which includes irrigation engineering.

Tuition fees amounting to £E20 ($80) are charged, but approximately 40 percent of the students are exempt. Applications are received from all sections of the country, as the school in Cairo is the only one of this type in Egypt. Boys from trade schools are selected on the basis of an entrance examination. Those from the third year of secondary schools are taken on the basis of promotion-examination marks, and boys who have completed four years of the secondary school are admitted on the basis of their certificate examination. The total enrollment in 1945–46 was 920— 564 in the five-year course and 356 in the three-year course. Of the first-year students in the five-year course, 112 had come from trade schools and 53 from secondary schools.

SCHOOL OF APPLIED ARTS

The School of Applied Arts in Cairo accepts students from the third year of secondary schools. Specializations include weaving, printing on cloth, rug designs, carpentry, wall decoration and stained glass, plaster-casting and decoration, wrought iron, wood- and ivory-carving, art metal-work, silversmithing and enamel-work, and photography. The present program provides a five-year course. This school was not visited by the American Council Commission.

SECONDARY AND VOCATIONAL EDUCATION

Schools of homemaking

Schools of homemaking were established for the purpose of teaching graduates of elementary schools how to protect the health of the family and raise the general standard of living. No tuition fee is charged, and girls are admitted on the basis of entrance examinations conducted by the school. The program is four years in length and gives practical and theoretical courses in home economics and needlework which occupy more than a third of the scheduled periods in each year. Other courses are in religion, Arabic, singing, penmanship, history, geography, arithmetic, science, hygiene, drawing, and physical training. Throughout the course effort is made to increase knowledge and develop habits which will improve the living conditions of Egypt's poorer families. In 1944–45 there were 16 of these schools, with a total enrollment of 1,784 girls.

Schools of embroidery arts

Schools of embroidery and needlework are technical schools which prepare girls for employment in these fields or to teach these subjects in elementary and primary schools. They offer a four-year program for girls holding the primary-school certificate. Tuition fees vary from £E4 ($16) to £E6 ($24), but free lunches are served five days of the week.

The program includes religion, Arabic, French, cutting, sewing, embroidery, dressmaking, knitting, drawing, bookkeeping and business practice, laundry, and physical training. French and drawing courses are correlated with the technical training. Graduates are capable of making all their own clothes and have little difficulty in obtaining employment in dressmaking establishments.

Advanced schools of the same type have been established in Alexandria and Cairo. These have a three-year program and prepare teachers for technical, primary, and secondary schools in addition to increasing the skill of those who wish better employment or hope to establish their own dressmaking shops. Except for one period a week of drawing in the first year and three periods of teaching methods in the third year, the entire time of the girls is spent in cutting, sewing, embroidering, and knitting. Students are allowed to make their own clothes in school, but most of the work is for individuals who engage the services of the school. Materials are usually provided by the patron; charges are to cover the cost of making the article ordered. The girls receive a proportion of the income from this source; the amount received by each girl in the course of the year exceeds the tuition fee of £E6 ($24).

A similar type of technical training for graduates of elementary schools is provided in workshops that are frequently attached to a higher technical school of embroidery, as is the case at Alexandria. These workshops give training in knitting, embroidery, and lace-making but no instruction in related or general subjects. No fees are charged; but once the girls have completed the learning stage, 40 percent of the value of the work which they produce is retained by the Ministry to cover in part the expenses of maintaining the workshop, and the balance is received by the girls.

FEMININE CULTURE SCHOOLS

Feminine culture schools were first established in 1937 and are designed to prepare primary-school graduates for the management of their homes. The program combines cultural courses with courses in domestic arts and child care. The course is six years in length, divided into two stages—a primary stage of four years and an advanced stage of two years. In the primary stage the course is largely cultural, including religion, Arabic, a first foreign language, history, geography, science, mathematics (household accounts), civics, and psychology, to which are added on the practical side courses in child welfare, hygiene and nursing, embroidery and dressmaking, and domestic science. Courses are also given in art, gymnastics, music, and gardening. The total number of periods per week is thirty-eight. In the advanced stage half of a total of thirty-six periods is given to Arabic and a first and second (optional) foreign language, while for the other half girls choose three of the following subjects: art, domestic science, child care, science, sewing and cutting, embroidery, and music. If a girl does not wish to study a second foreign language, she may choose a fourth subject from the list. Fees totaling £E14.5 ($58) are charged, but exemptions or partial exemptions are given on the basis of standing in the primary-school examinations. In 1942–43 there were 6 schools of this type with 694 girls enrolled. It was reported that the number of schools had increased to 13 by 1946.

Chapter 4

HIGHER EDUCATION AND EDUCATIONAL MISSIONS

*A*LTHOUGH various institutions of higher education developed in Egypt during the course of the nineteenth century, it was not until 1906 that the idea of establishing an Egyptian university was born. In that year a number of prominent Egyptians met under the presidency of Sa'id Zaghlul Pasha to consider the project. A committee was formed with Prince Ahmad Fuad Pasha, later King Fuad I, as chairman. Subscriptions and donations were collected from the general public, and a princess of the royal family donated farm lands to the project. A school of arts opened under the name of the Egyptian University at the close of 1908. Foreign visiting professors were invited to teach, and Egyptian students were sent abroad to prepare for teaching at the new University.

For fifteen years the Egyptian University remained a private institution, struggling under the handicap of inadequate funds. This situation gave rise to the idea of founding a state university, and in 1917 the Ministry of Education set up a commission to prepare a plan. The authorities of the Egyptian University, on the basis of the report made by the commission in 1921, decided to transfer the University to the government. A royal decree of March 11, 1925, provided for the foundation of a state university under the name "Egyptian University," which should include four Faculties (colleges): of Arts from the original University; of Science, to be created; of Law, incorporating the School of Law founded by Isma'il Pasha in 1866; and of Medicine, incorporating the venerable School of Medicine and Pharmacy which Muhammad 'Ali Pasha had founded in 1827. Another law, passed in August 1935, incorporated the existing School of Engineering, the Higher School of Agriculture, and the Higher School of Commerce as Faculties (colleges) of the University and included the School of Veterinary Medicine as a school. Thus evolved the first modern Egyptian university, the name of which was changed in 1940 to Fuad I University in memory of the king who had had so much to do with its creation.

In 1938, branches of the Faculties of Law and Literature were opened in Alexandria. By 1942 these branches, together with Faculties of Science, Medicine, Engineering, Commerce, and Agriculture, were converted into Faruq I University, the second state university in Egypt. With the increasing demand for higher education, there is talk of establishing a third at Asyut.

During the year 1945–46 steps were being taken to include Dar al-'Ulum, the institution that trains teachers of Arabic, within the University. Legislation was being passed through Parliament for that purpose.[1]

Fuad I University

Fuad I University now occupies a large site at Gizah, on the outskirts of Cairo, west of the Nile, and near the grounds upon which the Faculties of Engineering and Agriculture and the School of Veterinary Medicine had been built. Imposing buildings have been erected to accommodate the Faculties of Arts, Law, Science, and Commerce; they are grouped about a central administration building that has a spacious assembly hall. A separate building houses the University library. The campus includes a large playing field with a grandstand. Upper classes, graduate sections, and research laboratories of the Faculty of Science occupy part of the Za'faran Palace at 'Abbasiyah in the northeastern part of Cairo, pending completion of adequate buildings at Gizah. The Faculty of Medicine occupies its own historic site and buildings on Qasr al-'Ayni Street and has a large new hospital on nearby Rawdah Island in the Nile.

ORGANIZATION OF THE UNIVERSITY

The University is administered by a chancellor (*mudir*), a University administrative council, and a University council. Each Faculty (school) is administered by its own dean and Faculty council.

The chancellor, appointed by royal decree upon the recommendation of the Minister of Education, is responsible for the administration of the University, represents it before other bodies, and presides over the two University councils—unless the Minister of Education, who is the supreme head of the University, is present. The chancellor appoints minor clerical officials of the University and is responsible for preparing the budget. He is assisted by a secretary general, and a vice chancellor acts in his absence.

[1] The legislation passed, and Dar al-'Ulum graduates now receive a bachelor's degree from the University, and have the option of entering the Higher Institute of Education for professional training as fully qualified teachers of Arabic in Egyptian schools.

Above: Basketmaking in a school for the blind, Cairo
Below: Extracurricular activity group making perfumes in a primary school, Cairo

Above: A Boy Scout outing in the gardens of the Barrage, Egypt
Below: Girl Guides playing basketball, primary school, Cairo

The University administrative council is composed of the chancellor, the Under Secretaries of State for Education and Finance, the deans of the Faculties, and four members appointed by royal decree on recommendation of the Ministry of Education. It has control of the financial business of the University, building projects and maintenance, and deals with the annual budget and all appointments, promotions, transfers, and discipline of professors and teaching staff. The University council includes all the members of the administrative council and, in addition, two professors from each Faculty, the latter being elected by the Faculty council for three-year terms. It considers questions pertaining to the creation of new professorships, transfer of professors, the general organization of academic work, granting of degrees and diplomas, conduct of examinations, admission regulations, student discipline, fees, exemptions, and scholarships, and determination of the functions of higher University officials. Except for questions required by law to be decided by royal decree or by the Council of Ministers or the Minister of Education, the decisions of the two councils are final. They must, however, be reported to the Minister of Education within eight days.

The dean of each Faculty is appointed for a three-year term by the Minister of Education from a list of three professors recommended by the Faculty council. The Faculty council consists of the dean, the professors, and assistant professors. It supervises the academic work, examinations, and the general operation of the Faculty under the supervision of the two University councils. It is consulted before the University administrative council recommends professors and teachers to the Minister for appointment.

The teaching staff is made up of professors, assistant professors, and lecturers. Demonstrators, usually university graduates who act as laboratory or class assistants, are not considered regular members of the teaching staff, and they usually engage in graduate studies while working. Except in surgery, dental surgery, and pharmacy, where a master's degree is sufficient, a doctorate is a basic requirement for appointment as a lecturer. A candidate for an assistant professorship must have spent at least four years as a lecturer and must either have had eight years in government service or else ten years must have elapsed since he received his B.A. or *licence* degree. To be appointed a professor, the candidate must have spent four years as assistant professor and either twelve years in government service or fourteen years must have elapsed since his graduation. Moreover, lecturers and assistant professors must have made significant and original contributions in their fields to achieve promotion. Disciplinary matters affecting the staff are handled by a special board composed of the chancellor and deans of the Faculties.

In the last decade the number of Egyptian professors has increased so that they are now in the majority in almost all the Faculties, and all the deans are Egyptian. This is the natural outcome of the government's policy of sending students abroad for training in highly technical subjects. However, there is no intention of eliminating foreign professors; and it is a matter of policy to continue engaging a number of them, partly to maintain a high standard at the University and partly to benefit from the knowledge of persons prominent in some highly specialized subjects. Some foreign professors are employed on a permanent basis, others as visiting professors for a definite period. In 1944–45 there were seven visiting professors in five Faculties.

The University is financed principally from public funds and fees. A comparatively small income is received from property and other sources. It is a corporate body empowered by its charter to receive grants and contributions; to buy, hold, or sell property. The estimated budget for 1945–46 was £E949,600 (about $3,798,000). Of this total £E698,100 came as a grant from the government, £E210,000 from tuition and other fees, £E13,000 from property, and £E30,500 from miscellaneous sources.

The University library has about 300,000 volumes. Books are acquired by purchase and by donation. A prince of the royal family presented the library with a valuable and extensive collection of geographical and travel books containing many rare items. The library has a valuable collection of Arabic manuscripts and facilities for photostating them. It subscribes to many general and scientific periodicals from various parts of the world. Departmental libraries are maintained for each Faculty, some of them having tens of thousands of volumes.

There were 10,478 students in 1945–46 as compared with 10,001 in the previous year. Distribution by Faculties is shown in Table 14.

The number of women students has been increasing steadily since 1935–36, when there were only 165 women out of a total of 7,017 students registered in five Faculties: Arts, Science, Medicine, Law, and Commerce. In 1945–46 there were 634 women (not counting nurses) out of 10,188, with women registered in seven of the eight Faculties. All Faculties now admit women students.

The number of foreign students, too, has been increasing, 391 students from twenty-four countries being registered in 1944–45. The largest number came from Iraq, 94; followed by Syria, 75; Palestine, 66; Sudan, 52; Arabia, 28; Lebanon, 22; and Transjordan, 15. Other Arab countries of

HIGHER EDUCATION AND EDUCATIONAL MISSIONS

Asia and North Africa contributed 19, making a total of 369 non-Egyptian Arabic-speaking students. The other 22 foreign students came from various other countries in Asia, Africa, and Europe, with 1 from the United States. Foreign students had increased to 470 in 1945–46. In the spirit of the times and with the growth in prestige of the Arab League, Fuad I University is becoming in a true sense an Arab university.

Admission is granted to Egyptian students on the basis of the final Egyptian secondary-school certificate. At present students who hold sec-

TABLE 14
Distribution of Students by Faculties,
Fuad I University, Egypt, 1945–46*

Faculty	Enrollment, 1945–46			Graduates, 1945		
	Men	Women	Total	Men	Women	Total
Arts................	771	333	1,104	174	21	195
Science.............	613	38	651	95	12	107
Law................	1,433	30	1,463	242	2	244
Engineering.........	1,642	3	1,645	160	...	160
Medicine............	2,198	462†	2,660†	167	9‡	176§
Agriculture.........	1,147	26	1,173	266	...	266
Commerce...........	1,566	32	1,598	67	...	67
Veterinary medicine..	184	...	184	4	...	4
Total...........	9,554	924†	10,478†	1,175	44‡	1,219§

* Figures from *A Statement about Fuad I University*, a pamphlet published by the University on the occasion of the visit of King Ibn Sa'ud, January 1946. (In Arabic.)
† Includes 290 student nurses.
‡ Does not include nurses.
§ Composed of 110 graduates in medicine, 4 in dentistry, and 53 in pharmacy in the Faculty of Medicine.

ondary-school certificates of the governments of Iraq, Syria, Lebanon, Palestine, and Turkey are accepted without further requirements. Otherwise, foreign applicants for admission must apply to the Committee on the Equivalence of Degrees in the Ministry of Education to get recognition of their secondary-school studies. In the case of certificates from Sudan and Aden, which are based on the Oxford and Cambridge examinations, students must have passed four subjects exclusive of Arabic with the rating of "good," and must pass an examination in Arabic equivalent to that of the last year of the Egyptian secondary school.

In addition to the regular students who have satisfied the admission requirements and are working for degrees, there are special students who audit classes without receiving academic recognition. The special student does not have to comply with any admission requirements and pays £E2 ($8.00) for each course attended. The University issues such students a certificate stating what courses they have attended on this basis.

Tuition fees begin with £E20 ($80) in the Faculty of Arts and the

School of Pharmacy, rise to £E25 ($100) for Commerce and Veterinary Medicine, to £E30 ($120) for Science, Law, and Dentistry, to £E40 ($160) for Engineering and Agriculture, and reach £E45 ($180) in the Faculty of Medicine. Postgraduate fees are lower, £E4 in Arts, £E20 in Science, and £E10–£E15 in the other Faculties. In addition, every student pays £E1 each for membership in the Students' Union and for medical care, and PT50 ($2.00) as a library fee. There are no exemptions from these small fees, but students of high standing in the general secondary-school examination who are unable to pay tuition may apply for exemption from tuition fees. Exempted students are expected to maintain a high average. The Faculties of Arts and Science have special undergraduate scholarships available on the basis of a special examination. These scholarships carry exemption from fees and a cash sum of £E30 ($120) for one year for first- and second-year students, and for two years for third-year students. Graduate scholarships of £E120 ($480) for graduate work in Egypt and £E600 ($2,400) for graduate study abroad are available to students who stand high in their *licence,* or Bachelor of Science, examination and who have maintained a good record throughout their undergraduate course.

Men students from other parts of the country have to find board and lodgings as best they can, as the University provides no accommodations for men. However, it maintains a home in which all out-of-town women students are required to reside; this is under the administration of the Faculty of Arts, but serves women of all Faculties. A project was started in 1946 to develop a "University City," a residential quarter for students; public contributions are being solicited, and the foundation stone has been laid by King Faruq.

THE PROGRAMS OF THE FACULTIES

This account of the programs of the different Faculties is based on such catalogs and courses of study as exist, on visits of the American Council Commission to each Faculty, on discussions with the deans and other officials, and on the laws and regulations governing the Faculties. Each Faculty has its own organic law passed by Parliament and its internal regulations issued by royal decree.

The Faculty of Arts occupies two buildings on the central University campus and one outside. Its four-year course leads to the degree of *Licence* in Letters, and it offers three graduate courses leading to the master's and doctor's degrees: Oriental languages, archeology, and journalism. Undergraduate and postgraduate work is provided in seven departments: Arabic,

European languages with specialization in English or French, the classics, history, geography, and philosophy. Only students who choose French as their first foreign language in secondary schools are allowed to enroll in the French department; otherwise, the students have a choice of the departments of the Faculty.

Actual differentiation of courses begins with the second year. While first-year entering students are asked to indicate their choice of department within the Faculty, they share a common program during the first year and hence are able to postpone final decision until the year is completed. The first-year program for all comprises twenty hours a week of courses in Arabic, English, French, Latin, history, geography, and philosophy. A few more hours are given in the subject of the student's initial choice, but every student is exposed in this first year to all categories of learning within the Faculty. Beginning with the second year, with his choice of specialization final, the student follows a set course which offers little choice in subject matter. In the third year better students are allowed to apply for honors (*imtiyaz*) and take special additional courses appropriate to the department of their specialization. Very few students achieve the *Licence* in Letters with honors; in 1942–43 only 12 of 204 applicants were successful. Grades for all are based on written, or written and oral, examinations conducted by committees which may contain external examiners. Students are graded as "very poor," "poor," "satisfactory," "good," "very good," and "excellent." An average of "satisfactory" with no work of "very poor" in any one subject is required for passing. Students are not allowed to repeat the work of any year, except the final one, more than once without a special decision of the Faculty council. A second failure in the final year requires a decision of the University council acting upon the opinion of the Faculty council to permit the student to try again.

Postgraduate work toward the degree of Master of Arts is ordinarily allowed only to honor graduates. Under special conditions and with the approval of the Faculty concerned and the University council, a student passing with an average of "good" is permitted to work for his master's degree if he has written papers proving that he is of the appropriate intellectual caliber. The course is two years, the first devoted to further studies and the second to the thesis, which is written under the sponsorship of a professor and must be original. The student must pass a written and an oral examination in the subjects related to his thesis, must have attended 75 percent of the required lectures, and must defend his thesis before a board before he is awarded the master's degree. This degree may be granted with first- or second-class honors, which ranking, together with the subject of the thesis, is inscribed upon the diploma.

The Graduate Institute of Archeology (Egyptian and Islamic) gives three-year courses leading to a diploma in either Egyptian or Islamic archeology. The Graduate Institute of Oriental Languages gives courses of three years in each of the Semitic languages, the dialects of Arabic, and the languages of the Islamic states, leading to a diploma in any one of these fields. The Graduate Institute of Editing, Translation, and Journalism offers a two-year course for which a diploma in journalism is granted.

To matriculate for the degree of Doctor in Letters, a student must possess the master's degree, or, if he is in archeology, he must have the diploma in archeology, which leads to the degree of Doctor in Archeology. Exceptions are made if a student with a *licence* either has other degrees or has produced research deemed equivalent to that involved in acquiring a master's degree. Work preliminary to granting the doctor's degree usually takes two years and includes a thesis which constitutes a significant contribution to its field. The thesis is written in Arabic with an adequate digest in a foreign language, although a thesis about a foreign language, with the approval of the Faculty, may be written in that language, with an adequate digest in Arabic. The thesis must be sponsored by a professor and defended before a committee under the chairmanship of the dean; before the degree is granted the thesis must be printed and fifty copies deposited with the Faculty.

The Faculty of Science offers a four-year course in pure science leading to the degree of Bachelor of Science and a one-year preliminary natural-science course for students intending to enter the Schools of Medicine, Pharmacy, or Dentistry. Its graduate division offers a one-year course leading to diplomas in meteorology and geophysics in addition to the regular courses leading to the degrees of Master of Science, Doctor of Philosophy, and Doctor of Science.

The Faculty has departments in pure mathematics, applied mathematics, astronomy, physics, chemistry, botany, zoology, entomology, and geology. Teaching is mainly in English, but some courses are given in Arabic. Courses in English with special reference to scientific literature are given in the first two years of undergraduate work. French or German is taught in the fourth year of the course for B.S. candidates, and additional work in one of these languages is required of candidates for the M.S. degree.

The undergraduate course for the B.S. follows closely the pattern of the same course in English universities. In his first year the student chooses four subjects grouped in one of the following ways:

I	II	III	IV
Pure mathematics	Physics	Chemistry	Pure mathematics
Applied mathematics	Chemistry	Geology	Applied mathematics
Physics	Botany	Botany	Physics
Chemistry	Zoology	Zoology	Geology

In his second year he drops one of the four subjects and keeps three in any of six different combinations, or any combination approved by the Faculty council. In the third and fourth years, a student may work for the B.S. (general) or, with the approval of the Faculty council, for the B.S. (special). In the general course, he takes two of the three subjects studied in the second year as his principal subjects. The third subject he takes as a subsidiary subject. Having passed his final examinations, he receives his B.S. (general) degree in one of four classes: First- or Second-Class Honors, or Third- or Fourth-Class degrees. If he works for the B.S. (special) degree, a student may choose in his fourth year one of the following subjects: mathematics, astronomy, physics, chemistry, botany, zoology, or geology and pursue courses in that subject throughout the year. First- and Second-Class Honors are granted only to candidates of the B.S. (special) degree.

Examinations must be passed at the end of each of the undergraduate years for promotion to the next year. A student failing in one or more subjects in the first two years may present himself for re-examination in the fall; but if he fails in the fall, he is required to repeat the year in all subjects. The third- and fourth-year students must pass examinations in both principal and subsidiary subjects; but if they fail in a subsidiary course in the third year, they are allowed to proceed with fourth-year work pending re-examination in the subject in which they failed. A fourth-year candidate is allowed to present himself for re-examination in a subject or subjects in which he failed provided he repeats the courses assigned by the Faculty council. No student is allowed to repeat a year more than once. Examinations for the B.S. degree are conducted by a board under the chairmanship of the dean with internal examiners from the Faculty and external examiners from British universities.

The degree of Master of Science is granted to bearers of the B.S. who have completed two additional years of approved courses and research and presented a satisfactory thesis. Part of the work for this degree may be conducted in some other institution that is recognized by the University. The degree of Doctor of Philosophy may be achieved with one year and a thesis by holders of the master's degree or by three years of research plus a thesis by holders of the bachelor's degree. A candidate for the degree of Doctor of Science must be either a graduate of Fuad I University with an M.S. dating back two years or a graduate in science or medicine who has done postgraduate work in Egypt for not less than five years. He is required to present his published work to a committee of two examiners appointed by the Faculty council. In addition, he may submit unpublished work to support his candidacy and must state which parts of his works he considers original. The work must be considered of Doctor of Science standard by both examiners.

Theses for degrees of Master of Science, Doctor of Philosophy, and Doctor of Science are usually submitted to examiners in the British Isles.

The Faculty of Science, now quartered partly at Gizah on the main University campus and partly at 'Abbasiyah, has a new building in process of construction at Gizah that will presumably permit accommodation of the entire Faculty on the new site. This Faculty has an extensive library, with many English, French, and German accessions, and departmental libraries well equipped with advanced books and periodicals which are available to students from the third year upward. An additional facility is its Marine Biological Station at Ghardaqa on the Red Sea which includes equipment for research and a comprehensive library of books, reports of expeditions in the Indian Ocean and the Red Sea, and important periodicals and reprints from periodicals.

The Faculty of Medicine is the oldest of the schools included in the University, having been founded outside Cairo by Muhammad 'Ali Pasha in 1827 and transferred to its present historic site on Qasr al-'Ayni Street in Cairo in 1837. The latter site had been used as an army hospital by the French expedition under Napoleon in 1798–1801. The Faculty and its scientists have been associated with some important discoveries in medicine, notably the discovery of the parasite Bilharzia. Aside from buildings which house the classrooms, laboratories, museums, and library, the Faculty occupies the old Qasr al-'Ayni Hospital, with 1,174 beds, the new Fuad I Hospital on Rawdah Island, with 1,216 beds and space for 200 to 300 more, the Children's Hospital, with 181 beds, and, for the postgraduate practice of woman doctors, the Kitchener Memorial Hospital.

The Faculty of Medicine includes four schools: the Medical School, with 1,459 students; the School of Pharmacy, with 283 students; the Dental School, with 60 students; and the School of Nurses with 290 students —all figures are for the year 1945–46. The first three schools share the preliminary classes maintained within the Faculty of Science, which had 568 students in the same year.

HIGHER EDUCATION AND EDUCATIONAL MISSIONS

The Medical School offers a course of five and a half years. A great deal of practical work in the hospitals and clinics of the Faculty is required, including six months each in the medical, surgical, and obstetrics-gynecological wards, three months in the ophthalmological wards, and one and one-half months each in the orthopedic, neurological, tubercular, and genito-urinary wards. Three examinations are held, one at the end of the second year, one at the end of the third, and the final-degree examination. The examinations are very exacting, and usually a large number of students fail in the final examinations; only 80 out of 210 candidates passed in the examinations held in January 1946. Examiners are both internal and external, the latter being principally British. Successful candidates are granted the degree of Bachelor of Medicine and Surgery.

Two graduate degrees are granted, that of Master of Surgery and that of Doctor of Medicine. The former is given in one of six surgical or allied subjects to candidates who have spent at least three years at a recognized hospital and who have passed the required examinations. The latter is given in one of the following subjects: general medicine, diseases of children, tropical medicine, and public health. The candidate must have had five years in private practice, or three years at a recognized hospital, or two years at a teaching hospital and must pass required examinations. The School of Medicine also grants about twenty types of postgraduate diplomas in various branches of medicine, surgery, public health, and medical science, requiring studies of six months to two years.

The School of Pharmacy offers a course of three years beyond the preliminary year, leading to the degree of Bachelor of Pharmacy. The degree of Master of Pharmacy is granted to candidates who have had two years of experience as demonstrators in the pertinent subjects in a recognized school of pharmacy, medicine, or science and who pass the required examination or submit an adequate thesis.

The School of Dental Surgery gives a course of four years above the preliminary year leading to the degree of Bachelor of Dental Surgery. An examination is held at the end of each year. A shorter course is offered for students who already hold a medical degree or diploma. The degree of Master of Dental Surgery is granted to candidates who have completed requirements comparable to those for the degree of Master of Surgery.

The School of Nursing offers a course of thirty-six months to girls who have completed the primary school. A preliminary apprenticeship of six weeks is required. Graduates of the School of Nursing who wish to become midwives spend an additional twelve months taking theoretical and practical work in midwifery. The Kitchener Memorial Hospital in

Cairo offers a special course of one year in midwifery for which only ability to read and write is required. Such students graduate as assistant midwives.

The Faculty of Engineering, the second oldest higher institution in Egypt, occupies a set of buildings on a site of its own at Gizah not far from the central University campus and to the southeast of it. It has six departments which give courses leading to the bachelor's degree: civil engineering, architecture, mechanical engineering, electrical engineering, industrial chemistry, and mining engineering. In addition, it offers work leading toward the degrees of Master of Engineering, Master of Architecture, and Doctor of Philosophy.

The undergraduate course consists of one year of preparatory work, which is the same for all except industrial-chemistry students, and four years of specialization. The Faculty adheres to a policy of eliminating the weaker students in the preparatory class, which may result in the elimination of 40 percent of the class. Failure in subsequent years is not common, and about 90 percent of the fourth-year students pass their examinations and receive their degrees. Examinations for all years except the fourth are held by committees of the teaching staff. The final examinations are conducted by committees of internal and external examiners.

Conditions for granting the degrees of Master of Engineering or of Architecture and of Doctor of Philosophy are somewhat similar to those in the Faculty of Science. A thesis required for the degree of Doctor of Philosophy must be approved by the sponsoring professor and a committee of three professors and then submitted to an external examiner. In 1945 18 master's degrees and 3 doctorates were granted.

The Faculty is well equipped. In addition to laboratories for ordinary purposes and twelve different types of workshops, it has the following laboratories: heat-transmission research, sound, irrigation research, concrete research, soil-mechanics and foundation research, testing of materials, hydraulics, road and asphalt, internal-combustion engines, steam and refrigeration, telecommunications, electrical measurements, high voltage, and machinery. Also, it has an extensive library of about 45,000 volumes and as many as 118 European and American periodicals on its subscription list.

The Faculty of Law, third oldest of the present faculties, is situated on the main campus and gives a four-year course leading to the *Licence* in Law degree. Like many other law colleges in the Near East, it bears a French imprint. In each of the four years, two specified legal subjects are studied in French. In addition to general courses in the French language, economics and finance, introduction to the study of law, and Roman law, it offers courses in Islamic law, constitutional law, criminal law, civil law, public and private international law, commercial law, and legal procedure. To pass, a student must not fall below 50 percent in any subject in the first three years or below 60 percent in the final examinations for the *licence*. Undergraduate instruction is a combination of lecture periods, tutoring periods, and seminars. The student is required to join one seminar class each year and attend it regularly. The bearer of a law degree from a foreign institution must pass written and oral equivalence examinations in four subjects: Muslim law; legal, civil, and commercial procedure; criminal law—penal code and criminal investigation; and the organization of administration and justice, as well as administrative and financial law.

To earn the degree of Doctor of Law, the candidate must spend a year on each of two subjects in the following group of four: private law, public law, political economy, and Muslim law. The successful candidate receives a diploma of higher studies in each of the two fields of his choice, which together with an acceptable dissertation on an approved subject entitles him to receive the doctorate.

The Faculty maintains three postgraduate institutes which award diplomas: (1) the Institute of Criminal Studies gives a two-year course to bearers of the *Licence* in Law or its equivalent; (2) the Institute of Administrative Studies gives a one-year course above the *licence;* and (3) the Institute of Economic and Financial Studies gives a one-year course in either economics or finance to bearers of the *Licence* in Law or the Bachelor of Commerce degree.

The library of the Faculty contains 26,000 volumes, 7,000 of which are in Arabic; the rest are in French, English, German, Dutch, Italian, and Spanish. In addition, it has some 10,000 doctoral dissertations from abroad. It receives about 130 periodicals in law, economics, and sociology. The professors of the Faculty issue a review known as *The Review of Law and Economics,* which appears seven times a year and carries original articles in Arabic, French, and English.

The Faculty of Agriculture, founded as a school in 1890, became a higher institution in 1911–12 and was drawn into the University in 1935. It occupies a set of buildings on its own grounds, south of the main University campus in Gizah. It has large farm lands, including a dairy, and extensive laboratories for the various scientific and agricultural subjects; its dairy laboratory includes a refrigeration plant.

The undergraduate course of four years leading to the Bachelor of

Agriculture degree consists of scientific studies relating to agriculture and animal husbandry and modern economic and industrial problems and devices, including cooperatives. The weekly timetable allots twelve to fourteen periods to lectures and twenty-one or twenty-two periods to practical and laboratory work. Graduate work for the M.S. and Ph.D. degrees, each requiring two years of work, was instituted in 1944, but at the time of the American Council Commission's visit in 1946, no one had achieved the doctorate.

Graduates of the Faculty of Agriculture, being the most numerous within the University, have had difficulty in obtaining employment. At present the supply of technically trained advanced students of agriculture exceeds the demand for their services on big agricultural projects or in agricultural companies. The students have been demanding that the government grant graduates newly reclaimed agricultural land; but even if the government made the grants, it is doubtful if many of the graduates could finance the venture. Some graduates have recently begun to go into the teaching profession.

The Faculty of Commerce, originally the Higher School of Commerce, joined the University in 1935 and occupies a building on the main University campus. It offers a four-year course leading to the Bachelor of Commerce degree and a two-year graduate course which, with an original thesis, ends in the Master of Commerce degree.

The first two years of the undergraduate course give to all students alike a foundation in economics, economic geography, corporation law, contracts, accounting, business administration, and both English and French. In the third and fourth years the students specialize in either commerce and economics or in political science.

The School of Veterinary Medicine, which joined the University in 1935, occupies a site south of the central campus. Its course of five years leads to the degree of Bachelor of Veterinary Medicine. Holders of this degree, by doing two years of postgraduate work and preparing a thesis, may achieve the degree of Master of Veterinary Medicine. Candidates for the doctorate must have the master's degree and present an original dissertation. In 1945–46 there were 32 students working for the master's degree.

The school has a veterinary hospital, an extensive museum of animal pathology, an X-ray institute, and well-equipped laboratories, particularly for physiology, osteology, and anatomy.

Graduates of this school are in general absorbed into government service.

Faruq I University

In 1938 Fuad I University established branches of its Faculties of Arts and Law in Alexandria. In 1942 this nucleus, with five additional Faculties—Science, Engineering, Medicine, Agriculture, and Commerce—was legally constituted Faruq I University, Egypt's second state university.

This University, having been projected into a wartime world, with Egypt a center of military operations and communication with the outside world curtailed, has had a handicapped infancy. It has suffered from a lack of books, equipment, and professors; and with building construction at a standstill, its seven Faculties are spread over six different makeshift accommodations in Alexandria and its environs. The administration occupies a rented palace; the Faculties of Arts and Commerce are in old buildings on the Mahmudiyah Canal; the Faculties of Law and Science use old buildings of the 'Abbasiyah school; the Faculty of Engineering functions in the workshops of the al-'Urwat al-Wuthqah, a philanthropic society; the Faculty of Medicine carries on in the government hospital; the Faculty of Agriculture is situated on the outskirts of the town of Damanhur, some miles to the southeast of Alexandria. However, two lots of land, not far apart and totaling eighty-nine feddans, or nearly one hundred acres, have been acquired in Alexandria. Plans for the establishment of a University campus are under way.

During the war years, professors and other teachers were drawn from Fuad I University, various government departments, and other walks of life; it was impossible to obtain foreign professors at that time. As soon as the war ended in Europe, arrangements were made to bring in a number of European and American professors, and it was expected that some of them would be on hand during the year 1946–47. Both universities have been sending a number of students abroad to study for advanced degrees, preparatory to assuming teaching and research posts upon their return to Egypt.

ORGANIZATION OF THE UNIVERSITY

The organization of Faruq I University is similar to that of Fuad I. However, Faruq I has a single University council which combines the functions of the two councils at Fuad I. This council is made up of the chancellor as chairman, the vice chancellor, the deans of the Faculties, one professor from each Faculty (chosen by the Faculty council), a representative of the Ministry of Education, and the mayor of Alexandria. It supervises the business and administrative affairs of the University and also academic matters. Except for matters which require legislation or decision of the Council of Ministers or which fall within the jurisdiction of the Minister of Education, the decisions of the University council are final.

The chancellor is appointed by royal decree upon the recommendation of the Minister of Education. Whereas at Fuad I the vice chancellor is a dean selected by the University council simply to act for the chancellor in the latter's absence, the vice chancellor at Faruq I is appointed by the Minister of Education and is considered an official of the University administration. Similarly, the deans at Faruq I are not nominated by the Faculty council as at Fuad I, but are appointed for three-year terms by the Minister of Education from the five senior professors of each Faculty. A dean cannot be removed from office before the expiration of his term except by a decision of the Minister of Education showing cause. Two years must pass before a dean so removed may be reappointed. In other details the two universities have the same pattern of organization.

Financially Faruq I is more dependent upon the government than is Fuad I. Its estimated budget for 1945–46 was £E506,100, derived as follows:

Source	Budget
Tuition and library fees	£E102,400
Miscellaneous receipts	11,200
Grant from Ministry of Education	£E342,500
Grant from the government for cost of living allowances	50,000
Total grant from government	392,500
Total budget	£E506,100

This budget is more than six times the initial one of 1942–43. Starting with an actual expenditure of £E79,802, the budget jumped to £E273,146 in 1943–44, and to an estimated expenditure of £E392,300 in 1944–45. This rapid rise in cost has been necessitated by an equally rapid increase in the number of students and staff and by the fact that laboratories, lecture halls, study-rooms, and the library had to be equipped under conditions of wartime scarcity. It is estimated that the building of the new campus will cost approximately £E5,000,000 or about $20,000,000.

Admission of students is based on the secondary-school certificate or its equivalent. The University authorities are trying to give Faruq I a national character by admitting students from the entire country rather than just from the Alexandria area and the northern delta. There is a tendency

HIGHER EDUCATION AND EDUCATIONAL MISSIONS

on the part of students refused admission at Fuad I University to apply for admission at Faruq I. The latter had an enrollment in 1944–45 of 3,034 students, 111 of whom were foreign. Distribution by Faculty was as follows for that year:

Faculty	Enrollment
Arts	286
Science	343
Law	1,084
Medicine	520
Agriculture	204
Engineering	429
Commerce	168
Total	3,034

At the time of the Commission's visit in late 1945, only the Faculties of Arts, Law, and Medicine had had graduates. The other Faculties, which started their first year in 1942–43, were to graduate their first classes in the summer of 1946. Graduate work was being undertaken on a small scale by the older Faculties, particularly by the Faculty of Arts. In most cases the programs of the various Faculties have not yet definitely crystallized, but have thus far followed with minor variations the programs of Fuad I University, a natural enough circumstance since so many of the staff members have been drawn from the older university.

Progress in Higher Education

The preceding account of the two universities makes it clear that, although of recent development, university education has made great strides in the last twenty years. Progress is indicated not only by the ever-increasing number of students and the rapid increase in budgetary provisions for university education, but also by the caliber of the research and publications produced by members of the staff and by graduate students and published in many instances in scientific journals abroad. That Egypt is determined to give its deserving young people the best in university education is evident in the generous provisions made for the two universities, the high standard of buildings and equipment, and in the eagerness to obtain the services of outstanding foreign professors.

It is early to expect these young universities to strike out boldly in new directions in matters of organization and administration or to have perfected the adaptation of their programs to the needs of the country. It must be remembered that the inspiration for methods of university education in Egypt has thus far come from France and Great Britain. The French pattern is seen in the Faculties of Arts and of Law, especially in the latter, while British influence is seen in the other Faculties, particularly those of Science, Medicine, and Engineering. The Faruq I University, starting anew, has a splendid opportunity to attempt new methods of organization and teaching.

Student discipline offers a serious problem to both universities, principally in regard to student strikes and demonstrations. Students may strike and conduct demonstrations for political reasons, as they did in connection with the demand for British evacuation of Egypt. However, students may strike to modify academic conditions as well. At Faruq I students of the Faculty of Agriculture struck to demand certain concessions from the government as to employment and the granting of new lands to graduates. Special police under orders of the University authorities are delegated to keep order within the campuses.

Higher Institute of Agriculture

The Higher Institute of Agriculture, founded in 1942 at Shabin al-Kom, gives a course parallel to that of the undergraduate Faculties of Agriculture in the two universities. While the course at the universities is designed to prepare scientific and research workers in agriculture, the Institute is designed to prepare workers in practical agriculture. Students are admitted from the scientific sections of the secondary school after a personal interview. The length of the course in the Institute is four years with specialization in the fourth year in farm management, horticulture, and agricultural industries. The number of students in 1945–46 was 148, of whom two-thirds were boarders. Fees are £E25 for day students and £E40 for boarders, with about 10 percent of the enrollment exempt from fees on the basis of high standing in the secondary-school examination.

One distinctive feature of the instructional program is the regular use of extensive excursions to various parts of Egypt. These take place during the month of January and the months of June and July each year. Intensive studies are made of one area, including land reclamation, rice- and cotton-growing, various types of crops, and life of the farmers. In this way it is expected that each student will gain comprehensive knowledge of the practical problems of agriculture in Egypt. In the first two years each student is assigned a plot of land which he must develop in such a way as to be economically profitable. A degree of Bachelor of Science in Agriculture is given to successful candidates in the final examinations.

Higher School of Finance and Commerce

Another institute of postsecondary level outside the universities is the Higher School of Finance and Commerce in Cairo. It gives a four-year course above the secondary school which is of a more practical nature than the University course in commerce. Examinations for the diploma are given in the Arabic language, first and second foreign languages, translation from and into English, typewriting in Arabic and the first foreign language, business methods and accounting in the same two languages, business arithmetic, political economy, and law. This School was not visited by the American Council Commission.

Higher School of Fine Arts

The Higher School of Fine Arts in Cairo provides training in architecture, painting, sculpture, decorative arts, and engraving in a five-year course which for architecture is above the complete secondary-school program (five years) and for the other specializations is above the general course (four years) of the secondary schools. A graduate of the general course may be accepted for specialization in architecture if he holds a diploma of the School of Arts and Trades or an equivalent certificate. All students have to pass an entrance examination mainly designed to test their aptitude in drawing. Successful students receive a diploma in their specializations. The Higher School of Fine Arts was not visited by the American Council commission.

Educational Missions

The idea of sending students abroad was first developed into policy of the government by Muhammad 'Ali Pasha, founder of the present ruling dynasty of Egypt. Eager to establish a modern state having a strong army, Muhammad 'Ali sent young men abroad to study as early as 1813. In the course of his long rule he sent as many as 319 students abroad at a cost to his treasury of £E273,360.[2] The first missions were sent to Italy, but later France became the principal center of foreign study for Egyptian youth, and a special house with a French director and Egyptian supervisors was maintained for the students in Paris. Some missions were sent to England and Austria. In Europe the subjects of study were military and naval training, engineering, medicine, pharmacy, and arts and crafts ranging from printing to carpentry.

[2] Amin Sami Pasha, *Education in Egypt* (Cairo: al-Ma'arif Press, 1917), p. 7. (In Arabic.)

Muhammad 'Ali used the students thus trained to replace European officials and teachers in his departments and schools, to lead and organize his army, and to serve the army and the country as doctors, engineers, and technicians. Some translated books into Arabic and Turkish for use in the schools. Many former mission students assumed important positions in the service of the state and contributed to the renaissance of modern Egypt.

The policy of sending educational missions to foreign countries was continued under Muhammad 'Ali's successors. 'Abbas I sent 61 students; Sa'id, 57; Isma'il Pasha, 162 in his sixteen-year reign; and Tawfiq Pasha, from 1879 to 1882, sent 33.[3] In 1882, however, with the beginning of the British occupation, Egyptian policies underwent a drastic change. Strict economy was observed in all departments of government, and in the remaining years of Tawfiq's rule, 1882–88, only 9 students were sent abroad for study.[4] In 1888 the Council of Ministers decided to send no more students to study at government expense in foreign countries until the number already abroad should be reduced to 10 and from that point on to send only 2 a year. At the time more Egyptian students studying abroad were doing so at their own expense than at the expense of the state, and the Council thought the money used on missions should be spent for expanding educational facilities at home.[5]

This policy, nominally in force for more than twenty years, was not consistently carried out, for by 1908 there were 42 Egyptians studying abroad at government expense. In 1909 the government, wanting to educate men who could teach advanced subjects in Arabic at its higher institutions, decided to expand the educational missions. By 1914 there were about 750 Egyptian students in foreign countries; of these some 50 were studying at government expense.[6] The movement of students toward European institutions of learning was given additional impetus in 1925, when the necessity of creating a highly specialized Egyptian faculty for the new state Egyptian University compelled the government to expand the program of educational missions. During the eighteen years of King Fuad's rule, which ended with his death in 1936, 1,794 students were sent abroad on government missions.

By this time the nature of foreign missions had altered considerably. Early nineteenth-century students went forth with the minimum of educa-

[3] Ahmad 'Izzat 'Abd al-Karim, *History of Education in Egypt:* I, *The Age of 'Abbas and Sa'id*, 165, 273; and II, *The Age of Isma'il*, 775 (Cairo: Ministry of Education, 1945). (In Arabic.)

[4] Yacoub Artin Pasha, *L'Instruction Publique en Egypte* (Paris: Ernest Leroux, 1889), Annexe E, p. 209.

[5] 'Abd al-Karim, *op. cit.*, II, *The Age of Isma'il*, 597.

[6] Amin Sami, *op. cit.*, p. 73.

HIGHER EDUCATION AND EDUCATIONAL MISSIONS

tion and only slight acquaintance with the language of the country in which they were going to study. Regulations adopted in 1924 stipulated that students were to be sent only for degrees higher than those existing in Egypt. Thus, missions came to be composed principally of graduate students. However, the regulations are not too consistently followed, as the government continues to send a number of students abroad for graduate degrees which are offered by the two Egyptian universities, notably the M.S., Ph.D., and Dr.Sci.

The fact that 444 students were sent abroad at government expense between 1935 and 1938 indicates the growth of this program. The war brought mission movements virtually to a standstill, and only 20 new students were sent out of the country between 1939–44. In pre-war days the students were distributed in England, France, Germany, Italy, Belgium, Holland, Denmark, and the United States. In many years the number of students studying at their own expense abroad has exceeded the number of mission students.

Wartime interruption of the missions and absorption of many former mission students into work outside the teaching profession created a shortage of faculty members at the two Egyptian universities, particularly at Faruq I. Consequently, a vigorous mission program was instigated at the close of the war, and the 1945–46 mission had a total of 357 students, including those left over from previous years. Of these, 242 were new to the mission. It was planned to send an additional 209 in 1946–47, but not all of these had been sent by the middle of October 1946. At that time 522 students were actually in missions, which were distributed by country as follows:

Great Britain	244
United States	187
France	53
Switzerland	35
Italy	3
Total	522

It will be noticed that the largest number of students is sent to Great Britain. This has been more or less the case since the turn of the century when British influence in education became paramount. The United States, to which no more than 5 students had been sent in pre-war years, has now suddenly assumed second place, with 187 students, and, according to the Egyptian Education Bureau in Washington, D.C., there were in January 1947 an additional 53 students studying at their own expense in the United States. The number of mission students would undoubtedly be higher were it not for difficulties of transportation, exchange, and especially the difficulty of obtaining admission for the students in suitable American institutions. Since most students are sent to take graduate work in highly specialized fields, the Egyptian government is naturally desirous of sending them to the best institutions where they can work under professors of world renown; otherwise, it would not be worth while to send them, for the Egyptian universities now offer work in most fields.

The list of subjects assigned to the 242 students sent out in 1945–46 is illuminating and gives a very good idea of the desire for specialists in Egypt. One to 10 students may be assigned in each field.

In the arts, students were commissioned to study principles of education, methods of teaching science, social studies, mathematics, literature and English, sociology, philosophy, psychology, experimental and abnormal psychology, Arabic, hieroglyphics, Semitics, comparative literature, classical studies; ancient, medieval, and modern history; human, regional, and physical geography; and paleography.

In the field of law and politics students were to study civil law, criminal law, administrative law, constitutional law, commercial and maritime law, general and special international law, political economy, financial legislation and public finance, political science, and international relations.

In finance, students were to specialize in business management, industrial management, banking, various fields of statistics, accounting, insurance accounting, public finance, social economics, taxation, tourist trade and hotel-keeping.

Specialization in the fields of science and mathematics included higher mathematics, the astronomy of the universe, applied mathematics, pure mathematics, mathematical statistics, physics, electromagnetic waves, wave mechanics, hydrodynamics, spectrum analysis, astronomy, meteorology, the chemistry of alcoholic drinks, organic chemistry, biochemistry, metallurgy, fuels and fuel analysis, petrology, botany, marine biology, entomology, embryology, cytology, experimental zoology, paleontology, microscopic paleontology, mycology, genetics, the making of animal and plant models, and the manufacture of porcelain.

In pharmacy and medicine, students were to specialize in bacteriology and veterinary bacteriology, dermatology, industrial diseases, radiology and repair of radiological instruments, therapeutic chemistry, venereal-disease control, dentistry, dental mechanics, dental anatomy, histology, pediatrics, general surgery, physical chemistry, experimental and photographic pathology, materia medica, pharmaceutical chemistry, and nutrition.

HIGHER EDUCATION AND EDUCATIONAL MISSIONS 93

Extensive fields were covered in engineering and technology: reinforced concrete, internal-combustion engines, mining chemistry, electrical engineering, telephone engineering and acoustics, mining surveying, mining engineering, hospital construction, water power, control of water courses, hydraulic research, drinking-water engineering, city lighting, sewage systems, construction engineering, automobile engineering, foundation and geological mechanics, road paving, marine engineering and shipbuilding, mechanical engineering of ships, lighthouses and wireless direction, electrical instruments and their designs, technology and factory administration, strength of materials, hydraulics, architecture, radio engineering, electrical acoustics, air conditioning, metallurgy, surveying, and town-planning.

In agriculture, the students were to take up medical botany, agricultural machinery, agricultural buildings, soil survey and analysis, agricultural geology, classification of soils, horticulture, domestic animals and their diseases, technology of nutrition, physiology of crops, plant-breeding, virus diseases, agricultural experimentation, agricultural economics, animal husbandry, and animal-feeding.

Finally, a group of miscellaneous subjects included music, eurythmics, art, drawing for photomechanical printing, color photoengraving, printing and binding, manual arts, home economics, dress designing, archeological reconstruction, and physical education.

This list suggests the variety of subjects pursued in foreign countries by Egyptian government students. Gone are the days when missions were primarily intended for the purpose of preparing teachers. Today, in addition to preparing university professors, men are being trained to undertake the exploitation of Egypt's resources and to help in the solution of its vital problems.

An advisory committee composed of representatives of the Ministry of Education, the two universities, and the nine other ministries decides on the subjects to be studied by the missions, the selection of students, and the general mission policies. Each year the Government Missions Advisory Committee publishes a list of the subjects for foreign study, the number of students required for each subject, and invites applications. Students must fulfill certain conditions of scholastic standing, age, health, and vision. Applicants are subjected to a medical examination and must present themselves to the committee for interview. A student must possess the highest degree granted by the Egyptian government institutions in the subject in which he wishes to specialize abroad. Government officials sent on missions retain their re-employment and promotion rights. Students may be nominated for study abroad by the various ministries and universities but the final selection is made by the Government Missions Advisory Committee.

The government pays travel expenses to destination, a monthly allowance for living expenses beginning with the day of the student's departure from Egypt, tuition fees, expenses of any special study trips recommended by the university, and medical fees and expenses including hospitalization. In return, the student undertakes to complete his studies in the specified period, to maintain good behavior, and to serve for a period of seven years the ministry responsible for sending him or at least in some government service. Woman students are required to serve only three years. A student failing in his studies for reasons other than health may have the period of his contract extended for no more than one year.

In 1945–46 the budget for educational missions was £E157,500 (approximately $630,000).[7] This was more than doubled in the projected budget for 1946–47, £E336,500 ($1,346,000) being the amount set.

Education mission offices are maintained by the Egyptian government in Paris, London, Geneva, Rome, and Washington. The directors of these offices have charge of all the affairs of government students in the country concerned. They arrange for admission of the students to specific universities, visit the students to follow their progress and report findings to the Ministry of Education, and have charge of all financial arrangements affecting the students. They also supervise nongovernment students who have agreed to live under government supervision. This latter arrangement is usually made by the parent or guardian, who deposits money in the Ministry of Education to be paid out to the student by the missions office on the same basis as allowances are paid to mission students.

[7] This budget does not include the administrative expenses of the Egyptian Education Bureaus in Europe and in America. The administrative expenses of the Bureau in Washington, D.C., from April 1947 to March 1948 were $78,125.19. The amount spent on government missions in the U.S.A. for the same period was $723,130.14, and the funds spent on private students for the same period were $619,783.33. Thus the total expended for these three items for the year was $1,491,048.66. (The foregoing data are from the Egyptian Education Bureau, Washington.)

Chapter 5

INSTITUTIONS FOR TEACHER TRAINING

*I*NSTITUTIONS for the training of teachers have, for the most part, developed as a particular type of school experienced a shortage of teachers or as a new type of school was established. Courses in such institutions have been shortened at need and lengthened when an emergency was less acute.

Training Schools for Elementary Teachers

There are separate schools for training men and women for teaching in the elementary schools. The course for men is six years in length; for women who have had a two-year course above the regular elementary school the course is five years. Some of the training schools for women include an advanced course of two years, graduates of which may be assigned to teach in primary schools for girls. Students are accepted on the basis of an entrance examination conducted by the elementary-training school and in addition must pass a medical examination. There are many more applicants than can be accommodated. The faculties of these schools have received their preparation in postsecondary schools and hold a bachelor's degree or its equivalent. The schools charge no fees, and those for women usually have boarding departments for girls from the villages. In 1945–46 there were 9 schools for men and 8 for women distributed throughout the provinces.

The program of studies for these training schools includes advanced courses of the primary school and lower courses of the secondary school with a different time allotment; and, in the upper years there are courses in psychology, principles and practices of education, special methods of teaching and practice teaching. The schools for women include courses in needlework, laundry-work, and housekeeping, including cooking. The pattern of courses is equally set for men and for women: no election of courses or specialization is permitted. Student organizations are considered ample outlets for special interests and abilities. Excursions to points of interest in the vicinity are arranged by the school.

Training Colleges for Primary Teachers

In the fall of 1945 a new type of training school for teachers of primary schools for boys was opened in four centers: Cairo, Alexandria, Shabin al-Kom, and Asyut. This type of training school was established to meet the increased demand for primary-school teachers which resulted from the elimination of fees from primary schools and the consequent increase in enrollment. At present, the course is two years in length and admits students who hold the Secondary-School Certificate, General Section, which is obtained after four years of secondary education. Applicants were selected on the basis of a personal interview, standing in the certificate examination, age (recent secondary-school graduates being preferred), and physical fitness. In one school only a fifth of the applicants were admitted. No fees for tuition or boarding expenses are charged. The aim of these schools is to prepare class teachers, rather than subject specialists, for the new primary schools which may replace the elementary and primary schools to form a common school for all Egyptian children.

There is a uniform program for all students; it includes courses in Arabic, English, mathematics, history, civics, geography, science, drawing, handwork, pedagogy, special methods in teaching, hygiene, physical training, and practice teaching. Practice teaching is done in each year in the public and private primary schools in the vicinity. It is planned to provide some of these training schools with sufficient land to make possible practical training in agriculture to prepare teachers for work in rural areas.

Higher Institute for Women Teachers

The Higher Institute for Women Teachers, in Cairo, prepares women to teach domestic science, physical training, art, or music. The regular course is five years in length, with the first year considered as a preparatory year. Girls who have passed the public examination given at the end of their fifth year (general course) in secondary school are eligible for admission. However, a special five-year secondary-school program is provided in the music section for girls who wish to specialize in music but hold only the primary-school certificate. A second special section in art provides for the education of artists in a five-year course above the five-year secondary course for girls. This art course devotes its first three years to general courses and studio work in painting, design, sculpture, anatomy, and history of art, and its last two to specialization in painting, sculpture, or design. A third special section provides a one-year course in domestic science for girls interested in homemaking who have finished three years

INSTITUTIONS FOR TEACHER TRAINING

of secondary school or its equivalent. No tuition fees are charged those preparing to teach, but girls in the special sections in music, art, and domestic science are required to pay fees ranging from £E14 ($56) to £E20 ($80) a year. In 1945–46 approximately 300 girls were enrolled in the school, the sections in domestic science and art having the largest number of students.

The curriculum for the preparatory year in the domestic science, physical training, and music sections is similar to that for the orientation year of the secondary school, with minor changes dictated by the field of specialization. In the art section the program for this first year is similar to the orientation program in mathematics. In the remaining four years courses are uniform for all students within a section, with little attention given to subjects outside the field of specialization. Professional subjects, in general taught in the third and fourth years of the regular course, include principles of education, psychology, special methods of teaching, and practice teaching. The total number of hours assigned to professional subjects varies from fifteen in the art section to twenty-five in the music section. Laboratories, studios, and play areas provide facilities for extensive practical work in each field of specialization.

Dar al-'Ulum

Dar al-'Ulum was founded in 1873 at Cairo for the purpose of training *qadis* (judges) for the Shar' (Courts of Personal Statute) and teachers for the secondary schools. It was found advisable to establish a separate school for *qadis* in 1907, consequently the Dar al-'Ulum has been continued as a training school for teachers, now specializing in the training of teachers of Arabic for all levels of education. Some graduates have become professors of Arabic in higher institutions. Admission is based on graduation from al-Azhar secondary schools where students get a firm grounding in Arabic, the Koran, and Muslim religion. An entrance examination, both oral and written, covers those fields. There is also a medical examination. No fees are charged, and day students receive £E3 per month in addition to their lunches. In 1945–46 there were 343 students, of whom 28 were boarders. Students were drawn from all parts of Egypt, while 5 came from other Arab countries.

Formerly the course in Dar al-'Ulum was six years in length with concentration on professional training for teaching in the last two years. Beginning with 1945–46 graduates of the four-year course were admitted to the Institute of Education for Men for a professional course of two years. Dar al-'Ulum itself has been added to Fuad I University as one of its Faculties.

An intensive study in the four-year course is made of the various branches of Arabic including grammar, rhetoric, literature, philosophy, oral and written composition, prosody, and penmanship. A little less than half (twelve to fourteen hours) of the total program of thirty hours per week is given to these studies. In addition, courses are given in the related subjects of history and geography of Islam, Muslim theology, dogma, and law, the interpretation of the Koran and the traditions (Sayings of the Prophet), logic, history of religion and philosophy, Semitic and Oriental languages, foreign literature, and English. Finally, there are courses in sociology, general science, and physical education.

The Institutes of Education

The institutes of education for men and for women are professional training schools for teachers. They offer two-year postgraduate courses to holders of the *licence,* or bachelor's degree, and certain other courses. They are separate from the universities, both institutes having their own governing bodies which operate under the general supervision of the Ministry of Education.

THE INSTITUTE OF EDUCATION FOR MEN

The Institute of Education for Men was founded in 1929 at the suggestion of the late Professor Edouard Claparède of the University of Geneva. The newly reorganized Egyptian University had just begun to produce graduates, and the Institute was designed to give holders of the first university degree a two-year professional course. The Higher Training College, which had been training teachers for primary and secondary schools since 1880, had ceased accepting new students and was being abolished. In the beginning the new Institute of Education for Men had two sections, one for university graduates, as described, and the other for graduates of secondary schools. The latter offered a course of one preparatory year and two professional years for the training of primary-school teachers. In 1937 the primary-teachers section was abolished and the course for university graduates was reduced to one year for the preparation of both primary- and secondary-school teachers. However, in 1941 it was decided that the year course was inadequate for professional training of teachers, and the postgraduate professional course of two years was made the standard preparation for both primary- and secondary-school teachers

INSTITUTIONS FOR TEACHER TRAINING

until 1945–46, when the new teachers colleges for primary teachers were opened. The Institute is located in an old Isma'il palace in the Orman gardens at Gizah, not far from the University.

In addition to the postgraduate course of two years, the Institute at present offers a two-year course for teachers of art, admitting graduates from the Higher Institute of Fine Arts, and a three-year course for teachers of physical education, admitting graduates of the secondary school. The Institute has also added an advanced course of two years which is open to students who hold the diploma of the Institute, leading to the degree of Master of Arts granted by Fuad I University.

The postuniversity course for secondary-school teachers stresses psychology, and a psychological laboratory and a psychological clinic are maintained. Courses are given in experimental pedagogy, principles of education, methods, history of educational theories, and school and social hygiene. In addition, one lecture a week is on general scientific knowledge, and there is a one-year course known as "Survey of New Publications." Each student is supposed to devote three hours a week to practical hobbies, which range from typewriting to dramatics, and one hour to physical education.

One day a week throughout the two years is set aside for practice teaching in Cairo's primary and secondary schools. The Institute maintains three model schools, one of which, the Orman School, is on the campus and has a kindergarten and primary school; the other two are the Primary and Secondary Model Schools at Qubbah. In the first ten weeks of the first year "critic lessons" are given before the students; the group observes and then discusses the demonstration lesson. The students then teach one day a week for about nine weeks, after which they teach full time for three weeks, being observed by the school principal and the Institute teachers of methods. In the second year individual teaching for one day a week continues during the first month after which each student has two weeks of continuous teaching, both assignments being in the primary school. Practice in secondary schools starts later in the second year with four weeks of critic teaching, followed by individual practice by the student for four weeks and culminating in three weeks of continuous teaching in secondary schools. Each student has to pass a qualifying examination for teaching. The examiners are the principal of the school in which the student has taught, instructors of methods from the Institute, and an inspector from the Ministry.

Promotion from the first to the second year is based on the quality of the three or more term papers and on examinations. At the end of the second year a final examination is held in which the professional subjects are grouped into five papers. In order to pass, the student must receive a minimum of 350 out of the maximum of 700 marks possible. Practice teaching counts a minimum of 120 marks, term papers and the final examination papers supplying the balance. Upon graduation the student is granted the diploma of the Institute of Education, which makes him eligible to teach in primary and secondary schools. However, a severe shortage of teachers in the secondary schools in recent years has resulted in most of the Institute graduates—especially those in science and mathematics—going into secondary-school teaching.

The two-year course, originally restricted to students from the Faculties of Arts and of Science, because of lack of recruits from the Faculty of Science recently began admitting students from the Faculty of Agriculture. In 1945–46 graduates of Dar al-'Ulum, the institute for teachers of Arabic, were admitted.

Graduates holding the diploma of the Institute of Education or its equivalent with distinction, other holders of the diploma approved by the Council on Higher Studies on the basis of three years of teaching experience in public schools or other schools that are inspected by the Ministry of Education are eligible to pursue advanced studies leading to the Master of Arts degree. The candidate for the M.A. must be registered in the Division of Advanced Studies of the Institute for a period of two years, the first being devoted to required courses and final examinations (in which he must receive at least 70 percent) and the second to writing an original thesis on a subject which has been approved by the Council of the Faculty of Arts of the University and the Council of Advanced Studies of the Institute. Joint committees composed of representatives from both Institute and Faculty of Arts pass on the thesis and hold the written examinations.

The two-year course for teachers of art accepts graduates of the Higher Institute of Fine Arts and also of certain sections of the Institute of Applied Art in Cairo. In addition to courses in psychology and educational theory and methods of teaching art including practice teaching, the students study various fields of the arts, library work, biology, Arabic, English, physical education, and school hygiene.

The Institute maintains evening classes for teachers of art, limiting attendance to 25; these classes run ten hours a week for a year and are in art, decorative art, handicrafts, education, psychology, and methods. A special certificate is granted to successful candidates who have attended at least 75 percent of the classes.

INSTITUTIONS FOR TEACHER TRAINING

The three-year physical-education section, which admits graduates of secondary schools, includes in its program courses in games, gymnastics, swimming, eurythmics, the history and theory of various phases of physical education, anatomy, physiology, hygiene and first aid, corrective exercises and massage, theory and practice of education, psychology, special methods and practice teaching, Arabic, English, library work, and handicrafts. Elective courses are offered in fencing, boxing, tennis, wrestling, and exercises on special gymnastic equipment.

The Institute has been maintaining a branch of its literary section in Alexandria, the enrollment being 30 students. It is expected that, with the development of Faruq I University in Alexandria and the increasing demand for teachers, this branch will develop into a separate institute.

The distribution of students in the different sections is shown in Table 15. In addition, there were 16 students working for the M.A. degree, 8 in

TABLE 15
Enrollment in Institute of Education for Men, Cairo, 1945–46

Year	Literary	Scientific	Dar al-'Ulum	Art	Physical Education	Total
First..........	72	61	45	20	31	229
Second........	56	31	38	22	21	168
Third.........	...	...	...	...	21	21
Total......	128	92	83	42	73	418

the first and 8 in the second year. Of the total number of 434 students, 118 were boarders. Education at the Institute is free, as are board and lodging to all who apply. Day students receive £E3 a month toward their maintenance.

In order to attract more students into the teaching of mathematics, the Institute offers a scholarship of £E16 per year and exemption from tuition fees to undergraduate students registered in the Faculty of Science at the University. Such students must have graduated from the mathematics section of the secondary school with an average of 65 or higher in the public secondary-school examination, and they must agree to include pure and applied mathematics and physics in their studies of the first two years in the University. Also they agree that they will enter the Institute of Education for Men after graduation from the University and that they will serve as teachers for five years in the schools of the Ministry of Education after receiving the diploma of the Institute.

THE INSTITUTE OF EDUCATION FOR WOMEN

Occupying rented buildings in the fashionable Zamalik quarter of Cairo, the Institute of Education for Women, like the one for men, offers a two-year professional course to bearers of the first university degree. The small number of university graduates registered at the Institute for Women, however, has forced the Institute to maintain a four-year course for the preparation of primary-school teachers which admits graduates of the secondary schools—the type of course which the Institute for Men abolished in 1937. The two-year course resembles that at the Institute for Men, but is not divided into sections. In 1945–46 there were only 10 students registered in the first year and 11 in the second. The Institute maintains no model schools, but the students do practice teaching in the girls schools of the city.

The four-year course for primary-school teachers is divided into a literary, a scientific, and a kindergarten section. The literary section is subdivided into a section for Arabic and one for a European language; the two are identical in every respect except for the difference in language. The scientific- and literary-section programs of the first two years stress subject-matter courses; in the third year there is a mixture of subject-matter and professional courses, and in the final year the entire program is devoted to professional courses. The course for kindergarten teachers includes Arabic and religion, a European language, history, geography, and nature study in the first two years, with Arabic continued in the third year. Free and rhythmic games, music and singing, drawing, manual training, and story-telling are spread over the four years, while the courses in education, psychology, kindergarten methods, and practice teaching are concentrated in the last two years. Practice teaching follows the same pattern for all sections, with four hours weekly devoted to individual teaching and criticism in the first two years, continuous practice of four weeks in the third year and of six weeks in the fourth year.

In 1945–46 there were 123 students registered in the four-year course, giving the Institute a total of 144 students, 60 of whom were boarders. Here, too, tuition, board, and lodging are free, and day students receive £E3 a month for maintenance. In return, the students are under contract to serve the Ministry of Education for five years after graduation.

The Institute is headed by a British woman,[1] and, except for the teachers of Arabic, the teaching staff is composed almost entirely of Egyptian graduates of British universities.

[1] Since retired. In 1948 the head of the Women's Institute was Madame Asma Fahmy, an Egyptian lady and a graduate of the University of London.

Chapter 6

AL-AZHAR AND ITS INSTITUTIONS OF MUHAMMADAN LEARNING

THE VENERABLE MOSQUE of al-Azhar is the oldest existing Muslim university in the world. It was founded by the Fatimids soon after their conquest of Egypt. Its foundation stone was laid in 359 A.H. (970 A.D.), and it was opened for services in 361 A.H. (972 A.D.).[1] From being an important center of instruction in Muslim law and religion and the Arabic language, al-Azhar, with the passage of centuries, has become the unrivaled institution of Islamic learning, receiving students from all parts of the Muslim world.

Al-Azhar now includes three higher Faculties (Arabic, Theology, and Muslim Law) and nine institutes, seven of which consist of primary and secondary sections, and two, of primary sections only. These institutes are located in Cairo, Alexandria, Tanta, Zaqaziq, Shabin al-Kom, Asyut, Dassuq, Damietta, and Qina. In addition, a traditional "general section," which accepts unclassified students, is still maintained. Altogether al-Azhar in 1945–46 had an enrollment of 14,402 students, distributed as follows:

Division	Enrollment
Primary sections	5,729
Secondary sections	4,678
General section	1,422
Higher Faculties	
Faculty of Arabic 1,162	
Faculty of Muslim Law 873	
Faculty of Theology 538	2,573
Total	14,402

In that year there were 814 foreign students from more than thirty countries, including Syria, Lebanon, Palestine, Transjordan, North Africa (Tripoli, Tunisia, Algeria, and Spanish and French Morocco), Hijaz, Yaman, Sudan and Darfur, Turkey, Kurdistan, Turkestan, Iraq,

---

[1] "Al-Azhar," *Encyclopedia of Islam* (Leyden: 1913), I, 532–39.

Iran, Afghanistan, India, Java and the rest of Melanesia and the Malay States, and China. Among European countries represented are Russia, Poland, Yugoslavia, Albania, and Hungary.[2]

In the course of centuries al-Azhar evolved its own pattern of organization, curriculum, and methods of teaching which grew into the cherished tradition of the institution. Prior to the twentieth century students were admitted at almost any age and with little regard to preparation. Usually, however, students had previously learned the Koran by heart in a *kuttab* or under a private teacher and knew the rudiments of reading, writing, and arithmetic. Once admitted to al-Azhar, the student could continue along this road to learning almost indefinitely, some spending twenty or more years in study. Each student chose the subjects and the professors, or *shaykhs,* he preferred and proceeded at his own pace. No tuition was charged, and many students, particularly foreigners, found free lodging in the resident quarters (*riwaqs*) of al-Azhar with allowances for food to help in their maintenance. The *riwaqs* exist to this day, the name of each designating the region from which the occupants come. Living accommodations are available for students not only in the twenty-nine surviving *riwaqs,* but also in modern buildings constructed for the institutes in Cairo, Alexandria, Zaqaziq, and Asyut. These quarters are usually full and have a capacity of about 2,000 students.

Teaching took the form of lectures by *shaykhs* and *'ulama* (plural of *'alim,* or savant), with free questioning and discussion by students sometimes turning into the scholastic disputations typical of medieval institutions of learning in Europe. Prescribed books by old authorities were studied, many having been written by Azharite professors of bygone centuries. A student might receive a paper from his *shaykh* certifying that the former had read and mastered a specific book. The curriculum consisted largely of studying books and their commentaries, and the level of progress was indicated by the books a student was studying.

Goals at al-Azhar were intangible: there was no graduation, no granting of diplomas or degrees. Students might leave at any point. If not very far advanced, they were likely to be absorbed in various walks of life including teaching in *kuttabs.* The more advanced were likely to become preachers, *imams* of mosques, or judges in Egypt or elsewhere. Many continued their studies until they felt competent to become teachers at al-Azhar. They then started lecturing, and if they attracted increasing

[2] Figures obtained from the Directorate of Registration at al-Azhar as of December 1945 and January 1946.

AL-AZHAR AND ITS INSTITUTIONS

numbers of students, they would be licensed by the rector of al-Azhar and so eventually come to be counted among the *'ulama* of the institution. The rector, whose office is considered the highest religious office in Egypt, was chosen from among the more celebrated and devout *'ulama* of al-Azhar, receiving his appointment from the supreme government authority in the country.

A reform movement began in the latter half of the nineteenth century, and under the Khedive Isma'il certain legislation was formulated to modernize al-Azhar. Legislation on this subject has continued to the present day, the most important of the laws being those of 1911 and 1936. The former created a supreme council for al-Azhar and also the Body of Prominent 'Ulama from which the Grand Shaykh (rector) of al-Azhar is chosen; in addition, it attempted to systematize the studies of the institution by dividing them into successive stages and introducing new subjects.[3] The law of 1936, still in force, completed the reorganization of al-Azhar.

By provision of the law of 1936 the Grand Shaykh of al-Azhar is the supreme religious leader and chief supervisor of the conduct of all religious (Muslim) men, both in and out of al-Azhar. He is also the actual and general executor of all laws, royal decrees, and other regulations pertaining to al-Azhar. He appoints and dismisses the *shaykhs* of the *riwaqs* according to internal regulations and conditions attached to endowments. He, himself, is chosen from among the Body of Prominent 'Ulama and is appointed by royal order. He is assisted by a vice rector who is chosen in the same way.

The Body of Prominent 'Ulama is composed of thirty *'ulama* occupying teaching chairs and is presided over by the Grand Shaykh of al-Azhar. To qualify for membership in this body a man must be at least forty-five years of age, known for his rectitude and devoutness, bearing the degree of savant (*'alimiyah*) with the title of professor (*ustadh*), and must have occupied a teaching post with one of the Faculties for ten years, or the post of *mufti* (expounder of Muslim law) or the post of judge in a Muslim law court, or a post of learning in the administration of al-Azhar for fifteen years. If he fills these requirements, he must then present a dissertation which must be approved by a committee of ten chosen by the Body of Prominent 'Ulama, after which he is elected to membership by a three-fourths majority of the body and formally appointed a member by

---

[3] Muhammad Khalid Hassanein Bey, *Reform at al-Azhar University* (Cairo: 1940) pp. 5–6.

royal order. In December 1945, after considerable controversy, the law was amended to permit choosing a member of the Body of Prominent 'Ulama—and consequently the Grand Shaykh himself—from the faculties of the two modern state universities.

Al-Azhar also has a Supreme Council which is composed of the Grand Shaykh as chairman, the Vice Shaykh, the Grand Mufti of Egypt, the *shaykhs* of the three Faculties, the Under Secretaries of the Ministries of Justice, Waqf, Education, and Finance, two members of the Body of Prominent 'Ulama (appointed for two years), and two persons experienced in education (also appointed for two years). The Supreme Council, meeting at least once a month, is the seat of administrative and academic authority in al-Azhar. It prepares the budget and accepts endowments, initiates laws or decrees pertaining to the institution, lays down internal regulations, approves appointments of staff, programs of study, and types of diplomas and degrees, and considers all that is laid before it by the Grand Shaykh.

Each of the three Faculties of al-Azhar is headed by a *shaykh* and a Faculty council. The *shaykh* must be one of the 'Ulama and is appointed by royal order. The council is composed of the *shaykh* as chairman, two full professors chosen by the teaching staff, and two outsiders with experience in education chosen by the Supreme Council and appointed for two years by royal decree. The Faculty council makes recommendations for teaching appointments, prepares the budget and internal regulations, and recommends programs of study, textbooks, the yearly calendar, dates and committees for examinations, and the number of students to be admitted each year.

The teaching staff of each Faculty consists of instructors, assistant professors, and professors occupying chairs. An instructor must hold the degree of *'alimiyah* with the title of professor (*ustadh*) from al-Azhar or from an equivalent institution. The assistant professor must, in addition, have served not less than five years as instructor in a Faculty of al-Azhar or an equivalent institution. The professor occupying a chair must have served for five years as an assistant professor in a Faculty of al-Azhar or the equivalent. There are thirty professorial chairs: eleven in the Faculty of Muslim Law, ten in the Faculty of Theology, and nine in the Faculty of Arabic.

Al-Azhar has three main sources of income: (1) income from endowments; (2) grants from the Ministries of Finance and Waqf; and (3) miscellaneous incomes and grants. Its budget in 1940 was £E336,300, and in 1945, £E742,000.

AL-AZHAR AND ITS INSTITUTIONS

Programs of Study

Study at al-Azhar, apart from the general section, is now separated into definite stages of education, each being subdivided into grades which terminate in examinations that lead to promotion or to the certificates or degrees granted by al-Azhar. Teaching is carried on in modern classrooms with desks.

THE PRIMARY STAGE

The lowest or primary stage, conducted in institutes in Cairo and other large cities in Egypt, admits students at the age of twelve who have memorized the entire Koran and who pass an examination in reading, writing, dictation, and arithmetic. There is also a medical examination. The four-year program includes study of Muslim law (*fiqh*) according to the four main Sunni schools, monotheistic divinity (*tawhid*), the life of the Prophet and his companions, intonation (*tajwid*) of the Koran, Arabic reading, grammar, morphology, dictation, composition, memorizing, calligraphy, history, geography, arithmetic, geometry, algebra, hygiene, and drawing. On completion of this stage, the student receives the Certificate of Primary Studies.

THE SECONDARY STAGE

The secondary stage has a five-year program offering the following studies: Muslim law, commentaries on the Koran, tradition, monotheistic divinity, Arabic grammar and morphology, rhetoric, composition, history of Arabic literature, prosody and rhyme, reading and memorization, logic, physics, chemistry, biology, history, and geography. The graduate is granted the Certificate of Secondary Studies. Questions for the final examinations for both fourth primary and fifth secondary years are set at al-Azhar in Cairo for all institutes, and the papers are sent to Cairo for correction.

THE HIGHER FACULTIES

Undergraduate and postgraduate work is conducted in the Faculties of Muslim Law, Theology, and Arabic. Undergraduate work continues for four years and leads to the Higher Diploma. Postgraduate work of two years leads to the *'alimiyah* with a *licence,* and of five to seven years to the *'alimiyah* with the title of professor.

In the *Faculty of Muslim Law* the undergraduate course concentrates on commentaries on the Koran, principles of Muslim law and its interpretation by various schools, history of Islamic jurisprudence, logic, and philosophy; students may elect English or French. The graduate is awarded the Higher Diploma in Muslim Law. The two-year graduate course includes study of the laws and statutes of the Muslim law courts and of Waqf, tutelage courts and the Crown Council, legal testaments, legal procedures and exercises in them, a study of cases involving principles, legal policy, private international law, history of jurisprudence and the judges of Islam, constitutional law of the state, principles of economics, and lectures on medicine and astronomy. A foreign language, if elected in undergraduate years, may be continued. The student is granted the degree of *'alimiyah* with a *Licence* in Muslim Law, which entitles him to occupy a post in the Muslim law courts, to become a *mufti,* or to practice as a lawyer before the Muslim law courts and the tutelage councils, which decide on tutelage over orphans.

The Faculty of Theology. The undergraduate course offers the following subjects: monotheistic divinity, commentaries on the Koran, the traditions (including texts, men, and terminology), logic, ethics, philosophy, an abbreviated course in Muslim law, history of Islam, psychology, and either English or French. The graduate receives the Higher Diploma in Theology. If he wishes to continue, he takes a two-year postgraduate course, studying the Koran and its sciences (that is, the body and learning that grew around the Koran), preaching for the sake of God, public speaking and debating, Muslim schools of thought and of law with their histories, heresies, and customs, more of the foreign language begun in undergraduate years, and an Oriental language. This course leads to the degree of *'alimiyah* with a *licence,* which entitles him to become a preacher and counselor.

The Faculty of the Arabic Language. The undergraduate course leading to the Higher Diploma in the Arabic Language consists of Arabic grammar, morphology, etymology, vocabulary, composition, rhetoric, literature and its history, prosody and rhyme, commentaries on the Koran, abbreviated courses in Muslim law, the traditions, logic, philosophy, and reading, and an elective course in French or English. If the bearer of this diploma wishes to become a teacher of Arabic, he spends two years studying psychology, principles of education, school organization, general methods, history of education, special methods, practice teaching, ethics, school hygiene, drawing, calligraphy, physical education, and the foreign language studied previously. On passing examinations, he receives the *Licence* of Teaching, qualifying him to teach Arabic in both religious and government schools.

The degree of professor

A candidate for the degree of *'alimiyah* with the title of professor in any of the three Faculties must have the Higher Diploma of that Faculty, must pursue advanced studies in the field he chooses, pass an examination in them not earlier than four and not later than seven years after commencing these studies, and must present a dissertation in not less than one year after passing the advanced examinations. The Faculty of Muslim Law has a set program which all candidates for the Degree of Professor follow. In the Faculty of Theology, the candidate may choose one of three fields of specialization: (1) monotheistic divinity and philosophy; (2) the Koran and the traditions; or (3) the history of Islam. The Faculty of the Arabic Language offers specialization in either grammar or rhetoric. Having achieved the degree and title of professor, the scholar is qualified to teach his specialty in the Faculties of both al-Azhar and the government universities. This ultimate degree conferred by al-Azhar approximates the doctorate conferred by Western universities, just as the Higher Diploma and the *'alimiyah* with a *licence* correspond to the degree of bachelor and master, respectively.

Students graduating from the various Faculties and institutes of al-Azhar in 1945 were distributed as follows:

Degree	Number of Graduates
'Alimiyah with Degree of Professor	38
'Alimiyah with *Licence* in Law	106
'Alimiyah with *Licence* to Preach	35
'Alimiyah with *Licence* of Teaching	222
Higher Diploma in Muslim Law	137
Higher Diploma in Theology	139
Higher Diploma in Arabic	80
Total of degrees	757
Secondary certificate	582
Primary certificate	677
Total certificates	1,259
GRAND TOTAL OF GRADUATES	2,016

The general sections of al-Azhar are maintained side by side with the more regularized form of teaching in the primary and secondary institutes and the mosques. Here the students cluster on the floor of the mosque around a learned professor who lectures to them. These sections are designed as much to cater to the unclassified students who want to learn religion and Arabic as to maintain the quaint traditional form of teaching which has come down through the ages. More than half of the foreign students of al-Azhar (484 out of 814) were registered in the general section in 1945–46.

The above survey of education at al-Azhar shows that, while keeping the traditional Islamic and Arabic studies and keeping the spirit in which these studies are taught intact, al-Azhar has introduced in the last two generations considerable change in its administration, in its organization and methods of teaching, and has introduced many new studies such as history, geography, the sciences, mathematics, foreign languages, and even drawing.

Chapter 7

PRIVATE AND FOREIGN SCHOOLS

For the past century government, or public, education in Egypt has been supplemented by private and foreign institutions at most levels, such extension of educational opportunity being regarded with tolerance if not always with unqualified enthusiasm by the government.

Private schools must be registered, their staff, program, and physical facilities approved, and they are subject to government inspection. Some are operated for profit as private ventures by individuals, while others are established and administered by organizations interested in providing for a religious group or for a foreign community. Most of these schools accept pupils of other denominations or nationalities.

Foreign schools have been established for the most part by religious interests, usually as mission schools. Protestant schools are maintained by the American United Presbyterian Mission and the Church Missionary Society of England, while Roman Catholic schools have been established by French and Italian religious orders. In addition, there are lay schools for British, American, French, Italian, and Greek children. Table 16 gives the enrollment in private, foreign, and government schools for 1942–43, showing that approximately 25 percent of all pupils in elementary (including all levels below the secondary) schools were in private and foreign schools, but slightly more than 50 percent of secondary-school pupils were in such schools. Detailed statistics for that year show that in primary schools alone, 25 percent of the pupils were in government schools, 27 percent in foreign schools, and 48 percent in private schools. Unpublished statistics for 1944–45 show that government and private schools had increased their enrollments partly at the expense of foreign schools. This situation developed from the government's action in eliminating fees in its own primary schools and granting subsidies to private and foreign schools which agreed to eliminate fees. More private than foreign schools accepted the subsidies in lieu of tuition fees. Approximately 80 percent of all children in private elementary schools are in Muslim private schools or those maintained by

TABLE 16

ENROLLMENT IN EGYPTIAN SCHOOLS UNDER PUBLIC, PRIVATE, AND FOREIGN CONTROL, 1942–43*

Schools	Enrollment Boys	Girls	Total
Elementary:†			
Public	558,688	459,355	1,018,043
Private	224,851	63,614	288,465
Foreign	21,437	31,949	53,386
Total	804,976	554,918	1,359,894
Secondary:			
Public	23,860	2,260	26,120
Private	15,264	1,176	16,440
Foreign	6,422	4,317	10,739
Total	45,546	7,753	53,299
Vocational and technical:‡			
Public	34,498	7,950	42,448
Private	3,990	2,901	6,891
Foreign	2,900	1,635	4,535
Total	41,388	12,486	53,874
Higher:			
Public	10,807	1,196	12,003
Private	...	...	...
Foreign	409	110	519
Total	11,216	1,306	12,522
GRAND TOTAL	903,126	576,463	1,479,589

* Derived from *Statistique Scolaire, 1942–43* (Cairo: Imprimerie Nationale, Egyptian Government, Ministry of Finance, Statistical Department, 1945), pp. 160–63.
† Includes elementary, compulsory, kindergarten, preparatory, and primary schools.
‡ Includes agriculture, commerce, and teacher training schools.

Muslim benevolent societies; nearly 15 percent are in Coptic schools. Foreign schools have provided relatively more places for girls in primary and secondary education than have either private or government schools; they emphasize primary and secondary programs, though some schools have commercial-study and teacher-training specialization.

Programs of study in private schools follow the government pattern quite closely, although more time may be devoted to the study of religion in the sectarian schools. Foreign schools usually offer the pupil a choice between following a program consistent with that of the government and directed toward the public examinations or taking a parallel course in preparation for advanced study abroad. Instruction in foreign schools is in the native language of the foreign country except in courses in other languages. In most of these schools Arabic is taught at least to children from Arabic-speaking homes, but the standard is generally lower than that of the government schools, in which Arabic is the medium of instruction.

American and English schools make a point of preparing their students for matriculation in higher institutions abroad. Foreign schools vary considerably in the proportion of Egyptians in their student bodies. American schools were first, with 8,073 Egyptians in a total enrollment of 8,719 in 1942–43. French schools were next, with 23,053 Egyptians out of 30,259; English schools had 5,522 out of 9,239; Italian schools had 4,518 out of 8,757; Greek schools had only 512 Egyptians out of 9,973 pupils.

Foreign schools are usually housed in buildings designed for school purposes, some of them modern and possessing the best features of current school architecture. Play areas are frequently large enough to permit basketball, volleyball, and football—less frequently tennis. Science laboratories and good libraries are usually provided.

In the three months of the American Council Commission's visit in Egypt it was not possible to visit even one school of each type under private or foreign control, and it happened that more American schools than those of other nationalities were visited. It should not be assumed that a school or type of organization that is omitted is unimportant. No attempt is made in this report to evaluate the contributions made by the foreign and private schools either as a whole or in individual cases, such a project being incompatible with the limitations of time and scope placed upon the Commission.

American United Presbyterian Mission Schools

The American United Presbyterian Mission began work in Egypt in 1854. Its objectives were then and continue to be the development in Egypt of an educated leadership for the church, together with improving the understanding of the Christian faith by its adherents and a demonstration that Christianity means unselfish service to all men regardless of race or creed. To reach these objectives, the Mission has established training schools for religious workers, carried general education into villages and smaller towns where no schools existed, encouraged the education of girls and young women, provided physical and athletic training, and recently has conducted experimentation in rural education and the improvement of dairy cattle through the importation of Jersey stock. It has been the practice of the Mission to turn over the administration of individual schools to the Evangelical Church of Egypt whenever this has been practicable.

Asyut College

Asyut College, founded in 1865, serves as the center of the American Mission's educational activity in Upper Egypt. Although at one time some postsecondary work was offered, the present program follows closely the government program for secondary education and prepares the boys for both parts of the Egyptian Secondary-School Certificate examination. The College has extensive and beautiful grounds on the outskirts of the city of Asyut. Science laboratories, a large library, classrooms, assembly rooms, lecture halls, boarding facilities, faculty quarters, and a dairy occupy the various buildings of the campus. In 1945–46 there were 394 pupils enrolled. There were 157 boarders, and an additional 32 were living in college buildings in the city on a cooperative basis, furnishing and preparing their own food and caring for their quarters. The dairy, started in 1928 as an experiment in breeding Egyptian cattle with registered Jerseys, has been extremely successful. It is planned to develop it into an institute where boys may be trained in the fundamental principles of modern dairy farming. In addition, the College administers a primary school, housed in buildings in the city; in 1945–46 there were 445 boys enrolled in the two kindergarten and four primary grades. No tuition is charged in this lower school as the Ministry of Education grants a subsidy.

PRESSLEY MEMORIAL INSTITUTE

The Pressley Memorial Institute in Asyut, founded in the same year as Asyut College, is a school for girls providing a three-year kindergarten, four-year primary-, and five-year secondary-school course. The sixth year of secondary education required of girls is given at Asyut College, the laboratories of which are used by girls in the last three years of the secondary school. The program approximates that of government schools for girls, but provides additional opportunities in instrumental and vocal music. The girls are prepared for the public examinations. A teacher-training section was discontinued during the war. The 1945–46 enrollment for the entire institute was 510 with a nearly equal division among the three parts of the school. The school is housed in a modern building and provided with extensive gardens and play areas which are arranged to avoid interference by one age group with another.

THE AMERICAN COLLEGE FOR GIRLS IN CAIRO

Founded in 1861 as a primary school, the American College for Girls in Cairo has expanded until it now includes all levels from prekindergarten through the junior college. In 1945–46 the total enrollment was 771— prekindergarten, 44; kindergarten, 189; primary school, 247; secondary school, 251; junior college, 40. Included in the primary enrollment is a group of 44 irregular students whose preparation has been deficient in some subjects, usually English, and who, after a period of intensive study

PRIVATE AND FOREIGN SCHOOLS

in the field of deficiency, will be placed in the proper class of the secondary school. In the secondary and junior-college departments instruction is in English. More time is devoted to studying English in the primary and kindergarten departments than government schools provide. No attempt is made to follow the program prescribed by the Ministry though care is taken to provide adequate instruction in the Arabic language for girls from Arabic-speaking countries, and much time is devoted to the history and geography of Egypt and the Middle East. Considerable emphasis is placed upon music and homemaking, including child care. Opportunity is given, particularly in the junior-college years, for girls to become aware of the social and economic problems of Egypt through formal study and practical experience with local orphanages, social-service centers, and village welfare activities. Classwork is supplemented by the activities of organized groups and societies. An extensive library from which alumnae as well as students may borrow books contributes to the subsequent development of graduates.

The American University at Cairo

An institution growing out of the activities of the American Mission, but administered by an independent board of trustees in the United States, is the American University at Cairo. It was founded in 1920, with parallel secondary sections, one leading to the government examinations and the other preparing students for advanced institutions in which English is the language of instruction. These sections are still maintained, but the program of the University has been expanded to include a College of Arts and Science, a School of Oriental Studies, a department of education, and a division of extension. The College of Arts and Science offers courses in social science, science and mathematics, journalism, and education, all leading to the Bachelor of Arts degree of American-college standard. The School of Oriental Studies serves missionaries, businessmen, and research students, providing courses in the Arabic language and literature, Turkish, Hebrew, Persian, Ethiopic, history and religion of Islam, and general study of the political, economic, and social development of Egypt and the Middle East. The program of the department of education is planned to meet the needs of teachers in service and accepts as candidates for the Bachelor of Arts in Education holders of a teacher's diploma and of the Egyptian baccalaureate degree. The department of education sponsors the publication of the *Journal of Modern Education,* a professional magazine in Arabic widely read in the Arabic-speaking world.

The activities supervised by the division of extension and the average attendance at such activities are listed in Table 17. The program of the division of extension is designed to stimulate cultural and social-welfare development in Egypt, and the response of individuals, organizations, and government officials and agencies has been encouraging. Although it is difficult to identify influences of such complex activities, Egyptian leaders consider that the division of extension has made significant contributions to the cultural and intellectual life of Cairo and to the stimulation of training in social-welfare work and of progressive social thinking.

Enrollment in the American section of the University preparatory school

TABLE 17
ACTIVITIES AND ATTENDANCE OF THE DIVISION OF EXTENSION OF THE AMERICAN UNIVERSITY AT CAIRO, 1944–45

Type of Activity	Number	Average Attendance
Public lectures	22	353
Forums	16	109
Educational films	25	952
Children's films	6	581
Alumni films	6	657
King of Kings*	16	1,033

* Religious film produced by Cecil de Mille and shown by special permission of the Egyptian government to audiences composed mainly of Christians.

in 1945–46 was 166 men and in the Egyptian section, 143 men. The College of Arts and Sciences had 104 men and 28 women, and the department of education 48 men and 21 women.

Other Foreign Schools

It has been indicated in other parts of this report that Egyptian intellectual, cultural, and social life has been strongly influenced by the French since the Napoleonic invasion of 1798. More schools emphasizing French language and literature have been established than has been the case with any other foreign nation, and at present the French schools of Egypt have a higher attendance than any of the other foreign institutions. The schools have been established and maintained by lay, as well as religious, groups. The Saint Marc School for Boys in Alexandria, representative of French schools in Egypt, was established by the Lazarists in 1847, but was soon taken over by the Christian Brothers. It is housed in one of the most modern and well-equipped school buildings in Egypt and prepares boys for government-certificate examinations, French certificate examinations, and commercial life, as well as offering a special pre-engineering course. High standards are maintained in Arabic and English, but the language of general instruction is French. The primary school follows the

PRIVATE AND FOREIGN SCHOOLS

Egyptian government program in one section and the French syllabus in another. Tuition is charged in this school, but eight years of free instruction are offered in another school under the same administration. Saint Marc has also a postprimary intermediate class for students who require special instruction in French; as soon as their deficiency is eliminated, they are reclassified into appropriate classes.

The French School of Law in Cairo is a part of the University of Paris. Only men students holding an Egyptian or French *baccalauréat* are eligible for admission. It has enjoyed prestige and has rendered valuable services in the past in training personnel for the Mixed Courts. According to the Montreaux convention signed in May 1937 the Mixed Courts will cease to exist by 1949, and the influence of the French School of Law is on the wane. Its courses are held in the evening. The course extends over a period of three to four years, at the end of which a candidate is required to take his final examination in Paris (this rule, however, was relaxed, for obvious reasons, during the two World Wars). The American Council Commission did not visit this school.

Victoria College, founded in Alexandria by British lay interests in 1902, is now administered by a board of governors composed of representatives of various British agencies in Egypt. It has trained leaders for all the countries of the Near East. The program provides instruction from kindergarten to the Higher Certificate examination. Instruction is chiefly in English, but the standard in Arabic is such that boys are prepared to continue their studies in the Egyptian universities. Major emphasis, however, is upon preparing boys for entrance to British universities. The physical facilities of the College were taken over by the military during the war but have been returned, and extensive plans for improving and expanding buildings and equipment are now being developed. English, Arabic, and French are the languages stressed, and boys from non-Arabic-speaking homes are required to study Latin. Teachers, aside from foreign-language instructors, are British. A branch of Victoria College was established in Cairo during World War II.

Informal Educational Agencies

The Young Men's Christian Association in Cairo and Alexandria, with a total membership in 1945–46 of 3,400, conducts a vigorous educational program. It offers a three-year secretarial training course for young men. Clubs organized for underprivileged boys in Cairo and Alexandria have a combined membership of 700 boys: the one in Cairo trains young men to become leaders in work with boys. The library of the YMCA renders extensive service to members, especially to those who are college and university students. The organization sponsors debates, lectures, discussion groups, and meetings of book-review clubs. In 1945 more than one hundred such events had a total attendance of 5,000.

In Cairo, Alexandria, Asyut, Minyah, Tanta, Mahalla al-Kubra, and Zaqaziq, the British Council sponsors institutes which offer classes in subjects required by the external examinations of London University, arranges lectures and discussions, and provides concerts and educational films for members and invited guests. A rapidly growing library with reading rooms is meeting a real need of young Egyptian men and women.

The library of the United States Information Service, established in 1945, is providing a large collection of recent books for the use of Egyptian readers. The Cairo Library Association was formed in the spring of 1945 to develop interlibrary exchange of information, materials, professional library literature, and ideas. Initially the members were librarians of English and American libraries, but it was anticipated that the Association will draw in librarians of all important libraries in Cairo. The Association keeps a union list of periodicals received regularly by member-libraries and has prepared and distributed a union catalog of reference materials.

Educational opportunities are further supplemented by a variety of child-welfare agencies. Some of these are administered by individuals from other countries who have missionary leanings, as is the case with the Asyut Orphanage, which was founded and has been supported and supervised largely by the individual efforts of Miss Lillian Trasher since 1910. As many as 1,000 orphans, boys and girls, have been cared for in this remarkable institution financed by contributions from the United States and Egypt. Some institutions are supported by religious benevolent associations, some by educational institutions, and others by departments of the Egyptian government. These institutions provide some formal instruction, but stress physical welfare and the development of manual skills which will help the orphan get employment. There are many institutions of different types which provide some opportunity for orphaned children to receive an education. All institutions soliciting funds from the public are required to register with the appropriate department of the Ministry of Social Affairs, and their budgets and services are regularly inspected.

Part Two

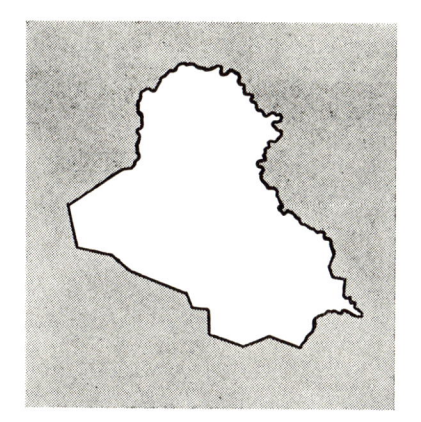

IRAQ

IRAQ

Population: *4,000,000 in 1943 (estimate).*

Area: *175,000 square miles.*

Form of government: *Iraq is a constitutional, hereditary monarchy, with a representative government. Legislative power is vested in two houses of Parliament: the Senate and the Chamber of Deputies. Deputies are elected by male suffrage; senators are appointed by the King.*

Principal occupations: *Agriculture, oil, mining, commerce and trade, finance, services, professions.*

Principal exports: *Oil, dates, wheat, barley, corn, licorice, wool, cotton, hides, sheep, goats, horses, cattle.*

Principal imports: *Cotton, silk, woolen textiles, machinery, motor cars, sugar, metals, timber.*

Monetary unit: *Dinar (approximately $4.045).*

Chapter 8

ORGANIZATION AND ADMINISTRATION OF THE EDUCATIONAL SYSTEM

THE PUBLIC-SCHOOL system is an integral part of the government in Iraq, being under the control of the Ministry of Education. It attempts to reach all levels from kindergarten through institutions of higher learning, embracing specialized instruction as well as general culture Like other departments of the Iraqi government, the administration of the public-school system is highly centralized, and the Ministry of Education not only issues regulations, instructions, and orders, but also is responsible for the appointment, promotion, and dismissal of teachers, the founding, financial support, and closing of public schools, the determination of curriculums and textbooks, the training of teachers, and the formulation and grading of public examinations. This intensive government control to a large extent determines the policies, curriculums, and methods of private and foreign schools. The regulations of the Ministry of Education went through repeated revisions in the period from 1933 to 1945.[1]

The Ministry of Education

The Minister of Education, a Cabinet member, is the supreme head of the Ministry. He is responsible for its administration and for the satisfactory performance of various duties by all of its officials. All orders, decisions, and instructions are issued in his name and executed under his supervision and control. All new appointments, promotions, and dismissals require his approval, as does the expenditure of sums exceeding 37.5 dinars (about $150). Under the Minister are the Director General of Antiquities, the Director General of Education, the deans of the Law College and of the Higher Teachers College, the Technical Adviser, and the chief of the Private Bureau. (See Chart III.) The latter is a comparatively minor

[1] Another revision took place in the summer of 1946, nine months after the American Council Commission left Iraq.

official who acts as secretary to the Minister. The Director General of Antiquities has charge of all the museums and the archeological activities conducted by his department and also supervises the work of foreign archeological expeditions and the preservation of monuments and remains of historical value. Although an agency for informal education, the Antiquities Department is not an integral part of the educational system.

In the days of the mandate a British adviser was attached to the Ministry of Education, but the office was abolished after 1930, prior to the termination of the mandate. It was re-established in 1943. The function of the adviser was to render an opinion on questions referred to him by the Minister and to make recommendations for the improvement of the work of the Ministry. The post of adviser was abolished in 1946.

The deans of the Law College and of the Higher Teachers College are directly responsible to the Minister for the proper functioning of their respective institutions. Both colleges are run under the supervision of their own faculty councils, whose decisions are subject to the approval of the Minister. They develop their own curriculums and conduct their own examinations. The faculty council of the Law College recommends candidates for its teaching posts, but in the Higher Teachers College this function is performed by the dean.

The Minister serves also as president of the Advisory Council on Education, a body created by the regulations of 1943 and consisting of the Minister, the Director General of Education, the Technical Adviser, the Director General of Antiquities, the deans of the Law College and of the Higher Teachers College, and four permanent members appointed—one each—by the Ministers of Finance, Communications and Works, Social Affairs, and Economics. All these persons meeting together elect four private citizens known for their experience and interest in education to supplement their number. The council meets at least twice a year, in October and April, and makes recommendations to the Minister of Education.

THE DIRECTOR GENERAL OF EDUCATION

The Director General of Education is the real administrative head of the public-school system. He is expected to be a man of experience in educational administration and in matters of teaching in the schools. He is responsible to the Minister for the proper operation and inspection of all the schools in order to insure that all Iraqi youth shall receive the right moral, intellectual, and physical education regardless of their race, lan-

Chart III

IRAQ: ADMINISTRATIVE ORGANIZATION OF THE MINISTRY OF EDUCATION, 1945–46

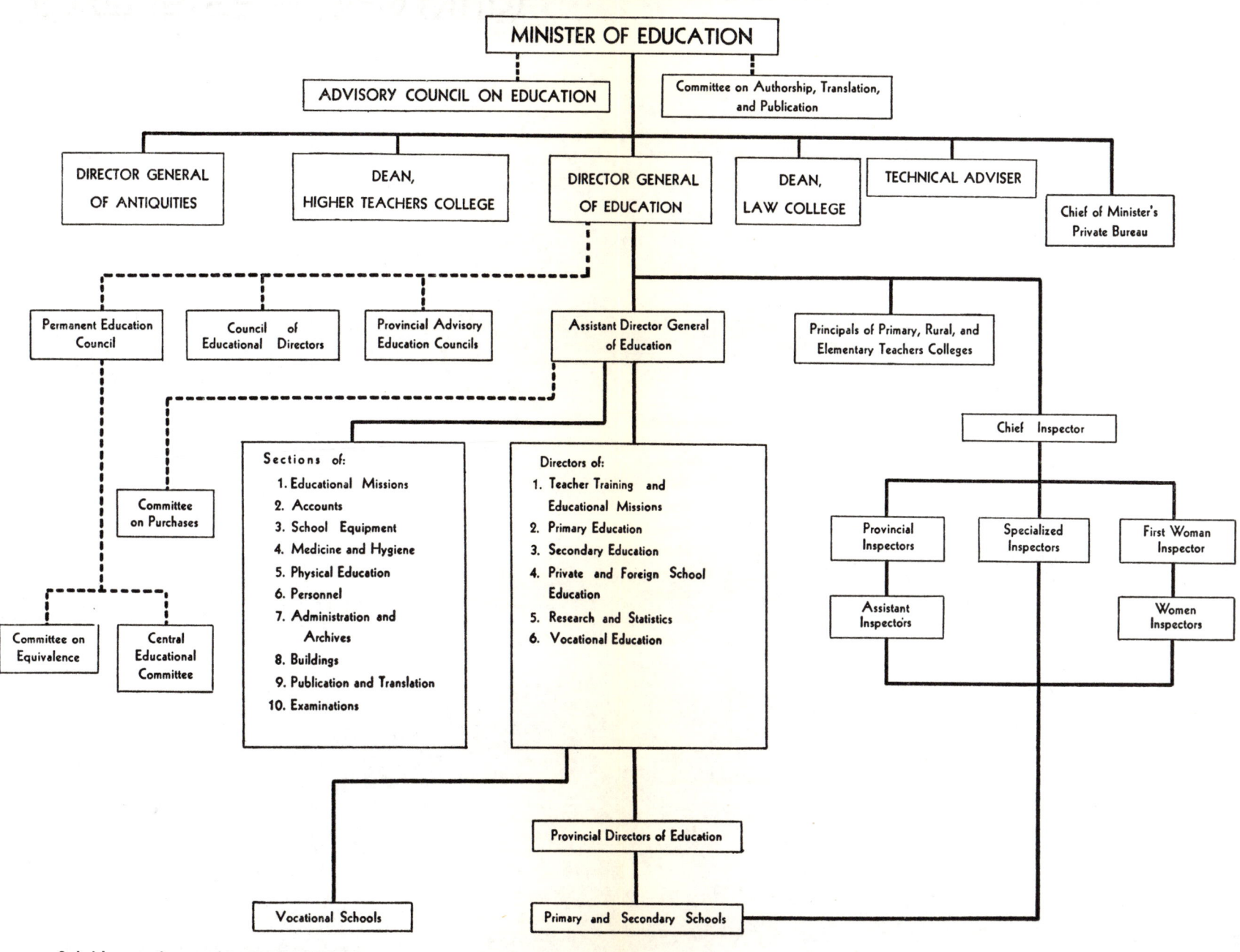

MINISTER OF EDUCATION

- ADVISORY COUNCIL ON EDUCATION
- Committee on Authorship, Translation, and Publication

Reporting to Minister of Education:
- DIRECTOR GENERAL OF ANTIQUITIES
- DEAN, HIGHER TEACHERS COLLEGE
- DIRECTOR GENERAL OF EDUCATION
- DEAN, LAW COLLEGE
- TECHNICAL ADVISER
- Chief of Minister's Private Bureau

Under Director General of Education:
- Permanent Education Council
- Council of Educational Directors
- Provincial Advisory Education Councils
- Assistant Director General of Education
- Principals of Primary, Rural, and Elementary Teachers Colleges

Under Permanent Education Council:
- Committee on Purchases
- Committee on Equivalence
- Central Educational Committee

Sections of:
1. Educational Missions
2. Accounts
3. School Equipment
4. Medicine and Hygiene
5. Physical Education
6. Personnel
7. Administration and Archives
8. Buildings
9. Publication and Translation
10. Examinations

Directors of:
1. Teacher Training and Educational Missions
2. Primary Education
3. Secondary Education
4. Private and Foreign School Education
5. Research and Statistics
6. Vocational Education

Chief Inspector
- Provincial Inspectors
  - Assistant Inspectors
- Specialized Inspectors
- First Woman Inspector
  - Women Inspectors

Provincial Directors of Education

Vocational Schools

Primary and Secondary Schools

——— Solid lines indicate administrative authority
- - - - Broken lines lead to councils and committees

guage, or any other difference. Actually, the Director General of Education is the key man of the Ministry. It is he who implements the policies initiated by the Minister or by himself or laid down in various councils and committees. As the Minister is the political head of the Ministry and usually changes with the changes in the administration, it devolves upon the Director General to provide the administrative and professional direction of the system as well as the continuity of policies desirable in any educational system. He is the equivalent of a permanent under secretary and is supposed to be professionally well trained. In practice, however, the Directors General have changed frequently, fourteen having held office between 1927 and 1945, with an average tenure of 15.5 months.

The Director General is aided by one assistant and by directors for each of the six fields of educational activity: primary education, secondary education, teacher training and educational missions abroad, vocational education, educational research and statistics, and private- and foreign-school education. The post of Director of Education for Women, established in 1934, was abolished the following year. The post of Director of Rural Education was twice instituted and abolished—in a country having 75 percent of its population rural. The Directorates of Teacher Training and of Private- and Foreign-School Education are recent innovations, originating in 1945.

Within the office of the Director General there are also ten sections which are shown in Chart III. Their titles are self-explanatory, but four require special comment.

The Publication and Translation Section has charge of the publication of all texts for public primary and secondary schools and of various other publications issued by the central office of the Ministry. At one time the publication of approved textbooks for public schools was left to the authors, who usually agreed with the Ministry about the sale price of the books. In 1935, however, the Ministry, in an attempt to produce textbooks more economically and adequately, inaugurated the policy of buying the authors' rights and publishing the books at its own expense. Although the policy has not been consistently followed, an appreciable number of approved texts are now published by the Ministry.

The Examinations Section has charge of all public examinations conducted at the end of the sixth grade of the primary school and the third and fifth years of the secondary school. Each year the section establishes committees for setting the questions and other committees for grading the papers. It keeps complete records of the results of the examinations.

The Educational Missions Section has charge of the affairs of students selected for study abroad at government expense and keeps records of all students who study abroad at their own expense.

The Medicine and Hygiene Section safeguards the health of the school children. It inspects school buildings, conducts regular health examinations of pupils, treats those who suffer from diseases, trains teachers in first aid and simple treatments, propagates health information, and supplies schools with drugs and first-aid materials. In addition, it gives physical examinations at government expense to all teachers and officials entering the service of the Ministry of Education and all students entering the various schools and colleges. This section has set itself the task of fighting the three endemic diseases—trachoma, malaria, and bilharziasis—prevalent among school children. In 1943–44, 67,415 pupils out of the total public-school registration of 104,359 were examined; and of those examined, 16,599 were found to have trachoma, while 3,253 suffered other eye diseases; 5,864 had malaria, and 1,299 had bilharziasis. Treatment of those afflicted with bilharziasis resulted in steady improvement. The fight against trachoma has proceeded systematically, and the percentage of school children suffering from it is being reduced. Much effort has been expended on the campaign against malaria in all the provinces. The Medicine and Hygiene Section began very humbly in 1931 with the appointment of one doctor. By 1942–43 it had twenty-one doctors, two dentists, ten women nurses for the provinces, and more than seventy other health workers. In 1943–44 it maintained twenty-nine clinics throughout the country, and more recently a special hospital for students was established in Baghdad. Treatment at the clinics and at the hospital is free.

PROVINCIAL DIRECTORS OF EDUCATION

There is a provincial director of education for each of the fourteen provinces of Iraq. He is responsible to the Director General for the proper functioning of all schools and educational institutions in his province with the exception of teacher-training colleges, some of the vocational and special schools, and higher institutions; these exceptions are the direct concern of the central office of the Ministry. It is the function of the provincial director to make sure that teaching in the schools within his jurisdiction is in accordance with accepted syllabuses, to supervise the behavior of teachers and education officers in his province, and to carry out instructions of the Director General. The regulations of 1945 provide for provincial advisory education councils under the chairmanship of the governor and with the director of education as secretary. These councils

ORGANIZATION AND ADMINISTRATION

were to act in an advisory capacity, reviewing the educational situation in the province and making proposals for the improvement and extension of education.

However, a new Provincial Administration Law, passed by Parliament in 1945, effective early in 1946, provides for a general provincial council in each province to meet yearly in the month of March. The councils are empowered to levy local taxes to support various local services, such as the opening of technical classes and schools, the teaching about industries that will fit the local needs, the establishment of agricultural schools, and the founding, administration, and supervision, according to the provisions of the Public Education Law, of primary schools and of schools for workers and illiterates. It is not yet clear what the relation will be between the provincial educational councils, provided for by the regulations of the Ministry of Education, and the general provincial councils provided for in the new Provincial Administration Law.

The inspectorate

Side by side with the administrative service is the inspectoral service headed by a chief inspector responsible to the Director General. Inspectors are of three kinds: specialized inspectors, provincial inspectors, and women inspectors. Those in the first category are specialists in subject-matter fields who visit classes and teachers in their own fields in intermediate and secondary schools, teacher-training colleges, and special schools on the secondary-school level. They report on the performance of individual teachers, as well as on the general situation with regard to textbooks, library books, equipment, and laboratories. There is also a specialized administrative inspector who inspects the general administration of the school systems of the provinces.

Provincial inspectors make their headquarters in the education offices of the provinces and visit primary and secondary schools, but not technical schools or teachers colleges. In the secondary schools these inspectors have to ask the help of specialized inspectors in matters concerning the various subject-matter fields. Provincial inspectors are under the jurisdiction of the chief inspector and are independent of the provincial director of education. Women inspectors visit and report on girls schools, under the direction of a first woman inspector.

Inspectors' reports are sent to the chief inspector with copies to the provincial directors of education, and the substance of the reports is sent to the individuals about whom the reports are made. The chief inspector presents semiannual reports to the Director General of Education, describing the condition of the schools, and he makes an annual report to the Minister. It is his duty to insure the proper inspection of schools, the dissemination of information about improved methods of teaching together with the giving of demonstration lessons before teachers, the inspection of extraclass and out-of-school activities, the behavior of both teachers and pupils, and the condition of school buildings, equipment, and furnishings.

Councils and Committees

In addition to the previously mentioned Advisory Council on Education, the provincial educational councils and the general provincial councils, there are various other councils and committees which carry on some of the most important work of the Ministry.

Foremost among these is the Permanent Education Council with its two committees, the Central Education Committee and the Committee on the Equivalence of Diplomas and Degrees. The Permanent Council, a kind of executive board for the Ministry, is composed of the Director General of Education as chairman, the Director of Antiquities, the deans of the Law College and the Higher Teachers College, and the chief inspector. The Technical Adviser may be invited to meetings, but has no vote. The council meets at least once a month at the request of the Minister to deal with the general policies and trends of education, curriculums, budget, educational missions, laws and regulations, and employment of foreign teachers, and acts upon decisions made by committees.

The Central Education Committee is composed of the Director General as chairman, the assistants to the Director General and the six directors of the various types of education. Its principal function is to do the groundwork for the Permanent Education Council as regards curriculums and educational missions; in addition, it sanctions the purchase of books for the public libraries. The Committee on the Equivalence of Diplomas and Degrees decides on the value of degrees and diplomas received abroad.

Another important body is the Council of the Provincial Educational Directors, which meets annually in the summer. It consists of the provincial directors, the higher officials of the Ministry of Education, the dean of the Higher Teachers College, and the principals of the primary-, elementary-, and rural-teachers colleges. Its chief function is to study the progress of education in the provinces and correlate the work of the central office with that of the regional offices. At its meetings the annual budget is apportioned among the provinces, new graduates of the teachers colleges are assigned to the several provinces, transfers of teachers from one province

ORGANIZATION AND ADMINISTRATION

to another are arranged, plans for new schools and classes are decided upon, and proposals, policy matters, complaints, and criticisms are discussed.

Finally must be mentioned the newly founded Committee on Authorship, Translation, and Publication, which is a self-perpetuating body of learned men forming a kind of academy. It may have a minimum of ten and a maximum of twenty members distributed among the various branches of learning. This committee endeavors to enrich the "Arabic Library" by translating important classics as well as modern books of science, technology, and general culture; to encourage original research and writing; to publish old Arabic manuscripts; and to standardize Arabic scientific terminology. The committee holds regular meetings to choose books to be translated or written, to select writers and translators, and to read and discuss the researches of members. It may give financial assistance to translators, authors, and publishers in the form of grants, purchase of copyrights, prizes, or any other manner considered advisable. It plans to establish contact with learned men and societies in Iraq and abroad, particularly throughout the Arabic world. Finally, it plans to publish its own bulletins and periodicals embodying the researches of its members.

Educational Finance

The Ministry of Education receives the third largest budgetary provision of all the departments of the Iraqi government, being exceeded only by the army and the police. The public educational institutions of Iraq are entirely supported by the central government. The provincial authorities contribute nothing to the school fund, nor do the municipal authorities except for occasional assistance given to poor pupils. For specific purposes, such as aid to poor students or enlargement or repair of a school, contributions are occasionally solicited from private citizens of a locality, under the auspices of the administrative and educational authorities. The schools may give dramatic performances and exhibits to secure funds for special needs. Except for these minor and irregular sources, the central government pays the whole cost of public education.

The percentage of the general budget allotted to education has fluctuated from year to year. Starting with 2.3 percent in 1920–21, it reached a maximum of 12.9 percent in 1938–39, declined again in the following years to 7.8 percent in 1944–45, and showed a slight rise to 8.6 percent in 1945–46. In absolute figures, however, the sums allotted to the Ministry of Education have risen consistently (except for 1923–24) from 130,360 dinars ($521,440) in 1920–21 to 1,630,800 dinars ($6,523,200) in 1945–46. The decline in the percentage in recent years shows that the increase in allotments to education did not keep pace with the increase in the expenditure of the government as a whole.

Of the total of 1,630,800 dinars allotted for the year 1945–46, 7.5 percent was to be spent on the central and provincial administration, including inspection, and 0.45 percent on books for public libraries and the activities of the Committee on Authorship, Translation, and Publication. The remainder, 92 percent, was to be spent on teaching and the schools. Expenditure on each type of education (primary, secondary, vocational, and teacher training) is left to the discretion of the Ministry. Deans of the higher colleges control the expenditure of their own budgets.

Expenditure is made according to the instructions of the Ministry of Finance. Within the limits of these instructions the Minister of Education can sanction expenditures up to 500 dinars ($2,000) on any single item, the Director General and the deans of the colleges up to 37.5 dinars ($150) and the provincial educational directors up to 15 dinars ($60). The principals of primary schools are allowed 300 fils ($1.20) and those of secondary schools 1.5 dinars ($6.00) for miscellaneous expenses each month. Beyond these sums, school principals have no authority to spend except by permission of the provincial director of education or of the Director General. Consequently, a great deal of correspondence goes on between the schools and the administration asking for money for anything that cannot be covered by the miscellaneous expenditure fund. School equipment, books for libraries, furniture, stationery, all come from the central or provincial education authority, and no principal is allowed to spend money on these items. A few principals have attempted to expand their school libraries by soliciting contributions from students using the libraries, but most of the schools resign themselves to the meager collection of books provided by the Ministry.

Educational Legislation

In general, education in Iraq is governed by the provisions of the Public Education Law of 1940. The law defines the functions of the Ministry of Education as the founding and maintenance of government schools of all types and levels; the supervision of private and foreign schools to direct them toward the general goals of the government schools; the organization of youth, particularly through military training, scouting, and physical education; and finally, the fostering of scientific and literary movements, the spread of general culture, and the liquidation of illiteracy. The law classifies the schools into primary, secondary, and higher institutions; according to purpose into schools of general culture and professional or

ORGANIZATION AND ADMINISTRATION

vocational schools; and according to control into government, private, and foreign schools. The law sets forth in a general way the conditions for admission of students to the various kinds of schools and of their promotion from one school level to another. It authorizes the Ministry of Education to declare attendance compulsory in those localities where adequate primary-school facilities exist. It defines the level of training required for teachers in each type of school, makes provisions for sending students abroad for study, and lays down rather careful stipulations for the supervision of private and foreign schools.

The Law on the Distribution of Grants-in-Aid to Private Schools and Institutions, enacted in 1926, stipulates that points to be considered in making grants are the standards of the school and the number of classes in it, quality of teaching, the number and preparation of the teachers, similarity of the syllabus to that of the public education system, the degree of the school's participation in public examinations—and the degree of success achieved by the students in such examinations—and the revenues and expenditures of the school. The recommendations of the regional educational director and the reports of the inspectors are taken into account, and the Ministry has the privilege of converting a sum granted into salaries to be paid to one or two teachers selected by the Ministry.

Other laws not primarily concerned with education have a definite bearing upon it. The Local Languages Law of 1931 defines the areas in northern Iraq where Kurdish, Turkish, or Arabic shall be the official language. In areas where any of these languages is that of the majority of the pupils, instruction in primary schools is in that language.

Teachers' salaries and pensions

The Civil Service Law of 1939, which applies to all government employees, governs the appointment, promotion, and dismissal of teachers. It links appointment and initial salaries to graduation from various levels of schools and makes promotion beyond 25 dinars ($100) conditional upon a university degree or a parallel examination. It allows teachers a vacation of three months annually, but also allows the Minister to ask any teacher to work without additional pay for a period not to exceed six weeks of that time. It provides for study leave with half pay for a maximum of two years, with an additional year at least three years after expiration of the first leave. Officials are allowed three months' sick leave at any one time on full pay and an additional three months at half pay. Men and women are paid equal salaries if their qualifications are equal.

The State Cadre Law of 1940 as amended by the Cadre Law of 1942 fixes the types of government posts existing in each Ministry, with the minimum and maximum pay for each type. Primary-school teachers begin with 6 to 12 dinars ($24 to $48) per month according to their qualifications, and may reach a maximum of 25 dinars ($100). Teachers on the secondary cadre, including teachers of primary- and rural-teachers colleges and of vocational schools, begin at 15 to 30 dinars ($60 to $120) per month, the latter sum being the initial salary of teachers holding doctorates of British, American, French, or Egyptian universities, but not of central European universities. The maximum for a secondary-school teacher is 40 dinars ($160), with the exception of principals and holders of the doctorate, who may reach 50 dinars ($200). Instructors at higher institutions start at 18 dinars ($72), which is the initial salary for a new appointee holding the B.A. degree or its equivalent; if they achieve full professorial rank, they may reach a maximum salary of 70 dinars ($280). This is the maximum salary paid ordinarily to a Director General and is the highest salary paid to a civil servant. A few posts exist at 80 dinars ($320) for directors general of a "distinguished grade"—mainly former ministers or directors general of long standing and service. The policy of including the full professors among the most highly paid civil servants was adopted in the amendments to the Cadre Law of 1942 to encourage some of the ablest men in the country to turn to scientific work. This policy has extended to a degree into secondary education to lessen the pay differential between secondary-school teachers and holders of official administrative posts in government offices. Provincial-education directors and inspectors may reach a maximum of 40 dinars ($160), and specialized inspectors, a maximum of 50 dinars ($200).

It will be seen that the civil service and the state cadre laws have on the whole made liberal provision for making teaching an attractive career for young men and young women. It is understood that amendments to the Civil Service Law are pending which will make educational service even more attractive, particularly in encouraging study abroad.

The Civil Pensions Law of 1940 provides that a civil servant of thirty years' service receives a retirement allowance equal to one-half of his average salary over the last seven years of his employment. A shorter or longer period of service pays proportionately. In case of death, the pension is paid to the wife and minor children in accordance with the inheritance law.

The Discipline of State Officials Law of 1936 provides for disciplinary boards in each Ministry to try officials, including teachers, for offenses com-

ORGANIZATION AND ADMINISTRATION

mitted in office. A Higher Disciplinary Board handles appeals and disputes regarding the rights of officials.

The Educational Ladder

The educational ladder in Iraq is based on a primary school, which children enter at the age of six and attend for six years, a secondary school of five years, and a number of colleges of three to six years; there are also numerous professional and vocational schools. (See Chart IV.) The secondary school is of two levels: an intermediate school of three years' duration is an approximation of the American junior-high school; a two-year preparatory school is a shorter version of the American senior-high school. Thus, Iraqi primary and secondary schools operate on the 6-3-2 plan as compared with the American 8-4 or 6-3-3 year plans. Below the primary-school level, a few kindergartens are maintained by the Ministry of Education or by some private agencies.

Public primary schools

The public primary school is free to all children who have reached the age of six years and offers a uniform curriculum extending over six grades. It is the common school which most Iraqi children, whatever their class, religion, or race, attend, and it is the medium through which the educational authorities of Iraq hope to develop a sense of citizenship and national unity. Attendance is compulsory wherever adequate facilities exist. Article 36 of the Public Education Law prohibits Iraqi children from attending foreign primary schools; and as native private schools follow rather closely the curriculum of the government schools, it is safe to conclude that all Iraqi children of primary school age who attend school at all receive a standard type of primary education.

The primary-school course ends in a special public primary examination, set by the Ministry for all the schools of Iraq. No pupil can be promoted to a postprimary school, whether public, private, or foreign, without first passing the public primary examination or presenting a certificate showing that he has pursued similar studies abroad.

Postprimary education

Of 5,416 graduates of primary schools in 1942–43, 4,214 pupils, or 77.6 percent, continued their education the following year. The great majority of these, 3,921 pupils, entered the intermediate schools, while the remainder, 293, entered some vocational or professional school. The boys

Chart IV

IRAQ: PUBLIC SCHOOL SYSTEM, 1945–46

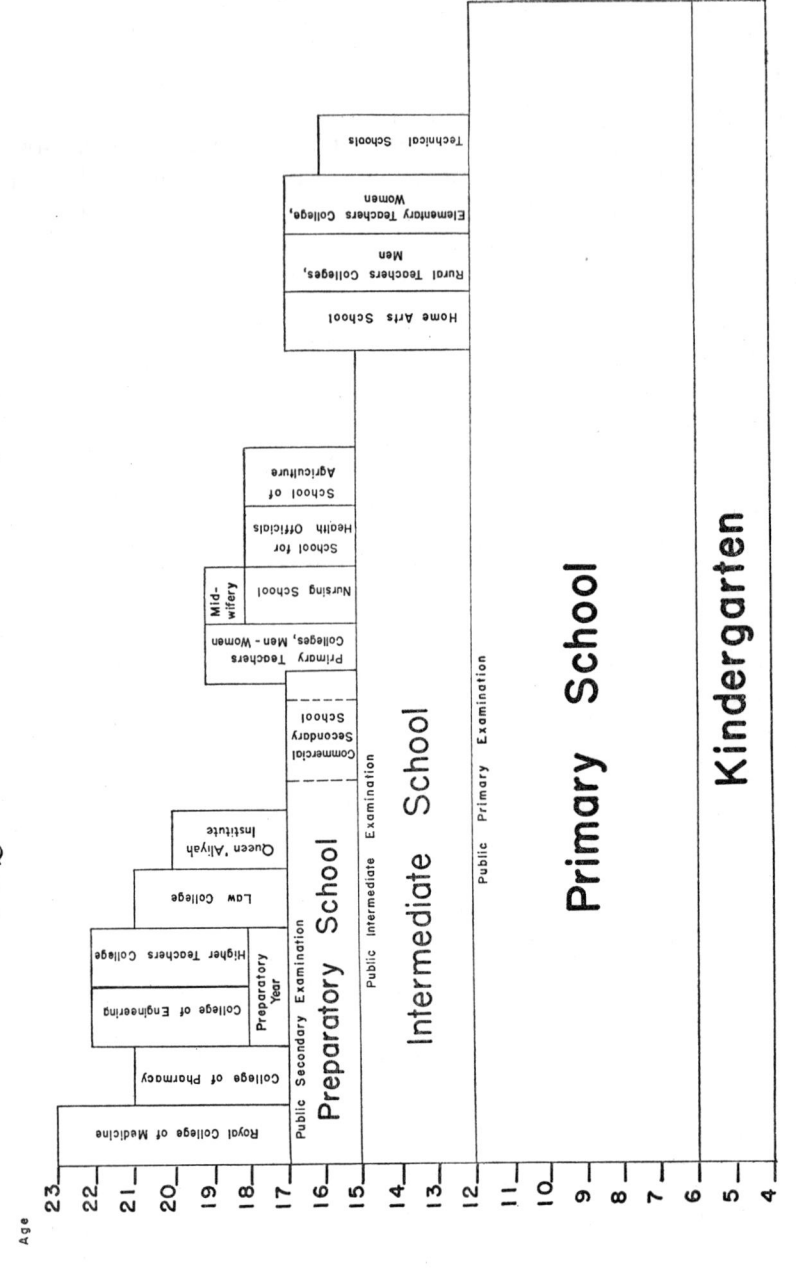

Age	
23	Royal College of Medicine
22	
21	College of Pharmacy
20	Higher Teachers College
19	College of Engineering
18	Law College / Preparatory Year
17	Queen 'Aliyah Institute
	Public Secondary Examination
16	Preparatory School
15	Commercial Secondary School
	Public Intermediate Examination
14	Primary Teachers Colleges, Men–Women / Midwifery / Nursing School / School for Health Officials / School of Agriculture
13	Intermediate School
12	Home Arts School / Rural Teachers Colleges, Men / Elementary Teachers College, Women / Technical Schools
	Public Primary Examination
11	
10	
9	Primary School
8	
7	
6	
5	Kindergarten
4	

ORGANIZATION AND ADMINISTRATION 133

enter the rural-teachers colleges or the technical schools, the girls the Elementary Teachers College for Women or the Home Arts School. Education in these vocational and professional schools is entirely at government expense—free tuition, board and lodging, books, medical care, some clothing, and travel between home and school being provided.

Most of the students passing the public intermediate-school examinations go on with their studies. Of 2,020 students who passed in 1943-44, 1,890, or 93.5 percent, entered postintermediate schools. The great majority of these, 1,738, or 86 percent, chose to complete their secondary-school course. The remaining 152 entered the primary-teachers colleges for men or women, or the schools of health workers, nursing, and agriculture. Study at these schools is entirely at government expense. The average preparatory school, that is, the upper part of the secondary school, offers the student a choice of two parallel courses, the literary or the scientific. Some preparatory schools have only one course, usually the literary. The Commercial Secondary School in Baghdad is a special type of preparatory school, offering a two-year commercial course. No student may pass from a secondary school to a higher institution unless he passes the public secondary-school examination, though expatriate students may substitute a certificate of equivalent study abroad.

Having completed his secondary education, an Iraqi student has a number of channels open to him. He may, of course, decide to go to work and leave school altogether. If he has done superior work in school, he has a chance of being sent on a government mission to study abroad. If he can afford it, he may study abroad at his own expense. Or he may apply for admission to one of the eight higher courses open to Iraqi students: the Royal College of Medicine, the College of Pharmacy, the College of Engineering, the Higher Teachers College, the Law College, the Primary Teachers College for Men, the Queen 'Aliyah Institute for Women, or the military and police colleges. All these institutions except the Primary Teachers College for Men and the military and police colleges are open to women students. Theoretically any graduate of the secondary school may be admitted to any of the colleges, but in practice only students who elected the scientific course in secondary school are admitted into the Colleges of Medicine, Pharmacy, and Engineering, and the scientific sections of the Higher Teachers College—with very rare exceptions in the last case. However, many students from the scientific course succeed in getting into the Law College and the literary section of the Higher Teachers College. Attendance drops after graduation from the secondary schools.

Of 1,011 graduates of secondary schools in 1942–43, only 470, or 46.5 percent, entered higher institutions in Iraq or went abroad to study. Admission to the colleges is based primarily upon scholastic standing and proportional representation of each province.

With the exception of the Law College,[2] instruction in the colleges is free, the student signing a contract to serve the government after graduation for a specified number of years. The Colleges of Medicine, Pharmacy, and Law have no boarding arrangements, but all other colleges maintain boarding departments at government expense. Other government aid for students studying at its expense includes books, medical care, travel, and in some cases clothing.

The Iraqi public-school system is essentially democratic in character, affording a large measure of equality of opportunity to students. It is largely a free system, fees charged in secondary schools being small and provision being made for a large percentage of exemptions for the poor student of little better than average standing.[3] Even higher education is almost entirely free, the Law College being the only important exception —and there the bright poor student is exempted from payment of fees. Moreover, the government has taken up the heavy burden of providing vocational and professional education entirely at its own expense.

Recently the Ministry of Education has taken steps to extend post-primary educational opportunities for village boys. Formerly the only courses available to poor village boys were in the rural-teachers colleges or the technical schools in Baghdad or Mosul. If a village boy wanted to proceed to the intermediate and secondary schools in the capitals of the provinces, he had to have means to support himself—and few did. In September 1945 the Ministry of Education adopted the policy of opening a boarding department in the capital of each province where 10 bright village boys can be taken annually at government expense and so allowed to pursue their secondary education. In addition, some of the brightest primary-school graduates are admitted annually from each province to King Faysal College for boys where they receive their secondary-school education in English at government expense. Some of the brighter girls from each province are admitted after graduation from the intermediate schools into the secondary section of the Queen 'Aliyah Institute at government expense.

---

[2] A College of Commerce was founded in 1946-47 and charges fees at the same rate as the College of Law—15 dinars ($60.00) per annum.

[3] Secondary-school fees were abolished entirely in 1946.

Public Examinations

An account of the educational ladder in Iraq is incomplete without reference to the public examinations which are held at the end of the primary, intermediate, and preparatory stages of schooling. These constitute a check by the Ministry on the standard of achievement of the schools and also serve to keep private and foreign schools in line with the programs and policies laid down by the Ministry. Government certificates issued on the basis of passing grades in these examinations are the only passport from one school level to the next in Iraq.

Regulations governing the public examinations were based on the Education Law of 1929 and, since their first issue in 1931, have been amended and revised many times. Current are the regulations of 1942 as amended in 1943, 1944, and 1945. According to these regulations, public primary examinations require papers in five subjects: Arabic, English, social studies, arithmetic and measurements, and object lessons (elementary science) and hygiene. Public intermediate examinations are in six subjects: Arabic, English, social studies, mathematics, biology and hygiene, physics and chemistry. In the public secondary-school (preparatory) examination the subjects are grouped into four categories: languages, social studies, mathematics, and the sciences. The examination is made up of seven papers, one in each language, and for the rest, two in each of two groups chosen by the student and one in the remaining group.

Students are admitted to the examinations either upon the recommendation of their schools or as outsiders. Schools, whether public, private, or foreign, are required to recommend only those students who have maintained a passing average in the final school year or who are delinquent because of failure in only one subject; they may not recommend students who failed in their yearly average. Students who wish to enter the public examinations as outsiders must first take a special examination in a public school according to a program determined by the Ministry; in addition, they must present a formal application to the provincial director of education before May 1 together with a character certificate. An outside student is charged 3 dinars ($12) for the intermediate examination and 5 dinars ($20) for the preparatory. No fees are charged for the primary examination. An outside student is not admitted to the intermediate examination unless he has passed the primary, or to the preparatory unless he has passed the intermediate. Students who have studied in recognized schools abroad, in vocational schools, or in private schools prior to the promulgation of the regulations are exempt from these last requirements.

Examinations of each type are held twice yearly, in the first half of June and in the second half of September. The second examination is held for the benefit of those who are delinquent in the June examination or who were absent from it for some valid reason. The passing mark is 50 percent in the individual subject and 60 for the general average. A delinquent is a student who receives below 50 in one or two subjects with his general average in the other subjects 60 or above, or who fails in one subject and whose general average is between 50 and 60, or who fails to achieve the average of 60 without having fallen below 50 in any single subject. Other failures may not be re-examined for a year.

In about the middle of the school year subject committees, composed of inspectors, specialized inspectors, and teachers—usually of schools of a higher level than that for which questions are being set, and of the teachers colleges—are formed to devise questions for the various levels. Final sets of questions are sent in sufficient number and in sealed packages to each examination center to be opened only by the director of the center and on the day of the particular examination. The number of examination centers for each level is determined on the basis of statistics provided by the provincial directors of education. Details of arrangements for staffing the centers are usually left to the provincial directors. The specialist marking committees are appointed usually on the basis of two committees for each subject on each level per center—though some subjects, Arabic and English for instance, occasionally need more. The directors of education or of the examination centers give each student a number which corresponds with the number of a seat in the examination hall.

The examination in a specific subject takes place simultaneously in all centers. The examinations are timed, usually two to three hours being allowed for six or seven questions. The director of the center collects and counts the books and sends them in sealed packages to the correction center. Correction centers for intermediate and preparatory levels are in Baghdad. Correction of the primary examinations is decentralized, each province having its own center.

In the correction center the upper left-hand corner of the cover of every notebook bearing the name and number of the student is turned and pasted over so that the notebook cannot be identified. The books are then given to the subject committee concerned, which meets in the correction building. No books are allowed out of the building, and no strangers are allowed in the building. The members of the committee distribute the questions among themselves, each marking his own questions, and the marks are then added up. A second committee rereads the books and

ORGANIZATION AND ADMINISTRATION

marks them independently. If there is a discrepancy of more than 10 between the two marks, the book is returned to the original committee. In case of no agreement on the mark, the two committees meet and mark the paper together. When the marking is completed, the covers of the books are opened and the results tabulated subject by subject by the director of the correction center and his assistants. The director is also responsible

TABLE 18
PUBLIC EXAMINATION RESULTS, IRAQ, 1944–45

STUDENTS	PUBLIC SCHOOLS Number	PUBLIC SCHOOLS Percentage	PRIVATE AND FOREIGN SCHOOLS Number	PRIVATE AND FOREIGN SCHOOLS Percentage	STUDENTS NOT ENROLLED IN SCHOOLS Number	STUDENTS NOT ENROLLED IN SCHOOLS Percentage	TOTAL Number	TOTAL Percentage
Primary examinations								
Number Entering	6,411	100.0	1,377	100.0	209	100.0	7,997	100.0
Number Passing	4,020	62.7	1,068	77.6	62	29.7	5,150	64.4
Number Failing	2,391	37.3	309	22.4	147	70.3	2,847	35.6
Intermediate examinations								
Number Entering	1,924	100.0	1,422	100.0	608	100.0	3,954	100.0
Number Passing	1,418	73.7	845	59.7	184	30.3	2,447	61.9
Number Failing	506	26.3	577	40.3	424	69.7	1,507	38.1
Preparatory examinations								
Number Entering								
Science	825	...	631	...	243	...	1,699	...
Literature	407	...	350	...	256	...	1,013	...
Commerce	16	...	...	...	6	...	22	...
Total	1,248	...	981	...	505	...	2,734	...
Number Passing								
Science	625	75.8	297	47.1	38	15.6	960	56.5
Literature	271	66.6	135	38.6	72	28.1	478	47.1
Commerce	15	93.8	...	...	4	66.7	19	86.3
Total	911	73.0	432	44.0	114	22.6	1,457	53.3
Number Failing								
Science	200	24.2	334	52.9	205	84.4	739	45.5
Literature	136	33.4	215	61.4	184	71.9	535	52.9
Commerce	1	6.2	...	...	2	33.3	3	13.7
Total	337	27.0	549	56.0	391	77.4	1,277	46.7

for making public the results of the examinations, usually during the first ten days of July, so that delinquent students have about two and a half months to prepare for the September examination.

Results of the public examinations for the primary, intermediate, and preparatory schools for the year 1944–45 are given in Table 18. It is apparent that for the year 1944–45 students of private and foreign schools did better in the primary examination than did the students of the public schools, while in the intermediate and preparatory examinations the public-school students did better. Students who prepare privately for the examinations are consistently the poorest on the average. The annual reports of the last four or five years show that these trends are not peculiar to any one year. The private and foreign primary schools, 52 in number, are only 11 percent of the total number of primary schools (479) in Iraq, and are mainly located in the larger cities where children come from better and more progressive homes. The 427 public schools are scattered all over Iraq, in remote villages and in small towns as well as in cities, and their pupils are drawn from all classes of the population.

The reason for the trend at the secondary-school level is quite different. Government intermediate and preparatory schools now admit students on the basis of their achievement and, furthermore, drop any student who fails twice in the same year's work. Those dropped, in an effort, in some cases, to save themselves from two years of military service as privates, enroll in the private schools, thus reducing the standing of the private schools. Naturally individual private schools maintain a good standard; conversely individual public schools make poor records.

On the average, about two-thirds of those who enter the public primary examinations and about three-fifths of those who enter the public intermediate and preparatory examinations pass, with percentages dropping as low as 32 percent and rising as high as 83 percent in some years. The results of the public examinations do not give a complete picture of failures, for since 1940 the schools have had authority to pass or fail students of their graduating classes prior to those examinations. An indication of the amount of failure at the school level is found in figures for the graduating classes of public schools in 1943-44: these were 22.5 percent for primary schools, 20.5 percent for intermediate schools, and 6.2 percent for preparatory schools. When the final results for that year are corrected in the light of these figures, it is found that of 8,758 pupils registered in the sixth grades of the public schools in May 1944, only 3,865 (44 percent) finally succeeded in passing the public examination; and of 2,885 students registered in the third year of the intermediate public schools, 1,286 (44.5 percent) passed the public examinations. Finally, of the 1,231 students in the fifth year of the public preparatory schools, 680 (55 percent) passed the public examinations.

Thus, it is seen that, generally speaking, fewer than half of the pupils in the top class actually graduate from the public schools. In other words, the public examinations at the end of each stage of the educational ladder act as real hurdles, and many students of low standing are eliminated or at least retarded.

ORGANIZATION AND ADMINISTRATION

Educational Statistics for Iraq

To complete the picture of education in Iraq, tables are included to give a statistical view of education as it is today in all types of educational institutions. For comparative purposes there are used whenever possible figures taken at ten-year intervals after 1920–21 and at yearly intervals after 1940, for the public-school system. Data for these tables were obtained from the reports of the Ministry of Education or from unpublished statistics in the possession of the Ministry.

Table 19 gives a general review of all education in Iraq, from which certain significant conclusions may be drawn. The public educational system has multiplied between 10 and 15 times its 1920 size and to between 2.5 and 6.5 times its 1930 size. Enrollments in private and foreign schools constitute a little less than one-fifth of the total enrollment. Private and foreign schools are only of kindergarten, primary, and secondary types, the government taking care of teacher training, vocational, and higher education. In 1944–45 there were 1,098 schools of all types, which employed 6,179 teachers and had a total enrollment of 139,111 students. World War II brought about a decline in enrollments of primary and secondary schools and of teachers colleges, but not in the number of schools or teachers. But the upward trend has already begun. Figures lately received from the Ministry of Education show that public primary-school enrollments in 1945–46 total 112,611, an increase of 15,596 pupils over the previous year.

The greatest gain in the last twenty-five years is registered in the enrollments of secondary and higher institutions, the former having multiplied 100 times and the latter 27.5 times since 1920.

The most concentrated efforts are still being directed toward primary education. Approximately ten-elevenths of the enrollment and nine-tenths of the schools and teachers in the public-school system are in primary education. The Ministry of Education considers that its first duty is to spread this basic education among the masses, founding secondary, vocational, and higher institutions only as the need of the country or insistent demand requires it to do so.

Expansion of the Public Primary-School System

In 1944–45 there were 878 public primary schools and kindergartens in Iraq, taught by 4,491 teachers and attended by 97,636 boys and girls. Table 20 shows the growth of the Iraqi public primary-school system since 1920. Comparing the year 1944–45 with 1930–31, we find that schools and pupils have increased about 3 times and teachers 3.6 times. For this

TABLE 19

Number of Schools, Teachers, and Pupils in Iraq, 1920–45, According to Level and Type of School

Year and Type of School	Primary Schools (Including Kindergartens) Number	Primary Schools Number of Teachers	Primary Schools Enrollment	Secondary Schools (Intermediate & Preparatory) Number	Secondary Schools Number of Teachers	Secondary Schools Enrollment	Teachers Colleges (Primary, Elementary, & Rural) Number	Teachers Colleges Number of Teachers	Teachers Colleges Enrollment	Vocational and Special Schools Number	Vocational and Special Schools Number of Teachers	Vocational and Special Schools Enrollment	Higher Institutions Number	Higher Institutions Number of Teachers	Higher Institutions Enrollment
Public schools:															
1920–21	88	486	8,001	3	34	110	1	...	91	1	...	80	1	...	65
1930–31	316	1,325	34,513	19	129	2,082	3	...	386	1	...	140	4	...	99
1940–41	735	3,525	90,794	56	472	13,969	4	86	2,119	4	58	464	4	37	907
1941–42	761	3,752	88,864	58	435	12,926	4	82	2,091	4	56	642	4	32	883
1942–43	788	3,979	87,445	60	471	11,191	5	88	1,754	6	63	804	5	40	898
1943–44	861	4,340	89,558	67	490	11,128	6	89	1,641	9*	82	1,163*	5	45	1,638
1944–45	878	4,491	97,636	71	539	11,309	7	94	1,344	7*	76	948	5	50	1,790
Private and foreign schools:															
1944–45	81	607	19,887	49	322	6,818	...	...	...	...	...	...	...	...	...
Total, public, private, and foreign schools:															
1944–45	959	5,098	116,902	120	861	18,127	7	94	1,344	7	76	948	5	50	1,790

* Includes School of Health Officials and School of Nursing, both of which are under the Ministry of Social Affairs. Comparative statistics are not available for previous years.

ORGANIZATION AND ADMINISTRATION

period girls schools have had a greater proportionate increase than the boys schools. Since 1930–31 girls schools and attendance have increased about 3.5 times and teachers 5.3 times. This growth is an encouraging sign. The old prejudice against female education has broken down in the larger cities and is weakening in even the most conservative centers.

The Iraqi primary school has now on the average one teacher more than it had fifteen years earlier, having a staff of five instead of four teachers. This is explained by the fact that for the past decade the Ministry of Education has made a vigorous effort to open new schools, increase the number of grades in existing schools, and train an adequate supply of teachers.

The increase in enrollment of girls is proportionately greater than that of boys. In 1930–31 girls totaled one-fifth of the primary-school enrollment, but in 1944–45 they constituted one-fourth.

The expansion of the public primary-school system can be considered in terms of the increase of pupils by grade. Table 21 shows the number of children in each grade for selected years between 1920 and 1945. Examination of the table reveals that in 1945 relatively more pupils were completing the primary-school course than had in 1930–31. While the number of first-grade pupils increased 2.13 times in the fourteen-year period, the number of sixth-grade pupils increased almost 6 times. Evidently the increase in the total number of primary-school pupils is not due merely to the fact that more children are entering the first grade, but also to the fact that a greater proportion are continuing in school.

This supposition is confirmed by the two sets of percentages shown at the bottom of the table. While the percentages for the first and second grades have declined, those for the other grades have increased, particularly in the upper grades. Whereas first-grade pupils constituted 42.6 percent of the total enrollment in 1930–31, they constituted only 32 percent in 1944–45. On the other hand, the percentage of sixth-grade pupils, having risen from 4.9 to 10.1, was more than doubled.

It is safe to conclude that the average primary-school-age child is getting more years of education than he got in previous years, but the process of lengthening the period of study of school-age children will have to go on for a long time before a more even distribution of pupils over the six grades will be achieved.

Between 1930 and 1945 secondary schools multiplied 3.7 times, rising from 19 to 71; the number of teachers multiplied 4.1 times, from 129 to 539; and pupils multiplied 5.5 times, increasing from 2,082 to 11,309 pupils. As is the case in primary education, the increase in girls enrolled in secondary schools is comparatively greater than the increase for boys.

TABLE 20
The Growth of Public Primary Education, Iraq, 1920–45

Year	Schools Boys	Schools Girls	Schools Coed.	Schools Total	Teachers Men	Teachers Women	Teachers Total	Pupils Boys	Pupils Girls	Pupils Coed.	Pupils Total
1920–21	...	...	...	88	...	...	486	...	...	...	8,001
1930–31	269	45	2*	316	1,075	249	1,325	27,467	6,753	293*	34,513
1938–39	560	145	34	739	2,263	886	3,149	69,505	23,105	4,009	96,620
1939–40	529	144	40	713	2,328	975	3,304	64,240	20,421	4,821	89,482
1940–41	543	145	47	735	2,462	1,063	3,525	64,112	20,029	6,653	90,794
1941–42	562	145	54	761	2,628	1,124	3,752	62,441	19,493	6,930	88,864
1942–43	590	146	52	788	2,827	1,152	3,979	61,697	19,031	6,717	87,445
1943–44	650	162	49	861	3,062	1,278	4,340	67,297†	22,261†	(6,227)†	89,558
1944–45	662	160	56	878	3,162	1,329	4,491	73,263†	24,373†	(8,512)†	97,636‡

* Kindergarten schools and kindergarten children, as no other coeducational schools existed then.
† Boys and girls in coeducational schools are included beginning with 1943–44, but are not included for the previous years. The figures in parentheses are included in the two preceding columns. In 1944–45 there were 4,322 boys and 4,190 girls in coeducational schools.
‡ Including 621 pupils in kindergartens.

TABLE 21
Enrollment of Pupils by Grades in Public Primary Schools, Iraq, 1920–45

Year	1st Grade	2nd Grade	3rd Grade	4th Grade	5th Grade	6th Grade	Total
1920–21	4,001	1,926	1,035	569	352	118	8,001
1930–31	14,575	7,756	4,858	3,118	2,282	1,631	34,220
1940–41	22,276	16,657	17,039	14,238	11,162	9,422	90,794
1941–42	23,768	15,892	14,935	13,990	11,400	8,879	88,864
1942–43	23,111	15,924	14,012	12,705	11,377	10,316	87,445
1943–44	25,753	16,432	14,308	12,251	11,242	9,572	89,558
1944–45	31,012	17,795	14,463	12,479	11,426	9,840	97,015
Ratio of 1944–45 enrollment to 1930–31 enrollment	2.13	2.30	2.97	4.00	5.00	5.82	2.8
Enrollment percentage for each grade, 1930–31	42.6	22.6	14.0	9.1	6.6	4.9	
Enrollment percentage for each grade, 1944–45	32.0	18.3	14.9	12.8	11.7	10.1	

ORGANIZATION AND ADMINISTRATION

This difference is due in part to the fact that girls secondary schools were not opened until 1929–30—and then were few in number—and in part to the fact that World War II caused less decline in the attendance of girls of this age.

At one time responsible authorities at the Ministry of Education named the ratio of 1:10 as proper between secondary and primary schools. This ratio has been approximated. In 1930–31 the number of secondary schools and of secondary-school pupils amounted to 6 percent of the total of primary schools and pupils. In 1944–45 these percentages had increased to 8.1 for schools, and 11.6 for pupils. In 1930–31 the number of secondary-school teachers equaled 9.7 percent of primary-school teachers. In 1944–45 secondary teachers equaled 12 percent of the total of primary teachers. This rise in the ratio was accomplished in spite of the rather rapid growth of primary education. The average secondary school, though having about 50 children more than the average primary school, is not unduly large, nor are the classes crowded, for the average number of students per class is about 31. The secondary-school regulations require that classes shall not exceed 40 students. Few, if any, classes are that large, while many classes have no more than 20 students. The increase in the number of teachers has kept up with that in the number of students.

The term "secondary school" is ambiguous: it may mean either an intermediate school or a preparatory school, or it may mean the two combined. The distribution of schools and pupils according to type is shown in Table 22.

TABLE 22
Enrollment in Secondary Schools, Iraq, 1944–45

Secondary Schools	No. of Schools			Enrollment		
	Boys	Girls	Total	Boys	Girls	Total
Intermediate schools..	32	17	49	6,579	2,015	8,594
Preparatory schools...	18	4	22	2,269	446	2,715
Total............	50	21	71	8,848	2,461	11,309

Thus, out of a total of 71 secondary schools there were only 22 preparatory schools leading to the final secondary-school certificate. The remaining 49 schools are intermediate schools, 12 of these being connected with the preparatory schools to make complete secondary schools of five years. So it may be said that in 1944–45 there were 59 secondary schools of which 12 were complete five-year schools, 10 were preparatory only, and 37 were intermediate only.

TABLE 23
Enrollment of Secondary-School Students by Years, Iraq, 1924–45

YEAR	1ST YEAR Boys	1ST YEAR Girls	1ST YEAR Total	2ND YEAR Boys	2ND YEAR Girls	2ND YEAR Total	3RD YEAR Boys	3RD YEAR Girls	3RD YEAR Total	4TH YEAR Boys	4TH YEAR Girls	4TH YEAR Total	5TH YEAR Boys	5TH YEAR Girls	5TH YEAR Total	TOTAL Boys	TOTAL Girls	TOTAL Total
1924–25*	240	...	240	86	...	86	55	...	55	24	...	24	...	...	...	405	...	405
1930–31*	898	165	1,063	589	11	600	262	...	262	157	...	157	...	...	...	1,906	176	2,082
1934–35	1,511	220	1,731	1,044	164	1,208	933	132	1,065	388	36	424	232	22	254	4,108	574	4,682
1940–41	3,055	876	3,931	3,269	727	3,996	3,349	593	3,942	951	164	1,115	870	115	985	11,494	2,475	13,969
1941–42	2,781	843	3,624	2,799	773	3,572	2,784	629	3,413	1,089	240	1,329	836	152	988	10,289	2,637	12,926
1942–43	1,575	514	2,089	2,602	755	3,357	2,810	677	3,487	851	120	971	1,068	219	1,287	8,906	2,285	11,191
1943–44	2,530	781	3,311	1,619	511	2,130	2,328	725	3,053	1,143	233	1,376	1,091	167	1,258	8,711	2,417	11,128
1944–45	2,820	809	3,629	1,916	628	2,544	1,843	578	2,421	1,189	236	1,425	1,080	210	1,290	8,848	2,461	11,309
Ratio of 1944–45 enrollment to 1934–35 enrollment	1.9	3.7	2.1	1.8	3.8	2.1	2.0	4.4	2.3	3.1	6.6	3.4	4.7	9.5	5.1	2.2	4.3	2.4
Enrollment percentage for each year, 1934–35	...	...	37.0	...	...	25.8	...	...	22.7	...	...	9.1	...	...	5.4	...	...	...
Enrollment percentage for each year, 1944–45	...	...	32.1	...	...	22.5	...	...	21.4	...	...	12.6	...	...	11.4	...	...	...

* Figures for the old four-year secondary school. The fifth year of the new five-year secondary school was not initiated until 1931–32.

ORGANIZATION AND ADMINISTRATION

INCREASE OF STUDENTS BY GRADES

Table 23 shows the increase in the number of students by grades in the public secondary schools from 1925–45. At the bottom of the table the progress made in the decade from 1934–35 to 1944–45 is shown in percentages.

As in the primary schools the rate of increase in the secondary schools rises with the grade: though attendance doubled in the first year, it increased by 5 times in the fifth year. The same phenomenon is apparent in the percent of the total of students in each grade. While percentages for the lower secondary grades have dropped slightly during the decade, those for the last two grades have risen from 14.5 to 24 percent of the total enrollment. Obviously more students are entering secondary schools now, and many more are attempting to finish. Again the rate of increase for girls is greater than that for boys.

ELIMINATION OF STUDENTS IN THE SECONDARY GRADES

However, though more students are staying with the secondary course to the end than did a decade ago, the ranks are thinned as a class moves upward. Taking, for example, the first-year class of 1940–41, which numbered 3,931 students, it is found that five years later they have been reduced to 1,290 in the fifth year in 1944–45, or 32.8 percent of those who were in the first year. The most drastic elimination takes place at the end of the third year because of the public intermediate examination. Of the 1,290 who were in the fifth year in 1944–45, only 1,248 entered the public secondary examination and of these 911 students passed. So only 23.2 percent of the students who entered upon secondary education five years earlier actually graduated. By that time, however, they were not the original group that started in the first year. Many of them dropped out through failure or other causes and were replaced by failures from the previous classes or entrants from the private schools. It can be safely concluded that the Iraqi secondary-school system is highly selective.

Chapter 9

PUBLIC PRIMARY EDUCATION

𝓕REE public primary education extends over six grades and is offered to any Iraqi child who has reached the age of six years. In theory, primary education is compulsory in areas where adequate facilities exist; in practice, in the few instances in which the Ministry of Education has declared attendance to be compulsory in given areas, social and economic conditions, together with inadequate planning, have made the ruling ineffective.

Except for certain modifications in schools in Kurdish or Turkish districts, or in the few so-called "model rural primary schools," the primary course is uniform throughout Iraq. Thus, a child moving from one district to another, from urban to rural or tribal district, is not handicapped by basic variation in the curriculum.

To a large extent, primary education segregates boys from girls, with boys schools taught by men and girls schools by women. The Ministry of Education, however, has made considerable progress in recent years, especially in the cities, in overcoming the traditional prejudice against coeducation. In 1933–34 the Ministry opened kindergartens, later called "junior schools," which admitted both boys and girls and employed women teachers. In the larger cities, particularly in Baghdad, the kindergartens soon were enlarged to include first- and second-grade classes. Rather hesitant about adding classes at first, the Ministry was encouraged by the popularity of this experiment to enlarge the program. By 1938–39 junior schools had sprung up in the capitals of almost all the provinces, and in spite of the war these schools continued to flourish, increasing in number and attendance until in 1944–45 there were 56 schools attended by 8,512 children, 4,322 boys and 4,190 girls. At the present time the typical junior school consists of the first four grades and parallels the work of those grades in the public primary school. A few junior schools offer a five- or six-year course. Apart from these planned coeducational schools, coeducation at the primary level is tolerated in many rural villages where no girls schools or only incomplete ones exist.

PUBLIC PRIMARY EDUCATION

Only six of the provinces include kindergarten classes with their junior schools; a total of 621 children, 265 boys and 356 girls, are registered in these classes. The Ministry of Education is most concerned with spreading basic elementary education and tends to leave nursery schools and kindergartens to private initiative. A few private or foreign kindergartens have been established in Baghdad.

Except for demonstration schools attached to the teachers colleges and administered jointly by the heads of the teachers colleges and the provincial directors of education, primary schools are under the authority of the latter officials. The public primary-school regulations authorize free primary instruction to children of all creeds and races who are between ages of six and fourteen and specify subjects to be taught and prohibit the use of textbooks that have not been approved by the Ministry of Education. Teachers and pupils are forbidden to engage in politics, and teachers may not engage in commerce or accept outside permanent or temporary employment without the approval of the provincial director of education. Teachers may not give private lessons to children of their own schools. They may do so to children of other schools only with the approval of the provincial director. At the time of admission to a school children must be free from disease and must present a certificate of vaccination against smallpox. Children admitted from *mulla* (*kuttab*) or private schools are examined and put in a suitable grade. Children transferring from one public school to another are supplied with certificates which place them in the same grade in the new school. Religious instruction given in any school is in the religion of the majority of the students; minority-group students are excused from attending classes for religious instruction.

The school year extends from September 15 to June 15. A ten-day vacation is given at midyear, and the schools enjoy the same holidays as do government offices. Children belonging to minority religions are allowed holidays for their important feasts. The whole school is closed for holidays of the majority religion. The school week is of six days with Friday free. There is a half-day session on Thursday, and Monday afternoon is devoted to school excursions, scouting, lectures, or other extracurricular activities. The school day of regular length consists of six lessons, four in the morning and two in the afternoon. The daily timetable is fixed in the regulations, and no principal is authorized to deviate from it.

The regulations lay down detailed instructions for conducting examinations in the school. These are given by the teachers under the general direction of the principal. In the first four grades the maximum grade is 10; in the fifth and sixth grades, 100. The pupil must not fall below 50 percent in any subject and must have an average of 60 percent in order to be promoted. If he fails in one subject, he may be re-examined at the reopening of school in September. Failure in two subjects entails repeating the year unless one of the subjects is physical education, penmanship, drawing, manual training, or singing. Daily marks must be recorded for children of the fifth and sixth grades; these are averaged with the marks on midyear and final examinations to obtain the final mark.

Authority in the school is concentrated in the hands of the principal. He is responsible for the proper functioning of the school and its discipline according to the regulations and instructions he receives from higher authority. Expulsion of a child from school must be agreed to by all the teachers sitting in committee and approved by the provincial director of education. With the approval of the director an expelled child may be admitted to another school after one year. In other cases the principal administers punishments. He supervises teaching, inspects books of both teachers and pupils to make sure that all is according to regulation, calls staff meetings for the discussion of school affairs, distributes the teaching load, makes the daily schedule, personally seeks the cooperation of parents in solving behavior problems of pupils, keeps accurate registers and accounts of textbook and stationery sales to students, corresponds with his director and provides him with numerous formal reports, registers, and tables, some monthly, some yearly. In addition, he usually teaches at least twelve periods a week.

Teachers are required to conduct their classes in accordance with prescribed syllabuses and instructions, prepare each lesson, keep books of lesson plans, and notebooks for registering marks and the progress of their pupils. Usually each has charge of a specific class and must, in addition, take his turn in the daily supervision of the school. Teachers must be good examples for their pupils and are held responsible for cleanliness of the pupils and for their behavior both in and out of school.

The Primary Course of Study

Iraq's first course of study consisted of a few mimeographed sheets written in Arabic and issued by the British education authorities in 1918. After the establishment of the national government, proposals of various curriculum committees resulted in a new course with instructions in 1922. A revision, based on suggestions from teachers in the field, was brought out in 1926 and remained in use for ten years. The 1936 revision simplified that of 1926 and moved upward in the grades some of the more difficult phases of subjects, particularly arithmetic, history, and geography. Further revisions were made in 1940 and 1943, the latter now being in force.

This current course of study states that the aim of primary education is "the diffusion of general culture among the rising generation, and providing this generation with the requirements of civilized life, *e.g.,* general information, correct thinking, a strong body, sound character, high ideals, good taste, a working hand, and loyalty and sacrifice to the country and nation." The teacher is bidden to provide useful, correct information, making it as practical as possible and relating it to the environment of the child, and to correlate the subjects which he teaches with those taught by his colleagues. The course of study for each subject is prefaced by directions to the teachers. The course of study contains a completely rewritten English syllabus; otherwise, the most drastic changes were made in the syllabuses of history and geography which shift emphasis from world events and geography to Arab and local history and geography. Table 24 below

TABLE 24
Public Primary-School Program of Studies, Iraq, 1945–46

Subjects	1st Grade	2nd Grade	3rd Grade	4th Grade	5th Grade	6th Grade
Religion and Koran	4	4	3	3	2	2
Arabic language and penmanship	11	12	10	10	6	6
English	...	...	...	...	6	6
Arithmetic and mensuration	6	6	6	6	5	5
Object lessons and hygiene	2	2	2	2	2	2
Geography and history	...	...	4	4	4	4
Moral and civic duties	...	...	...	1	1	1
Drawing and manual arts	3	3	4	4	4	4
Physical education and singing	4	3	3	2	2	2
Total	30	30	32	32	32	32

shows the program of studies and the number of class periods devoted to each subject.

The course of study in *religion* consists of two parts, the Koran and religious information. The Koran is given a first reading in the first four grades and reread in the fifth and sixth grades with correct intonation (*tajwid*). Parts are memorized in each of the six years. Religious information includes a study of the main tenets of Islam relative to God, the prophets, especially Muhammad, explanation of important traditions (*al-Hadith*), and ethical principles.

Arabic includes reading, oral and written composition, memorization, dictation, grammar, and handwriting. Reading starts in a phonetic primer that has been in use for about twenty-five years, though experiments have been conducted in a few schools in applying the sentence method to Arabic. Each grade has a reader approved by the Ministry which is usually read and reread. Hardly any other reading is done. Writing goes hand in hand with reading. Memorizing begins in the first grade and continues with selections of increasing difficulty through the six grades. Oral composition also starts in the first grade and is supplemented with written composition beginning with the fourth. Grammar is begun formally in the fourth grade, and by the sixth the basic rules are covered and applied. Dictation —usually of prose selections, rarely of words—is given throughout the course. Formal teaching of handwriting continues from the second through the sixth grades emphasizing two styles of writing, the *naskhi* and the *ruq'i*.

The course in *English* is more in the nature of suggestions to teachers, emphasizing that grammar is a means to an end, good comprehension, and correct expression. Grammar rules are not to be memorized but applied. Too much emphasis on vocabulary is not necessary, but emphasis is given to the construction of correct sentences so that such construction becomes a habit. Comprehension tests are to be given at frequent intervals and not only words but idioms dealt with. Composition is different from sentence drill in that it helps the child to express his own ideas accurately and well. The teachers are enjoined to supplement classwork with special activities, such as an English-speaking group, an English magazine, and dramatics. Special aids have been and are being prepared to help the Iraqi primary-school teacher of English.

In *arithmetic* and measurement, work starts with the fundamental addition and subtraction combinations. In multiplication the product is not more than 20, and in division numbers up to 20 are divided into equal parts. Counting reaches up to 100. On this basis more complicated operations are taken up in each grade; the multiplication table is learned up to 10×10 in the third grade and to 12×12 in the fourth. Decimals and common fractions start in the fourth grade and are completed in the next. In the fifth grade the children learn the reading and writing of numbers involving millions and start on the factoring of numbers. More complicated common fractions are given, and ratio and proportion are begun and completed in the sixth grade where interest and profit are taken up with some attention to saving and savings accounts.

Parallel with arithmetic go also the study of the Iraqi currency (beginning with the second grade), notions of time and the calendar, the metric system,

PUBLIC PRIMARY EDUCATION

and later the English measures of weight and length—the inch and foot. Geometry is introduced with the drawing of different kinds of lines, and goes on to the drawing of circles and plane geometrical figures, to working out the areas of these figures, and finally leads to the recognition of solid figures and the lateral areas and volumes of only the cube and the prism.

Courses in *object lessons* and *hygiene* are given in every year throughout the primary school. Starting with personal habits, hygiene develops into a simple study of human anatomy and physiological functions, the study of simple principles of nutrition, the common diseases in Iraq, infection, and public hygiene and first aid. Object lessons concern themselves with the study of objects used in the environment, of common domestic and wild animals and their uses, the common plants, flowers, trees, and fruits, rudiments of agriculture, and a simple classification of mammals, and end in the sixth grade with a study of air, water, heat, magnetism, and light.

History starts formally in the third grade with a study of primitive man, and discovery of fire and agriculture, the domestication of animals, and the growth of the family into the tribe. In the fourth grade the study of important personalities in the history of Iraq from ancient times to the present is made involving a description of life in each period to which the men belonged. The fifth and sixth grades are taken up with the study of the history of the Arabs from the pre-Islamic period to the present.

Informal *geography* starts in the first two grades with taking notice of the classroom, the school, the home, the road from home to school, and the like. This is expanded in the third grade to a study of the locality and its connection with the surrounding country, the four seasons, the weather, means of communication, and the tribes. In the fourth grade, land features of various parts of Iraq are studied, through the device of imaginary trips to those sections, which emphasize that Iraq is part of the Arab world and of Asia. The fifth and sixth grades are given a more systematic study— the fifth to physical geography, the continents, and important countries of the world, and the sixth to the geography of Iraq, the Arab world in Asia and Africa, Turkey, and India.

The study of *moral and civic duties* begins in the fourth grade with attention on the pupil and the school, home life, and pupil and society, the nation, and the patriotic duties of the pupil. In the fifth grade are studied general concepts of the state, the people, the government and its powers, while in the sixth grade this is more specifically applied to Iraq with special reference to public health at the end of the course.

Drawing starts in the first two grades with the drawing of simple objects and ornamentation, continues in the next two grades with drawing from nature and some composition, and in the last two grades special attention is given to Arab ornamental designs. The work is mainly conventional, and lacks vitality and originality.

In *manual arts* the boys work with colored paper, cardboard, plasticine, straw and palm leaves, and wood, making toylike things, leading to more useful objects later. The girls concentrate on needlework and embroidery, knitting, and making such things as doilies, aprons, and baby clothes. They also learn how to wash and clean clothes, polish windows and furniture, and prepare the tea table. They study other home economics subjects.

Physical education programs differ for boys and girls. Boys engage in athletic exercises, classroom games, rhythmic movements and games, and later organized games such as basketball, volleyball, and soccer. Competitive sports meets between schools are held in the larger cities. For the girls, appropriate exercises and games are provided. Singing is confined almost exclusively to national songs.

Description of the Iraqi Public Primary School

It may be worth while to close this part of the report with a description of the primary school, both segregated and coeducational, as the American Council Commission saw it function in the eight provinces (*liwas*) included in its itinerary. It is impossible to give an account that would apply in all its details to all public primary schools, but traits common to all are numerous enough to warrant the conclusion that there is a general type of Iraqi primary school which can be described.

BUILDINGS

About 60 percent of the schools are housed in public buildings built either by the government or by local subscription. A number of public schools for Christian children are housed in buildings owned by various sects. These schools were previously parochial schools administered by religious communities and were willingly given over to the government in accordance with an agreement in 1921 between the Department of Education and the communities. By the terms of this agreement the communities were to supply the buildings, and the government would pay the salaries of the teachers, supply and equip the schools, and assume administrative responsibility. The remaining 40 percent of the primary schools are housed in rented buildings, usually former residences. Rented buildings converted

PUBLIC PRIMARY EDUCATION

to use as schools are found principally in the cities of Mosul, Baghdad, and Basrah and most of the capitals of the provinces.

A government primary school built within the last twelve to fifteen years in the cities usually has ten to twelve rooms about 5×7 meters (16.4×22.96 feet) or 5.5×8 meters (18.04×26.24 feet). In addition, there may be two to four smaller rooms used as offices or storerooms. Toilet facilities are outside the building. Drinking water is in large earthenware containers provided with taps from which the children can drink. School buildings need improved plumbing and sanitary facilities, but the country as a whole suffers from a lack of skilled plumbers.

School buildings dating from the twenties are not as good as the more recently constructed ones, being less substantial and having smaller rooms. There are a few exceptions to this rule in the provinces of Basrah and 'Amarah where the erection of some schools was financed by the Maud[1] Memorial Fund and subscriptions collected by a particularly energetic governor of 'Amarah. Some buildings show signs of the rapid growth of the system, having started as two- or three-room constructions and then having a room or two added as needed.

The typical village school building has four to eight small, narrow, inadequately lighted and ventilated rooms. Some schoolrooms visited by the Commission were absolutely dark. Some first-grade rooms were badly overcrowded; in one instance the children had overflowed to the floor and filled the windows. Poor construction materials are often used for village schools, especially when hurriedly built by local authorities. Dripping ceilings were a commonplace. Some rural schools in the south, particularly in the province of 'Amarah, were housed in reed huts. After 1934, however, the government built a number of village schools of from two to six rooms of standard size with adequate lighting and ventilation.

The large number of rented houses serving as school buildings in urban Iraq is explained in terms of the growth of the school system which has been so rapid that the building program fell far short. Most of the rented buildings are not suitable for school purposes, the rooms being too small for classroom use. Play space is limited to the central courtyard, which is usually small. Repairs and readjustments are neglected because owners are reluctant to spend money on the property since prewar rental ceilings have been maintained by law. Government-owned schools, too, have deteriorated in the war years.

---

[1] The name of the British general who conquered Baghdad from the Turks in 1917.

Equipment

First- and second-grade rooms are normally furnished with tables at each of which two children are seated. The chairs, though easily movable, are usually set in rows. In the middle grades the typical desk has a small, narrow, backless bench attached to it and accommodates two children—though in crowded classrooms there may be three children to a desk. In the upper grades individual desks with fixed seats are common.

Most schools are supplied with Arabic maps of the continents and with French—or sometimes English—charts for use in conversation lessons. The larger and older schools are equipped with French natural-history charts and closets of miscellaneous, simple laboratory materials. There is little if any equipment for manual arts, drawing, music, and singing.

The older schools have libraries of 300 to 350 books and pamphlets. The newer the school, the smaller the library. The book collection is a mixture of old textbooks, courses of study, books on teaching method, and some travel books. Children's books are few. The same books are found in most schools because schools are almost entirely dependent upon the Ministry for their library collections. This "library" is kept in a closet in the principal's office, and in most schools visited by the Commission it seemed to be used very little by either teachers or pupils. A couple of refreshing exceptions to the rule were found in Baghdad in schools connected with the teachers colleges, where a definite effort had been made by the staff to collect reference books and children's literature in both English and Arabic, the purchases having been made out of small contributions from the children.

The Children

There are more over-age children in Iraqi primary schools than in European or American schools. This is due not only to retardation in learning, but also the lack of compulsory-attendance requirements results in many children entering school late. Usually there are more overage children in village schools than in city schools.

School children are encouraged to wear Western dress, and in the cities most of them do, but in rural districts and small communities native dress is common. Many rural children are too poor to buy either shoes or essential books and stationery. The Ministry has recently undertaken to provide needy children with free books, which are returned to the school at the end of the year. Children of more prosperous parents may either buy or rent their schoolbooks.

In 1943 an attempt was made in the province of 'Amarah to provide a

PUBLIC PRIMARY EDUCATION

simple meal for poor children, using funds collected by subscription. This experiment resulted in a marked rise in attendance, but unfortunately the effort was not sustained in the years that followed. Frequently money raised by dramatic shows is spent on clothing for poorer children. The standard of cleanliness was found to be lower among rural children than among city children. In one village school first-grade children were being given a practical lesson in the use of soap; those whose use of it was ineffective were sent back to the water tap to clean their hands and faces. The Commission found this a refreshing departure from the predominantly academic and detached-from-life atmosphere of the schools.

THE SCHOOL DAY

The school day begins with a general lineup of the pupils in the courtyard of the school at 8:15 A.M. The children are grouped by class and inspected for cleanliness of face and hands and general neatness. Inspection is followed by a song or two sung by the whole school, and, if time permits, by the recitation of a poem or piece of prose. Lessons begin at half-past eight.

The daily schedule is usually so arranged that arithmetic, Arabic, and English lessons are taught in the early hours of the morning, while such subjects as art, singing, manual arts, and physical education come toward noon or in the afternoon. The first two periods of the day are forty-five minutes in length, the next two are of forty minutes. Ten-minute recesses occur between periods and a fifteen-minute recess is given in midmorning between the second and third periods. Absences are noted in registers provided by the Ministry.

The morning session of the school ends about noon, and the afternoon session starts at 2 P.M., with another lineup of the children. There are two forty-minute periods in the afternoon, so that school is out at about 3:30. Some schools have after-school games under the direction of the athletics teacher, who may or may not be assisted by other teachers.

METHODS OF TEACHING

Teachers are required by the regulations to prepare each of their daily lessons, and lesson-plan books are furnished them by the Ministry. The Commission saw a number of these plan books, but the "planning" was scarcely more than a mention of the date, grade, and topic to be taught.

Methods of teaching in the primary schools are fairly uniform. The teacher is in the center of the stage and keeps the initiative throughout the lesson. Occasionally teachers lecture to their pupils, especially in history or geography, but the question-and-answer technique is the most commonly used, particularly in the teaching of language and arithmetic. The children rarely take the initiative in the classroom, and they are not encouraged to inquire about things which interest them. Questions of a type to provoke original thought are rare. Thus, teaching in these schools is principally a matter of presenting facts and demanding that they be memorized, this in spite of the fact that the primary course of study eschews such practice. A few schools, chiefly those attached to teachers colleges, have developed small projects using the more progressive methods, and have succeeded in arousing the pupils to activity.

A short description of the methods used in some of the subjects taught may be of profit. First-grade reading is taught from a primer based on the phonetic method. Each page contains words related by sound, but having no meaningful connection. The words are chosen for their phonetic characteristics and with no regard to their frequency in speech or to any other criterion. After about ten of these pages the words are supplemented by a few sentences which also are constructed from words chosen for their phonetic characteristics and which rarely have any meaningful connection with each other. The last few pages of the primer contain a few simple stories, each of which fills a page. The phonetic method has been in use since 1922-23, with the use of a primer which has been revised many times. Experiments in the use of connected sentences and stories from the beginning of reading have been conducted in schools connected with the teachers colleges, but even though they have met with a large measure of success, there has thus far been no sign of intention to generalize the method.

In other grades little reading is done outside the set of readers approved by the Ministry—except in some of the demonstration schools of the teachers colleges. Little if any silent reading is done. Usually the teacher reads the selection aloud to the class, explaining difficult words and sentences; then the pupils read it aloud in turn. This procedure is rarely modified except for an occasional dramatization of a story.

Arabic grammar is taught largely by the inductive method. Examples are written on the blackboard, discussed and compared, and the grammatical rule extracted and written on the blackboard. A summary of rules developed is made toward the end of the lesson; and if there is enough time, exercises follow the summary; if not, the exercises are left until the next lesson. They are taken from textbooks which are imported from Egypt and are likely to be limited in number and variety. Arabic grammar presents a number of complexities which are difficult to master in the primary grades. Some schools in the larger towns issue school magazines in Arabic, written largely by the children under the direction of their teachers.

In arithmetic, work starts by taking each of the numbers 1 to 9 in succession and performing the four fundamental operations with them. Recently the study of the number combinations has been introduced, but the traditional approach to arithmetic has not been abandoned. In more advanced work textbooks on the American plan and written by a man trained in America are used. Exercises on the number combinations and on Iraqi currency—which is a good introduction to the decimal system—with exercise sheets and simple life-like problems are emphasized. The older methods with more difficult problems are still in use, however. The method of solving problems is so slow that not more than five or six problems can be solved in a forty-five-minute period.

In elementary science charts and pictures are used as visual aids. In studying a common animal such as the dog, the picture of a dog is hung in front of the class; the students then learn that the dog is a mammal of the canine family with certain characteristics and is of use in guarding house or tent. In the same way they learn about other creatures, from whale to fly. Nature excursions are rare. Elementary agriculture, too, is taught within the walls of the classroom and on paper. Recently the new model-farm schools are attempting to teach practical agriculture.

The teaching of English has improved considerably through the efforts of the English Committee, which is composed of British and Iraqi teachers of English. Fawcett's *Oxford English Course for Foreign Children* is used, with reading and language books for each grade which emphasize types of sentences to be constructed. Additional class activities include simple conversation and simple compositions. Some schools have begun to issue magazines in English under the guidance of their teachers, and English songs and plays are taught.

TEACHERS

After graduating from a teachers college, a teacher is assigned to a certain province and is appointed by its director of education to a school. Effort is made to appoint as many teachers as possible to their home provinces, but since some provinces are oversupplied and others undersupplied with teachers, this is not always possible. A teacher appointed away from his province usually tries to obtain an appointment nearer home.

Frequent transfers are the rule among primary-school teachers and principals; especially is this true of the teachers of rural and small-town schools, but even in the city schools there is much shifting about. The

American Council Commission visited some schools in which the majority of teachers had been recently transferred, and in one province about a third of the principals had been shifted before the start of the school year. This practice makes for instability and lack of continuity of policy in the school and at the same time destroys personal interest on the part of teachers and principals in their own schools. As it is, teachers and principals tend to lay the blame for the shortcomings of the school on the shoulders of their predecessors. Responsibility for good or bad school management is lost, and it is difficult for the Ministry to appraise the work of the teachers. Appraisal is made by inspectors on the basis of short visits and reports of the conduct of the teachers rather than on long-term achievement.

No one cause explains the frequency of transfers, but a variety of reasons may be found. Among these are lack of cooperation or personal quarrels among teachers or between teachers and their principals and differences between teachers and the local populations or the administrative authorities, the fact that transfers drag other transfers in their trail, and the fact that dissatisfaction with their posts leads teachers to exert continuous pressure on the educational authorities for transfers to more favorable situations. Some of this is a natural and legitimate desire for advancement, but much of it arises from nostalgia for the home province or from the extreme discomfort of living in an outlying village. It is impossible to deny that most of the outlying villages lack the simplest and most necessary amenities of life: satisfactory living quarters are unavailable; there are frequently no facilities for buying fresh meat and vegetables or for medical care. Under such conditions conscientious work and professional enthusiasm do not flourish, however capable and well-intentioned the teacher may be.

A housing program for village teachers and their families would go a long way toward solving this problem and toward raising the morale of the teaching profession. The dividend secured in increase in teaching efficiency would be worth the cost. Moreover, at least some of the expense could be recovered in the form of rent.

SALARIES AND PROMOTIONS

Graduates of rural- and elementary-teachers colleges have a beginning salary of eight dinars ($32) per month; graduates of the three-year course in the primary-teachers colleges begin at ten dinars ($40) per month; and graduates of the four-year course—two years beyond secondary—receive 12 dinars ($48) per month. Salaries are paid for all twelve months, and teachers have a three-month summer vacation.

PUBLIC PRIMARY EDUCATION

The following is the distribution according to salary of the public primary-school teachers and principals of Iraq as of October 21, 1945:

Monthly Salary	Number of Teachers
6 dinars ($24)	119
8 dinars ($32)	1,033
10 dinars ($40)	749
12 dinars ($48)	1,434
15 dinars ($60)	1,112
18 dinars ($72)	182
21 dinars ($84)	39
25 dinars ($100)	1
Total number of teachers	4,669

Average monthly salary, 10.8 dinars ($43.20)

Like other state officials, teachers are supposed to be promoted at two-year intervals as long as their salaries are below 15 dinars ($60), and at three-year intervals thereafter. Such promotions, however, are conditional upon the existence of vacancies in the primary cadre. The maximum salary for a primary-school teacher is 25 dinars ($100), though as recently as 1945 only one primary teacher or principal had reached that figure since that grade had been established only a short while. Promotion is by recommendation of a special promotion committee of the Ministry. The length of time that has elapsed since the last promotion and length of service seem to be the main factors considered by this committee. Quality of work and behavior are negative rather than positive factors in determining promotions: poor work and behavior may retard promotion, but a teacher of outstanding ability is rarely given preference over a teacher of commonplace ability but more years of service.

During the war years promotions were fairly regular, and the Commission found only one primary teacher in the schools visited whose promotion had been delayed because of a reprimand. All others stated that they had been promoted within the last two or three years. Before the war, budgetary limitations delayed promotions of primary teachers for as long as four or five years. During World War II the government started to pay war allowances to government officials at a rate which increased as the salary bracket lowered and which was higher for married officials with children than for unmarried officials. The rate has been approximately 80 percent of the lower-grade salaries. While the war allowances taken in conjunction with promotions doubled the prewar incomes of most teachers, the rise in cost of living to 5 or 6 times the prewar cost leaves the financial condition of teachers unsatisfactory. Unquestionably economic necessity urged a number of primary teachers to leave their profession for more lucrative jobs during the war, and the Ministry of Education lost many good teachers.

PRESERVICE AND IN-SERVICE TRAINING OF TEACHERS

The Ottoman Turks had maintained 3 teachers colleges, 1 in each of the larger cities of Iraq. Two of these were established after 1910 and had produced only a small number of teachers by the time World War I began in 1914. Moreover, these teachers were trained to teach in Turkish and were unfamiliar with literary Arabic. When the British occupied Basrah in 1915, they were moved by the paucity of teachers to start a short training course for a few young men at the American School for Boys. In Baghdad the supply of teachers was inadequate, and most of those available were considered unsatisfactory—whether for political or academic reasons—by the authorities. A three-month training course was started for anybody who was available. Out of this emergency beginning there later developed the Primary Teachers College for Men. First the course was lengthened to six months, then gradually to four years above primary school. In 1929 it was made two years, and later three years, above intermediate school. Finally, it was changed to a two-year course above secondary education. Parallel with this school was the "elementary course" for teachers which was started with two years and was lengthened to three years above primary school before it was metamorphosed into the present rural-teachers college with its five-year course above primary school. The teachers colleges for women had a similar course of development, though a later start.

All these shades of training are reflected in the composition of the present teaching body—with some additional varieties. Early in the twenties the authorities were forced to utilize disbanded officers from the Turkish army as teachers or principals. Later secondary- or even intermediate-school graduates as well as people who had a background of "private study" and products of private schools were appointed.

Table 25 gives the distribution of primary-school teachers in government schools according to qualifications.

The table shows that more than 85 percent of the teachers have had some sort of professional training, while the remainder have had none. However, both groups contain numerous teachers who have not even completed the secondary school. Graduates of the teachers colleges themselves are of widely varying standards. These facts suggest the need of a vigor-

TABLE 25
Public Primary Teachers Classified According to Qualifications, Iraq, 1945–46

Qualification	Men	Women	Total
Professionally trained:			
One year above primary	28	40	68
Two years above primary	235	124	359
Three years above primary	311	236	547
Four years above primary	717	382	1,099
Five years above primary	349	...	349
Two years above intermediate	13	43	56
Three years above intermediate	772	165	937
Two years above secondary	103	50	153
Secondary plus professional course	350	71	421
Total, professionally trained	2,878	1,111	3,989
Not professionally trained:			
'Al al-Bayt University (religious)	12	...	12
Secondary	111	62	173
School of Agriculture	21	...	21
Home Arts School	...	87	87
Dar al-'Ulum (religious)	69	...	69
Technical school	23	...	23
American high school	8	21	29
Other, less than secondary	133	79	212
Private study	53	1	54
Total, not professionally trained	430	250	680
Grand Total	3,308	1,361	4,669

ous program of in-service training for teachers. There have been attempts to provide such training. As early as 1929 a short summer course of two weeks was held and attended by about 30 teachers. In 1935 a six-week summer course was given for 200 teachers and a two-week course for teachers of beginning reading. Summer and one-year professional courses have been held for the rapid conversion of secondary-school graduates into primary teachers. In recent years summer courses and camps for physical-education teachers and courses for teachers of English have been given.

Little is done by way of effective supervision and guidance of young teachers by capable principals and supervisors. Taken as a group the public primary-school teachers of Iraq are very young: the great majority of them graduated from their schools after 1930. However, they do not exhibit such vitality and interest in their work as is expected of youth, especially youth caught up in a pioneer movement to carry knowledge to the remote corners of their country. It is necessary to inspire these young teachers with a sense of the importance of their work, of the unique circumstances and opportunities it provides for participation in the creation of a new society.

Chapter 10

SECONDARY AND VOCATIONAL EDUCATION

*U*NDER OTTOMAN rule Iraq had secondary schools for boys in Baghdad, Mosul, Basrah, Kirkuk, and Sulaymaniyah. These schools prepared students for advanced study in Istanbul or to enter the Law College in Baghdad. Most students who went to Istanbul attended the Military College; others entered the colleges of medicine, law, or civil administration.

After World War I secondary education developed slowly, the first classes being started in Baghdad, Mosul, and Basrah in 1920 and the first graduation taking place in 1924. It was 1930 before secondary classes for girls were started in the same cities. After the passing of the Education Law of 1929, the secondary course was lengthened from four to five years, with an intermediate stage of three years and a senior stage of two years, each stage concluding with public examinations.

Although coeducation is spreading in the primary schools and is an accomplished fact in all the higher institutions except the College of Engineering, it does not exist at the secondary-school level. The somewhat rapid expansion of secondary-school education for girls and the shortage of women teachers have compelled the Ministry of Education to use men teachers to complete the staffs of some girls schools. Except in one or two localities this practice has not met with opposition, and it has allowed a more rapid development of secondary schools for girls than would otherwise have been possible.

All public secondary schools in the country are now under the jurisdiction of the provincial directors, who inspect them administratively and are responsible for their equipment and general operation. The Director General of Education, however, controls the distribution, appointment, and transfer of secondary-school teachers, since it is considered necessary, at least for the present, for a central agency to distribute teachers according to their specialties and according to the needs of the individual schools.

The Iraqi Military Service Law exempts secondary-school and college students until graduation, after which they receive nine months of training as reserve officers instead of having to serve two years as privates, as do nonstudents. The application of this law has considerably popularized secondary education. The resulting expansion of schools at this level is not so apparent in the public secondary schools for boys, as expansion is controlled by budgetary limitations, but the effect upon private and foreign schools has been pronounced. In 1944–45 these private and foreign secondary schools for boys numbered 47 as compared with 50 public secondary schools for boys. Thus, it is apparent that the private secondary schools are competing with the public system. The Military Service Law brought into the public secondary school many inferior students whose principal interest was escape and who failed in their studies repeatedly. To avert the danger of having the public schools filled with laggards who lowered the standards and often became behavior problems, it was ruled that a student who failed the same grade twice should be dropped. Many of these failures from the public-school system contributed to the expansion of the private schools, which tend to have somewhat flexible standards.

Except for a short interval the Ministry of Education has maintained evening secondary-school classes since 1924. However, private night schools have become more numerous than the government ones.

Secondary Education

Secondary schools are governed by the Public Secondary School Regulations, which have undergone many revisions since they were first issued in 1930. The latest revision took place in 1944.

These regulations divide the secondary schools into the three-year intermediate course and the two-year preparatory course and empower the Ministry of Education to open evening classes in secondary schools and to establish boarding sections in provincial capitals for impoverished bright students. The regulations make the public examinations the basis for admission to foreign and private as well as to public secondary schools, and in the event that more students apply for admission to the intermediate section than can be accommodated, selection is made on the basis of preference being given to public primary-school graduates. Fees are set at 3 dinars ($12) for the intermediate school and 4 dinars ($16) for the preparatory school, yearly, payable in two installments. However, students having one brother or sister in secondary or higher schools pay only half the fees, those having two brothers or sisters in these schools pay one-third, and so on. Thus, a parent pays the full rate for only one child. The Ministry of Education is authorized to determine evening-school fees according to the type of school and class. Three categories of students are exempt from fees: (1) poor students of good behavior who secure an average of 65 percent in the public-school examinations; (2) any student of good behavior who makes an average of 85 percent; (3) children of government officials and employees whose salaries do not exceed 15 dinars ($60) a month. On this basis 26 percent of students in public secondary schools were exempt from fees in 1943–44. In individual provinces, however, the percentage of exemptions varied from 45 percent in Karbala down to 17 percent in Basrah. Students exempted from fees are supplied with free books, stationery, and other equipment.[1]

The maximum number permitted in a class by the regulations is 40 students, and the Ministry is instructed to reduce this number gradually to 30. Registration begins on the first Saturday in September, delinquent examinations are held on the second Saturday, and classes begin on the third Saturday. No student may be admitted after October 1 except in case of illness or of transfer from other schools.

Administration of the secondary school is in the hands of a principal, who may have one or more assistants and clerks, depending on the size of the school. If the school maintains a boarding department, there is a resident master to supervise sleeping and eating arrangements and the work of servants, and the principal appoints a resident teacher for every 50 students. A resident teacher eats with the students and supervises their social, moral, and hygienic life. For the day school, the principal appoints a form teacher for every class or section, who acts as adviser to the students. The school doctor examines the students twice a year and treats them in case of illness.

The maximum teaching load in the intermediate school is twenty-four periods a week; in the preparatory school it is twenty-two. For extra pay a teacher may assume up to six additional periods. Teachers are expected to supervise students in extracurricular work and leisure hours. Each school has a general teachers council which meets at least once a month, and there are committees responsible for discipline, purchases, school activities, and for studies and examinations. There are five committees for studies and examinations—one each for Arabic, English, mathematics, science, and social studies. They meet at least once every two months to consider ways of improving the teaching in the school, and at the end of the year each study committee acts as an examining committee, setting questions and

---

[1] Secondary-school fees were abolished in public schools in 1946.

SECONDARY AND VOCATIONAL EDUCATION

marking papers jointly and submitting a final report on examination results to the principal.

The class teacher conducts quizzes and topical tests and midyear examinations, but final examinations are given by the study committees. These are confidential, with numbers substituted for names on the examination books, and those who mark the books are not supposed to know the identity of the student whose book is being corrected. The passing mark for individual subjects is 50—except in religion, which must be 60. The final yearly mark for any subject is determined by dividing averages of daily and topical tests plus the midyear examination mark by three and then adding this quotient to the final examination mark and dividing by two. To pass, a student must not fall below 50 in any individual subject and must have a general average of 60. A delinquent student may sit for re-examination in September in subjects in which he has failed or hopes to raise his mark. Third- and fifth-year students do not take the final school examinations because they sit for public intermediate or secondary examinations.

The last section of the regulations deals with discipline and student behavior. As incentives to study and good behavior, prize awards to the best student in a class and to the best class, public commendation of leading students, and appointment of such students as monitors of their classes are mentioned. Various punishments are specified, ranging from an oral warning by the principal to expulsion. Expulsion, however, is valid for only one year, at the end of which the Ministry of Education may look into the case with a view to reinstating the pupil. Cheating in the topical tests or in the midyear examination is punished by a zero in that examination, but a student caught cheating in any final examination is failed in the whole year's work. Corporal punishment and other harsh methods of dealing with students are expressly forbidden.

While the secondary-school regulations are similar in spirit and import to those of the primary school, a few differences exist. Primary education is free to all, while secondary education operates on the basis of low fees with extensive exemption granted poor boys and girls of little more than average record. As a group, secondary-school teachers enjoy a greater freedom of action within the school than do primary teachers; their teachers council has greater powers and they have the nucleus of an academic organization within the school. However, secondary-school teachers, as well as primary, have little opportunity to deviate from the prescribed courses of study and textbooks. The primary-school teacher is essentially a grade teacher, while the secondary-school teacher is a subject teacher. Secondary schools are inspected administratively by the provincial director of education or by an inspector who specialized in the administration of secondary schools, and by inspectors who specialize in the various subjects.

THE SECONDARY PROGRAM OF STUDIES

A secondary-school program was first published in 1926 and provided for a four-year course. After the lengthening of the secondary course to five years in two stages, a temporary intermediate program was issued in 1929, and in 1931–32 the new course for the upper two years was issued. This program attempted a departure from the earlier type of specialization in either the literary or the scientific section by permitting four types of specialization—literary, social studies, science, and mathematics. There was also an innovation in the form of a course to study Iraq in all phases of its political, economic, and social life. The four parallel courses and the study of contemporary Iraq aroused a great controversy and resulted in a revision of the secondary-school program in 1936 which returned to the two parallel curriculums of scientific and literary subjects and abolished the study of contemporary Iraq as being too controversial. Two other revisions were made in 1940 and in 1943. These revisions attempted to unify the literary and scientific curriculums for girls schools; but the present program, that of 1943, follows the same lines for girls as for boys except that girls have two additional periods per week for home arts and needlework, and in the fourth and fifth years have two and four periods respectively in child education instead of the study of Iraq, now permitted again in the fourth and fifth years. Table 26 shows the distribution of periods for the various subjects according to the new intermediate and secondary courses of study.

The content of the courses in *religion, Arabic, history, geography, civics, mathematics* (arithmetic, plane and solid geometry, algebra, and trigonometry) is similar to the secondary-school program in Egypt (see pages 58–63) except that in history, civics, and geography special attention is given to national interests and conditions.

In the preparatory stage a course in the economic and social conditions of Iraq may be considered as a continuation of the civics course or, better, as a social-science course. A more extensive version of it is given over a two-year period for the literary section, while the scientific section for boys takes it for only one year. This subject is not given to the scientific section for girls. The course covers extensive ground, including the situation and climate of Iraq, the population and its racial and social composition, Iraq's recent political history and international status, its administrative organization and problems, the status of woman and the family, the land problem, irrigation, agriculture, industry, trade and other economic phases of Iraqi

TABLE 26
The Secondary-School Program of Studies, 1943 Revision, Iraq

SUBJECT	Periods per Week						
	Intermediate			Preparatory			
	1st Year	2nd Year	3rd Year	4th Year		5th Year	
				Literary	Scientific	Literary	Scientific
Religion................	1	1	1	...	...	...	...
Arabic.................	6	6	6	7	5	7	5
English................	6	6	6	7	6	7	6
Translation.............	...	...	...	1	1	1	1
History................	2	2	3	4	...	4	...
Geography..............	2	2	2	2	...	3	...
Civics and ethics........	...	2	1	...	...	...	...
Study of Iraq...........	...	...	...	2	2*	2	...
Economics..............	...	...	...	...	...	3*	...
Arithmetic..............	4	2	...	...	...	...	...
Algebra................	...	2	3	...	2	...	2
Geometry...............	2	2	3	...	...	...	3
Trigonometry............	...	...	...	...	3	...	...
General mathematics.....	...	...	...	2	...	2	...
General science.........	6	...	...	4	...	...	...
Physics................	...	...	3	...	...	...	7
Chemistry..............	...	3	...	...	5	...	...
Biology................	...	2	...	...	5	...	5
Hygiene................	...	...	2	...	...	...	...
Drawing................	2	1	1	1	1	1	1
Child care and psychology...	...	...	...	...	2†	4†	...
Physical education.......	2	2	2	2	2	2‡	2
Home arts and needlework...	2†	2†	2†	2†	2†	2†	2†
Total, Boys............	33	33	33	32	32	32	32
Total, Girls...........	35	35	35	34	34	34	34

* Boys only.
† Girls only.
‡ Girls have only one period of physical education.

life, the hygienic situation and problems, the cultural development of Iraq, the problems of illiteracy, education of girls, types of educational institutions, and a discussion of the main educational problems of Iraq. The students are to be encouraged to select topics for individual study and write themes about them.

A very extensive *science* program is provided on the intermediate and preparatory levels. The program begins with a course in general science in the first year, the inspiration for which is American in origin. This course takes up a study of air, water, heat, fuel, weather and climate, the solar system and the stars, plant and animal life, hygiene, electricity and magnetism, and light and sound. A practical program is provided mainly by demonstration and observation.

In the second year a course in *biology* and a course in *chemistry* are given. What is studied in chemistry is related as far as possible to the more practical phases as found in the environment, for example, the making of soap, matches, and brick. Laboratory-work topics are specified for performance by the students in addition to the demonstrations by the teacher.

The course in *physics* in the third year is more comprehensive than in the other Arab countries studied, and in the scientific section, fifth year, an expanded treatment is given in seven periods a week. A more extended treatment of chemistry and biology is also given in the fourth year of the scientific section, biology now being divided into botany and zoology. Toward the end of the biology course a study is made of animal cells and fission, body and reproductive cells, Mendelian and non-Mendelian heredity, variation and mutation, and finally the theory of organic evolution. In all the science courses laboratory experiments are performed by the students in the fourth and fifth preparatory years.

The course in economics in the fifth year of the literary section goes over the usual ground but in an abbreviated form, and attention is given to economic conditions in Iraq—its monetary system, baking, trade, business and industry, and natural resources.

The course in *child care* for girls of the fourth-year science program comprises the care of the mother, the child's room, his cleanliness and feeding, the child's exercise, his development and weight, children's diseases and bodily defects; also home-nursing and first aid. The latter includes study of the patient's room and his bed, observation of his temperature, pulse, respiration, urine and excretion, prevention of some of the infectious diseases, first aid for burns, wounds, sprains, fractures, bites, gas poisoning, bleeding, sunstroke, electric shock, and of entry of foreign matter into the body.

In addition, the fifth-year literary section for girls includes a course in child psychology and development in mind and body, learning and habit formation, motivation, the child's toys and games, imagination, stories and story-telling, the child's questions, social behavior of children, mental hygiene, children's problems, child study, and child guidance.

The course in *manual arts* and *home economics* for girls comprises sewing, embroidery, knitting, cooking, and home cleaning in a more developed form than in the primary years.

The courses in *drawing* and *physical education* are of the same nature as in earlier years but in a more advanced form.

Description of the Public Secondary Schools

BUILDINGS

Secondary schools on the whole have better buildings than the primary schools. Whenever there is a building program, the secondary schools

Above: Recess at the rural school used as a demonstration and practice school by the students of the Rural Teachers College, Rustumiyah, Iraq
Below: Secondary school for girls, Baghdad, Iraq

Above: A laboratory class in chemistry, Higher Teachers College, Baghdad, Iraq
Below: A reading class in the first grade of the Mamuniyah School, Baghdad

SECONDARY AND VOCATIONAL EDUCATION

usually hold the priority over primary schools. If a good building is vacant it is usually the secondary school that gets the preference. Thus, in all parts of Iraq most intermediate and preparatory schools are housed in comparatively new buildings, with fairly large classrooms ($16\frac{1}{2} \times 23\frac{1}{2}$ feet), and with laboratories of larger size. An intermediate school usually has one common laboratory or science room. The better preparatory schools, such as the Central Preparatory School in Baghdad, have separate laboratories for physics, chemistry, and biology, with storerooms attached and with a machine for producing gas. Secondary schools are also more favored with a larger amount of space for playgrounds than primary schools have.

Equipment

The same is also true with regard to furniture and equipment. There are three types of classroom seats: desks, with seats attached, for one or for two students, and a tablet armchair for a single student much like the ones in American advanced classrooms, though not as good in quality. Blackboards are made of wood and are usually small and inadequate, often definitely bad. However, a new kind of plaster built-in blackboard large enough to fill the entire front wall, and sometimes the side walls too, was first used at the Higher Teachers College, and its use is spreading in the secondary schools. Laboratory equipment is supplied to intermediate schools from the central store of the Ministry of Education according to a standard list drawn up by the Ministry. A much larger collection of laboratory equipment is usually sent to the preparatory schools. The older schools are better equipped than the others, while some of the schools that were started during World War II or shortly before are meagerly supplied. Arabic maps are imported from England or from Egypt. Most of the laboratory equipment was imported from France and England and some from Germany. As there is no central workshop for repairing laboratory equipment and as most teachers have no experience in repair work, laboratory instruments tend to get out of order rather quickly, which results in a great deal of waste. For this reason and because of the great amount of dust in the Iraqi air, equipment acquires a dilapidated look which requires an extraordinary amount of care on the part of the teacher to avoid. The fact that teachers change frequently is an additional factor in the lack of care that is apparent in laboratory equipment.

Teaching and method

Methods of teaching in secondary schools do not differ in their essentials from those of the primary schools. In the main they are based on the initiative and activity of the teacher in class. Great stress is laid on the teacher's explanation in class by inductive, deductive, lecture, and demonstration methods according to the subject. Not enough emphasis is laid on student activity which should develop understanding and knowledge of what the students are studying. They, therefore, come to rely on the teacher for clarifying the subject. Theirs is to learn what has been explained and be ready to recite it back when required. In this way the "spoon-feeding" of the primary school is carried over to the secondary school, and the students do not as a rule acquire a habit of self-reliance and self-instruction.

It is largely a textbook method of teaching. The textbooks are chosen by the Ministry of Education and are uniform for all public schools and most of the private schools, which usually choose to follow the government program. The textbook is followed closely lesson by lesson and chapter by chapter, the students relying on it and on the teacher's explanation in preparing their lessons. Little, if any, reading is done outside the textbook, since most of the teachers do not assign reference work. It is the rare teacher who tries to stimulate students' interest in reading outside magazines and books, fiction or otherwise.

Intermediate-school libraries are small and on the whole little used, except where an enterprising principal or teacher tries to take charge of it and encourage students to read. Preparatory-school libraries are usually larger and in the case of the older schools may exceed 1,000 books.

In the field of science, demonstration by the teacher predominates in the intermediate schools. This is limited sometimes by the equipment as well as by lack of ingenuity of the teacher. The latter is particularly true in the field of biology where, if charts and models are not existent, the enterprising teacher can find a great deal of material in nature. Some good teachers, however, have made their own biology charts, and in one instance a teacher of biology with artistic talent produced a large number of excellent charts. In the preparatory schools more individual work is carried by the students where equipment is adequate. A great deal of room for improvement exists in the care of the laboratory equipment, in a much greater use of it, in working out laboratory manuals for secondary schools, and in general in greater effort to make the laboratory the center of science teaching. At the same time more excursions for nature study and for visits to establishments of scientific interest are needed.

EXTRACURRICULAR ACTIVITIES AND SPORTS

Extracurricular activities are becoming more popular in the secondary schools, though not to the same extent as in some more advanced countries.

SECONDARY AND VOCATIONAL EDUCATION

Perhaps the most common activity is some form of Arabic club or society. English societies are also springing up, especially in the preparatory schools. Occasionally schools put on dramatic performances, the revenue from which usually is spent in helping clothe poor students. Some of the schools issue magazines which vary from handwritten sheets hung on the walls or bulletin boards, to mimeographed or printed magazines. Most of these are in Arabic, but some are also in English. Occasionally a school may issue a yearbook or a book of essays by students on various subjects, mainly literary.

Much greater activity in the field of sports is manifest. Aside from the regular class periods devoted partly to formal exercises and partly to such games as basketball and volleyball, most of the schools have interclass and interschool competitions in soccer, basketball, and volleyball. The interschool competition usually culminates in a championship series which ends in games played at Baghdad by the finalists. Similar competitions in track and field events lead to a final field day in which secondary schools from all over Iraq participate, with a shield, cups, and medals distributed by the King or a member of the royal family.

Excursions of various sorts are popular in the schools. Some of these are of a general character, such as visits to the archeological sites which abound in Iraq, to the oil fields, the main dams, and the like. Others are of a sporting character, such as bicycle trips, hiking trips, and camping trips. In the summer the Department of Physical Education of the Ministry of Education maintains a number of swimming centers and some summer camps for the benefit of schoolboys. This program has for the last few years culminated in a camping visit to the summer resort at Salah al-Din in the northern mountains, at the expense of H.R.H. the Regent, for some of the boys of high scholastic standing.

Teachers

Teachers of secondary and vocational schools and of rural- and primary-teachers colleges are all put in one category known as the "secondary cadre." For its supply of secondary-school teachers, Iraq has relied on four main sources: (1) importation of teachers from abroad, mainly from Syria, Lebanon, Palestine, Transjordan, and Egypt, but also from England; (2) Iraqi graduates of foreign universities and colleges, whether studying at their own expense or as members of the government missions; (3) graduates of the Higher Teachers College, whether in the first stage (1923–31) or the second stage (1935——) of its existence; and (4) teachers advanced from the primary cadre because of their ability, notably in Arabic. This last practice has now been stopped.

Non-Iraqi teachers have been employed for secondary and allied schools since 1919. At that time there were almost no Iraqi secondary-school teachers with university degrees. Recourse was, therefore, had to teachers mainly from Syria and Lebanon. Later teachers from Palestine and Egypt were imported in large numbers, and at one time non-Iraqi teachers outnumbered the Iraqis in the secondary schools.

TABLE 27

SECONDARY-SCHOOL TEACHERS CLASSIFIED ACCORDING TO QUALIFICATIONS, IRAQ, 1946

Qualification	Men	Women	Total
Doctor of Philosophy	2	...	2
Master of Arts or Science	10	5	15
Licence, Higher Teachers College	267	41	308
Bachelor of Arts, American University of Beirut and United States institutions	63	21	84
Degrees from other universities and colleges	26	5	31
Higher Teachers College (one, two, and three years)	85	...	85
American Junior College	5	22	27
Vocational studies above secondary school	11	...	11
Primary teachers colleges, secondary certificates and their equivalent	19	4	23
Vocational schools above primary level	13	2	15
"Private" study	12	...	12
Total	513	100	613

The reopening of the Higher Teachers College in 1935 has to a large extent remedied the shortage of men teachers and caused a sharp decline in the employment of non-Iraqi teachers at the secondary level. The need for women teachers is still great. There were in 1945–46 some forty vacancies for women in the secondary schools, and attempts were being made to fill them with teachers from Syria, Lebanon, and Egypt. When unsuccessful, the authorities were obliged either to make temporary use of women primary teachers in the secondary schools or to use men in girls schools.

The shortage of women teachers and the need for training them at a faster rate than is possible at the Higher Teachers College has led to the establishment of the Queen 'Aliyah Institute for Women, which gives a three-year course above the secondary school. It is designed to attract girls who find the five-year course at the Higher Teachers College too long as well as girls whose parents are reluctant to send them to a coeducational institution. At the same time the Ministry keeps up its missions abroad from which some students return as teachers in the secondary schools.

Table 27 shows the distribution of Iraqi teachers on the secondary cadre according to their qualifications as of January 12, 1946. Part-time lecturers and non-Iraqi teachers are not included.

SECONDARY AND VOCATIONAL EDUCATION

Of the total of 613 teachers on the secondary cadre, 440, or 71.7 percent, have had degrees based on four or more years of college or university study; 123, or 20.1 percent, have had one, two, or three years of study above the secondary school; and 50, or 8.2 percent, are of secondary or lower standard. Of these, all of the Higher Teachers College graduates and some of the other university graduates have had professional education.

Besides the Iraqi teachers there is a fairly large, but diminishing, number of non-Iraqi teachers on the secondary cadre. These numbered 125 teachers in 1944–45 of whom 80 were men and 45 were women. In addition, an undetermined number of part-time teachers is employed. These are paid by the hour and are not included in the cadre.

Secondary-school teachers' salaries as of January 12, 1946, were as follows; salaries being paid on a twelve-month basis:

Monthly Salary	Number of Teachers
8–12 dinars ($32–$48)	9
15 dinars ($60)	16
18 dinars ($72)	312
21 dinars ($85)	156
25 dinars ($100)	47
30 dinars ($120)	46
35 dinars ($140)	19
40 dinars ($160)	2
Total number of teachers	613

The average salary of the Iraqi secondary-school teacher was 20.6 dinars ($82.40). These salaries do not include cost-of-living allowances. The salaries may appear low, but they should be compared with the maximum civil service salary (for professors and directors general) of 70 dinars ($280), with a few "distinguished grade" posts at 80 dinars ($320). The large number of salaries at the intermediate level is partially explained by the fact that the majority of the teachers are young and have entered the service rather recently. Of the 613 teachers, 492, or 80 percent, entered the service in the last ten years; 389, or 63 percent, in the last five years. The average service of secondary teachers of Iraq in 1946 was only 6.7 years.

SPECIAL TYPES OF SECONDARY SCHOOLS

Before closing this section on secondary-school education, mention must be made of two special types of secondary schools—King Faysal College and the secondary section of Queen 'Aliyah Institute which bring together boarding students from all the provinces of Iraq.

King Faysal College was established to provide secondary education at government expense for boys of high ability regardless of their economic status or place of residence. Boarding facilities are provided, and, although the school is located in Baghdad, no day pupils are admitted. Under a first plan, initiated in 1940–41, graduates of intermediate schools were admitted and given the last two years of the secondary-school program plus an additional year to improve their English and provide some orientation in postsecondary opportunities for study. In 1944–45 this plan was abandoned, and since that time the boys are selected from the 5 or more applicants from each of the fourteen provinces on a basis of high standing in the public primary examination. Other factors considered are age (boys of twelve and thirteen years are preferred), alertness and promise as judged by oral tests and personal interviews, physical condition, and personal appearance. The 3 top applicants are selected from each province, and any vacancies remaining are filled with the best applicants available, regardless of residence.

In addition to these boys who are educated and supported at government expense, about 10 boys, who pay fees of 60 dinars ($240) a year, are admitted to each class. These paying pupils are held to minimum standards only, but frequently find these difficult.

The fundamental purpose of the College is the provision of general education on broad cultural lines under circumstances which afford the advantages of communal life and preparation for higher education in Western universities. The curriculum is similar to that of government intermediate and secondary schools, although instruction—except in courses in Arabic language, literature, and history—is in English. The students, since they are on the whole a superior group, have little difficulty in maintaining a high standing in the public intermediate- and secondary-school examinations, which they are obliged to take in Arabic.

The secondary section of the Queen 'Aliyah Institute was opened in the fall of 1945 to provide opportunity for completion of secondary-school education by girls who are from provinces which have no preparatory schools for girls. It was hoped that this would provide a larger supply of girls to enter the Queen 'Aliyah Institute and the various higher institutions of medicine, pharmacy, and law and the Higher Teachers College. The course is identical to that of the preparatory school and is conducted in Arabic. Tuition, board, and lodging are entirely at government expense. Admission is from the intermediate school, after which the girls take a preparatory course of two years' length. Fifty-four students were admitted in 1945, of whom 24 were in the scientific section and 30 in the literary

SECONDARY AND VOCATIONAL EDUCATION

section. This policy is likely to remain in force until the Ministry of Education has enough women teachers to permit establishing a girls secondary school in each province.

Vocational Education

Iraq has a variety of postprimary schools aside from the regular intermediate and secondary schools and the institutions which train teachers for secondary schools. These special schools are designed to fill the country's need for skilled workers—mechanical, clerical, and professional—and range from simple trade schools, requiring only a public primary-school certificate for admission, to the College of Law and the Royal College of Medicine. Because of the shortage of trained workers and professional people, the government offers training in these institutions free, in most cases, to qualified applicants. (The colleges preparing professional workers will be described in the next chapter.)

TECHNICAL SCHOOLS

Technical education on a trade-school level is provided in Baghdad, Mosul, and Kirkuk for boys who have passed the public primary-school examinations. This is a four-year course, and the schools at Baghdad and Mosul have a registration of approximately 100 boys each. The school at Kirkuk was opened in the fall of 1945. Provision has been made for 400 boarding students at Baghdad; but since these facilities are in excess of the present enrollment, they are being utilized by boys from the Commercial High School and by students in the preparatory year of the Higher Teachers College. No fees are charged, and boarding students receive clothing and laundry service as well as board and room without charge. The Mosul school has no boarding students at present, though facilities are available.

In spite of such favorable provisions, enrollment in these schools is low. The advantages offered seem to be in large part nullified by the Compulsory Military Service Law which does not treat the graduates of vocational schools in the same way as those of secondary schools but requires them to spend two years in the military service as privates. Students, therefore, prefer to go to secondary schools because after graduation they can enter the reserve officers training course of nine months.

The school at Mosul provides training in weaving, carpentry, machine-shop practice, motor-car repair, and electrical wiring. During each of the first and second years twenty-two hours per week are devoted to theoretical work, and twenty hours are spent in the shops. The student in his first year works in each of the different trades to acquire a basis for choosing the one he will follow. In the third year theory occupies fourteen hours and shopwork twenty-eight hours weekly, while in the fourth year the distribution is fifteen hours for theory and twenty-seven for practical work.

All shops seemed to be well equipped except the electrical shop, which in 1945 was a recent establishment and suffered because of the difficulty of obtaining suitable materials and equipment under war conditions. The machine-shop was congested and poorly lighted, but, in general, though classrooms and shops were small, the small enrollment prevented serious crowding. Instructional materials were available in mechanical drawing, and there were excellent models for the study of internal-combustion engines.

The director's tabulation of present occupations of graduates from 1928–40 inclusive showed that of 84 graduates, 68 were engaged in the occupations for which the school had prepared them, while 16 had taken up other types of work.

The Technical School in Baghdad is housed in modern buildings with ample classrooms for theoretical instruction and large, relatively light, extensively equipped workshops. Physical facilities would accommodate five or six times the number of students enrolled in 1945–46.

The present program at Baghdad provides for twenty-eight hours per week of theoretical work for the first two years—mathematics, five; English, five; Arabic, four; history, two; geography, two; science, four; mechanical drawing, four; and physical education, 1—and fourteen hours of practical work. In the first year the shopwork consists of carpentry with hand tools and sheet metal work. In the second year the students work in the machine-shop, and in shops providing experience in sheet metal, blacksmithing, foundry, electricity, carpentry, and building. Theoretical work in the third and fourth years is reduced to fourteen hours and shopwork is increased to twenty-eight hours a week. The student specializes in his last two years in the building trades (carpentry, furniture construction and repair, plumbing and electric wiring), heavy engineering (blacksmithing, sheet metal work, and foundry) or light engineering (fitting, turning, electric welding, automobile repair, tractors, and internal-combustion engines). It is considered necessary for a graduate to work with an experienced workman for two or three years before setting out independently.

The major needs of the school as expressed or implied are a teaching staff that is adequate in training and number, means of attracting boys of aptitude and interest to the school, reclassification of the school to give it

SECONDARY AND VOCATIONAL EDUCATION

equal status with secondary schools, a placement and follow-up service for graduates, and careful study of Iraq's needs in the field of technical education at the level of this type of school.

HOME ARTS SCHOOL

The Home Arts School in Baghdad admits girls who hold a Primary-School Certificate. A new program introduced in 1945 has the dual purpose of fitting girls to be intelligent homemakers and at the same time preparing them to teach in primary and intermediate schools, so that more of cooking, sewing, child care, and health matters may be taught in these schools. This program follows in general the intermediate- and secondary-school syllabuses, but is seven years in length instead of five. The additional time is spent on courses in dressmaking, cooking, drawing and design, child care, health, hygiene, and sanitation.

Of the 134 girls enrolled in the fall of 1945, 53 were boarding students. The capacity of the boarding department is 72. The majority of the girls are from the Baghdad area although efforts are made to enroll girls from all sections of Iraq. The school is housed in a modern building with large, well-lighted classrooms and workrooms. It is well equipped for its specialized courses and presents annual public exhibitions and style shows. This School appears to be filling a real need, and the girls show genuine interest in the program.

THE COMMERCIAL SECONDARY SCHOOL

The Commercial Secondary School in Baghdad admits boys who hold the Intermediate-School Certificate and provides two years' training for junior clerkships. Selection is based on quality of work in the intermediate-school examination, interest in the commercial field, and geographical representation. In the year 1945–46 there were 52 boarding students out of a total enrollment of 91. Tuition and boarding costs are paid by the government. Bank officials, merchants, and heads of government departments have cooperated in the development of this school, and there is active demand for the services of its graduates, although some continue their education in the Law College.

The faculty consists of five full-time teachers including the principal and four part-time lecturers secured from the Supply Department of the government, a bank, and a business firm. The part-time instructors were added to the faculty to insure that training would be consistent with current Iraqi business practice. In 1945 an English section was opened to increase the student's facility in that language.

Interest in this School has fluctuated in recent years with frequent changes of policy relative to its status, prerequisite training, and program. The program of studies, given in Table 28, is designed to meet the needs of both pupils and employers more satisfactorily and should increase the popularity of the School.

At present the Commercial Secondary School is the only vocational school which offers opportunity for study parallel with the secondary-school program. This School has had a checkered history in the last eight or nine years. Established and abolished more than once, it sometimes strove to be

TABLE 28

Program of Studies for the Commercial Secondary School, Baghdad, 1945–46

Subjects	1st Year Arabic Section	1st Year English Section	2nd Year
Arabic	5	5	4
English	6	6	6
Bookkeeping	4	4	4
Typing	9	6	9
Business methods, Arabic	2	2	3
Business methods, English	2	2	3
Commercial law	...	...	2
Commercial arithmetic	3	5	3
Economics	2	2	2
Geography	...	4	...
Commercial geography	3	...	...
Physical training	1	1	1
Total	37	37	37

a complete secondary commercial course; at other times it was reduced to an intermediate course; and at still others it functioned as one of the sections of the Central Secondary School in Baghdad. In 1945 it was an independent preparatory school of two years above the intermediate level, giving a special course that leads to a Commercial Certificate of secondary-school level and appeared to be attracting the appropriate type of student.

The school of agriculture

The School of Agriculture, located near Baghdad, has accommodations for 200 students—nearly twice as many as were enrolled in 1945. It offers a three-year course above the intermediate school, and student enrollment is according to geographical distribution. A school of agriculture had been established in 1928 by the Department of Agriculture, but was abolished in 1930 because of lack of students.

Apparently there is little demand for trained agriculturists except in

SECONDARY AND VOCATIONAL EDUCATION

government employment where vacancies are fewer than applicants. In 1945, 30 out of 48 graduates of the School were employed by the Department of Agriculture, 17 by the Ministry of Education, and 1 was at home, occupation unknown. Many of those employed in the Ministry of Education are teaching in the model-farm schools, a new type of primary school.

The first- and second-year students in the School of Agriculture have a thirty-six-hour week. In the first year they study Arabic language, English, physics, chemistry, agronomy, botany, zoology, practical agriculture, surveying, and carpentry. In the second year they study Arabic, English, organic chemistry, insects, bees, animal-breeding, irrigation, agricultural machinery, practical agriculture, vegetables, meteorology, carpentry, and veterinary medicine. In the third year the program is increased to thirty-eight hours a week and consists of English, soils, agricultural economics, cooperatives, agricultural accounting, plant products, dairying, plant diseases, agricultural machinery, practical agriculture, fruits, flowers, carpentry, and chicken-breeding. There is no organized physical education, but the students play basketball and volleyball in their leisure time. There is a supervised-study period of two hours each night. All students live at the college at government expense.

Plans are underway to introduce some of the vocational and special types of education into the secondary-school system. The central idea is to have vocational schools offer programs of secondary standard, combining academic and vocational subjects. These courses would lead, through public examination, to Intermediate-School and Secondary-School Certificates. As the combination of the two programs requires more time, the Higher Committee on Studies and Curricula has decided to have a six-year secondary vocational school, with four years of intermediate and two of preparatory work. The plan embraces the technical, agricultural, commercial, and home-arts schools and may eventually include the Fine Arts School.

Students who pass the public primary-school examination will be admitted at government expense and first given a two-year vocational and academic program. At the end of two years those who pass a selective examination conducted by the Ministry in both types of study and who show promise of benefiting from a full secondary course will be given another two years leading to the public intermediate-school examination. Those who pass the intermediate examination will continue with a higher vocational-preparatory course of two years ending with a vocational-secondary certificate entitling the student to admission to higher institutions of the same type. Students who fail the second-year examination will be given a purely vocational course lasting two years and leading to a vocational certificate.

It is hoped that this arrangement will attract the intelligent student with vocational aptitudes. It will open to him opportunities for higher education and will entitle him to Reserve officers training instead of compulsory service as a private; it will also make him eligible for study abroad. At the same time, it is designed to produce a more cultured type of artisan. Details of the scheme had not been worked out in 1945.

Chapter II

THE EDUCATION OF TEACHERS

Primary Teachers

*I*RAQ has two types of institutions for the training of primary-school teachers: primary-teachers colleges which prepare urban teachers, and rural and elementary colleges for the training of rural teachers. In either type, men and women students are segregated in separate colleges. The programs of primary- and rural-teachers colleges differ in important respects.

PRIMARY-TEACHERS COLLEGES

Iraq's two primary-teachers colleges, one for men and one for women, are in Baghdad. The College for Men has for the past few years offered two courses, a four-year course for graduates of intermediate schools and a two-year course for secondary-school graduates. Recently the four-year course has been reduced to three years. Intermittently there has been a section for the preparation of primary-school English teachers. The program of studies in the three-year course is similar to that of the secondary schools except for the inclusion of two periods per week in the first year and three in the second of principles of education and seven periods per week of educational psychology and teaching methods in the final year. The two-year course substitutes four periods per week of educational psychology in the first year for some of the academic studies of the secondary school, and in the second year two periods per week of philosophy of education and six of teaching methods.

Students are admitted largely on the basis of their achievements in the public intermediate- and secondary-school examinations. Other factors considered are distribution according to provinces, medical-examination report, and results on an admittedly inadequate entrance examination to discover the aptitudes of the students. The question of distribution according to province is vital in all teachers colleges since some provinces have desperate need of more teachers and since great pressure is applied by teachers working outside their home province to return to them. At the beginning of the 1945–46 school year there were 44 students enrolled in the two-year course and 181 in the three-year course, while about 50 applicants for admission had been rejected.

As in other teachers colleges, most students are boarders at government expense and pay no fees. The government provides them with clothing, books, stationery, medical care, and fares for their trips between their home towns and Baghdad. Only a small charge of 500 fils ($2.00) is made for physical education. About 50 Arab students from abroad—from such places as Alexandretta, Hadramaut, and far away Java—board at the Primary Teachers College for Men while pursuing their studies in other institutions of learning in Baghdad.

The courses in education cannot be said to provide adequate professional preparation for teaching. Three months of the final year are devoted to practice teaching. At first it takes the form of individual lessons conducted by the student-teachers in the demonstration school in the presence of their instructor and the rest of the education class. Later the student-teachers are distributed throughout the Baghdad primary schools for boys to teach full time for a period of two or three weeks.

The staff includes a director, an assistant director, a boarding master, twenty-three instructors, five part-time lecturers, and a librarian. Only the teachers of education and psychology are professionally trained.

The Primary Teachers College for Women has now been superseded by the Queen 'Aliyah Institute. Formerly the College, like that for men, gave the four-year course above the intermediate school, and the two-year course above the secondary school. As now reorganized under the name of the Queen 'Aliyah Institute,[1] it is comprised of three sections: (1) A boarding secondary school admitting girl graduates of intermediate schools from all provinces. This section, which has already been dealt with under secondary education, has superseded the four-year course. Girls passing their secondary-school examinations are entitled to admission to the higher colleges or to the other two sections of the Institute to be mentioned immediately. (2) A three-year course admitting girl graduates of secondary schools to prepare them for intermediate-school teaching. This will be dealt with later in the discussion of the education of secondary-school teachers. (3) The old two-year course for the education of primary-school teachers, which more directly concerns us here.

Originally the two-year course was made up of two sections, the scientific and the literary. Later a course for the preparation of English teachers was

---

[1] See pp. 196–97 for a further description of the Queen 'Aliyah Institute.

THE EDUCATION OF TEACHERS

substituted for the literary course. In 1945–46 the authorities, realizing that specialization along literary and scientific lines was undesirable for primary teachers, established a new general course for primary teachers as given in Table 29. There were 96 students enrolled in the two-year course in 1945–46.

TABLE 29

Program of Studies for Primary Teachers, Queen 'Aliyah Institute, Iraq, 1945–46

Subject	Hours per Week	
	1st Year	2nd Year
Religion	1	1
Arabic	5	5
English	3	3
Psychology and education	6	8
History	2	2
Geography	2	2
Mathematics	2	2
Science	4	3
Drawing and manual arts	4	4
Physical education and singing	2	2
Hygiene	1	1
Total	32	33

The training of primary-school teachers for the cities has been the subject of controversy for the last two or three years and has more than once engaged the attention of the Higher Committee on Studies and Curricula in its meetings. There are two divergent points of view. There are those who believe that two parallel courses should be maintained, leading to diplomas of equal value: one should be a four-year course for intermediate-school graduates, with the first two years similar to the secondary-school course, the third and fourth years being the same as the regular two-year course offered to secondary-school graduates. The other point of view protests the four-year course as too expensive and of too high a standard considering the great number of teachers needed for the task of putting every child in school, and considering also the fact that a higher level of training requires a higher rate of pay than the country can afford. It is suggested, therefore, that only the three-year course above intermediate school should be maintained and that emphasis should be laid on rural-teachers colleges, which have a lower standard that results in lower salaries being paid to their graduates. Both factions agree that institution of the two-year course above secondary school would probably be unsuccessful since secondary-school graduates prefer to apply for educational missions abroad, entrance into the higher institutions, or even ordinary clerical jobs rather than to enter the Primary Teachers College. Consequently the quality of students entering this course has been poor, and it seems advisable to preserve the policy of admission from intermediate school for some time to come.

RURAL- AND ELEMENTARY-TEACHERS COLLEGES

The forerunner of the present rural-teachers colleges was an "elementary section" opened in 1923 at the old Primary Teachers College and offering a two-year training course to primary-school graduates. Even that requirement was not strictly applied because of the scarcity of applicants and the need for teachers. This course was considered sufficient for a village teacher. In 1929 it was lengthened to three years, but was abolished in 1931 as being of too low a standard.

In 1934 the need for teachers and the emphasis laid upon rural education by the Monroe Commission's report[2] led to the establishment of the Rural Teachers College. The rural teacher was to be not only a teacher, but also an agriculturist and a social and health worker who should undertake the work of rural reconstruction through the school. Courses were adopted in consideration of this theory: practical and theoretical training in agriculture, hygiene, first aid and simple medical treatment, sociology, and visits to villages were started. The application of this idea has been attempted with varying degrees of success in the last twelve years. The course was developed into a four-year and later a five-year course above primary school. The practice of admitting pupils direct from primary school has been maintained in order to insure a supply of village boys who are presumably willing to return to the village upon graduation, thus solving the problem of the city dweller's reluctance to teach in outlying small villages.

The first of these rural-teachers colleges was established at a camp near Shatrah, on the Gharraf River in southern Iraq. Later it was transferred to the large government farm at Rustumiyah, where students had admirable opportunity for agricultural training, though opportunities for social and health work and practice teaching were limited, there being few rural settlements near the farm. In the attempt to turn out a large number of teachers, the Ministry of Education allowed this rural college to grow very large and unwieldy, more than 1,000 students being registered at one

[2] A commission of American educators, under the chairmanship of Paul Monroe, which was invited by the Iraq government to study the educational system of Iraq and make recommendations for its improvement. Cf. *Report of the Educational Inquiry Commission* (Baghdad: The Government Press, 1932).

THE EDUCATION OF TEACHERS

time. The size and the lack of preparation of the faculty to handle the creative kind of program planned militated against converting into practice the theory which underlay the founding of the college.

Later an attempt was made to limit the number of students at Rustumiyah, and 2 other rural-teachers colleges were opened, 1 in 1943 at Mahawil, in the province of Hillah, the other in 1944 at Ba'qubah, in the province of Diyala. A fourth college for men is projected for Shaqlawah, in the province of Arbil, to prepare teachers for schools in the mountainous districts of the north.

Table 30 offers some statistics for the three rural teachers colleges of Iraq in 1944–45.

TABLE 30
RURAL-TEACHERS COLLEGE ENROLLMENT, IRAQ, 1944–45*

COLLEGE	NO. OF CLASSES & DIVISIONS	NO. OF FULL-TIME TEACHERS	ENROLLMENT					
			1st Year	2nd Year	3rd Year	4th Year	5th Year	Total
Rustumiyah...	17	31	...	79	97	152	191	519
Mahawil......	5	9	101	50	...	...	...	151
Ba'qubah.....	3	6	78	...	...	...	...	78
Total.....	25	46	179	129	97	152	191	748

* Data supplied by the Statistical Bureau of the Ministry of Education.

The combined registration of the 3 colleges in 1944–45 was smaller than that of Rustumiyah alone in its peak years. However, it is hoped that with the addition of the projected rural-teachers college the 4 will meet the requirements of normal expansion in the primary-school system.

The College at Rustumiyah had 430 students when it was visited by the American Council Commission in the fall of 1945. A selection committee at the Ministry of Education together with the principals of the colleges concerned selects the students and distributes them among the colleges. As in the other teachers colleges, selection is made on the basis of the school record, distribution according to provinces, a medical examination, and an interview. Students from villages are preferred; in fact, city students are not usually admitted. All students are maintained at government expense.

The first three years of this five-year course follow the intermediate curriculum, adding six hours a week of theoretical and practical agriculture and three hours of drawing, singing, and games. In the third year algebra replaces athletics, and a course in hygiene and first aid is given. The thirty-nine-period week is divided between theoretical and practical pursuits, twenty-eight periods for the former, eleven for the latter. The fourth-

and fifth-year programs, while continuing work in academic subjects, include courses in social affairs of Iraq, poultry-breeding, dairying, carpentry, and blacksmithing, principles of education and psychology, teaching methods, and practice teaching. In all these courses emphasis is upon the problems and needs of rural teachers of primary schools in Iraqi villages.

By a recent ruling students who have completed the fourth year are required to pass the public intermediate-school examinations before they can register for the fifth year. The professional courses are concentrated in the last two years; practice teaching is limited to the fifth year, beginning in a rural school connected with the college and ending with full-time practice in a village school during April. Methods instructors visit the student-teachers to appraise their work and give them assistance.

The staff of the College at Rustumiyah consists of the principal, who is a graduate of the old Higher Teachers College, and twenty-four instructors, of whom nineteen are graduates of the four-year course at the Higher Teachers College, four are graduates of Fuad I University in Cairo, and one is a graduate of the American University of Beirut. All graduates of the Higher Teachers College have had some professional training as prospective secondary-school teachers, but three of them—the teachers of psychology and education—are graduates of the Division of Education which existed at that College from 1937–42 and have had more intensive educational training.

Rustumiyah is situated on an extensive farm about 14 kilometers (8.7 miles) south of Baghdad on the Diyala River. Originally an experimental farm belonging to the Department of Agriculture, it was transferred in 1934 to the Ministry of Education. In addition to the original building which formerly housed the School of Agriculture (1928–30), there are now large dormitories with dining-rooms and an assembly hall, and extensive bungalows have been built to serve as classrooms. The College has a small library and large playing fields.

It was recently suggested by the Higher Committee on Studies and Curricula that the course for rural teachers should be lengthened to six years, with the first four years devoted to intermediate-school studies plus agricultural and hygiene classes and the upper two years devoted to studies of standard secondary and professional training. It was felt that such a plan for rural teachers would provide them with the equivalent of a secondary-school diploma and so open opportunities for the ambitious to pursue further study. At the same time it would attract a better type of student—the village boy who would like to attend a secondary school but is unable to do so because of lack of facilities in his village. The suggestion

THE EDUCATION OF TEACHERS

was opposed on the grounds that its adoption would make the course unduly long at a time when the Ministry of Education is in great need of primary teachers and that it would raise the level of salaries beyond the capacity of the budget of the Ministry.

THE ELEMENTARY TEACHERS COLLEGE FOR WOMEN

The Elementary Teachers College for Women made its first appearance in 1934 in Diwaniyah, where an uncongenial environment brought its performance to an early end. It reopened as a branch of the Primary Teachers College for Women in Baghdad, but was later separated from that institution. It offers a course of four years to girl graduates of the primary school and is designed to prepare women teachers for rural primary schools. In its first three years this College follows the course of the intermediate schools except that it substitutes general-science courses for the separate science courses of the intermediate school. In the fourth year the program is as follows:

Subject	Periods per week
Psychology	2
General education and method	2
Practice teaching	3
Methods of teaching primary subjects	5
Arabic	6
English	4
Algebra	2
Geometry	2
History	2
Geography	2
Science	3
Drawing	1
Sewing	2
Singing and physical education	1
Total	37

It is apparent that the course of study is little adapted to the College's objective of fitting women to teach in the rural districts. It is a regular academic course combined with a few professional classes. As a result both types of instruction are weak and the curriculum is overcrowded, fourteen subjects being taught in one year.

The course is being lengthened to five years, and the students are to be required to pass the public intermediate-school examination before being admitted to the fourth year. The first graduating class to complete the new five-year program will be that of 1948.

At the time of the American Council Commission's visit (1945) the College had 212 students, almost all of them boarders at government expense. The attempt to admit only village girls is less successful than the similar policy in the rural-teachers colleges for men because there are fewer village schools for girls to supply candidates and because of the prejudice of parents against sending girls away from home. There is a staff of thirteen, including the principal and assistant principal. Of this number, five have had some professional training. The College is housed in a large quadrangle, one part of which is occupied by a practice school and a kindergarten.

The Education of Secondary-School Teachers

Teachers for intermediate and secondary schools are now educated at the Higher Teachers College, the three-year course at the Queen 'Aliyah Institute for women teachers, and at the Physical Education Institute.

THE HIGHER TEACHERS COLLEGE

The Higher Teachers College originated in evening classes which were opened for primary-school teachers in 1923 in order to prepare them to teach in secondary schools. This was later turned into a full-time boarding college giving a course of two years above the secondary school, divided into a literary and a scientific section. The College was abolished in 1931 as being of a low standard and having an inadequate staff. The need for secondary-school teachers made the Ministry of Education reopen the College in 1935, with a course of two years which was lengthened to three in 1937 and to four in 1939. In 1943 it was decided to add a preparatory year taught exclusively in English.[3] Women students were first admitted in 1937 and now constitute about one-third of the enrollment.

Buildings and grounds.—The Higher Teachers College is housed in two large, modern buildings on the northern outskirts of Baghdad with ample space for additional buildings, playgrounds, and gardens.

One building houses administrative offices, classrooms, and an assembly hall. The other houses the dormitory, the dining-room, reception rooms, the College library, and, until a special science building is erected, the physics and chemistry laboratories. Women students live in a rented house

---

[3] Word has recently been received that the preparatory year has been dropped and the program again reduced to four years. As no details of the new program were available, the description of the program as it was being executed and planned at the time of the visit of the American Council Commission has been maintained.

THE EDUCATION OF TEACHERS

about a mile from the College. It is planned to build a special women's dormitory closer to the College.

Students.—In October 1945 when the American Council Commission visited the Higher Teachers College, there were four classes: preparatory, first, second, and fourth years. The fourth-year class was the last following the old four-year program. The remaining three classes were following the five-year program. Of the total registration of about 357 students it was expected that about 120 would be women, an increase of about 20 women students over the previous year. Students registered in the College were distributed as shown in Table 31.

TABLE 31
Enrollment in Higher Teachers College, Baghdad, 1945–46

Year*	Literary	Social Studies	English	Chemistry —Biology	Physics— Mathematics	Total
Preparatory year....	...	...	...	...	...	130
1st year...........	17	19	12	20	14	82
2nd year...........	12	10	8	18	8	56
4th year...........	20	17	9	25	18	89
Total..........	...	...	...	...	...	357

* There was no third-year class in 1945–46 because of the change of length of course from four to five years.

Students are admitted on the basis of standing in the public secondary-school examination, distribution by provinces, health, and personal interview by the admission committee. Tuition, board and lodging, books, and medical care are free. Boarding students sign a contract with the Ministry, agreeing to serve the Ministry two years for every year spent at the College or pay 50 dinars ($200) for each year of study. Day students agree to teach one year for each year of study or forfeit 25 dinars ($100) per year of study.

Curriculum.—The distribution of subjects and periods is shown in Tables 32 and 33. The preparatory year has two parallel courses, the literary and the scientific. Both sections study the same courses in Arabic and English. However, in the English course students are grouped into A, B, and C sections, according to ability, each taking a course corresponding to its ability. Students wishing to become teachers of English must be members of section A or else stand very high in section B.

Preparatory students of the literary section take, in addition to English and Arabic, a three-period course in general mathematics and four-period courses in ancient history, modern history, and geography, whereas the scientific section concentrates on mathematics, physics, and chemistry. All

TABLE 32

Program of Study of the Higher Teachers College for Arabic, English, and Social Studies Sections, Iraq, 1945

Hours per Week

Subject	Preparatory Year (Common)	Arabic Section				English Section						Social Studies Section						
		1st Year	2nd Year	3rd Year	4th Year	1st Year	2nd Year	3rd Year	4th Year	1st Year	2nd Year	3rd Year Major			4th Year Major		
												Arab History	Modern History	Geography	Arab History	Modern History	Geography
Arabic	7	8	7	8	8	3	3	3	…	…	…	…	…	…	…	…	…
English	6	3	3	3	…	10*	10*	10*	8	5	…	…	…	…	…	…	…
Psychology	…	…	3	4	…2	…	3	4	2	…	3	…	…	…	2	2	2
Education and practice teaching	…	…	…	4	7	…	5	4	7	…	5	4	4	4	7	7	7
Educational biology	…	3	…	…	…	3	…	…	…	3	…	…	…	…	…	…	…
Hygiene	…	2	…	…	…	2	…	…	…	2	…	…	…	…	…	…	…
Ethics	…	…	…	…	1	…	…	…	1	…	…	…	…	…	1	1	1
General mathematics	3	…	…	…	…	…	…	…	…	…	…	…	…	…	…	…	…
Ancient history	4	…	…	…	…	…	…	…	…	…	…	3	3	3	2	2	2
Modern history	4	…	4	…	…	…	…	…	…	4	5	…	6	…	…	6	…
Arabic history	…	…	…	…	…	…	…	…	…	4	5	6	3†	9§	6	…	6
Geography	4	2†	…	…	…	2†	…	…	…	5	5	3†	…	…	…	…	…
French or Latin	…	3	3	3	3	3	3	3	3	…	…	…	…	2	…	…	…
Economics	…	…	…	…	…	…	…	…	…	…	…	2	2	…	…	…	…
Government	…	…	…	…	…	…	…	…	…	…	…	…	…	…	3	3	3
Sociology	…	…	…	…	…	…	…	…	…	…	…	…	…	…	…	…	…
Translation	…	…	…	…	…	1	1	…	…	…	…	…	…	…	…	…	…
Total	28	25	25	22‖	21‖	24	25	24	21	23	23	22	22	22	21	21	21

* Including British history and institutions.
† Geography of the Arabic world.
‡ Geography of the British Commonwealth.
§ Includes three hours of geography of the Arabic world.
‖ Two three-hour courses in Syriac required in addition from students hoping to become candidates for fellowships abroad.

TABLE 33

Program of Study of the Higher Teachers College for Chemistry-Biology and Physics-Mathematics Sections, Iraq, 1945

			Hours per Week								
			Chemistry-Biology Section					Physics-Mathematics Section			
Subject	Preparatory Year (Common)	1st Year	2nd Year	3rd Year Major		4th Year Major		1st Year	2nd Year	3rd Year	4th Year Major	
				Chemistry	Biology	Chemistry	Biology				Mathematics	Physics
Arabic	7	...	...	...	...	...	...	...	...	...	...	...
English	6	5	...	...	...	...	...	5	...	...	...	...
Psychology	...	...	3	4	4	2	2	...	3	4	2	2
Education and practice teaching	...	...	5	4	4	7	7	...	5	4	7	7
Educational biology	...	3	...	...	...	...	...	3	...	...	...	...
Ethics	...	...	...	...	...	1	1	...	...	...	1	1
Physics	4	4	...	...	...	...	...	4	7	7	...	7
Mathematics	7	3	6	...	...	...	...	6	6	6	6	3
Chemistry	4	5	6	10	4	12	...	5	...	...	...	...
Zoology	...	4	6	6 or 6	6	...	6	...	...	...	...	...
Botany	...	4	...	2	2	...	6	...	...	...	...	...
Biological theories	...	...	...	...	...	3	3	...	...	...	...	...
Anatomy, physiology, and hygiene	...	...	...	...	...	...	...	...	3	4	4	4
Mechanics (applied mathematics)	...	...	...	...	...	...	...	3	2	...	...	...
Hygiene	...	...	...	...	...	...	...	...	...	...	...	...
Total	28	28	26	26	26	25	25	26	26	25	20	24

teaching is in English. The College regards the preparatory class as a means of discovering material unsuitable for higher training. Any student who fails in more than two subjects in this preparatory year is dropped. Between 18 and 25 percent in the class usually fails. A minimum grade of 60 in any subject and a general average of 65 are required. A student failing more than once at any time in his college career is dropped—unless he is a fourth-year student on the point of graduation, in which case he has another chance.

Having survived the preparatory course, the student may choose one of five parallel courses: Arabic, English, social studies, chemistry-biology, or physics-mathematics. All courses in every section are required. They have in common courses in English, educational psychology, education and practice teaching, educational biology, hygiene, and ethics. Only the courses in educational psychology and in education need be described briefly here.

In educational psychology students study a general course in psychology in the first year, a course in child and adolescent psychology in the second year, a course in mental and educational measurements in the third year, and a course in mental hygiene and behavior problems in the fourth. Studies in education include in the second year a general course in secondary education and visits to schools. In the third year courses in special methods and in the philosophy of education, based on Dewey's *Democracy and Education,* are given. Preliminary practice teaching consists of individual lessons given by the student-teachers in the presence of their fellow-students. These lessons are later discussed in class. In the fourth year the methods course is continued with three weeks of practice teaching in the demonstration school under the supervision of a training teacher. The instructors in methods are expected to visit the student-teachers about once a week. Early in April the student-teachers are assigned to the intermediate schools of Baghdad for an additional three weeks of practice teaching. During this period the student-teacher conducts two or three lessons a day by agreement with the subject teachers in the school. Specialized-methods courses are given in the teaching of four subjects: Arabic, English to foreigners, social studies, and science and mathematics.

In addition to the courses that are common to all and require a total of thirty-six hours out of the general total for four years' study of eighty-nine to one hundred and five hours (one hundred seventy-eight to two hundred ten semester hours), each section follows its own more or less specialized courses. In general, the first two years are intended for surveying the fields of study and the last two years for increased specialization in the field of the student's choice. Exceptions to this rule are the Arabic and English

THE EDUCATION OF TEACHERS

sections, which require all students to take the same courses throughout.

The courses of the Arabic section are designed to give the student a specialist's knowledge of Arabic grammar and literature, sufficient familiarity with English language and literature to be at home in this language, and a basic knowledge of either French or Latin.

Courses of the English section are designed to produce a competent teacher of English. The curriculum stresses language and literature, but includes courses in British history and institutions and in the geography of the British Commonwealth. Here, as in the Arabic section, French or Latin is required, partly to deepen the student's understanding of the English language and partly to introduce him to a second Western literature. By direction of their English professors, most of the students elect Latin.

In the social-studies section, survey courses of college level are given in the first two years in Arabic history, modern European history, and geography, to provide the student with a basis for teaching these subjects in intermediate schools. In the last two years the student elects one of these subjects and takes advanced courses in it. All students are required to take two courses in ancient history—one an advanced course in the ancient history of Iraq (Babylonia and Assyria) and the other in that of Greece and Rome—one course in sociology, and one course in either government or economics.

In the chemistry-biology section the students take a general college course in physics in the preparatory and first years, and one general course in higher mathematics which includes the elementary concepts of the calculus needed in advanced chemical or biological work. The courses in chemistry, starting with the preparatory years, are designed to acquaint the student with inorganic and organic chemistry, with qualitative analysis and elements of physical chemistry. Survey courses in zoology and botany are given in the first two years. In the third year the student may specialize in chemistry or in biology. If he chooses chemistry, he studies quantitative volumetric and gravimetric analysis, industrial chemistry, and advanced physical chemistry; in addition, he studies either zoology or botany in his third year. If he chooses biology as his field of specialization, he studies theoretical biology, a course in anatomy, physiology, and hygiene, and has two years each of zoology and botany.

Students in the physics-mathematics section probably have the heaviest and hardest course in the College. All take four years of mechanics. They have a common program in physics and mathematics through the third year with only minor differentiation in the fourth. The courses in physics, beginning with the second year, cover the usual branches of the subject in detail and lead up to an ultimate course in the later discoveries concerning the atom. Mathematics courses begin with elementary calculus, analytical geometry, and higher algebra, continue with advanced courses in these subjects, and end up with differential equations and interpolation in the fourth year.

Before graduation a student from any section must write two theses—one in the field of education or psychology, the other on a subject within the field of his specialization—and pass a comprehensive oral examination in both fields.

Equipment.—The fact that the Higher Teachers College was just getting re-established at the outbreak of World War II subjected it to delays and shortages in equipment. However, the government was rather generous in its budgetary allotment, and every attempt was made to equip it as well as possible.

Laboratories were started from nothing in the summer of 1937, only two years before the war. Large orders for equipment placed in England and various European countries gradually materialized, so that by 1941 the laboratories were supplied with essential, if not adequate, apparatus, chemicals, glassware, microscopes and slides, charts, and specimens. During the last year of the war the shortage of chemicals was felt, and the increase in number of students made the number of available microscopes inadequate. In 1945 the College was in great need of a workshop for repairing scientific apparatus and trained technicians to do the work.

For geography a good collection of Arabic, English, and German maps and globes has been brought together. Maps of Iraq of various scales have been supplied by the Iraqi Survey Department. There is a small geological collection, and a biological museum is contemplated.

The library grew from about 500 volues in 1937 to 9,252 in October 1945. About two-thirds of the books are in English; the rest, except for a few hundred in French and Turkish, are in Arabic. In spite of the difficulties of importing books in wartime, the library managed to add from 1,200 to 1,500 volumes to its collection yearly. The library has a fairly representative list of periodicals, but it was impossible during the war to get American magazines regularly, and there are many gaps in the files. Almost all the important Arabic periodicals are received and about 35 English and American periodicals. The Dewey Decimal system of classification is used. Work was proceeding in 1945 on a card catalog of authors, subjects, and titles.

Students make heavy use of library books for reference and assigned reading, but borrow few books for their own enjoyment.

Staff and administration.—In 1945–46 the staff of the Higher Teachers

THE EDUCATION OF TEACHERS

College, consisting of the dean, professors, associate professors, assistant professors, instructors, lecturers, assistant instructors, and demonstrators, totaled forty. The faculty is drawn from Iraq, Lebanon, Egypt, England, and, in one instance, the United States. Professional qualifications are as follows:

Ph.D. or D.Litt. from the United States, England, or France	8
M.A. or M.S. from the United States, England, Egypt, or American University of Beirut	10
B.A. or B.Sc. from England or American University of Beirut	9
M.D.	1
Licence in Letters from Egypt	1
Licence in Law and old scholastic study of Arabic, Baghdad	1
Diploma of Dar al-'Ulum, Cairo	2
Diploma of Higher Teachers College, Egypt	1
Licence in Science or Letters, Higher Teachers College, Baghdad	7
Total	40

Difficulty in obtaining professors of scientific subjects from Egypt in 1944 and 1945 resulted in chairs of physics, chemistry, botany, and mathematics becoming vacant. Part-time lecturers, of whom there were fifteen in November 1945, were carrying on part of the work in these subjects.

The College is administered by a dean who is appointed by royal decree from among the professors of education at the College. He is responsible directly to the Minister of Education. He is assisted by an assistant dean for administrative affairs and an assistant dean for student affairs, both chosen from the College faculty and appointed by the Minister of Education upon their nomination by the dean.

The College faculty, or council of professors, composed of all members of the staff except the assistant instructors, is the body which controls the general policies of the institution and sets its curriculums. Its decisions are subject to the approval of the Minister, but actually the institution enjoys a considerable amount of autonomy. Each department constitutes a committee of all who teach in it under the chairmanship of the professor. One departmental committee may embrace more than one subject of the curriculum. The six committees—educaton, Arabic, English, social studies, chemistry-biology, and physics-mathematics—meet at the request of their chairmen to consider proposed modifications in the curriculum, contents of the courses, textbooks, progress of students, distribution of teaching loads, and plans for future development. The council of professors approves and coordinates all recommendations for curricular changes and must endorse all final marks before these can be given to the students. The teaching load varies from six periods a week as a minimum for professors to twelve periods as a maximum for instructors.

Student life and activities.—Most of the men students and about half the women are boarders, their accommodations being in dormitories, for private rooms do not exist. A student committee, elected each term, looks after the physical arrangements, setting down the weekly menu, superintending the reception of provisions from the contractor, and supervising kitchen and dining-room. It has the power to reject any food supply that it considers unfit, and the contractor is obliged to replace it.

There are various student societies and clubs that hold regular meetings and receptions. Some societies, such as the Arab Culture Society, the English Society, the Social Science Society, the Science Society, and the Art Society, follow subject lines. The Mirth and Entertainment Society occasionally holds parties at which skits and comic plays are presented, and there is a more serious dramatic group. The Cooperative Society, established with capital collected from selling shares to students, maintains a shop on the campus, chiefly for selling tea, coffee, and other refreshments. At the end of each year profits are distributed to the students. Recently a Students' Union was started to coordinate the activities of students and societies and to represent student interests before the College administration. Its members are elected from the student body and serve on a committee with two faculty members who are appointed by the dean. The Students' Union developed plans for issuing a College magazine, the first numbers of which have already appeared. It is hoped that the Students' Union will so develop as to increase the measure of self-government enjoyed by the students.

The athletics program is limited by the nature of the College grounds, which are not yet well prepared for sports. However, soccer is played to some extent, and among indoor games basketball and volleyball, ping-pong, and badminton are popular. Competitions between classes and between individuals are common, and there are occasional intercollegiate competitions. Track and field sports occupy some of the students part of the year, and an annual field-day competition among the higher colleges has been held for the last five years.

THE QUEEN 'ALIYAH INSTITUTE FOR WOMEN TEACHERS

The reorganization of the Primary Teachers College for Women as the Queen 'Aliyah Institute in October 1945, which opened a three-year course for training intermediate-school teachers, was an attempt to overcome the shortage of women teachers for intermediate schools at a time when it was

THE EDUCATION OF TEACHERS

difficult to get women teachers from Syria, Lebanon, and Egypt and when the number of women students at the Higher Teachers College was inadequate to meet the demand. It was hoped that the shorter, three-year course would attract girls who could not afford the five-year course of the Higher Teachers College and that its segregated character would appeal to conservative parents who distrusted coeducation.

In October 1945, 35 graduates of secondary schools had been admitted into the literary section and 26 into the scientific section. An additional 10 were on the waiting list. In order to speed up the process of graduation, 27 other students, who had had a year beyond secondary school, were advanced to form a second-year literary section of 16 and a second-year scientific section of 11. Thus, the total number of students was 88. The first graduation was expected in June 1947.

Table 34 shows the program of studies at the Institute:

TABLE 34

PROGRAM OF STUDIES, QUEEN 'ALIYAH INSTITUTE FOR WOMEN TEACHERS, IRAQ, 1945–46

Subjects	Literary Section 1st Year	Literary Section 2nd Year	Literary Section 3rd Year	Scientific Section 1st Year	Scientific Section 2nd Year	Scientific Section 3rd Year
Arabic	7	7	7	5	3	2
English	5	4	3	3	3	...
Education (general)	2	...	...	2	...	...
Child and adolescent psychology	2	...	...	2	...	...
General method	...	4	...	...	4	...
Educational psychology	...	2	...	...	2	...
Special methods	...	...	4	...	...	4
Philosophy of education	...	...	4	...	...	4
History	6	6	3	...	...	...
Geography	4	4	3	...	...	...
Social science and civics	...	...	2	...	...	...
Hygiene and physiology	...	...	1	...	...	2
Mathematics	...	...	...	7	6	6
Chemistry	...	...	...	5	5	5
Physics	...	...	...	4	4	4
Biology (zoology and botany)	...	...	...	4	4	3
Total	26	27	27	32	31	30

The Institute is staffed largely by men, four of whom are full-time instructors. There are twenty part-time lecturers, drawn chiefly from the Higher Teachers College. The Institute is housed on the premises of the old Primary Teachers College for Women, whose principal became the director of the Institute. It is expected that arrangements will be made in the future to permit graduates of the Institute to finish their studies at the Higher Teachers College.

THE PHYSICAL EDUCATION INSTITUTE

The Physical Education Institute offers a one-year course to men interested in teaching physical education in intermediate or secondary schools or in supervising playground or sports programs. In 1945–46 there were 20 students, 18 of whom were graduates of the rural-teachers college and 2 were secondary-school graduates who were preparing to teach in Jewish schools. All were boarding students.

In 1945–46 a director, one full-time teacher, and four part-time teachers conducted the program, which provided instruction in Olympic games, rules, gymnastics, principles of teaching, wrestling and boxing, English, Arabic, administration, hygiene and first aid, extracurricular games, scouting, and small games. The weekly schedule provides for forty periods of theory and practical work. Equipment and play areas were ample for the needs of the number enrolled. The Institute is located near the public stadium, which is large enough for three football games to be played simultaneously. A large and well-constructed swimming pool is available for instruction and recreation.

Chapter 12

HIGHER EDUCATION AND EDUCATIONAL MISSIONS

*T*HERE IS AS YET no university in Iraq. At least two attempts were made in 1943 and 1945 to incorporate the present colleges into a university, but neither attempt went beyond producing a draft charter and a draft law for the proposed university. Higher education as it now stands, therefore, is provided in separate colleges directed towards education for the professions. These are the Higher Teachers College, the Royal College of Medicine (with which is included the College of Pharmacy), the Law College, and the College of Engineering. To these must be added the three-year course of the Queen 'Aliyah Institute. No liberal-arts college existed at the time of the visit of the American Council Commission. The Higher Teachers College comes nearest to a liberal-arts college of the American type, combining academic and professional education as American colleges often do. There are, however, at least two important differences. The College is exclusively for the education of teachers; and, instead of a fluid elective system where individual courses may be combined in almost infinite alternatives, selection is limited to five parallel programs, the courses in which are almost all required.

The Higher Teachers College and the Queen 'Aliyah Institute have already been dealt with in the discussion of teacher education in the preceding chapter. The present chapter will describe the other colleges and educational missions abroad.

The Royal College of Medicine and Associated Schools

The Royal College of Medicine has associated with it under the same dean, the College of Pharmacy, the School of Nursing, and the School of Health Officials.

The Royal College of Medicine, established in Baghdad on the grounds of the Royal Hospital in 1927, provides the only medical training available in Iraq. The course is six years in length including one year of internship. New students are selected on the basis of the public secondary-school examination results, geographical distribution, age, minority representation, personal interviews, medical examination, and a special oral and written examination in English.

Tuition is free to students who sign a contract to serve for a period of four years after graduation in the Department of Public Health or for a period of fifteen years with the army. However, all students are required to pay a fee of 4 dinars ($16) per year and to buy their own textbooks. A limited number of students pay their own tuition fees, amounting to about $160 a year, but even they may be required to practice in villages for a period of six years. Because of the dearth of medical service in villages and rural areas, proposed legislation would require all graduates to serve outside the cities for a definite period after graduation.

In 1945–46 the student body totaled 312 men and women, with 93 (including 19 repeating) in the first year, 43 in the second, 39 in the third, 41 each in the fourth and fifth, and 55 in the sixth. Students make their own living arrangements as the College has no boarding provisions. Classes and laboratories are held daily except on Friday, though part or all of Thursday afternoon is often free.

The first-year program consists of lectures and laboratory work in anatomy, chemistry, biology, and physics. Second-year students do theoretical and practical work in anatomy, physiology, and biochemistry and begin work in elementary clinics. The third year provides experience in the hospital wards and lectures and laboratory work in bacteriology, pathology, orthopedics, junior medicine, junior surgery, materia medica, and dispensing. The fourth year provides for continuation of work in wards, a study of sanitary administration, public health, obstetrics and gynecology, clinical therapeutics, skin diseases, senior medicine, senior surgery, and lectures and demonstrations in forensic medicine. Senior medicine and surgery are continued in the fifth year; approximately one-fourth of the student's time is spent in the wards, with children's diseases, mental diseases, ear, nose, and throat diseases, operative surgery, ophthalmology, radiology, anesthetics, and venereal diseases occupying the balance of his time. In the sixth year the student has lectures and practice in hematology and medical ethics, but most of his time is consumed by practical training with major emphasis on the medical and surgical services. The academic year of not less than thirty weeks is divided into three terms. Instruction is in English.

Administration of the College of Medicine is carried on, under the Ministry of Social Affairs, by the dean of the faculty, assisted by the board of studies and a council. The council includes the dean of the faculty of medicine as chairman, the director of the School of Pharmacy, and five

Above: A first grade in a village primary school, Za'faraniyah, Iraq
Below: The sixth grade in the same school. Note the small size of the class due to drop-outs

Above: The circulation desk of the library of Baghdad College at the end of the day, Baghdad, Iraq.
Below: Snack-time at the kindergarten of the demonstration school of the Elementary Teachers College for Women, Baghdad, Iraq.

professors of the medical college who are nominated by the board of studies and approved by the Minister of Social Affairs. Members of the faculty have received their medical training at universities and hospitals in England, Egypt, Turkey, Paris, and Beirut.

The College is housed in a modern building specially built for it with fairly extensive laboratories, dissection rooms, and lecture halls, large enough to accommodate 60 to 70 students in each of the six years. In addition, the College enjoys the extensive facilities of the teaching hospital on the grounds of which it is situated. This largest of Iraq's hospitals has 600 beds in large wards and semiprivate and private rooms, thus accommodating patients of all classes. As the hospital receives patients not only from the Baghdad area, but also from all parts of Iraq, students have a chance of seeing a very large and representative variety of cases and diseases. The hospital has a very large outpatient clinic occupying a two-story building and some annexes where more than 700,000 new cases are treated each year. Next to the College building is the large building housing the pathological and bacteriological institutes and the antirabic and vaccine-production institutes. On the same grounds is also the extensive X-ray building with facilities for both X-ray diagnosis and therapy, including fluoroscopy and radium therapy. All these facilities form part of the teaching facilities of the College.

THE COLLEGE OF PHARMACY

The College of Pharmacy, included for administrative purposes in the Royal College of Medicine, was established in 1936 and provides graduates of the secondary school with a four-year course leading to a Diploma of Pharmaceutical Chemist. In 1945–46 the enrollment was 98, with the four classes about equal in size. Upon graduation the student spends six months in practical work with a registered pharmacist and three months in a government dispensary. Students are admitted on the basis of a medical examination, public secondary-school examinations, personal interview, and geographical and minority distribution. Those who sign a contract to serve the Department of Health for four years after graduation are exempt from all fees except an instruction fee of 3 dinars ($12) yearly. Tuition fees for others are 33 dinars ($132) per year.

The College is administered by the dean assisted by a college board composed of permanent professors and lecturers. Members of the teaching staff are nominated by the dean, subject to the approval of the college board and confirmation by the Director General of Health.

The curriculum includes botany, general chemistry, business methods and bookkeeping, physics, and zoology in the first year; analytical chemistry, pharmacy, pharmacognosy and pharmaceutical botany, inorganic materia medica, and organic chemistry in the second; organic pharmaceutical chemistry, biochemistry, pharmacy, organic materia medica, and pharmaceutical physiology in the third; and microscopic pharmacognosy, toxicology, inorganic pharmaceutical chemistry, pharmacy, bacteriology and parasitology, and hygiene and first aid in the fourth. There are fourteen hours of lectures and sixteen of laboratory per week in the first year, twelve of lectures and sixteen of laboratory in the second and third years, and ten of lectures and twenty-four of laboratory in the fourth. A student must not fall below the mark of 50 percent in any subject in the yearly final examinations or below 65 as an average. First-year students are allowed to repeat in the event of failure, but a second failure results in dismissal from the College. The nine-month practice period ends in oral and practical examinations which the student must pass, and he must also receive a favorable report from the supervisory pharmacist before he is granted his diploma and may work independently as a pharmacist.

THE SCHOOL OF NURSING

The School of Nursing is under the general administration of the dean of the College of Medicine, but has a principal as the immediate head. Instruction is in Arabic and English and is given by doctors associated with the College of Medicine or the Royal Hospital. It is a three-year course, and admission is limited to those who have an Intermediate-School Certificate or its equivalent. Applicants must be between eighteen and twenty-three years of age and are selected on the basis of their school records, public-examination results, and medical examinations. Students must sign a contract to work in a government hospital for four years upon graduation, but while they attend school all their expenses are paid and they receive an allowance of 1.5 dinars ($6.00) per month during the first year, 2 dinars ($8.00) during the second, and 2.5 dinars ($10) the third. A vacation of one month is granted during the period of July through September when no classes are held. Students are on duty in the Royal Hospital from seven to ten each morning and for two hours in the afternoon. Formal lectures are given daily from ten to twelve. A graduate may be released from the obligation to serve in a government hospital by paying 200 dinars ($800) to the government. In 1945–46 there were 33 girls enrolled in each the first and the third year classes and 20 in the second.

Subjects of instruction for the first year are anatomy and physiology, elementary science (including hygiene, sanitation, and bacteriology), food values and invalid cooking, theoretical and practical nursing and first aid; for the second and third years, anatomy, physiology, elementary science, gynecology, surgery and medicine, and theoretical and practical nursing. Specialization in midwifery requires an additional year of study.

THE SCHOOL OF HEALTH OFFICIALS

The School of Health Officials was established to relieve the pressing need for medical service. Graduates of intermediate schools are enrolled in a two-year course, at the end of which they are given nine months of practical experience in a government dispensary or clinic. Thus trained, health officials may be assigned to assist medical officers or be sent to outlying villages to work under the supervision of a district medical officer. They are considered to be qualified in first aid, minor surgery, and diagnosis and treatment of common diseases. On independent duty they are placed in charge of government dispensaries where treatment is free. They are responsible for the collection and reporting of data on diseases and health conditions.

No tuition fees are charged, since the student agrees to work for four years in the government health service, but in the absence of boarding facilities the student must pay for all living expenses. His salary in his first appointment is eight dinars ($32) a month, but it has been recommended that this be increased to 10 dinars ($40) after one year of practice. In 1945–46 there were 28 students in the first-year class and 26 in the second. The second-year class of that year was the first for which completion of the nine-month practice training was required.

The first-year students study inorganic and organic chemistry, materia medica, public health, bacteriology, anatomy, internal diseases (general), surgery (general), nursing, and English. In the first half of the second year they study dispensing, medical accounting, public health, skin and venereal diseases, materia medica, dentistry, endemic diseases, the ear, nose, and throat, ophthalmology, internal diseases (special), surgery (special), English, and health laws. The second half of the year is spent in practical study in the various clinics of the hospital. Having fulfilled all requirements mentioned, the student receives the Certificate of Health Official. It has been recommended that this certificate should be rated with that of the secondary school for purposes of admission to the School of Pharmacy and the College of Medicine. It is assumed that the School of Health Officials will be discontinued when Iraq has sufficient fully qualified doctors to answer all needs. However, at the present time doctors avoid village practice because of the unsatisfactory living conditions and the inability of the villagers to pay even nominal fees for private treatment.

The Law College

The Law College, located in Baghdad, serves the entire country. Its four-year course is open to men and women who hold the secondary-school certificate. The enrollment by class was in 1945–46: first year, 394; second year, 313; third year, 258; fourth year, 119. At that time the teaching staff consisted of twelve full-time members and eight part-time. Lack of classroom space necessitated parallel sessions in morning and afternoon. Fees of 15 dinars ($60) are charged all students except those who are certified to be poor or who maintain an average of 80 or higher in their marks. The high mark keeps the exemptions made on that basis at a minimum.

The first-year student takes three-hour courses in principles of law and history of Roman law, two-hour courses in constitutional law, criminal law, economics, and civil and religious law, and six hours of English a week. In the second year he takes four hours each of civil and religious law and of English, three each of economics and public international law, and two each of theory of obligations, administrative law, and criminal law. In the third year the number of weekly lectures is reduced to seventeen with six hours for Muhammadan civil law, three for public finance, and two each to theory of obligations, civil court procedure, commercial law, and criminal court procedure. In the fourth year two specializations are available, one to prepare lawyers and judges, the other to prepare local government administrators. The two groups have in common courses in Muhammadan law, land law, procedure of judgments, private international law, commercial law, Muhammadan jurisprudence, and application of criminal and civil law, totaling sixteen hours a week. The prospective judges take, in addition, two hours weekly in criminal investigation, two in legal medicine, and one in criminal psychology; the future administrators take one hour of administrative law, two of financial law, one in diplomacy, political science, and history of politics, and one in statistics.

The library, though well supplied with books in English, French, and Arabic, has yet to be organized for effective use, and it has been reported that few of the students are sufficiently well grounded in English and French to utilize the sources in these languages. The addition of a preparatory year to the course with instruction in English to overcome this deficiency has been suggested.

Students are selected on the basis of their standing in the public secondary-school examination, marks in English, geographical distribution, personal interview, and an entrance examination in English. Because of the large number of applicants from the city of Baghdad, it is sometimes necessary to limit admission to secondary-school graduates of the preceding year. The staff and the physical facilities, as well as the curriculum, are admittedly inadequate to meet the needs of the students now in attendance. It is anticipated that the establishment of a college of arts and sciences will relieve the pressure for admission to the Law College.

The College of Engineering

At the time of the American Council Commission's visit in the fall of 1945, the College of Engineering was in its second year of operation under a reorganized plan which had added a preparatory year to the old four-year course. There were 159 students, of whom 106 were boarders. Distribution by class was as follows: preparatory, 70; first-year college, 31; second-year, 6 (failures under the old plan); third-year, 33; fourth-year, 19. Only students who achieved an average grade of 70 or higher in mathematics and physics in the public secondary-school examinations may apply for admission. Final selection is made on the basis of medical examination, personal interview, proficiency in English, and geographical distribution.

The College is administered by a director under the general supervision of the Minister of Communications and Public Works. However, it is recognized that a governing body which includes professional engineers and also employers of engineers is desirable. Such a body would be more competent to evaluate a recent proposal to coordinate all technical education under a plan which would presumably improve trade training and at the same time open an opportunity for the more promising student to reach the College of Engineering and specialize in civil, mechanical, or electrical engineering. At present the College trains only civil engineers.

The curriculum provides for instruction in mathematics, English, physics, chemistry, descriptive geometry, machine drawing, and workshop in the preparatory year. Instruction throughout the College is mostly in English because most texts and references are in that language. The first-year program consists of mathematics, English, physics, descriptive geometry, machine drawing, mechanics, geology, surveying and workshop; the second year, mathematics, machine drawing, graphics, strength of materials, theory of structures, hydraulics, heat engines, theory of machines, electrical engineering, and surveying; the third, strength of materials, theory of structures, hydraulics, surveying, building construction, soil mechanics, irrigation, railways, roads, and economics; the fourth, strength of materials, theory of structures, hydraulics, surveying, municipal engineering (water supply and sewage disposal), estimating (specifications and contracts), engineering law, and design (structures, irrigation works, and buildings). Lectures and practical work total from twenty-eight to thirty-two hours per week. This curriculum will be expanded when specialization in mechanical and electrical engineering is added.

No tuition or boarding fees are charged, but students sign a contract to work for a period of five years after graduation in the Department of Public Works. During this period of employment they are paid on the same scale as other government officials with similar preparation and experience.

Educational Missions

It was in 1921, just after the foundation of the national government and the accession of King Faysal I to the throne of Iraq, that the Ministry of Education proposed sending qualified students abroad to study. That year nine of the brighter boys were picked from the secondary schools, six of whom were sent to the American University of Beirut in Lebanon and three to England. Of these, two were to study medicine in England, one was later to study agriculture in the United States, and six were to prepare for high-school teaching. From the first, the idea of educational missions was to train specialists to meet Iraq's needs in the fields of health, education, and agriculture.

Needs multiplied until foreign educational missions were projected in no less than forty-six of the most diverse subjects. These included various sciences and subjects necessary to teaching, such as physics, chemistry, biology, mathematics, history, geography, Arabic, and English. Students were sent to study education, psychology, and kindergarten methods, chiefly in America. Agriculture was studied almost entirely in America. Students went abroad to study all types of engineering, surveying, architecture, the social sciences, modern business practice, astronomy, geology, meteorology, and law. The establishment of the Royal College of Medicine at Baghdad in 1927 almost stopped the movement of medical students to foreign universities, except for graduate study, but they continued to go abroad to study dentistry and veterinary science. They went on missions to study technical trades, archeology, Islamic art, physical education, printing, library science, and home economics. For the study of painting, sculpture, and music they were sent principally to France and Italy.

As the fields to be studied on mission became more numerous, so did the

HIGHER EDUCATION AND EDUCATIONAL MISSIONS

number of students sent. The number of students supported wholly or almost wholly by the government rose from 9 in 1921 to 93 in 1928–29 and reached the peak figure of 238 in 1939–40. It declined because of World War II to 114 in 1943–44, but began to increase in 1945. Altogether more than 700 students have been sent abroad for study in the last quarter-century. The number of students who studied abroad at their own expense is at least as large.

Missions have been sent to eleven different countries, Lebanon receiving the most because of the popularity of the American University of Beirut. This University has not only prepared a large number of teachers for the Iraqi secondary schools; it has also served as a station for students going to America, to improve their English and prepare them for advanced study in the United States. After Lebanon, England receives the most, then Egypt, and in order, the United States, Switzerland, France, Germany, Sweden, Turkey, Italy, and India. World War II limited the missions for the most part to Lebanon and Egypt.

The first mission students returned to Iraq in 1926 and were absorbed by the secondary schools and the Primary Teachers College. Since then hundreds of students have returned. Most of them and most of the students who studied abroad at their own expense have gone into government posts where they are helping to fill a great need. At least 4 have attained cabinet rank, while many have become directors general of various departments and members of Parliament. The largest number have gone into teaching or administrative posts in the Ministry of Education. The next largest group are in technical posts in engineering or agriculture. Others are scattered throughout the ministries, having begun their careers as teachers and transferred from the Ministry of Education.

The budget for educational missions began in a modest way in 1921 and reached its highest peak of 62,000 dinars ($248,000) in 1938–39. It declined to 45,000 dinars ($180,000) in the war years, but is now expected to be increased. For a full-scholarship student the government pays nearly all his necessary expenses, including tuition fees, travel expenses to and from his place of study, an adequate monthly allowance for living expenses—varying from country to country—and an allowance for books and medical care. Any major medical treatment or surgery is also paid for by the government. A former government official sent on a mission receives, in addition to these benefits, one-third of his former salary to help support his family. In return for all this, the student signs a contract which commits him to serve the government one year for each year of study. In case of default or of failure to complete his studies, he must reimburse the government for all expenditure in his behalf. This system allows many a bright but impoverished student to achieve a kind of education and career that unaided he could never have had.

Regulations govern the selection of students and other aspects of this program. The latest revision of the regulations was in 1942, and, according to these, a student to be eligible must be at least a secondary-school graduate with an average of no less than 66 in the public examination and of no less than 75 percent in the subject of his specialization; he must pass a medical examination and be interviewed by the selection committee, which looks into his credentials and into a confidential report from his former school principal. To qualify for postgraduate study abroad, a student must have attained first- or second-class honors in his undergraduate course.

The Council of Ministers determines the number of students to be sent every year and the fields to be studied, basing the decisions on statements of the various ministries and departments concerning their needs. With the growth of the various colleges in Iraq, more emphasis is being placed upon postgraduate study to prepare advanced specialists. In undergraduate work there is a good deal of concentration on the various branches of engineering and technology.

Chapter 13

PRIVATE AND FOREIGN SCHOOLS

Two TYPES of schools function outside the government system: private schools, which are owned and operated by Iraqi citizens, either individual or in association; and foreign schools, which are owned and operated by foreign individuals or groups. Since Iraqi parents are forbidden by law to send their children to foreign primary schools, there are no foreign schools below the intermediate level in Iraq, with the exception of 5 primary schools for Iranian boys. Table 35 presents enrollment figures for all types of primary and seconday schools in Iraq as of 1945–46.

Both private and foreign schools are obliged to conform to governmental regulations and to have governmental approval of housing, qualifications of teachers, curriculums, and textbooks. They must follow the government's courses of study for Arabic language and social studies, and teachers of these subjects are appointed by the Ministry of Education. Admission to the first and fourth years of secondary schools is conditional upon having passed the public primary- and intermediate-school examinations.

Curriculums for both private and foreign schools follow those of the government schools so that pupils will not be handicapped in the public examinations. Since all foreign secondary schools are American, English is emphasized, and in the last two years of the course some subjects are taught in that language. The private schools for Jews teach Hebrew language and literature in the primary sections and English and French language and literature in the secondary schools. The better students in the Jewish schools are prepared to take the examinations for French certificates, as are pupils in the schools which were founded as French missionary schools.

Private schools fall into three categories: private ventures, schools maintained by associations interested in raising the standard of national culture, and sectarian schools. The private ventures are conducted for profit and appeal especially to pupils who do not find places in the government schools. Associations that maintain schools are usually composed of citizens

TABLE 35

ENROLLMENT IN PRIMARY AND SECONDARY SCHOOLS IN IRAQ, CLASSIFIED ACCORDING TO CONTROL, 1945–46

Types of Schools	No. of Schools Boys	Girls	Coeducational	Enrollment Boys	Girls
Primary:					
Private................	36	25	17	12,776*	7,977*
Foreign................	5	...	...	917	...
Government					
Day..................	681	155	56	84,229†	27,458†
Evening..............	21	...	...	4,285	...
Total..............	743	180	73	102,207	35,435
Secondary:					
Private					
Intermediate only					
Day..................	8	6	...	885	584
Evening..............	4	...	...	356	...
Preparatory only					
Day..................	1	...	...	209	...
Evening..............	1	...	...	157	...
Complete					
Day..................	5	1	...	1,507	136
Evening..............	13	...	...	2,983	...
Total..............	32	7	...	6,097	720
Foreign:					
Intermediate only.......	2	...	...	114	...
Complete..............	2	1	...	582	127
Total..............	4	1	...	696	127
Government:					
Intermediate only.......	18	17	...	3,673	1,938
Preparatory only.......	3	2	...	1,114	380
Complete..............	15	3	...	4,697	608
Total..............	36	22	...	9,484	2,926
GRAND TOTAL..............	815	210	73	118,484	39,208

* Of these, 2,579 boys and 2,326 girls were in coeducational schools.
† Of these, 4,199 boys and 4,368 girls were in coeducational schools.

who are desirous of enlarging upon the educational provisions made by the government. Associations of this sort sprang up in the early twenties and continue to look after the cultural welfare of their members through the establishment of libraries, public lectures, discussion groups, and publications, in addition to schools. Such an association is the Tafayyud Society in Baghdad, which maintains kindergartens, primary schools, and a day and an evening secondary school in that city and has recently established intermediate schools in six towns in central Iraq. The Teachers Association in 1945 started evening secondary schools for boys in Baghdad,

PRIVATE AND FOREIGN SCHOOLS

Mosul, and Basrah and a day secondary school for girls in Baghdad.

The Jewish communities in Baghdad, Mosul, and Basrah are typical of associations primarily interested in the education and welfare of their own religious group. Both free and tuition schools of kindergarten, primary, and secondary level are administered by the community councils, and it is thought that nearly all Jewish children have a chance to become at least literate. In addition to full day and evening schools, which bear resemblance to government schools of equal level, these communities have workshops for poorer children. These provide training in sewing and crafts, and elementary work in reading, mathematics, and religious literature. In the early twenties these communities took over the administration of the Alliance Israelite Universelle schools, which now supply teachers for the communities. Teachers of such schools are paid by the local community. Other religious groups, such as the Assyrians, Syrian Orthodox, Syrian Catholics, Roman Catholics, Chaldeans, and Armenians, also maintain schools.

Iraq's only foreign primary schools are the 5 which provide instruction for Iranian boys from families of merchants and craftsmen who have long been residents of Iraq. These schools are located in Baghdad, Basrah, Karbala, and Najaf. There is also an intermediate Iranian school in Basrah.

All other foreign schools are controlled and financed by American agencies. Basrah has an intermediate school of this type, and Baghdad has 3 complete secondary schools, 2 for boys and 1 for girls.

The oldest of these schools is the American School for Boys in Basrah, founded by the Dutch Reform Mission early in this century. Its principal, Dr. John Van Ess, author of *Meet the Arab*,[1] has long been associated with education in Iraq, having served as its first Director of Education during the British occupation in 1915. This School provides education through the third year of the secondary course for poorer boys from Basrah and the surrounding villages. It stresses both high academic standards and the development of high moral character, and its graduates are in demand in business enterprises of the vicinity. The School opens its extensive play areas to poor boys who live near the school and provides one of its buildings for use as a recreation center by former students and their friends. Elementary instruction in the first four grades is provided for girls; both the girls school and the primary section of the school for boys are classified as private schools and have Iraqi citizens as their principals. More advanced instruction is offered girls on an informal basis through the Young Woman's Club.

[1] New York: John Day Co., 1943.

The American School for Boys in Baghdad was founded by the Dutch Reform Mission, but is at present under an independent board of trustees of which Lowell Thomas is president. Dr. and Mrs. Calvin K. Staudt, associated with the School since its founding a quarter of a century ago, have not only made it possible for boys to qualify for the Secondary-School Certificate examination, but have also done much to develop good character and good will among the diverse groups that attend the School. High standards are maintaned in the Arabic language, but special attention is given to strengthening oral and written English. Certain subjects, such as science, mathematics, and general history are taught in the last two years through the medium of English so that graduates will be better equipped to continue their education at the American University of Beirut or in Western universities. Pupils of the School are not under obligation to take the public Secondary-School Certificate examination in order to graduate. The School has a variety of student activities and organizations, which include Arabic and English dramatic societies, an international relations club, a chorus, assemblies, a brotherhood, sports field days and intramural athletic contests, oratorical contests, and Sunday evening religious services. Recently (1945) it became a member of the Near East Colleges Association, and is being developed into a college. A boys primary school is maintained under an Iraqi principal.

The American School for Girls was founded in Baghdad in 1925 by the United Mission of Mesopotamia. A six-year primary school, under an Iraqi principal, is followed by a five-year secondary school under the supervision of an American principal. The program of the School parallels the government program, and pupils regularly take the appropriate public examinations. Here, too, the use of the English language is stressed, and graduates are fitted for higher education in English and American institutions.

The most recently established American school in Iraq is the Baghdad College for Boys, founded by American Jesuits in 1932 and now under the supervision of Rev. Francis B. Sargeant, S.J. The aim of the school is to provide a good secondary education under Catholic auspices. Located at the northern edge of Baghdad, this school is housed in the most modern school buildings in all Iraq and has extensive play areas that are ample for athletic activities. It has boarding facilities, and in 1945–46 70 of the 418 boys enrolled were boarders. The fact that fees are comparatively high determines that most of the students will be of the upper middle class. The majority are from Christian families, but other religions are represented. The program follows the public-school program rather closely,

PRIVATE AND FOREIGN SCHOOLS

and the boys take the public certificate examinations. Instruction in mathematics and science and some other subjects is in English, but care is taken to cover the appropriate vocabularies in Arabic. An extensively equipped laboratory makes individual experiment possible in physics, chemistry, and biology. A large library circulates many books for collateral reading. Informal organizations include religious groups, the International Relations Club, various sports associations, a debating society, and a staff which publishes a school paper.

Another foreign agency which is making an important contribution to education in Iraq is the British Council. Institutes have been established in Baghdad, Basrah, Mosul, and Kirkuk in which young men and young women are given an opportunity to prepare for proficiency examinations in English as well as for the London matriculation and intermediate examinations. Classes are held in the mornings for women and in the late afternoons and evenings for men. Fees are nominal and the classes are popular. A model kindergarten has also been established in Baghdad which is attended largely by children of English-speaking parents. Clubs which have both social and educational aims have been established in the larger cities. Lecture series, musical evenings, and discussion programs are regularly scheduled for these clubs. Educational films are distributed to schools and organizations in Baghdad. Although not a responsibility of the British Council, the reading rooms established in the smaller towns and larger villages by the Public Relations Department of the British Embassy are much used. Current magazines in English and Arabic are regularly supplied to these reading rooms and a small library of selected titles is available. A radio is usually supplied also.

Part Three

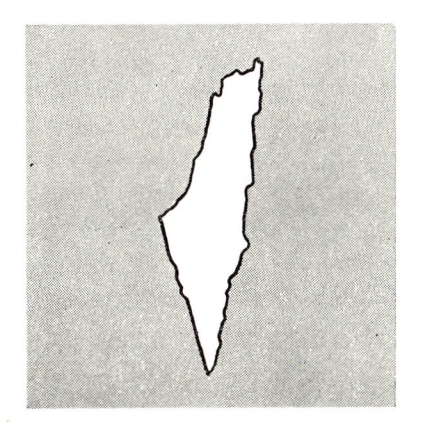

PALESTINE

PALESTINE

Population: *1,887,214 (December 31, 1946).*

Area: *10,434 square miles.*

Form of government: *(At the time of the visit of the American Council Commission in 1946) Under mandate of Great Britain, governed by a High Commissioner appointed by the King of England.*

Principal occupations: *Agriculture, industry, commerce, finance, professions.*

Principal exports: *Citrus fruits, soap and edible oils, potash, bromine, knitted goods and apparel, artificial teeth, polished diamonds, kerosene, benzine, hides and skins, chocolate.*

Principal imports: *Industrial machinery, iron bars and rods, apparel, cotton goods, wool yarn, wood, fuel oil, seeds, animal feed, food products, cattle, sheep, goats.*

Monetary unit: *Palestinian pound (£P) equivalent to approximately $4.03.*

Chapter 14

ORGANIZATION AND ADMINISTRATION OF THE GOVERNMENT (ARAB) EDUCATIONAL SYSTEM

THERE ARE TWO public educational systems in Palestine, one for Arabs and one for Jews.[1] The Arab system is administered by the Government Department of Education, the Jewish by the Educational Committee of the Vaad Leumi (General Council of the Jewish Community in Palestine). In addition, there are numerous private schools for Arabs and for Jews.

The two public systems have only slight contact with each other. The Government Department of Education has a legal right of registration of schools and of supervision over all schools that receive government assistance, including the Jewish public schools. It grants to the Jewish system an annual subsidy, most of which is given in a lump sum to the Vaad Leumi. The Government Department of Education includes on its staff a Jewish Assistant Director with Jewish inspectors who inspect Jewish schools and deal with matters pertaining to Jewish education; also the Department conducts public examinations which are open to students of Jewish as well as Arab schools, both public and private. In all other respects the two systems are separate, each following its own aims, plans, and methods. Therefore, they will be dealt with as separate systems in this report.

The organization of the Government Department of Education is shown in Chart V. At the head is a British Director of Education responsible to the Chief Secretary of the Palestine government. Powers pertaining to educational matters are strongly concentrated in the office of the Director, and the system is thoroughly centralized. Most of the funds for the Government system are derived from government revenues. Major lines of educational policy, appointment, promotion, and dismissal of teachers, sanctioning of new public schools, approval of textbooks, and the preparation and marking of secondary-school examinations are all decided

---

[1] The reader is reminded that this volume reports a survey made in 1946.

Chart V

PALESTINE: ADMINISTRATIVE ORGANIZATION OF THE GOVERNMENT (ARAB) DEPARTMENT OF EDUCATION, 1946

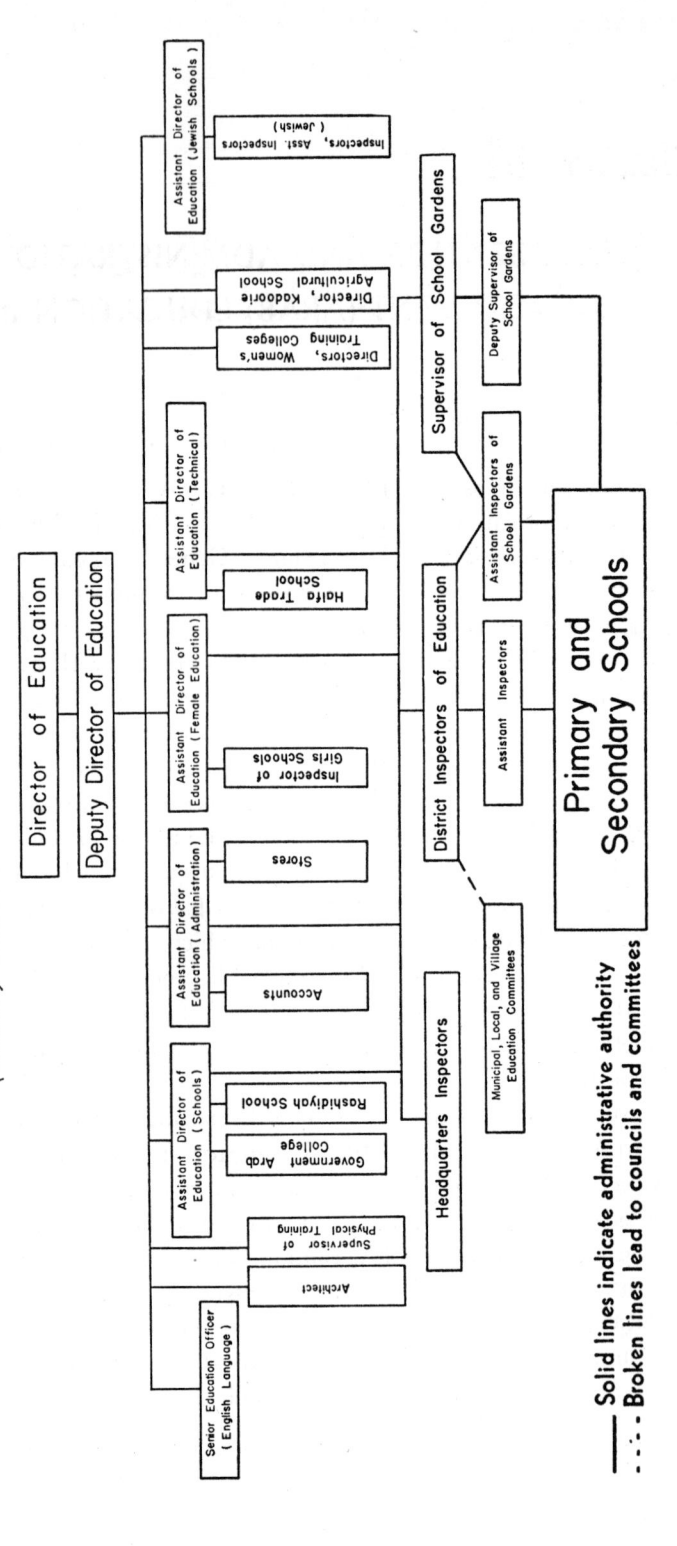

— Solid lines indicate administrative authority
- - - Broken lines lead to councils and committees

ORGANIZATION AND ADMINISTRATION

within the central office of the Government Department. Thus, the government system of public education (for Arabs) in Palestine is similar in its centralization to the public education systems of other Arabic-speaking countries. The Director of Education is assisted by a British Deputy Director and five assistant directors.

The Assistant Director of Education for Schools deals with professional and pedagogical questions and is responsible for the curriculum and textbooks; he is also director of the Government Arab College—the institution for training Arab men teachers—and has jurisdiction over the Rashidiyah School in Jerusalem, which is one of the two complete government secondary schools for boys (the other being the Amiriyah School in Jaffa[2]).

The Assistant Director of Education for Administration is responsible for the appointment, promotion, and dismissal of teachers, and for budgetary matters. He also has charge of accounts and stores, and must see that schools are adequately supplied with equipment and textbooks.

At the time of the visit of the American Council Commission in 1946, a British woman had been appointed Assistant Director of Education for Female Education, but had not taken up her duties. She was to be assisted by a woman inspector of girls schools.

The Assistant Director of Education for Technical Education, a British officer, serves also as director of the Haifa Technical School, the only government trade school in the country, and has charge of all prevocational education in elementary schools.

The Assistant Director of Education for Jewish Schools is assisted by seven Jewish inspectors who visit Jewish schools and report their findings. Neither the inspectors nor their superior may take any executive action with regard to Jewish schools—executive power resides with the educational authorities of the Vaad Leumi. The Jewish officials within the Department of Education have no concern with matters of Arab education, and no Arab officials interfere with matters of Jewish education.

There are three officials in addition to the assistant directors who report directly to the Director or Deputy Director of Education. These are the supervisor of physical training, the architect—for whom budgetary provision had been approved, though the office had not yet been filled in March 1946—and the senior education officer, who deals with all matters relating to the teaching of English—curriculum, textbooks, and methods.

The Director and Deputy Director of Education have additional respon-

---

[2] The Government Arab College maintains two upper classes of the secondary school, thus making three schools for Arabs with upper secondary classes.

sibilities in connection with three specific schools: the Teachers Training College for Women in Jerusalem, the Rural Training Center for Women at Ramallah, a few miles north of Jerusalem, and the Kadoorie Agricultural School at Tulkarm,[3] which is the only agricultural school for Arab students in the country and which also prepares teachers of agriculture for the rural schools of Arab Palestine.[4]

Next to the assistant directors and immediately attached to them according to field of specialization are the district inspectors of education, the supervisor of school gardens, and the headquarters inspectors.

Administration

District inspectors of education are actually administrators of provincial education. The six administrative districts of Palestine are grouped for educational purposes into four areas, each of which is administered by a district inspector. These educational districts are: the Jerusalem area, comprising the administrative district of Jerusalem, with headquarters at Jerusalem; the southern area, comprising the Southern and Lydda districts, with headquarters at Jaffa; the Samaria area, comprising the district of the same name, with headquarters in Nablus; and the Galilee area, comprising the districts of Haifa and Galilee, with headquarters in Haifa. Each district inspector has two assistant inspectors and an assistant inspector of school gardens. All four visit schools and classes and supervise instruction. All Arab public schools in Palestine (except those previously mentioned which are attached to a higher authority) come under the jurisdiction of the district inspectors of education. Certain matters beyond the jurisdiction of the district inspectors are referred to the central office; such matters include questions of appointment and promotion of teachers, opening of new schools or classes, admission of free pupils, most expenditures and supplies, and curriculum and textbooks. The district inspectors also act as liaison officers with municipal, local, and village councils with respect to educational affairs. The district inspector is usually an official member of the educational committees of these councils, but may delegate another person to attend meetings in his stead.

The supervisor of school gardens and his deputy have charge of the 238 school gardens which in January 1946 existed in the Arab rural schools. The supervisors lay down plans for expanding these gardens and

[3] There is also a Kadoorie Agricultural School for Jewish students at Mount Tabor (see p. 288).
[4] The teacher-training course was subsequently discontinued.

ORGANIZATION AND ADMINISTRATION

devise curriculums and approve textbooks for agricultural instruction in elementary and secondary rural schools. They keep in constant touch with the field, either personally or through assistant inspectors of school gardens.

Six headquarters inspectors, each specializing in one or more subjects, inspect the schools both administratively and professionally, recommending modifications in curriculum or textbooks in their respective fields. Each has certain administrative duties in the central office. Questions coming from district inspectors are referred first to the appropriate headquarters inspector, who may in certain instances take direct action and in others must refer the matter to higher authority.

Municipal and other local councils have been taking an increasing interest in education, and most of them now have educational committees formed in accordance with the provision of the Education Ordinance of 1933. Local authorities concentrate most of their efforts on the provision and maintenance of school buildings, but in numerous instances such councils have appointed teachers to schools in their localities at local expense, and a few municipalities have even established schools of their own. The municipality of Jaffa, the largest Arab city of Palestine, has its own school inspector. Ordinarily local authorities do not interfere in the professional aspects of their schools, as all Arab public schools follow the directives of the Department of Education.

Educational Finance

The Government Department of Education makes the major financial provision for the public-school system for Arabs and contributes to the support of the Jewish public-school system and to certain private schools. The budget allotment for education in the fiscal year 1945–46 was £P762,208[5] ($3,048,832), or 3.7 percent of the general budget of £P20,572,552 ($82,290,208). Table 36 shows the constant growth of the educational budget over a period of twenty-six years; it shows also that this has not kept pace with the growth of the total budget of Palestine. The government authorities do not deny that the lack of budgetary provision for education is perhaps the greatest obstacle to development of the Arab public-school system. Yearly about 8,000 applicants are refused admission to the elementary schools because of lack of places. In the upper elementary

---

[5] The rate of exchange of Palestinian pounds (£P) during World War II was established at $4.06. Since it varies slightly from time to time, $4 will be used in reducing Palestinian figures to approximate American dollars.

grades a rigid selection of pupils is practiced to save places for the younger pupils.[6]

The distribution of the educational budget between Arab and Jewish schools is roughly on the basis of three to one, which is approximately the ratio between the number of children of school age, five to fifteen years,

TABLE 36

RELATION OF EDUCATIONAL BUDGET TO TOTAL BUDGET, PALESTINE, 1920–21 TO 1945–46

YEAR	TOTAL BUDGET Palestinian Currency	TOTAL BUDGET American Dollars	EDUCATIONAL BUDGET Palestinian Currency	EDUCATIONAL BUDGET American Dollars	PERCENTAGE
1920–21	...	...	£E 78,000*	$ 312,000	...
1925–26	£E 2,040,332*	$ 8,161,328	£P 101,392*	405,568	4.96
1931	£P 2,374,866	9,499,464	146,988	587,952	6.19
1935–36	4,236,202	16,944,808	221,087	884,348	5.22
1940–41	7,450,355	29,801,420	302,079	1,208,316	4.05
1941–42	7,463,602	29,854,408	385,204†	1,540,816	5.16
1942–43	10,253,283	41,013,132	458,322†	1,833,288	4.47
1943–44	14,819,250	59,277,000	652,157†	2,608,628	4.40
1944–45	18,196,594	72,786,376	711,916†	2,847,664	3.91
1945–46	20,572,522	82,290,088	1,037,208†	4,148,832‡	5.04

* £E means Egyptian pound. The Palestinian pound was not established until later.
† These figures include compensatory allowances for the wartime rise in the cost of living. In 1945–46 the compensatory allowance to education amounted to 4.2 percent of the compensatory allowance of the total government budget, which was estimated at £P2,600,000 (approximately $10,400,000). The actual educational budget for 1945–46 was £P762,208 (approximately $3,048,832).
‡ Estimated.

in the two communities. The division of the budget between the two school systems for 1944–45 is given below; figures include expenditures by the Departments of Public Works and Agriculture on schools.

Allocated to	Budget	
Administration and inspectorate (Arab and Jewish)	£P 44,229	($ 176,916)
Arab schools (including grants to private schools)	537,751	(2,151,004)
Jewish schools (including grants to private schools	157,935	(631,740)
Miscellaneous	2,487	(9,948)
Total	£P742,402	($2,969,608)

The Department of Education is not the sole support of even the Arab public-school system. Budgetary limitations on funds for village school buildings and for hiring new teachers have forced Arab villagers who

[6] Jerome Farrell, *Education in Palestine, General Survey 1936–45* (Jerusalem: 1945), pp. 3–4; Jibrail Katul, *Education in Palestine*, p. 11; Government of Palestine, *A Survey of Palestine*, prepared in December 1945 and January 1946 for the information of the Anglo-American Committee of Inquiry (Jerusalem: Government Printer, 1946), p. 641.

ORGANIZATION AND ADMINISTRATION

wanted new schools to raise funds for buildings and equipment and—in the event that the government did not provide sufficient teachers—the pay of teachers as well. From April 1941 to the end of August 1945 Arab villages raised £P325,120 ($1,300,480) for the expansion of their educational facilities. Of this sum, £P121,395 ($485,580) was spent on school buildings; during this period, the central government spent only £P23,720 ($94,880) on village school buildings. The government makes no provision for furniture for village schools, but contributes books and part of the teaching materials. Some of the larger municipalities levy local rates as authorized by the Education Ordinance and have built some of their schools and appointed their own teachers. In January 1946 there were 346 public-school teachers, among a total of 2,156, on the payrolls of village and town local authorities. In addition, some of the local authorities maintain, fully or in part, hostels for elementary- and secondary-school students.

Teachers salaries and promotions

A single salary scale prevails for all teachers and personnel of the nonclerical technical staff of the Department of Education, both men and women. Personnel with equal academic and professional qualifications receive equal pay.

Lowest on the scale are "supernumerary teachers." These teachers are uncertificated—they lack even the Secondary-School Certificate. They receive an initial salary of £P60 ($240) per annum, with an annual increment of £P6 until their annual salary is £P96 ($384). Such teachers cannot progress further unless they acquire higher qualifications.

The next category, grade four, is for teachers who have no university degree but who have at least a Secondary-School Certificate. The salary range is £P96–£P192 ($384–$768) with an annual increment of £P8. For teachers of Arabic, the initial salary varies from £P96 ($384) for those having only a Secondary-School Certificate to £P152 ($608) for graduates of Dar al-'Ulum in Cairo. At certain points teachers are barred from further promotion unless they pass prescribed examinations or take up further study in approved institutions in Palestine or abroad. Teachers holding only a Secondary-School Certificate or a Palestine or London Matriculation Certificate, or their equivalent, reach the limit of £P104 ($416) annual salary. To progress beyond this point, they must pass the Teachers Lower Certificate examination, Part I, an examination in educational theory and practice. Graduates of the lower teacher-training institutions, which give professional training but are considered below the Secondary-School Certificate standard in subject training, stop at £P144 ($576) until they take the Teachers Lower Certificate examination, Part II, a subject-matter examination, or make up any deficiencies they may have in certain subjects. Manual-arts teachers who are graduates of the Haifa Technical School or a similar school are also stopped at £P144 until they pass the Teachers Lower Certificate examination, Part I. Having passed these examinations, all these types of teachers may proceed unhindered to a maximum annual salary of £P192 ($768).

Between grade four and grade three—the latter, holders of the first university degree—is another type of teacher whose qualifications are higher than the Secondary-School Certificate but lower than the first university degree. This class includes graduates of the Government Arab College and the Teachers Training College for Women, both of which give professional and subject-matter training, the former two years and the latter one year above secondary school. Such teachers start at £P136 and £P120 ($544 and $480) respectively and stop at £P192 ($768) unless they pass certain parts of the Teachers Higher Certificate examination. Similarly Dar al-'Ulum graduates who start at £P152 ($608) may not progress beyond £P192 ($768) without passing the Teachers Higher Certificate examination.[7] All teachers are thus required to achieve the intermediate standard, equivalent to about two years of university study, and to reach a higher standard in educational theory and practice before entering the next grade, starting at £P200 ($800). Exceptions are made for graduates of the American University of Beirut, who start in grade four at £P140 ($560) and may proceed to grade three without examination, and for bearers of the Palestine Diploma of Arts and Sciences, who start at £P152 ($608).

Grade three is for all teachers who have fulfilled all the requirements of the Teachers Higher Certificate examination. They may or may not be university graduates. They begin at £P200 ($800) and, according to qualifications, work up at the rate of £P8 per annum to £P280 ($1,120), or at the rate of £P10 to £P300 ($1,200). Without acquiring a university degree they may not rise above £P300 per annum. This grade includes graduates from various foreign universities (with the exception of Oxford, Cambridge, and London), at £P224 ($896) per annum; they may be promoted to grade two without examination.

Grade two is limited to university graduates and bearers of the Palestine Diploma in Arts and Sciences. The lowest salary is £P300 a year. Annual increments are £P12, £P15, and £P20, with limits on annual salaries of

[7] For details of this examination, see pp. 234-35.

ORGANIZATION AND ADMINISTRATION

£P420, £P480, and £P500 ($2,000) respectively. For most teachers the limits of this grade represent the maximum which they may attain as teachers in Palestine. For graduates of Oxford, Cambridge, and London Universities the initial salary is usually £P336 ($1,344).

Grade one, with an initial salary of £P480 ($1,920), annual increments of £P20, and a maximum yearly salary of £P600 ($2,400) holds only teachers who have graduated from Oxford, Cambridge, or London Universities, and inspectors and assistant inspectors who are graduates of any recognized university. The maximum salary of £P600 a year is, at the present time, the highest pay available to any teacher in the Government school system of Palestine.

Above the numbered grades are four grades for higher officials of the Department of Education. The grade of Senior Education Officer, starting at £P600 with increments of £P25 a year to the maximum salary of £P800 ($3,200), is for district inspectors of education and for selected headquarters inspectors, the selection being made on the basis of efficiency and length of service in grade one. The grade of Assistant Director of Education, starting at £P800 with annual increments of £P25, has a maximum of £P1,000 ($4,000). The grade of Deputy Director of Education carries a fixed annual salary of £P1,000. The Director of Education has a fixed salary of £P1,350 ($5,400). The last two grades are reserved for British officials. All British officials receive in addition to regular pay an "expatriation allowance" ranging from £P100 a year for those of lower salary to £P200 for the Director of Education.

During the latter years of World War II compensatory allowances were added to the basic salaries of all government employees to cover rising war prices. The allowances were made in accordance with an ascending scale of six steps determined by the number of the employee's dependents and his basic salary if between £P2 and £P15. Thus, a porter with a monthly salary of £P2 ($8.00) received an additional minimum allowance of £P1.778 ($7.12) if unmarried, and a maximum of £P11.258 ($45) if married and the father of four or more children. An employee with a monthly basic salary of £P15 ($60) received an additional minimum allowance of £P9.480 ($37.92) if single and a maximum allowance of £P18.960 ($75.84) if married and the father or four or more children.

The salary scale for women teachers is the same as for men, but women are required to resign if they marry.

The following figures represent the distribution of teachers in the various levels for the year 1945–46:

Rank	No. of Teachers
Supernumerary teachers at £P60–£P96 ($240–$384)	266
Grade four at £P60–£P192 ($240–$768)	1,285
Grade three at £P200–£P300 ($800–$1,200)	219
Grade two at £P300–£P500 ($1,200–$2,000)	20
Grade one at £P480–£P600 ($1,920–$2,400)*	54

* Includes some inspectors and assistant inspectors.

PENSIONS AND RETIREMENT

Palestine has two forms of retirement compensation for government teachers—a pension system and a provident-fund system.

Under the pension system, certified teachers with approved efficiency records, occupying posts declared pensionable by the High Commissioner in Council, and in service on or before March 31, 1943, are eligible for participation in the pension plan after a probation period of three years. Teachers appointed after March 31, 1943, are not eligible unless their salaries are £P300 ($1,200) or more a year. Qualified teachers may be granted a pension after ten years of service. The amount of pension is calculated on the basis of one-sixtieth of his salary at retirement times the number of years in service. A teacher of thirty years' service is entitled to a pension equal to half his last annual salary. The pension allowance, however, may not exceed two-thirds the highest pensionable salary received by the teacher during his term of service.

Teachers appointed after March 31, 1943, whose salaries are not less than £P60 ($240) and no more than £P300 ($1,200) have the benefit of the provident fund. Under this system a teacher pays the treasurer 5 percent of his monthly salary, and the government pays an identical sum; this fund gathers interest at 3 percent. On leaving the service the teacher receives the amount standing to his credit.

At marriage or resignation, women who have taught five years or more are entitled, if occupying a pensionable office, to a gratuity of one-half month's salary for every six months of service up to a maximum of the equivalent of twelve months' pay.

Educational Legislation

Education in Palestine is subject to the Education Ordinance of 1933 and the regulations attached to it. The ordinance classifies public schools according to the principal language of instruction—into Arabic schools established by the government, and Hebrew schools declared public by the Director of Education in a special schedule attached to the law. The Director of Education is required to consult with any local authority or association

ORGANIZATION AND ADMINISTRATION

that maintains a school with regard to matters pertaining to the school. A nongovernment school must be registered at the Department of Education within a month after its opening, and a representative must be appointed to represent its interests to the Director. The Director of Health or any medical or sanitary officer authorized by him may visit the school, and, on the basis of his report, the Director of Education may require the manager of a school to effect repairs recommended by the sanitary officer. In case of default, the High Commissioner, after three months, may close the school. All schools except nonassisted schools are subject to government inspection, and nonassisted schools may be visited by Department of Education officials after reasonable notice. These schools are required to furnish visiting officials with information upon demand, but the officials have no authority to interfere with internal administration or curriculum of the schools.

No one is allowed to teach in a public or assisted school without a license procured by registering with the Department. The Director of Education may demand the dismissal of a teacher who has been convicted of bad morals or seditious teaching after inquiry by a judge. A school not properly registered or one conducted in a manner contrary to public morals and order or one that retains a teacher whose dismissal has been demanded by the Director of Education may be closed by the High Commissioner.

The ordinance provides for the establishment of local education authorities. Every municipal or other local council approved by the High Commissioner constitutes a local education authority, which establishes a committee of not more than thirteen members for a municipality or local-council area and of not more than seven members for a village. These committees are composed of three categories of members: (1) members of the municipal or local council; (2) some members drawn from the locality, and (3) an official of the central administration, the district inspector of education, and the headmaster of a public school in the area. The last two are Arabs for Arabic schools and Jews for Jewish schools. The local education authorities may impose an education tax, subject to the approval of the district commissioner, "which shall be a surcharge upon any rate, tax, tithe, or due assessed and collected by the government or the local authority under the terms of any law in force from time to time." If a local education authority fails to collect a rate adequate to maintain the schools, the High Commissioner has power to impose and collect a rate as if it were a government tax.

Local education authorities are charged to provide, at the request of the Director of Education, lands, school buildings, playgrounds, sanitary and hygienic conveniences, and other apparatus for schools. They may be required to provide free tuition, materials, and books for poor students, equipment and furniture for the school, and an adequate teaching staff, and to pay such teachers as are not pensionable government officials and also to pay the government treasurer the monthly 5 percent on such teachers' salaries to make up the required provident fund.

Local education authorities may make an agreement for the maintenance of a community (denominational) school. In this event a joint committee is formed of three members from the community and one from the local education authority to manage the school. The school is then considered a public school. The proprietors are responsible for the maintenance of school buildings and grounds; other expenses are provided for according to arrangements worked out between the local education authority and the Director of Education. Children of other denominations may be accepted up to a maximum of 25 percent to fill vacant places, subject to the consent of the committee on management of the school. No child may be required to attend religious instruction contrary to the desire of his father. Children of minority faiths may have religious instruction of their own at the expense of their communities.

Any school managed by a registered public body or association other than a local education authority may, if recognized by the government, be registered as a public school. Certain conditions have to be met to obtain such recognition. It must be shown that the number of places in other public schools is inadequate; the medium of instruction must be one of the three official languages (English, Arabic, Hebrew) or Greek or Armenian; the syllabus must be approved by the Director of Education; the teachers' salary scale must not be lower than the minimum paid by the government; no teacher may be appointed or dismissed or punished with more than a reprimand without the approval of the Director of Education; the school must pay to the government the required provident-fund contribution for nonpensionable teachers; fees charged by the school must be approved by the Director of Education; finally, a number of free places must be provided. These provisions place the school largely under the authority of the Department of Education.

The Arab Educational Ladder

The Arab public-school system of Palestine forms a single, and quite simple ladder, shown in Chart VI. It rises from a kindergarten of one year (almost exclusively for girls) through an elementary school of seven years, a secondary school of four years, or, more frequently, of fewer years, 2 higher institutions for boys, and 2 schools for the training of women teach-

Chart VI

PALESTINE: THE GOVERNMENT (ARAB)
SCHOOL SYSTEM, 1946

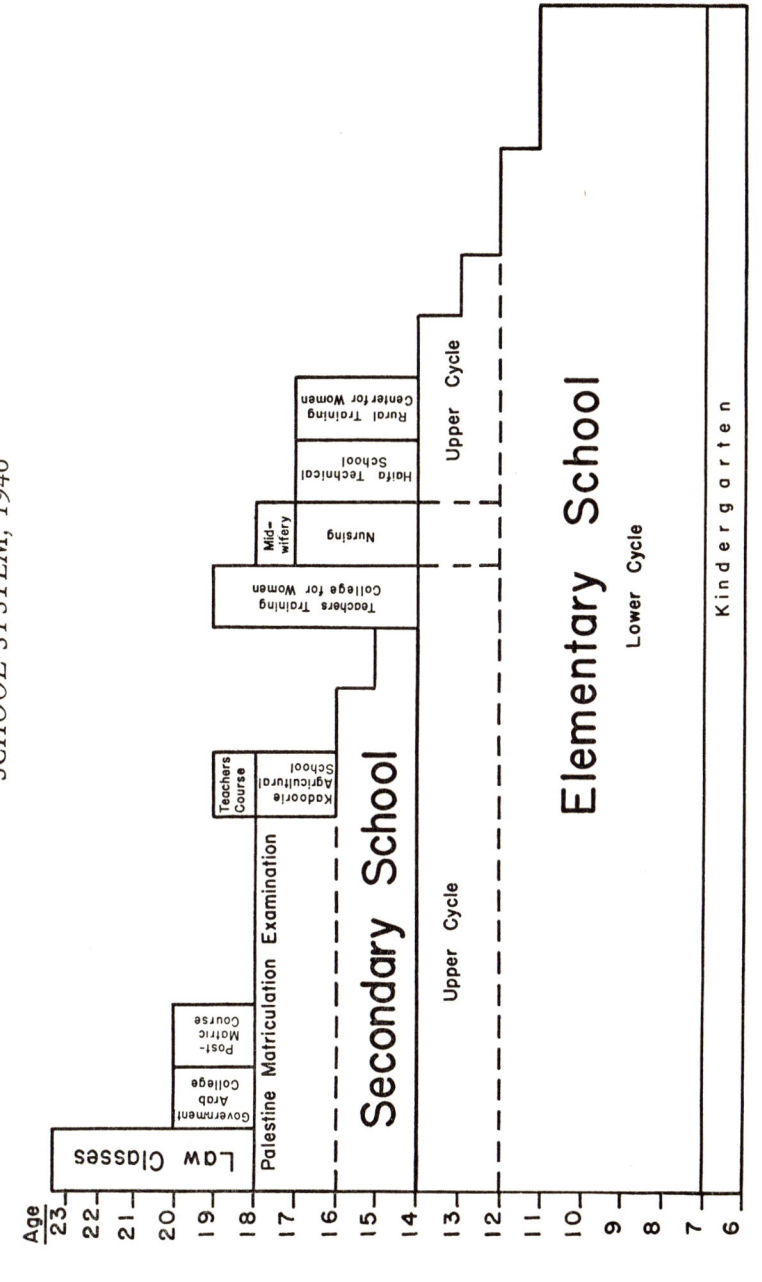

ers. Boys and girls attend separate elementary and secondary schools. The only professional education given other than teacher-training, is the five-year program of the Law Classes, which admit students from the secondary schools. The Kadoorie Agricultural School at Tulkarm admits boys from the second year of the secondary school, and the Haifa Technical School admits boys from the top class of the elementary school. Training for nurses is provided for both Arab and Jewish girls by government and mission hospitals. All of these schools will be described hereafter.

There are only three complete four-year public secondary schools for Arab boys in the country. There are thirteen schools having two secondary years, most of these being combined with some elementary grades (three of the thirteen are for girls). In addition, there are five elementary schools for boys which have added the first secondary-school class. Some of these one- and two-year schools offer courses in agriculture, including work in school gardens, along with the regular secondary program.

The two higher institutions for boys are the Arab College and the Rashidiyah School, both situated in Jerusalem. The Rashidiyah School is in fact a complete four-year secondary school with a two-year postmatriculation course of purely academic subjects. The Arab College combines academic subjects with professional education for teaching, and graduates are expected to teach in a government school. Upon completion of the course at either of these institutions, the student may present himself for the Palestine intermediate or the London University intermediate examination. This exhausts the opportunity of study within Palestine for Arab students. However, the superior student has a chance of being sent on scholarship to England if the need for teachers in the two colleges and the upper years of the secondary school is great.

Upon completion of elementary school, girls may enter one of the three two-year secondary schools situated in Jerusalem, Jaffa, and Nablus, or one of the two institutions for training teachers—the Teachers Training College for Women, in Jerusalem, or the Rural Training Center for Women, in Ramallah, for the training of rural teachers.

The public-school system for Arabs is essentially an elementary-school system to which are attached a few institutions designed to supply it with teachers. Of 82,775 students registered in 1946 in public schools conducted by the government or by local authorities under the supervision of the government, 80,901, or 97.8 percent, were in the kindergartens and elementary schools. The remaining 1,874 boys and girls, constituting 2.2 percent of the total, were distributed through all other types of schools:

ORGANIZATION AND ADMINISTRATION

secondary, teacher-training, agricultural, and technical, and the one two-year postmatriculation institution—Rashidiyah School.

In 1945–46 only 932 pupils, or 42 percent of the 2,211 pupils who had been registered in the seventh grade the previous year, were registered in the first secondary year or its equivalent. The remainder went to private schools or dropped out of school altogether—though a few may have been allowed to repeat the seventh grade.

Government Examinations

The Government Department of Education conducts five types of examinations: (1) the Palestine matriculation examination; (2) the Secondary-School Certificate examination; (3) the intermediate examination; (4) the Higher Certificate examination; and (5) the Diploma examination. In addition, the Department supervises examinations held in Palestine by the University of London and other British institutions. The Palestine Board of Higher Studies, formed in 1923, has charge of all these examinations. Its chairman is the Director of Education, and it is composed of representatives from the American School of Archaeology and various foreign educational institutions, government officials, and other persons interested in academic education in Palestine.

THE MATRICULATION EXAMINATION

The Palestine matriculation examination was first held in 1924 for 27 candidates, 9 of whom passed. It is held only once a year, beginning the first Monday in July. The candidate must be at least sixteen years old; he may be entered by a school or he may enter independently. Subjects are grouped into seven fields (common to the Secondary-School Certificate examination as well as the matriculation examination) as follows:

Group 1. Principal languages: English A, Arabic A, and Hebrew A. (The "A" indicates that the examination is designed for candidates whose mother-tongue is the language concerned and is the highest in standard of the language examinations.)
Group 2. Elementary mathematics.
Group 3. General history.
Group 4. Additional languages: Arabic and Hebrew are offered in three descending levels of difficulty, A-1, B-1, and B-2. English may be offered in two levels, A or B. Other languages which may be offered are Armenian (classical and modern), French, German, Italian, Latin, Greek (classical or classical and modern), and additional Hebrew.

Group 5. General physics. Additional physics, special physics in three parts (I: mechanics and hydrostatics; II: heat, light, and sound; III: electricity and magnetism), chemistry, botany, zoology, biology, geography, domestic science (for girls), and additional history.
Group 6. Religious knowledge: Jewish, Christian, and Muslim.
Group 7. Additional subject: physiology and hygiene.

The candidate must choose one subject in each group from 1 to 5, and a sixth subject in either group 4 or group 5. Each subject requires from one to three papers. He must satisfy the examiners in all six subjects. He is not allowed to choose the same language in groups 1 and 4 or to choose any subject in special physics if he has already chosen general or additional physics, or to choose biology if he has previously chosen botany or zoology. However, he may offer additional Hebrew if he has chosen Hebrew A from group 1 and either English or Arabic in group 4. Students may choose additional subjects from groups 6 and 7 to satisfy requirements of certain universities, but these do not count in the six required for the Matriculation Certificate. The names of these additional subjects will, however, be inscribed upon the certificate.

The examination may be taken in English, Arabic, or Hebrew, according to the candidate's choice of principal language in group 1. He is not obliged to choose his mother-tongue, but if he does he must achieve the highest standard. An Arab or a Hebrew candidate may offer a lower level if he can prove that Arabic or Hebrew is not his mother-tongue and that he studied in a school where some other language was the medium of instruction. All examinations except in modern languages, Latin, and Greek must be answered in the principal language. Modern languages are answered in their own medium. Biblical Hebrew and classical Arabic must be answered in the principal language chosen from group 1. Latin and classical Greek must be answered either in the principal language chosen or (if the candidate has chosen Arabic or Hebrew as his principal language) in English. Some practical work may be asked in the science examinations.

The Secondary-School Certificate Examination

The first Secondary-School Certificates were awarded in 1930. The examination for the certificate is conducted in much the same way as the matriculation examination except that the standard required is lower and the candidate has more freedom of choice. The student may choose his six subjects from any group, the only requirement being that he must take one in group 1. A candidate for this examination must not be more than twenty years of age and must be presented by a school, with a statement from the school that he has studied courses in the language of instruction, in one other language, in history, in mathematics, and in at least one science.

Results of the 1945 examinations are shown in Table 37.

TABLE 37

Results of Secondary-School Certificate Examination According to Language Medium, Palestine, 1945*

Medium	Number Taking Examinations	Passed Matriculation Examination Number	Passed Matriculation Examination Percentage	Passed School Certificate Examination Number	Passed School Certificate Examination Percentage	Failed Number	Failed Percentage
Arabic....	148	71	48.0	57	38	20	14.0
English...	81	34	42.0	34	42	13	16.0
Hebrew...	115	28	24.5	44	38	43	37.5

* Data supplied by the Department of Education.

The higher percentage of failure among candidates in the Hebrew medium is probably due to the lower age range of the candidates. As might be expected, since they are a highly selected group, the government school students make the highest record; students from nongovernment schools take second place, and unattached candidates have the poorest average. This is shown in Table 38.

TABLE 38

Results of Secondary-School Certificate Examination According to Type of School, Palestine, 1944

Type of School	Number Taking Examinations	Passed Matriculation Examination	Passed School Certificate Examination	Failed Number	Failed Percentage
Government schools........	85	60	21	4	4.7
Nongovernment schools....	259	88	109	62	23.0
Unattached candidates.....	44	12	...	32	72.7

Intermediate examinations

The intermediate examination is the first part of the examinations for the Diploma in Arts and Sciences, granted by the Department of Education as the equivalent of the Bachelor of Arts degree. Candidates holding the Palestine Matriculation certificate or its equivalent may sit for the intermediate examination if they are registered in a school which provides postmatriculation studies or if they have previously attended such a school and are presented by its principal. The examination may be taken in any one of the three official languages of Palestine and is held at the same time as the matriculation examination. Its subjects are in six groups. Group 1 contains English and either Arabic A or Hebrew A. Group 2 is history, which is divided into periods, each of which counts as a separate subject. Group 3 is history, philosophy, archeology, geography, and logic. Group 4 is pure and applied mathematics. Group 5 is classical and modern languages, including Armenian, Arabic B, and Hebrew B. Group 6 is physics, chemistry, biology, geology, and geography.

To pass, a candidate must satisfy the examiners in English and in either Arabic or Hebrew. If his mother-tongue is neither of the latter languages, he may substitute a modern language of Group 5. In addition, he must offer three other subjects, one being either history or mathematics, the other two to be chosen from any of the groups, though he is limited to two subjects in history. A student who offers two subjects in science and two in mathematics may be exempt from offering his mother-tongue. Aside from the languages, the choice is between a literary and scientific group of subjects. This organization is in line with the present division of courses at the Arab College and the Rashidiyah School.

The English examination consists of five papers; the Arabic examination, four; and the Hebrew examination, four. Examinations in all three are advanced in standard. History includes ancient history to Alexander, Greece and Rome, and Europe and the Near East from Constantine to 1500 A.D. Special episodes within these periods may be taken as separate subjects. The archeology of Palestine requires two papers. Pure mathematics includes two papers in advanced algebra, plane and solid geometry, and trigonometry as well as on coordinate geometry and elementary calculus. Applied mathematics includes two papers on statics, dynamics, and hydrostatics. Examinations in modern languages consist of two papers and an oral examination. General physics (not including mechanics) and chemistry require two papers each and inspection of the candidate's laboratory notebooks. For geography one paper in general and one in regional geography are required, and a third is devoted to mapwork. Candidates for the intermediate examination have been offered by the Arab College since 1941 and by the Rashidiyah School since 1944. As they are selected candidates, they usually all pass. Rashidiyah School prepares for the University of London intermediate also.

THE TEACHERS HIGHER CERTIFICATE EXAMINATION

The Higher Certificate examination, based on the same syllabus as the intermediate examination, is less exacting. Additional subjects may be included if application is made to the Board of Higher Studies early in the school year preceding that in which the examination is to be held. The examination is designed for candidates who have continued school after passing the matriculation examination and have taken studies of approximately intermediate-examination standard. Three subjects are required but with no particular grouping, and there are language tests in English and either Hebrew or Arabic. The language examinations are simpler than those of the intermediate examination, consisting of an essay and translation from English to the mother-tongue and vice versa. A candidate may offer up to five subjects in addition to the language tests.

This examination is in two parts: Part I, *a* and *b,* is in educational theory and practice, from which graduates of teacher-training colleges are exempted, but *c,* in the content of elementary- and secondary-school syllabuses, is required of all; Part II, a subject-matter examination of the University of London or Palestine intermediate-examination standard, is required of all except graduates of the Government Arab College of the class of 1943 or later.

DIPLOMA EXAMINATION

The Diploma examination, which is of the standard of an English Bachelor of Arts degree, was first held in 1929 and consists of subjects grouped under arts and under science. Only students who have passed the intermediate examination are allowed to sit for the Diploma examination. Candidates in arts must pass a six-paper examination in English and a similar one in Arabic or Hebrew. They must sit for two additional subjects if one is in the classics or for three if none is in the classics. Subjects included are as follows: general and special periods in history, archeology, and anthropology; history of political ideas; pedagogy; history of philosophy; languages (Arabic B, Hebrew B, French, German, and Armenian); and the classics, including classical history. Candidates offering in science must also satisfy the examiners in English and in either Arabic or Hebrew. If neither Arabic nor Hebrew is their mother-tongue, they may substitute either French or German. In addition, they offer three subjects, two of which must be chosen from the following: pure mathematics, applied mathematics, physics, chemistry, and biology. The third subject may be chosen from the foregoing or from astronomy, geology, geography, history of science, mathematics, and pedagogy.

The Diploma examination is held only upon application of a candidate, and very few candidates had applied in the period from 1929 to 1946.

EXAMINATIONS FOR FOREIGN INSTITUTIONS

The Department of Education, in addition to conducting its own examinations, supervises qualifying examinations held in Palestine by various British institutions, among which are London, Oxford, and Cambridge Universities, the London Association of Certified Accountants, Institute of Fire Engineers, Royal Aeronautical Society, and Institute of British Radio Engineers.

Expansion of the Arab Educational System

Table 39 represents an attempt to summarize statistically the development of the government public-school system for Arabs since the end of World War I. Beginning in 1919 with 171 schools, 408 teachers, and 10,662 students, it grew rapidly for a two-year period, adding 140 new schools, 231 teachers, and about 9,000 pupils. There followed a decade of relative stagnation, during which the number of schools remained virtually at a standstill—and in some years acually declined—the number of teachers increased very slowly, and the number of students was augmented by only about 500 a year. Lack of budgetary provision for educational expansion was largely responsible for this period of arrested development.

In 1933 the government, acting upon the recommendations of a committee of inquiry, laid down a five-year plan which was applied for only three years but which pushed the number of schools to 384 in 1935–36, the number of teachers to 1,148, and student registration to 42,765—an increase of about 18,000 over 1932. There followed another period of

TABLE 39

DEVELOPMENT OF THE ARAB PUBLIC-SCHOOL SYSTEM, PALESTINE, 1920–46

YEAR	NUMBER OF SCHOOLS	NUMBER OF TEACHERS	ENROLLMENT Boys	Girls	Total
1919–20	171	408	8,419	2,243	10,662
1920–21	244	525	13,656	2,786	16,442
1921–22	311	639	16,606	3,033	19,639
1925–26	314	687	16,146	3,591	19,737
1930–31	308	744	19,346	4,942	24,288
1931–32	305	783	19,658	5,179	24,837
1935–36	384	1,148	33,053	9,712	42,765
1938–39	395	1,312	39,702	10,318	50,020
1939–40	402	1,340	42,219	12,148	54,367
1940–41	403	1,364	42,244	12,314	56,558
1942–43	403	1,452	45,603	12,722	58,325
1943–44	458	1,729	50,450	14,340	64,790
1944–45	478	1,872	56,359	15,303	71,662
1945–46	504	2,156	65,828	16,947	82,775

stagnation, seven years in duration. The early years of this period, 1936-39, were marked by acute civil disturbances in Palestine; the final years were marked by World War II when expenditures on military operations made heavy inroads on Palestinian funds to the detriment of the social services. However, while school buildings remained numerically fixed, students kept increasing in number. The increase for this seven-year period was about 16,000. New rooms were added to existing schools at the expense of the local authorities, some new teachers were appointed, and classes were filled to more than capacity.

Naturally, this situation could not continue indefinitely, nor could the overwhelming demand of the Arab population for education be ignored. Accordingly, a new period of expansion set in and in the three years following 1943, 100 new schools were established, the number of teachers was increased by 700, and the number of pupils by about 24,000. However, the supply of educational facilities continues to fall far short of the ever-increasing demand motivated by the new Arab awakening. Recent years have witnessed a growing measure of participation in the educational effort by both local municipalities and the Arab populace in general. This participation manifests itself in the vigorous school-building activity carried on largely at the expense of the local authorities and supported by contributions from the people, in the collection of education taxes by a number of municipalities, and in the willingness of local authorities to finance new schools and pay additional teachers. In the last five years about 200 new schoolrooms were built and, in 1945-46, 346 teachers were being paid by the local authorities.

It is pertinent, at this point, to raise the question of what progress the public education system for Arabs has made toward its goal of universal education. There are about 300,000 boys and girls in Arab Palestine between the ages of five and fifteen. In 1945-46 there were about 119,000 children in kindergartens and elementary schools—private as well as public—in Arab Palestine, or approximately 40 percent of the children in the five- to fifteen-year age group.

However, if the hypothesis of the Government Department of Education that universal elementary education should be achieved through the five-year elementary school is accepted, the picture is brighter. It was estimated that on October 1, 1945, there were 156,098 Arab boys and girls in the six- to eleven-year age group. In November of the same year there were 71,663 boys and girls in the lower five grades of the public elementary school. Adding to this number the approximately 25,000 children in the corresponding grades of private schools, we find that about 96,000

Arab children, or about 62 percent of all children, in that age group were attending this basic school. Among the countries covered in this report, Palestine offers the second highest ratio between school attendance and school-age group, the highest being in Lebanon.

Table 40 shows the distribution of pupils by grades in the public schools

TABLE 40

DISTRIBUTION OF PUPILS BY GRADES, ARAB PUBLIC SCHOOLS, PALESTINE, 1944 AND 1945*

GRADES	ENROLLMENT, NOVEMBER 1944			ENROLLMENT, NOVEMBER 1945		
	Boys	Girls	Total	Boys	Girls	Total
Kindergarten	6	1,837	1,843	9	1,851	1,860
Elementary						
1	13,161	3,616	16,777	15,332	3,719	19,051
2	11,759	3,067	14,826	13,534	3,302	16,836
3	10,470	2,584	13,054	11,865	2,859	14,724
4	9,346	1,981	11,327	10,497	2,200	12,697
5	5,784	1,263	7,047	6,932	1,423	8,355
6	3,204	734	3,938	3,884	791	4,675
7	1,764	447	2,211	2,297	506	2,803
Secondary						
1	465	107	572	661	135	796
2	288	59	347	388	93	481
3	107	33	140	140	33	173
4	83	13	96	105	20	125
5	21	19	40	33	15	48
6	16	...	16	15	...	15
Technical	64	...	64	71	...	71
Agricultural	69	...	69	65	...	65
Total	56,607	15,760	72,367	65,828	16,947	82,775

* Data supplied by the Government Department of Education.

for the years 1944–45 and 1945–46. Comparison of the enrollment in classes in 1944 with that in the next classes in 1945 shows little elimination of pupils in the first four years of the elementary school. The sharp decline in numbers between the fourth and fifth grades is largely due to the fact that about half of the rural schools do not go beyond the fourth grade. Beginning with the sixth grade, the selective principle applied with increasing strictness brings registration almost to a vanishing point in the final year of postelementary education. It will be noticed that there was a gain in total registration of more than 10,000 in 1945–46.

Chapter 15

PUBLIC AND PRIVATE SCHOOLS FOR ARABS

*P*UBLIC KINDERGARTENS, found only in girls schools but admitting a few boys under six, give some instruction in reading and arithmetic, but emphasize helping the child to bridge the gap between home and school. The average age is six to seven years. However, some are as young as three and others as old as nine. Much attention is given to group games, stories, free play, and the development of personal habits of cleanliness. The aim of the kindergarten is the adjustment of the child to participation in a social group of his contemporaries. There were 1,860 children in the kindergartens of the Arab public-school system in 1944-45, only 9 of whom were boys.

Public Elementary Schools

The elementary school in Palestine has a seven-year course and in theory admits beginners who are seven years old. However, in practice, children from five to twelve are found in the first grade. Although most children enter directly from the home, some of the boys come from the *kuttabs* (native religious schools) and some of the girls from the kindergartens. The elementary school is divided into two stages or cycles.

The first stage consists of the first five grades in town schools and the first four grades in village schools. It would be incorrect to assume that villages have only four-grade schools, since almost half of the schools outside of the main towns have five or more grades. The elementary school in its lower five-year section is the vehicle with which the government hopes to stamp out illiteracy. Progress toward the realization of this goal is slow because of inadequate funds. This lower school is at present free, but economically incapable of admitting more than 60 percent of its applicants—a figure that does not take account of children in remote villages who do not apply because there is no school in their locality.[1] Out of

---

[1] Jerome Farrell, "Arab Public Education in Palestine," (Typewritten memorandum dated May 10, 1945); Farrell, *Education in Palestine, General Survey, 1936-45* (Jerusalem: 1945), p. 3.

79,141 children enrolled in public elementary schools in 1945–46, according to statistics supplied by the Government Department of Education, 71,663 were in the lower section. No selection is practiced in this section, admission to the first grade being strictly by priority of application. Every elementary-school principal is required to keep a register of rejected pupils for use in deciding subsequent priorities. As the demand for education is great and the number of places limited, the omission of tests of ability as a basis for admission has led to large classes in the lower stage. One repetition of a grade is permitted, but failures are not extensive. The authorities believe that, given adequate funds, a very near approach to universal elementary education based on the lower school could be achieved among the Arabs without compulsion.

In the higher section, which comprises the sixth and seventh grades, the limited number of places available requires a very strict selection of students. Statistics for November 1945 show 8,355 pupils in the fifth grade; the number drops abruptly to 4,675 in the sixth, and to 2,803 in the seventh, making a total of 7,478 in the higher section as against 71,663 in the lower. Promotion to the sixth grade is on the basis of merit and age. A pupil in the fifth grade of a town school or the fourth grade of a rural school who will be fourteen before the coming October and who is not eligible for promotion is automatically dropped. In the higher section, repetition of a grade is allowed only on grounds of prolonged illness or of age below the norm for the grade—indicating too rapid acceleration. Dismissal of the dullard and the idler is justified on the ground that in a system of limited facilities a repeater wastes public money by depriving a worthier child of a place in the school. Although repeaters may aggregate 12 to 18 percent of the enrollment in the lower classes in boys schools, they drop to from 3 to 6 percent in the sixth and seventh grades respectively, to 1 percent or less in the first two secondary years, and disappear altogether in the last two secondary years and the two postmatriculation classes. Repeaters among girls are even rarer than among boys.

A fee of £P1.5 (about $6.00) is charged in the sixth and seventh grades, but no competent pupil is barred from school because of inability to pay a fee. Pupils barred from the higher cycle because of low grades sometimes enter private schools, which charge higher tuition fees but practice little or no selection.

In rural Palestine an attempt is made to maintain a complete seven-grade elementary school in any strategically placed large village which is surrounded by small villages having schools of four or five grades. Better pupils from the smaller villages may then be admitted to the larger school.

PUBLIC AND PRIVATE SCHOOLS FOR ARABS

To help rural boys to complete their elementary education, boarding departments are being opened in a number of large village or rural town schools. Four hostels had been established prior to 1940, one of which, at Beersheba, provides living quarters for Bedouin boys. Nine additional hostels were established between 1940 and 1945. The hostels are small, the capacity of the entire thirteen being 459 boys in 1945. Rented houses, abandoned municipal offices, and former military quarters are utilized as hostels under the supervision of the local school authorities. The hostels are maintained by fees and by contributions from the municipalities and the Department of Education. Scholarships which include maintenance are offered to needy students by the Department.

An official report shows that in 1945–46 there were 374 village schools in Palestine with the following grade distribution:

Grade Distribution	No. of Schools
Schools with one grade	2
Schools with two grades	5
Schools with three grades	26
Schools with four grades	161
Schools with five grades	66
Schools with six grades	31
Schools with seven grades	83
Total	374

In addition to the above, there are 48 village schools maintained by local education authorities, increasing the total to 422. There are also eleven rural towns where upper elementary classes and one or two secondary classes are maintained, raising the number of schools in rural areas with seven classes to 94. In rural areas the principal emphasis is laid on the four-year elementary school. Very few schools have less than four grades. It was found that of 33 such schools in 1945, 27 had been in existence only one to three years and thus had not yet had a chance to develop a fourth grade.

Palestine alone of the countries studied in this report holds no public examinations for pupils concluding their elementary schooling.

THE ELEMENTARY COURSE OF STUDY

The elementary-school program of studies is established by the Department of Education, but modifications, subject to the approval of district inspectors, are permitted to meet local needs in rural areas. Local programs are adjusted to the presence or absence of school gardens, workshops, and teachers trained in special fields. The standard program of studies is given in Table 41. Two periods of theoretical and practical agriculture are added in the fourth and fifth grades and three in the sixth and seventh grades in schools that have school gardens.

TABLE 41

ELEMENTARY-SCHOOL PROGRAM OF STUDIES FOR ARABS, PALESTINE, 1945–46

| SUBJECTS | PERIODS* PER WEEK |||||||
	1st Grade	2nd Grade	3rd Grade	4th Grade	5th Grade	6th Grade	7th Grade
Arabic	14	11	12	8	8	8	8
English	...	...	...	8	8	8	8
Mathematics	5	5	5	5	5	6	6
Hygiene and nature study	...	3	3	2	2	2	2
Religion	5	5	5	4	4	3	3
History and geography	2	2	3	4	4	4	4
Manual training or domestic science	2	2	2	2	2	2	2
Drawing	2	2	2	1	1	1	1
Physical training	...	...	3	1	1	1	1
Total	30	30	35	35	35	35	35

* Periods are thirty minutes in length in first grade, forty-five in all others.

The first-grade course in the *Arabic language* proceeds in the usual form —reading from a simple book, conversation on familiar topics, the writing of characters of the alphabet and familiar words, and recitation of short easy pieces from the prescribed reader. Memorization of poetry and prose begins in the second grade (ten lines of each required), and *nashkh,* the most common script, is taught. Silent reading with comprehension tests is introduced in the third grade, memorization increased to at least thirty lines of poetry and twenty of prose, and *ruq'ah* script is added. The study of the fundamentals of grammar begins in the fourth year, formal grammar in the fifth. Memorization, dictation, and composition increase in difficulty through the fifth, sixth, and seventh grades. In the seventh grade special emphasis is placed upon syntax. Some fifty supplementary readers are prescribed for silent reading from the third through the seventh grades, but their use had to be curtailed during the war owing to the shortage of paper.

The *English language* is introduced in the fourth grade with a direct and conversational method. In the first half-year a conversational reader—either Morris, *An English Course for Foreign Children,*[2] Books I and II, or Bentwick, *English for Beginners,*[3] Parts I and II—is used, after which

[2] New York: Macmillan Co.
[3] New York: Longmans, Green & Co.

PUBLIC AND PRIVATE SCHOOLS FOR ARABS

West's *New Method Reader I: Alternative Edition*[4] and supplementary books are studied. Pupils are expected to complete readers one through seven together with supplementary books in the elementary school. In the early stages Arabic equivalents of English words are used, but translation is avoided. The main objects in the teaching of English are ease of silent reading involving the acquisition of a large passive vocabulary; correctness, rather than ease, of written composition, and correctness of oral expression and pronunciation.[5] The style of handwriting taught is "cursive script," which in its early stages resembles print. At the beginning of the seventh grade and thereafter disjointed handwriting is not permitted.

Attention is given to instruction in grammar beginning in the second year of the study of English—fifth grade—but systematic and formal study of grammar is postponed until the fourth year when Tipping's *English Grammar for Beginners*[6] is studied.

Recitations of selections from prose and poetry are required beginning with the third year—sixth grade. Selections are taken from the readers and supplementary books. The supplementary books include simplified editions of *The Deerslayer, The Cloister and the Hearth, Quentin Durward* in the third year, and *King Solomon's Mines, Treasure Island, Ivanhoe,* and *Silas Marner* in the fourth year. Additional books are available in most schools for pupils who wish to carry on voluntary collateral reading. Much recitation and reading in unison are used to increase the amount of practice for each pupil. The classes are sometimes divided into paired groups with one pupil asking questions and the second giving the answers. Since this is done simultaneously in a number of groups in the classroom, a visitor may get the impression of great noise and confusion. The pupils seem to be less disturbed and to enjoy the activity.

The study of *mathematics* emphasizes logical form, accuracy, and neatness in all written number work. At the lower levels there is much practice in oral work, and practical demonstrations with familiar objects are employed. The content of the courses from first grade through fourth grade is similar to the conventional outline year by year as described for the Egyptian elementary program in chapter 2. However, while elementary mathematics ends with the fourth year in Egypt, there is a fifth grade in Palestine, in which work with fractions and decimals becomes more complex, and the pupils study square root, ratios as fractions, and give some attention to averages.

---

[4] New York: Longmans, Green & Co.
[5] *Instructions for the Teaching of English in Government (Arab) Elementary Schools* (Jerusalem: The Modern Press, 1944), p. 7.
[6] New York: Macmillan Co.

In the upper division of the elementary school, sixth-grade pupils study the metric system in detail, the English monetary system, simple equations and formulas, simple and compound proportion and proportional parts and averages, simple exercises on percentages, and simple interest. They are taught to use instruments and to develop geometric ideas inductively and by observation of carefully drawn figures. In the seventh grade the pupils study square root, profit and loss, commission, insurance, simple and compound interest, debit and credit accounts, bank discount, use of checks and bills, easy problems on stocks and shares, and a slightly more advanced kind of theoretical and demonstrative geometry.

Systematic study of *science* (hygiene, nature study, and elementary science) begins in the second grade, though even kindergarten children have their attention called to objects and living things in their environment. The course is designed to interest children in nature, arouse their curiosity, and develop their powers of observation and perception. Small museums are found in many schools. Through the second and third grades they are taught health habits and the importance of cleanliness, and study common domestic and wild animals, birds, and insects. They are introduced to elementary gardening in the third grade, and in the fourth grade emphasis is upon the importance of plants, animals, and minerals to the economic life of Palestine, and industries of the country are studied. In this grade the children learn more about anatomy and the functions of various parts of the body, simple first aid, and something about the safe handling of milk and food and the methods of obtaining pure water.

More formal study of the *biological sciences* begins in the fifth grade with the classification of animal and plant life and the study of types, and education in hygiene proceeds to an elementary study of the nervous system, how to combat common diseases (such as trachoma and malaria), methods of using disinfectants and antiseptics, etc.

The *physical sciences* are introduced in the sixth grade and continue in the seventh grade. More advanced subjects in hygiene and the biological sciences are also studied in the seventh grade, including the functions of the skin and kidneys, the effects of alcoholic beverages, the prevention and transmission of serious diseases, and advanced first aid.

The study of *religion* is similar in all Arab public schools, and covers memorization of the Koran, study of the life and teachings of the Prophet, and the required practices in prayer, fasting, and pilgrimages. Non-Muslim pupils are not required to attend classes in the Muslim religion; if a Christian teacher is available, Christian religious instruction is given. In schools with Christian majorities the situation is reversed. There are three

PUBLIC AND PRIVATE SCHOOLS FOR ARABS

approved syllabuses of the Christian religion: nondenominational, Greek Orthodox, and Catholic. The last is a syllabus for the Latin (Roman) and Greek (Uniate) Catholics. Religious instruction in schools is given only by the schoolteachers. If no suitable teacher is available, arrangements are made for the pupils to attend classes elsewhere for instruction by a clergyman of the appropriate sect.

As far as possible, teaching of *history* and *geography* is coordinated in all grades. The work is organized in three cycles, the first including grades one and two; the second, the next three grades; and the third, the sixth and seventh grades. The content of the course is similar to standard outlines for the different levels, with the substitution of Palestine in the emphasis that is customarily given to the study of the native country. History and civics are correlated, with emphasis upon comparative government.

School gardening or *elementary agriculture* has become an important activity in both rural and town schools. In 1945 more than half the elementary schools had gardens, with a total acreage of 680. Boys get theoretical and practical training in making terraces and preparing ground for planting, cultivating, and harvesting cereals and vegetables. They learn pruning and grafting of fruit trees, and many schools have nurseries which supply other schools and neighboring farmers with small trees. Poultry-raising and beekeeping are included in the program of some schools. Each upper-grade pupil has a plot for which he takes complete responsibility. Other plots, particularly in schools with large gardens, are cared for by groups of pupils as communal activities. The pupils get experience also in raising flowers in plots arranged to improve the appearance of the schools.

Other standard subjects include courses in manual training and domestic science, drawing, and physical training, following the conventional pattern through the grades, making use of native materials with which to work, and organized with regard to the age and ability of pupils. (See description of similar courses in Egypt, chapter 2.) In physical training, the upper grades have formal drills with planned exercises, and sports days among groups of schools arouse great interest as culminating activities of the year's work.

SCHOOL BUILDINGS AND GROUNDS

Construction of school buildings has been greatly retarded by lack of funds. Many elementary schools occupy former dwellings, and some are in buildings formerly used as military establishments or local government offices. New buildings that have been financed by the Department of Education are designed to permit expansion by the addition of wings or stories. Such buildings are of stone, with floors and stairways of tile or cement. The standard classroom is about 24 feet 6 inches by 23 feet and is furnished with double benches and desks with hinged tops or an open shelf. The blackboard is painted plaster or wood. Playground space is usually small, and, as it is rarely paved or graveled, it is dusty in dry weather and very muddy during the rainy season. Most schools have developed attractive flower gardens, shrubs, rock gardens, and trees. Village schools for the most part have been constructed by funds raised locally. Those of more than one room are built as a row of rooms opening upon a south porch—a type of construction that makes future addition of rooms or wings relatively easy. Outside latrines are common. Running water is available in some schools and is used for irrigation in many of the school gardens. In other schools wells have been dug to insure a water supply for the school and its garden. Some schools are supplied with pumps.

Public Secondary Schools

As shown in Chart VI (page 229), secondary education in government schools for Arabs in its complete form consists of a four-year course above the elementary school with separate schools for boys and girls. However, there are only three complete public secondary schools for Arab boys in Palestine—the Arab College and Rashidiyah School, both in Jerusalem, and both also providing two years of postmatriculation work, and a school at Jaffa, which graduated its first regular four-year class in 1946. (The school at Jaffa had previously offered a two-year commercial course above the second year of secondary school.) There are 13 schools having two secondary years (3 of the 13 being for girls), and there are 5 elementary schools for boys which have added the first secondary-school class.

The only four-year secondary schools open to girls are those in connection with the two schools of teacher training—the Teachers Training College for Women, in Jerusalem, and the Rural Training Center for Women, in Ramallah. The school in Jerusalem has a five-year program, four of secondary education and one of professional training to prepare teachers for urban elementary schools. The Ramallah Training Center was a three-year course above the elementary school at the time of the visit of the American Council Commission, but a fourth year was to be added in 1946–47. The Center prepares teachers for rural schools for girls. Two-year secondary courses for girls existed in Jerusalem, Jaffa, and Nablus.

Secondary education for Arabs in government schools is limited to a highly selected group. The selective principle begins to function at the

PUBLIC AND PRIVATE SCHOOLS FOR ARABS

end of the fifth elementary grade and becomes increasingly rigid at the end of the seventh grade. Selection is based upon age and class standing. All the secondary schools, except the one at Jaffa, have boarding departments and receive pupils from other parts of the country. Tuition and boarding fees are low, and exemptions from all or part of the fees are made for bright pupils without financial resources. A few of the town elementary schools include one or two years of the secondary course, from which the best pupils are transferred to a complete secondary school.

THE SECONDARY PROGRAM OF STUDIES

The secondary school program is designed primarily to prepare pupils for the Palestine matriculation examination, previously described. Those

TABLE 42

PROGRAM OF STUDIES FOR ARAB SECONDARY SCHOOLS, PALESTINE, 1945–46

Subjects	1st Year	2nd Year	3rd Year Literary Section	3rd Year Scientific Section	4th Year Literary Section	4th Year Scientific Section
Muhammadan law and religion	1	1	2	2	2	2
Arabic	7	7	5	5	5	5
English	8	8	8	8	8	8
Elementary mathematics	...	...	5	5	4	4
Arithmetic	2	2	...	...	...	...
Geometry	2	2	...	...	...	...
Algebra	3	3	...	...	...	...
Additional mathematics	...	...	...	5	...	5
Physics	3	3	5	5	5	5
Chemistry	1	1	...	3	...	3
Botany	1	...	...	...	...	...
Zoology	...	1	...	...	...	...
Latin or Greek	...	...	4	...	4	...
History	3	3	3	3	4	4
Geography	2	2	3	...	3	...
Drawing	1	1	...	...	...	...
Physical training	1	1	...	...	...	...
Manual training	...	...	2	2	2	2
Preparation	...	...	2	1	2	1
Total	35	35	39	39	39	39

who pass with distinction are awarded the Palestine Matriculation Certificate; those who pass at a somewhat lower standard receive the Palestine Secondary-School Certificate. Minor variations in program exist in different schools—for instance, the course for girls is modified to permit study of the domestic arts and sciences—but the general pattern is shown in Table 42.

Arabic and English, the courses for which the most time is allowed, include the study of composition and précis writing, grammar, translation, and literature of appropriate difficulty and content.

In *English literature,* the students study Shakespeare's *Hamlet, Macbeth, Richard II, Henry IV, Henry V,* and *King John;* selections from A. S. Collins' *Treasury of English Prose,* including works of Ascham, Sidney, Jonson, Milton, Dryden, Addison, Burke, Hazlitt, De Quincey, Huxley, Chesterton, and Churchill. Selections from *Essential Poetry* by A. A. Mendilow and D. Melitzky (published by Aaronson in Jerusalem) are studied, including poems by Milton, Dryden, Pope, Gray, Wordsworth, Byron, Keats, and Tennyson.

Mathematics is studied in parallel classes rather than in sequence. In arithmetic the elementary-school subjects are reviewed, and more difficult problems and irregular figures in mensuration are added. Topics in algebra include quadratic equations, graphs of functions of first and second degree, roots, maxima and minima, fractional and negative indices, and logarithms to the base 10. The scope in geometry is equivalent to the first four books and book six of Euclid, including loci and areas of triangles and parallelograms of which the bases and altitudes have commensurable lengths. Work in trigonometry includes the functions of simple angles and their application to the solution of right-angle triangles. Additional mathematics for the third- and fourth-year students of the scientific section provides more advanced study in algebra, geometry, trigonometry, coordinate geometry, and calculus.

General physics includes the usual topics in mechanics, heat, light, sound, electricity, and magnetism; both qualitative and quantitative aspects are studied, and laboratory work is emphasized.

Chemistry covers elementary inorganic chemistry, and laboratory work and practical applications are stressed.

Botany ranges through morphology, physiology, and classification and uses of plants, and students are expected at the end of the course to be able to recognize at least 100 of the common plants of Palestine, including 30 trees.

The year of *zoology* includes general principles of animal life, growth and metamorphosis, structure and mode of life of types within the different orders with their distinguishing features.

In *Latin* the students progress through the elementary study of the language to reading selections from Lucretius, Catullus, Vergil, Horace, Seneca, Ovid, and Martial.

Elementary *Greek* is followed by the reading of Plato's *Apology* and Euripides' *Hippolytus.*

Above: The Arab College, Jerusalem, Palestine. (Photo by Schwartz. Courtesy of Public Information Office, Government of Palestine.)
Below: The Kadoorie Agricultural School (Arab), Tulkarm, Palestine

Above: Arab boy at blackboard in a primary school, Palestine. (Photo by Schwartz, Jerusalem.)
Below: A Government village school (Arab), showing part of the school garden, Palestine. (Photo by Schwartz, Jerusalem.)

BETWEEN CLASSES AT A GOVERNMENT VILLAGE SCHOOL (ARAB), PALESTINE

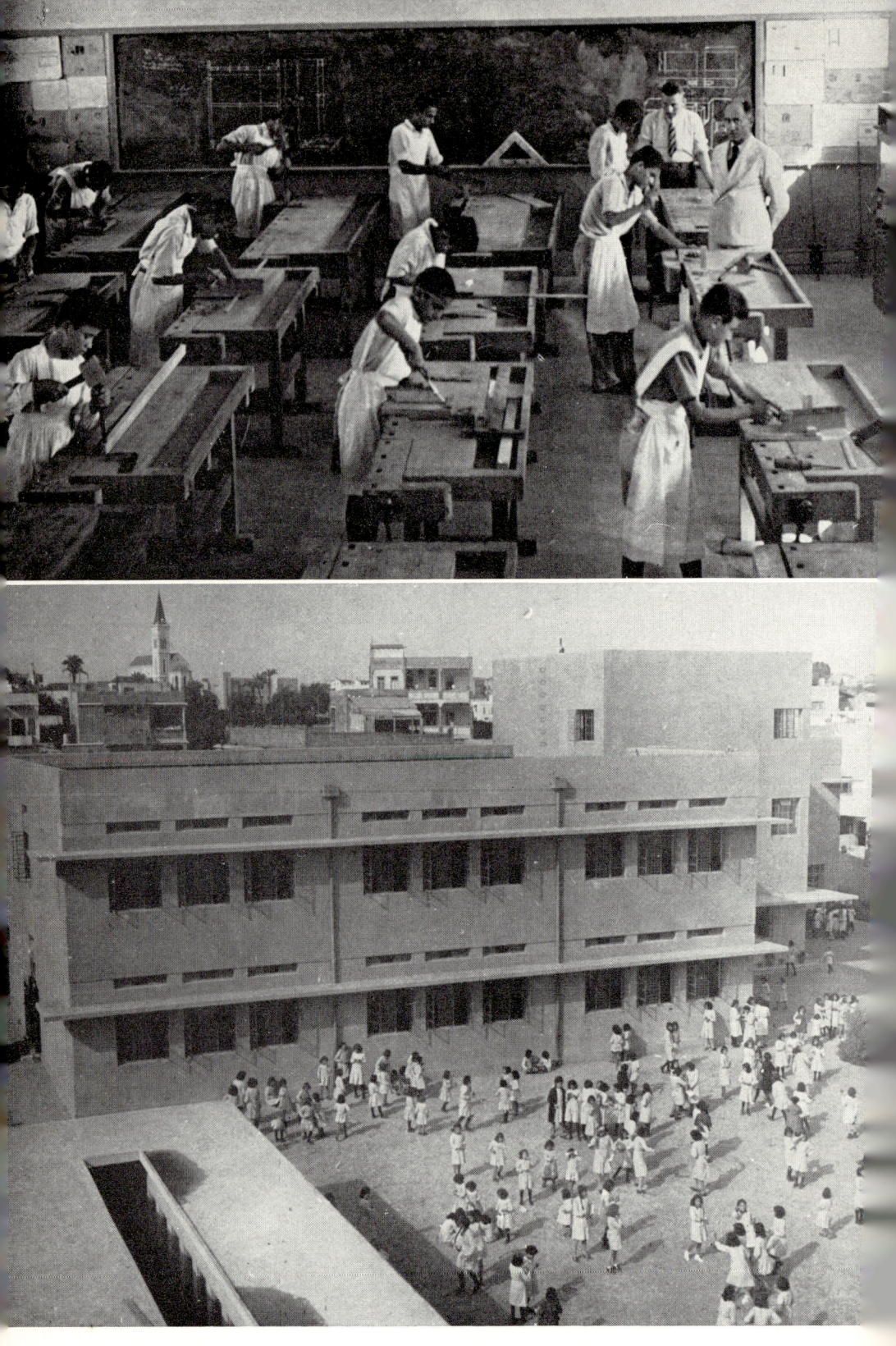

Above: A class in industrial arts, Government secondary school for boys (Arab), Jaffa
Below: Recess at the Government primary school for girls (Arab), Jaffa

Although the *history* program emphasizes Arab history in its proper chronological order, it takes up ancient, medieval, modern, and English history in successive years.

Geography, which is correlated as much as possible with history, deals with sea basins, their coasts and hinterlands rather than with land masses.

Postmatriculation Study

Qualified students are provided with two years of postsecondary study at the Arab College and at Rashidiyah School (both in Jerusalem), the course being divided into literary and scientific sections. At the Arab College all postmatriculation students study Arabic language and literature, English, theoretical and practical pedagogy, logic, philosophy, hygiene, the elementary-school syllabus, and manual training. In addition, literary-section students take special courses in history, Latin or Greek, and philosophy, and those in the scientific section take pure and applied mathematics and the history of science. After this two-year program the student is prepared to teach in the elementary and lower secondary schools of Palestine or to proceed to English universities, Egyptian universities, or the American University of Beirut. The program at the Rashidiyah School omits professional preparation of teachers and includes premedical and pre-engineering subjects. In 1945–46 the Arab College had 19 students enrolled in its postmatriculation course, Rashidiyah School, 26; total enrollment for each school in that year was 88 and 310 respectively.

The Teachers Training College for Women, in Jerusalem, provides a fifth year of professional training for teachers after the four-year secondary course. Fifth-year study includes psychology, principles of education, history of education, methods of teaching the different elementary-school subjects and review of the subject matter of such subjects, and practice teaching. The total enrollment of the College in 1945–46 was 104 girls, 15 of whom were registered in the fifth-year course.

The Rural Training Center for Women,[7] at Ramallah, originally a three-year course above the elementary school, was to add a fourth year in 1946–47. Tuition and board are free, though a small fee is charged for school activities. Pupils are accepted from all parts of Palestine. In 1945–46 the total enrollment was 35. Each year the girls study the following subjects at increasingly higher levels: Arabic and English language and literature, mathematics, history, geography, science, hygiene, child welfare, religion, agriculture, drawing, sewing, theoretical and practical

---

[7] Not of postmatriculation standard but included here because it is a parallel institution in function.

housecraft, cooking, laundry, physical training, and singing. In the second and third years the program includes psychology and methods of teaching. It was planned that the fourth year, which had not been introduced at the time of the American Council Commission's visit, would provide professional training, history of education, special methods of teaching elementary-school subjects, and practice teaching, as well as additional work in academic fields. In this school the practical aspects of subjects are emphasized, and special attention is given to agriculture and poultry-raising.

Nursing Education

Training for nurses is provided for both Arab and Jewish girls under government auspices in seven government hospitals and seven mission hospitals. Instruction in the government hospitals is in English, and ability to speak, read, and write English is the only academic entrance requirement, although girls are expected, but not required, to have completed the elementary-school course. The nursing course is three years in length. The nursing profession has not developed any great popularity in the country, and applicants are few in spite of the fact that students receive a small stipend in addition to maintenance. Only 18 girls were in training in 1945–46 in the Government Hospital in Jerusalem. The training is largely practical, with five hours a week devoted to lectures. There are lectures on principles and practices of nursing each year. In addition the first-year program includes anatomy, physiology, and hygiene; the second, anatomy, physiology, infectious fevers, spread of infection, tropical diseases, and bacteriology; and the third, medicine, surgery, obstetrics and gynecology, and infant and child care. A fourth year provides opportunity to specialize in midwifery, mental diseases, child welfare, or ophthalmology.

Vocational Training for Boys

The Haifa Technical School has had an interrupted career. The physical plant, relatively well equipped and with sufficient land for expansion, was established in 1936. Almost immediately, however, all facilities were taken over by the military during the disturbances of 1936–39 and were retained during World War II. The School was returned to the Department of Education in 1945. All pupils are boarders. They pay a total fee of £P12 ($48) a year for tuition, board, room, and laundry. The study program includes Arabic and English languages and literatures, technology and trade theory, freehand and mechanical drawing, workshop mathematics, science, and workshop practice. The course is three years in length, each year having forty-five periods per week. Workshop practice consumes eighteen periods the first year, twenty-seven the second, and thirty-three the third. Boys are selected on a basis of class standing in the elementary school and a personal interview by the director of the Technical School. Approximately one-sixth of those considered acceptable in terms of their elementary-school record were approved for admission in 1945. The School offers elementary trade training in fitting and machinery, carpentry and joinery, blacksmithing and welding, and automobile repair and maintenance. There were plans to extend the program to include training of electricians and builders. It is expected that graduates will eventually reach the foreman status in industry. Of recent graduates about one-third are working in the oil refinery, one-third in War Department workshops, and the remainder are teaching or are in private employment.

TRAINING IN AGRICULTURE

The Kadoorie Agricultural School at Tulkarm provides a two-year course for Arab boys who have completed two years of secondary school; at the time of the visit of the American Council Commission in 1946 it provided a third year for training men teachers of agriculture, but the teacher-training course was subsequently discontinued. The School was occupied by military forces during the disturbances of 1936–39 and World War II, and some parts of the School farm had not yet been released in the spring of 1946. Originally under the government Department of Agriculture, the School was transferred in 1944 to the Department of Education. It was planned to convert the general course to a three-year program, with a fourth year for teachers, beginning with 1946–47. In 1945–46 the first-year program included botany, chemistry, physics, zoology, physiology, Arabic, English, agricultural mathematics, horticulture, vegetable-growing, agriculture, poultry-raising, animal husbandry, agricultural economics, and drawing. Second-year students took field and fodder products, farm management, cooperatives, animal husbandry, plant protection, soils and fertilizers, irrigation, drainage and terracing, botany, horticulture, vegetable-growing, chemistry, surveying, bookkeeping, and poultry-raising. The year of professional training for teachers consisted of general methods of teaching, classroom management, model lessons, drawing, study of the syllabus of the elementary school, methods of teaching agriculture, and practice teaching. Five afternoons a week are devoted to practical agriculture in each of the three years.

In 1945–46 there were 11 in the class for teachers and 51 in the first two classes. All pupils are boarders and are selected on the basis of their records in the secondary schools. In 1945–46 it was necessary to refuse admission to two-thirds of the qualified applicants because of lack of accommodations. Total annual fees amount to £P24 ($96), but approximately 30 percent of the pupils are exempt. The school has 150 acres of land, 110 of which are being farmed. Of the 27 graduates in 1945, 23 are teaching, 1 is employed by the Department of Agriculture, 2 had formed a partnership to operate a dairy, and 1 was unemployed in 1946. It was reported that out of a total of 120 graduates, only 2 were working as agriculturists. The small number engaged in farming is attributed to the difficulty in raising capital to purchase land and equipment.

Law Classes

Aside from the two-year courses of postmatriculation study at the Arab College and at Rashidiyah, the only opportunity for higher public education is provided in the Law Classes, which are administered by a board of fourteen members called the "Law Council." The council is responsible for appointing examiners, forming a disciplinary court for lawyers, approving credentials of foreign lawyers, and registering Muhammadan law counselors.

The course is five years in length, with examinations at the end of the second, fourth, and fifth years. Applicants with a London or Palestine Matriculation Certificate or the Secondary-School Certificate with credit in five subjects or the equivalent are admitted. Some officials of the police department, general administration, and courts are admitted on the recommendation of their department heads and without the minimum requirements; however, such students must pass the matriculation examination before they are permitted to practice as lawyers.

Classes are held from five to eight in the evening, four nights a week. Fees are £P12 ($48) a year. In 1945–46 there were 553 students enrolled, including 20 Jewish girls. Lectures are in English, Arabic, and Hebrew. Subjects studied in the first two years are civil law, criminal code, jurisprudence, law contracts, constitutional law, Ottoman land law, law of religious endowments (*waqf*), political science, and religious (*shari'ah*) law (optional). Third- and fourth-year students take law of evidence, commercial law, private and public international law, law of torts, forensic medicine, and legal history. Successful candidates in the intermediate examination, given at the end of the fourth year, are permitted to work as solicitors, but are not permitted to plead before the courts. The Diploma examination at the end of the fifth year is on civil and criminal procedures, Palestinian ordinances, legal drafting, and bookkeeping. Graduates must practice with a lawyer for two years before being permitted to plead before the courts.

Private and Foreign Schools

Since private schools for Jews are part of the Hebrew system, they are included in the description of that system and will not be discussed here. Private schools, whether for Jews, Christians, or Muslims, may be classified as "assisted" and "nonassisted" schools.

In 1942–43, the latest year for which detailed statistics were available, there were 236 private schools, Muslim and Christian, enrolling 20,334 pupils—13,071 boys and 7,263 girls—which were receiving small grants-in-aid from the government. There were 322 schools with 20,141 pupils—11,942 boys and 8,199 girls—which did not receive aid. Most of the unaided schools were kindergartens and elementary schools, and those of Christian denominations were in the majority. Private schools have considerable freedom to develop their own programs, but tend to follow the government pattern quite closely, since most private-school pupils prepare for the government examinations. Increasingly, however, foreign-school pupils are substituting the London matriculation examination for the Palestine examination.

Most private and foreign secondary schools include elementary classes, and foreign schools usually begin a foreign language (the native language of the country of origin of the founders) in a lower grade than is the case in government schools. In many of the foreign secondary schools this foreign language becomes the language of instruction for much of the work in the upper grades.

Foreign schools have been established by missionary groups of many nationalities including British, American, French, German, and Russian. Usually they were started to emphasize religious education, but some, such as the Syrian Orphanage, were started to provide practical training in preparation for earning a living in a trade. The contribution of both private and foreign schools has been significant. Limitations of time made it impossible for the American Council Commission to visit many examples of either type.

The Friends Schools for boys and girls at Ramallah are providing a somewhat freer type of education on an American model. Buildings and grounds are designed for school activities. The programs of the schools follow the government plan, but instruction in most of the classes of the secondary school, other than Arabic, is in English. Many of the students are preparing for advanced work in the American colleges at Beirut. Work in the boys school begins with the fifth grade of the elementary school and ends with the fourth year of the secondary. Boys in grades one through four are taught in the school for girls. The girls school had, in 1946, a kindergarten, seven elementary grades, and three years of secondary school. There were 95 boarders in the girls school, 3 of whom were from Ethiopia, while the boys school had 100 boarders. A number of the boarders in each school were from Transjordan.

The Terra Sancta College for boys in Jerusalem is administered by American Franciscans. It has a kindergarten, seven elementary grades, and four secondary years. In 1946 there were 335 boys in the kindergarten and elementary school and 170 in the secondary school. The building, erected in 1926, was constructed for use as a school and is well equipped. Instruction is in Arabic in the elementary school and in English in the secondary school. French and Hebrew are offered in addition to the government program. The school prepares boys for the Palestine matriculation examination, which they usually take in English. The majority of the boys are Christians, but a considerable number of Muslims and Jews are also enrolled.

The Najah College at Nablus and the Rawdat al-Ma'arif in Jerusalem are two private schools which the American Council Commission visited. Both are schools for boys and offer kindergarten, seven years of elementary school, and four years of secondary. They have boarding departments with approximately 100 boarders each. Instruction is in Arabic, and emphasis is placed upon the literature and history of the Arabs and the Muslim religion. They were established, partly, at least, to provide an alternative opportunity to the foreign missionary schools. Their objective is to provide education of a high standard for leaders with strong national aspirations.

Two more agencies provide educational opportunities on a more informal basis. The Young Men's Christian Association in Jerusalem has a beautiful physical plant, centrally located, which serves as a cultural center for Jerusalem. Excellent equipment is available for an extensive physical-activity program, and a large auditorium is popular for many types of activities. There were 423 public programs held in the auditorium in 1945. The facilities of the building are used by 125 different organizations. Classes are held in languages, including English at six levels, Arabic, French, Hebrew, German, Spanish, Russian, and Italian; matriculation classes in mathematics, physics, and chemistry; commercial subjects—shorthand, typing, and bookkeeping; lecture courses in art and modern history; music, with classes in fundamentals of music and a chorus; tutorial classes for adults, organized by Edwin Samuel; and a school for government messengers. There are 1,900 members of the Association from thirty-four different national backgrounds. The second agency, the British Council, has institutes in the principal cities of Palestine where instruction in English and other matriculation subjects is given in the late afternoon and evening. The Institute of Higher Studies in Jerusalem, also sponsored by the British Council, prepares students for the London intermediate examination.

The Department of Social Welfare of the government of Palestine supervises education and care of children and young persons in 28 institutions for Arabs enrolling a total of 1,940 pupils, and 102 institutions for Jews having a total of 5,136 pupils. Approximately 40 percent of the pupils in both Arab and Jewish institutions are girls. The institutions for Arabs provide for social cases (delinquents), orphans, and physical defectives (largely the blind) and are administered by voluntary societies, religious bodies, and by the government. A relatively small number of the pupils (136) receive their education in schools outside the institutions. The institutions for Jews provide for social cases, immigrant children (mostly orphans), orphans, mental and physical defectives, and neglected children. These are maintained by voluntary lay and religious groups and societies, private individuals, the Jewish community (through the Vaad Leumi), and municipal agencies. Slightly more than one-third (1,731) of the children receive their education in schools outside the institutions.

Chapter 16

THE HEBREW EDUCATIONAL SYSTEM

MODERN HEBREW education in Palestine was initiated in the second half of the nineteenth century by European Jews who became interested in the welfare of Palestinian Jews, numbering about 25,000 at that time. Schools were founded by individuals, Jewish philanthropic societies, and, significantly, by Jewish national organizations that sprang up in tzarist Russia during the eighties and aimed at Jewish colonization in Palestine and the revival of the Jewish tradition there.

While most of these schools used the language of their founders' country, some—notably those fostered by societies of Russian origin, the Hovevei Israel and the Bilu, which were interested in bringing about a revival of the Hebrew language—began to teach school subjects in Hebrew. As Hebrew up to that time had been the language of religious liturgy and literature, but not that of everyday speech, its revival required considerable effort. Textbooks had to be written and terms for scientific concepts had to be coined before Hebrew could become the medium of instruction. It was natural that the advocates of teaching in Hebrew should sooner or later come into conflict with some of those who taught in the vernacular languages. Such a conflict, developing shortly before World War I, led to the foundation of a Jewish Board of Education (Vaad Hachinuch), which in 1914 assumed control of 12 schools in which all instruction was in Hebrew. Financial support was shared by Jewish settlers in Palestine and the Zionist Organization. From this nucleus the present Zionist school system developed.

At first only elementary schools were established, but in 1905 the world's first Hebrew secondary school, the Hertzliah Gymnasium, was opened in Tel-Aviv. Soon a second, the Hebrew Gymnasium, opened in Jerusalem, and in 1912 foundations were laid for the Haifa Technion.[1]

[1] Much of the information on the Hebrew educational system in Palestine is based on the following references: Executive of the Vaad Leumi, *Memorandum Submitted to the Commission of Enquiry into the Jewish Education System* (Mimeographed; Jerusalem: Vaad Leumi, 1945), pp. 1–4; Noah Nardi, *Education in Palestine, 1920–1945* (Washington, D.C.: Zionist Organization of America, 1945), pp. 17–19; Isaac B. Berkson, "Zionist School

THE HEBREW EDUCATIONAL SYSTEM

After World War I and the promise of the Balfour Declaration to facilitate the establishment of a National Home for Jews in Palestine, the Zionist schools increased rapidly in number. Many schools controlled by other associations transferred to the Zionist Executive, which now established a Department of Education in Palestine. In 1918–19 Palestine had 94 Jewish schools enrolling a total of 10,172 pupils. Thus, it happened that the Zionist Executive assumed responsibility for the majority of Jewish schools in Palestine while the government took over administration of the Arab public-school system which had previously been maintained by the Ottoman government. Out of this situation developed Palestine's dual educational system.

In the early days of the mandate the Palestine government classed schools administered by the Zionist Executive with private schools and allowed them the small grants it allowed other private schools on the basis of 200 mils per pupil per year, a sum equal at that time to little more than a dollar. The Jewish community, however, claimed the right under Article 15 of the mandate to maintain its own schools in its own language and secured governmental recognition of the Zionist educational system as the Jewish public-school system. As a result the grant was substantially increased, to £E20,000 ($80,000) annually. In 1932 the Jewish school system was transferred from the Jewish Agency—which had taken over from the Zionist Executive—to the Vaad Leumi, the National Council of Palestine Jews. Thus, the main responsibility for the control and support of the Jewish public-school system, after it had been borne for some years by international Jewry, was assumed by the Palestinian Jews.

Administration

In theory the Government Department of Education has supreme authority over all education in Palestine; in practice the government has no direct administrative control over Jewish educational institutions. The Education Ordinance of 1933 authorizes the Government Department of Education to inspect and supervise schools, and the Department includes a Jewish Assistant Director of Education to advise the Director of Education on Jewish school matters and five (to be increased to seven) Jewish inspectors who may visit grant-aided Jewish schools. The government grants the Vaad Leumi Department of Education an annual lump sum for the support of Jewish public schools, and the Vaad Leumi controls the

System," in I. L. Kandel, ed., *Educational Yearbook of the International Institute of Teachers College, Columbia University, 1928* (New York: Bureau of Publications, Teachers College, Columbia University, 1929), pp. 177–79.

distribution. The Government Department of Education, empowered by the Education Ordinance to license teachers, rarely exercises this right with respect to Jewish teachers.

Actual responsibility for the Jewish public education system rests with the Vaad Leumi as the executive council of the Elected Assembly representing the registered Jewish community of Palestine (Kneseth-Israel). However, the Jewish Agency, which handed over that responsibility to the Vaad Leumi in 1932, declared that it would continue, as the representative of world Jewry, to share responsibility for the Jewish educational system in Palestine and to give financial assistance within the limits of its ability. Accordingly, the Jewish Agency makes a substantial annual grant to the Vaad Leumi and has one representative on the Executive Education Committee of the Vaad Leumi. In addition, the Zionist Organization of America, one of the Jewish Agency's most active sections in the Jewish National Home movement, maintains its own education committee, which concerns itself with Jewish education in the United States and elsewhere, including Palestine.

The administrative organization of the Jewish public-school system is shown in Chart VII. Supreme authority rests with the Vaad Leumi, which is responsible to the Elected Assembly representing Palestinian Jews. Three distinct parties are represented in the assembly: the General Party, a middle-of-the-road group; the Labor Party, the leftists; and the Mizrahi Party, composed of Orthodox Jews who have agreed to join the Zionist movement. It is important to bear these parties in mind, as the political divisions and ideologies within the community are reflected in the educational organization and in the curriculum of the school system.[2] Control of the administration is in the hands of three other bodies, the Executive Education Committee, the Board of Education (Vaad Hachinuch), and the Government Department of Education. In addition, there are three school councils—one for each of the political trends—and the local education authorities.

The Executive Education Committee of the Vaad Leumi consists of six members; three are representatives of the Vaad Leumi (one for each party or trend); one representative of the Jewish Agency; one representative of the Tel-Aviv municipality; and one representative of the central administration of the rural schools. A representative of the Government Department of Education is an advisory member, but he has no vote. This Committee decides all matters of policy and finance, but its important decisions, such as the approval of the budget and the appointment of the Director

---

[2] For further description of the differences between the schools, see p. 278.

Chart VII

PALESTINE: ADMINISTRATIVE ORGANIZATION OF THE
HEBREW PUBLIC SCHOOL SYSTEM, 1946

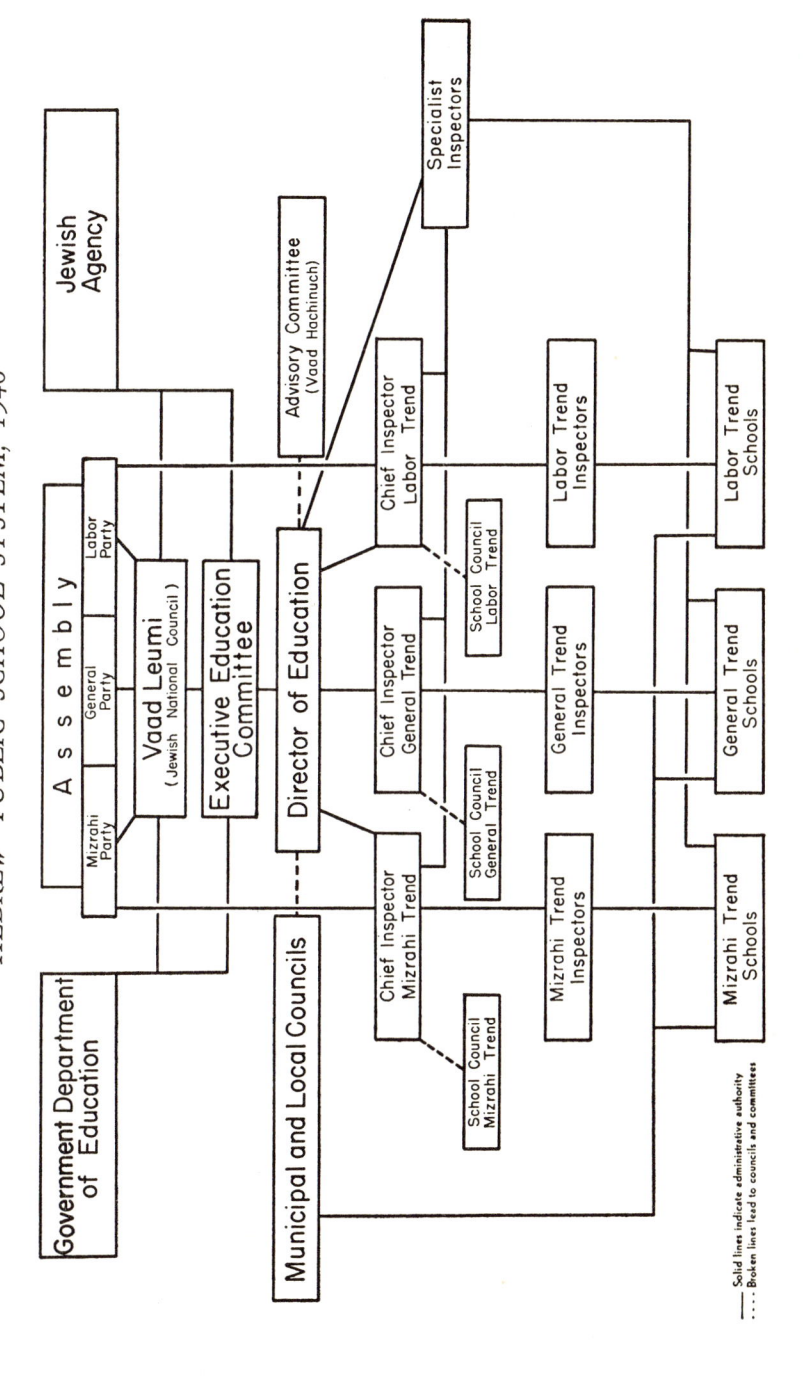

—— Solid lines indicate administrative authority
···· Broken lines lead to councils and committees

of Education, are subject to the approval of the Vaad Leumi. The Director's appointment must be approved also by the Jewish Agency.

The Board of Education (Vaad Hachinuch) was formed in 1914 to administer Zionist schools, which had at that time begun to teach all subjects in Hebrew. Since its administrative functions were assumed by the Executive Education Committee (in 1932), its functions have been advisory, dealing with questions of curriculum, teaching, and purely educational affairs common to the three trends. It is composed of thirteen members including the Director of Education as chairman. Other members are: four from the General Trend, two each from the Mizrahi and Labor Trends, three from the Teachers Organization, one nominated by the Hebrew University, and one by the Executive Education Committee.

The Department of Education is the executive body responsible for conducting the school system. Its Director has the over-all administration and supervision of the Jewish public education system; appointed by the Vaad Leumi with the concurrence of the Jewish Agency, he answers to both bodies for carrying out their policies and those of the Executive Education Committee. The Director has three chief inspectors, one for each trend, who organize inspection within their trends and deal with school affairs therein, including appointment of headmasters, teachers, and inspectors subject to the approval of the Director. The chief inspectors have both administrative and supervisory duties and are in effect assistant directors. In another sense, however, they are more than assistants, for in matters affecting any one of the trends, the Director may not take action without first consulting the chief inspector of that trend. Conversely, the chief inspector may not take action without the approval of the Director. In cases of disagreement the matter is referred to the Executive Education Committee for decision. Decisions in matters affecting all the trends are made in a meeting of the Director and the three chief inspectors, and in case of disagreement the Director's decision prevails.

Each trend has, for the further protection of its interests, a school council made up of nine members, with the chief inspector as chairman. Members are appointed by the trend organization concerned. Aside from the chief inspector there are the three trend representatives on the Executive Education Committee and the Advisory Education Board, three teachers from schools of the trend, a representative of parents in urban areas, and a representative of parents in rural areas. Through their chief inspectors these councils submit recommendations to the Executive Education Committee for the appointment of trend inspectors and to the Director of Education for the appointment and dismissal of teachers. In addition,

THE HEBREW EDUCATIONAL SYSTEM

they decide on curriculums to be used in the trend schools after securing the approval of the Advisory Education Board and the Director of Education.

The Vaad Leumi employs thirty inspectors, eight of whom are women. Six of the women are kindergarten inspectors, the other two are inspectors of special subjects. Of the twenty-two men inspectors, two are inspectors of secondary schools for the General Trend, thirteen are trend elementary-school inspectors, and seven are specialist inspectors. Trend inspectors visit only schools of their own trend, but specialist inspectors visit schools of all trends. The Mizrahi and Labor inspectors visit both elementary and secondary schools of their trends. The inspectors not only supervise teaching, but also make recommendations regarding teachers and principals and perform various administrative duties. There are no district inspectors. All inspectors report to the central office. The municipality of Tel-Aviv employs its own inspectors who function apart from those of the Vaad Leumi. The Government Department of Education has its own Jewish inspectors who visit Jewish schools regularly. Thus, there is a dual inspection system of Jewish schools.

It may be recalled that the Education Ordinance of 1933 set up procedures for creating local education authorities and empowering them to register land in their names for school purposes and to levy an education rate, or tax. In cities and villages of mixed population, two education committees may be set up, one for the Arab and one for the Jewish schools. The local Jewish authorities own most of their school land and buildings, and the number of such authorities levying local education rates is on the increase. Concerning other educational functions of the local authorities there is no standard practice. In Tel-Aviv, for instance, where the city pays most of the cost of education and receives a comparatively small grant from the Vaad Leumi, the local education committee exercises considerable authority, maintaining and inspecting schools and appointing and dismissing teachers with the approval of the Vaad Leumi Department of Education. However, in newly established small settlements, the community may furnish a school building, and the Vaad Leumi or the community may provide the teachers and pay them. In some communal settlements teachers who are members of the settlement are treated as other residents and receive no pay; in such settlements the school is usually an integral part of all phases of community life.

The general organization of the Jewish public-school system is marked by a good deal of flexibility. Local education authorities are taking an increasing share of responsibility, and the three trends enjoy considerable freedom and, indeed, authority to recommend their own inspectors, principals, and teachers and to decide curricular matters. In contrast to the Arab public-school system, the Jewish system is rather thoroughly decentralized and allows freedom for individual and group initiative without much interference from above. Only on this basis was it possible, in the last twenty-five years, to induce the conservative Mizrahi and the leftist Histadruth (Labor organization) to bring their schools within the Jewish public-school system.

This system has not escaped criticism from various sources. Some Jewish educators, feeling that a more unified curriculum is desirable, regard with disfavor the reflection of factional differences in the schools.[3] The Government Director of Education stated his criticisms and recommendations in two messages addressed to the chairman of the Executive Education Committee of the Vaad Leumi.[4] His contentions are summarized in the following paragraph.

The three-party system prevents the Vaad Leumi Director of Education from being master in his own house. It is a wasteful system in which inspectors may inspect only schools of their own category and in which the effective voice in the appointment of teachers is that of the party councils whereas the teachers are supposed to be employees of the Vaad Leumi, which is responsible for their salaries and pensions. Moreover, teacher training under the three trends is not as efficiently carried out as it should be, and a sound financial policy for the system cannot be followed as long as trend councils, with or without connivance on the part of trend inspectors, open unnecessary schools and classes, financially committing the Government Department of Education to expenditures in excess of its funds. To quote the Government Director: "All important matters in the Department are decided by a committee of four persons, the Vaad Leumi director with three inspectors, each of whom owes primary allegiance neither to the director nor through him to the Vaad but to the 'category' which he represents. Unity has one certain vote only, and whatever the inspectors may feel about each other's distinctive views, two at least are almost inevitably supporters of separation." He contended that variation of the curriculum to suit the convictions of the three parties could be accomplished without prejudice to a unified and efficient system of administration, proposing an administrative cadre in which inspectors should be weaned from their party affiliations and in which sole responsible administrative authority in the central office would rest with the Director of Education and his deputy, subject to the instructions of the Executive of the Vaad Leumi. At the same time safeguards could be established to maintain the special character of the sectional schools.

[3] Nardi, *op. cit.*, pp. 235–44.
[4] Jerome Farrell, "Jewish Educational Administrative Reform," *Palestine Review*, Vol. IV, No. 35 (Jerusalem), March 29, 1940, pp. 431–35; *Memorandum of the Director of Education on Organization of the Hebrew Public School System, Delivered to the Chairman of the Vaad Leumi Executive Education Committee on 1st July, 1940* (Jerusalem: Government Press, 1940), 11 pp.

THE HEBREW EDUCATIONAL SYSTEM

The Commission of Enquiry sent by the British Colonial Secretary to investigate the Jewish system of education in Palestine agreed in general with the views of the Government Director of Education. The Commission was headed by Sir Arnold McNair, a well-known English educational leader, and included among its four other members Sir Leon Simon, a prominent English Jew who stands high in Zionist circles. In its report the Commission deplored the fact that education, which in most countries is a unifying force, is in Palestine "separatist" in its effects. "The two main systems—the Jewish and the Arab, or Government, system—have no contact with one another."[5] Moreover, partisan influences within the Jewish system went beyond separatism in the form of the three trends and tended to develop "sub-trends within some of the trends. Recent history has shown the danger of enabling political parties to control or influence curriculum and teaching in the schools, and the Jewish public-school system stands in this danger today."[6] On the subject of administration, the Commission recommended a system of checks and balances created to satisfy mutual lack of confidence rather than one of individual personal responsibility. It considered that local education authorities, as a rapidly developing factor, should occupy a more prominent position in the administrative set-up. It made recommendations designed to weaken the influence of the trends and to strengthen that of the local authorities, and to put more effective control in the hands of the Director of Education.

Educational Finance

At the close of World War I the Zionist Organization bore the brunt of the cost of the Jewish system of education; in 1918–19 it paid £P65,844 ($273,376), or 88.7 percent, of the total expenditure on Jewish education, while the Jewish community together with other sources paid only £P8,348 ($33,392), or 11.3 percent. The sum paid out by the Zionist Organization increased annually until 1922–23, when the Palestinian Jewish community had recovered sufficiently from the war to increase its contribution to the support of the schools. From that point on the share of the Zionist Organization decreased. At about the same time the government began to contribute small sums toward the maintenance of the school system, gradually increasing the grants as the years passed. These facts are revealed in Table 43.

[5] Great Britain, Colonial Office, *The System of Education of the Jewish Community in Palestine,* Report of the Commission of Enquiry Appointed by the Secretary of State for the Colonies in 1945, Sir Arnold McNair, Chairman (London: H.M. Stationery Office, 1946), Colonial No. 201, pp. 6–7.
[6] *Ibid.,* p. 16.

TABLE 43

Sources of Income for the Maintenance of the Jewish Public-School System, Palestine, 1918–45*

Year	Zionist Organization (Jewish Agency) £P	Dollars	Per cent	Palestinian Government £P	Dollars	Per cent	Jewish Community and Other Sources £P	Dollars	Per cent	Total £P	Dollars
1918–19	£P 65,844	$263,376	88.7	£P ...	$ ...	...	£P 8,343	$ 33,372	11.3	£P 74,187	$296,748
1920–21	113,539	454,156	77.0	2,238	8,952	1.5	31,796	127,184	21.5	147,573	590,292
1930–31	75,271	301,084	40.8	19,175	76,700	10.4	90,177	360,708	48.8	184,623	738,492
1940–41	35,000	140,000	6.8	56,000	224,000	10.9	421,500	1,686,000	82.3	512,500	2,050,000
1944–45	116,760	467,040	7.9	127,082†	508,328	8.5	1,245,721‡	4,982,884	83.6	1,489,563	5,958,252

* Executive of the Vaad Leumi, *Memorandum Submitted to the Commission of Enquiry into the Jewish Education System* (Mimeographed; Jerusalem: Vaad Leumi, 1945), p. 63, except for 1944–45, figures for which are taken from Great Britain, Colonial Office, *The System of Education of the Jewish Community in Palestine*, Report of the Commission of Enquiry Appointed by the Secretary of State for the Colonies in 1945, Sir Arnold McNair, Chairman (London: H.M. Stationery Office, 1946), Colonial No. 201, p. 49.
† Includes £P55,000 ($220,000) cost-of-living allowances.
‡ Includes £P15,412 ($61,648) paid by the government as arrears from previous years.

THE HEBREW EDUCATIONAL SYSTEM

From a position of virtual dependence upon the Zionist Organization for maintenance of its public-school system in 1918, the Palestinian Jewish community has, in the course of twenty-seven years, traveled a long way toward self-support in education. In that period it has increased its share from 11.3 percent of the total cost of education to 83.6 percent. The contribution of the Jewish Agency, although greater now than that of the Zionist Organization in the peak year of 1920–21, represents only 7.9 percent of the total cost, while the government's substantial grant constitutes only 8.5 percent of the total.

The 1944–45 contribution of the Jewish community can be traced to the following sources:

Sources	Contribution	
Vaad Leumi (general funds)	£P 4,000	($ 16,000)
Deficit to be met by Vaad Leumi Department of Education*	37,721	(150,884)
Local authorities and local Jewish Communities	556,000	(2,224,000)
School fees	584,000	(2,336,000)
Unclassified	64,000	(256,000)
Total	£P1,245,721	($4,982,884)

* Including £P16,412 ($65,648) arrears from previous years paid by the government.

The contributions of the local authorities and communities and the school fees provide the greater share. The fees, which constitute the largest item of all, are collected for every type of school, including the elementary, with the exception of the elementary schools in Tel-Aviv which are tax-supported and collect only a registration fee. The schools in the communal settlements charge no fees except to outsiders. Otherwise the elementary-school fees constitute from 25 to 32 percent of the elementary-education expenditure; and, in the elementary classes attached to secondary schools, 94 percent.

Both the Vaad Leumi and the Jewish community have protested the system's heavy reliance upon the collection of fees, especially in elementary schools, which in most civilized countries are free and tax-supported. The McNair Commission suggested that the burden of the fees for elementary education, now borne by individual parents, should be more generally distributed by rates collected by local authorities, and it commended the municipality of Tel-Aviv for the step it had taken in that direction.[7] However, the Jewish educational authorities argue that the fee

[7] *Ibid.*, pp. 50–51.

policy is necessitated by the inadequacy of the government's grants-in-aid,[8] and challenge the governmental allocation of funds between the Arab and the Jewish systems.

Allocation of expenditure within the Jewish public education system for 1944–45 was estimated as follows:[9]

Allocated to	Expenditure	
Central (Vaad Leumi) and local administration	£P 89,563	($ 358,252)
Kindergartens	150,000	(600,000)
Elementary schools	850,000	(3,400,000)
Secondary schools	270,000	(1,080,000)
Teachers colleges	40,000	(160,000)
Vocational schools	50,000	(200,000)
Continuation classes	30,000	(120,000)
Evening classes	10,000	(40,000)
Total	£P1,489,563	($5,958,252)

Further study of Table 43 on sources of income for the Jewish educational system reveals that the budget has grown to twenty times its 1918–19 size and ten times its 1920–21 size. This growth is attributable to three principal factors: (1) the rapid increase in Jewish population, largely the result of immigration, until it was in 1944–45 about ten times its 1918 figure; (2) the affiliation with the public-school system of a large number of schools that were formerly outside it; and (3) wartime inflation, which was mainly responsible for the trebling of the budget between 1941–45.

However, the budget of the Vaad Leumi Department of Education does not cover the entire cost of the schools for which it is more or less responsible. In fact, it was estimated that the budget actually provides £P340,000 ($1,360,000), or less than 25 percent of the estimated total cost for 1944–45, and that it receives most of this sum from the government Department of Education (£P127,082, or $508,328) and from the Jewish Agency (£P116,760, approximately $467,040), the rest of the income being derived from fees from schools (£P584,000, approximately $2,336,000), contributions by local authorities (£P556,000, or $2,224,000), the Vaad Leumi general funds (£P4,000, or $16,000), and miscellaneous sources (£P64,000, or $256,000). A deficit of £P37,721 or $150,884 was expected. The major portion of funds provided in the budget is handled by the local authorities.

For budgetary purposes, schools are divided into three categories: (1)

---

[8] Executive of the Vaad Leumi, *op. cit.*, p. 3; Nardi, *op. cit.*, pp. 227–33.
[9] Great Britain, Colonial Office, *op. cit.*, p. 49.

THE HEBREW EDUCATIONAL SYSTEM

schools owned and supported by the Vaad Leumi—most of the public schools in Jerusalem, Haifa, Tiberias, and Safad, the Mizrahi teachers colleges in Jerusalem, and schools for workers' children in Tel-Aviv and Petah-Tikvah belong in this category; (2) schools nominally owned by Vaad Leumi but actually supported by local authorities, although the Vaad Leumi is the ultimate guarantor for the payment of teachers' salaries and makes grants-in-aid to the local authorities; and (3) schools owned and supported by newly founded settlements and receiving only minor grants from the Vaad Leumi, which does not guarantee salaries of the teachers—after a period of trial (usually not more than two years) these schools are transferred into category 2. There is an additional group of schools which are owned and maintained privately with no financial assistance from the Vaad Leumi, but which have affiliated themselves with the Vaad Leumi and are supervised by it.

The relative strength of these four categories of schools is indicated by pupil enrollment in each in 1942–43.[10]

Schools	Enrollment
Maintained by Vaad Leumi	10,630
Maintained by local authorities	36,340
Assisted	2,206
Private affiliated	17,563
Total	66,739

Relative expenditure of the categories—grouped somewhat differently—was as follows in the same year, 1942–43:[11]

Category	Expenditure		Enrollment
Vaad Leumi	£P138,000	($ 552,000)	10,630
Local education authorities	465,000	(1,860,000)	43,953
Private affiliated	217,000	(868,000)	12,156
Total	£P820,000	($3,280,000)	66,739

For the last few years the Jewish educational system has been operating on an increasing financial deficit, which in 1944 amounted to £P49,111 ($196,444). Moreover, the Jewish Department of Education has been obliged to borrow from the Teachers Pension Fund a sum which, with

---

[10] *Ibid.*, p. 47. Quoted by the McNair Commission from a report by A. Ulitzer and L. Kroner, presented to the Vaad Leumi, on the financial and administrative situation in the Jewish school system.

[11] Government of Palestine, "The Social Services," *A Survey of Palestine,* Report for the Anglo-American Committee of Enquiry (Jerusalem: Government Printer, 1946), chap. xvi, p. 669.

interest, totaled £P53,041 ($212,164) in 1943–44. In all, the Department's indebtedness came in that year to £P102,152 (about $408,000). At one time in the late twenties, teachers went without pay for as long as six months, and during the recent war failure to adjust teachers' pay to rising prices led to strikes which resulted in raising the salary scale of teachers throughout the system and increasing the financial burden of the Department of Education.

Jewish educational leaders have been urging the government to increase its grant to Jewish education to ease this financial strain. They have challenged the formula on which the government bases the apportionment of funds for the schooling of children between five and fifteen years of age. In 1945–46 it was estimated that there were about 300,000 Arab children as compared with about 100,000 Jewish children in this age group. The Jewish leaders argue that hardly more than a third of the Arab children are actually in school, while the Jews make every effort to approximate universal elementary education for their children, and that government grants should, therefore, take into account the number of children actually in attendance.

The Government Department of Education maintains that such a basis for calculation would be unjust to the Arabs, whose yearning for education remains unsatisfied because of inadequate budgetary provision. Thousands of Arab children are denied admission to primary schools yearly—10,079 in 1945–46—in localities that have schools. An unknown number do not apply for admission simply because no schools exist in their localities. There are instances of villages gathering contributions and building a school only to be told that no teachers are available because of budgetary limitations. Therefore, the government maintains that any additional sums available should go to provide places for Arab children who are being refused, and the Jewish system benefits in the meantime from the increased allotments in the ratio of Jewish to Arab children of school age.

The McNair Commission recognized the financial problem of the Hebrew educational system, admitting that the Jewish community bore a heavy burden of school fees in addition to taxes, but did not see its way to suggesting any amendment to the formula. Given the assumption that Palestine's paramount educational need is universal literacy, the Commission concluded, "the logical method of distributing the money available for education is to divide it between the two communities in the ratio of their school-age population." It went on to point out that the chief problem was posed, not by the formula, but by the inadequacy of the government's budgetary provision for education.[12]

[12] Great Britain, Colonial Office, *op. cit.*, pp. 51–58.

THE HEBREW EDUCATIONAL SYSTEM

Teachers' Salaries and Pensions

The scale of salaries for Vaad Leumi teachers which was in force at the beginning of World War II classified elementary-school teachers into three groups with maximum and minimum monthly salaries as follows:

Elementary-School Teachers	Minimum	Maximum
Teachers in grades one to four	£P 8 ($32.00)	£P14.4 ($ 57.60)
Graduates of teachers colleges	10 (40.00)	18.0 (72.00)
University graduates with training in education	14 (56.00)	26.0 (104.00)

With wartime inflation these salaries became inadequate, but financial difficulties of the Vaad Leumi Department of Education and its differences with the government Department of Education over the salary scale prevented adjustment of the salary scale until 1943–44, when a special wages commission, one member of which was a government representative, was appointed to draw up proposals for a new scale. The commission recommended raising the salaries of the groups of teachers to minimums of £P10, £P12, and £P16 and maximums of £P17, £P20, and £P28 respectively and increasing family allowances from £P1 to £P1.5 per dependent. In addition, it recommended a special qualifying examination to raise salaries of teachers of long service to £P24 instead of the customary £P20. Delay in the application of this new scale led to a teachers' strike at the beginning of the school year 1944–45. The strike lasted for more than a month and was settled by the acceptance of the recommended scale with an alteration in the maximum basic salary of graduates of teachers colleges (the largest group of teachers) to £P21 with a special allowance of an additional £P1 a month. Cost-of-living allowances were on the same scale as obtained for officials of Jewish national institutions. In addition, salaries for the previous year of 1943–44 were amended by a special grant of £P2 a month and a two weeks' salary plus family allowances. This scale was to be in force for the year in progress, 1944–45. For 1945–46 further amendment of the scale was made by raising the special allowance from £P1 to £P2 a month. As it now stands, the scale starts with an initial monthly salary for a teachers-college graduate of £P12 plus £P2 special allowance and leads to £P21 plus £P2 for a teacher of nineteen or more years of service. In addition, a married teacher gets £P1.5 for his wife and also for each child, so that a teacher of nineteen years or more of service who has a wife and three children receives £P29 ($116) a month. Additional cost-of-living allowances may reach up to £P16.218 ($64.87) for a teachers-college graduate who has a wife and two children.

Recent salary scales have been agreed to only on a year-to-year basis.

The Teachers Organization is pressing for a basic salary scale of £P15–£P30 plus family allowances of £P2 for each dependent and a cost-of-living allowance equal to that of other employees of Jewish national institutions. The teachers are showing determination to be treated as other Vaad Leumi officials are treated, and it is probable that other revisions of the scale will result in yet higher pay, despite the deficit in the Vaad Leumi educational budget.

Secondary-school teachers have in general fared better than elementary-school teachers. The Vaad Leumi maintains no secondary schools; and owing to the fact that all secondary schools are private, fee-charging institutions, there is no standard scale for the teachers. Most schools, however, have accepted the demand of the Teachers Organization for a scale beginning with a basic salary of £P20 and rising to £P35, plus a family allowance of £P2 per dependent and a cost-of-living allowance of 50 percent of the salary if such an allowance is higher than the rate paid to officials of the Vaad Leumi.

A pension fund has been set up to which teachers contribute 5 percent of their salaries and the Vaad Leumi a matching sum. For the last few years, however, the Vaad Leumi has not only ceased making its own contributions to the fund, but also has been financially pressed into borrowing the pension deductions from the teachers salaries.[13] By 1943–44 the indebtedness of the Department of Education to the pension fund had mounted to £P53,041 ($212,164). However, it was making payments to pensioners out of its current budget, including cost-of-living allowances, and an actuarial study of the pension fund was being conducted with a view to establishing a solvent pension plan.

The Hebrew Educational Ladder

In the broadest sense, the Hebrew educational system in Palestine comprises kindergartens, elementary and secondary schools, teachers colleges, vocational schools, the Hebrew University, and the Haifa Technion, and, in addition, continuation evening classes for workers and elementary evening classes for underprivileged boys and girls who are obliged to work during the day. Some of these schools have affiliated themselves with the Vaad Leumi system and are subject to departmental inspection, while others maintain a strictly private character and have to rely largely on fees for support. It is only by taking account of the Hebrew educational institu-

---

[13] *Ibid.*, p. 84, quoting the report by Ulitzer and Kroner on the finances of the Department of Education of the Vaad Leumi.

THE HEBREW EDUCATIONAL SYSTEM

tions in all their variety that it is possible to give a meaningful picture of the educational ladder.

The ladder of Hebrew education is shown in Chart VIII. At the bottom is the kindergarten, usually a two-year course for children of four to six years of age, but sometimes accepting children of three, and at least one kinder-

Chart VIII
PALESTINE: HEBREW SCHOOL SYSTEM, 1946

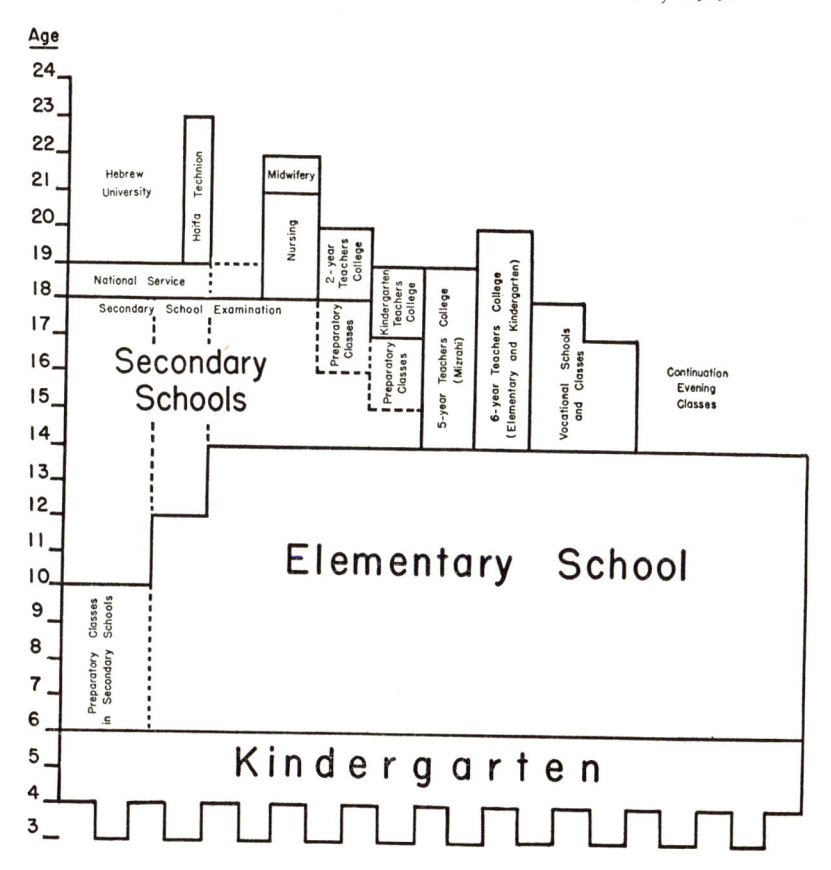

garten in Tel-Aviv takes children of two. Kindergartens are neither maintained nor assisted by the Vaad Leumi Department of Education. Most of them are separated from elementary schools and charge fees that may run as high as £P30 ($120) a year. Tel-Aviv, some other municipalities, and communal settlements, however, maintain kindergartens and kindergarten classes in connection with elementary schools.

The fact that more than 17,000 children were attending Jewish kindergartens in 1944-45 suggests the popularity of the kindergarten with the Jewish population. The number enrolled constitutes the great majority of children of kindergarten age in Jewish Palestine.

The combined length of elementary and secondary education is twelve years for children between the ages of six and eighteen. In general, the elementary school maintains an eight-year course, and the secondary school is of four years' duration. However, there are secondary schools which begin at fifth-grade level, maintaining the first four grades as a preparatory course, and a few which begin at seventh-grade level. Thus, there are three types of school organization—the 8-4, the 4-8, and the 6-6.

The pupil who finishes the eight elementary grades and is able to continue his education may enter either a secondary school, or one of the teachers colleges, or a vocational school.

To graduate from secondary school, the student must pass a combined school and external (Vaad Leumi Department of Education) examination, which will be described later. To the graduate Palestine offers further education in one of the Faculties (colleges) of the Hebrew University, in the Haifa Technion, or in a two-year teachers college. The Hebrew University and the Haifa Technion will not admit him, however, unless he agrees to spend at least six months in national service at the end of his course.

If the secondary-school graduate takes and passes the Palestine matriculation examination, he may enter the Law Classes in Jerusalem, for which the Vaad Leumi Department of Education examination is not recognized.

Vaad Leumi Examinations

The Vaad Leumi Department of Education, like the Government Department of Education, conducts a variety of examinations for the school system under its jurisdiction.

SCHOLARSHIP EXAMINATIONS

In the last few years the Vaad Leumi Department of Education has been conducting scholarship examinations for graduates of elementary schools to assist superior students of no financial resources to continue school. Candidates are admitted to the examination upon recommendation of their principals if they have achieved an average of 80 or higher in their eighth-grade work. The examination is in Hebrew composition, the Bible, mathematics, and English. Students are ranked according to the total number of marks obtained in all four subjects, and scholarships are awarded to the top-ranking students.

THE HEBREW EDUCATIONAL SYSTEM

SECONDARY EXAMINATIONS

Students completing their secondary-school studies take a combined internal and external examination: internal in that it is conducted within the school, external in that the questions are set and the papers read by committees set up by the Vaad Leumi Department of Education. Secondary-school inspectors, together with perhaps as many as sixty outsiders drawn from the Hebrew University, teachers colleges, and other sources, are grouped into subject committees, each with its chief examiner. Questions are usually set by the chief examiner, approved by the committee, and finally approved by the Jewish Director of Education. The examinations are held simultaneously in all the larger schools and in centers created for smaller schools. The papers for each subject are distributed among the members of the appropriate committee, each member reading his share, and the chief examiner rereading all.

The final secondary-school examination is in seven subjects, four being mandatory: Hebrew composition, the Bible, English, and mathematics. In addition, literary-course students take examinations in the Talmud, Hebrew literature, and history; and science students take examinations in higher mathematics, physics, and chemistry; students interested in biology may substitute it for physics. Certain schools require an additional paper in Arabic, French, economics, or Palestinography. At the agricultural secondary school at Pardes-Hannah, the examination in mathematics is taken at the end of the eleventh grade, while biology, chemistry, and agriculture examinations are held at the end of the twelfth.

The passing mark is 60 percent, but a student may pass with 50 in one subject—as long as it is not Hebrew. Those who fail in one or two subjects in the June examinations are given a chance to repeat those subject examinations at midyear. Results of the 1945 Hebrew secondary-school final examinations were as follows:

Section	Entered	Passed	Failed	Percentage Failing
Humanities	358	296	62	17.3
Science and biology	254	228	26	10.2

In addition to the final secondary-school examinations, the Department sets an earlier examination at the end of the tenth grade, consisting of three papers: in the Bible, Hebrew grammar, and English grammar. In schools recognized by the Department, the papers are corrected by the local teachers; in others they are read by the local subject teacher in conjunction with an external examiner appointed by the Department.

TEACHERS COLLEGE EXAMINATIONS

The Vaad Leumi Department of Education also examines students graduating from teachers colleges. In colleges providing a two-year course above the secondary school, students are examined in Hebrew composition, Hebrew grammar, education, and actual teaching. The passing grade is 60 except in Hebrew composition and actual teaching, in which it is 70. The examinations are more comprehensive in the colleges which accept elementary-school graduates and give five- or six-year courses: students are examined in Hebrew grammar, Hebrew composition, the Bible, English, history, literature, education, and practical teaching, and those planning to go to the Hebrew University must take mathematics also. Mizrahi teachers colleges substitute the Talmud for literature. Kindergarten teachers take additional examinations in hygiene, kindergarten theory, and psychology. The examining committees are composed of internal and external examiners with an inspector from the Department on each.

Expansion of Jewish Education

Tables 44 and 45 offer statistical summaries of the development of the Jewish educational system in the last quarter-century.

Table 44 gives an idea of the quantitative growth of the Jewish public and private schools, the number of pupils in them, and the number of pupils in non-Jewish schools. The public schools increased from 137 in 1920–21 to 651 in 1944–45, their teachers from 533 to 3,652, and their pupils from 12,830 to 79,441; in other terms, public schools multiplied 4.7 times, teachers 5.8 times, and pupils 6.2 times in that period. Since 1930–31 the schools have multiplied 2.8 times, teachers 4 times, and pupils 3.5 times. These figures show that there are on the whole more pupils per school than formerly. In the case of private schools, lack of figures for 1920 prevents comparison with that year; in 1922 there were 5,689 pupils in Jewish private schools. Compared with 1930–31, private schools have increased from 117 to 324, their pupils from 11,447 to 24,858 (1943–44 figures), and their teachers from 632 to 1,593 (1942–43 figures). Thus, schools have multiplied 2.7 times and pupils 2.1 times (4.4 times since 1922). The rate of increase in number of private schools has kept pace with that of the public schools, but in number of pupils it has fallen behind. The number of Jewish pupils in non-Jewish schools has doubled in fourteen years. No comparable number of non-Jewish pupils attend Jewish schools; the number fluctuated between 21 and 26 pupils a year between 1939 and 1943.

TABLE 44

Number of Jewish Schools, Teachers, and Pupils, Palestine, 1920–45, According to Type of Control*

YEAR	PUBLIC SCHOOLS			PRIVATE SCHOOLS			JEWISH ENROLLMENT IN NON-JEWISH SCHOOLS	TOTAL		
	Schools	Teachers	Enrollment	Schools	Teachers	Enrollment		Schools	Teachers	Enrollment
1920–21	137	533	12,830	...	...	11,447	725	347	1,529	34,705
1930–31	230	897	22,533	117	632	23,880	1,022	701	3,986	83,594
1940–41	403	2,296	58,692	298	1,690	23,961	1,277	746	4,060	88,045
1941–42	437	2,367	62,807	309	1,693	23,649	1,366	780	4,208	91,754
1942–43	483	2,615	66,739	297	1,593	24,858	1,478†	903	...	99,440
1943–44	579	3,324	73,104	324	...	...	...	...	...	...
1944–45	651	3,652	79,441	...	...	...	...	...	...	...

* Statistics for the public schools, teachers, and pupils, from Executive of the Vaad Leumi, *Memorandum*, Appendix 8, p. 69. Those for the number of schools supplied by the Vaad Leumi Department of Education. Statistics for private schools and Jewish pupils in non-Jewish schools are taken from Government of Palestine, Department of Education, *Statistical Tables and Diagrams for the Scholastic Year 1942–43* (Jerusalem: Government Press), p. 25 except those for 1943–44 which were taken from Great Britain, Colonial Office, *The System of Education of the Jewish Community in Palestine*, Appendix II, Tables A and B, pp. 100–1, and from Government of Palestine, *A Survey of Palestine*, Report for the Anglo-American Committee of Enquiry (Jerusalem: Government Printer, 1946), p. 668.
† Includes a few non-Jewish pupils, probably no more than from twenty to thirty pupils.

TABLE 45

Number of Teachers and Pupils in Jewish Public Schools, Palestine, 1920–45, According to Level of School*

YEAR	KINDERGARTENS		ELEMENTARY SCHOOLS		SECONDARY SCHOOLS		VOCATIONAL SCHOOLS		TEACHERS COLLEGES		TOTAL	
	Teachers	Enrollment	Teachers	Enrollment	Teachers	Enrollment	Teachers	Enrollment	Teachers	Enrollment	Teachers	Enrollment
1920–21	127	2,713	305	8,368	63	992	10	532	28	225	533	12,830
1930–31	177	5,000	544	15,031	86	1,489	45	513	45	500	897	22,533
1940–41	228	6,211	1,569	44,818	382	6,307	39	539	78	817	2,296	58,692
1941–42	267	7,398	1,510	46,690	474	7,335	41	609	75	775	2,367	62,807
1942–43	308	8,485	1,638	49,181	528	7,846	47	603	94	624	2,615	66,739
1943–44	410	11,049	2,175	51,672	567	8,929	65	734	107	720	3,324	73,104
1944–45	469	12,490	2,422	55,471	613	9,527	41	1,067	107	886	3,652	79,441

* From Executive of the Vaad Leumi, *Memorandum*, Appendix 8, p. 69.

Totaling all categories of Jewish schools and pupils, there were, in 1943–44, 903 Jewish schools with 99,440 Jewish pupils in Palestine. The latter number represents 19 percent of the Jewish population of the country as compared with 22 percent in 1922. The principal reason for the steady increase in schools, teachers, and pupils is, of course, the growth of the Jewish population, chiefly by immigration. Whether the decline in the percentage ratio of school pupils to general population is due to a decline in birth rate or to a larger proportion of adults among the new immigrants, or to a lag in school attendance, or to a combination of all these factors cannot be determined. Secondary schools show the greatest expansion, with approximately a tenfold increase of teachers and pupils. Elementary schools are next with teachers increasing 7.9 times and pupils 6.6 times since 1920–21. Roughly speaking, kindergartens and teachers colleges show a fourfold increase, and enrollment in vocational schools has doubled. Most of the vocational-school enrollment is in private vocational schools.

TABLE 46
JEWISH PRIVATE-SCHOOL ENROLLMENT, PALESTINE, 1943–44*

Type of School	Enrollment	Percentage
Kindergarten	4,534	18.2
Elementary: grades one through seven†	13,163	52.9
Secondary: grades eight through eleven†	1,565	6.3
Teachers colleges, including twelfth grade†	329	1.3
Vocational	4,521	18.2
Special	746	3.0
Total	24,858	99.9

* Figures are from Government of Palestine, *A Survey of Palestine*, p. 668.
† Statistics for elementary and secondary schools and teachers colleges are not quite comparable with those of the Jewish public schools because the government uses a different classification from Vaad Leumi, counting the eighth grade as first-year secondary and including the twelfth grade with the teachers college.

Teacher increase has kept pace with enrollment in secondary schools and teachers colleges, so that the teacher-pupil ratio has not changed materially during the period covered. The lowest pupil-teacher ratio, 8, is in the teachers colleges, with that of the secondary school, 15.5, next. The increase in number of teachers in the elementary and vocational schools has outstripped enrollment, reducing pupil-teacher ratio from about 27 to 23 in the former and cutting it in half (from 50 to 26) in the vocational schools. In the kindergartens the increase in number of teachers has lagged behind the enrollment with the result that there are 5 more children per teacher, 26 instead of 21, than formerly.

Average class size has increased substantially in both teachers colleges,

THE HEBREW EDUCATIONAL SYSTEM

20 to 34, and secondary schools, 24 to 31. The rise for kindergartens is more moderate—22 to 26. Elementary-school classes have stayed about the same on the average, while vocational-school classes have been cut drastically in size—an indication of less crowded conditions in workshops.

Enrollment in private Jewish schools in 1943–44 is shown in Table 46.

Private-school enrollment is about 25 percent of the total enrollment in all Jewish schools in Palestine. Kindergartens and vocational schools occupy a relatively higher position in the private than in the public schools, having 18.2 percent each of the total enrollment. Indeed, enrollment in private vocational schools is more than 4 times that in public vocational schools. Elementary-school enrollment is 52.9 percent of the total as compared with 59.8 percent in the public schools, while private secondary schools have only 6.3 percent as compared with 11.9 percent in the public secondary schools.

Chapter 17

THE JEWISH SCHOOLS AND THEIR PROGRAMS

*T*HE DISTINCTIVE feature of Jewish schools in Palestine is the use of the Hebrew language as the medium of instruction in all subjects except English, French, and Arabic. At all levels much emphasis is given religious instruction and the background and development of Zionism.

As previously stated, schools of the Hebrew system are classified in three categories, or trends, in accordance with the party membership of the parents: General, Mizrahi, and Labor. These trends differ in educational, religious, and political ideals. Supporters of the General Trend believe that the spirit of the Jewish religious tradition should guide educational work, but that the observance of religious commandments should be left to the parents and home. The aim of the General-Trend schools is to give pupils a nationalist-Zionist education combined with progressive humanitarian ideals. About 53 percent of Jewish pupils are in schools of the General Trend. Schools of the Mizrahi (Orthodox-Zionist) Trend provide their pupils with a general education, but stress religious education. The children are taught to carry out the precepts of the Jewish religion, and all teachers are required to be Orthodox. About 24 percent of the pupils in the Jewish public-education system are in Mizrahi schools. Labor-Trend schools synthesize general national ideology and the principles of the Jewish labor movement in Palestine. Besides providing general and religious studies common to schools of all trends, Labor-Trend schools seek to inculcate a love of manual work in the children; many offer special training in handicrafts and agriculture. Much attention is given to developing knowledge and understanding of the history and philosophy of the labor movement in other countries as well as in Palestine, and also to creating an understanding of the importance of expanding Jewish activity to include work in the soil and in factories, and of counteracting the traditional overcrowding of commercial, banking, and professional fields. About 23 percent of Jewish public-school pupils are in these schools.

THE JEWISH SCHOOLS AND THEIR PROGRAMS

Kindergartens

In Jewish Palestine, where parents have come from such diverse cultures and backgrounds and speak so many languages, the kindergarten has special significance as a unifying force in the lives of small children. It bridges the gap between home and school and has been especially effective in accustoming children from homes where languages other than Hebrew are spoken to the language in which they will receive instruction for the rest of their school days.

There are kindergartens of every description, ranging from crowded rooms that are poorly equipped and inadequately ventilated in the old city of Jerusalem to well-arranged, extensively equipped modern institutions in Tel-Aviv. Some are little more than day nurseries which solve child-care problems for working mothers and may represent an improvement over the home environment of the child. The highest type is a model school used in training kindergarten teachers. Some kindergartens are attached to elementary schools; most of them are separate institutions. In 1944–45 there were 339 kindergartens associated with the Vaad Leumi Department of Education, with an enrollment of 12,490 children; other kindergartens not supervised by Vaad Leumi had an estimated enrollment of about 5,000.

In communal settlements, babies are placed in the nursery of the children's section (commonly called the "children's village") soon after birth to remain until their formal education is completed—normally at the end of the eighth grade. Parents are permitted to visit their children at certain hours each day, but the care and training of the children from birth to adolescence are provided by the trained personnel of the children's village.

Elementary Schools

Elementary education is not compulsory for either Jews or Arabs in Palestine. Although great effort is made to insure that all Jewish children have at least eight years of schooling, and the percentage of school-age children attending school is undoubtedly higher among the Jews of Palestine than among any other people of the six countries studied by the American Council Commission, it is estimated that there are about 3,000 Jewish children in Palestine who do not go to school. Most of these are in the oriental Jewish communities, principally in Jerusalem. In 1944–45 there were 269 Jewish public elementary schools with 55,471 pupils.

The lack of a compulsory-attendance law also results in curtailing school life for many children, as is shown by the enrollment by grade in the public elementary schools for 1942–43 and 1944–45:[1]

Grade	Enrollment 1942–43	Enrollment 1944–45
A	9,025	9,863
B	7,953	9,082
C	7,037	9,567
D	6,131	8,511
E	5,601	7,228
F	5,261	5,952
G	4,921	4,957
H	4,219	4,596
Total	50,148	59,756

Eighth-grade enrollment diminishes to less than one-half of first-grade enrollment. This phenomenon is common to elementary education in all of the six countries studied. Normal retardation, of course, accounts for part of this decrease in number of pupils, but there is no doubt that the decrease is largely due to pupils dropping out of school for one cause or another. While it is impossible to analyze all factors that cause children to leave school prematurely, it is safe to say that the economic status of the family is a major factor, especially as fees are charged in most elementary schools.

In general, the elementary school maintains an eight-year course, with classes designated by the letters A through H in the Hebrew alphabet. As previously stated, schools of the Hebrew system are classified in three categories or trends in accordance with the party membership of the parents: General, Mizrahi, and Labor.

THE ELEMENTARY PROGRAM OF STUDIES

Table 47 presents the program of studies for boys in General-Trend elementary schools.

In girls schools the program includes three hours of handwork and sewing in each grade beginning with the third. Time for these subjects is obtained by slight reductions in time allowed for Bible, Hebrew, arithmetic, drawing and modeling, singing, and gardening. The Mizrahi schools for boys add two periods to the school week in grades five and six and three in grades seven and eight, and devote almost three times as many

---

[1] Data for 1942–43 from Government of Palestine, Department of Education, *Statistical Tables and Diagrams for the Scholastic Year 1942–43*, pp. 14–15; data for 1944–45 supplied by Vaad Leumi Department of Education.

Above: Jewish school children planting trees during Arbor Day celebration, Beisan, Palestine. (Jewish National Fund photo.)
Below: A class out-of-doors in a Jewish colony, Tel Joseph, Palestine. (Jewish National Fund photo.)

Above: The playground of a p[r]
school in a Jewish colony, Pal[estine].
(Jewish National Fund photo.)
Below: The seminary for the trai[ning of]
Jewish teachers for schools of th[e Gen]eral Trend, Tel-Aviv, Palestine. [(Jew]ish National Fund photo.)

Above: The library of the Hebrew University, Jerusalem. (Jewish National Fund photo.)
Below: The Jewish Technical Institute (Technion), Haifa, Palestine. (Jewish National Fund photo.)

Above: A class in farm machinery repair, School of Agriculture, Mikveh Israel, Palestine. (Jewish National Fund photo.)
Below: A demonstration in a course in bee-keeping in a Jewish school, Palestine. (Photo by Schwartz.)

THE JEWISH SCHOOLS AND THEIR PROGRAMS

TABLE 47
Program of Studies in Hebrew Boys Elementary Schools, General Trend, Palestine, 1945–46

Subject	1st Grade*	2nd Grade*	3rd Grade	4th Grade	5th Grade	6th Grade	7th Grade	8th Grade
Bible	...	...	6	5	6	5	5	4
Hebrew	...	...	6	7	5	4	4	5
Mishnah	...	...	...	...	...	...	2	2
Palestinography: geography and nature study	...	...	6	4	4	4	4	4
History	...	...	...	...	2	2	3	3
Arithmetic	...	...	4	4	5	5	5	5
Drawing and modeling	...	...	...	2	2	2	2	2
Singing	...	...	2	2	2	2	1	1
Gardening	...	...	...	2	2	2	1	1
Physical training	...	...	2	2	2	2	2	2
English	...	...	...	...	5	5	4	4
Total	24*	24*	26	28	33	33	33	33

* Assignment of periods in the first two grades is determined by each school.

TABLE 48
Program of Studies in Elementary Schools of the Labor Trend, Palestine, 1945–46

Subject	1st Grade*	2nd Grade*	3rd Grade	4th Grade	5th Grade	6th Grade	7th Grade	8th Grade
Reading (literature)	...	...	7	7	4	4	3	3
Language (grammar, writing)	...	...	...	...	2	2	2	2
Ancient literature	...	...	...	...	...	...	1	1
Bible	...	...	3	4	4	4	3	3
Talk on social matters	...	...	...	...	1	2	2	2
Palestinography	...	...	4	2	1	...	...	...
Jewish affairs, Zionism, labor movement	...	...	...	...	...	...	1	2
Geography	...	...	...	...	2	2	2	2
Nature study	...	...	...	3	3	4	4	4
Jewish and general history	...	...	...	...	...	2	3	3
History of Culture and ancient history	...	...	...	1	1	...	...	...
Arithmetic and algebra	...	...	5	5	6	5	4	4
Physical labor: sewing, handwork, gardening, and farming	...	...	5	5	6	6	7	7
Drawing and modeling	...	...	2	2	2	2	2	1
Singing	...	...	2	2	1	1	1	1
Physical training	...	...	2	2	2	2	2	2
English	...	...	...	...	5	5	4	4
Total	29	29	30	33	40	41	41	41

* Assignment of periods in the first two grades is determined by each school.

hours to religious subjects as do schools of the General Trend. Mizrahi girls schools have the same number of hours in the school week as General-Trend schools for girls, but devote more time to religion.

Nearly all Labor-Trend elementary schools are coeducational, and the only differentiation made on the basis of sex in the program of studies shown in Table 48 is in handwork.

The Labor-Trend schools average slightly more than six hours above General-Trend schools in length of work-week, and the former devote less time to religion and much more to manual work.

The course of study for each trend is developed by a central education committee of the trend under the general supervision of the Vaad Leumi Department of Education. Subjects common to all schools follow, in general, the same course and use the same textbooks.

Palestinography, or study of the "Homeland," is stressed in all schools. The early grades study geographical features of home, school, and the immediate environment. Festivals, memorial days, and religious customs are discussed and celebrated. Communications, population distribution and characteristics, climate, location of offices of public services, plant and animal life of the vicinity, local history and legend, map-reading, and important characteristics of naturally defined areas of Palestine, are studied in detail. In more advanced grades a similar approach is made to the Arab countries surrounding Palestine and to the countries of the Mediterranean. This course is designed to develop an intelligent understanding of and a support for the Zionist ambitions in regard to a National Home in Palestine.

In *history,* major stress is on the activities of the Jews through the ages. Bible study begins with simple stories told or read in the first two grades and progresses to the more difficult books, including the study of commentaries in the higher grades. Mishnah includes the study of the sayings of religious leaders in the first few centuries of the Christian era. The course in Hebrew contains much study of religious literature.

Nature study is planned as a practical course. Much of the work is based upon direct observation, and there is correlation with the course in Palestinography. Attention is given to good health habits and to acquiring an understanding of the functions and care of the human body. Practical work in school gardens and on farms is correlated with the course in nature study, and there are frequent trips to points of educational significance.

To increase opportunity for practical *manual work* for boys without resorting to uneconomical shops in individual schools, handicraft centers have recently been established in Jerusalem. Boys in the upper grades of various schools go to these centers for an entire morning or afternoon of work in wood or sheet metal. Sewing for girls provides training in making and repairing simple clothing. In the upper grades some attention is given to design, knitting, and embroidery for decoration of blouses and frocks.

In some schools, especially in localities of mixed population, the study of *Arabic* is introduced in the two upper grades. Spoken, rather than written or classical, Arabic is emphasized to provide the pupils with a basis of communication with Arab neighbors.

Although cooking is not named in the program of studies, it receives much attention of a very practical and effective kind. Instruction is provided in connection with the Hadassah (Women's Zionist Organization of America) school-luncheon projects started by Miss Henrietta Szold in 1925. Since 1939 they have been carried on by the combined efforts and support of the Hadassah and the social-service department of the Vaad Leumi. The primary purpose of the project was to provide hot lunches for needy and undernourished children, but the educational value appears no less important. Nearly every school that has an adequate number of pupils in the three highest grades to warrant the provision of a cooking teacher has its own kitchen where each day a different group of eight pupils—boys and girls in coeducational schools—work under the direction of the cooking teacher and prepare a school meal for from 150 to 250 fellow-pupils. The heavy work in the kitchen is done by paid workers. Notebooks of recipes and menus are kept by all pupils who work in the kitchen. Rotation of duty brings each group into the kitchen about once in every three weeks. Kitchen squad members are held responsible for making up all work missed because of absence from regular classwork. During their last three years in elementary school, pupils spend approximately thirty-six school days in the kitchen where, guided by the teacher, they acquire considerable knowledge of cooking. In addition, about half of the pupils are taught the theory of nutrition for an hour a week by the cooking teacher. More than 29,000 children are receiving a wholesome, balanced, and nourishing noonday meal. Some nonneedy children are permitted to have these meals on a paying basis. Schools which have no kitchens have meals sent in either from a nearby school kitchen or from one of the four central kitchens located in different parts of Palestine: these provide daily lunches for 8,300 children. Since 1940–41, the teaching of domestic science in centers equipped by Hadassah has been provided for eighth-grade girls. Girls in 24 schools are now receiving such instruction.[2]

[2] Much of the description of the cooking course is taken from a memorandum prepared by Mrs. S. Bavly, present director of the Hadassah school-luncheon project.

A special department of the Hadassah provides doctors and nurses who give annual physical examinations, provide treatments and medical care, give or assist with health instruction, and inspect general health and sanitary conditions in the schools. A milk project provides a daily glass of milk at very low cost during one of the recesses to every child in schools supervised by the Vaad Leumi. This special attention to the health of school children has paid dividends, especially in the marked drop in the incidence of trachoma.

There is great variety in the physical facilities of the schools. Some schools are housed in rented private dwellings, dark, poorly ventilated, and ill-suited to school purposes; others are in large, airy, attractive modern school buildings such as one finds in Tel-Aviv or in the settlements. City schools are crowded so that in some schools multiple shifts are arranged to provide space for all the children. In most settlement schools classes are small and physical facilities adequate. Newer schools in cities and settlements have space available for play areas and stress physical activity and development of healthy bodies. School furniture and equipment, especially in newer schools—except for certain shortages caused by the war—are, in general, adequate. Individual desks or tables and chairs are common.

In recent years a number of clubs have been formed to care for children of working parents. These children have quarters in school buildings or in rented houses under the supervision of leaders—frequently students in higher institutions. Provision is made for supervised study, games, handicrafts, and recreational reading, and a nourishing meal is furnished in the evening before the children go to their homes. Playing fields under the supervision of trained physical-education leaders provide additional facilities for healthful recreation. Summer camps provide similar accommodations in the holiday period.

To provide for boys and girls who are obliged to work for a living before completing their elementary education, evening classes have been established in the cities, especially in Jerusalem and Tel-Aviv. Such classes usually begin at six and continue until nine in the evenings. There is an intermission during which a meal which the pupils have helped to prepare is served. Approximately 1,600 boys and girls are taking advantage of this opportunity to complete an elementary course.

Secondary Schools

Secondary schools of the Jewish system in Palestine usually include a full elementary section, making a twelve-year program. The first four grades are called a "preparatory section," and the secondary section has eight grades, its first grade corresponding to the fifth grade in an ordinary elementary school, and its fifth grade corresponding to the first year of the usual secondary school. Pupils who complete the eight-year elementary school may enter the fifth year of this eight-year secondary school, but it is reported that there are some difficulties in adjusting to the program. Some secondary schools are four years in length, admitting graduates of the eight-year elementary school. A recent tendency has been to classify the first six years of the twelve-year secondary school as preparatory and the last six as secondary, and to complicate things still further, at least one communal settlement central school (Mishmar HaEmek) has a five-year secondary program, based on principles of progressive education, above a six-year elementary school.

With the exception of one public secondary school recently opened by the Tel-Aviv municipality and not yet complete, all secondary schools in the Jewish system are independent and charge fees. There are 28 secondary schools affiliated with the Vaad Leumi and thus subject to its inspection. Twenty were classified as General Trend, 4 as Labor, and 4 as Mizrahi. Fees averaged £P28.5 ($114) in 1943–44, but are sometimes as high as £P55 ($220) per year. Many students are partially or totally exempted from fees. In recent years and at the suggestion of the Government Director of Education,[3] the Vaad Leumi Department of Education started giving scholarships of £P20 to worthy students who stand high in a competitive examination (the scholarships are discontinued if the student fails to maintain a high standing in school). About 400 students sit for this examination each year. These scholarships are for both secondary and vocational schools. The total number of scholarships awarded between the years 1942 and 1945 was 278, and in 1945–46, 120 were added to this number. These scholarships constitute the only financial link between the Vaad Leumi Department of Education and the secondary schools. With the exception of the scholarship students and certain students exempted from payment of fees by the schools, secondary-school pupils pay substantial sums for the privilege of attending school.

Of the 28 secondary schools affiliated with the Vaad Leumi Department of Education, 17 maintained preparatory classes. In 1944–45 secondary-school enrollment was 9,527 pupils, of whom 4,205 were in the lower eight elementary grades attached to the schools, and 5,322 were in the

---

[3] Farrell, *Memorandum of the Director of Education on Organization of the Hebrew Public School System, Delivered to the Chairman of the Vaad Leumi Executive Education Committee on 1st July, 1940* (Jerusalem: Government Press, 1940), p. 10.

upper four years of secondary school. The 15 private secondary schools not affiliated with the Vaad Leumi Department of Education had a total enrollment in 1942–43 of 3,169, with 1,796 enrolled in elementary and 1,373 in secondary classes. It may be said that of approximately 100,000 pupils in all types of public and private Jewish schools in Palestine about 7 percent are in the four-year secondary course.

The student has some choice of program in his final two years of secondary education. Most of the schools divide into literary and scientific sections at this point. Some are developing a biological section. One secondary school at Pardes-Hannah offers theoretical and practical training in agriculture, and Tel-Aviv has a commercial secondary school.

The program of studies of the Hertzliah Gymnasium (secondary school), founded in 1906, is given in Table 49. This school is reported to be the first modern Hebrew secondary school in the world. Its program is not presented as a typical program, but as an early attempt to harmonize the demands of Western academic training with the peculiar requirements of the Zionist program in Palestine. The program of the first four years is not included since it is similar to the program of the elementary schools of the General Trend.

The only exception to the general rule that all instruction is in Hebrew is the Evelina de Rothschild School for Girls, where instruction is in English.

Examinations which must be passed by secondary-school students have been described in chapter 16. Since the Palestine government does not recognize the Hebrew Secondary-School Certificate, it is necessary for students who wish to continue their education in the Government Law Classes to pass the Palestine matriculation examination and receive the Palestine Matriculation Certificate. In 1945 there were 115 Jewish candidates for this certificate, 28 of whom received it, and 44 who did not reach this highest standard were awarded the Government Secondary-School Certificate.

At the end of the secondary-school course all physically fit boys and girls spend a year in Jewish national service. This custom was established to relieve the labor shortage in the settlements and to provide the young with a practical introduction to life in the colonies.

Vocational Schools

Vocational education for Palestinian Jews began with the establishment of the Mikveh-Israel Agricultural School in 1870. This school was founded by the Alliance Israelite Universelles (a French organization for the extension and improvement of modern education for Jews throughout the world) to train Jewish agricultural workers for Palestine before the Jews

TABLE 49

Program of Studies of Hertzliah Secondary School, Tel-Aviv, 1945-46

Subjects	1st Year	2nd Year	3rd Year	4th Year	5th Year	6th Year A*	6th Year M*	6th Year L*	7th Year A*	7th Year M*	7th Year L*	8th Year A*	8th Year M*	8th Year L*
Bible.............	4	4	4	4	3	3	3	3	3	3	3	4	4	4
Talmud...........	2	2	2	2	2	2	2	2			2			4
Grammar..........					2	2	2	2						
Hebrew...........	4	4	4	4	3	3	3	3	4	4	4	5	5	6
General literature..											2			2
Algebra and geometry.	4	4	4	4	5	4	4	4	3	4	3	4	6	4
Physics...........					3†	2	2	2	2	5‡	2	2	5	1
Chemistry.........						2	2	2	2	4‡	1	2	2	
History...........		2	2	2	2	2	2	2	2	2	3	1	1	4
Geography.........	2	2	2	2					2	2	2		3	2
Natural science....	2	2	2	2	1				2	2	2	4	1	1
Drawing...........	2	2	2	2			1	1						
Descriptive geometry.														
English...........	5	4	4	4	5	5	5	5	5	5	5	6	6	6
Arabic or French...					3	3	3	3	3	3	3			
Music.............	2	2	2	2	1		1	1			1			
Handicrafts.......	4§	3§	3§	3§										
Physical training..	2	2	2	2	2	2	2	2	2	2	2	1	2	2
Soil science.......												4		
General agriculture.						6			6			3		
Total.............	33	33	33	33	34	36	34	34	36	36‡	35	36	35	36

* A refers to agriculture specialization, M to mathematical, and L refers to literary.
† Includes 1 hour of mathematical geography.
‡ Includes 2 hours combined laboratory, physics and chemistry.
§ Handicrafts include sewing, binding, carpentry, and horticulture.

had acquired a single agricultural settlement in the country. Instruction for the first fifty years was in French, but after World War I changed to Hebrew. Although fees are charged, nearly half of the students are exempted from half of all tuition. About 650 acres (2,600 dunums) of land given by the Turkish government provides opportunity for instruction, production, research, and experimental programs. At the time of the American Council Commission's visit (1946) approximately 450 students, including 250 refugees, were enrolled in the three-year course of the School. The regular course accepts boys and girls who have completed the eight-year elementary school or its equivalent. There is a special two-year course for students who have completed two years of the secondary school.

The first two years of the regular course offer a common training in general and technical subjects. Third-year students may specialize in field crops, vegetables, poultry, fruit trees, landscape gardening, nurseries, beekeeping, dairying, or sheep-raising. In general, half of each day is spent in class and half in practical enterprises.

Other important agricultural schools for Jewish students are the Kadoorie School at Mount Tabor, founded with funds from a bequest of Sir Eli Kadoorie, a wealthy Baghdad Jew, an agricultural school for girls at Nahalal, and an agricultural secondary school at Pardes-Hannah. The last named offers a complete secondary-school education in addition to vocational education. In 1943–44 there were 17 agricultural schools for Jews in Palestine with a total of 2,019 students; some of these schools are of elementary-school standard.

There are 16 trade or vocational schools in the Jewish educational system, but only 9, with 1,067 students, are affiliated with the Vaad Leumi. Schools offering technical training are in Tel-Aviv, Jerusalem, Haifa, Safad, and other communities. These schools admit elementary-school graduates to a three-year course that allows boys to specialize in the metal trades, carpentry, building, and seafaring, and girls to specialize in domestic science, sewing and weaving, and commercial subjects. Most of these schools belong to the Labor Trend and are supported in part by the Histadruth, the Jewish labor organization.

The Max Pine Vocational School for boys in Tel-Aviv started as an evening school in 1928 and opened day classes in 1933. In 1945–46 there were 324 boys enrolled in its three-year course. The course is common in the first year, but in the second and third specialization is offered in fitting, electricity, and auto mechanics. In 1945–46 there were 57 third-year students specializing in fitting, 28 in electricity, and 18 in auto mechanics. There are evening classes to accommodate 300 apprentices. Approximately half of a 45-hour week is devoted to general and theoretical work and one-half to shopwork. General subjects include Hebrew, history, sociology and demography of the Jews, mathematics, physical training, and hygiene. Of 313 boys graduated up to the time of the American Council Commission's visit, 158 were working in city factories in Palestine, 41 in settlements, 87 were in the army in technical jobs, 7 were studying engineering, and 20 were either dead or their occupations were unknown. The school is supported chiefly by tuition fees, but receives some income from the Histadruth, the municipality of Tel-Aviv, sale of its shop products, and a small grant from the Government Department of Education. Applicants are subjected to a battery of psychological aptitude tests used as a basis for admission and also as a basis for selection of specialization.

The Hadassah founded a similar school for girls in Jerusalem in 1942. A four-year course above the elementary school is provided for about 200 girls. They have a choice of three fields of specialization—cooking and domestic science, sewing (including arts and crafts, and weaving), and commercial training. The first graduating class (1946) was divided 11, 16, and 13 among these specializations. The school is housed in buildings formerly occupied by the Hadassah Hospital. Somewhat more than half of the school week—which is forty-two periods for sewing and domestic science specialists, and thirty-eight for those in the commercial course—is spent in vocational or technical subjects and practical work, the remainder on general subjects, which include Bible, English, Arabic—for commercial pupils—civics, gymnastics, and singing. This school is a unit in the Brandeis Vocational Center, which includes, in addition, the Julian Mack School and Workshops, a progressive elementary school for underprivileged children, the Vocational Guidance Center, and the Apprenticeship Training School (precision instruments). The Vocational Guidance Center is a service center for school children, working youth, and returning soldiers. General intelligence and performance tests are administered to individuals and groups, and professional guidance is given. A general testing program is administered to all eighth-grade children in Jewish schools in Jerusalem. The Center conducts entrance examinations for a school for backward children, two vocational schools, a school of nursing, a social-service school, and a secondary school. It is engaged in standardizing original and translated tests in Hebrew. A similar center has recently been established in Tel-Aviv.

Technical vocational training is provided in two schools for Jews at Haifa—one high school and one higher institution. The Technical High School offers three- and four-year courses above the elementary school in metal-work, electrical work, auto mechanics, and woodwork, and a special two-year course is open to boys who have finished two years of secondary school. The school week is divided about evenly between general courses and practical work in the shops of the Haifa Technion, the higher institute of technology (described on page 295). The Nautical School trains navigators and marine engineers in a four-year course above elementary school. External examinations are administered under the auspices of the London Board of Trade. In 1945–46 there were 275 enrolled in the Technical High School and 90 in the Nautical School.

Nursing Education

Training of Jewish nurses takes place chiefly in Jewish hospitals, the largest of which is the Hadassah Hospital in Jerusalem. There are 4 Jewish training centers in Palestine, but the program of only one, the Henrietta Szold Hadassah School of Nursing, will be described here.

The course is three years in length for girls who have graduated from an approved secondary school or who hold a Matriculation Certificate or who have successfully completed a seven-year course in the gymnasium type of school. Instruction is in Hebrew, and a small tuition fee is charged, although students receive maintenance. The minimum age for admission is nineteen, and applicants are selected on the basis of a questionnaire, personal interview, and physical examination. Student nurses are exempted from the year of national service. Representatives of the school canvass graduating classes in secondary schools to recruit for the training program. In 1945–46 there were 87 girls training in this School of Nursing, distributed about equally among the three classes. The capacity of the school is 90, although this number was exceeded during the war years. The working day consists of two-and-one-half hours of lectures and class discussions and eight hours of practical work. Every effort is made to correlate the practical work with classroom work. Opportunities for specialization are provided in six-month graduate courses in midwifery, public-health nursing, and physiotherapy. External examinations for graduates are supervised by the Government Department of Health. The School of Nursing has the modern and extensive facilities of the Hadassah Hospital for practical work.

Teacher-Training Colleges

Of Palestine's 5 teacher-training colleges for Jews, 2 are for teachers in the General Trend, 2 for Mizrahi, and 1 for Labor. In 1944–45 the total enrollment in teacher-training classes was 886. Three of the colleges offer five- or six-year courses above the elementary school. The first four years approximate the work of the secondary school and the additional years provide professional training. The other two colleges admit secondary-school graduates to a two-year course that is designed to give professional training and to extend the students' knowledge of Hebrew language and literature. Schools of the General and Labor Trends are coeducational; the Mizrahi Trend segregates its students. There are two special schools, a General Trend and a Mizrahi, and a special section of the Tel-Aviv Training College for the training of kindergarten teachers. Recently a preparatory class was added to the Beth HaKerem Training College in Jerusalem for the benefit of applicants from abroad or from the smaller schools of Palestine who have deficiencies to make up. The deficiencies are usually in Hebrew or English. Model schools for demonstration and practice teaching are attached to or associated with each of the training colleges. These teacher-training institutions of Jewish Palestine have assumed a much more important role in supplying teachers since Nazi persecution of European Jewry arose. Previously many, if not most, of the teachers in Jewish Palestine received their preparation in European institutions.

Final external examinations are a condition of graduation in all the teacher-training institutions. Students are examined in pedagogy, psychology, and hygiene and are required to teach model lessons before an external board of examiners. In addition, graduates of the seminary at Beth HaKerem are required to submit an essay on an educational subject. The preparation of this essay usually requires a year or more after graduation. In 1945 a study of the activities of all graduates of this institution from 1936 to 1945 showed that of 329 graduates, 226 were teaching or doing closely related work in Palestine, 44 were in the armed services, 6 were on leave from teaching, 20 had shifted to other occupations, 3 were dead, 24 had never taught, 2 were teaching in other countries, and the present occupations of 6 were unknown.

Higher Education

Above the secondary school and apart from teacher-training schools there are 2 institutions of Jewish higher education, the Hebrew University at Jerusalem and the Technion at Haifa.

THE HEBREW UNIVERSITY

Hebrew University, the capstone of Hebrew education for the entire world, was formally opened on April 1, 1925. The idea of such a university was first advanced by Dr. Hermann Schapira, professor of mathematics at the University of Heidelberg, in 1882. Legal restrictions placed upon attendance of Jewish students at higher institutions in some eastern European countries helped to rally supporters for Dr. Schapira's idea. The foundation stone was laid in July 1918. Instruction began in 1923 with the establishment of a Chemistry Institute. Before the formal opening of the University in 1925, the Microbiological Institute and the Institute of Jewish Studies also were started. It was realized that a complete university of high standard does not spring up overnight and that it would be wise to limit first efforts to a few research institutes. Emphasis was placed upon research to solve problems of major importance in the development of the Jewish community in Palestine. These problems have been concerned with health, agriculture, irrigation, Jewish history, language and literature, sanitation, economics, and geology.

Increase in anti-Semitism, reduction in educational opportunities for Jews in Europe, and increased pressure from Palestinian Jews who desired higher education caused the authorities to inaugurate regular instruction for students. At present such instruction is provided in a Faculty of Humanities, a Faculty of Science, and a School of Agriculture. A Pre-Faculty of Medicine provides opportunities for postgraduate study and research, and in the near future it is expected to develop into a complete School of Medicine.

The Faculty of Humanities has three divisions—the School of Oriental Studies, the group of general humanities, and the department of education —and in addition, the Institute of Jewish Studies. The School of Oriental Studies offers three major subjects: Islamic culture, Arabic language and literature, and Semitic philology; and two minor subjects: archeology of the Near East and Egyptology. General humanities includes four major subjects: archeology, history, classics, and philosophy; and four minor subjects: Palestinian archeology, French civilization, Romance philology, and cultural sociology. The department of education gives courses in three principal subjects: principles of education, educational methods and administration, and psychology. The Institute of Jewish Studies provides for instruction in six major subjects: Hebrew philology, Bible, Talmud, Hebrew literature, Jewish philosophy and mysticism, and Jewish history and sociology.

The Faculty of Science offers instruction in seven major subjects: mathematics, physics, chemistry, biochemistry, zoology, botany, bacteriology and hygiene. Minor subjects are parasitology and geology, and additional lecture courses are given in meteorology, climatology, and physiology.

The School of Agriculture, in cooperation with the Agricultural Research Station of the Jewish Agency in Rehovoth, has a five-year course.

THE JEWISH SCHOOLS AND THEIR PROGRAMS

After studying principally natural sciences for two years in the University proper, the student spends a year in practical work in the settlements under the supervision of the Research Station and the last two years of the course at Rehovoth in specialized laboratory work.

The Pre-Faculty of Medicine offers advanced research opportunities to doctors in the following fields: bacteriology and hygiene, parasitology, physiology, pathological physiology, cancer research, hormone research, pathological anatomy, and, in cooperation with the Rothschild-Hadassah University Hospital, seven clinical subjects: internal medicine, surgery, pediatrics, obstetrics and gynecology, dermatology and venereology, ophthalmology, and X-ray and radiotherapy. The projected complete School of Medicine will include two years of premedical work, five of medical study, and a year or two of internship.

The University's four-year courses in the humanities and science lead to the Master of Arts and the Master of Science degrees. Candidates must satisfy examiners in one major and two minor subjects, presenting a thesis in the major subject and passing both oral and written examinations. The Ph.D. is granted to the holder of the master's degree in either field after two additional years of study. A special five-year course provided through cooperation of the Faculties of Humanities and Science and the department of education admits graduates of approved secondary schools in Palestine or equivalent accredited foreign schools and candidates who pass entrance examinations to become teachers in upper elementary and secondary schools. Successful completion of this course is recognized by a diploma. The department of education has a three-year graduate course for holders of the master's degree from either Faculty and upon completion of the course confers the Certificate of Pedagogical Studies. Tuition fees vary from £P20 ($80) in the Faculty of Humanities to £P70 ($280) in the Faculty of Science.

Hebrew University is located on the beautiful Mount Scopus site where extensive acreage is available for expansion. Buildings are planned to give maximum utilization for efficient study and instruction. The modern and well-equipped Hadassah Hospital is easily accessible to the students. The Jewish National and University Library, a collection of more than 400,000 volumes, is housed in a large modern building centrally located on the campus and provides extensive collections of botanical, zoological, geological, and archeological materials. The Museum of Biblical and Talmudic Botany and Jewish and Arab Plant Lore is housed in the large hall of the open-air theater.

All instruction, except in some aspects of the study of foreign languages, is in Hebrew. The University has contributed heavily to the simplification and to the extension of vocabulary of the Hebrew language to meet modern conditions. The faculty, in 1944–45 consisting of thirty-seven professors, thirty-eight lecturers, twenty-three assistants, and sixty instructors, had been recruited from European countries, England, and the United States. The variety of points of view represented in the faculty has been productive of a unique organization and favors the development of a dynamic philosophy of higher education.

The Hebrew University is an independent institution administered by a board of governors representing the following elements: the Jewish community of Palestine, Societies of Friends of the Hebrew University throughout the world, the Zionist Organization, the Jewish academic world, and the University's principal financial supporters. Most of the money for capital and current expenses has come from foreign contributions. The direct administration of the University is the function of the Executive Committee, which consists of a group of men of public standing and experience in business, an administrative group appointed by the board of governors, and an elected group from the staff of the University. The chairman is appointed by the board of governors and is head of the University administration. The University president, elected by the board of governors, presides at the annual opening ceremony and at the graduation ceremony and acts as director of the Hebrew University Press Association. The administrator (chairman of the Executive) is the chief official of the University administration. Academic affairs of the University are in the hands of the senate, consisting of the professors and the representatives of lecturers and assistants. The rector, who is academic head of the University and represents it in all academic matters, is elected by the senate for a period of two years with the possibility of one re-election; he is chairman of the senate and of its standing committee and is an ex officio member of the Executive Committee. The Faculty of Humanities, the Faculty of Science, and the Pre-Faculty of Medicine have boards composed of the professors of each Faculty and all the lecturers who are engaged in teaching. The Faculty boards deal with all matters relating to instruction and particularly with the syllabuses.

In 1945–46 there were approximately 650 regular students registered at the University—350 in the Faculty of Humanities, 250 in the Faculty of Science, and 50 in the School of Agriculture. Since its founding the University has conferred about 500 master's and 50 Doctor of Philosophy degrees. The latest available analysis of the student body, made in 1940–

41, showed 72 percent to be men and 28 percent women. In that year more than half of the students had entered from secondary schools in which the language of instruction was not Hebrew, and about a third were graduates of Hebrew secondary schools in Palestine. The countries from which most students had come were: Poland, 20 percent; Germany and Austria, 18 percent; Czechoslovakia, 11 percent; Rumania, 6 percent; and Hungary, 5.5 percent. The average age of students was 23.64 years.

THE TECHNION AT HAIFA

The Technion, Hebrew Institute of Technology, which was founded in 1912 but not opened until January 1925, is the only higher technical school in Palestine. In 1946 technical training was offered in civil engineering, architecture, industrial engineering (with specialization in mechanical or electrical engineering in the last two years), and chemical engineering. The four-year course admits graduates of secondary schools or holders of certificates of matriculation standard. Instruction in all specializations is in Hebrew. Diplomas with the degree of engineer are granted to candidates who pass an external examination which is set and marked by a board made up of government officials and representatives of the Jewish Agency and local professional societies. Questions and problems are selected by the board from a collection submitted by the teaching staff. The examinations are usually held in March of each year for students who completed their formal instruction the previous June.

The Technion is financed largely by tuition fees, although small grants have been made by the Palestine government and the Jewish Agency. Fees and income from property, workshops, and laboratories provide about 65 percent of the total budget. The annual tuition fee is £P45 ($180), plus an additional fee of £P5 ($20) charged for chemical engineering.

In 1945–46 the Technion (exclusive of the Technical High School and the Nautical School) operated on a budget of £P56,000 ($224,000). In that year the total registration was 459: 175 first-year students, 130 second, 105 third, and 49 fourth. Industrial engineering is the most popular course, with 208 students; civil engineering is next with 130. Extensive opportunities for practical training and research are provided in the fourteen laboratories and workshops of the Technion. A testing laboratory for building materials is used for instructional purposes but also serves the government departments and private construction firms. The workshops, which produce a variety of needed articles, contributed important products for the armed forces during World War II.

Other Hebrew Schools and Cultural Associations

The Talmud Torahs, private schools which emphasize instruction in religion and private elementary education for religious leaders, are the most conservative and orthodox of Jewish educational institutions. The language of instruction may be Yiddish, Arabic, or Hebrew. In recent years some of these schools have received government grants and have reorganized on a more modern basis and raised their standards. In 1944 there were 73 of these schools with 8,234 pupils; 28 of these schools (enrolling 4,826 pupils) were receiving government grants. Such schools are comparable to the Muhammadan *kuttabs*.

Art and music education for relatively small groups is provided by art schools and conservatories in Jerusalem and Tel-Aviv. Dramatic arts are encouraged by the Habimah Theater, a cooperative society of actors, and the Ohel Theater. The Matate, a satirical theater of the European type, engages in candid commentary on social and political problems touching the Jewish community. The Art Theater of the Kindergarten Teachers Society brings the drama to the educational system.

A notable Jewish cultural institution is the Palestine Symphony Orchestra, which is managed by the Palestine Orchestra Trust and employs some seventy musicians. From time to time it has been conducted by some of the world's greatest conductors. The Palestine Folk Opera produces works of both Jewish and non-Jewish composers. Other organized bodies of note are the Palestine Oratorio Society, the "Music for the People" Association, and the choir of the Great Synagogue in Tel-Aviv. There are numerous small musical groups, many specializing in chamber music.

Cultivation of distinctively Jewish qualities is perhaps most pronounced in the literary field. There are associations concerned with the structure of the Hebrew language, notably the Hebrew Language Committee, and the Vaad Halashon, a body dedicated to modernizing the Hebrew vocabulary. Many famous literary works have been translated into Hebrew, and there is a substantial output of original works of distinction. Numerous literary prizes have been founded, among them the Bialik and Tchernokowsky prizes for poetry and the Dizengoff, Rabbi Kook, and Professor Clausner prizes for other forms of literature.

Part Four

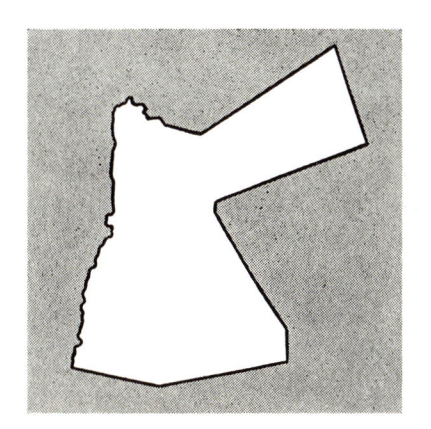

TRANSJORDAN

TRANSJORDAN

Population: *400,000 in 1946 (estimated).*

Area: *33,750 square miles (estimated).*

Form of government: *A constitutional, hereditary monarchy. Legislative power is vested in the National Assembly and the King. The National Assembly consists of the Councils of Notables (the Senate), appointed by the King, and the Chamber of Deputies, composed of elected representatives.*

For purposes of general administration, Transjordan is divided into the Desert Area and four divisions, known as "liwas," each under a governor.

Principal occupations: *Agriculture, animal breeding, industry (limited).*

Principal exports: *Wheat, barley, raisins, skins, hides, wool, sheep, goats, cattle.*

Principal imports: *Manufactured articles, especially textiles, foodstuffs, benzine, kerosene, animals.*

Monetary unit: *Palestinian pound (£P) equivalent to approximately $4.03.*

Chapter 18

ORGANIZATION AND ADMINISTRATION OF THE EDUCATIONAL SYSTEM

THE PUBLIC educational system of Transjordan is largely a development of the period between the two World Wars. Before the First World War, the Turks had no more than a handful of elementary schools of five grades for boys in the larger towns. No school for girls existed. Transjordan was at that time an outlying part of the vilayet of Damascus and as such received even less attention in the matter of education than the neglected vilayets of the Ottoman Empire.

With the rise of the amirate of Transjordan in 1921, there gradually developed a small school system which now comprises 73 schools and 9,874 pupils. Nine of the schools are for girls, all elementary, with 1,956 pupils; 1 is a technical school for boys; and 4 schools are for boys, combining secondary with elementary classes. The rest are elementary town and village schools for boys.

Administration

The public educational system of Transjordan is administered by the Ministry of Education, which is charged with the direction, supervision, and inspection of all government schools, and with the supervision and inspection of nongovernment schools. The Minister is a member of the Cabinet. He is assisted by a Director General of Education who is the executive head of the public-school system. Under the Director General are three district inspectors, one of whom has the rank of senior inspector. These inspectors correspond to the three districts of 'Ajlun, Balqa (in which 'Amman is situated), and the combined southern districts of Karak and Ma'an. Although assigned to these three districts, the inspectors actually have their headquarters at the capital, 'Amman. They are charged with inspecting the public and private elementary schools of their districts and share among themselves the inspection of secondary schools, each taking certain subjects. The senior inspector supervises the teaching of Arabic and religion, the second inspector visits English and social-studies classes, and the third has charge of science and mathematics. The duties of the inspectors, however, are not confined to class visiting, but also involve general administrative inspection of schools, including the application of the education laws, registers, school premises, distribution of pupils by grades, the timetables, the register of marks, and other similar duties. Inspectors are also charged with presenting confidential reports about school principals and teachers, giving their opinions about reports sent by school principals about their teachers, presenting recommendations concerning the appointment, promotion, transfer, and discipline of teachers, the opening of new schools, and the composition of the staff of each school under their jurisdiction.

A special fourth inspector supervises the school gardens. The central office has in addition, a chief clerk, an accountant, a storekeeper, and some clerks. The administrative organization is shown in Chart IX.

Chart IX

TRANSJORDAN: ADMINISTRATIVE ORGANIZATION OF MINISTRY OF EDUCATION, 1946

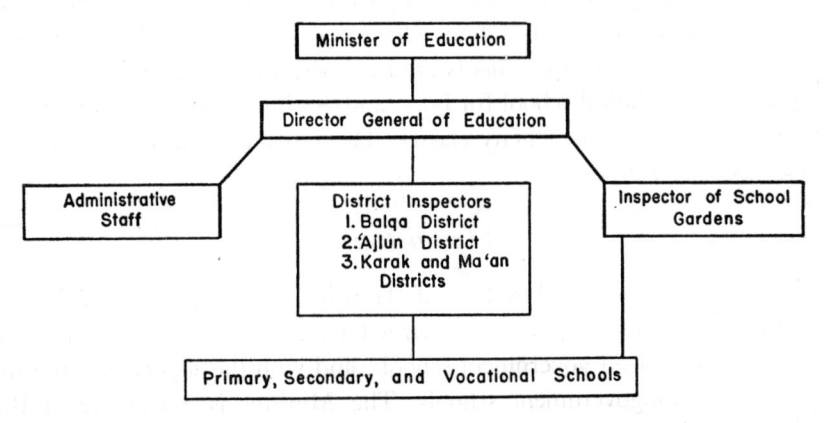

```
                    Minister of Education
                              |
                  Director General of Education
                              |
   ┌──────────────────────────┼──────────────────────────┐
Administrative          District Inspectors         Inspector of School
    Staff                1. Balqa District              Gardens
                         2. 'Ajlun District
                         3. Karak and Ma'an
                            Districts
                              |
              Primary, Secondary, and Vocational Schools
```

Educational Finance

The financial support of public education in Transjordan is borne almost wholly by the central treasury. Table 50 shows the financial provisions in the annual budgets for the span of twenty-two years.

It is clear that as the general budget rose during the war years there was no corresponding increase in the budget for education, and that, therefore, the proportionate amount spent on education declined sharply. The whole educational provision is no more than £P35,248, which represents 1.1 percent of the general budget. It is not too much to say that had the proportion remained at about 6 percent, as it was over several years, the sum would have been nearly sufficient to provide for universal elementary education.

TABLE 50

TOTAL BUDGET AND ESTIMATES FOR EDUCATION, TRANSJORDAN, 1924–46

Financial Year	Total Estimates	Education Estimates	Percentage
1924–25	£P 274,868*	£P14,771	5.4
1928–29	318,950	22,582	7.1
1930–31	350,532	23,482	6.7
1939–40	599,338	28,911	4.8
1941–42	1,183,155	29,542	2.5
1942–43	1,423,349	31,432	2.2
1943–44	2,062,290	33,366	1.6
1944–45	3,252,334	33,478	1.0
1945–46	3,249,000	35,248	1.1

* A Palestinian pound is equivalent to slightly more than $4.00.

A 1937 amendment to the Turkish Elementary Education Law of 1329 A.H. (1914) provided for a municipal education tax. This has so far been imposed in seven municipalities, and a total of twenty teachers has been appointed in the public schools and paid from municipal revenues derived from this tax. The appointment of these teachers made it possible to add sixth and seventh grades to many of the local schools.

According to the old Turkish law, the school building in the rural districts must be provided by the village authorities. The Ministry of Education must provide the rest—school furniture, equipment, cost of upkeep, and teachers' salaries. In the cities the cost of rental is borne by the Ministry of Education. All of the school buildings in Transjordan, except five, are rented.

Teachers are employed on the same basis as other civil servants. The Transjordan civil service is divided into four classes and ten grades as follows:

Class	Grade	Monthly Salary Range
I	1	£P58–64
	2	48–56
	3	38–46
	4	32–36
II	5	26–31
	6	21–25
III	7	17–20
	8	13–16
IV	9	9–12
	10	6–8

In addition, there is a temporary grade to which a salary of £P5 or less is attached. Appointment to this grade is upon the recommendation of the Director General of Education and the approval of the Minister. Officials and teachers in classes three and four are appointed upon the recommendation of the Director General, but with the approval of the Prime Minister. Officials of classes one and two are appointed upon recommendation of the Ministry concerned, with approval of the Council of Ministers and the King. At the time of the visit of the American Council Commission, the post of Director General of Education was scheduled on grade two of the civil service, the senior inspector was in grade four, and the other inspectors were in grade five.

Teachers with the degree of B.A. or its equivalent are first appointed in grade seven. Those who have finished the junior year at the American University of Beirut are appointed in grade eight; students who have finished the sophomore year of the American University of Beirut and graduates of the American Junior College for Women, in Beirut, and of the Arab College of Jerusalem are appointed in grade nine. Holders of the Transjordan Matriculation Certificate are put in grade ten on first appointment.

Promotions of teachers have lately been so rare that out of thirteen teachers with B.A. degrees who were teaching in the secondary schools, only four remained. The other nine left teaching for more lucrative jobs.

Educational Legislation

Until recently education in Transjordan was legally subject to the provisions of the education laws of the Ottoman regime. These were superseded, however, by the new regulations passed in 1939. Education Regulation No. 1 for the year 1939 concerning the organization of the educational system provides that the administration of the educational services must be conducted with the knowledge of the officials of the central office, the inspectors, the local administrative officials, the municipal committees in towns, and educational committees in the villages. The Departments of Health, Public Works, and Agriculture are enjoined to cooperate with the Ministry of Education, each in its own field. Regulations further prescribe the administrative framework for education already described. They stipulate that students for the educational missions are to be chosen by a committee of inspectors under the chairmanship of the Minister (later changed to the Director General) of Education. The Minister may also select specialists and principals of secondary schools to assist inspectors in work within their districts.

ORGANIZATION AND ADMINISTRATION

Education Regulation No. 2 for the year 1939 laid down the fundamental lines of educational organization. The functions of the Ministry of Education are defined as "the foundation, administration, and inspection of public schools, general supervision over private schools, encouragement of scientific and literary activities and of scouting and physical education in the schools, promoting fine arts, control of public morals, and concerning itself with all that pertains to public education and culture." Schools are classed as rural elementary, elementary, primary, secondary, and specialized.

The regulations set down the main features of elementary, secondary, and specialized education. Rural and town elementary education is free, and elementary education is compulsory for boys and girls in localities defined by the government. The conditions for admission to each type of school and for the granting of certificates are specified. Private schools cannot be opened without the permission of the Minister of Education. Private-school teachers must be licensed to teach by the Ministry. The teaching of Arabic and of the history and geography of the Arab world, including Transjordanian history and geography, are obligatory. Arabic lessons must be no less than five periods a week in elementary classes, and four periods in secondary classes. Teachers of elementary schools must be graduates of elementary- and primary-teachers colleges, while those of secondary schools must be graduates of a higher-teachers college (neither type of teachers college exists in Transjordan and, therefore, teachers must be prepared in neighboring countries). However, in case of lack of qualified teachers the Minister is empowered to choose people from a lower grade on a temporary appointment. Such temporary appointees cannot be confirmed in the service unless they spend three years in teaching during which they study special educational courses, and unless the Director General deems them worthy for teaching. Similarly, teachers of physical education and other special subjects may be appointed if deemed competent in their subjects without regard to other requirements.

The regulations provide for a public secondary examination, while an amendment passed in 1944 sets up a similar examination at the end of the primary school leading to the primary-school certificate. The above-mentioned Regulations Nos. 1 and 2 for the year 1939 abolish all previous Turkish laws on education.

Regulation No. 1 for the year 1945 for private schools defines these schools as those founded by a Transjordanian or foreign individual, group, or sect and supported by their owners from their own funds or from fees, donations, or religious endowment. Private schools may be opened only by permission of the Ministry of Education. The list of teachers, the courses of study, and the books must first be approved. The Ministry, also, is to endorse the diplomas and certificates of the teachers. Teachers are not to encroach on the freedom of religion and are to refrain from teaching beliefs which contradict the beliefs of the children who do not belong to the religion or sect of the school; nor are they to teach beliefs in opposition to the constitution of the state. No coeducational school may be opened beyond the third elementary grade, and no men may be appointed as teachers in girls schools even on a temporary appointment. Corporal punishment is prohibited. Schools are subject to examination by inspectors, doctors, and architects of the Ministry of Education. Authorities of the school must present to the inspectors all information required, and send to the Ministry of Education within three months after the opening of each school year statistics of the distribution of pupils by classes, ages, and religions. A full personal register for each pupil must be kept. The program for any ceremony, public meeting, or graduation exercises must be submitted to the local authorities for approval at least a week before the meeting.

The Educational Ladder

The educational ladder in Transjordan is very similar to that of Palestine, although somewhat simpler. The two countries were in the last quarter of a century under the same mandatary; thus, it is to be expected that similarities should exist.

Chart X shows the design of the system. The primary schools are of

Chart X
TRANSJORDAN: PUBLIC SCHOOL SYSTEM, 1945-46

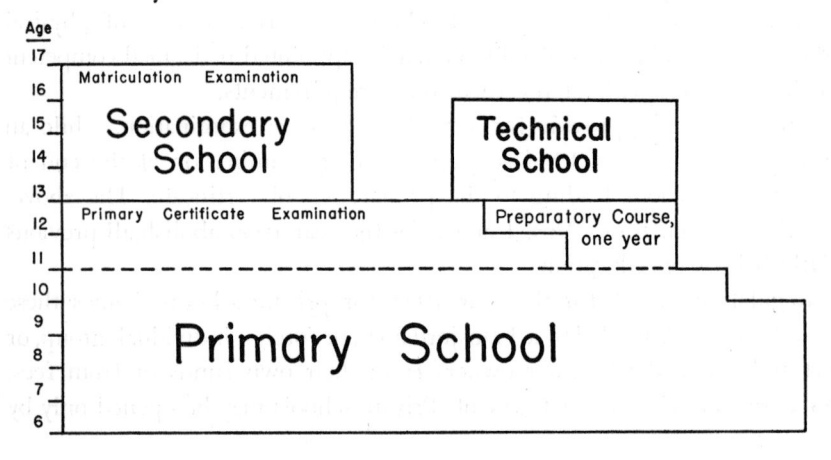

seven grades, divided into a lower cycle of five grades known as the elementary cycle and a higher cycle of two grades. Schools in the towns are either complete primary with seven grades or elementary with five grades. In the villages most schools are of four grades (as in Palestine) and are known as village elementary schools. In 1945–46 there were in Transjordan 12 complete public city primary schools of seven grades and 7 city elementary schools of four or five grades. In the same year there were 44 village schools of which 1 was of two grades, 1 of three, and 42 of four grades. In addition, there was 1 school for Bedouins.

To be admitted to the first grade, a pupil must have completed his sixth year of age, and not exceeded his eighth. A pupil is not allowed to repeat a grade more than twice and is dropped from a primary or elementary school if he has completed his fifteenth year of age. Previously pupils were graduated from the primary school on the basis of school examinations, but beginning with 1944–45 the primary-school certificate was granted only after a public examination.

Secondary schools are of four years in two stages—an intermediate stage and an upper stage, each of two years. Annual fees of £P2 for the intermediate stage and of £P3 for the upper stage are charged. Students are not admitted if they have completed their sixteenth year of age, and no student is allowed to repeat a year more than once. Secondary education ends with the Transjordan matriculation examination conducted by the Ministry of Education. In 1945–46 there were 4 public secondary schools, 1 of two years at Karak, 2 of three years (one at 'Amman and one at Irbid), and 1 complete school of four years at al-Salt. It was hoped that at least the 'Amman school would be extended to four years by 1946–47.

There is no public secondary school for girls in Transjordan, and the education of girls in the public schools, therefore, reaches only to the end of primary school. There is, however, 1 secondary school for girls, reaching to the third secondary year, which is maintained by the Church of England Missionary Society.

Parallel with the secondary school, is the Technical School at 'Amman. Here pupils may pursue a four-year course in carpentry (including upholstery), and blacksmithing.

No postsecondary schools exist. Students either are sent by the government to study outside Transjordan or go at their own expense. Educational missions have been sent to the American Universities at Beirut and Cairo. The British Council helped send 5 students to universities in England and Scotland. Some have been sent to Palestine to the Arab College and the Teachers Training College for Women in Jerusalem, to the Agricultural

School at Tulkarm, and to the English Girls College and the Schmidt College in Jerusalem. Twenty-three have been sent for agricultural training at the Near East Foundation Farm at Tha'labayah, Lebanon. Two boys were sent to the Higher Teachers College in Baghdad. Students may also go at their own expense to the American University of Beirut, the Syrian University in Damascus, the Egyptian universities, and other institutions abroad. In addition, the government has sent students for short courses in village welfare service in Lebanon, or in scouting in Palestine. During the period from 1927 to 1946 a total of 103 mission students, including 5 sent to England and Scotland by the British Council, have been sent to other countries to study for varying lengths of time. Of this total at least 12 were girls.

The Development of the System

Table 51 shows statistically the development of the public educational system in Transjordan between 1922–23 and 1945–46.

TABLE 51

Number of Public Schools, Teachers, and Pupils, in Transjordan, 1922–46

Year	Number of Schools	Number of Teachers	Enrollment Boys	Girls	Total	Average Number of Pupils per Teacher
1922–23	44	81	2,998	318	3,316	43.4
1930–31	54	122	4,110	588	4,698	40.5
1940–41	74	184	8,255	1,895	10,150	56.7
1941–42	74	184	8,365	1,999	10,364	56.1
1942–43	74	186	7,955	1,897	9,852	52.3
1943–44	73	188	7,750	1,857	9,607	50.0
1944–45	73	197	7,645	1,844	9,489	47.7
1945–46	73	199	7,918	1,956	9,874	49.2

In the first nine years, schools increased by less than 25 percent, or at the rate of approximately one school a year, while the number of teachers increased by 50 percent and pupils by slightly less than that. In another ten years, by 1940–41, schools had increased by 37 percent over the previous decade, teachers by 50 percent, while the number of pupils had more than doubled since 1930–31. It is to be noted that the number of girls increased at a more rapid rate during the decade. Since 1940–41 the number of schools has been at a standstill, the number of teachers has increased slightly, and the number of pupils showed some drop during the war years. Evidently the number of pupils has been increasing at a more rapid rate than that of schools or teachers, so that the number of pupils per teacher has correspondingly risen from 43.4 in 1922–23 to 56.7 in

1940, and had come down to 49.2 in 1945–46. Some classes are too large for efficient teaching.

In 1945–46, there were 73 public schools of all types, with 199 teachers (including 38 women), and 9,874 pupils, of whom 1,956 were girls. In the same year there were 100 nongovernment schools of which 64 were for boys; 21, for girls; and 15, coeducational. These were manned by 251 teachers, of whom 95 were women, and attended by 6,472 pupils, of whom 2,640 were girls. Thus, the total number of pupils in both public and private schools was 16,346, of whom 4,596 were girls. It is noteworthy that there were more private than public schools and that more girls were in private than in public schools.

TABLE 52
Enrollment by Grades in Public Schools, Transjordan, 1945–46

Grade	Primary and Secondary Schools	Technical Schools
Elementary		
1	2,254	...
2	2,064	...
3	1,815	...
4	1,576	...
5	795	...
Primary		
6	575	...
7	357	...
Secondary		
1	138	26
2	99	20
3	93	19
4	36	7
Total	9,802	72

It is not possible to give accurately the ratio between children attending schools and the total number of children of school age. A rough calculation on the basis of a five-year school shows it to be between 26 and 28 percent. This ratio is higher for boys than for girls. Among the Christian communities there is approximately universal attendance in elementary schools for children of school age.

Distribution of pupils according to classes in public schools shows the same tendency of gradual elimination of pupils as in the other Arab countries. Table 52 shows the enrollment by grades for public schools for 1945–46.

A sharp decline in numbers occurs between the fourth and fifth grades, largely due to the fact that half the public schools do not go beyond the fourth elementary grade. As in Palestine, very few pupils reach the top secondary classes, but, unlike Palestine, there seems to be no express policy of strict selection of pupils after the fifth grade. The process of elimination seems to take place naturally, partly due to the small number of complete primary and secondary schools.

An analysis of the statistics of attendance by types of schools reveals the following:

Type of School	Enrollment
City primary and elementary schools	6,321
Rural elementary schools	3,099
The Tribal School	16
Secondary schools	366
The Technical School	72
Total	9,874

Attendance in primary and elementary schools is divided in the proportion of two in the cities to one in the villages, although the ratio for the general population is more nearly the reverse. The number of secondary-school pupils is 3.8 percent of the number of primary- and elementary-school pupils.

Public Examinations

The public primary-school examination was instituted for the first time in 1944–45. This examination is open to all those who wish to sit for it. Application of pupils are sent through the schools, while independent applicants send their applications direct to the Ministry of Education. A fee of £P2 is charged. A committee is appointed by the Minister with the Director General of Education as chairman and with its membership made up of the inspectors and selected members. The committee chooses those who are to formulate the questions and those who are to be supervisors of the examinations and readers of examination papers. It sets down the rules for the examinations and summarizes the results. The results are not considered final until approved by the Minister.

The examination covers the topics taught in the upper two classes of the primary schools and is comprised of Arabic, English, arithmetic and geometry, history, geography, and science. Muslim boys take an examination in religion, while non-Muslims take an examination in agriculture. Girls take domestic science and child care instead of science, and non-Muslim girls take nursing instead of religion.

The passing mark is 60 for each subject. Pupils failing in more than one subject are considered failures. Those failing in one subject must, in order

ORGANIZATION AND ADMINISTRATION

to pass, have secured a mark near the passing mark in that subject. The examination is held only once a year. A student who has failed, therefore, may present himself again only in the following year. Pupils passing the examination are granted the Transjordan Certificate of Primary Examinations. Only holders of this certificate may be admitted to the public secondary schools.

In 1944–45, 224 boys and 42 girls took the primary-school examinations. Of these, 118 boys (52.6 percent) and 26 girls (61.9 percent) passed, and 106 boys and 16 girls failed. Reference to Table 52 reveals that a large number of pupils eligible to take the examination did not attempt it.

The Transjordan examination for the secondary-school certificate is conducted, in the same way as the primary examination, by a committee under the chairmanship of the Director General of Education. It is based on the program of the four years of secondary school. It comprises five

TABLE 53
Results of Public Secondary-School Examinations, Transjordan, 1940–45

Year	Number Entering	Number Passing	Number Failing	Percentage Passing
1940–41	64	59	5	92.2
1941–42	57	57	0	100.0
1942–43	41	33	8	80.5
1943–44	66	12	54	18.5
1944–45	55	14	41	25.4

required subjects—Arabic, English, mathematics, physics, and history. Muslim students are, in addition, required to take an examination in religion and one other of the elective subjects. Non-Muslims have to take two of these electives. The electives are botany and zoology together, general geography, and geography of the Mediterranean Sea.

The examination is held only once a year. The passing mark is 60 for each subject. A student failing in more than one subject is considered to have failed the examination, while one failing in one subject may be considered to have passed if his mark in the subject is not much below the passing mark. Successful students are granted the Transjordan Certificate of Secondary Examinations.

Table 53 shows the results of the secondary-school examinations for the five years 1940–45.

The proportion of passing students fluctuates considerably from year to year, having varied from 18 to 100 percent in the five-year period 1940–45.

Chapter 19

THE SCHOOLS OF TRANSJORDAN

THE PUBLIC, or government, education system of Transjordan consists of a seven-year primary school and a four-year secondary school leading to a public matriculation examination. There are no kindergartens in the public-school system as yet, although children younger than six may go to *kuttabs* (traditional religious schools, not included in the public-school system, which teach beginning reading and writing, but which emphasize religious instruction). In some villages the schools are incomplete, offering courses which vary from two to five years in length and frequently combining classes. In 1945–46 there were 44 such schools, all for boys, with 3,115 pupils registered. Girls are sometimes permitted to attend the first three grades of the elementary school for boys.

Elementary schools are housed in rented buildings, usually former dwellings. The increase in interest in school attendance during the last few years has been paralleled by increases in the size of classes so that at present most rooms are crowded. Most of the classes in primary schools in cities have more than 60 boys in each class and in at least 1 school there are 91 enrolled in one class in the second grade. Playground space is limited. Thirty-four of the village schools have school gardens varying in size from one and one-half to five acres.

Secondary schools are in rented or government buildings. The new building at Irbid is modern in design and construction and is surrounded by ample playground space. Classes are not large, and rooms are not crowded in secondary schools.

The Primary Course of Study

The Program of studies for primary schools for boys is given in Table 54. Slight differences appear in the distribution of periods in girls schools to provide one period per week in domestic science in the sixth and seventh grades, one period per week in child care in the seventh, and one period per week for nursing instruction in the sixth and seventh grades, and a total of thirteen hours for handwork distributed over grades two to seven. The total number of periods per week for girls is the same as for boys except that the girls have two additional periods in grades two and three and one additional period in grades four and five. In the program for five-year village schools, the length of the periods assigned to religion, Arabic, English, and geography is reduced slightly in order to provide theoretical and practical agriculture for six periods per week in the third, five in the fourth, and four in the fifth grade. If no garden is available, the periods assigned to practical agriculture are distributed to the basic subjects.

TABLE 54
Program of Studies in Primary Schools for Boys, Transjordan, 1945–46

Subject	\multicolumn{7}{c}{Periods* per Week}
	1st Grade	2nd Grade	3rd Grade	4th Grade	5th Grade	6th Grade	7th Grade
Koran and religion	4	5	5	4	4	4	3
Arabic	12	12	12	9	9	9	8
English	...	...	...	7	7	7	7
Arithmetic	5	5	5	5	5	4	4
Geometry	...	...	...	...	...	1	1
History	...	1	1	2	2	2	3
Geography	...	1	1	2	2	2	2
Civics	...	...	...	...	...	...	1
Science	...	1	2	2	2	2	2
Agriculture	...	...	...	...	...	1	1
Physical training and singing	2	1	1	1	1	1	1
Drawing and handwork	1	1	1	1	1	1	1
Total	24	26	28	33	33	34	34

* Periods are of 45-minute length.

The course of study in the *Koran* and *religion* provides for the memorization of parts of the Koran, beginning with about 150 lines in the first grade and requiring the learning of complete chapters in the sixth and seventh grades. Simple stories of the life of the Prophet and a study of his sayings are begun in the first year and continue for the entire course. By the end of the seventh year pupils are expected to know all the requirements of the Muhammadan religion relating to prayers, fasting, ablutions, feast days, pilgrimage, and responsibilities to the poor. Character traits such as honesty, truthfulness, attitudes toward parents, obedience, self-control, and kindness to animals are discussed and emphasized. Attention is given to an elementary study of the history of Islam, personal status (such as marriage, divorce, and inheritance), beliefs, and the lives of the prophets, including Adam, Abraham, Moses, and Jesus.

The course of study in *Arabic* includes the study of colloquial and classical Arabic. Attention is given to reading, writing, memorization, grammar, and composition, with materials selected which are considered appropriate for the age level involved. Dictation is frequently used as a method of instruction. Both personal and business letters are studied in the seventh year. Pupils are encouraged to read books and magazines and to use the library. Much of the material used in reading is derived from religious literature.

The study of *history* begins in the second grade and is correlated in that grade with geography. Simple stories of important figures during the early Islamic period serve as content in the second year. The lives of King Husayn and his sons are studied in some detail in this year. The course is continued in the third year with a more detailed study of the important events during the lifetime of Muhammad. From the fourth to the sixth years inclusive a systematic study is made of Arab history from the death of Muhammad to the period of the Crusades. In the seventh year a rapid survey is made of the history of the Near East from the time of the ancient Egyptians to the present.

Geography in the second year includes a study of the physical features of the pupil's village or city; definitions of such terms as mountain, valley, sea, lake, river; development of knowledge about day and night, the cardinal directions, the seasons, and means of communication in and between population centers. The earth and its movements are studied in the third year. Other topics include maps and the globe; definitions of such terms as island, peninsula, strait, canal, and cape; and the geographical features of Transjordan. The geography of Syria, Lebanon, Iraq, and Palestine is studied in the fourth year as well as such general topics as volcanoes and earthquakes, latitude and longitude, and phenomena of the atmosphere. Asia, Europe, and Africa are considered in the fifth year, and North, Central, and South America and Australia in the sixth. The emphasis in the seventh year is on the Mediterranean basin and a review of the geography of the Near East.

The course of study in *civics* in the seventh grade provides for the study of the family, the nation, development of government, the rights and responsibilities of citizens, and the constitution of Transjordan. Attention is given to both local and central organization and administration of the affairs of the country. The relationships between the executive, legislative, and judicial bodies are studied.

General Science begins in the second grade with observation and discussion of common animals and plants in the child's environment. The importance of cleanliness of body, clothing, and living spaces is emphasized. The relationship of wholesome food, fresh air, and exercise to good health is stressed. These topics are continued in the third grade with more details

Above: The new secondary school for boys, Irbid, Transjordan
Below: Recess at the secondary school for boys, Irbid

THE SCHOOLS OF TRANSJORDAN

regarding good health habits and care of the eyes, nose, and ears. Discussion of common industries and occupations with attention to materials used is included in this grade. In the fourth grade domestic animals are studied, with special attention to their commercial value, and wild animals such as the lion, tiger, and elephant are discussed. Plants and trees of commercial value, including olive and almond trees, grape vines, wheat, and watermelon, are studied in this year. Rocks and minerals are identified, and their uses and importance explained. The skeleton and muscular, digestive, and circulatory systems of man are studied. Some common illnesses and their causes, and first-aid treatment are considered. The major topics of the fifth year are the less common animals of land and sea; structure of typical plants; introduction to elementary factors in agriculture such as function of plowing, importance of irrigation, and uses of common instruments or tools; and the human nervous system. In the sixth year more emphasis is placed upon physical principles, such as air pressure; size, weight, and density of substances; evaporation and melting; and meteorological phenomena such as fog, rain, hail, and snow. The human circulatory system is studied in considerable detail. Chemistry and its uses are introduced in the course of study in the seventh year. Differences between elements, mixtures, and compounds are explained. Chemical properties of common substances such as sulphuric acid, iron, lead, mercury, air, water, carbon are illustrated and explained. Respiratory systems in plants and animals are studied and compared. Importance of a balanced diet is stressed. Some of the elementary ideas about electricity together with such phenomena as lightning are included. Sound and light are also studied in this year. Contagious diseases, methods of transmission of disease, and further study of first aid are considered.

The course in *agriculture* for village schools from the third to the seventh years attempts to give modern theories together with much practice in the school gardens. Effort is made to make the course as practical as possible and to provide the basis for improvement of agriculture in the village areas. Vegetables, flowers, fruit trees, beekeeping, animal-breeding, poultry, plant and animal pests and diseases, grafting, pruning, and dairying are studied during the five-year period.

The Michael West series of New Method Readers is used in the course in *English* which begins in the fourth grade and continues through the seventh. The readers and companion books through reader five are expected to be completed by the end of the seventh grade. The introductory texts, however, are the *First Year English* by Morris and part of the second book by the same author.

The course in *arithmetic* for the first grade provides for learning to read and write numbers up to 10, exercises in addition and subtraction of numbers to 10, and adding equal numbers as an introduction to the multiplication tables. By the end of the year pupils are expected to carry out the four fundamental operations with numbers up to 20. In addition to reviewing the first year's work, the second year's work includes operations with numbers up to 100, multiplication tables to 6×6, writing numbers to 500, and an explanation of the simplest fractions such as one-half and one-fourth. Multiplication tables, including 12×12, are learned in the third year. The decimal system is studied intensively in this year, and written problems are begun. Measures of time, length, and weight and more difficult and complex fractions are also studied in the third year. Reading and writing numbers up to 1,000,000 and multiplication and division by numbers with two or more digits are carried out in the fourth year. Problems involving units of time, the metric system, and Palestinian money are included. Addition and subtraction with compound numbers are studied in the fourth year. The fifth-year course includes a review of the four fundamental operations with whole numbers, fractions, and decimals; conversion of common fractions to decimals and vice versa; ratio and proportion; and areas of square and rectangular figures. In the sixth year, local, metric, and English measures, including money, are introduced, together with problems requiring conversion from one system to another. Problems involving simple, direct, and inverse proportion are solved. Commercial arithmetic involving percentage, simple and compound interest, profit and loss, insurance, and simple bookkeeping and elementary business practice comprise the content for the seventh year.

The relatively small amount of time allotted to *geometry* in the sixth and seventh years permits little more than an introduction to intuitive geometry and simple constructions. Elementary characteristics of circles, squares, rectangles, and parallelograms are discovered. Ability to compute the areas of these figures and the volume of the corresponding solids is developed.

At the end of the seventh grade of the primary school a public certificate examination is given to those pupils who have completed the course and who apply.

Since there are no teacher-training institutions in Transjordan, most of the elementary-school teachers in schools for boys are holders of Matriculation, or secondary-school, Certificates, although some have not completed their secondary-school course. In the schools for girls, especially in the smaller cities, most of the teachers have completed only the elementary-school course. In the larger cities, teachers in girls schools have received additional training, usually in Jerusalem or in Beirut.

THE SCHOOLS OF TRANSJORDAN

Secondary Education

Secondary education for boys was provided under government auspices in 4 schools in Transjordan in 1945–46. These schools were located at al-Salt, 'Amman, Irbid, and Karak. Only the school at al-Salt provided the complete four-year program, but it was expected that the schools at Irbid and 'Amman would offer complete programs in 1946–47, and the one at Karak, in the following year. The total enrollment in the 4 schools in 1945–46 was 366 boys. There are no government secondary schools for girls. Preparation for government employment or higher education is the primary objective of the secondary schools. Government employment includes teaching, as well as clerkships in government departments. A determined effort has been made during the last few years to avoid the development of a group of unemployed secondary-school graduates.

THE PROGRAM OF STUDIES

The program of studies is comprised of a uniform course of four years' duration, upon successful completion of which the student presents himself for the public government Matriculation, or secondary-school, Certificate examination. The details of the program of studies are given in Table 55.

Somewhat detailed courses of study have been prepared for each of the subjects. A brief summary of the more important topics is given below.

Reading of the *Koran* forms the basis of the study in religion during

TABLE 55
PROGRAM OF STUDIES FOR SECONDARY SCHOOLS FOR BOYS, TRANSJORDAN, 1945–46

Subject	Periods* per Week			
	1st Year	2nd Year	3rd Year	4th Year
Koran and religion	2	2	1	1
Arabic	7	7	8	6
English†	7	7	7	7
Arithmetic	2	2	...	...
Algebra	3	3	2	2
Geometry	3	3	2	3
Trigonometry	...	...	1	...
History	3	3	3	3
Geography	2	2	2	2
Physics	2	3	5	5
Chemistry	1	...	3	3
Botany	...	...	...	1
Zoology	...	...	...	1
Agriculture	2	2	...	...
Total	34	34	34	34

* Periods are of 45-minute length.
† Between 5 and 10 minutes are taken from reading lessons for dictation.

the first three years. Directions relative to ablutions, prayer, fasting, charity, and pilgrimages are reviewed and emphasized. The four important sects of Islam are described and their differences explained. Quotations from the Koran are used to explain standards of behavior and relations to others. In the fourth year, major emphasis is placed upon developing an understanding of personal status (marriage, divorce, inheritance, and family relationship) as provided for in Muslim law. The bases of good government as found in the Muhammadan religion are studied.

The study of *Arabic* continues to improve the quality of written and oral expression, in addition to which attention is given to furthering knowledge of the historical development of Arabic literature, with special emphasis upon the 'Abbasid Period. An analytical study of the contributions of the Arabs to literature is made. Memorization of selections from poetry and prose is required.

In *English,* the sixth and seventh readers of the Michael West series form the basis of the work in the first year of the secondary school. More attention is given to silent reading of simplified or abridged editions of standard prose such as *Don Quixote, Ivanhoe, The Cloister and the Hearth,* and to anthologies of English poetry in the last three years. Systematic study of grammar is carried out in all four years.

The course of study for *history* in the first year provides for the study of ancient times up to the invasion of the barbarians, with special emphasis on the development of civilization in Egypt, the Near East, Greece, and Rome. Study of the Middle Ages from the barbarian invasion to the French Revolution is indicated for the second year, special attention being given to the part which the Arabs played in this period. Modern history from the French Revolution to the present is studied in the third year, and an intensive study of the history of the Arabs from earliest times to the present is made in the fourth year.

In the first year of *geography,* after a brief review of the material studied in the elementary school, attention is directed to the geographical features of Asia and especially the Middle East. Such topics as location, climate, natural resources, size, population, important cities, agriculture and industry, exports and imports, transportation, and government are considered for each political division. Europe and Africa are the regions studied in the second year, North and South America and Australia in the third year, while in the fourth year Syria, the Arabian peninsula, Iraq, and the Mediterranean basin are studied intensively.

The history of *agriculture* receives some attention in the first year, but major emphasis is upon such topics as forests, beekeeping, milk production, water supply, irrigation, plants and their requirements for growth, field crops, and rabbit-breeding. Gardening, cattle- and sheep-raising, insects and their control, fertilizers, fruit trees, experimental agriculture, and floriculture are the topics receiving most attention in the second year.

In *arithmetic,* written problems involving the four fundamental operations, determination of the highest common factor and the lowest common multiple, ordinary and decimal fractions including conversion of one to the other, and ratio and proportion are included in the first-year course. Some business arithmetic involving percentage, profit and loss, insurance, and simple interest is studied in the first year also. In the second year the course includes a review of ratio and proportion, English and metric systems of measure, English and Palestinian monetary systems, square and cube roots, area and volume of common surfaces and solids, compound interest, and stocks and bonds.

In *algebra,* the major topics in the first year are fundamental operations with algebraic expressions, factoring, fractions, and problems with three unknown quantities; in the second year, simple and complex fractions, factors of the sum and difference of quantities to the third power, and quadratic equations; in the third year, more difficult factoring, theory of exponents, indices, logarithms and graphs; and in the fourth year, solution of equations by the use of graphs, and a review of the work of previous years with more difficult problems.

Trigonometry is taught for one hour a week during the third year. Elementary facts are studied regarding measurement of angles, relationships of length of sides to angles in triangles, trigonometric ratios for angles of 0, 15, 30, 45, 60, and 90 degrees, and problems involving the computation of sides and angles of right triangles are solved.

The course of study for *physics* for the first year includes measurement using the metric system, density, mechanics of liquids and gases, atmospheric pressure, temperature and laws of expansion; second year, magnetism, static and current electricity, batteries, electricity in the atmosphere, electric bells, telephone, telegraph and microphone, elementary principles and applications of sound and light; in the third year, simple machines, force and motion, work and energy, freezing, evaporation, humidity, and advanced work in sound, magnetism, and electricity; and in the fourth year, nature and characteristics of light, optics, analysis of light, electric current and its magnetic, mechanical, and chemical effects, electrons, radio, and a review of previous work in physics.

Chemistry is studied in the first, third, and fourth years. The introduction in the first year includes the study of differences between physical and chemical changes, compounds and mixtures, oxidation and combustion, composition of air, production and characteristics of oxygen, hydrogen, and nitrogen, composition and properties of water, and the study of nitrogen, carbon, acids, and salts. In the third year the topics studied are atomic weights, Dalton's Theory, important chlorides, nitrogen and the production of ammonia, manufacture of ice, nitric acid, fertilizers, sulphur and its compounds, silica, and carbon. The topics studied in the fourth year are: chemical theories and laws; characteristic properties and compounds of sodium, potassium, calcium, magnesium, copper, silver, iron, and aluminum; preparation and properties of cement, steel, alcohol, ether, sugar, and starch. An introduction to the chemistry of photography is given.

Relatively little attention is given to the *biological sciences* in the secondary-school program. Only two periods per week in the last year are provided for the study of botany and zoology. The course in botany includes the study of the cell, germination of seeds and growth of plants, respiration, food requirements, storage of food, reproduction, grafting and pruning, and method of classification. In zoology the topics studied are: general characteristics of animals, the cell, food and nutrition, digestive, circulatory, respiratory, and nervous systems of animals, reproduction, classification, and a detailed study of the skeleton of the rabbit.

Laboratory work does not seem to have an important place in the teaching of science in the government secondary schools. Supplies and equipment are limited partly because it has been difficult to secure needed material during the war. Proper rooms for laboratories were not available in most of the schools, and existing equipment did not appear to be used extensively.

Informal student activities take the form of Boy Scout organizations, literary societies (usually limited to Arabic), cultural societies, and sports including soccer and basketball.

Since there is no institution of higher education in Transjordan, most teachers who have received training beyond the secondary school have studied in Palestine, Lebanon, Egypt, or Iraq.

Vocational Education

The only vocational education in Transjordan is given in the Technical School in 'Amman. There were 72 boys enrolled in this School in 1945–46, of whom 40 were boarding students. No fees are charged although boarding students must furnish their own clothing and their beds and bedcoverings. The vocational course is three years in length for those who have completed the primary-school course of seven years. Since in many towns and villages only five years of elementary school are offered, a preparatory year is given for those who have completed only five or six years of the elementary school. In 1945–46, 26 of the 72 students were in the preparatory class.

The program of studies for the preparatory years includes Arabic (nine periods per week), arithmetic (six), geometry (three), physics (four), geography (two), general drawing (five), and shop orientation (five). The courses in these subjects are selected from the corresponding courses for the sixth and seventh grades of the elementary school and are designed to give in one year what is most necessary in the preparation for work in the Technical School.

There are two specializations in the Technical School—blacksmithing, including turning and fitting, and carpentry, including upholstering. Blacksmithing was more popular in 1945–46, having an enrollment of 30 boys, as compared to 15 in carpentry. Prior to the war a third specialization in bamboo-chair making and basketry was offered, but it had to be discontinued when materials were not available.

Instruction is carried out largely in the shops, with only one or two hours a day given over to mechanical drawing and theory. A series of practical projects of graduated difficulty is used as the basis of instruction. An exhibit of the students' work is held annually, at which time the objects are sold and the income is used for the support of the School. It was reported that graduates have little difficulty in finding employment with the Iraq Petroleum Company, the army, or in local repair shops.

Nongovernment Schools

Public education in Transjordan is supplemented by provision for education under private, usually religious, auspices. Catholic schools under the Latin Patriarchate of Jerusalem have the largest number of pupils, 2,731; Muslim schools have 1,429 pupils; Greek Orthodox, 1,247; Protestants, 843; and other religious groups or individuals provide for 222. Of the total of 6,472 pupils in nongovernment schools, 3,832 are boys and 2,640 are girls. Approximately two-thirds, 4,345, of the total in nongovernment schools are Christians. All but two of the schools are elementary or primary schools which follow more or less closely the government program of studies and prepare for the public primary-school certificate examination. Some have kindergartens and accept pupils below the age of six. Fifteen of them have boys and girls in the same classes for the kindergartens and first three grades. Most of the schools are housed in buildings constructed as private dwellings or in parts of church buildings or adjacent quarters. Some, such as the Catholic School and the Church of England Missionary Society School for Girls in 'Amman, begin the study of a foreign language, English, as early as the kindergarten.

The only secondary education for girls in all Transjordan is provided in the Church Missionary Society School for Girls in 'Amman. This School, founded as an elementary school in 1927, is now providing three years of a secondary-school program. In 1945–46 there were 9 girls in the first year, 6 in the second, and 4 in the third. Girls who wish to continue their education after finishing the third year usually go to the American Junior College in Beirut or to schools in Palestine. In addition to the secondary school, there is a kindergarten and seven grades of elementary education which provided for 225 pupils in 1945–46. There were 75 boys enrolled in the kindergarten and the first three grades. The program of studies in the elementary school is not greatly different from the program in government schools except that the study of the Scriptures takes the place of the Koran and Muslim religion, and English is studied from five to seven periods in each year, including the kindergarten. In the program for the secondary years the major change consists of substituting domestic science, sewing, singing, biology, games, and Scriptures for the physics, chemistry, and Koran in the government course. The school week is forty-three periods including three periods for games, as compared to thirty-four periods in public schools. The study of Arabic is emphasized throughout the entire elementary- and secondary-school course. Extraclass activities include a fortnightly cinema provided by the British Council, a Christian Endeavor Society, and a literary society, each of which meets weekly, and an annual school outing. Fees for day pupils vary from £P12 ($48) in the kindergarten to £P18 ($72) in the secondary school. There were 14 boarders in 1945–46 who paid an additional fee of £P48 ($192). The School has an attractive building and site in a residential section of 'Amman. Recent additions to the original building have reduced the congestion, but many requests of boarding students have to be refused because of lack of space. A large playing field adjacent to the school building is much used. The student body is divided into six houses which compete in intramural games.

The Bishop's School, located a short distance from the Church Missionary Society School for Girls on the same ridge high above the city of 'Amman, was founded in 1936 to provide elementary and secondary education for boys. The present program (1946) begins with the fourth grade of the elementary school and finishes with the fourth year of the secondary school—a total of eight years. The total enrollment in 1945–46

THE SCHOOLS OF TRANSJORDAN

was 212 boys, of whom 97 were in the secondary school. There is a tendency for boys to leave at the end of the third year to enter as freshmen at the American University of Beirut. Boys who complete the fourth year and pass the Transjordan matriculation examination are accepted as sophomores at A.U.B. Tuition fees vary from £P18 ($72) in the elementary classes to £P24 ($96) in the secondary classes. Boarding students pay £P66 ($264) in addition. The program of the School is similar to the government program although some of the subjects are taught in English instead of Arabic. Much emphasis, however, is laid on a high standard in Arabic. Students prepare for the London, as well as the Transjordan matriculation, examinations. In addition to the regular program of the School, informal activities include a literary society, Boy Scout troops, the YMCA, a hiking club, Sunday school, and a choir. A magazine containing articles in English and Arabic is published at the end of each school year. Of the 10 graduates of the class of 1945, 4 continued their work at the American University of Beirut, 1 is teaching in a government secondary school, and 5 are employed in government offices or in business.

The Bishop's School has attractive stone buildings which were constructed for the School. Classrooms are not large, but since classes are restricted in size they seem quite satisfactory. An area adjoining the buildings has been leveled off to form a football field and tennis courts. The boys seem much interested in sports activities. A cooperative society of present and former pupils operates a shop where sweets, stationery, and other requirements of boys are met.

Part Five

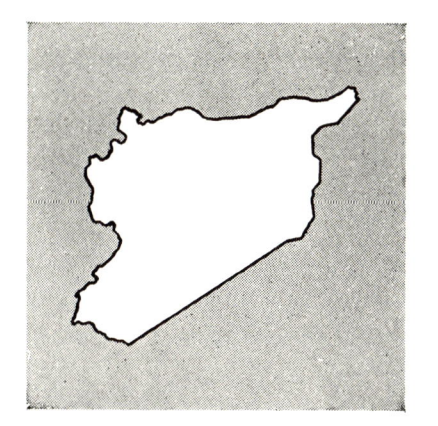

SYRIA

SYRIA

Population: *3,300,000 at the end of 1946 (estimate).*

Area: *171,104 square kilometers (66,063 square miles).*

Form of government: *Republic. President is elected for five years by the Chamber of Deputies (unicameral). Members of the Chamber of Deputies are elected by universal male suffrage. The Prime Minister is selected by the President. The Prime Minister nominates members of his Council of Ministers (cabinet), who are appointed by the President but responsible to the Chamber of Deputies.*

Principal occupations: *Agriculture, trade, professions, industry.*

Principal exports: *Cereals, fruits and nuts, meats, wool and hides, textiles.*

Principal imports: *Manufactured wares, mineral and chemical products, fuels, cotton goods, woolen textiles, foodstuffs (meats, fruits, rice, sugar, spices).*

Monetary unit: *Syro-Lebanese pound (£S) equivalent to $0.4576.*

Chapter 20

ORGANIZATION AND ADMINISTRATION OF THE EDUCATIONAL SYSTEM

*E*DUCATION in Syria underwent a process of radical change in the years 1943–46. As Syria was under French mandate prior to World War II, the educational system had been gradually shaped after the French model with a twelve-year ladder of general education involving a primary-certificate examination, an examination for the *brevet,* and examinations for the *Baccalauréat,* First and Second Parts, the former divided into scientific and literary sections, and the latter into mathematics and philosophy sections. While instruction was in Arabic, French occupied a prominent place in the curriculum. The French adviser to the Ministry of Education wielded decisive influence over the educational decisions of the Ministry. Almost all educational missions were sent to France, and French-trained Syrians held the key positions in administration and teaching.

With the declaration of the independence of Syria in 1941 and the holding of new elections which resulted in a nationalist victory, it was natural that the new Syrian government should wish to pursue a national policy in education, free from French influences, and calculated primarily to develop a Syrian-Arab type of education.

In order to do this, the Syrian government procured the services of the well-known Arab educator, Sati' al-Husri, a man of outstanding ability who, after making a special study of Swiss, French, and Belgian education, had become the most prominent educator in Turkey prior to 1914. After the separation of the Arab provinces from Turkey he joined the short-lived Arab government of the late King Faysal in Syria as its Minister of Education. Upon the fall of this government he accompanied King Faysal to Iraq where he became Director General of Education, laying the main foundation of the Iraqi educational system and continuing to exercise considerable influence on that system until 1936. He left Iraq in 1941 to reside in Lebanon, and since he was of Syrian origin, he was invited by the Syrian government to study its educational system and report on possible reforms. He brought to his task a decided nationalist outlook and considerable experience with the problems of education in the Near East. His sixteen reports, written between March and July 1944, have been published in one volume.[1] The recommendations of these reports served with very slight changes as the basis for the new educational organization in Syria, and inspired the laws and regulations which are now in force. The new policies constituted a sharp turn from French educational policies as they had been applied in Syria and caused considerable controversy and some armed conflict as late as 1945.

One of the causes of contention was the new education law (No. 121, "Embodying the Organization of Public Education") which was passed in December 1944. It provided, among other things, that no foreign language was to be taught in elementary schools. This meant the abolition of French from elementary schools, where it had formerly been required. The new law provided that a first foreign language was to be taught beginning with the first secondary year and a second foreign language beginning with the fifth year. Students were given their choice, thus putting French on an equal footing with any other foreign language—notably English, which was becoming increasingly popular.

The Franco-Syrian clash of May 1945, when the French bombarded Damascus, resulted in the boycotting of French schools by the Syrian population, and they were compelled to close. As the year 1945–46 approached, French schools were told that to be allowed to reopen they would be required to register with the Ministry of Education, submit to supervision by the Ministry, follow the syllabuses of the Ministry in the teaching of the Arabic language, Arab history and geography, and comply with certain other conditions. Almost all French schools failed to do this and, therefore, remained closed. A few schools formerly registered as French now registered as national schools, put a Syrian citizen at the head of the school, and were allowed to open. These were usually schools run by Syrian monks or sisters.

The closing of the French schools, which had an enrollment of 19,503 in 1944–45, created a serious situation for the Ministry of Education. Thousands of students were confronted with the possibility of not being able to attend school, at the same time that the demand for education was increasing rapidly. The government, therefore, took drastic measures. A special budget annex was passed. Six new secondary schools and 52 new

---

[1] Sati' al-Husri, *Reports on the State of Education in Syria and Recommendations for Its Reform* (Damascus: Ministry of Education, Republic of Syria, Dar al-Hilal Press, 1944) 304 pp. (In Arabic.) Most of the statistical data on education in this chapter come from the al-Husri reports unless otherwise identified.

elementary schools are opened throughout the country. In addition, new classes and divisions were opened in the existing schools. Private schools were encouraged to open new classes, and special financial aid was offered for the opening of new private schools. Naturally, most of this effort was spent in the larger cities where most of the French schools had existed. Public secondary-school enrollment increased by 1,930 students in the six cities of Damascus, Aleppo, Latakia, Homs, Hama, and Tartus. Public primary schools had an increase of 6,718 pupils in the same cities, excepting Tartus. Private schools also registered large increases, an increase of 2,458 pupils taking place in the private primary schools of Damascus alone.

It is claimed that these measures dealt with the situation effectively enough to accommodate almost all the children who applied. Some secondary-school students, uncertain of being admitted to schools in Syria, arranged early to go to school in Lebanon. Because many of the measures were hastily improvised, they left something to be desired, but the emergency created by the closing of the French schools was met. It is with this state of emergency and the radical departure from French methods and influence in mind that the following description of the Syrian school system should be read.

Administration

The administration of public education in Syria, as in the other Arab countries, is centralized and is controlled by the Ministry of Education. The Ministry provides almost all the money for public schools, educates and appoints the teachers, establishes the curriculum, prescribes the textbooks, and holds public examinations at the end of the primary, intermediate, and secondary courses.

The organization of the Ministry of Education and its departments is set down in a special decree (No. 224, "Embodying the Organization of the Ministry of Education") and a special law (No. 202, "Limiting the Number of Officials of the Ministry of Education"), both of which were issued in 1945. The organization is shown in Chart XI. At the head is the Minister of Education, who is a member of the Cabinet and is responsible to Parliament for the educational policies of his Ministry, and, with the aid of the Director General of Education, for the proper execution of the laws and regulations. All decisions and instructions are issued in his name and executed under his supervision. The Minister has his own Private Bureau which handles his appointments, correspondence, and controls all papers and documents entering or leaving his office.

Next in authority to the Minister is a Director General of Education,

Chart XI

SYRIA: ADMINISTRATIVE ORGANIZATION OF THE MINISTRY OF EDUCATION, 1946

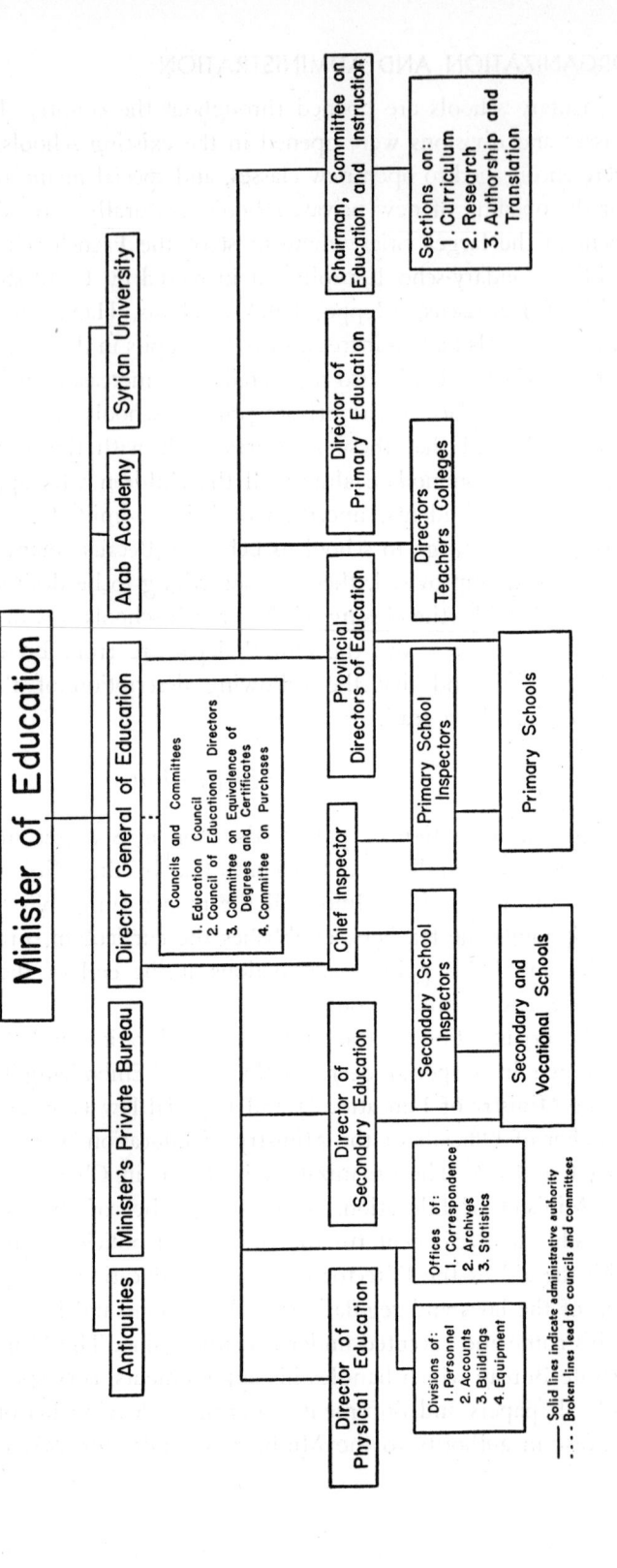

Minister of Education

Reporting to the Minister:
- Antiquities
- Minister's Private Bureau
- Director General of Education
- Arab Academy
- Syrian University

Councils and Committees (linked to Director General of Education):
1. Education Council
2. Council of Educational Directors
3. Committee on Equivalence of Degrees and Certificates
4. Committee on Purchases

Under Director General of Education:
- Director of Physical Education
- Director of Secondary Education
- Chief Inspector
- Provincial Directors of Education
- Director of Primary Education
- Chairman, Committee on Education and Instruction

Director of Physical Education

Divisions of:
1. Personnel
2. Accounts
3. Buildings
4. Equipment

Director of Secondary Education

Offices of:
1. Correspondence
2. Archives
3. Statistics

- Secondary School Inspectors
- Secondary and Vocational Schools

Chief Inspector
- Primary School Inspectors
- Primary Schools

Provincial Directors of Education

Director of Primary Education
- Directors Teachers Colleges

Chairman, Committee on Education and Instruction

Sections on:
1. Curriculum
2. Research
3. Authorship and Translation

——— Solid lines indicate administrative authority
· · · · Broken lines lead to councils and committees

who is the administrative head of all the departments of the Ministry and supervises the work of all the department officials and the proper operation of the schools. He appoints the officials of the central office and specialists in secondary and vocational education belonging to the second and third grades in the salary scale, and recommends to the Minister the appointment of officials of the higher grades. He is empowered to issue general notices and administrative instructions to help clarify ministerial instructions and to facilitate the running of his departments.

The Director General is assisted by three directors: the Director of Secondary Education who has charge of the affairs of all intermediate, preparatory, and vocational schools; the Director of Primary Education, who supervises primary and elementary schools; and the Director of Physical Education, who assists the Director General in organizing physical education, including scouting activities, sports, and organized games in and out of school.

Seven divisions and bureaus conduct the everyday business of the Ministry. The Division of Personnel keeps a complete register of all that pertains to the officials and teachers of the Ministry of Education. The Division of Accounts supervises the accounts of all departments, prepares budget estimates and is responsible for the execution of the budget law. The Division of Buildings, headed by an architect, draws the plans for school buildings and supervises all construction, repairs, and maintenance work in schools belonging to the Ministry. The Division of Equipment has charge of the central stores of the Ministry, of keeping textbooks and school furniture and equipment until they are distributed to the schools. In addition, there are the three bureaus of Correspondence, Archives, and Statistics, the functions of which are sufficiently indicated by their titles.

There are ten provincial directors of education, one each for the city of Damascus, Damascus Province (excluding the city), Hawran, Jabal Druze, Homs, Hama, Latakia, Aleppo, Jazirah, and Euphrates Provinces. These directors have charge mainly of primary education in their provinces and of supervising private schools. They are under the double jurisdiction of the Ministry of Education, from which they receive their instructions and approval of their proposals, and of the governor of their province, through whom they issue their orders and conduct their correspondence with higher authorities. The powers of the provincial directors of education during the regime of the French mandate were very limited. They were then called inspectors of education. Even the appointment of a janitor to a post already provided for in the budget needed to be referred through the governor to the Ministries of Education and Finance and was not final until taken cognizance of by them and published in the Official Journal. Even the salary of the janitor was not paid until this publication took place, which sometimes stretched into months. This procedure resulted in delays in the appointment of teachers and was detrimental to their financial position and their morale. Efforts are now being made to expedite this procedure.

Side by side with the administrative machinery stands the inspectoral staff. Headed by a chief inspector, it consists of two types of inspectors—secondary and primary. The basic duties of inspectors are defined as supervising the work of principals and teachers of schools, guiding them into the better interpretation and application of programs and curriculum, showing them better methods of teaching, correcting their mistakes, and orienting their activities. They are further charged with keeping the Ministry informed of the conditions of teaching in the schools, the needs of the schools, and the activities and abilities of teachers and principals. They study the educational needs of the cities and villages and do publicity work for education among the people.

Secondary inspectors are appointed on the basis of the subjects in which they have specialized. They have their headquarters in Damascus and are sent to inspect schools according to a plan worked out by the central office. At the time of the visit of the American Council Commission, the inspectors of secondary schools were visiting schools as a team, each inspecting his own subject or subjects in the same school.

Primary inspectors are not expected to be specialists in any one school subject. One or more are attached to each province and inspect the schools of that province according to a program worked out with the director of education of the province. Special inspectors may be appointed for the special subjects—for example, physical education, manual arts, agriculture—and for private and foreign schools in the larger towns where these abound. Inspectors' reports are submitted in two copies, one for the provincial director of education, and one for the chief inspector's office at the Ministry. The provincial director then takes such action as he sees fit, based upon the report.

A third department of the Ministry under the Director General is the Committee on Education and Instruction. It is made up of a chairman and three permanent members, with power to elect other workers from among the officials, inspectors, and teaching staff of the Ministry. The committee is a professional body which is put in charge of making school curriculums, laying down educational policies and plans as well as school regulations; selecting suitable textbooks and books for school and public libraries;

ORGANIZATION AND ADMINISTRATION

writing and translating books and articles and issuing educational periodicals; collecting information about educational systems abroad for the benefit of the Ministry and the school system and for the purpose of establishing the equivalence of degrees and diplomas; preparing and studying statistics about the school system; preparing plans and courses for teachers institutes and conferences; conducting educational experiments; and, finally, studying any professional question laid before it by the Ministry. The committee is supposed to include a representative of each of the important fields of specialization, each mastering "one of the languages of world culture to ensure that the committee shall have access to the most important cultural and educational publications appearing in Europe or America." Each member is required to teach no more than four periods a week in one of the teachers colleges and is empowered to visit schools. The committee is divided into three sections: one on curriculum, one on educational research, and one on translation and authorship.

In addition to the three main divisions of the Ministry of Education there are two councils and two committees provided for in the decree, with other committees to be formed by administrative order when necessary. These are the Education Council, the Council of Directors of Education, the Committee on the Equivalence of Degrees, and the Committee on Purchases.

The Education Council is composed of the Director General of Education as chairman, the chairman of the Committee on Education and Instruction, the Inspector General, and the section Directors of Primary, Secondary, and Physical Education. Its function is to pass on proposals coming from the appropriate departments with regard to curriculum, textbooks, the budget, proposed laws and regulations, and any other matter submitted to it by the Minister.

The Council of Directors of Education meets under the chairmanship of the Director General of Education and is made up of the Inspector General, the Directors of Primary, Secondary, and Physical Education, and the provincial directors of education. It meets once a year to discuss the school staffs and the educational needs of the provinces, to pass on proposals for opening new schools and expanding existing ones, distribution of teachers, and allocation of the budget among the provinces.

The Committee on the Equivalence of Degrees meets under the chairmanship of the Director General, and has as its members the chairman of the Committee on Education and Instruction, the Inspector General, the Director of Secondary Education, and a representative of the Syrian University. The committee makes its decisions on the basis of reports submitted to it by the Section of Educational Research of the Committee on Education and Instruction.

The Committee on Purchases is under the chairmanship of the accountant of the Ministry, with two other members appointed by the Director General of Education. It has charge of all buying of equipment, of receiving bids, and of preparing the contracts of the Ministry.

Beside the Directorate General of Education and its branches covering the system of public education for the entire country, three other institutions and agencies are connected directly with the Minister of Education:

1. The Department of Antiquities is headed by a director who is under the jurisdiction of the Minister. It has charge of the museum of antiquities, supervises all excavations, and preserves archeological sites. Its regulations are incorporated in Decree No. 352 (1945) "Embodying the Regulations of the Directorate of Antiquities."

2. The Syrian University, which until 1946 consisted of the Faculties of Medicine and Law, was in the process of reorganization at the time of the visit of the American Council Commission. It is described in chapter 22.

3. The Arab Academy, which was founded during the Arab government regime following World War I, is a body of learned Arabists, which has its own assembly of members in Syria and corresponding members in other Arabic and Islamic countries as well as among orientalists. It holds public lectures, issues a magazine known as the *Review of the Arab Academy* which appeared first in 1920 and in which are published the researches and studies of its members. It also maintains a public library which contains about 20,000 printed books and more than 4,000 Arabic manuscripts. The Academy has at times attempted to lay down Arabic equivalents to modern scientific terms.

Educational Finance

Educational finance in Syria is centralized. The bulk of the expenditure on the schools and their equipment, on the salaries of teachers and janitors, comes from the budget of the Ministry of Education, which is a part of the general budget of the Syrian Republic. The Ottoman Education Laws of 1869 and 1913, which had remained the basic education laws during the French-mandate period, had provided that the expenditures of elementary schools should be borne by the local authorities. This, however, remained more a theoretical than a practical possibility in most of the Ottoman Empire. In Syria, some school buildings were provided—in Turkish, as in French, days—by the central governments, some by the localities or

ORGANIZATION AND ADMINISTRATION

municipalities, and the majority were, and are still, rented buildings, the rent being paid from the central budget. Salaries and other expenses are also paid from the funds of the Ministry of Education.

Table 56 gives a picture of the growth of the educational budget since

TABLE 56
Growth of the Educational Budget, Syria, 1923–46

Year	General Budget	Educational Budget	Percent of General Budget	Number of Government Schools	Enrollment in Government Schools
1923*	£S 3,970,640†	£S 361,914	9.1	310	22,443
1931*	11,932,693	1,170,892	9.8	479	45,491
1941†	13,603,100	2,272,623	16.7	...	...
1945‡	103,678,000	9,953,568	9.6	694	93,727
1946‡	129,704,000	14,127,388	10.9	...	...

* Actual expenditure. Figures from the annual *Rapports sur la Situation de la Syrie et du Liban* (published by the French Government).
† The rate of exchange of the Syro-Lebanese pound was £S2.18 to the dollar in 1946.
‡ Estimates. Figures from the Ministry of Education.

the early days of the French mandate. Although the table shows a very large increase in budget allotments for education from £S361,914 in 1923 to £S14,127,388 in 1946, these figures should not be taken at their face value. The Syro-Lebanese currency, being based on the franc, had fluctuated in value along with the franc until 1943. Moreover, the increased amounts for 1945 and 1946 show clearly the influence of inflation. The budgetary provisions, therefore, are not based on the same rates of value. For this reason it would not be correct to say that the budgetary provision for education in 1946 was about thirty-nine times that of 1923. About the only thing that can be said is that the Syrian government, anxious in this era of independence to expand public education, is giving generously to the Ministry of Education. A budget of about £S16,000,000 was planned for 1947.

It will be seen from Table 56 that the percentage of the educational budget to the general budget has fluctuated from 9.1 to 16.7. In spite of the rapid increase in the general budget, the educational budget, while growing remarkably in the last four years, did not keep pace with the general budget. The percentages declined from 16.7 in 1941 to 9.6 in 1945 and picked up somewhat in 1946. This is a phenomenon that has been common in most of the other Arab states in the last few years. The 1945 budget was supporting 694 public schools of all types and 93,727 pupils in these schools, representing respectively 2.2 and 4.2 times the number of public schools and number of pupils in 1923.

The distribution of the budget over the various fields of public education in 1945 is shown in Table 57.

In the year 1944–45 there were 85,540 pupils in the public primary schools and 6,331 in the public secondary and teacher-training institutions. Thus, the average per pupil cost of a public primary school was £S61 (about $28) while that for a secondary or teachers-college pupil was £S278.6 (about $127.30). The latter figure includes the expenditure for boarding students both in some of the secondary schools and in the teach-

TABLE 57
BUDGET OF THE MINISTRY OF EDUCATION, SYRIA, 1945

Allocated to	Amount	Percent
Administration	£S 402,052	4.0
Primary education	5,220,000	52.5
Secondary and teacher education	1,763,720	17.7
Vocational education	630,596	6.3
Higher education and other cultural institutions	1,937,200	19.5
Total	£S9,953,568	100.0

ers colleges. Primary education is free. In secondary education fees are charged at the rate of £S48 for intermediate schools and £S60 for secondary schools (upper two classes) with exemptions to be detailed later. Boarding students pay a fee of £S300 in addition. In vocational schools no tuition fees are charged, but boarding students pay a boarding fee of £S240 per year, although some students receive free board and lodging. Education in the teachers colleges is entirely free, students not only receiving free board and room, but also £S15 a month for pocket expenses. Day students receive £S50 a month toward their board and lodging and £15 for pocket expenses. In the Syrian University tuition fees of £S120 are charged, but with about 25 percent of the students exempted. Additional fees are levied for the library and for physical education.

Revenue from fees goes to the Treasury and cannot be used directly by the schools or the Ministry of Education. Expenditure follows strictly the provisions of the budget.

The financial problem which public education in Syria faces is the same as that of the other Arab countries—to find the funds necessary to put into effect a program of universal education. So long as almost total reliance is placed on the central government budget, little hope can be entertained of reaching that goal. With the budget of the central government so pressed by the requirements of the various departments and agencies of the state, it is not possible to expect more than a limited increase in the budget provisions for education. The proposal, therefore, has been made that the way out of this situation is by the imposition of a special education tax levied by the local authorities.[2] This could be done in two stages, first by making the local communities pay for the erection of school buildings and later by making them bear all other expenses, including the salaries of teachers. Steps were being taken in 1946 to put the first stage into operation.

TEACHERS' SALARIES

At the time of the visit of the American Council Commission in April 1946 the decree law governing the appointment, promotion, and salaries of teachers was on the point of being superseded by new decrees which were then in the making. A short sketch of the old decree law (No. 163, dated August 11, 1943) will be presented here in order to give an idea of the kind of practice which prevailed under French auspices and which is bound to leave its effect on the grading of teachers for some time. This will be followed by a summary of the new decrees defining the new cadres of the Ministry of Education.

The old decree law differentiates between the categories of teachers and of principals of schools, giving the latter a separate scale which was higher than that of the teachers. Teachers proper were divided into two categories: secondary (called professors) and primary teachers.

Secondary teachers were classified into six groups: head professor, group one professor, group two professor, group three professor, associate professor, and assistant professor. Each of these groups was further subdivided into four grades—distinguished, first, second, and third. This made a total of twenty-four grades for secondary-school teachers, for which the monthly salaries of the lowest grade ranged from a minimum £S60 ($27.50) to a maximum of £S75 ($34.40), and of the highest grade, a minimum of £S185 ($84.80) to a maximum of £S215 ($99). Grades and professorial groups overlapped in the salaries assigned to them to such an extent that the maximums and the minimums of three out of four grades in every group were the same as those of three grades in the next higher or lower group. This made a very complicated system.

Secondary teachers' salaries and their classification were closely linked with French degrees and diplomas. Each of the types of professors had to have one or more of the certificates of higher education leading to the *Licence ès Lettres* or *ès Sciences*.[3] In order to be appointed to the lowest secondary-school teaching post—that of associate professor—a candidate had to possess one certificate. One additional certificate was added for each of the four higher posts mentioned above until five certificates and a state or university doctorate were required for the head professors. As no colleges of arts and sciences existed at the Syrian Uni-

[2] Al-Husri, *op. cit.*, pp. 263–65.
[3] The *Licences ès Lettres* and *ès Sciences* are the first French university degrees. An undergraduate student had to secure certificates in four fields before he became eligible automatically for the *licence*.

versity, the medical and law degrees of this institution were equated to four and three certificates respectively. In order to occupy the three higher ranks of secondary-school teaching, therefore, a candidate had to go to France to secure the required certificates. Degrees from other countries were equated, by a special committee if necessary, but holders of French or Syrian degrees or certificates were given an advantage. Although the decree law was extremely detailed and explicit, it gave no bases for the equation of well-known degrees from other countries. The degree of Bachelor of Arts of the American University of Beirut (an institution recognized in America as a Class A institution) was recognized as equivalent only to the secondary-school *Baccalauréat,* Second Part, a fact which barred its holders from teaching in the public secondary schools.

The same method of classification and assignment of salaries was followed in the case of primary teachers. These teachers were grouped into seven groups of four grades each. The upper three groups were reserved for graduates of primary-, elementary-, and "practical" teachers colleges in descending order, while the lower four groups were open to candidates who had only the second *baccalauréat,* first *baccalauréat,* or the primary-school certificate with four years of secondary work, again in descending order. Each grade had its minimum and its maximum. The lowest grade carried a minimum salary of £S33 ($15) and a maximum of £S42 ($19), and the highest grade carried a minimum of £S97.5 ($44.70) and a maximum of £S120 ($55). Salaries of women teachers were fixed consistently one grade lower than those for the men even though they had the same qualifications.

A special cadre was drawn up for secondary- and primary-school principals, the former in four groups of four grades each, and the latter in two groups of four grades each. As in the case of the teachers, each grade for the principals had a maximum and a minimum. The lowest grade for a secondary-school principal carried a minimum of £S97.50 ($44.70) and a maximum of £S130 ($55), while the highest grade of principals received a minimum of £S205 ($94) and a maximum of £S247.50 ($113.50). Differentiation among principals was not on the basis of academic or professional qualifications, or on experience and length of service, or on tested ability, but on the type of school administered—whether a primary-, elementary-, or vocational-teachers college, a secondary or a vocational school, and whether it was a day or a boarding school, and if a day school whether it had more or less than 300 students.

Primary-school principals were classified into two groups of four grades each. The higher group was for principals of large schools of ten or more classrooms and the lower group was for smaller schools of at least five classrooms. The range in salaries was £S70 to £S100 ($32 to $45.80) for the lowest grade, and £S112.50 to £S150 ($51.60 to $68.80) for the highest grade. Like the grades and the salaries of the secondary-school teachers, those for primary teachers and for principals greatly overlap one another.

It would take too long to give even a summary of the rest of the decree law, the details of which fill seventeen large pages, each of two columns of small print, dealing with conditions of choice of teachers, the types of studies and combinations of studies recognized, the conditions and emoluments of part-time teaching and supervising of students in the schools, and so on.

In his *Reports on the State of Education in Syria*[4] Sati' al-Husri levels a number of criticisms at the decree summarized above and makes certain recommendations. As his criticisms and suggestions point the direction which reform of this phase of the Syrian educational system is taking, a summary is given.

1. Exception is taken to the close tying-up of grades and salaries to the French type of diplomas and degrees on the ground that the French practice of accumulating certificates toward the degree of *licence* is not found in most other countries; indeed, it is the exception. To base teachers' appointments on it, therefore, is to create unnecessary difficulties in the way of dealing with degrees secured from other sources. Moreover, the certificates in French higher education have value only as leading to the degree of *licence* and should not be considered as separate entities or stages which would entitle a person to take teaching positions as laid down in the decree. In another connection the writer warns against blind imitation of one system of education (in this case the French) and declares that Syrian education had been for a quarter of a century under the monopoly of the French type of educational organization. He advocates a diversification of the sources of educational ideas from different countries with the idea ultimately of creating "a special Syrian-Arab type of educational organization."[5]

2. The decree, in overemphasizing certificates, gave little if any weight to the teacher's length of service and experience and to his ability and enthusiasm in his teaching. This tends to discourage the good teacher and creates a current of dissatisfaction among teachers. Any arrangement for the service of teachers should take account of these factors.

3. It makes a special classification for principals, distinct from teachers, with a considerable difference in salaries. This is not based on a sound educational principle and would tend to draw the best teachers toward school administration, to the detriment of good teaching and scholarship. Besides, to base the classification of principals on the sizes of the schools and not on ability and qualifications is not in the public interest, for a small but important school may require the appointment of one of the ablest men among principals.

4. There is no justification for setting the salaries of women teachers at a lower rate than those of the men. Salaries should be according to qualifications regardless of the teacher's sex. Otherwise, an injustice would be done to women at a time when more women are needed in teaching and should be encouraged to get into the profession.

5. The practice of promoting primary-school teachers into the field of teaching in secondary schools under the title of "assistant professors" is one of the main factors of weakness in this field, particularly when these are confirmed in their new positions. A better practice would be to keep them as teachers "delegated" from the primary schools until such time as the need for them ceases, or until special courses and classes are opened to enable them to raise their level.

6. Finally, the system of overlapping groups and grades is very confused and

[4] Al-Husri, *op. cit.*, pp. 11–32.
[5] *Ibid.*, pp. 47–49.

confusing and should be replaced by a simpler system where the various grades meet end-on, providing a consecutive scale.

Sati' al-Husri's criticisms have provided some of the bases for the new cadres of the Ministry of Education. These were passed shortly after the Commission of the American Council on Education left the Near East.[6] They were based on the *Basic Officials' Law* which had been passed earlier in the year and which lays down a new basic salary scale for all officials.

The new law divides state officials into twelve levels, from the eleventh at the lowest to the first, with a "distinguished" level on top. Each of these levels is divided into three grades with a minimum and a maximum salary. The minimums and maximums for each level, however, usually do not overlap, but meet end to end. Thus, the lowest level, the eleventh, is divided into three grades as follows:

Grade	Monthly Salary	
Grade 3 (minimum)	£S30	($13.76)
Grade 2	35	(16.05)
Grade 1 (maximum)	40	(18.35)

This increment continues at the rate of £S5 for each grade up to the sixth level, then at the rate of £S10 through the fifth, at the rate of £S15 through the third, of £S25 in the second, of £S30 in the first, and £S40 in the "distinguished" level. The salaries for this last level are:

Grade	Monthly Salary	
Grade 3 (minimum)	£S420	($192.66)
Grade 2	460	(211.00)
Grade 1 (maximum)	500	(229.39)

Thus, the lowest official in the state receives a basic salary of £S30 ($13.76) a month, and the highest receives £S500 ($229.39) a month.

According to the new decrees embodying the education cadres mentioned above, primary-school teachers are classified into five ranks, of which the tenth level (minimum salary, £S45) is their lowest appointment, and they may reach up to the fourth level (maximum salary, £S175). Graduates of the primary-teachers colleges are first appointed in the middle grade of the eighth level (£S75), graduates of secondary schools in the lowest grade of the ninth level (£S55), and graduates of intermediate and vocational schools in the lowest grade of the tenth level (£S45). Only graduates of teachers colleges may be promoted beyond the eighth

[6] Legislative Decree No. 61, dated October 20, 1946, "Embodying the Cadre of the Officials of Primary and Secondary Education"; and Legislative Decree No. 62, dated October 21, 1946), "Embodying the Cadre of the Officials of Secondary and Vocational Education," *Official Gazette of the Syrian Republic*, Vol. XXIV, No. 44, October 21, 1945, pp. 1479–83.

ORGANIZATION AND ADMINISTRATION

level without taking competitive examinations. The others must pass theoretical and practical professional examinations before they may be promoted beyond the eighth level. Salary scales are the same for men and women, and for teachers and principals. A principal, however, is given an additional allowance.

Secondary- and vocational-school teachers are classified into seven ranks and may be appointed, depending on their qualifications, at the bottom of the seventh level (minimum salary £S85) and may reach up to the second level (maximum salary £S290). To be appointed to the secondary or vocational schools, a candidate must hold a university degree beyond a secondary-school certificate. The bearer of a doctorate in literature or in science based on a *licence,* or master's degree, in arts or science may be initially appointed in the middle grade of the fourth level (£S150). The holder of a *licence,* or a master's degree, in arts or science may be appointed in the lowest grade of the fourth level (£S145), while the holder of a B.A. honors degree from an American university is first appointed at the highest grade of the fifth level (£S130). Candidates without these qualifications may be appointed when need arises after passing a competitive examination, provided they are either graduates of secondary schools who have had at least two years of university studies or are graduates of primary-teachers colleges who have had at least five years of experience in teaching, or are secondary-school graduates with at least six years of teaching experience. These may be first appointed only in the lowest grade of the seventh level (£S85) and cannot be promoted beyond the sixth level except after passing a further examination. The same salary schedule prevails for men and women, and for principals and teachers. Principals of boarding schools and their assistants, however, receive an allowance for their added responsibilities.

Both primary- and secondary-school teachers may receive leave for study without pay in order to improve themselves professionally. Any diploma or degree which they might receive as a result entitles them to corresponding increases in salary. The two decrees provide for commissions which will study the individual cases of every teacher and regrade him or her according to the new scale.

Owing to the wartime inflation, however, teachers, like all government officials, were given cost-of-living allowances. In 1946 these were 180 percent for £S40 or below, 120 percent for salaries between £S41 and £S80, 90 percent for salaries between £S81 and £S150, and 45 percent for any salary of £S151 or above. In addition, there were allowances for a wife and children. Thus, the salary of £S40 rises to £S112, while the highest salary paid, £S500, becomes £S912.5 ($418.57), not including allowances for the wife and children.

A system of pensions for government officials provides for a pension amounting to half the average final salary after thirty years of service. Teachers automatically fall under this plan.

Educational Legislation

Five articles of the Syrian Constitution (Articles 19–23) deal with education. The freedom of education is guaranteed in so far as it is not contrary to public order and good morals and is not detrimental to the dignity of the country or of religion. Education is directed to raise the moral and intellectual standard of the people on lines best suited to the national characteristics, and to promote concord and a fraternal spirit among all citizens. Primary education is compulsory for all Syrians of both sexes and is free of charge in the public schools. The curriculum for public education is laid down by law in order to insure educational uniformity. All schools are placed under government supervision.

The provisional Ottoman Education Law of 1913 had never been completely superseded during the French mandate. The law of July 6, 1933, "Fixing the Orders and Stages of Public Education," and the various decrees and orders (*arrêtés*) issued during the mandate regime had determined the educational ladder, set down the curriculum, the public-examinations regulations, the internal administration of schools, the supervision of private and foreign schools, the sending of educational missions abroad, and various other aspects of education, repealing in each case the corresponding sections of the Ottoman law.[7]

The 1943 education law represents a somewhat radical departure from the law of 1933 and the collection of decrees and orders (*arrêtés*) which governed education under the mandate. Since it sets down the main provisions upon which the new educational structure has been and is being laid, a summary of it is given here.

The law defines the basic function of the Ministry of Education as "giving a good education to the new generation—in all aspects, physical, moral, and intellectual—in order that each of its individuals will grow with

[7] Excepting the orders regulating archeology (1933), the Syrian University (1926), and the Arab Academy (1943) which are to keep their force in so far as they do not conflict with the new law, until changed in their turn. The order regulating archeology was later superseded by Decree No. 352, "Embodying the Regulations of the Directorate of Archeology" (1945), while that regulating the University was superseded by Law No. 269 (1940) and Decree No. 40 (1945).

a strong body, good character, and sound thinking, loving his country, proud of his nationality, conscious of his duties, equipped with the knowledge which he needs in his life, capable of serving his country with his mental and physical powers, and with his productive efforts."

The activities of the Ministry of Education are defined as: (1) establishing and administering public educational institutions of all types and grades; (2) supervising private and foreign educational institutions and directing their activities toward the basic aims of public schools; (3) fighting illiteracy, and disseminating culture among all the people; (4) stimulating the energies of youth and organizing their affairs by encouraging sporting and scouting activities in and out of school; (5) stimulating scientific and literary movements through the founding and expanding of public libraries, scientific museums, publishing old and new books, organizing broadcasts, public lectures, pageants, founding and encouraging academies, societies and clubs, and aiding individual efforts in science and literature; (6) fostering economic education by strengthening the love of work and production in students and youth; (7) fostering fine arts in and out of school; (8) preserving the national antiquities and directing all matters of archeology; and (9) strengthening cultural ties between Syria and its sister-Arab countries with a view to creating a unified culture for the Arab world.

The law divides education into three main levels: primary (five years), secondary (six years), and higher education. Provision is made for special schools for children who have not attained primary-school age. Higher education is to be at the Syrian University and its colleges, the proposed Higher Teachers College and its branches, and any other specialized institutions. The organization of the University is laid down in a special law. The education law of 1943 provides that the Ministry of Education may found higher colleges independent of the University.

Schools are further divided, according to aim, into schools of general culture and specialized schools, such as schools of agriculture, industry, commerce, and fine arts. Vocational education is to be provided in special classes or schools of all levels, some being complementary to primary education, others parallel to intermediate or secondary schools, while still others would be higher institutions.

Three kinds of institutions for the education of teachers are contemplated in the law: elementary-, primary-, and higher-teachers colleges. The first would prepare teachers for elementary and rural schools; the second would prepare them for primary schools; and the third would prepare them for intermediate schools. In addition, the Ministry of Education may create special classes or courses annexed to the teachers colleges, or above vocational schools, for the preparation of teachers of special subjects—for example, art, physical education, manual arts, and home economics. No teachers may be employed in elementary and primary schools unless they are graduates of elementary- and primary-teachers colleges. In case of need, however, secondary-school graduates may be employed on a temporary basis, but may not be confirmed in their posts unless or until they have had the required teachers training and have passed a special examination in subjects of education and methods of teaching. Only graduates of the Higher Teachers College or of higher institutions in which they specialized in the subjects they are to teach may be appointed to intermediate and preparatory schools, except in case of emergency need, when temporary appointments may be made. Only candidates who have received a doctor's degree may be appointed to teach in higher institutions. Teachers of special subjects, such as physical education, art, music, home economics, manual arts, may be appointed regardless of the academic level they have reached provided they pass a special examination of aptitude in their subjects.

Teachers are prohibited from disseminating teachings leading to the corruption of character and to dissension, or teachings which are an affront to the dignity of the Syrian people and the Arab nation, or which make of education a means for political or partisan propaganda.

Finally, the law sets down the provisions for private and foreign schools of any kind or at any level, as follows: Written permission of the Ministry of Education is required before any such school may be established; all such schools must submit to the supervision of the Ministry of Education from all points of view—hygienic, educational, and moral; classes opened by individuals or groups for the teaching of one or more subjects (including languages or technical subjects) are regarded as schools, must secure permission, and are subject to supervision. The teaching of the Arabic language, Arabic history, and the geography of the Arab world, according to the course formulated by the Ministry of Education, is compulsory in all private and foreign primary and secondary schools. Private schools are forbidden to receive assistance from foreign sources except with the knowledge and approval of the Ministry of Education.

The Educational Ladder

The educational ladder in Syria, built upon the new education law, is shown in Chart XII. A comparison of certain features of the old 1933 law and the new 1943 law will help to bring out the salient points of the

Chart XII

SYRIA: PUBLIC SCHOOL SYSTEM, 1946

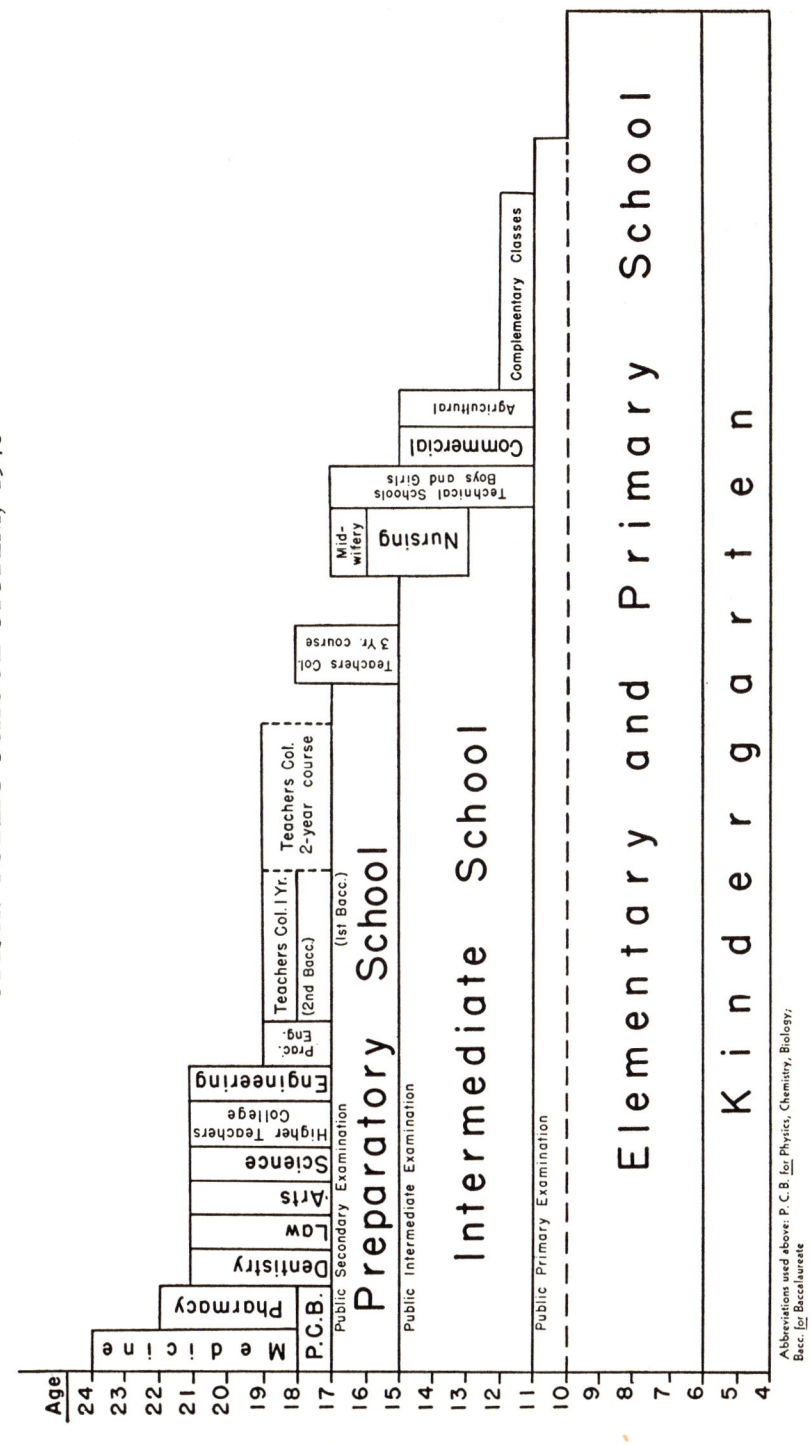

Age	
24	Medicine
23	
22	Pharmacy
21	
20	Dentistry / Law / Arts / Science / Higher Teachers College / Engineering
19	P.C.B.
18	Prac. Eng. / Teachers Col. 2-year course / Teachers Col. 1 Yr.
17	(1st Bacc) / (2nd Bacc)
16	Public Secondary Examination — Preparatory School
15	Teachers Col. 3 Yr. course
14	Public Intermediate Examination
13	Midwifery / Nursing — Intermediate School
12	Technical Schools Boys and Girls
11	Commercial / Agricultural
10	Public Primary Examination — Complementary Classes
9	
8	Elementary and Primary School
7	
6	
5	Kindergarten
4	

Abbreviations used above: P. C. B. *for* Physics, Chemistry, Biology; Bacc. *for* Baccalaureate reorganization. Both laws provide that primary education shall be compulsory and free.

The total period of primary education under the 1943 law is five years, the first four of which constitute a special cycle known as "elementary." While the old law differentiated between an elementary school of four years without French and a primary school of five years with two years of French, the new plan abolishes the teaching of French in the primary grades and makes the curriculum of the first four grades of both types of schools identical. The pupil finishing elementary school under the old regime had to repeat the fourth primary year if he wanted any further education; now he may transfer from the fourth elementary to the fifth primary grade without loss of time.

To enter the first grade of the elementary school, a pupil must have completed his sixth year of age. A basic curriculum is set down for elementary and primary schools, but this is to be adapted to the needs of the different sexes, on the one hand, and to the needs of urban and rural localities on the other. Although no foreign language may be taught in primary schools, the Ministry of Education may annex to any school in the cities a complementary class in which a foreign language and principles of keeping accounts are taught for the benefit of children who do not intend to proceed to secondary education.

Secondary education has been made more accessible. Formerly, a pupil was required to have attained a grade of *assez bien* (fairly good) in the primary-school certificate examination, or must have gone through an additional (sixth) primary year. Now, admission to a secondary school is open to all bearers of the Certificate of Primary Studies without regard to grade. A wide system of exemption from fees adds further to the accessibility of secondary education. This exemption may be made for as many as one-third or more of the student body, and may involve free board and lodging for promising out-of-town students.

Secondary education has been shortened from seven to six years, making the total of primary and secondary schooling eleven years, which is in line with the rest of the Arab countries studied in this report except Lebanon, which has kept its twelve-year system.

The six-year secondary school is divided into two stages: the first four years constitute the "intermediate" stage, the last two years, the "preparatory" stage. The preparatory stage is divided into literary and scientific sections, with different curriculums. Both stages lead to public examinations, which, if passed by the student, entitle him to the Certificates of Completion of Intermediate or Preparatory Studies respectively. The Ministry may add commercial, agricultural, and technical classes to any intermediate school if the need arises.

Under the French mandate, postprimary education was a two-ladder system. In addition to the secondary-school program which led to the University, two types of complementary courses were provided: a general complementary course of four years without a second foreign language, and professional complementary courses. The first led to the *Brevet* of General Complementary Education, after public examination. The professional complementary courses were of two types: one provided for a preparatory year followed by a program of from one to three years, leading to a professional (vocational) *brevet*. The other, following the four-year elementary school, gave a practical training of one to four years, ending in a Certificate of Practical Complementary Education. Holders of the two types of *brevets* and of the certificate were eligible for admission to technical schools, which usually gave a course of three years.

In practice, however, many of the "general complementary" schools were in reality incomplete secondary schools, having a curriculum identical with the corresponding secondary-school classes. The new law does away with the complementary courses.

A primary-school graduate may, therefore, either pursue a single-track secondary education or may enter one of the vocational schools.

The abolition of the teaching of French from the primary school has naturally affected foreign languages in the secondary school. Previously French was taught throughout the secondary school in continuation of its teaching in the last two primary years. A second foreign language was begun in the third secondary year. The new law gives the student the freedom to choose his foreign languages, one beginning in the first and the other in the fifth year of the secondary school, with the result that the overwhelming majority are now choosing English as a first language. Out of 1,000 pupils entering the first secondary year in Damascus in 1945–46, it was reported that only 37 chose French, the rest English. There arose, therefore, a great demand for teachers of English, a demand which cannot be satisfactorily met for the present.

Under the 1933 law there was a first *baccalauréat* examination at the end of the sixth year and a second *baccalauréat* examination at the end of the seventh; under the 1943 law there is an intermediate examination after four years, and a further examination after another two years upon the completion of the preparatory stage.

The division of studies into literary and scientific sections in the fifth and sixth years is maintained, but the sections of philosophy and mathematics in the seventh year disappear with the abolition of that year in the shortening of the total secondary program from seven to six years.

There are two outlets for the graduate of the intermediate stage who does not go on to complete the full secondary-school program: (1) teachers colleges for both boys and girls, or (2) the School of Nursing, connected with the Faculty of Medicine of the Syrian University, for girls.

The situation in teachers colleges is in a state of transition. Previously a one-year course was offered for elementary-school teachers open to holders of the *brevet* or first *baccalauréat,* and another one-year course for primary-school and complementary-school teachers open to students holding the second *baccalauréat*. Later each of these courses was lengthened to two years. With the reorganization in 1943, three types of teacher-training courses are being maintained: (1) One year of professional education after the second *baccalauréat*. This was expected to disappear with the graduation of the last class of philosophy and mathematics in June 1946. (2) Two years after the first *baccalauréat* or after the sixth-year secondary course, offering a professional education for prospective teachers. (3) A three-year course after the intermediate-school certificate (old *brevet*). It is hoped that the latter type will become the standard course for the education of teachers, although the second course is likely to be continued for some time, owing to the shortage of teachers.

Finally, graduates of the full secondary program may go into the various colleges of the Syrian University, pursuing academic courses or one of the professional or technical fields—medicine, with its branches of dentistry, pharmacy, and nursing; law; engineering; or teacher-training. Requirements for admission, course of study, and examinations are discussed in chapter 22.

The reorganization of Syrian education did not come to pass without dissenting voices, mainly from individuals with a French educational background. Fear was expressed that the shortening of the secondary school from seven to six years would result in lowering the standard of Syrian general education. The fear was also expressed that, in attempting to preserve the main body of the seventh-year course (philosophy, mathematics), the new provisional course had introduced these subjects into the lower years, thus unduly crowding the course in these years, making it hard, if not impossible, for the teachers to cover all the ground adequately.

In answer to these criticisms it was pointed out that the former twelve-year combined-primary-and-secondary educational system in Syria is one year more than in Egypt, Palestine, and Iraq, among the Arabic countries, and Turkey, Denmark, Rumania, Spain, Brazil, and a number of other countries. The twelve-year period in France and thirteen in Germany are due to the great attention paid there to the classics, the teaching of which is equal to more than a year. Moreover, the seventh-year course gave eleven out of twenty-four hours to the study of philosophy, a subject not given in secondary schools in many countries because it is believed to be beyond the capacity of most secondary-school students. Even where it is given, the time for it is much less than eleven periods a week, and Syria needs to give to the subject no more than three or four periods a week.[8]

The abolition of French from the primary-school curriculum, although it has had a much more favorable reception, has also been criticized. It is pointed out that the teaching of French in Syria is already much weaker than in Lebanon, where French is taught beginning in the first grade (even in the kindergarten), and many subjects, notably science and mathematics, are taught in French. Even in the period when French was required in the primary school, it was not begun until the fourth grade, and since the teaching was entirely in Arabic, students had little practice in the use of French.

A number of reasons are given for the abolition of French in the primary schools. The primary curriculum is very crowded and needs to be lightened. As the teaching of a foreign language at such an early age is considered by some to be educationally unsound, it is only natural that thought should be directed toward postponing its beginning to the later, more logical stage of secondary education. It is pointed out that few countries teach a foreign language in the primary school.

Public Examinations

Before the recent reorganization of education in Syria, there were four main public examinations held by the Ministry of Education. These were the examinations leading to the Certificate of Primary Studies, the *Brevet* of General Complementary Education, the *Baccalauréat,* First Part, and the *Baccalauréat,* Second Part. These were regulated by decrees and orders (*arrêtés*)[9] setting down the rules of the examinations. In addition, there were ministerial examinations for the vocational complementary education leading to the Industrial and Commercial *Brevets* and examinations for

[8] Al-Husri, *op. cit.,* pp. 113–20.
[9] Arrêté No. 29, "Certificat d'Etudes Primaires," of February 28, 1927 (in French and Arabic); Decree No. 68 of January 25, 1941, "Règlement du Brevet d'Enseignement Complémentaire Général" (in French); and Decree No. 242, "Regulations of the Syrian Baccalauréat of Secondary Education," dated March 9, 1938, supplemented by Decree No. 244 dated March 10, 1938.

the certificate of aptitude for primary and elementary teachers and for graduation from teachers colleges.

Examinations were both oral and written. There were six written and four oral primary examinations. Four of the written and two of the oral had to do with the Arabic and the French languages. No student was admitted to the oral examination unless he had passed the written examinations. Marks were on the basis of 10 for each subject; and, in order to pass, the student had to obtain half the total marks of all the subjects together and not receive a zero in any subject.

For the general *brevet* there were five written and six oral examinations. For the first *baccalauréat* there were four written and eight oral examinations for the literary and for the scientific sections. Examinations were weighted 1, 1.5, 2, or 3, depending upon the subject and the section. In the second *baccalauréat* there were three written and six oral examinations for the philosophy and for the mathematics sections. In all three secondary examinations marking was on the basis of 0 to 20. In order to pass, a student had to get an average of 50 percent and not receive a zero in any subject.

This examination system had been criticized[10] in that it gave too important a place to oral examinations, a fact which made strict evaluation of the students' work difficult, if not impossible, particularly since so many committees in various localities examined in the same subject, with all the differences in standards and tastes of the committees and the individuals composing them. The public examination is supposed to be an objective check on the work of the schools and the learning of the students; yet such a system made objectivity extremely difficult to achieve. Furthermore, the marking system was such that a student might be extremely weak in one, two, or even three subjects—receiving marks only slightly above zero in them—and yet through high marks in the other subjects reach the 50 percent required to pass. This gave the opportunity to many students, particularly in private and foreign schools, to pass in spite of their extreme weakness in the national language—Arabic.

The weighting of the subjects also followed a strange pattern. The total number of marks for oral and written primary examinations was 110, of which 35 were given to Arabic and 35 to French; 20 to mathematics; only 10 to object lessons, agriculture, and hygiene combined; and 10 to history and geography combined. In the written examinations for the *brevet*, 60 marks were given to Arabic, 40 to French, 40 to arithmetic, and nothing

[10] Al-Husri, *op. cit.*, pp. 233–42.

ORGANIZATION AND ADMINISTRATION 349

to science and history. Yet, in the oral examinations for the same stage the total mark for all the sciences was not equal to that of drawing, while that for history and geography was equal to drawing.

Accordingly, the new regulations for public examinations have attempted to eliminate these features and others besides.[11] Three, instead of four, examinations were prescribed—the primary, the intermediate, and the secondary. All examinations are to be written. The primary examination comprises six papers—Arabic grammar and dictation, Arabic composition, civics and ethics, history and geography, arithmetic and elements of geometry, and object lessons and hygiene.

The intermediate examination includes eight papers—Arabic grammar and literature, Arabic composition, first foreign language, civic and legal information, history and geography, mathematics, physics and chemistry, and biology and hygiene.

The secondary-school examination (given to three different sections) comprises eight papers. Each section has papers in the first foreign language, the second foreign language, and logic and psychology. In addition, the literary section has Arabic literature, history, geography, science, and general mathematics. The section for girls combines history and geography in one paper and adds child care and nursing. In addition to the subjects common to all, the scientific section has Arabic composition, history and geography, mathematics, physics and chemistry, and biology and hygiene. The papers are marked on the basis of 100. A student receiving a total of 60 and a mark of at least 40 in each subject passes.

Only one primary-school examination is held each year. Two are held each year for the intermediate and secondary stages, one in June and one in September. Students failing in two subjects or in the total may be reexamined in September, but students failing in more than two subjects or in one subject and the total have to repeat the year. In order to avoid too sudden a change from the old system to the new one, a transitory arrangement was worked out whereby lower standards were set for 1945 and 1946, the new standards going into effect in 1947. Thus, in 1945 the passing mark was to be 15 percent for each subject, and 40 for the total, while in 1946 it was to be 30 for each subject and 50 for the total.

[11] Decree No. 149, "Embodying the Public Examinations Regulations for the Certificate of Primary Studies"; Decree No. 150, "Embodying the Public Examinations Regulations for the Certificate of Intermediate Studies"; and Decree No. 151, "Embodying the Public Examinations Regulations for the Certificate of Secondary Studies," all dated February 6, 1945.

The questions are set by the Committee on Education and Instruction of the Ministry of Education and remain confidential to the day of the examination. The papers are marked by committees.

The public-examination results for 1943 and 1945 are given in Table 58. It will be noticed that the results for 1945 follow the same

TABLE 58
RESULTS OF PUBLIC EXAMINATIONS, SYRIA, 1943 AND 1945

TYPE OF EXAMINATION	1943			1945		
	Entered	Passed	Percent Passing	Entered	Passed	Percent Passing
Primary examination....	6,033	3,743	62.0	7,042	4,011	56.9
Brevet (intermediate)....	1,661	554	33.3	1,517	810	53.3
Baccalauréat, Part I.....	1,222	267	21.8	976	558	57.2
Baccalauréat, Part II....	744	125	16.8	604	370	61.1

classification that prevailed previously, as the new regulations did not come into full force until 1947.

It will be noticed that in the old system the percentage of those passing decreased steadily as the level of the examination rose. Whether this will be true under the new policy it is impossible to tell. The examinations in 1945 took place under exceptional circumstances; owing to the Franco-Syrian clash in May of that year, no examinations were held in June but were postponed until the fall.

Development and Extent of the Educational System

Table 59 shows the relative growth of public, private, and foreign schools and enrollments during the past quarter of a century. It was not possible to secure statistics for the years prior to 1923, nor were separate figures for boys and girls available for the early years. Information about the number of men and women teachers was not available for the years prior to 1943–44. In spite of these gaps, however, the table gives a fairly accurate idea about the expansion of education in the period following World War I, up to and including World War II.[12]

Table 59 shows that the schools increased from 562 to 1,165, and the enrollment from 53,403 to 162,818 between 1924 and 1945. Thus, while the schools are only two times their original number, the enrollment

[12] In their annual reports to the League of Nations, the French had kept separate statistics for Syria, Latakia, Jabal Druze, and Alexandretta. The latter has since been lost to Turkey. As the present Republic of Syria includes all the first three, the statistics for them have been combined throughout.

has nearly trebled. As compared with 1931, the schools increased 31 percent and the pupils 88 percent.

Of the three categories of schools, the public schools had the highest rate of increase. Compared with 1924 the number of public schools has more than doubled, while the pupil enrollment has almost quadrupled

TABLE 59
GROWTH OF SYRIAN EDUCATION, 1923–45*

YEAR	PUBLIC SCHOOLS Number of Schools	PUBLIC SCHOOLS Enrollment	PRIVATE SCHOOLS Number of Schools	PRIVATE SCHOOLS Enrollment	FOREIGN SCHOOLS Number of Schools	FOREIGN SCHOOLS Enrollment	TOTAL Number of Schools	TOTAL Enrollment
1923	310	22,443†	190†	22,584‡	Not available		...	...
1924	334	25,045	206‡	26,455‡	22§	1,903§	562	53,403
1931	479	45,491	246	25,318	160	17,038	885	87,847
1941–42	626	76,852	331	42,213	168	22,950	1,125	142,015
1943–44	664	83,186	311	40,983	155	22,529	1,130	146,698
1944–45	694	93,717	311	45,214	160	23,887	1,165	162,818

* Data for 1923, 1924, and 1931 from French annual reports to the League of Nations (1926, p. 34; 1931, p. 203). Data for 1941–42 from Conseil Supérieur des Intérêts Communs, *Recueil de Statistiques de la Syrie et du Liban, 1942–43* (Beirut: Imprimerie Catholique, 1945), pp. 24–25 and 38.
Data for 1943–44, from Sati' al-Husri, *Reports* . . . , 1944, pp. 63–66.
Data for 1944–45 supplied by the Ministry of Education.
† Not including the Syrian University.
‡ Including French schools.
§ Not including French schools. In later years French schools were included in the foreign group.

(374 percent). Compared with 1931, the public schools have increased by almost half their number (145 percent), while the number of pupils has slightly more than doubled.

It is not possible to determine accurately the growth of private and foreign schools separately, owing to the fact that, in the early years of 1923 and 1924, the reports of the French authorities included the French schools among the native private schools, and included only non-French schools in the foreign category. This was changed later. Taking the private and foreign schools together, we find that there were 228 such schools enrolling 28,358 pupils in 1924, compared with 471 schools and 69,101 pupils in 1944–45, an increase to 206 and 243 percent respectively. Comparing 1944–45 with 1931, the number of private schools increased by 65, bringing them to 126 percent, and by 19,896 pupils, raising the enrollment to 178 percent. The number of foreign schools has remained static, while enrollments have increased by 6,849, an increase to 140 percent. Compared with 1941, however, enrollments in foreign schools have only slightly increased. With the closing of the French schools in 1945–46, the number of foreign schools must have declined sharply because in 1944–45 the French schools constituted 74 percent of the foreign schools, and 82 percent of foreign-school enrollment. Thereafter most pupils went to public schools.

In 1924, enrollment in the public schools constituted less than half (46.9 percent) of the total enrollment in all schools. Enrollments in private and foreign schools together were more numerous, constituting 53.1 percent. This situation was reversed in 1944–45 when public schools enrolled 57.5 percent of the total; private schools, 27.8 percent; and foreign schools, 14.7 percent. The preponderance of the public-school enrollment was probably even more accentuated after the closing of the French schools in 1945–46, with the private schools also gaining considerably. This lead of both public and private schools will probably continue even if the French schools reopen, since many so-called "foreign" schools have joined the ranks of the private schools, and a large proportion of pupils who have transferred to government or native private schools are likely to stay there.

DISTRIBUTION OF SCHOOLS BY TYPES

Table 60 gives the latest available data about the number of schools and of pupils distributed according to the types of schools—primary, secondary, vocational, teacher training, and higher—and according to the authority controlling the schools—public, private, and foreign.

There were in 1944–45 as many as 1,072 primary schools, of which 658 were public, 287 private, and 127 foreign schools. The public schools were attended by 85,540 children as against 43,010 in the private and 19,878 in the foreign schools. These represented 57.6, 29.0, and 13.4 percent respectively of the total primary-school enrollment. Of the total enrollment in all types of schools and educational institutions, that in primary schools represented 91.1 percent. In other words, less than one-tenth of the enrollment were in secondary schools, vocational schools, teachers colleges, and the University. It will be noticed that in the government schools boys and girls were taught in separate primary schools, while in the private and foreign schools there were two practices, separate schools and coeducational schools. There were 128 coeducational primary schools in existence during the year. Foreign schools on the whole were the larger, having an average enrollment of 156 pupils, closely followed by the private schools with an average enrollment of 153. Public primary schools had an average enrollment of 130. This is because private and foreign schools are situated in the larger urban centers for the most part, while many of the public schools are in sparsely populated rural districts.

There were 69 secondary schools in Syria in 1944–45, of which 22, or fewer than one-third, were public, 17 private, and 30 foreign. Nevertheless, the public schools accounted for more than half the student body (6,047 students, or 52.2 percent), while private schools had 1,743 stu-

ORGANIZATION AND ADMINISTRATION

TABLE 60
Syrian Schools Classified According to Type of School and Type of Control, 1944–45*

Type of School	Number of Schools				Enrollment			
	Boys	Girls	Coeducational	Total	Boys	Girls	Total	Percent
Primary and intermediate:								
Public	542	116	...	658	63,755	21,785	85,540	57.6
Private	158	40	89	287	28,800	14,210	43,010	29.0
Foreign	50	38	39	127	9,942	9,936	19,878	13.4
Total	750	194	128	1,072	102,497	45,931	148,428	91.1
Secondary:								
Public	14	8	...	22	4,557	1,490	6,047	52.2
Private	8	7	2	17	1,283	460	1,743	15.0
Foreign	9	14	7	30	2,639	1,163	3,802	32.8
Total	31	29	9	69	8,479	3,113	11,592	7.2
Vocational								
Public	4	1	...	5	812	199	1,011	60.2
Private	6	1	...	7	444	17	461	27.4
Foreign	2	1	...	3	101	106	207	12.3
Total	12	3	...	15	1,357	322	1,679	1.0
Teachers College (public)	2	2	...	4	153	131	284	0.2
Syrian University (public)	4	1	...	5	766	69	835	0.5
Grand Total	799	229	137	1,165	113,252	49,566	162,818	100.0
Summary:								
All public schools	566	128	...	694	70,043	23,674	93,717	57.5
All private schools	172	48	91	311	30,527	14,687	45,214	27.8
All foreign schools	61	53	46	160	12,682	11,205	23,887	14.7

* Figures supplied by Ministry of Education.

dents (15 percent), and foreign schools, 3,802 (32.8 percent). Public schools were either for boys or for girls, but a few private and foreign schools were coeducational. Government schools, with an average enrollment of 275, were larger on the whole than either private schools (with an enrollment per school of 102 students), or foreign schools (with an enrollment of 127 per school). One of the reasons for that situation is probably that the public schools charge much lower fees and have a substantial percentage of exempted students.

A further scrutiny of Table 60 shows an interesting fact about the relative number of boys and girls in public, private, and foreign schools. In the public schools the ratio of girls to boys is roughly 1 to 3, while in the private schools it is approximately 1 to 2, and in foreign schools the two sexes are almost equally represented. It is interesting to speculate upon the reason for this phenomenon. One reason is the fact that there are a number of French Catholic orders of nuns which maintain schools patronized by Christians and non-Christians owing to the strict education and discipline exercised over the girls. Another reason lies in the fact that most of the pupils of foreign schools (77 percent) in 1942–43 were Christians and Jews, and it is a well-known fact that the education of girls is the more popular among these two groups—primary education among them is, in fact, almost universal, particularly in the cities where most of the foreign schools are located. This fact is further supported by the figures for foreign primary schools, which show that 19,878 pupils are almost equally divided between the two sexes—the difference is only six pupils—a phenomenon familiar where universal education prevails. Secondary education for girls, however, is much less popular, the girls forming only 30 percent of the total number of students in foreign secondary schools.

In addition to the regular graded schools, there were in Syria, according to Ministry of Education statistics, 1,229 ungraded schools, or *kuttabs,* enrolling 34,440 children. Of these 292 were for girls, enrolling 6,190 pupils. Presumably these figures are for the year 1943–44.[13]

In the vocational-education field the public schools lead with 1,011 students, or 60.2 percent, in 5 schools. Of the 7 private schools with a total enrollment of 461, or 27.4 percent, 5 schools are not, strictly speaking, vocational. They are religious and Muhammadan law schools, enrolling 424 students. This leaves 2 vocational schools with a total enrollment of 37 pupils. Three foreign schools give vocational training to 206 pupils, or 12.3 percent of the total.

There were 4 teachers colleges for educating teachers for the primary and elementary schools—2 for men and 2 for women—enrolling 284 students. This is a great advance over the previous year when there were only 78 students.[14]

Finally there is the Syrian University with its Schools of Medicine, Dentistry, Pharmacy, Nursing, and Law, with 834 students, of whom 69 are women in the School of Nursing.

TEACHERS

As has already been mentioned, statistics for teachers are difficult to secure. Only figures for primary public-school teachers in the year 1944–45 were available to the American Council Commission. These numbered 2,140 and were distributed as follows:

[13] Al-Husri, *op. cit.*, p. 65.
[14] *Ibid.*, p. 54.

ORGANIZATION AND ADMINISTRATION 355

Teachers	Full time	Part time	Total
Men	1,411	95	1,506
Women	585	49	634
Total	1,996	144	2,140

Some figures were available, however, for the year 1943–44. There were in that year 2,239 teachers in all types of public schools except the University, distributed as follows:

Distribution of Teachers	Number of Teachers
Delegated to the central administration	50
Primary-school teachers	1,856
Secondary-school and teachers-college teachers	255
Vocational-school teachers	78
Total	2,239

Evidently the number of primary-school teachers gained considerably in one year, although it is difficult to determine accurately the amount of gain owing to the fact that some teachers, both primary and secondary, were delegated to the central administration, while others taught only part time.

Chapter 21

PUBLIC PRIMARY, SECONDARY, AND VOCATIONAL SCHOOLS

The Kindergarten

KINDERGARTEN education in Syria is still in its infancy. In 1944–45 there were 267 children—all girls—in the *classes enfantines* in connection with girls primary schools. These were in 4 schools, thus making an average of 47 children in each school.

In 1945–46 the Ministry of Education opened 2 new kindergartens, in Damascus and Aleppo. Both were visited briefly by the American Council Commission. They take children usually from four to six years of age, although the one at Aleppo was accepting children of two and one-half years of age. The children are kept busy with toys, singing and dancing, games, drawing, and similar activities. Care was being taken to teach the children habits of cleanliness. Some Montessori material, or an imitation of it, was being used. Some rudiments of reading without formal class teaching are included in the program. Each of the kindergartens had one teacher trained in France. The others were trained as primary teachers in the Teachers College for Women at Damascus.

Primary Education

Primary education is free in the public schools. It is also supposed to be compulsory, although this is more of a hope than a reality. The new education law, in setting down the principle of compulsion, provides that the principle may be applied in places decided upon by the Ministry of Education when adequate facilities exist. In his *Reports* Sati' al-Husri says that in drafting the new education law he was obliged to write the principle of compulsion into the law out of deference to the constitution which declares that primary education shall be compulsory. He knew, however, that the present number of schools is far from being adequate for requiring compulsory attendance in primary schools. Because the government budget will not be able to bear the expenses of compulsory primary schooling, he therefore exhorts the government to embark upon a program of local taxation for the maintenance of primary schools.

But how far is Syria from compulsory attendance? Only a rough estimate can be made as there is no census showing the various age groups in Syria. If it is assumed that the ratio of children of school age (in Syria, age six to eleven) is the same as that in Egypt, then the total number of children of school age would be about 13 percent of the total population, which was estimated in 1942–43 at about 3,000,000 people including the tribes.[1] This would give a total of about 390,000 children between the ages of six and eleven. As there were in 1944–45 about 148,000 children in primary schools of all kinds, this would leave 242,000 children without regular graded schooling. Children in primary schools therefore represent roughly 38 percent of the total number of children of school age. Even if the 34,000 children in the ungraded *kuttabs* were to be taken into account, this would bring the total number of children attending schools to 182,000, or 45.6 percent of children of school age. There will still be 208,000 children left who are growing up in illiteracy, and for whom schools are needed.

Primary education is offered either in primary schools of five years or in elementary schools of four years. The former are largely in the cities and larger centers, while the latter are mostly in the rural districts. Five-year primary schools do, of course, exist in the rural areas as well, particularly in the larger villages. In practice, however, schools of from one to five classes exist, as is shown by the following tabulation (figures supplied by the Ministry of Education):

Type of School	Boys	Girls	Total
Schools of one grade	11	2	13
Schools of two grades	55	8	63
Schools of three grades	177	30	207
Schools of four grades	97	14	111
Schools of five grades	202	62	264
Total	542	116	658

Thus, only 264 public schools out of 658, or 40 percent, are complete with five grades. Another 111, or about 17 percent, could be considered *complete* elementary schools, bringing the total of complete primary and elementary schools to 375, or 57 percent. The remaining 43 percent have from one to three grades. The average number of grades in Syrian public primary schools is 3.8 grades.

[1] Conseil Supérieur des Intérêts Communs, *Recueil de Statistiques de la Syrie et du Liban, 1942–43* (Beirut: Imprimerie Catholique, 1945), pp. 9, 14, 15.

It is, therefore, to be expected that pupil registration in the various primary grades would show a drastic decline as one moves up the grades, and, indeed, such is the case. Statistics are not available for grade registration over a period of years which would enable us to calculate the amount of yearly elimination from grade to grade. The number of pupils in each of the five grades in 1944–45 are given in Table 61:

TABLE 61
ENROLLMENT BY GRADES IN PUBLIC PRIMARY SCHOOLS, SYRIA, 1944–45*

GRADE	ENROLLMENT			NUMBER OF SECTIONS	PUPILS PER SECTION
	Boys	Girls	Total		
Classe enfantine....	...	267	267	4	47
First grade........	27,221	9,871	37,092	1,017	36
Second grade......	13,703	4,670	18,373	721	25
Third grade........	10,588	3,287	13,875	629	22
Fourth grade......	7,347	2,247	9,594	441	21
Fifth grade........	4,896	1,443	6,339	315	20
Total.........	63,755	21,785	85,540	3,127	27†

* Supplied by the Ministry of Education.
† Average.

Forty-three percent of the children are in the first grade, as compared with only 7 percent in the fifth. Children in the second grade number one-half of those in the first. From the second grade on, the number of children is cut in half every other grade. This phenomenon, which seems to be the rule wherever universal education is not enforced, has been observed with various degrees of intensity in all the countries studied in this report.

Table 61 brings out another characteristic—the declining size of classes from first to fifth grade. The average size of a class declines from 36 in the first grade to 20 in the fifth grade. This shows that not only do classes become fewer as we move up the grades, but they are attended by fewer pupils. The American Council Commission found classes that were as large as 91 in the lower grades and as small as 3 in the higher.

THE PRIMARY PROGRAM OF STUDIES

The primary course of study was in process of change at the time of the visit of the American Council Commission. A detailed new syllabus had been worked out only for history, geography, civics and ethics, and object lessons. Presumably these were considered the subjects most urgently in need of revision, while the other subjects were to follow the lines prescribed by the old course of study.[2]

[2] Detailed description of the content of subject courses will not be given here, except as attention will be called to the differences between the old and the new program in the

Table 62 gives the new distribution of periods assigned to the various subjects, which had been in effect since November 1945, the date of the delayed opening of the schools. All periods are of forty-five minutes each. The school day consists of four periods in the morning and two in the afternoon, with a half-holiday on Thursday and a full holiday on Friday.

It will be noted from Table 62 that under the old course of study *history* did not begin until the third grade. The new program provides for incidental teaching of history in the first two grades. In the third grade, the

TABLE 62
Primary Course of Study for Syrian Public Schools, 1945–46

Subject	1st Grade	2nd Grade	3rd Grade	4th Grade	5th Grade
Religion and Koran	4	4	4	3	3
Arabic	13	13	9	8	8
Arithmetic and geometry	5	5	5	5	5
Object lessons	4	4	4	4	4
History	...	...	2	2	2
Geography	...	...	2	2	2
Civics and ethics	...	...	...	2	2
Handwriting	...	2	2	2	2
Drawing and handwork	3	2	2	2	2
Physical education and singing	3	2	2	2	2
Free activities	2	2	2	2	2
Total	34	34	34	34	34

children are introduced to modern Arab heroes and other great men through short biographies and work back to the Prophet Muhammad and the famous men and women of early Arab history. A few non-Arab kings and statesmen of ancient and modern times are included. With the biographies, a description of life in Babylon, Syria, Arabia, and Egypt is woven in. Systematic teaching of history begins in the fourth grade with generalizations about primitive society, the beginning of civilization, the domestication of animals, early human inventions, the rise of the family, the tribe, and the state. History of the Arabs through the Umayyad period is taken up in the fourth grade and is completed to modern times in the fifth. In the fifth grade reference is made to the rise of modern nations and imperialism and the development of democracy, and this is connected with modern Arab history.

The teaching of *geography* has also been advanced a grade. Under the new course of study incidental teaching of geography begins in the second

---

revised syllabuses for the four subjects mentioned. In general, the content of courses in the lower grades is similar in all the Arab countries except that the history and geography of each country is given special attention in the schools of that country.

grade, dealing with the school, the quarter, the village or town, and the surrounding plains, mountains, and rivers. Systematic geography begins in the third grade, with some study of the sun, moon, and earth. Maps of the class, the school, and the locality are made, showing the roads connecting the community with the outside. Actual trips are sometimes made to the surrounding country and imaginary trips to the rest of the Arab world in Asia and Africa. In the fourth grade, fundamental concepts of physical geography are given, with a brief study of outstanding countries on each continent. The fifth grade is devoted to a more detailed study of the geography of Syria, Lebanon, Palestine, and Transjordan, and a less detailed study of the rest of the Arab world.

Civics and ethics begin in the fourth grade and include man's duties to himself, his family, to others, to his country and countrymen, and to animals. In the fifth grade a study is made of the machinery of government, and the administrative divisions of Syria, Syrians abroad and foreigners in Syria, and the main types of government.

The new courses on Observation of the Environment and Object Lessons are a compound of two parts—the observation of nature (*science and hygiene*) and the observation of the environment (social and civic). It begins in the first grade with simple topics on personal cleanliness, the home and the school, and continues through the fifth grade, each year adding more complex subjects. Fifth grade subjects include physics, physiology, zoology, and botany and agriculture.

In general, the content of courses in *arithmetic, home economics, manual arts, drawing, music,* and *physical education* is similar to the primary course of study for Egypt, previously described.

An adaptation of the course of study for a three-year rural school cut down the periods for religion, civics, drawing, manual arts, and object lessons, adds more time for Arabic and arithmetic and prescribes six hours of practical agriculture a week. The American Council Commission visited a rural school of this kind near Homs, which had a garden of about one and a half acres. No special training in agriculture was given, and the teacher relied on his readings in a textbook and on the experience of the school janitor who was a farmer.

Teaching, Textbooks, and School Activities

It is difficult to give an adequate idea about classroom teaching in a whole country which has hundreds of schools. Some very good teaching was witnessed in a number of schools, such as in the practice school of the Teachers College for Men in Damascus, among others, while teaching in

Class in Arabic at Damascus College, Damascus, Syria

Above: Teacher (at right) and part of the top class of the primary school for girls, Suwayda, Syria
Below: A former French army barracks now used for a government school for boys, Suwayda

other schools, particularly in the villages, left much to be desired. The American Council Commission is under the impression that most of the better teachers are concentrated in the larger centers, while the tendency is to push the indifferent teachers to the outer regions.

Teaching is conducted mainly through inductive and deductive development lessons and through questions and answers. Through the use of readers and textbooks and discussion in class, subject matter is methodically imparted to the children. The teacher is the prime mover, and few, if any, classroom activities are initiated by the children. Children often write summaries down in their notebooks, and care is taken in true French style that the notebooks are kept clean and orderly. Occasionally, as in object lessons, material is brought in for observation, and charts and maps are used. Homework is assigned beginning in the first grade.

Readers and textbooks for the various subjects have been written in Arabic by Syrian authors, most of whom are in the public-school system. These follow mainly French models. Only textbooks approved by the Ministry of Education may be used in the public schools, and these are published by their authors. High prices prevailed during World War II and the period immediately following. Pupils buy their own books, although poor pupils are often helped by a cooperative society in the school.

The prevailing practice is to have the teacher responsible for his or her own class. In many schools, however, work in the fourth and fifth grades (and some in the third) is distributed among teachers by subjects. In village schools a teacher may have to take more than one class, or even a whole school. In this case, however, the school rarely exceeds three grades. The art of simultaneous teaching of more than one class is far from being perfected, and in most schools the Commission found the teachers teaching one group while the other students sat idle. Occasionally a teacher would give one item to one group, move to the next group for a few minutes, and then move back to the first group, the other group being idle in the meantime. Thus, the teacher would go back and forth many times in a period of forty-five minutes. Clearly, training in the use of simultaneous teaching would greatly improve the efficiency of the village schools.

A check-up conducted in a number of schools revealed that a majority of the children in the first grade, notably in the smaller centers, spent more than one year in that grade. The class is often unofficially divided into two or more sections, usually studying in the same room, and an advanced section may be reading in the first-grade reader in a place thirty to fifty pages ahead of a lower group. It seemed to be taken for granted that most of the pupils of the lower group would not be promoted to the second grade at the end of the year, while a check-up of the advanced group showed that most of the children had been in the lower group the previous year.

Another quick check-up in the fifth grade of a few schools showed that children take from five to seven years to finish the primary school. Among 88 fifth-grade boys in one school the age range was eleven to seventeen. One school principal estimated that 25 percent of the children spend more than five years in the primary school. Others put it at a higher figure.

The school year now begins on October 1 and ends in mid-June, although the schools did not open in 1945 until late in November, owing to the emergency created by the closing of the French schools. The daily timetable is as follows:

> 8:00–11:45 A.M. Morning session of four periods of forty-five minutes each, with recesses of fifteen minutes between
> 11:45 A.M.–1:45 P.M. Lunch
> 1:45–3:30 P.M. Afternoon session of two periods and one recess

In the fasting month of Ramadan certain lessons are cut down and only a morning session is held.

Attendance in village schools increases gradually from October to January, usually remains high in January, February, and March, and begins to decline in April, and in some schools may be extremely low in the last two months of the school year when children may be working in the fields with their parents.

As regards extracurricular activities, many schools, especially in the cities, have cooperative welfare societies to which children make voluntary contributions to help the poorer pupils. Some schools have Scout troops. Many schools make excursions to the cities or to the surrounding country, while celebrations, parties, and dramatic performances are held in many of the larger schools.

Teachers

There were 1,996 full-time teachers in 658 public primary schools in 1944–45, compared with 1,856 in 639 schools in the previous year. This makes an average of three teachers per school for the whole country in 1944–45, compared with 2.9 teachers per school in the previous year. The following is the distribution of schools according to the number of teachers in them.[3]

[3] Figures supplied by the Ministry of Education.

PRIMARY, SECONDARY, AND VOCATIONAL SCHOOLS

Type of School	Number of Schools
Schools with one teacher	345
Schools with two teachers	90
Schools with three teachers	40
Schools with four teachers	17
Schools with five teachers	42
Schools with six teachers	38
Schools with seven teachers	24
Schools with eight teachers	16
Schools with nine teachers	10
Schools with ten teachers	6
Schools with more than ten teachers	30
Total	658

More than half of the schools (52.4 percent) are one-teacher schools, while the number of schools with a full complement of teachers (five or more) is 166, or 25.2 percent.

Light may also be shed upon primary education by an examination of the qualifications of primary-school teachers. The following data are for 1943–44:[4]

Qualification	Number of Teachers
Graduates of teachers colleges or holders of teaching diploma	820
Law College graduates	10
Agricultural School (Salamiyah)	13
Higher School of Literature	18
Baccalauréat, Second Part	93
Baccalauréat, First Part	225
Brevet (General, Technical, or Commercial)	159
Total	1,338

As the number of teachers was 1,856 in 1943, this leaves 518 teachers unaccounted for, presumably because their qualifications were even lower than the *brevet* (roughly equivalent to a junior-high-school certificate).

BUILDINGS AND EQUIPMENT

A large number of primary schools, particularly in the cities, are in rented buildings. Most of these are houses built to accommodate families, although some of the old-style houses are spacious and have large courtyards. Ordinarily the rooms planned as lodging quarters are too small for

---

[4] Sati' al-Husri, *Reports on the State of Education in Syria and Recommendations for Its Reform* (Damascus: 1944), p. 132.

a class of thirty or forty, and classes either become crowded or have to be adjusted to the rooms. Rented buildings range from the large houses that may be found in Damascus, Homs, Hama, and Aleppo, to the small village houses which are little more than huts. Primary-school buildings may be owned by the government, but the number of these is comparatively small. Many schools in cities and in villages are owned by municipalities or are rented by the municipalities as their contribution to the maintenance of the schools. Sanitary conditions, lighting, and ventilation may be fair in government-owned buildings and in some of the rented ones, but they are often inadequate.

The usual classroom desk is built with seats attached to accommodate two children, and is frequently a local product. The seats may or may not have backs, and in the latter case the children rest their backs either against the wall or against the desk immediately behind them. In a crowded school a desk for two may be occupied by three or even four pupils. The desks are in various degrees of preservation, some being new, while others appear to have been in use a long time.

Some of the larger primary schools in the cities are well stocked with instructional materials and equipment such as maps in French or Arabic, natural-history charts imported from Egypt, story pictures. In some schools there is a variety of instructional materials made by the teachers. The village schools are not so well supplied.

Libraries, when they exist, are very small and little used by the children. Very little money is given by the Ministry of Education for the purchase of library books. Occasionally books are sent to the schools by the Ministry.

The schools are run on the most economical lines. Very little money is allowed for the everyday running of the schools. The principal or head teacher has to spend out of his own pocket or borrow from the welfare society's fund. Only after receipts for the expenditure are presented and approved by higher authority is the money refunded by the Treasury.

Secondary Education

As has already been stated, secondary education was shortened from seven to six years under the new plan of organization. In the earlier course the first four years led to the examination for the *brevet* certificate, and were followed by two years in the scientific or literary section, which ended in the first *baccalauréat* examination. The new plan calls simply for an intermediate stage of four years leading to the intermediate examination, and a preparatory stage of two years divided into a scientific and a literary section and leading to the Secondary-School Certificate examination.

New regulations for secondary schools were issued between February and December 1945.[5] The regulations declare that the aim of education is (*a*) to develop a cultured élite by inculcating on adolescents and youth the fundamental information and general culture which they need in their life; and (*b*) to prepare these adolescents and youth for vocational studies, on the one hand, and higher studies, on the other. Admission of students to the first year of the intermediate stage requires the possession of the government primary-school certificate. A student must be of good character and must be no less than ten and no more than fifteen years old. Admission to the preparatory stage requires the possession of the government intermediate-school certificate. The student must be of good character and no less than fourteen and no more than twenty years old. The school year begins on October 1 and ends on June 15. Schools are in session five and a half days a week, Thursday afternoons and Fridays being holidays. In addition, schools are closed on official holidays and for two weeks after midyear examinations.

A new plan for school examinations provides for three kinds—daily oral or written quizzes, midyear, and final examinations. The midyear examination papers are to be corrected by the class teacher, but final examination papers are to be read by a committee of which the class teacher is a member. All midyear and final examinations are written except those in languages, which are oral as well. Marks are on the scale of 100. The results of the quizzes for the first and second terms are averaged separately, added to the results of the midyear examination, and divided by three. The resulting mark is added to that of the final examination and divided by two. In order to pass, a student must have a general average of 50 or more, and a grade of 50 in each subject. If he has a general average of 50 and less than 50 in one or two subjects, he may be re-examined in those subjects. Otherwise he fails. As these passing marks are much higher than those previously prevailing, a transitional scheme of passing marks higher than those previously set but lower than the new marks was to be used until the end of 1945–46.

[5] These are contained in *Regulations for Intermediate and Secondary Schools and Teachers Colleges* (Damascus: Government Press, 1945), 51 pp., and comprise Decree No. 1415, dated December 17, 1945, "Embodying the Secondary School Regulations"; Decree No. 183, dated February 20, 1945, "Embodying the Futuwah Regulations for the Preparation of Secondary School Students for Military Life"; Law No. 201, dated September 19, 1945, "Embodying the Organization of Secondary Schools"; Decree No. 1304, dated November 13, 1945, "Embodying Fixing the Maximum Teaching Load for Intermediate, Secondary, and Vocational Schools, and the Fees Thereof." (In Arabic.)

These are the highlights of the new secondary-school regulations. In addition, the regulations give detailed provisions for admission of pupils and their transfer from one school to another, duties of students, absences, courses of study, and methods of teaching. The teachers are exhorted to use "active" methods in teaching and not to have students be mere listeners, and to encourage them to engage in free activities, such as reading, art, sculpture, music, and dramatics, in order to promote initiative and creativeness. In girls schools, studies are directed toward home needs and the "duties of motherhood." The regulations also set down provisions for the discipline of pupils, for the guidance of the administrative and teaching staffs as well as school committees and councils, and for relations with the parents. A staff council must meet at least three times a year, and subject committees must meet once a month. A disciplinary committee and a purchasing committee are also provided for.

A special decree prescribes compulsory military training for boys in the fifth and sixth years, and empowers the Ministry of Education to arrange for military training groups in nonpublic schools requesting it, and in the University.

Another decree abolishes the posts of special monitors (*surveillants*) for keeping order and discipline in the schools, which hitherto had been the practice borrowed from France, and puts the responsibility for discipline and order on the principals, their assistants, and the teachers.

Another decree fixes the maximum teaching load for teachers in secondary and vocational schools. Teachers of the special subjects, such as art, music, manual arts, physical education, domestic science, penmanship, and typing, teach up to twenty-four periods a week. Teachers of the other subjects in intermediate and vocational schools have a maximum load of twenty periods a week, while those teaching in preparatory classes and teachers colleges have a load of eighteen periods. Principals and their assistants are also required to teach a minimum ranging from three periods a week for a principal of a boarding school to ten periods for an assistant principal in a day intermediate or vocational school.

THE SECONDARY COURSE OF STUDY

The time allotment for the various subjects of the secondary course of study is given in Table 63. A total of thirty-four periods a week is maintained throughout the six years. Each period is forty-five minutes. The program for the first four years is the same for all students except that girls receive instruction in domestic science whereas boys are allowed periods for free activities. A choice between French and English is allowed in foreign languages.

TABLE 63

THE NEW PROGRAM OF STUDIES FOR SECONDARY SCHOOLS, SYRIA, 1945–46

| | \multicolumn{4}{c|}{Intermediate} | \multicolumn{4}{c|}{Preparatory: Boys} | \multicolumn{2}{c}{Preparatory: Girls} |
| | | | | | \multicolumn{2}{c|}{Literary Section} | \multicolumn{2}{c|}{Scientific Section} | | |
Subject	1st Year	2nd Year	3rd Year	4th Year	5th Year	6th Year	5th Year	6th Year	5th Year	6th Year
Religion and Koran	1	1	1	1	1	1	1	1	1	1
Arabic language and literature	7	6	6	6	6	6	4	4	5	4
First foreign language*	8	7	7	6	5	4	5	4	5	4
History	3	3	3	3	4	4	…	3	4	4
Geography	…	2	2	2	2	3	2	…	2	…
Ethics and legal and civic information	…	…	…	3	…	…	…	…	…	…
Mathematics	4	4	4	5	3	3	6	6	3	3
Science	4	4	6	6	3	4	6	7	3	4
Second foreign language*	…	…	…	…	5	4	5	4	5	4
Principles of science and logic	…	…	…	…	2	…	2	…	2	…
Psychology	…	…	…	…	…	3	…	3	…	3
Child care and nursing	…	…	…	…	…	…	…	…	…	3
Drawing	2	2	2	…	…	…	…	…	…	…
Physical education	2	2	1	1	…	…	…	…	1	1
Music	1	1	…	…	…	…	…	…	1	1
Free activities for boys } Domestic science for girls }	2	2	2	1	…	…	…	…	2	2
Futuwah (drill) and military information	…	…	…	…	3	2	3	2	…	…
Total	34	34	34	34	34	34	34	34	34	34

* Choice is made between English and French. The language chosen in the intermediate stage becomes the first foreign language for the preparatory stage.

In the preparatory stage boys and girls have different courses. Boys may choose either a literary or scientific course, in which the subjects taught are the same but with a difference in the amount of time devoted to them. Both sections take the same courses in foreign languages, logic, and psychology. The literary section emphasizes and gives more time to Arabic, history, and geography, while the science section takes more mathematics and science. Military training and lectures on military subjects are given to the boys. All girls take the same course, which includes two hours of domestic science each week in each year, with a correspondingly smaller amount of time devoted to geography and science than is given the boys. A second foreign language is introduced for all students in the fifth year.

A brief summary of the courses of study in the secondary school is given below, and the most important differences between the old and the new courses are indicated.

In *Arabic,* reading and literature are made the center around which the other subjects revolve. A smaller number of poets and writers are studied than in the old course, but more of the works of each are studied. Composition is stressed throughout the six years, while grammar is meant to be simpler and more practical than under the old course. Prosody, rhetoric, and elocution are given in the fifth and sixth years of the literary section; in the scientific section, emphasis is laid upon scientific reading material in these years.

In *geography,* Asia and Oceania are taught in the second year, and Europe and America in the third year. In the fourth year, Africa and the Arab countries in Africa and Asia are studied in detail. In the fifth year, general physical, human, and economic geography is taken up by both the literary and scientific sections, while in the sixth year, the literary section studies the Arab world again as well as the geography of the great powers.

History begins with prehistory and ancient history in the first year; the second and third years are entirely devoted to the history of the Arabs; the fourth year is devoted mainly to European history to the present time, although some time is given to Arab civilization at its height, the downfall of the 'Abbasid Empire, and to the Arab countries between the two World Wars. In the preparatory years, the fifth-year literary section studies the history of civilization with emphasis upon Arab and modern civilizations, and in the sixth year both sections take modern history and the history of the movement for independence in the Arab world.

In the field of *science,* the first year is devoted entirely to a general course aimed at building a common foundation for the later study of physics, chemistry, zoology, botany, and physical geography. In the second year, mechanics and sound are studied in physics in two periods, while elements of zoology and botany are taken up in the other two. Heat and light are taken in third-year physics, and nonmetals are studied in chemistry. Finally, in the fourth year, electricity and magnetism are taken in physics, metals and organic compounds in chemistry, and anatomy and physiology. In the scientific section of the preparatory stage, the physics and chemistry studies of the intermediate stage are expanded and completed in the fifth year, while, in the sixth, advanced studies in the vibratory and periodic motions and in the theories behind modern inventions complete the physics course. In the literary section, also, the fifth-year class studies an expanded course in physics and chemistry. The study of science in the secondary schools is largely theoretical—the laboratory equipment is generally deficient. The students rarely do experiments by themselves, even in the advanced classes; whatever laboratory work exists is usually in the form of demonstrations by the teacher.

In *mathematics* the first year is given entirely to arithmetic, while the second, third, and fourth years are taken up with algebra and plane geometry. In the fourth year, elements of logarithms, trigonometric functions and graphs and their applications to surveying and statistics are included. In the preparatory stage, the literary section has a course in general mathematics which includes elements of trigonometry, further applications to statistics and surveying, and astronomy. The scientific section completes the study of algebra and geometry by taking advanced topics in each, including solid geometry. It also takes mechanics, trigonometry, the elements of analytical geometry, and astronomy.

The courses in the principles of *science* and *logic* and in *psychology* in the old course of study for the philosophy section (seventh year) are transferred to the fifth and sixth years. In the old course the philosophy section took eleven periods a week of philosophy (logic, psychology, ethics, and metaphysics); the mathematics section took four hours a week of philosophy, which included only logic and ethics. The new course of study provides for only logic and psychology, together with principles of scientific method to be taken by both the literary and the scientific section.

The details of the courses for *English* and *French* had not been made public at the time the American Council Commission was in Syria.

The new course of study for secondary schools has been criticized in certain quarters because it has attempted to condense a seven-year program into six years, with a consequent crowding of the curriculum which will make it difficult for the teachers to finish the course and for the students to digest the subjects. To this criticism it is answered that some subjects—philosophy, for example—have been abolished and others reduced. The second foreign language has been abolished for the last three years of the intermediate school and now only begins in the fifth year. It is claimed that formerly a disproportionate amount of time was taken by the examinations at the beginning and the end of the year. Much less time is now taken by the examinations so that somewhere between a half and a full academic year is saved and is available for teaching purposes.

ADMISSION AND EDUCATIONAL OPPORTUNITY

Admission to the secondary school was formerly open to holders of the primary-school certificate provided they had passed their examination with a grade of *bien* (good) or *assez bien* (fairly good). In this way admission to the secondary school was limited. Under the reorganization these limitations have been abolished, and the way is open to all who wish to enter, provided they can pay the fees. The fees are not exorbitant, being £S48 ($21.60) in the intermediate, and £S60 ($27.27) in the preparatory schools. Even here, however, there is a wide range of exemptions. Children of teachers or of government employees receiving less than £S50 a month are exempt. Students are also exempt if their marks are high enough in the public examinations. A reduction of 30 percent of the fees is made to children of officials having a monthly salary of £S50–£S100. By order of the Ministry of Education no fees were charged in the two secondary schools of the Jabal Druze. In practice, about one-third of the student body receives exemptions. In addition, brothers pay less. One additional brother pays two-thirds of the fees, two additional brothers pay one-half each, and three additional brothers pay one-fourth each.

Students coming from localities where there is no secondary school, or the local school is incomplete, go usually to Damascus or Aleppo where boarding departments are maintained in both the boys and the girls secondary schools. Here, again, help is given to the deserving poor student through provision for free board or free lunches. In Aleppo, out of 247 boarding students in the public secondary school for boys, 92 received free board; and out of 140 students who ate only lunch at school, 58 received it free. The proportions were even higher in the Aleppo public secondary school for girls, where 24 boarders received their board free as compared with 29 girls who paid. Twenty-two had free lunch as compared with 10 who paid.

It is clear that an effort is being made to help the underprivileged child

PRIMARY, SECONDARY, AND VOCATIONAL SCHOOLS

to pursue his education further, and to equalize educational opportunity. How far these efforts are effective in the rural communities is another matter. Inquiry at some of the village schools showed that very few pupils from them had gone on to secondary schools.

Teachers, classes, and school activities

There were 255 secondary-school teachers in the Syrian public schools in 1943–44. The following is a tabulation of their qualifications.[6]

Qualifications	Number of Teachers
Doctorates (of which 7 were in medicine)	17
Licence ès Lettres or *ès Sciences* from France	35
Licence in Letters from Fuad I University, Cairo	5
Master of Arts from the American University of Beirut, or from America	14
Licence in Law	17
Higher School of Letters	11
Teachers College at Istanbul	2
Total	101

The remainder (154 persons) have varied qualifications. It will be noticed that while many teachers of the secondary cadre hold higher degrees, few of them are professionally trained. Many teachers have formerly been in primary schools and were promoted to teach in secondary classes.

The same phenomenon of the decrease in the number of students as they rise in their grades which was noticed in the primary school is noticeable in secondary and vocational schools, as is shown by the figures for 1944–45 (Table 64) which were supplied by the Ministry of Education:

TABLE 64

DISTRIBUTION OF PUPILS IN CLASSES IN SECONDARY AND VOCATIONAL SCHOOLS, SYRIA, 1944–45

Class	Boys	Girls	Total
Preparatory class (vocational)	340	93	433
First year	1,863	604	2,467
Second year	1,103	393	1,496
Third year	742	291	1,033
Fourth year	446	193	639
Fifth year	356	52	408
Sixth year	234	47	281
Philosophy and mathematics	285	16	301
Total	5,369	1,689	7,058

[6] Al-Husri, *op. cit.*, pp. 131–34.

While there were 2,467 students in the first year, there were only 301 in the seventh year. Most classes have between 30 and 40 pupils, but classes with as low as 11 students and as high as 70 students were seen by the American Council Commission. Crowded classes, however, are rare in the secondary schools.

Attendance is quite regular, but it tends to drop sharply toward the end of the year, the students preferring to prepare for their final examinations at home.

School activities are on the whole encouraged, although schools differ in this respect. In addition to the regular athletic classes and the compulsory *Futuwah* (military training), schools engage in a number of organized games, mainly football, basketball, volleyball, and in some cases tennis. A number of schools have Scout troops. School groups also conduct picnics and excursions. Student clubs are more numerous in larger schools than in the smaller ones. The most common is the cooperative welfare society, which gathers contributions from students, teachers, and occasionally from the general public, for the help of poorer students. There are also clubs for Arabic, music, dramatics, and other such activities. Some schools and their clubs issue student magazines. The teachers usually play a leading role in these activities, serving as sponsors and in some schools as chairmen.

Perhaps a word regarding the opportunities open to the secondary-school graduate will be in order. In Syria proper a graduate may go to the Syrian University or to the two-year course in teacher training. The latter is the course most of the girls follow. However, a number of opportunities exist outside Syria where the second *baccalauréat* was considered to be of a high standard. Previously it was accepted in France and students holding it were permitted to enter French higher institutions. Whether the new certificate, with one less year of schooling, will be considered of the same level remains to be seen, although it is hardly likely under the circumstances. Both the American University and the Université St. Joseph in Beirut accepted it; the former required an examination in English but admitted students to the sophomore and even to the junior year. The latter accepted it for the purposes of entrance to its Faculties of Medicine, Law, and Engineering. The Egyptian Ministry of Education also recognized it for entrance to the Universities of Fuad I and Faruq I and other higher institutions.

Buildings and Equipment

Secondary schools are more fortunate than primary schools with regard to their buildings. The boys schools are usually more favored as to buildings than are the girls schools. Of 14 secondary schools visited by the American Council Commission, 7 were government-owned, including 2 confiscated French barracks at Suwayda in Jabal Druze; 2 belonged to local municipalities; and 5 were rented. Undoubtedly, the best secondary-school buildings seen by the Commission in Syria were those of the Damascus and Aleppo boys schools. A fine new building for the boys secondary school at Homs was in the process of construction.

In libraries, also, the secondary schools are more favored. There is a wide range, however, in the number of books—from about 25 or 30 books in the library of the intermediate school for boys at Suwayda to about 7,000 volumes in the library of the secondary school for boys in Damascus. The books are almost entirely in French and Arabic. Large collections of French literary works and French textbooks exist at both Damascus and Aleppo boys schools. A number of Arabic magazines are subscribed to, and formerly a number of French magazines as well. The British Council recently gave small collections of English books to the libraries of some of the schools. The Damascus school for boys has a full-time librarian. Usually there is little space for reading in the libraries, and students borrow books at specified times, sometimes paying deposits for the books borrowed. More freedom in the system of borrowing, more space for reading in the libraries, and more encouragement by teachers and all concerned seem to be necessary for making the school library play a more important part in the educational programs of the schools.

The situation with regard to desks and furniture is much the same as that in primary school except that the quality of the desks is better, and few, if any, desks accommodate more than two pupils.

Vocational Schools

There were 6 public vocational schools in Syria at the time of the visit of the American Council Commission: the Technical (trade) School for boys, the Technical School for girls, and the Commercial School for boys, all in Damascus; the Technical School for boys, and the Commercial School for boys, both in Aleppo, and the Agricultural School at Salamiyah, east of Hama. The last named is under the jurisdiction of the Ministry of National Economy. Four of the six schools were visited by the Commission—the Technical School for boys and the Commercial School for boys at Damascus were not visited.

All of the vocational schools (except the school of agriculture) give a course of four years above the primary-school certificate. Formerly they formed part of the plan for complementary education, which was of two kinds: general complementary, restricted to general cultural courses, and vocational complementary, combining cultural and trade education. A certificate known as the general *brevet* was given at the end of the general course after the student had passed a public examination, and "vocational *brevets*,"—Technical, Commercial, or Agricultural—were given at the end of the vocational courses after public examinations.

The attempt to make the vocational schools a part of the complementary education had resulted in a heavy overloading of the course of study, and the students were working and studying for forty-six periods a week in the technical schools besides which there were additional study periods that were compulsory for boarding students. After the abolition of the complementary system in the new educational organization the vocational schools were considered as independent schools, and an attempt was made to lighten their programs.

The number of students in the public vocational schools in 1943–44 was 1,024, and in the following year, 1,011. A summary description of the schools visited by the Commission will perhaps give the best picture of public vocational education in Syria.

THE TECHNICAL SCHOOL FOR BOYS

The Technical School for boys at Aleppo dated back to 1900 when it was founded in connection with an orphanage, with the idea of providing trade education for orphans. Its connection with the orphanage was severed in 1924–25.[7] It had 148 students in 1945–46, of whom 73 were boarders. Eleven of these paid annually a sum of £S240 (about $108.00) for their board, and the other 62 had free board at the expense of the state. The boarding students come from the outer districts of the governorate of Aleppo as well as from the governorates of Homs, Hama, Latakia, and Dayr al-Zur. Thus, about one-half of the student body is from outside Aleppo, and an attempt is being made to give opportunity for vocational education to students from the smaller towns. No tuition fee is charged.

The new program of study, issued in November 1945, covers four years and combines general cultural with vocational work. It includes religion, civics, Arabic, a foreign language, mathematics, physics, history, geography, physical education, industrial drawing, technology, and shopwork. In the first year, which is a preparatory year, the shopwork is common for all

[7] This conception of technical education as primarily suited to orphans is of long standing and has persisted until lately in the Damascus technical schools for boys and for girls. In recent years steps have been taken to separate the orphanages from the technical schools in that city.

students. Specialization begins in the second year. Eight lines of specialization are provided: turning, fitting, foundry, auto and motor mechanics, blacksmithing, carpentry, wood-carving, and weaving. All students in the first six sections take welding as well. The auto-mechanics section is the most popular with the students, and most of them would take it up if allowed. Wood-carving is the least popular. In order to keep a balance between the various sections, therefore, the School has to apply some pressure on some of the students. Shopwork ranged from fourteen periods a week in the first year to twenty-two periods a week in the fourth year.

The School occupies a government building originally built as an elementary school by the Turks. It has fairly well-equipped fitting, turning, and carpentry shops. Most of the equipment was acquired twenty years ago, and few, if any, additions or replacements have been made. The new budget provided £S40,000 (about $18,200) for new equipment and raw materials. In addition, £S25,000 (about $11,400) was provided as working capital. Out of the profits from products sold or services rendered, it is planned to add a certain proportion to capital and to credit the remainder to the students. This would accumulate during their stay in school, and would be given to them at the time of their graduation to serve as their working capital. A law legalizing this procedure (Law No. 254) was passed on June 4, 1946.[8] In this way it is hoped to put the school and its other sister schools on a profit-making basis as far as that is compatible with instructional purposes.

Of the 12 students who were graduated from the Aleppo school in the previous year, 1 was working in the railways, 1 in the fire department, 1 in the Department of Supplies, 3 were primary-school teachers, 2 were working independently, and 4 were unemployed.

THE TECHNICAL SCHOOL FOR GIRLS

The Technical School for girls in Damascus was also originally started as an orphanage primary school. The Technical School proper began in 1938–39, and the first four of the primary grades were removed elsewhere. It was hoped to remove the fifth grade in 1946–47. Most of the students of the School still come from the orphanage, after having received their primary-school certificate. In 1945–46 the School had 118 students of whom 20 were free boarding students, and 2 were paying boarders. No

---

[8] Sati' al-Husri, *Reports on the Conditions of Education in Syria during the Year 1945* (Damascus: Government Press, 1946), p. 133. This is a sequel to his earlier reports already referred to, which were published in 1944. They attempt to show the progress made in the reorganization of Syrian education.

tuition fee is charged. The boarding fee is the same as in all other boarding public schools.

The course of four years provides instruction in religion, Arabic, a foreign language, mathematics, general science, physics, chemistry, biology (including hygiene), "industrial science," history, geography, civics, music, physical education, and drawing. In addition, courses in home economics, nursing, and child care are given. As many as thirteen subjects may be given in one year in a program that totals forty periods a week. Practical work ranges from ten periods in the first year to eighteen periods in the fourth. Specialization is afforded in any one of five departments—dressmaking, embroidery, lacework, decorative art, and rug-making. In the first year the students make the round of all the five trades. Specialization begins in the second year. Dressmaking is the most popular trade chosen, followed by embroidery. Decorative art is the least popular.

Most of the students provide their own materials and are allowed to keep the product. If the material is provided by the School, the work is kept by the School.

No information was available on the activities of graduates.

THE COMMERCIAL SCHOOL FOR BOYS

The Commercial School for boys in Aleppo (like its sister-school in Damascus, which was not visited by the Commission) was founded in 1933. Fittingly enough it occupies part of an old *khan* (inn) built in 1740 for foreign merchants trading in Aleppo. It had an enrollment in 1945–46 of 65 students. In contrast with the Technical School, it has only 4 students from outside Aleppo and is entirely a day school for which no tuition is charged. Only 2 new students had applied for admission at the beginning of the year; accordingly, there was no first class. A first-year secondary was opened in connection with the School, and students who are not exempt pay tuition as in the rest of the secondary schools. The reasons given for the lack of new applicants for the Commercial School were two: (1) the opening of the secondary schools virtually to all graduates of the primary school and a wide range of exemption from fees make students prefer to go to the secondary schools; (2) the benefits for the graduates have been limited and not encouraging. As the students are graduated young, firms are not usually inclined to employ them at such an early age.

The program of studies is of four years' duration, and is comprised of religion, Arabic, foreign language and translation, history, geography, mathematics, science, civics (including ethical, legal, and economic information), drawing, penmanship, and physical education. The commercial studies, which start in the second year, range from eight subjects in the second year, to thirteen in the fourth year, and include commercial law, merchandising, typing, bookkeeping, and practical work in business firms. The total number of periods is thirty-four per week.

The school has a small library of commercial books and some Arabic and French typewriters.

Of the 5 students who were graduated in the previous year 3 were in the Department of Supply, 1 was studying in secondary school, and 1 was teaching in a primary school.

THE SALAMIYAH AGRICULTURAL SCHOOL

The Salamiyah Agricultural School is situated on a farm near the village of Salamiyah to the east of the city of Hama. The School was founded by the Turks in 1910, but had been closed in 1932 and was reopened in 1943 by the Ministry of National Economy, which now administers it.

Minimum preparation for admission is completion of the primary school, but between 30 and 40 percent of those admitted have held the *brevet*. Fifty-four students were registered at the school in 1945–46—23 in the first and 31 in the second year. All students are boarders. Of these, 33 are free boarders, paying nothing for tuition or board. The other 21 each pay £S300 a year (about $136.40).

The course of study extends over two years. It is comprised of civics, history, geometry, topography, hygiene, agricultural geography, agricultural and business arithmetic, mechanics, agricultural bookkeeping, physics and chemistry applied to agriculture, botany, zoology, and agriculture. The last mentioned includes general agriculture, agriculture of special crops, vegetable gardening, domestic animals, farm machinery, farm buildings, agricultural law, political and agricultural economy, geology, poultry, forestry, aviculture, silkworm raising, plant diseases, entomology, and veterinary science. To each of these, a certain number of lectures is allotted, ranging from ten to forty-five.

The School owns two plots of farm lands of 1,000 and 2,500 *dunams* (a *dunam* is a Turkish unit of land measurement). It has a number of buildings and barns, most of which were erected in the period of Turkish rule. It seemed to be fairly well equipped with farm machinery, including a harvesting and threshing combine and a cotton gin. It provides its own electric power. The farms have extensive fields for raising grain, vegetables, and fruits. There is also an extensive nursery and a variety of shade trees. Irrigation is provided from underground canals bringing water from a distance, a system which has come down from ancient times and which abounds in the district. They are similar to the *kahrizes* of northern Iraq.

Practical agricultural training takes place every day, the first- and second-year students alternating in the mornings and afternoons. Students, working in groups of four or five, are assigned a specific type of work, such as nursery or vegetable gardening, each day. Thus, they go the round of each type of activity during the week and come back to the same activities the next week. No individual plots are assigned to the students.

Chapter 22

HIGHER EDUCATION AND THE EDUCATION OF TEACHERS

Syrian University

UNTIL OCTOBER 1946 the Syrian University consisted of the Faculties of Medicine and of Law. The Faculty of Medicine was founded in 1901 and the Faculty of Law in 1912, both by the Ottoman government. Both Faculties were closed toward the end of the First World War, but were reopened by the Arab government in 1919 as separate schools. In 1923 they were joined to form the Syrian University which also included the Arab Academy and the Antiquities Department. These latter two institutions were separated from the University in 1928, and a Higher School of Letters, offering a three-year course, was added in the same year. The Higher School of Letters was abolished in 1933. This left the original two Faculties of Medicine and of Law as the only branches of the University.

At the time of the visit of the American Council Commission, the reorganization of Syrian education was beginning to affect the University. A former Egyptian Minister of Education, Dr. Abd al-Razzaq al-Sanhuri Pasha, who had previously been dean of the Faculty of Law at Fuad I University, was responsible for developing plans for the reorganization of the University, which include the founding of new Faculties. It was planned to open initially Faculties of Letters, Science, and Engineering, and a Higher Teachers College. The Faculty of Engineering was to be in Aleppo while the others were to be in Damascus. Faculties of Agriculture and Commerce may be opened later. The reorganization plan was established by Decree No. 40, dated September 11, 1946, "Embodying the Cadre of the Syrian University." The first students were admitted to the new Faculties in October 1946.

The administration of the University is entrusted to a president who is appointed by a decree of the Council of Ministers acting upon the recommendation of the Minister of Education. The president presides over the University council unless the Minister of Education, who is the supreme head of the University, is present. The University council consists of the deans of the Faculties and the directors of independent institutes, of one professor representing each Faculty (chosen by the respective Faculty councils for a term of two years), a representative of the Ministry of Education appointed for a term of two years, and three members with experience in higher education appointed by the Minister of Education for a term of two years. The University council acts upon the annual budget and the final accounting, the granting of degrees and diplomas recommended by the Faculty councils, the granting of honorary degrees, the setting down of the regulations for the University's educational missions as well as approving of the students chosen to go abroad and the conditions under which they are sent. The University council further acts upon the appointment, promotion, or transfer of any of the members of the teaching staff or their delegation to another university or department inside or outside the country.

The Faculties are administered by deans appointed for three years by presidential decree upon the recommendation of the Minister of Education who in turn avails himself of the advice of the Faculty council concerned. The dean is chosen from the professors occupying chairs of the Faculty and may not be removed until his term expires unless a special presidential decree is issued for removing him at the request of the Minister of Education after consulting the University council. The dean presides over the Faculty council which consists of professors occupying chairs, other full professors, assistant professors, and three members from outside the Faculty who have special knowledge of the subjects taught at the Faculty. These latter members are appointed for a term of two years by the Minister of Education acting upon the recommendation of the University council after due consultation with the Faculty council. The Faculty council is entrusted with the running of all affairs of the Faculty except those specifically entrusted to other bodies. It usually meets once a month.

The members of the teaching staff are classified as professors occupying chairs, professors, assistant professors, and lecturers. Teaching assistants, laboratory assistants, and demonstrators are not considered as members of the teaching staff. In addition, visiting professors and part-time lecturers may be employed by decision of the University council acting upon the recommendation of the Faculty council concerned. If foreign visiting professors or part-time lecturers are needed, the approval of the Council of Ministers must be secured.

To be appointed as an assistant or a demonstrator, a candidate must hold a *licence,* a bachelor's, or an M.D. degree. He must have gained these degrees with honors; otherwise, he must pass a competitive examination before his appointment. A year after his appointment he may be sent by the University on a mission for study abroad. While on the mission he receives his full salary and, for purposes of promotion and pension, is considered in the service of the University.

Lecturers must hold a doctorate. For the Faculty of Medicine a diploma of specialization as designated by the University council must be added to the qualifications. Assistant professors and professors must, in addition, have made significant contributions in their fields and have served for at least four years as lecturers and assistant professors respectively.

Such is the new plan for the administrative organization of the Syrian University. As is to be expected, it shows in most points the influence of the organization prevailing at the public universities of Egypt.

THE FACULTY OF MEDICINE

The Faculty of Medicine, the oldest of the institutions included in the Syrian University, is situated a short distance from the right bank of the Barada River which flows through Damascus. Here one University administration building, including a lecture hall, has been built in the same compound with the hospital and the public clinics. The School of Dentistry and some of the laboratories of the Faculty, together with the University library, are situated on the premises of the old religious school of Sultan Sulayman.

The Faculty of Medicine is made up of four schools: Medicine, Pharmacy, Dentistry, and Nursing. The Schools of Medicine and Pharmacy require for admission, in addition to the second *baccalauréat* or its equivalent, a year of science study known as the P.C.B. year (physics, chemistry, biology). This is borrowed from the French plan of medical education, as indeed are the main features of medical education in Syria. The School of Dentistry admits students directly after graduation from the secondary school, while the School of Nursing requires three years of secondary schooling, but if not enough girls apply, a lower standard is accepted.

The Faculty of Medicine gives a course of five years leading to the degree of Doctor of Medicine. A further year of internship in the University hospital or another approved hospital is required before a candidate is allowed to practice. This makes a total of seven years beyond the secondary school.

In the first two years the curriculum consists of the usual basic subjects— anatomy, physiology, histology and embryology, medical physics and chemistry, and elementary diagnosis. In accordance with the French plan of medical education, clinical work begins with the first year. In the third and fourth years, pathology, parasitology, internal medicine, surgery, experimental medicine, obstetrics, minor surgery, therapeutics, and materia medica are given. Practical work in the clinics and the hospital continues and includes bedside study of the specialized subjects in medicine—skin and venereal diseases, psychiatry, diseases of the nose, ear, and throat, children's diseases, and tropical and infectious diseases. In the fifth year, hygiene, legal medicine, medical ethics, therapeutics, and materia medica are studied.

Examinations are written, oral, and clinical, given at the end of every year and prior to the granting of the degree. The examinations are conducted by committees of professors, which included French professors in the days of the mandate. Most of the professors of the Faculty have been educated or have had their specialization in France.

The course in the School of Pharmacy requires, in addition to the P.C.B. year, a year of practical apprenticeship in an approved pharmacy prior to admission to the School. Here the apprentice takes notes on all prescriptions filled and methods used, and before entering the School of Pharmacy has to pass a written and practical examination based on his experience of the previous year. He then enters a three-year course of theoretical and practical subjects in pharmacy and allied sciences, leading to practical and theoretical examinations at the end of every year and at the end of the third year.

The course in dentistry requires no P.C.B. preparatory year and consists of four years of study above the secondary-school studies. The course includes a study of "descriptive" anatomy, anatomy of the teeth, physiology, histology, bacteriology, inorganic, organic, and analytical chemistry, biochemistry, dental surgery and minor surgery, crowns and bridges, fillings, anesthesia, X-ray, and other allied subjects. Yearly and final examinations are both theoretical and practical and lead to the degree of Doctor of Dental Surgery.

The School of Nursing and Midwifery as envisaged in the decree embodying its new regulations accepts unmarried girls between the ages of seventeen and thirty who have finished the third secondary year, or, if sufficient applicants are not available with this preparation, girls who have had some study beyond the primary school and who pass an entrance examination. The course for nurses is of three years. Students may be day or boarding students. A fourth year is provided for those interested in midwifery. Students in midwifery must be boarders. Six hours a day of practical nursing and, later, midwifery are required throughout the four years, plus five to seven hours a week of study in anatomy, physiology, hygiene, bacteriology, parasitology, pharmacology, chemistry, the anatomy of the female genital organs, midwifery, legal medicine and ethics, and brief courses in the various types of diseases. Practical and theoretical yearly and final examinations lead to the diploma in nursing or in nursing and midwifery.

The Faculty of Medicine has one hospital of 160 beds and another with 60 beds in obstetrics. It has also an outpatient clinic. The School of Dentistry has 13 dental chairs. Laboratories in chemistry, physics, anatomy, biochemistry, histopathology, and other subjects are located mostly in the nearby old building of the religious school of Sultan Sulayman. The laboratories on the whole are of modest proportions and the building is unfit for them.

THE FACULTY OF LAW

The Faculty of Law gives a course of three years above the second *baccalauréat*. With the shortening of the secondary course it is hoped to lengthen the course to four years. Students are prepared to be lawyers, judges in civil courts, and judges in Shar' (Muslim law) courts. Many of the graduates become government officials. The examinations leading to the degree of *Licence* in Law are conducted by committees consisting usually of two professors and a prominent judge, lawyer, or government official for each of the subjects. These external examiners are appointed by the Minister of Education. Graduates must work in a law office for two years before being licensed to practice before the courts. The government when endeavoring to fill a legal office holds its own special examinations which in the case of filling a vacancy in the Shar' courts include examinations in Muslim law.

Study at the Faculty of Law relies heavily on lectures. A student is permitted to absent himself from up to 50 percent of the lectures. A long period is allowed at the end of the year for the final examinations. Naturally, cramming at the end of the year is the prevailing practice.

The University library consists of 12,000 volumes, mainly in Arabic, French, and English. Books may be read in the library and are lent outside the library only to members of the teaching staff.

Student registration in 1945–46 was as follows:

Faculty	Enrollment
Medicine	256
Pharmacy	59
Dentistry	32
Nursing and midwifery	49
P.C.B. class	103
Law	541
Total	1,040

About one-third of the student body was from other countries, mainly Arab.

Teaching at the Syrian University is conducted entirely in Arabic. The Faculty of Medicine is the only such faculty in the Arabic world which teaches in Arabic.

Educational Missions

Educational missions were sent chiefly to France prior to World War II. With the French government as mandatary power, with French advisers to the Ministry of Education, and with the Syrian educational system following French educational methods and ideas, this was to be expected. As has already been said, graduates of French universities and institutions were shown a decided preference in appointments to posts in the Ministry of Education. The situation was not different in other departments of the government. It was only natural, therefore, that even students going abroad for study at their own expense usually preferred to go to France.

Even in 1943–44, when the French grip on Syria had loosened, 58 out of a toal of 101 students on educational missions were studying in France; most of them had begun their study in the prewar period. Of the other 43, there were 37 in Egypt and 6 in Beirut.

For the year 1946–47 it was planned to send 120 students abroad. None of these was being sent to France, partly because of the aversion to the French that has developed in Syria, and partly because the new Secondary-School Certificate is no longer recognized in France. Most of the students were being sent by the Ministry of Education. The remainder were being sent by other ministries. The countries to which the students are being sent are Belgium, Switzerland (evidently taking the place of France), Great Britain, the United States, and Egypt. Only a few are destined to study in Great Britain or the United States largely because of the difficulty of securing admission to American and British universities. The subjects to be studied cover a wide range and include the various branches of engineering, architecture, technical education, agriculture, irrigation, mathematics, the sciences, finance, medicine, public and school health, law, archeology, Semitics, history, English, education, commerce, and Arabic literature.

The Education of Teachers

The education of teachers in Syria has gone through a number of stages. In the latest of these, two kinds of teachers colleges were maintained: the elementary-teachers college, which accepted students holding either the first *baccalauréat* or the *brevet* and gave them a course of one year; and the primary-teachers college which accepted holders of the second *baccalauréat* and gave them a course of one year. Later each of these courses was lengthened to two years. In addition, special examinations were held for the granting of the Certificate of Efficiency in Teaching. A total of 809 men and 242 women had been graduated from the teachers colleges or had received the Certificate of Efficiency in Teaching between 1919 and 1943. During the latter year there were 35 students in the Primary Teachers College for Men in Damascus, 13 in the Teachers College for Women in the same city, and 16 in the Elementary Teachers College for Men in Aleppo—a total of 64 students. In view of the great need for teachers, these numbers were wholly inadequate.[1]

Steps were therefore taken to increase the enrollment and to open a Teachers College for Women in Aleppo, bringing the total number of teachers colleges to four. Enrollment in 1944–45 increased to 153 men and 131 women students, a total of 284, and in the following year the American Council Commission found 162 men and 215 women in the four colleges, a total of 377 students.

At the present time the education of teachers is in the transition stage. As indicated before, three types of courses are being offered.[2] A professional course of one year is given, to which holders of the second *baccalauréat* are admitted. This course which is given only in the Damascus teachers colleges for men and women is expected to disappear with the disappearance of the second *baccalauréat*. In 1945–46 there were 17 men and 16 women registered in this course.

The second course is one of two years above the first *baccalauréat* or above the new Secondary-School Certificate. This is also a professional course which was started in 1944–45, with the first class graduating in June 1946. It was hoped that this course would attract more students than the previous one, since holders of the second *baccalauréat* are in demand in various fields which normally they would prefer to teaching. With the offering of a two-year education at the expense of the state it was thought that this course would attract more students. In 1945–46, the enrollment

[1] Sati' al-Husri, *Reports* . . . 1944, pp. 132–34 and 137–38.
[2] See Decree No. 1144, dated October 23, 1944, "Embodying the Amendment of the Regulations of Teachers Colleges for Men and Women," and Decree No. 182, dated February 20, 1945, "Embodying the Regulations for Primary Teachers Colleges for Men and Women," both in Ministry of Education, *Regulations for Intermediate and Secondary Schools and Teachers Colleges* (Damascus: Government Press, 1945), pp. 34–51.

in the two-year course was 41 men and 47 women, all in the Damascus teachers colleges.

The third type is a three-year course admitting students from the intermediate school. This was also started in 1944–45 and was in its second year at the time of the visit of the Commission. The first class was to be graduated in June 1947. It was hoped that the course would attract an even larger number of students. In 1945–46 there were 263 students (104 were men and 159 women) taking the three-year course in the 4 teachers colleges. As this course promises to be the most extensive, and possibly the permanent, plan, its program of studies is given in Table 65.

TABLE 65
Program of Studies of the Three-Year Course for the Education of Teachers, Syria, 1946

Subject	Periods per Week		
	1st Year	2nd Year	3rd Year
Academic:			
Religion	1	1	...
Arabic language and literature	5	3	...
French and translation	5	3	...
History	3	2	2
Geography	2	2	...
Mathematics	4	4	...
Physics and chemistry	3	3	2
Biology, agriculture, and hygiene	3	3	3
Sociology	...	...	3
Professional:			
Psychology and logic	...	3	2
Methods of teaching	...	3	4
Practice teaching	...	...	8
Practical or artistic:			
Drawing	2	2	2
Manual arts	...	2	2
Physical education	2	...	...
Music	2	...	...
Arabic penmanship	2	...	...
Agricultural activities	...	3	6
Total	34	34	34

The course of study is divided into three parts: the academic subjects, the professional subjects, and the practical or artistic subjects. The academic subjects are largely concentrated in the first two years and aim at rounding out and replenishing the student's fund of knowledge gained in the intermediate school. The professional subjects begin in the second year. In the theoretical and practical teaching of agriculture, as well as in hygiene, some recognition seems to have been given to the possible needs of the rural-school teacher.

Practice teaching takes place in a special practice school. Individual

HIGHER EDUCATION AND EDUCATION OF TEACHERS

lessons are given by each student with his classmates observing him. These lessons are later criticized by the students and the teacher of method. In the second half of the year the student spends fifteen days in full-time teaching.

Admission of students is controlled by a committee consisting of the principal as chairman and two lecturers as members. Students are admitted on the basis of their standing in the previous public examinations, a medical examination, and an interview.

Education in the teachers colleges is free, including board and lodging. Day students are reimbursed for the value of board at the rate of £S50 ($22.70) a month. All students receive £S15 ($6.80) a month for expenses. All the four colleges have boarding departments. The following was the number of day and boarding students in each college for the year 1945–46:

College	Day	Boarding	Total
Damascus Teachers College for Men	62	67	129
Damascus Teachers College for Women	130	22	152
Aleppo Teachers College for Men	13	20	33
Aleppo Teachers College for Women	45	17	62
Total	250	126	376

Three of the colleges were housed with the secondary schools in government buildings, while the fourth, the Teachers College for Women in Damascus, was in a rented building. The 2 colleges at Aleppo are headed by the principals of the public secondary schools in that city.

Most of the staff of the teachers colleges also teach in the secondary schools. Their qualifications are generally the same as those of the secondary-school teachers, already mentioned. The lecturers in education, practice teaching, and psychology in most cases have been educated in France, although some have been educated in Germany and at the American University of Beirut.

Chapter 23

PRIVATE AND FOREIGN SCHOOLS

*P*RIOR TO the Franco-Syrian political crisis of May 1945, private and foreign schools provided for the education of approximately 42 percent[1] of the school enrollment of Syria, excluding the *kuttabs*, or ungraded Koran, schools. These schools include primary (with kindergarten), secondary, and vocational schools. No private or foreign teachers colleges or higher institutions exist, except the American Junior College at Aleppo. As this last was recognized as an institution equivalent to those institutions preparing for the second *baccalauréat,* it was not classified as a higher institution. Table 66 shows a comparison for 1944–45 of the number of institutions and enrollment in private and foreign schools with the public schools of their level.

In 1944–45 there were 685 public primary, secondary, and vocational schools with an enrollment of 92,598 students, compared to 306 private schools with an enrollment of 44,790 students, and 160 foreign schools with an enrollment of 23,887 students. Thus, public-school enrollment accounted for 57.4 percent of the total enrollment in these three types of schools, private schools accounted for 27.8 percent, and foreign schools for 14.8 percent.

One feature brought out by Table 66 is that, while the total enrollment of girls as compared with boys in the public schools was approximately in proportion of one to three, it was one to two in the private schools and nearly one to one in the foreign schools. Private and foreign schools were educating more girls than were public schools (25,892, as compared with 23,474). They were, however, educating considerably fewer boys (42,785, compared with 69,124). Not only was the proportion of girls schools to boys schools greater in the private and foreign schools, but there were a comparatively large number of coeducational private and foreign schools. None of the government schools, except the University, is coeducational.

Comparative figures are shown in the following tabulation:

---

[1] This is the second highest proportion of private- and public-school enrollment in the six Arab countries studied here, the first being Lebanon.

PRIVATE AND FOREIGN SCHOOLS

Administrative Control	Boys	Girls	Coeducational	Total
Public schools	560	125	..	685
Private schools	167	48	91	306
Foreign schools	61	53	46	160
Total	788	226	137	1,151

Another fact brought out by Table 66 is that while foreign schools occupied third place in number of institutions in the field of primary education, accounting for 13.5 percent of the enrollment as compared with 39 percent by the private schools, the situation was reversed in the field of secondary education where the foreign schools occupied second place with 32.9 percent of the secondary-school enrollment, while private schools held third place with only 15 percent. The same thing is true of the vocational schools, where foreign schools have 16.4 percent of the enrollment and private schools only 3 percent.

Most of the foreign schools were French schools as shown in Table 67. Thus 120 out of 160, or 75 percent of the schools, were French. These schools had an enrollment of 19,710 out of 23,887 pupils, or 82.9 percent of the total foreign-school enrollment. A number of the schools registered as foreign however, are in effect private schools registered as French by the French authorities in the days of the mandate. Of such a character are the schools of Alliance Israelite Universelle, which are locally supported and are occupying buildings built by the local Jews, and some of the local Catholic sectarian schools which for various reasons previously preferred to be classed as French schools. Similarly, but in a reverse way, some of the so-called "American" schools had first been established by American missionaries, but have now been transferred to the local Protestant communities, though they are still registered as American schools.

Such was the situation as regards private and foreign schools up to the Franco-Syrian crisis of May 1945. It was then that the French schools were boycotted and closed. They remained closed throughout the following year of 1945–46, except for a few schools which declared themselves to be really native schools, willing to accept the conditions set by the new education law, and appointed Syrian principals. They were then registered as private schools and allowed to open. The closing of the French schools naturally caused a rush on the public and private native schools. The measures taken by the Ministry of Education to deal with the situation have been indicated previously (pages 326–27). Here it is sufficient to say that the loss of the French schools meant the gain of the public and private schools. Accordingly, there was a sharp drop in the enrollment in foreign schools

TABLE 66

PUBLIC, PRIVATE, AND FOREIGN SCHOOLS AND THEIR ENROLLMENTS ON VARIOUS LEVELS, SYRIA, 1944-45

TYPE OF SCHOOL	PUBLIC SCHOOLS					PRIVATE SCHOOLS					FOREIGN SCHOOLS					GRAND TOTAL, ENROLLMENT
	No. of Schools	Enrollment				No. of Schools	Enrollment				No. of Schools	Enrollment				
		Boys	Girls	Total			Boys	Girls	Total			Boys	Girls	Total	
Primary....	658	63,755	21,785	85,540	287	28,800	14,210	43,010	127	9,942	9,936	19,878	148,428		
Percent...				57.5				29.0				13.5	100.0		
Secondary..	22	4,557	1,490	6,047	17	1,283	460	1,743	30	2,639	1,163	3,802	11,592		
Percent...				52.1				15.0				32.9	100.0		
Vocational..	5	812	199	1,011	2	20	17	37	3	101	106	207	1,255		
Percent...				80.6				3.0				16.4	100.0		
TOTAL......	685	69,124	23,474	92,598	306	30,103	14,687	44,790	160	12,682	11,205	23,887	161,275		
Percent...				57.4				27.8				14.8	100.0		

TABLE 67

FOREIGN SCHOOLS AND ENROLLMENT CLASSIFIED ACCORDING TO NATIONALITY OF GOVERNING BODY, SYRIA, 1944-45*

NATIONALITY	PRIMARY SCHOOLS				SECONDARY SCHOOLS				VOCATIONAL SCHOOLS				TOTAL	
	No. of Schools	Enrollment			No. of Schools	Enrollment			No. of Schools	Enrollment			No. of Schools	Enrollment
		Boys	Girls	Total		Boys	Girls	Total		Boys	Girls	Total		
French....	96	8,179	8,655	16,834	21	1,921	748	2,669	3	101	106	207	120	19,710
American..	18	1,273	699	1,972	6	678	312	990	...	...	...	...	24	2,962
British....	6	344	203	547	2	40	94	134	...	...	...	...	8	681
Danish....	6	136	359	495	1	...	9	9	...	...	...	...	7	504
Greek.....	1	10	20	30	...	...	...	...	...	...	...	...	1	30
Total.	127	9,942	9,936	19,878	30	2,639	1,163	3,802	3	101	106	207	160	23,887

* Data supplied by the Ministry of Education. See also Sati' al-Husri, *Reports on the Conditions of Education in Syria during the Year 1945* (Damascus: Government Press, 1946). pp. 52 and 56.

in 1945–46 with a corresponding drop in the percentage of foreign-school enrollment compared with the total primary- and secondary-school enrollment. This is clearly brought out in Table 68.

TABLE 68
COMPARISON OF ENROLLMENT IN PUBLIC, PRIVATE, AND FOREIGN SCHOOLS, SYRIA, 1944–45 AND 1945–46*

CONTROL	PRIMARY-SCHOOL ENROLLMENT				SECONDARY-SCHOOL ENROLLMENT			
	1944–45		1945–46		1944–45		1945–46	
	Pupils	Percent	Pupils	Percent	Pupils	Percent	Pupils	Percent
Public schools...	85,540	57.5	99,703	66.5	6,047	52.1	8,276	65.3
Private schools...	43,010	29.0	47,224	31.5	1,743	15.0	3,322	26.3
Foreign schools..	19,838	13.5	3,207	2.0	3,802	32.9	1,063	8.4
Total.......	148,388	100.0	150,134	100.0	11,592	100.0	12,661	100.0

* Figures from Sati' al-Husri, *Reports . . . , 1945*, pp. 136–38.

Enrollment in public primary schools increased by 14,163 in 1945–46 and its percentage of the total enrollment rose from 57.5 percent to 66.5 percent. The private-school enrollment increased by 4,214 pupils, and its percentage rose by 2.5 percent to 31.5 percent. At the same time the foreign schools lost 16,631 pupils, their percentage declining from 13.5 percent to 2 percent.

Similarly, the public secondary schools show an increase of 2,229 students and a rise in their percentage of 13.2, while the private secondary schools almost doubled their enrollment by adding 1,579 students and raising their percentage from 15 to 26.3. The foreign secondary schools lost 2,739 students, their percentage going down from 32.9 to 8.4. It is to be noted that in spite of the closing of more than 100 French schools, the total school enrollment in 1945–46 increased over the previous year. Primary schools show a net increase of 1,746 pupils, and secondary schools increased by 1,069 students. This would tend to show that as far as student registration is concerned, the crisis created by the closing of the French schools was fully met.

It is interesting to note that the decrease in the enrollment of the foreign schools is almost entirely due to the closing of the French schools. The schools of other nationalities remained largely unaffected as shown by the following figures of enrollment in non-French schools:

Year	Primary	Secondary
1944–45	3,044	1,133
1945–46	3,207	1,063
Gain or loss	+163	−70

The non-French primary schools increased by 163 pupils, while the secondary schools decreased by 70. It can, therefore, be said that enrollment in the other foreign schools remained substantially the same and that these schools were unaffected. The reaction was entirely against the French schools.

As all three foreign vocational schools had been French and had closed, there were no foreign vocational schools in 1945-46.

The future of the French schools remains uncertain. It is probable that those French schools which were originally Syrian schools will be registered as private schools, as indeed some have already been. The others, or at least some of them, will probably reopen, but with much less prestige and with reduced enrollment. It is reported that a few French schools were allowed to reopen in 1946-47.

The Franco-Syrian crisis and the new plan of the Ministry of Education to abolish the teaching of a foreign language in the primary schools created a problem for some of the private schools. Christian schools especially, largely in response to the demands of parents who are usually keen on their children's learning foreign languages, frequently start the teaching of French in the first grade and often even in the kindergarten. This they did even at the time when government schools started French in the fourth grade.

With the coming of the new regime of independence and the abolition of the foreign language from the primary-school curriculum, pressure was brought to bear upon the private schools to follow the lead of the public schools—or at least to postpone the teaching of the foreign language until the two upper grades. This, however, would put the private schools at a disadvantage with the foreign schools, almost all of which begin the teaching of the foreign language, usually French or English, very early. Representations were, therefore, made by some schools that if such a course were followed, the private schools would lose a large number of their pupils to the foreign schools, owing to the insistence of parents on their children's learning a foreign language. The representations of the schools were successful, at least temporarily. How permanent such an arrangement can be, and how far there will be a shift from French, which prevailed in most of the private Christian schools, to the English language is a matter of the future.

Grants-in-Aid

A decree was passed in March 1945 setting down the conditions for giving grants-in-aid to private schools and other cultural institutions.[2] This

---

[2] Decree No. 261, dated March 25, 1945, "Embodying the Regulations for Grants-in-Aid to Private Schools and to Cultural, Artistic, and Sporting Institutions."

ALEPPO COLLEGE, ALEPPO, SYRIA
This view shows the Arabic arched façade of the main classroom building

Above: One of the classroom buildings of the secondary school for boys, Homs, Syria
Below: A village primary school with a school garden, near Homs

decree, designed to encourage private individual and group effort "in the service of science, letters, fine arts, and physical education," provides that financial aid is to be given to private schools and educational institutions in proportion to their service to education and to their financial needs. Criteria are established to serve as a basis for the distribution of funds: (1) the level of the school and the number of its classes and pupils; (2) the standard of education provided; (3) the number of teachers, their qualifications and teaching ability; (4) the curriculum and the degree of its agreement with the public-school curriculum; (5) the number of students participating in the public examinations and the percentage of those passing; (6) the income and expenditures of the school; and (7) the fees levied upon students and the number of students exempted from the payment of fees.[3] Grants are to be allotted annually by the Education Council in the first half of August. The council's decisions in this matter must be based upon the reports of the inspectors and directors of education concerning each school. If necessary, the Ministry of Education may pay the grant in the form of salaries paid to teachers which it selects or appoints to the schools.

Bases are also laid down in the 1945 decree for the distribution of grants to cultural, artistic, and sporting societies and clubs.

This provision as to grants-in-aid was of great help to the Ministry of Education in its attempts to meet the crisis created by the closing of the French schools. The budgetary provisions for the grants were trebled by being increased from £S100,000 (about $45,450) to £S302,500 (about $137,500). Private schools were encouraged to open new classes to take in more pupils, and grants were given to stimulate the opening of new schools.

Private Schools

Private primary schools are usually classified in Syria by the denomination of the authorities controlling them. Table 69 shows the denominational distribution of private primary schools in Syria for 1944–45.

The data for the 9 private secondary and 8 intermediate schools, which have an enrollment of 1,743 students, are not given by denominations.

It does not, however, follow that all the schools classed as controlled by denominations are actually so. Many of them are really secular and are simply classified according to the sect of the controlling authority, following a custom started during the French mandate which emphasized sectarian matters as a policy. In actual fact private schools are of three main categories:

[3] Compare with Iraq, pp. 128–29.

sectarian schools, schools controlled by societies and groups, and schools controlled by individuals.

The first class of schools is that maintained by religious groups, the clergy, or by lay organizations having a religious motive. The second are conducted by groups having a philanthropic or national aim, often without regard to religious affiliation, and the last, those conducted by individuals, may be philanthropic or national in aim, but are often established to secure a livelihood or personal gain for the founder.

TABLE 69
Distribution of Private Primary Schools According to Religious Control, Syria, 1944–45*

Denomination of Controlling Authority	No. of Schools				Enrollment		
	Boys	Girls	Coeducational	Total	Boys	Girls	Total
Muslim	53	15	9	77	11,146	3,518	14,664
Catholic (Greek, Syrian, Chaldean, Maronite, and Armenian)	49	12	10	71	5,128	2,673	7,801
Orthodox (Greek, Syrian, and Armenian)	50	11	50	111	10,129	6,542	16,671
Protestant (Syrian and Armenian)	2	...	15	17	942	754	1,696
Jewish	3	...	1	4	822	24	846
Miscellaneous	1	2	4	7	633	699	1,332
Total	158	40	89	287	28,800	14,210	43,010

* Figures from Sati' al-Husri, *Reports* ... *1945*, pp. 43–44.

In the sectarian category fall the schools maintained by the Waqf department for the training of Muslim religious teachers as well as judges and clerks for the Muhammadan law courts. There are 5 of these schools, enrolling 424 students. Such schools are, however, actually public schools since they are supported by Waqf funds. The Ministry of Education pays nothing toward their maintenance and consequently classes them as private.

Some of the schools are of hardly more than primary standard. Two, however—1 in Damascus and 1 in Aleppo—are of a higher standard. The *Shari'ah* college in Damascus was founded by the Body of 'Ulama in 1942. It is still in the process of development. In 1945–46, it had 140 students, of whom 85 were boarders from the various parts of Syria. Admission is from the primary school, and the plan is to have a series of three courses, one above the other. The first course of six years would be a kind of religious secondary course to prepare clerks for the Muhammadan law courts and teachers of religion for the elementary schools. A higher course of four years would aim at training higher clerks for the courts, preachers, minor judges, and teachers of Arabic and religion for secondary schools. Finally, a special course of two years would prepare full judges and *muftis*. Eight of the proposed fourteen classes were in existence in 1945–46. The Aleppo school follows the same program. At the end of the first and second courses a public examination is held for which the questions are set by the professors of the 2 schools at Aleppo and Damascus sitting together.

The Damascus school is run by a board composed of the *qadi* (a judge of the canon law of Islam) as chairman, the *mufti* of the Republic, the *naqib* (dean or registrar), the directors of Waqf of the Republic and of Damascus, two representatives of the Ministry of Education, and finally the director and the secretary of the school. Education is entirely free, including the board and lodging of the boarding students.

A sectarian Muslim school of a different kind is the Islamiyah College in Aleppo maintained by a society of Muslims who support the idea of a modern education but who also believe in a sound Islamic religious education. Its sponsors believe that the curriculum of the modern schools errs in giving too little attention to Muslim religious education and to Muslim character. At the same time it is felt that it is necessary "to counteract the effects of foreign schools." A group of citizens mostly connected with the Muslim Orphanage of Aleppo got together and solicited the help of a devout Aleppo lady who gave them the funds for erecting a large building for the school on the outskirts of the city in 1943. The school in 1945–46 had 238 boys enrolled in fifth primary through the sixth secondary. It had 30 boarding students of whom 8 were from the Orphanage and were given their education and living free after passing a competitive examination. The remainder came from the districts of Aleppo province and paid for their tuition, food, and lodging at the rate of £S700 (about $318.00). Tuition for day students ranges from £S50 to £S160 ($22.70 to $72.00) with full exemption for 10 boys and half-exemption for another 51 boys.

The curriculum of the government schools is followed with the addition of more hours for the study of the Koran, religion, and Muslim character. The school is supported by contributions from the public, by grants from the central government and the municipality of Aleppo, and by fees.

The Christian sectarian schools follow two main types—the Greek Orthodox and the Roman Catholic.

The Orthodox schools are exemplified by the Greek Orthodox school in Damascus which was visited by the American Council Commission. This school and 5 other schools in Damascus are conducted by the denominational council of the Greek Orthodox church—a council which has control of the property, the finances, and the philanthropic and educational activities of the church. A board of five men, all laymen, is chosen by the council to have charge of the schools. These 6 schools make a complete kindergarten, primary, and secondary ladder by themselves, consisting of 2 boys primary schools, 2 girls primary schools (1 of which is topped by an intermediate section), a coeducational primary school, and a complete secondary school for boys. Girls leaving the girls intermediate may join the secondary classes at the boys secondary school, and in 1945–46 there were 5 girls who had done this.

The schools are supported by fees, by income from the church endowment and property, by grants from the government, and by contributions. The buildings are owned by the Greek Orthodox church and community. The student body, though predominately Greek Orthodox, has students from other denominations. The boys secondary school, for example, has about 40 Muslims, 25 Jews, and 20 Catholics. The teaching staff of the school is also mixed: 16 Greek Orthodox, 5 Muslims, 2 Jews, and 3 Catholics. Fees are £S6 to £S90 in the primary schools and £S20 to £S200 in the secondary schools.

All pupils whose families receive help from the welfare society of the Greek Orthodox community are exempt from fees. Other pupils pay according to ability after inquiry by the priests and the committee.

In general, the curriculum follows that of the government, but with two important differences. French is begun in the first primary grade, and English in the first secondary grade. Arabic reading is begun toward the end of the first kindergarten year and continued in the second kindergarten year. By the time the children enter first grade, they know how to read. The first grade is, therefore, in reality equivalent to the second grade of the government schools; and, although the primary school is nominally five years, it is in actual fact six years. The first-grade children appear to be above the average age. This procedure may perhaps have been necessitated by the early teaching of French.

The problem of teaching a multiplicity of languages in primary schools is found in an extreme form in Armenian schools. The largest Armenian community in Syria is in Aleppo where Armenians took refuge after the Armenian massacres in Turkey during the First World War. Anxious to preserve their national language and to know the language of the country of their adoption, they have had to teach both Arabic and Armenian. At the same time the advantages that accrued to those who knew French under the mandate made them introduce that language into their schools, while the fact that most Armenian youth who wanted to continue their education preferred an American school forced them to teach English as well.

This situation is well illustrated by the 2 Giligian primary schools in Aleppo—1 for boys and 1 for girls. Both are under the same principal. The boys school had in 1945–46 an attendance of 254 boys, while the girls school had 228 girls. The kindergarten department in connection with the latter had 240 boys and girls in four sections, one section of which had 72 children. Naturally, the teacher could do little more than watch over the children. In these schools Armenian is begun in the upper section of the kindergarten, Arabic in the first grade, English in the second grade, and French in the third. Previously, however, it was the practice to begin French in the first grade.

In order to provide for a program so heavily loaded with languages, each grade has an average of thirty-six to thirty-seven periods a week. The program also extends over six years instead of the usual five years of the public schools. The schools are housed in rented houses, and are supported mostly by fees ranging from £S30–£S60 a year. About 65 boys and girls are exempted. The government pays a grant of £S750 a year and the salary of one teacher which it supplies. The other teachers are graduates of American secondary schools, holders of the second *baccalauréat,* or women who have had some secondary studies. Two are from the Armenian secondary school in Istanbul, Turkey, while five men and women are graduates of the Armenian teachers college in Nicosia, Cyprus. This is an institution offering a course of three years above the secondary school for the education of teachers for Armenian schools.

While Orthodox schools are mostly controlled by laymen's councils of the community with the clergy in the background, the Catholic schools are controlled to a considerable extent and often directly by the clergy. The 3 Catholic private schools visited by the Commission in Syria were of this nature. A Catholic primary school in Aleppo was under the supervision of the Bishop of Aleppo and supported by him. The Maronite school for boys is headed by a priest and housed in a building belonging to the church. Its deficit is met by the Maronite welfare committee. A Maronite girls school in Latakia is conducted by the Maronite nuns of the Holy Family commonly known as the "nuns of 'Ibrin," a village in Lebanon where the mother convent is located. In all these schools French is stressed, except that the latter school by agreement with the government begins the teaching of French in the fourth grade.

The final type of private school is the nonsectarian school maintained either by groups and societies or by individuals.

An example of the former is the Dawhat al-Adab school for girls in Damascus, maintained by the society of the same name. It is a school founded by a group of society women of Damascus who thought that a school for society girls was needed. Hitherto such schools were mainly in the hands of nuns, while the government schools were open to all classes. An organization was, therefore, established in 1928 which opened the school in 1931. The school, which began in a small way, now has a kindergarten, a primary section, and a secondary section leading to the second *baccalauréat*. Although established for society girls, many girls from poorer homes are accepted. Comparatively high fees are charged, but 30 girls are fully exempt, and another 40 are partially exempt. Fees range between £S120 and £S200 a year. The school has a large budget of £S120,000 (about $54,550), toward which the government contributes £S20,000. The program followed is that of the government, with the addition of the English language. Special attention is paid to home economics, sewing, and embroidery. A number of student societies exist. An Arab society follows up the news of the Arab world; a cultural society holds lectures, invites speakers from outside, and takes care of the library; a cooperative society of the type found in many schools helps poorer students; and social committees help the needy in the city.

The individual private school is exemplified by the Scientific National College at Damascus, founded in 1907 by Dr. Munif Aidi, a professor of the Faculty of Medicine of Syrian University, and now administered by his son. It consists of a boys primary and secondary school, a girls primary and secondary school, and a coeducational kindergarten. These schools together have an enrollment of more than 1,000 students, of whom 109 are boarders. The schools have a budget of more than £S200,000. About 70 percent of the revenue is from fees, the government pays a subsidy of £S12,500, and contributions are solicited from the public. The Syrian government contributes five teachers without charge, while the Egyptian government contributes three.

The school has tried to fit its program to the demand. Prior to 1939, a section preparing students for the French *baccalauréat* examination existed side by side with the section preparing for the Syrian *baccalauréat*. Recently, with the disappearance of the French and the ascendance of the English, a section organized along the lines of the preparatory school of the American University of Beirut has been opened.

The school pays some attention to sports and games and has its own teams which play against other schools. It has a Boy Scout troop and a recently established Girl Guide troop. Student societies also exist.

PRIVATE AND FOREIGN SCHOOLS

In summary, it may be said that, while there are some good private schools, the general impression left on the visitor is one of precarious finance leading to makeshift arrangements, such as poor accommodations, small rooms, crowded classes, and, often, poorly qualified teachers. On the other hand, they make a more determined effort to keep in touch with the parents than do the public schools and are more careful about the teaching of languages. There is little, if any, original or creative planning being done in the private schools with regard to curriculum, methods, or organization. If they are not following the government curriculum, they are usually imitating one or the other of the foreign-school systems in the country, generally either the French or the American schools.

Foreign Schools

Foreign schools in Syria belong to five different nationalities: French, American, British, Danish, and Greek, named in the order of their numerical importance. Greek and Danish schools could not be visited by the Commission, the latter lying in eastern Syria outside of the Commission's itinerary. French schools were entirely closed during the whole year of 1945–46 and could not, therefore, be visited. The visits of the Commission were confined to 5 American schools in Damascus, Aleppo, and Latakia, and to a British school at Idlib, which lies between Aleppo and Latakia.

One originally French school, the Lazarist school for boys in Damascus, was visited. It is one of the oldest, if not the oldest existing school in that city. The Lazarist mission had been founded in Damascus in 1755, and the school had followed about two decades later. After a very long service of a century and a half, it had become part of the Catholic community of Damascus. When the Franco-Syrian crisis of 1945 took place, therefore, it had been registered as a native school and allowed to remain open. (A separate school for girls was also open, which included boys in the first grade.) The school, however, was running on a reduced scale, as it had opened late and many students had gone elsewhere. The morale seemed to be low, and there was an atmosphere of uncertainty about future developments.

The school consisted of five primary and four secondary grades. It had fourteen teachers, of whom eight were brothers. This is rather typical of French missionary schools in Syria and Lebanon run by the various Catholic orders of monks. In this way cost is reduced to a minimum. Teaching was being conducted in Arabic, except in science and mathematics in the upper classes, which were taught in French. The teaching of French started from the first primary grade. Otherwise, the school was following the government program. Fees of £S30–£S40 in the primary grades and of £S50–£S150 in secondary grades were being charged. About 100 students did not pay any fees, while others made partial payments. As the school was in intimate touch with the community, it had no difficulty in knowing the poorer pupils who needed to be exempted from fees. Fifteen students were boarders as compared with 73 in the previous year.

Most of the French schools are conducted by the various orders of monks or nuns such as the Jesuits, the Lazarists, or the teaching order of the Christian Brothers. There are, however, schools that belong to the French secular mission known as the Mission Laïque which had a number of schools in Syria, particularly in Aleppo, Damascus, and Tartus, on the seacoast between Tripoli and Latakia. Since the French schools almost invariably follow the French type of program, together with the government program, they are not usually different from the other French schools in Lebanon. A further description of them will, therefore, be found in chapter 26.

The British school for boys and girls at Idlib was founded in 1927 by the Irish Mission Board of the Reformed Presbyterian Church. It consists of one kindergarten and seven primary classes and in 1945–46 enrolled a total of 136 children, of whom 92 were boys and 44 were girls. The fees range from £S45 to £S108, paid in nine monthly installments. All teaching is done in Arabic, except in the seventh grade, where it is done in English. Previously, both French and English were taught, the former beginning with the second grade, and the latter with the fourth grade. French is being gradually eliminated, the seventh grade in 1946 being the last class to take it. English now begins informally in the kindergarten, and formal teaching of it begins in the second grade. The school was staffed with four full-time and two part-time teachers of whom one full-time woman teacher was British. She was the principal.

Five American schools were visited by the Commission: Damascus College, the American High Schools for Boys and Girls in Latakia, the American High School for Girls in Aleppo, and Aleppo College, which includes a high school for boys.

Damascus College was opened in the fall of 1945 by the American University of Beirut, on the basis of an understanding with the government, which was anxious, because of the closing of the French schools, to provide the best educational facilities possible. Accordingly, a high school was started in a rented building, the high rent being contributed by the government. Only the first two secondary classes were opened rather late in the year—after many likely students had registered elsewhere. The school had a staff of four full-time and two part-time teachers and a registration of 33 full-time day students in the first two classes. In addition, there were the two special English classes, one of which was for adults. It is hoped that this school will eventually develop into a junior college, drawing away from the University at Beirut some of the pressure of student applications. Teaching is conducted in English, and the program is the same as that of the preparatory school of the University in Beirut.

The two American schools, one for boys and one for girls, in Latakia are maintained by the Reformed Presbyterian Mission of North America and are under one administration. They were founded in 1860 and occupy buildings belonging to the Mission erected in the late eighties. The boys school had an elementary section of six grades enrolling 332 boys and a secondary section with four grades enrolling 74 students. The eleventh grade, which is the highest grade, was missing in 1945–46. The school had twelve teachers, of whom two were American. The government contributes two teachers but no financial aid. The girls school had a kindergarten with 121 boys and girls, and a school ordinarily of eleven grades of which only eight existed during 1945–46, enrolling 313 girls. Girls finishing the eighth grade may continue in the boys school. Three girls were doing so. The girls school had twelve teachers, of whom one was American. Fees ranged from £S36 to £S180 a year. Boarding fees were £S500. There were 24 boarders in the boys school, but none in the girls school.

The program is a modified American program of the college-preparatory type. English is begun in the fourth grade, and French in the third grade. All teaching is in Arabic in the first six grades and is changed to English at the beginning of the seventh grade. General and European history is taught. The schools have always prepared students for the government primary-school certificate examination. At one time they also prepared for the *brevet*, but this has been discontinued. The two schools aim to prepare students for Aleppo College and the American University of Beirut. The latter accepts their students upon examination. The schools have no laboratory. The boys school has a small library. A chapel service is held once a week. The student body is drawn from many of the religions and sects in Syria. Greek Orthodox students were the largest group (139), followed by Protestants (54), Muslims, Alawites, Maronites, Greek Catholics, Druzes, and Isma'iliyas.

The American High School for Girls in Aleppo is the combination of a Congregational Mission school at Marash, Turkey, before the First World War, and another Presbyterian school at Aleppo. Its educational policies are controlled by the educational committee of the Syrian Mission with headquarters in Beirut. The School has a kindergarten and classes from the first to the eleventh grade, with an elementary school of six years and a high school of five years. The total registration is 501 pupils. Boys are accepted in the kindergarten and the first two grades. A class in special English, which in 1945–46 enrolled 53 pupils, prepares students coming from other schools with little or no knowledge of English to be fitted into the proper grade. This is a provision found in many of the larger American schools in Syria and Lebanon. The School has twenty-eight teachers, of whom four are American. There are eight boarding students. Fees range from £S60 to £S200 a year. The student body stems from twelve denominations, the largest number of students being Muslim (174), followed by Armenian Orthodox (122), Greek Orthodox (52), Armenian Protestants, Greek Orthodox Protestants, Jews, Syrian Orthodox, Greek Catholic, Roman Catholic, Syrian Catholic, Armenian Catholic, and Maronites.

The language of teaching is Arabic in the elementary school and English in the high school. English is informally taught in the first grade, but regular teaching of it begins in the third grade. French is now begun in the fifth grade. Graduates of the School may go to the American Junior College for Women in Beirut and thence to the American University of Beirut. Some go into teaching.

The highest American institution in Syria at the present time is Aleppo College, situated in Aleppo, the largest urban center of Syria. Founded as Central Turkey College at 'Ayntab (Gaziantep), Turkey, in 1876, its work was cut short by the First World War. It was transferred to Aleppo and reopened as a high school in 1924. Another American high school, known as the North Syria High School for Boys, was established in 1927. These two institutions were combined as Aleppo College in 1937, occupying their two new buildings on the present site on the outskirts of Aleppo in 1940–41. Aleppo College consists of an elementary school, a secondary school, and a junior college.

The elementary school consists of four grades, from the third through the sixth. By an agreement with the American High School for Girls, boys are admitted to the kindergarten and the first two grades of that school, after which they are transferred to the boys school. The latter is not on the College campus, but is situated in the city. Teaching is conducted in Arabic.

The high school for boys consists of five grades (seven through eleven), each in two or three sections, and a special class designed to help students with a meager knowledge of English to fit themselves into the regular school and college classes. Only students with such intentions are admitted to it. These classes combined had an enrollment of 479 students, of whom 135 were in the special class. Instruction is entirely in English, except for the classes in the three languages of Arabic, French, and Armenian. The textbooks, except for those used in language instruction, are usually American. The Michael West series[4] of readers for foreign students with its accompanying simplified classics is used in the lower secondary classes. The program of studies is shown in Table 70.

TABLE 70
Program of Studies, High-School Section, Aleppo College, Syria, 1945–46

Subject	7th Year	8th Year	9th Year	10th Year	11th Year
English	5	5	4	4	3
Arabic	5	5	5	5	5
Arabic for Armenians	(5)*	(5)*	(5)*	(5)*	(5)*
Armenian	3	3	3	3	2
French	4	4	3	3	3
Algebra	...	...	4	...	4
Geometry	...	...	...	4	...
Arithmetic	4	4	...	...	...
Physics	...	...	...	...	6
Biology	...	...	...	4	...
Science	2	2	4	...	...
Geography	3	3	...	...	1
History	...	...	3	4	4
Bible	2	2	2	2	2
Home room	1	1	1	1	1
Athletics	2	2	2	2	2
Study period	8	6	6	5	6
Music	...	2	2	2	...
Total	39	39	39	39	39

* Omitted from totals.

It will be noticed that the program is quite heavily loaded with languages. Armenian is, however, compulsory only for Armenians. For the rest the course is of the college-preparatory type, but with an emphasis upon the teaching of the Bible, which is compulsory for all students whatever their religion or denomination. Special provision is made for the teaching of Arabic to Armenians, using classes in colloquial conversation and readers and books of a considerably lower grade than those used for Arabic-speaking students.

The junior college has 35 students in the freshman year and 27 in the sophomore year, all men. Teaching is in English. The course for freshmen

[4] A carefully graded series of readers, language books, and simplified supplementary readers written by the British educator Michael West and published by Longmans, Green & Co.

is the same for all students and consists of the study of English, Arabic, and Armenian (for Armenians), literature, a course in introductory college mathematics using an American text, a course in the history of the Arabs, and a course in religion.

The sophomore year is divided into three sections: arts, science, and engineering. All take philosophy and literature. The arts section takes, in addition, economics, political science, history (modern Europe), and religion. The science section takes mathematics (calculus), physics, and biology, the latter two with extensive laboratory work. The engineering section takes descriptive and solid geometry, calculus, physics, and drawing. The total number of hours are eighteen for the arts, twenty-three for science, and twenty-five for engineering.

The College occupies two fine buildings, one of which is for administration and instruction and the other for boarders. The campus, only recently established, affords a view of the city of Aleppo from the edge of the plateau on which the College is situated. Tuition fees, including health and laboratory fees, range from £S85 ($38.53) to £S455 ($206.82). The boarding fee is £S700 ($318.18). The College is considered to have the best science laboratories of any school in Syria. It has a library of 8,000 volumes which is extensively used by the students and friends of the College.

The College encourages athletics and extracurricular activities. It has its own teams for football, basketball, and volleyball, and fosters tennis and swimming. A Scout troop has existed for some time. A choir and a small orchestra provide mediums for the development of student talent in music and singing. Many student clubs function on the campus—a fine-arts club, international-relations club, and a Christian Endeavor Society. Literary evenings are held. A campus paper, the *College Herald,* and two class papers are issued in English. A literary review is printed once a year in Arabic, English, and Armenian.

Part Six

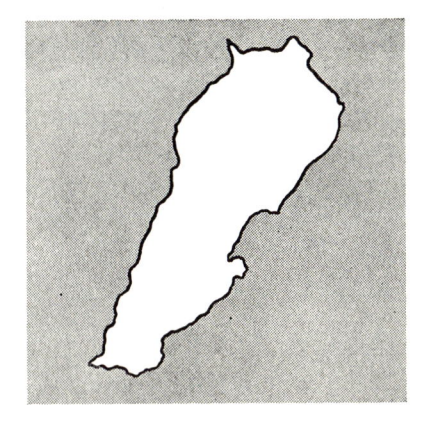

LEBANON

LEBANON

Population: *1,200,000 at the end of 1946 (estimate).*

Area: *10,170 square kilometers (3,926 square miles).*

Form of government: *Republic. President is elected for six years by the Chamber of Deputies (unicameral). Members of Chamber of Deputies are elected by universal male suffrage. The Prime Minister, selected by the President, nominates members of his Council of Ministers (cabinet) which are appointed by the President but are responsible to the Chamber of Deputies.*

Principal occupations: *Trade, agriculture, professions, industry.*

Principal exports: *Olive oil, oranges and other fruits, silk, textiles, wool and hides.*

Principal imports: *Manufactured wares, mineral and chemical products, fuels, foodstuffs (wheat, meats, vegetables, rice, sugar, spices), cotton goods, woolen textiles.*

Monetary unit: *Syro-Lebanese pound (£L) equivalent to $0.4576.*

Chapter 24

ORGANIZATION AND ADMINISTRATION OF THE EDUCATIONAL SYSTEM

TWO UNIQUE features of education in Lebanon distinguish it from education in the rest of the Arab world. Lebanon has the highest rate of literacy among the Arab states. It is estimated that between 70 and 75 percent of the children of primary-school age are attending school—a considerably higher rate than in the neighboring countries. This rate would have been higher had it not been for the addition to Lebanon after World War I of some regions which were much less advanced educationally than the original Mount Lebanon. Many village communities in Lebanon have what amounts to or approximates universal literacy.

The second remarkable fact is that this comparatively advanced stage has been accomplished largely through the efforts of private and foreign schools rather than through publicly supported schools. Indeed, before World War I, autonomous Lebanon had only one public school, the Daudiyah at 'Abay, which was supported by the Lebanese government for the education of the children of that predominantly Druze region.[1] The private and foreign schools were largely sectarian. This gave education in Lebanon a predominantly sectarian character, emphasizing sectarian differences, the remnants and effects of which are felt to this day.

Even in 1945–46 the number of pupils enrolled in the public schools was smaller than the number of those enrolled in either private schools or foreign schools. Higher education is conducted entirely in foreign institutions. Secondary education is shared between private and foreign schools, the Lebanese Ministry of National Education having no complete secondary schools. Primary education is conducted in all three types of schools—public, private, and foreign—with the public schools in the third place in enrollments. In addition to primary schools, the Ministry of Na-

[1] Government schools existed in those parts of the present Lebanese Republic which were parts of the neighboring Ottoman provinces. Among these were the cities of Beirut (now the capital of Lebanon), Tripoli, Sidon, and Tyre, as well as such districts as 'Akkar, Buqa', and Marju'yun.

407

tional Education conducts a few schools with complementary classes, two normal schools (one for men and one for women), a School of Arts and Crafts including a course in agriculture, and a conservatory of music.

The Lebanese public educational system, therefore, is by itself incomplete. Only by relating it to the systems of private and foreign schools—which roughly fall into two types, the French and the American-British—does it become a complete, though diversified, system. The description of education in Lebanon will have to follow a somewhat different pattern than the one used for the other school systems. A description of the organization, administration, and finance of public education will be followed by a description of the public primary and special schools and the public examinations. Next, there will be a description of the French, American, and British schools, which set the pattern for most if not all private schools, and the account will end with a consideration of the various types of private schools.

The Administration of Public Education

The administration of public education in Lebanon is centralized and is entrusted to the Ministry of National Education and Fine Arts. This is sketched in Chart XIII. The head of the Ministry is a member of the Council of Ministers and is responsible to the Lebanese Parliament. For the last few years the Minister of National Education has also occupied another ministerial chair, usually that of foreign affairs. He has, therefore, been able to give only part of his time to the Ministry of National Education.

Under the Minister is the Director General of Education, who is the permanent executive. At the time of the visit of the Commission of the American Council on Education, the Director General was also occupying an administrative position in the executive department of the Republic, and was giving only part of his time to his functions at the Ministry of Education.

The burden of the work of the Ministry of National Education, therefore, fell on the shoulders of the Chief of the Cabinet of the Ministry of Education who seemed in effect to be doing the main work of the Director General. During several visits by the Commission to the office of the Ministry in an effort to secure material for the present study, it found him in the process of supervising the preparation, administration, and correction of the public examinations, and working on the new decree concerning private schools and the passage of the decrees embodying the new

Chart XIII

LEBANON: ADMINISTRATIVE ORGANIZATION OF THE MINISTRY OF NATIONAL EDUCATION AND FINE ARTS, 1946

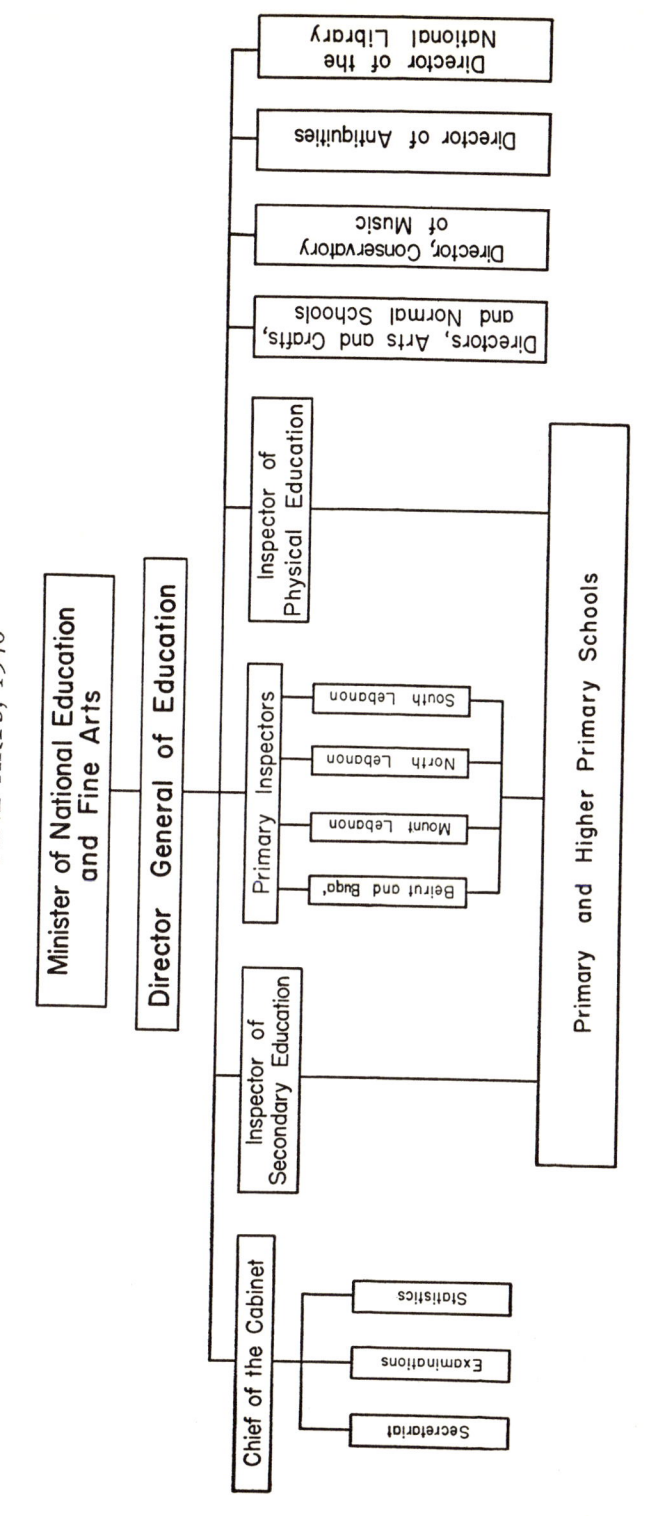

Minister of National Education and Fine Arts
│
Director General of Education
│
├── Inspector of Secondary Education
├── Primary Inspectors
│   ├── Beirut and Buqa'
│   ├── Mount Lebanon
│   ├── North Lebanon
│   └── South Lebanon
├── Inspector of Physical Education
├── Directors, Arts and Crafts, and Normal Schools
├── Director, Conservatory of Music
├── Director of Antiquities
└── Director of the National Library

Chief of the Cabinet
├── Secretariat
├── Examinations
└── Statistics

Primary and Higher Primary Schools

programs of study. His office was usually full of inspectors, heads of schools and other establishments of the Ministry, and of teachers and others who were trying to transact business with him in his official capacity.

The Chief of the Cabinet's office consists of three sections: (1) the Secretariat, which includes clerks and typists, one of whom acts as an accountant, while another has charge of the files and archives of the Ministry; (2) the Examinations Section, with two clerks, one of whom has charge of the stores; (3) the Statistical Section, with two clerks in charge.

Such is the constitution of the purely administrative side of the comparatively small central office of the Ministry in Beirut. The regional administration is in the hands of the four primary inspectors who have charge of the four regions into which Lebanon is divided for purposes of educational administration. These are: North Lebanon with Tripoli as a center; Mount Lebanon, which is the central portion of Lebanon facing the sea, with Ba'abdah, the old capital, as a center; Beirut and Buqa', which includes those sections of the country lying on the east side of the mountain range, with a center at Mu'allaqah Zahlah; and South Lebanon, which includes the southern provinces on both sides of the range, with a center in Sidon. Each region is headed by a chief, who, in addition to his duty of inspecting public and private schools, is in charge of all the administrative work. These regional offices are small, with the result that the administrative work of the inspector tends to reduce his inspectorial or supervisory work to a minimum.

Two other inspectors have their headquarters at the Ministry of National Education—the Inspector of Secondary Education and the Inspector of Physical Education. Since there are only a few incomplete public secondary schools, which in reality are upper primary schools (*écoles primaires supérieures*), the work of the Inspector of Secondary Education is primarily the inspection of private and foreign secondary schools. As in the days of the French mandate, when the foreign schools enjoyed a privileged position and were inspected by officials from the High Commissioner's Department of Education, the duties of an Inspector of Secondary Education have not been heavy. However, with the adoption of the new decree concerning private and foreign schools emphasizing the right of supervision by the Ministry of Education, the duties of the Inspector of Secondary Education are likely to grow. As his title implies, the duties of the Inspector of Physical Education are to supervise and encourage physical education and games, Scout activities, and various forms of sport inside and outside the schools.

ORGANIZATION AND ADMINISTRATION

Four schools, situated in Beirut, are directly connected with the Ministry. These are the School of Arts and Crafts which includes a section on agriculture, the Normal School for Men, the Normal School for Women, and the National Conservatory of Music. The Directorate of Antiquities and the Directorate of the National Library complete the list of the institutions directly connected with the Ministry of National Education.

Educational Finance

The support of public education comes almost entirely from the central budget of the government. Table 71 shows the growth of the educational budget in selected years of the last quarter of a century. This budget, which includes that of the Directorate of Antiquities, has ranged between 5.6 to 8.4 percent of the total budget of the state. The influence of wartime inflation can be seen from the almost sevenfold jump in the educational budget between 1941 and 1945, while in the corresponding period the number of schools increased from 267 to 308 and the enrollment from 21,056 to 30,113.

It was not possible to obtain the salary scale for public-school teachers. A scale set down by a government decree to serve for private and foreign schools fixes salaries at figures probably not very different from those paid in the public schools. The system of classifying teachers as instructors, assistant instructors, and teachers is almost identical with the public-school system. Instructors must be holders of university degrees, assistant instructors must have the *baccalauréat* or the Lebanese teaching certificate, and teachers must hold the Lebanese *brevet* or its equivalent. Monthly salaries for instructors range from £L75 to £L135 ($34 to $61), for assistant instructors from £L45 to £L85 ($20 to $39), and for teachers from £L35 to £L55 ($16 to $25). Salaries are paid for twelve months.

During World War II, cost-of-living allowances were added for government officials and teachers. These ranged from 250 percent for salaries that were £L40 a month or less, to 45 percent for the highest salaries paid by the state. In addition, married teachers received £L14 each for the wife and first child, and £L10 for each additional child up to five children.

A pension plan for government officials allows half the average salary for the last three years after thirty years of service. A person who has been in government service for thirty years and who has attained the age of fifty-five may ask to be retired or may be sent to retirement by the government after due investigation by a committee. Sixty-five is the latest age for retirement, though under special circumstances a person may be allowed to serve on a yearly basis up to the age of seventy.

TABLE 71

GROWTH OF THE EDUCATION BUDGET, LEBANON, 1921–45*

ALLOCATED TO	1921	1932	1939	1941	1945	1946 Budget	Percent of Total Educational Budget
			Education Budget				
Administration	£L 14,559	£L 19,510	£L 20,924	£L 14,180	£L 111,060	£L 150,433	3.2
Primary education	164,721	218,923	304,019	335,761	2,215,820	3,018,319	64.6
Technical education	...	...	74,399	83,027	325,336	309,741	6.6
Agricultural education	...	...	...	...	40,305	33,955	0.7
Fine arts education	...	3,750	4,327	5,315	25,204	25,204	0.5
Teacher education	...	...	...	...	...	121,556	2.6
Antiquities	...	17,716	84,373	55,439	439,901	479,133	10.2
National library	...	8,447	9,180	11,199	49,292	58,000	1.3
Grants and awards	...	20,500	42,000	44,925	324,200	475,100	10.2
Total education budget	£L 179,280	£L 288,846	£L 539,222	£L 549,946	£L 3,531,118	£L 4,671,441	99.9
			State Budget				
Total state budget	£L2,438,000	£L5,109,000	£L6,369,000	£L6,635,000	£L43,314,500	£L60,046,000	
Percent allotted to education from state budget	7.3	5.6	8.4	8.3	8.1	7.7	

* In Lebanese pounds (£L); one pound equals $0.45.

ORGANIZATION AND ADMINISTRATION

Educational Legislation

Article 10 of the Lebanese Constitution of May 23, 1926, guarantees freedom of teaching provided it does not transgress upon public order or morals and is not disrespectful of any religion or sect. It also guarantees the rights of the religious denominations to establish their own schools provided they are established in conformity with the regulations laid down by the state. This is the only article in the constitution dealing with education. Decrees regulating both public and private education are issued, as the need arises, by the President of the Republic acting upon the decision of the Council of Ministers. The main provisions of three of these decrees which were made available to the Commission of the American Council by the Ministry of Education will be summarized here. A fourth decree set up the administrative organization of the Ministry of Education, as already stated. The decrees establishing the new courses of study and the procedures governing examinations will be given in chapter xxv.

Legislative Decree No. 295, dated December 17, 1942, prescribes the conditions for the selection of the teaching staff of the Ministry of National Education and Fine Arts. This staff is divided into two parts: the staff for primary education and the staff for secondary and technical, or vocational, education. Primary-education staff members are classified upward as practicing teacher, teacher, assistant instructor, and inspector. The personnel of secondary and vocational education are classified as instructors and inspectors.

To be appointed a practicing teacher, a candidate must hold the *Baccalauréat,* Part II, or the *brevet.* Before he may be appointed to the grade of teacher, he must have passed through a probationary period of two years, or if he holds the Lebanese teaching diploma,[2] he may be appointed a full teacher after only one year of probation. The regular requirement for promotion to the sixth grade of teaching, which is the beginning grade for a full teacher, is that the candidate must have passed the two parts of the examination for the Lebanese teaching diploma.

To be appointed an assistant instructor, a candidate must be the principal of one of the higher primary schools, or hold the teaching diploma and have had five years of teaching in complementary classes, or have taught eight years in the classification of practicing teacher.

A secondary- or vocational-school instructor must hold a *Licence* in

---

[2] This is given either to students of the normal schools or to practicing or probationary teachers who have passed the two parts of the diploma examinations. The first part is the same as the examination for the first-year studies of the normal school, and the second part is the same as that for the second year.

Letters, Science, or Teaching, or an engineering diploma. He must spend one year on probation.

A primary-school inspector is chosen either from secondary-school instructors who have spent at least five years in service, or from assistant instructors of primary schools who have served for at least ten years.

Finally, secondary- and vocational-school inspectors are chosen from among the professors of higher institutions, or from secondary- or vocational-school instructors who have spent not less than ten years in service, or from primary inspectors who have spent not less than ten years in service and who have taken a higher degree.

Legislative Decree No. 212, of August 31, 1942, fixes the conditions of employment of private-school teachers. As already indicated, it classifies the teaching staff as instructors, assistant instructors, and teachers, and fixes the grades and salaries of each. Further, it specifies the principles of appointment, promotion, discipline, leaves of absence, and compensation upon dismissal. It fixes the teaching load for primary-school teachers at no less than thirty hours a week, for teachers of the upper primary or equivalent secondary classes at no less than twenty-four hours a week, and for upper secondary classes (*deuxième, première, philosophie et mathématique*) at no less than eighteen hours. It also specifies the cost-of-living allowances for teachers in private schools. These changed progressively with the rise of prices during the war.

Perhaps the most important educational legislation in Lebanon of recent years is Decree No. 7,000, of October 1, 1946, issued only a few days before the last member of the American Council Commission left Lebanon. It is concerned with the opening, running, and supervision of private schools and is based on a previous similar decree (No. 7,962, of May 1, 1931), though with a number of significant new features.

This decree defines a private school as any educational institution founded or administered by an individual, a society, or a mission. To open a school, an official permit must be secured in the form of a decree which is issued upon the recommendation of the Minister of National Education and Fine Arts. Only persons who have attained the age of eighteen and who hold an official school certificate may teach in a private school at any level. Only persons who hold at least the *Brevet Primaire Supérieur* or its equivalent may direct a primary school; and only those who hold at least a complete *baccalauréat* or a higher degree may direct a secondary school. These heads of schools must be at least twenty-one years of age.

An individual or a recognized association wishing to open a school must submit the name of the proposed principal, his qualifications, his certificate of good behavior, and the places of his residence during the last five years, as well as a plan of the building to be used, a certificate from the county doctor as to its sanitary arrangements, and another certificate from an architect (or master-mason in outlying villages) as to the soundness of the building. The principal must give an affidavit stating that the school will follow the official course of study. Before granting the permit, the Minister considers whether there is a need for the school. Any changes in the plan of organization of the school require repetition of all the processes indicated above. A school which does not open within two years of the date of issue of its permit has its permit withdrawn. Any school whose proprietor has no permit is closed.

Coeducation is permitted up to the age of eleven. Although the private and foreign schools are required to follow the official courses of study, the principals have a choice of methods of teaching. Only textbooks approved by the Minister of Education may be used in the teaching of history, geography, and moral, civic, and patriotic subjects, and any private school that uses a textbook banned by the Ministry is subject to the penalty of being closed.

Private schools, whether native or foreign, are subject to supervision by the Ministry of National Education. At the end of November of each year private-school principals must submit a register of the school staff and their qualifications, a detailed report on the condition of the school, and the number of pupils and the denominations to which they belong. Schools already having permits at the time of the issuance of the decree of October 1946 were required to register them before April 1947, after which date an unregistered school was subject to being closed.

The Educational Ladder

Schools in Lebanon, as already intimated, belong mainly to one of two types of educational organization: a French or an American type. The French type prevails in the government schools, in the large majority of foreign schools, and in some of the private schools—all culminating in the French Jesuit university known as the Université Saint-Joseph. The American type is found in the next largest group of foreign schools, the schools of the Protestant Synod, and in some of the private schools. These culminate in the American University of Beirut, the oldest existing institution of higher education in Lebanon (founded in 1866). A third type of organization comprising a small number of schools may be called the "British" type and is exemplified by the British-Syrian Training College for girls and the elementary schools for boys and girls attached to it.[3]

Which one of the types a particular pupil is likely to choose depends to a large extent upon his community background—more specifically his religious community background. A Catholic parent is likely to place his child in a Catholic foreign or native private school, which means that he receives the French brand of education. Greek or other Orthodox children, when they do not go to their own schools, are as likely to pick a French type as American or British types of school. When picking a French type, they usually prefer a lay-mission (Mission Laïque) school where they are not subjected to the intense religious teaching of the Catholic-mission schools. Most Protestant children go to Protestant schools which, with one notable exception (Le Collège Protestant Français) are of the American or British types. A Muslim parent usually would prefer to send his child to a Muslim school, which may be following plans of any of the types. The poorer Muslims often send their children to the government schools, which follow the French type of organization, or to the French lay-mission schools, or to the American or British types of school. The deciding factor is the absence or minimum of proselytization. Druzes, when they do not send their children to their own schools, usually send them to government schools, but they may choose American or British schools; the latter have had long-standing relations with the Druze community. Druzes also send their children to French schools and to some of the Muslim and Christian denominational schools. Thus, the choices of schools are to a large extent determined by sectarian considerations. This situation is a perpetuation of the status prevailing in the days of the Ottoman Empire, which was accentuated even further in the days of the French mandate. It is not likely to change appreciably until the government assumes greater responsibility for public education than it has hitherto.

Chart XIV attempts to depict the various educational systems in vogue in Lebanon. In general, two systems—the American and the French—go their own ways, using their own curriculums, their own methods, and, indeed, are guided by two distinct philosophies.[4] About the only link between the two types is the establishment by the American University of Beirut of a *Section Secondaire,* in which an adaptation of the French secondary program is followed and where the teaching is in French. Those who finish this program present themselves for the French or Lebanese

---

[3] There are, in addition, 1 Danish, 1 Swiss, and 1 Greek school. The American Council Commission was unable to visit any of these schools and, therefore, is not in a position to describe the type of organization they follow.

[4] For a description of French schools, see chap. xxvi; for American and British schools, chap. xxvii.

Chart XIV
LEBANON: EDUCATIONAL SYSTEM, 1946

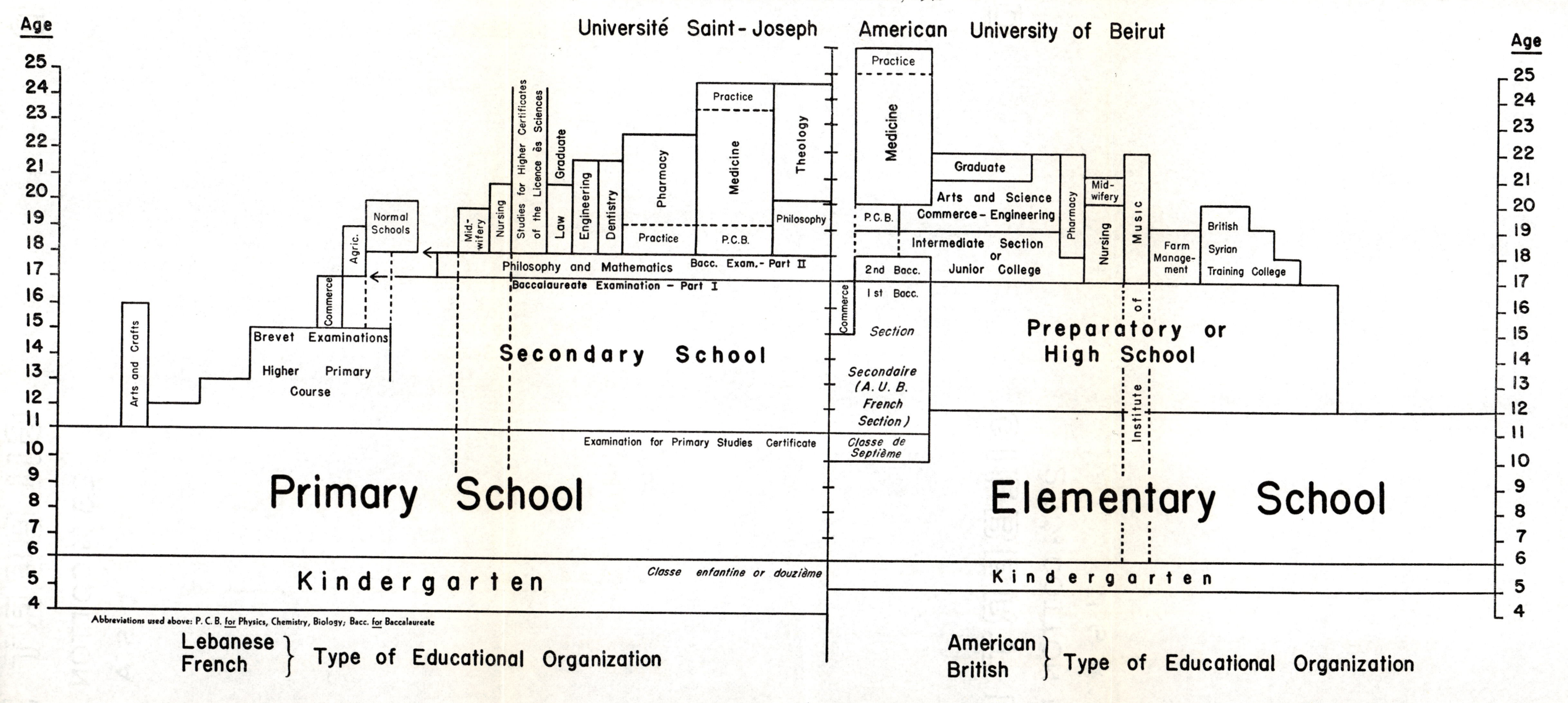

Abbreviations used above: P.C.B. for Physics, Chemistry, Biology; Bacc. for Baccalaureate

Lebanese / French } Type of Educational Organization

American / British } Type of Educational Organization

ORGANIZATION AND ADMINISTRATION 417

baccalauréat examinations (Parts I and II) and then become, as are other holders of the French or Lebanese *baccalauréat,* eligible for admission to the junior year of the School of Arts and Sciences of the University. The French and Lebanese authorities recognize the B.A. degree of the American University as only equivalent to the complete *baccalauréat.* As a rule the French schools give English as their second language. American and British schools give French as their second language: until recently they even started teaching French earlier than they did English.

PUBLIC SCHOOLS

In constructing Chart XIV, the new government course of study, which was announced in October 1946, was used. Until the new course is gradually put into operation in the next few years, however, the former course will still prevail in the public schools. This consists of a six-year primary school and a three-year higher primary school. The primary school is divided into three courses of two years each—the preparatory, elementary, and middle courses—and leads to the primary-studies certificate examination. If successful, a pupil may enter the higher course *(cours supérieur)* of one year, followed by the complementary course *(cours complémentaire)* of two years. This ends in the *brevet* examination. As the government maintains no complete secondary schools, a pupil who wishes to finish his secondary education has to transfer to a French-type secondary school, where he spends six to seven years, depending upon the class to which he is admitted. Though having no secondary schools, the Ministry of Education set a secondary course of study modeled after the French, but with the addition of Arabic, local history and geography, and Arabic philosophy. This course serves as the basis for the Lebanese *baccalauréat* examinations, Parts I and II. The course is uniform for all students until the ninth grade (called *classe de troisième*). It then divides into two sections—scientific and literary—for the two classes which follow, tenth and eleventh grades, after which the first *baccalauréat* examination takes place. In the final secondary year the students may enter either of two sections—the *classe de philosophie* or the *classe de mathématique*—and finally present themselves for the second part of the *baccalauréat* examination. The course also provides for a classical section starting with the *sixième* (sixth grade) in which an oriental or Western classical language is required.

The new course of study provides for a kindergarten of two years to which children may be admitted at as early an age as three, followed by a primary school of five, instead of six, years ending in the primary-studies certificate examination. Having passed that examination, a pupil may proceed either to the seven-year secondary school or the four-year higher primary school, or to the School of Arts and Crafts, which gives a course of four years. The program of the first two years of the higher primary school has been made identical with that of the first two years of the secondary school in order to facilitate transfer from one school to the other. Those students who pass the *brevet* examinations may enter one of two other government schools or courses. These are the agricultural course, which is now under the same administration as the School of Arts and Crafts, and the normal school for men or that for women. Entrance is by competitive examination. Students who have passed the first *baccalauréat* examination may also apply for admission to the agricultural course, while those who have passed the first or first and second *baccalauréat* examinations may apply for admission to the normal schools. These more advanced students are allowed 10 or 20 marks for their certificates, thus giving them an advantage in the total score which forms the basis of admission.

Education in the public schools is entirely free, the pupils providing their own books. Students in the School of Arts and Crafts, the agricultural course, and the normal schools may be boarding students at the expense of the government.

FRENCH SCHOOLS

The organization of the French schools in Lebanon is not very different from that of the public schools because the latter schools have been modeled after them. The French schools constitute a complete system from kindergarten to university. As a rule, a French institution has both the primary and secondary schools as one continuous school on the same premises.

The kindergarten class for three- and four-year-olds leads to a prefirst grade (called twelfth class—*douzième*), where some very rudimentary elements of reading and arithmetic are taught. The real first grade, however, is the eleventh class (*onzième*). The primary school extends from the eleventh through the seventh class, and is divided into a preparatory course of one year, an elementary course of two years, and a middle course (*cours moyen*) of two years. If the pupil remains in the same school to continue his secondary education, he need not take the primary-certificate examination. If he decides to take this examination, he usually has a choice of the French examination, formerly given by the Haut Commissariat and now by the Œuvres Françaises, or of the Lebanese examinations already mentioned. He may take these examinations after his seventh class or a year later, after the sixth class. If he passes these examinations, he may continue his education in the same school (the customary procedure)

ORGANIZATION AND ADMINISTRATION

or transfer to some other French or Lebanese school, or even to an American- or British-type school.

The secondary course which follows is of seven years, and prepares for the first and second *baccalauréats,* both French and Lebanese, and also for the *brevet* examination, both French and Lebanese. Some schools also prepared for the Syrian *baccalauréat* up to a very recent date.

After graduating from the secondary school and becoming a *bachelier,* the student has several choices for continuing his education. He may enter one of the two higher institutions in Lebanon—the French Jesuit Université Saint-Joseph or the American University of Beirut, or he may go abroad, especially to France, where both the Lebanese and French *baccalauréats* are recognized for admission to higher institutions. Comparatively few graduates of French secondary schools transfer to the American University.

The usual course for the graduate of a French or French-type secondary school is to enter the Université Saint-Joseph. Here he may pursue studies leading to the degree of *Licence ès Sciences* (though the University itself does not grant that degree), or he may enter one of the professional schools—the Faculty of Theology, Institute of Oriental Letters, Law School, Engineering School, or Faculty of Medicine with its divisions of pharmacy, dentistry, nursing, and midwifery. The requirements and courses are described on pages 473–78.

AMERICAN SCHOOLS

The American-type schools also constitute a complete ladder from kindergarten to university. The term is applied to the system of American nonsectarian and mission schools, together with the native private schools which follow the American pattern. At the top of the ladder is the American University of Beirut.

The ladder starts with a kindergarten of one year, which exists mainly in the girls schools. This is followed by an elementary school of six years, which may be for boys alone, or girls alone, or coeducational. Sometimes the lower classes are coeducational, the children separating after the second or third grade. The elementary school is followed by a five-year high, or preparatory, school which follows a uniform program throughout. The combined normal duration of the elementary and high school is eleven years, instead of the twelve of the French ladder. Some of the schools, however, have twelve grades, with the better students skipping directly from the sixth to the eighth grade, while the slower ones stay in the school for the entire twelve years.

A girl graduate of an American-type high school who wishes to continue her education may enter the American Junior College for Women situated in Beirut. Though included for convenience in Chart XIV under the American University of Beirut, it is an independent institution with a separate board of trustees. It offers a two-year course, which, if of an approved sequence, is accepted for admission to the junior year of the School of Arts and Sciences of the University. A woman student may enter the School of Nursing of the University, where, after a three-year course she receives the Nurses' diploma. An additional year of study leads to the diploma of midwifery. A graduate of the School of Nursing who is also a graduate of the American Junior College for Women may receive the B.A. degree by studying for one more year in the School of Arts and Sciences.

A male graduate from high school may enter the intermediate section (freshman and sophomore classes) of the School of Arts and Sciences. Here he may continue his college studies in the academic subjects, or take up farm management, pursue a business course, or, after the freshman year, enter the School of Pharmacy.

After finishing the intermediate section, the student may enter the junior year of the University where he is joined by the graduates of the American Junior College for Women and by the higher-ranking graduates of the *Section Secondaire* (the French-type secondary school established by the American University) or other holders of the French or Lebanese *baccalauréat*. Here he may take courses in the arts, the sciences, commerce, or engineering, or pursue an honors course. If he intends to study medicine, he enters the School of Medicine after his junior year.

The University Institute of Music has no specific requirement for admission beyond a practical examination to determine the class into which the student fits. The course is of seven years' duration, including a preparatory year for beginners. It is described further on pages 496–97.

British schools

British schools are comparatively few in number. They are described on pages 499–501.

The ladder consists of two years of kindergarten followed by a course of ten years covering the elementary-, middle-, and high-school standards (grades). The high-school certificate is recognized for entrance into the American Junior College for Women and to the School of Nursing of the American University of Beirut.

Such is the present situation with regard to the educational ladder of Lebanon—if ladder it can be called. It is a situation where two, or perhaps three, educational outlooks and philosophies emanating from abroad dominate the scene. Native schools, whether public or private, follow one or the other of these educational ideologies and systems. Owing to the policies followed by the French mandate between the two World Wars, the French type of school and curriculum is by far the most prevalent. nevertheless, the American type enjoys a certain vogue, largely owing, perhaps, to the prestige of the American University of Beirut, for which many a private school prepares its students.

The Growth of Education

The former autonomous province of Mount Lebanon had only one public school and relied on private and foreign schools to educate its children. The other parts of the present Lebanese Republic, which were parts of the vilayets of Beirut and Damascus and subject to the direct rule of the Ottoman government emanating from Istanbul, had public schools maintained by the Ottoman government through its departments of education in the provinces. These schools formed the nucleus of the new Lebanese public-school system when the former Ottoman cities and districts were added to Lebanon after 1920.

It was not possible to secure statistics of schools and attendance in Lebanon in the same detail as for the other Arab countries. All that could be secured from the Lebanese Ministry of Education was the total number of schools, teachers, and pupils for 1944-45 in the public, private, and foreign schools, together with the distribution of the pupils in the public schools according to sect. For the rest the American Council Commission had to glean whatever data it could find in the statistical annual for 1942–43, which was issued by the Council of General Interests for Syria and Lebanon, in the *Bulletin de l'Enseignement,* a periodical previously published by the Education Department of the Haut Commissariat, and the annual reports of the French Republic to the League of Nations on the situation in Syria and Lebanon. Even these, however, gave no figures as to the distribution of teachers and pupils by grades, or the number of complete and incomplete schools, and other useful figures which would permit a more intimate study of an educational system. Both the government and the Haut Commissariat's figures emphasize the sectarian distribution of schools and their pupils.

Table 72 shows the growth of education in Lebanon between 1924 and 1945 in public, private, and foreign schools.

It is evident from Table 72 that the public schools are in the minority. In 1944–45, there were only 308 public schools, in which 30,113 pupils

TABLE 72

NUMBER OF SCHOOLS AND PUPILS CLASSIFIED ACCORDING TO CONTROL, LEBANON, 1924–46

YEAR	PUBLIC SCHOOLS No.	PUBLIC SCHOOLS Enrollment	PRIVATE SCHOOLS No.	PRIVATE SCHOOLS Enrollment	FOREIGN SCHOOLS No.	FOREIGN SCHOOLS Enrollment	TOTAL No.	TOTAL Enrollment
1924	117	8,064	762*	52,705*	98†	6,614†	977	67,383
1930	129	13,632	767	49,197	410	36,153	1,306	98,982
1941–42	267	21,056	986	73,608	326	43,654	1,579	138,318
1944–45	308	30,113	963	71,524	326	43,065	1,596	144,702
1945–46	451	40,926	...	...	...	...	...	...

* Including French schools.
† Not including French schools. In later years French schools were included among the foreign schools.

were enrolled. This represents 19.3 percent of the total of 1,596 schools, and 20.9 percent of the total of 144,702 pupils. In sharp contrast, there were 963 private schools, enrolling 71,524 pupils, a percentage of 60.3 and 49.4 respectively. In other words, more than one-half of the schools were private schools, accommodating one-half of the school population of Lebanon. Foreign schools numbered 326 (20.4 percent) and enrolled 43,065 pupils (29.7 percent).

It is to be noticed, however, that the public schools have been increasing at a more rapid pace than the other schools owing to the vigorous policy followed by the Ministry of Education in opening new schools. In 1945–46 the number of schools reached 451 and of pupils 40,926, an increase of 143 schools and 10,813 pupils in a single year. This brought the number of public schools to approximately 4 times what they were in 1924, and the number of pupils to about 5 times. During the same period private and foreign schools reached 1.5 times their former number (860 to 1,289) while the number of pupils approximately doubled (59,319 to 114,589). It is to be noted that private and foreign schools have been at a standstill in the last few years. This may be due to the difficulties of the war period. It may, however, be possible that they have reached a saturation point; and with the end of the French mandate, which encouraged foreign schools (especially the French), and with a more vigorous educational policy by the Lebanese government, the next few years may witness a spurt in public education and a comparative lull in the numerical expansion of private and foreign schools.

The distribution of pupils according to sex is available only for public and foreign schools. No comparable figures of recent date have been found for private schools. The figures are as follows:

	PUBLIC SCHOOLS BOYS	PUBLIC SCHOOLS GIRLS	PUBLIC SCHOOLS TOTAL	FOREIGN SCHOOLS BOYS	FOREIGN SCHOOLS GIRLS	FOREIGN SCHOOLS TOTAL
1942–43	17,051	5,803	22,854	22,316	24,410	46,726
1945–46	30,361	9,965	40,326	...	...	...

ORGANIZATION AND ADMINISTRATION

In the public schools one out of every four pupils is a girl. In the foreign schools, including the large number of girls schools maintained by orders of nuns, the number of girls is greater than that of boys. The ratio of girls to boys in the private schools probably stands somewhere in between these two extremes.

In 1944–45 there was a total of 5,092 teachers in all types of schools in Lebanon. Of these, 887 were in public schools, teaching an average of 34 pupils each; 2,167 were in private schools, teaching an average of 33 pupils each; and 2,037 were in foreign schools, teaching an average of only 21 pupils each. The average number of pupils per teacher was markedly lower in the foreign schools partly because of the presence of higher institutions among them, and partly because many of them were run by orders of friars and nuns who received no salaries and cost only their maintenance. Such schools, therefore, could afford greater numbers of teachers.

Table 73 shows the distribution of schools and pupils according to types of schools in 1941–42, the latest year for which such figures could be obtained.

TABLE 73

DISTRIBUTION OF SCHOOLS AND PUPILS BY TYPE OF SCHOOL, LEBANON, 1941–42

Type of School	Public Schools Schools and Units	Public Schools Enrollment	Private Schools Schools and Units	Private Schools Enrollment	Foreign Schools Schools and Units	Foreign Schools Enrollment	Total Schools and Units	Total Enrollment
Primary and complementary	266	20,761	1,164	69,422	435	35,671	1,865	125,854
Normal and secondary	3	295	37	4,186	48	6,295	88	10,776
Higher institutions	...	...	...	...	25	1,688	25	1,688
Total	269	21,056	1,201	73,608	508	43,654	1,978	138,318

Public and private Lebanese schools were of the primary and secondary types. No public or private higher institutions existed. All public schools, except 3, were primary and complementary. The 3 exceptions were the 2 normal schools (1 for men and 1 for women) and the School of Arts and Crafts, all at Beirut. There were 37 private secondary schools, having an enrollment of 4,186 pupils; and 1,164 private primary units, enrolling 69,422 pupils. Among the foreign schools, there were 435 primary sections, enrolling 35,671 pupils; 48 secondary sections, enrolling 6,295 pupils; and 25 units of higher education (the American and French universities and their component schools and departments), enrolling 1,688 students. There were more foreign secondary schools than public and private secondary schools combined, with three-fifths of the total secondary-school enrollment.

The distribution of foreign schools according to nationality, and the number of boys and girls enrolled in them in 1942-43 (the latest figures available), are shown in Table 74.

TABLE 74

DISTRIBUTION AND SIZE OF FOREIGN SCHOOLS BY NATIONALITY, LEBANON, 1942–43

NATIONALITY	NO. OF SCHOOLS	ENROLLMENT Boys	Girls	Total
French	273	17,789	21,724	39,513
American	36	3,462	1,581	5,043
British	14	847	946	1,793
Danish	1	18	110	128
Greek	1	170	...	170
Swiss	1	30	49	79
Total	326	22,361	24,410	46,726

The largest group of foreign schools was the French, constituting 83 percent of all foreign schools and enrolling 84 percent of the total foreign-school enrollment. Far behind them trail the American schools, which constitute 11 percent of all foreign schools and educate about the same proportion of pupils. They are followed by the British schools, which constitute 4 percent of the total of foreign schools with the same percentage of the total enrollment. Denmark, Greece, and Switzerland are each represented by one school.

Finally, owing to the great stress laid in Lebanon on the sectarian distribution of school children and of the population in general, it seemed worth while to study the sectarian composition of the school population of

TABLE 75

SECTARIAN COMPOSITION OF THE SCHOOL ENROLLMENT OF LEBANON AS COMPARED WITH THE COMPOSITION OF THE GENERAL POPULATION, 1941–42

RELIGIOUS AFFILIATION	ESTIMATED POPULATION	PERCENT	Public Schools	Private Schools	Foreign Schools	Total	Percent	PERCENT OF ENROLLMENT TO POPULATION
Christian	585,443	53.0	6,783	53,274	36,606	96,663	69.9	15.8
Muslim	434,705	39.3	13,208	16,997	3,999	34,204	24.7	7.8
Druze	72,842	6.6	1,002	2,799	1,117	4,918	3.5	6.7
Jews	5,567	0.5	10	262	1,775	2,047	1.5	36.8
Miscellaneous	6,112	0.6	53	276	157	486	0.4	8.0
Total	1,104,669	100.0	21,056	73,608	43,654	138,318	100.0	12.5

ORGANIZATION AND ADMINISTRATION

Lebanon and compare it with the composition of the general population of the country. The matter is not without both educational and sociological interest. This is shown in Table 75.

Although the Christians of Lebanon constitute slightly more than one-half of the population, they have 70 percent of the total school enrollment of the country. The ratio of children in school to the Christian population is 15.8—which seems to show that the Christians are closely approaching universal literacy. It tends to confirm the statement made earlier, based on personal observation, that many a Christian village in Lebanon has achieved almost complete literacy. The Muslims, who make up 39.3 percent of the population, have 24.7 percent of the school enrollment. Their children constitute 7.8 percent of the total Muslim population. They seem to be half-way on the road to complete literacy. They are closely followed by the Druzes who have 6.7 percent of their population in the schools. As a community the Druzes make up 6.6 percent of the total population and have 3.5 percent of the total enrollment. The abnormal proportion of Jewish children in school compared with their population (36.8 percent) may be attributed either to the possibility that the figure given for the Jewish population is an underestimate or that Jewish students are coming from neighboring countries to study in Lebanon in such numbers as completely to upset the ratio. The Jews seem to have no problem of illiteracy.

Taking the total school enrollment and the total population of Lebanon, it is found that the former constitutes 12.5 percent of the latter—the highest percentage among the Arab countries.

Chapter 25

PUBLIC EDUCATION

To DESCRIBE the public schools of Lebanon is essentially to describe its primary and higher primary schools. At the time of the visit of the American Council Commission in 1945 the public primary school consisted of six grades. These were divided into three courses in the French fashion, the first two grades making up the preparatory course; the next two grades, the elementary course; and the last two grades, the middle course (*cours moyen*). The higher primary school consisted of three years, the first year of which was called the higher class, and the remaining two years were called the complementary classes (*classes complémentaires*). French was the only foreign language taught in the public schools and began with the first grade. The medium of instruction in the first four grades was Arabic, but children were required to study in French the arithmetic they learned in Arabic. In this way they were gradually inducted, from the first grade, into the study of subject matter through the medium of French. Beginning with the first year of the middle course (fifth grade), the study of object lessons was shifted to the medium of French, while arithmetic was carried through in both languages. Much the same pattern was kept in the classes of the higher primary school, science taking the place of object lessons. Drawing, manual arts, and physical education were allied to French, while singing was conducted in both languages.

The new course of study, issued in October 1946, shortens the length of the primary school from six to five years, gives the pupils the option of either French or English as the foreign language, and makes Arabic the language of instruction throughout the primary school. The teachers, however, are to "Habituate the pupils, beginning with the fourth year, in the understanding and use of scientific terms in French or English—according to the choice of the pupil—in arithmetic and object lessons." In the public examination at the end of the five-year course, the pupil may choose whether he will be examined in French or English.

Kindergartens

The kindergarten is of two years. In the first year special attention is paid to the cleanliness of the children and to teaching them games in the open air. They are given picture books and taught music and singing. They are taught the numbers from 1 to 10 and told moral stories relating to the members of the family.

In the second year, attention to cleanliness and the teaching of games, music, and singing are continued. A beginning is made in reading, and the children write the letters and words they learn. Elementary arithmetic is continued with objective practice on the four fundamental operations with numbers from 10 to 25. In object lessons short discussions of the pupils' environment are held, including such topics as furniture, equipment, clothing, and food. Moral precepts and love of one's country (taught by means of stories and conversations), patriotic songs, the Lebanese flag, the national anthem, and pictures portraying views of Lebanon, the president of the Republic, and famous Lebanese men, are included in the second year.

Primary Education

Education in the primary stage is said to have two functions: preparing pupils for life, and preparing them for the next stages of education. Though these may appear contradictory they have a common basis which is viewed as the real aim of primary education, namely, preparing the whole man, the thoughtful citizen, and the active member of society by providing him with spiritual, intellectual, and physical education. Spiritual education is based on the idea of God and His relation to creation, on respect for the human personality, on acceptance of the "hierarchy of values, rising from matter to mind to spirit," on the practice of noble virtues, and on the understanding of the duties and rights of man. Intellectual education is based on accustoming the pupil to correct thought and deduction, good observation and close attention, together with a body of information and practical methods which will enable him to deal with the everyday affairs of life. Finally, physical education aims at strengthening the body and helping it to grow through athletics. All these are to be accomplished by means that fit the level of the student, using tangible examples and avoiding going into abstractions and debatable issues in any detail.

Higher primary education is said not to differ in general aim from primary education except that orientation toward the more practical side of life becomes a fundamental aim. Students are prepared in this stage for vocational schools and professional schools for teachers and for entry into life. During the first two years, therefore, the teacher is to watch the interests of the pupil in order to direct him toward that line of specialization for which he is best suited.

The primary program of studies

The program for the first two years of the higher primary school is made identical with that of the first two years of the secondary program to allow the pupil to transfer without loss of time, and presumably to give him enough time to mature and for his abilities and interests to show themselves before he chooses his career. The last two years, however, differ from those of the secondary school in giving greater emphasis to the practical side of the studies. Translated into time distribution, this means one hour more to drawing and manual arts, and to science (physics, chemistry, and biology), and two hours more to mathematics in the higher primary course, while in the secondary course emphasis is laid on languages, history and geography, and morals and civics.

Table 76 shows the primary and higher primary program of studies which together make up a program of nine years.

A summary of the primary and higher primary courses of study, though separate units, will be given here in a combined form, partly to avoid repetition and partly to show the evolution of each subject through the grades.

Arabic

In the teaching of Arabic special attention is paid to the difference between the colloquial and the classical languages, and an effort made to bridge the gap between them by selecting, as far as possible, vocabulary from the colloquial and incorporating it in correct sentences in the classical style. Care is taken not to choose difficult and rare words far from the pupil's environment. In the higher primary school special emphasis is laid on composition and style on living topics, and on the development of taste in literature.

Arabic begins in the first grade with reading of elementary words and simple sentences in a method that seems to be a combination of a spelling and a phonetic method. Reading is accompanied by penmanship based on the lessons and by memorization of simple poems. In subsequent years read-

PUBLIC EDUCATION

ing of pieces with explanation of the meaning of words and comprehension is emphasized. The pieces are at first voweled to insure correct reading, but later unvoweled pieces are introduced. Selections from contemporary writers are chosen in the first two years of the higher primary school, while in the last two years selections from various periods of Arabic literature are chosen. Memorization continues throughout with poems and, later, prose

TABLE 76

Program of Studies for Primary and Higher Primary Schools, Lebanon, 1946

	Periods per Week				
Subjects	Primary School			Higher Primary School	
	1st Year	2nd and 3rd Years	4th and 5th Years	1st and 2nd Years	3rd and 4th Years
In Arabic:					
Religion	1	1	1	1	1
Moral and national lessons	1½	1	1	1½	1½
Reading, memorization, penmanship copying*	6	3½	2	3	} 5
Composition, grammar, dictation	...	3	...	3	
Grammar, dictation	...	...	2	...	
Composition, penmanship	...	...	2	...	
Object lessons, conversation, hygiene†	2	1½	2	...	...
Arithmetic	5	5	5	...	...
History, geography	...	2	2	2½	2½
Drawing, manual arts	2	2	2	2	3
Music, singing	2	1	1	1	1
Physical education	2½	2	2	2	2
In the foreign language:					
Reading, memorization, penmanship	} 5	} 5	2	3	} 5
Grammar, composition, dictation			...	3	
Grammar, dictation			1½	...	
Composition, penmanship			1½	...	
Optional in Arabic or the foreign language:					
Physics, chemistry, biology	...	...	...	4	4
Mathematics	...	...	...	4	5
Total	27	27	27	30	30

* Penmanship shifted to composition after third year. Copying eliminated.
† Periods assigned to conversation only in first year, hygiene added in fourth and fifth years.

pieces and proverbs of increasing difficulty. Dictation starts in the second grade with exercises already studied and continues later with unstudied selections through the third year of the higher course, with emphasis on the writing of the *hamzah*. Written composition starts in the second grade with exercises in sentence construction, leads to the writing of descriptions of simple events, stories, and letters; develops in the higher course into longer stories, writing about descriptive and moral topics, essays, development of themes, and translation. Conversation lessons are given in the second and third primary years and are based on the observation of the immediate environment of the children—the home, the school, familiar animals, flowers and plants, fairy tales, school picnics, and trips—and in the third grade on such topics as the seasons, the story of bread, the various trades, the mail, the cleaning of the streets, transportation, and dramatized stories. In the fourth and fifth years conversation is merged with the preliminary discussion of composition topics.

Grammar begins in the second grade with the parts of speech, the singular, dual, and plural, the masculine and feminine, proper and common nouns, the adjective, the pronoun, simple conjugation, and the subject and object. In each subsequent year these topics are expanded and new topics brought in, for example, the root verb and the derivative verb, the past, present, and imperative, and their conjugation, the verbal and the nominal sentences, the active and the passive, the adverbs of place and time, number, the demonstrative nouns, and types of nominal sentences. By the end of the third year of the higher primary school almost all the topics of grammar have been studied, and some of them repeatedly emphasized.

The Arabic course culminates in the fourth year of the higher primary course with a study of Arabic literature, heroic and lyric poetry, dramatics, philosophical poetry, the story, and description. Selections from the works of two prose writers and one poet of the 'Abbasid period are studied.

History and Geography

In teaching history and geography, the teacher is reminded that these subjects are of great use in developing patriotism and national spirit, that the two subjects are intimately related, that full use should be made of maps, particularly in the study of Lebanon's economic wealth and possibilities, and the lines of communication within Lebanon and between it and the Arab and other countries of the world. Special detail is to be given to the countries which have received Lebanese emigrants.

History and geography start informally in the first grade by reference to village life, the earth, the stars, and atmospheric phenomena. In the second and third years historical pictures and stories about Lebanon and the Arab countries are taken up. Beginning with the fourth year, history is divided into two parts: history of Lebanon and history of the rest of the world. In the fourth grade, early history of Lebanon is brought down to the end of the Byzantine period, and the history of the world to the discovery of America and the beginning of the Western nations is studied. In the fifth year Lebanese history to the present day is studied including relations with the Arab countries, while world history takes up the modern period including the French Revolution, the attempt at the unification of Europe, and modern discoveries.

In the higher primary course the history of the ancient peoples having relations with Lebanon is studied, including the Egyptians, the Babylonians, Assyrians and Chaldeans, the Aegeans, Hittites, Hebrews, Persians, Greeks, and the Romans; the growth of Christianity and the Byzantine empire. The ancient history of the Phoenicians—the early inhabitants of Lebanon—is then studied, with emphasis on their invention of the alphabet, their seafaring and trade, their founding of Carthage and other colonies around the Mediterranean. In the second year the course is divided into three parts: history of the Arabs down to the Mamluks, the invasions of Europe and the states growing out of these invasions, and Lebanon during the Arab period down to the Fatimids, the Crusades, and the final expulsion of the Crusaders. In the third year the Renaissance and the rise of the modern states in Europe are studied, together with the Ottoman conquest in the early 1500's, and the situation in Lebanon in Ottoman days down to the seventeenth century. Finally, in the fourth year European history is brought down to the First World War, the history of Lebanon in the Shihabi period, and during its autonomous regime after 1864, during World War I, the French mandate, and finally the establishment of the independent Republic of Lebanon in 1943.

Geography is taught informally through stories and pictures in the first two grades to develop basic concepts about the earth, the stars, the villages, mountains, plains, rivers, and many of the geographical features which are in the immediate environment. In the third year, physical geography of the five continents and the important nations in each are studied. The fourth year is given to brief survey of Lebanon, the Arab countries, and Turkey, Cyprus, and Greece, while in the fifth grade a more extended study of Lebanon is made, with brief studies of Italy, France, Spain, North Africa, and other important countries of the world. Lebanese migration to various countries is noted.

In the higher primary school, physical geography of the continents of Asia and Oceania is studied in the first year; in the second year, Europe and Africa with emphasis on the Mediterranean basin, noting physical and climatic characteristics, agricultural, mineral, and industrial regions, as well as political divisions; in the third year, North and South America; and in the fourth year, astronomical geography, a review of the five continents, a detailed study of Lebanon, and lines of communication, especially among the Arab countries, conclude the course.

Morals and Civics

The primary course in morals covers personal traits and general virtues such as cleanliness, good manners, obedience, justice, charity, moral courage, sacrifice for others, honesty, love of parents, respect for teachers, and cooperation with others. In civics, a beginning is made from the first grade by explaining words such as citizen, soldier, flag, state, minister, and similar familiar terms. In the second and third years such concepts as nation, people, administration, customs duties, public projects, prosecutor general, and juries are explained, while in the fourth and fifth years general principles about the form of the state, the distribution of powers to legislative, executive, and judicial branches, parliament, the courts, military service, taxation, elections, banks and currency, and similar topics are studied.

In the higher primary course a more rationalized study of morals is made with emphasis on the place of the mind, the will and discipline, the conscience, cooperative living and what it implies in respect for others, mutual aid and philanthropy, division of labor, the family in general and family life in Lebanon, and Lebanese society. The course in civics gives in much more expanded form the ideas about the state, the division of power, and the parliamentary system, which were touched upon in the primary school. In the third year, principles of freedom and equality are discussed in detail: personal freedom (inviolability of home and property), freedom of work, conscience, belief, assembly, teaching and of thought, speech, writing and publishing, equality in civic and political rights and public duties, and equality of men and women. In addition, the duties of the citizen, such as obedience to law and authority, paying taxes, and military service, are studied together with the Lebanese Constitution, its development and its latest amendments. In the fourth year, an extensive study of Lebanon is made, the elements constituting it, its international position before World War I and after, its relations with the states of the Arab League and the United Nations. A review is made of the forms of government in the modern history of Lebanon from the seventeenth century to the present day. The program ends with a study of the aims of education, the contribution of the Lebanese people to culture, and Lebanese emigration, its causes and effects, and some of the famous emigrants.

Foreign Languages

Foreign-language teaching in the primary grades is justified by the fact that Lebanon's geographical position is that of a bridge between East and

West, and that archeological excavations have shown Lebanon to have been multilingual from the very dawn of history. With present-day shortening of distances and mixture of cultures, Lebanon should not abandon its role in world culture which it has acquired by virtue of being open to both East and West. A foreign language must then be taught side by side with the Arabic language—and taught well, bearing in mind the cultural benefit accruing from such teaching. In the modern world, French and English have the greatest vogue and potential usefulness, and the student is given the choice of one of these languages. The teaching of both starts with the first grade.

In French, the children are supposed to learn to read simple material fluently by the end of the first grade. Vocabulary and language exercises are based on familiar topics, and simple conjugations are stressed. The writing of letters of the alphabet and familiar words is taught by dictation. In subsequent grades the students are taught the derivation of words and the construction of sentences, and are gradually introduced to new topics in grammar—conjugation of regular and irregular verbs, parsing and logical analysis—and they read selections from French literature. Written exercises are assigned regularly throughout the entire four years. By the end of the fifth grade the pupil is supposed to be able to write simple narratives, descriptions, and letters.

In the higher primary school, a review of grammar is followed by systematic study, including logical and grammatical analysis, and culminating in a study of prosody. Reading begins in the first year with literary selections from twentieth-century French writers and poets; in the second year, selections from the eighteenth- and nineteenth-century writers are studied; in the third year, writers of the seventeenth century; and in the fourth year all periods are studied, including the complete works of such authors as Corneille, Racine, Lamartine, Chateaubriand, Molière, and Victor Hugo. In the fourth year, selections for reading keep pace with a course in the history of French literature. Composition starts with narration, description, and letters and ends with literary analysis, criticism, imitation of literary pieces, the writing of themes and expansion of proverbs and maxims. Texts written for French children are used throughout.

English starts in the first grade with conversation about the immediate environment, the study of the sounds and the alphabet, and memorization of simple songs and poems. Both oral and silent reading from texts are emphasized beginning with the second grade. Special attention is paid to pronunciation, fluency, dramatization, and meanings of words in their context. Supplementary reading material is introduced in the fifth grade and conversation in English in class is encouraged. Composition ranges from answering questions on texts and using words in sentences in the third grade, to reproducing material read, telling and writing simple stories, and writing short compositions on easy subjects in the fifth grade. Grammar includes conjugation with emphasis on the verbs "to be" and "to have," the third person singular, plurals, the possessive case, affirmative, negative, interrogative, degrees of the adjective, irregular verbs, and all types of pronouns including the use of the relative pronoun. Throughout the course selections for memory work and dictation are based on the texts used. The books recommended are to be selected from those specially written for foreigners, viz., those by Michael West (in use also in Egypt and parts of India), by Morris (in use in Palestine), and by Leavitt (developed and used at the American University of Beirut and schools allied to it).

Mathematics

Arithmetic in the first grade starts with reading and writing numbers from 1 to 20 and then to 100, simple addition of numbers of one digit, subtracting numbers below 100, counting by twos, threes, fours, and fives as an introduction to multiplication, and the reverse of this process as an introduction to division. Second-grade teaching covers reading and writing numbers up to 1,000 and then to 10,000, adding and subtracting numbers of three digits, multiplying these numbers by 3, 4, and 5, and later by 6, 7, 8, and 9, dividing whole and decimal numbers by numbers from 2 to 9, exercises and problems on the four fundamental operations. In the third grade are taught addition of numbers of five or more digits, multiplication by numbers of three, four, and five digits, the multiplication table, division of whole and decimal numbers by two digits, introduction to the metric system of measures of length, weights, and capacity, the Lebanese currency up to 100 piasters, simple operations on buying, selling, and profit, and simple proportion. In the fourth and fifth grades are taught reading and writing of whole and decimal numbers, augmenting and diminishing numbers 10 and 100 times, the four fundamental operations with emphasis on mental arithmetic, divisibility by 2, 3, 4, 5, and 9 and the corresponding multiplication table, the highest common factor and lowest common multiple of two numbers only, common and decimal fractions, squaring numbers and the square root of whole numbers and fractions, a fuller study of the metric system; units of length, area, volume, and weight, density and specific gravity, the units of work and energy, compound numbers, measures of time, changing compound numbers to

PUBLIC EDUCATION

fractions, distance and speed, ratio and proportion, percentage, interest and discount, compounds and mixtures. Some notions of geometry are included in the fourth and fifth grades, including the various types of lines and angles, the circle, the compass and the protractor, the triangle and its parts, the right triangle, quadrilaterals, the areas of triangles and quadrilaterals, regular and irregular polygons. Arithmetic is continued in the four years of the higher primary school with a more extensive treatment of the primary-school topics and the addition of graphs, direct and inverse proportion, and practical applications.

Geometry is taught in each of the four years of the higher primary school. The first year is taken up with elementary geometry, finding the areas of geometrical figures, and the volumes of solids. The second year deals with the kinds of lines, angles, triangles, and quadrilaterals, their properties, their drawing, and some operations on them. The third year includes the following topics: the relationship between the circle and the straight line including the tangent, the arc, and the chord; the relationship between angles and circles, angles inside and outside the circle, arcs corresponding to an angle, quadrilaterals and polygons drawn within a circle; two tangents drawn from a point outside the circle; similar figures, triangles, and polygons. The fourth-year course is divided into plane and solid geometry. Plane geometry comprises metric relationships in the right triangle, in any triangle, and in the circle; the areas of polygons and the relationships between areas. In solid geometry are studied lines and planes, the intersection of planes, parallel and perpendicular lines and planes, solid angles, solid figures, their areas and volumes, the plane diameter, and the plane tangent to a sphere.

Algebra begins in the second year with elementary definitions, numerical values, negative numbers, the use of parentheses, reduction of terms, the four fundamental operations on one term and on many terms, equations of the first degree with one and two unknowns involving no fractions. In the third year the study of algebra is continued with fractions, their simplification and their addition, subtraction, multiplication, and division; the square roots, their simplification, and the four fundamental operations on them, changing a square root denominator to a nonsquare root denominator; equations of the first degree with one or more unknowns and with denominators; algebraic measures of vectors on a directed straight line; theory of Thales, finding the position of a point in a plane with rectangular coordinates; notions of variable, and function; the relations of $Y = ax$ and $Y = ax + b$ where a and b are numerical values. In the fourth year, study is given to equations of second degree with numerical coefficients, the relation between roots and coefficients, graphic representation of the functions $Y = ax^2$ and $Y = \dfrac{1}{x}$, and problems the solution of which leads to equations of the first or second degrees.

Object Lessons and Sciences

Object lessons begin in the first two grades with conversations about familiar objects in the environment and such topics as air, water, time and its divisions including the seasons, months, weeks, days, and reading the hours of the clock. In the third year, an elementary study is made of the body of man, of the domestic animals and the main differences among them, of common plants, of food and drink, of raw materials and the chief local manufactured products, and of the three elements of nature—air, water, and fire. These topics are reviewed and expanded in the fourth year with the addition of a study of useful and harmful animals and insects, the main families of plants, agricultural operations, types of rock, kinds of fuel, the common minerals, air, respiration, combustion, atmospheric pressure, and water, its uses and its three states. In the fifth year the subject is divided into topics in physics, chemistry, zoology, botany, and elementary notions of agriculture.

In the higher primary school this division into subjects is maintained under the headings of physics, chemistry, and natural science. The course outlines cover about twenty pages, and considerations of space make it impossible to summarize them in any detail. First-year physics consists of a brief survey of the subject. Mechanics of solids and liquids are studied in the second year, gases and heat in the third year, and light, magnetism, electricity, and sound in the fourth year—the whole having a practical bent with emphasis on the various instruments which show the application of physical laws (barometer, manometer, balance, thermometer, voltmeter, etc.).

In chemistry the first year is taken up with simple experiments on air, oxygen, hydrogen, water, carbon, with the preparation of oxygen, hydrogen, and carbonic gas, a brief study of sulphur, common salts, calcium carbonate and the main acids, bases and salts; properties of metals and alloys. In the second year systematic study is begun of physical and chemical phenomena, kinds of matter, chemical nomenclature, formulas and equations; combustion, oxygen, oxides, phosphorus, sulphur, carbon, calcium, sodium, acids and bases, iron, zinc, magnesium, water, hydrogen. In the third year some of the commonly used compounds of the elements

PUBLIC EDUCATION 437

mentioned above are studied while in the fourth year organic chemistry and the main organic compounds are taken up.

In natural science the first year is devoted to a general survey of the study of man, animals, plants, and geology. In the second year, botany and zoology are studied in greater detail, together with the classification of animals and plants. The third year is given to an extensive course in hygiene and another in geology, including the types of volcanic and sedimentary rocks, the influence of air, glaciers, rain and sea water, and living beings, the movement of the soil and earthquakes, volcanoes, geological strata and fossils, the geological ages, and finally, applications of geology to mining, public works, agriculture, and hygiene. The fourth year is given to a study of animal and plant anatomy and physiology.

Beginning with the fourth primary grade, the courses in science and mathematics may be given in either Arabic or French; schools have the option of teaching these subjects in either language and presumably in English as well.

Physical Education, Music, Drawing, Manual Arts

In physical education, the usual program for boys and girls in the primary and higher primary schools includes marching and running exercises, Swedish and gymnastic exercises, group games, ball games, dances, and corrective exercises.

Music consists of songs in Arabic and the foreign language, elements of musical notation and reading, the scales and the keys, culminating in the higher primary school in songs for one voice or in group songs with parts; recorded classical music with explanations by the teacher, the history of music and stories of the lives of famous composers, information on types of instrumental and vocal music, and types of musical instruments: string, brass, woodwind, and percussion instruments. With the training and equipment of the average Lebanese teacher it is doubtful if this program can be applied—indeed, it is the exceptional teacher that can apply it even in part.

Drawing in the primary school includes the drawing of geometrical figures, objects, animals, flowers, and some wooden or clay models. In the higher primary, three types of drawing are mentioned: artistic, decorative, and geometrical. The student is to be directed to whichever type he likes best.

The course in manual arts follows the traditional lines of paper-folding, cutting and pasting, and work in straw and clay. The girls learn to embroider, knit, weave a small rug, and do some needlework. Boys in the villages may take a course in agriculture and girls a course in home economics and elements of home nursing. The course in agriculture covers soils, irrigation, the raising of cereals, vegetables, and trees, and the care of animals. Theoretical and practical work are provided for. However, since the time allotted for drawing, manual arts, and agriculture combined is only two hours a week, and since very few if any schools have facilities for agriculture, the course is more an expression of a hope than a practical reality.

Description of Primary Schools

Of 23 government primary and higher primary schools in Lebanon visited by the American Council Commission, 10 were housed in buildings belonging to the government, 11 were in rented buildings, and 2 had been contributed by individuals or communities. Some of the government buildings, mostly those in the cities, had been built under the Ottoman regime, while others were built during the French mandate regime. In two instances in northern Lebanon modern buildings were being erected by the government. Rented buildings and some of the government buildings in the villages left much to be desired, their rooms being too small for the classes, which often were large.

The schools were poorly equipped. A few maps and charts were found in some schools, and one school had a very small laboratory. Libraries were noticed in two schools; these two libraries were being developed through the efforts of the principals and contributions from the pupils, the government sending a few books occasionally. Desks were of the fixed-seat variety designed to accommodate from two to four pupils. Often, however, they were used by from three to six or even more pupils. Most of the furniture showed signs of long use. Playing space was small, especially where the buildings are rented.

The school year of nine months begins about October 1 and lasts until the end of June. The school day consists of a morning session from 8 A.M. to 12:15 P.M., and an afternoon session from 2 to 4 P.M. Classes usually run in half-hour units.

THE TEACHERS

Schools in the cities are largely staffed with graduates of the 2 teachers colleges of Beirut—1 college exclusively for men and 1 for women. Some of the teachers—a small number—have passed the teachers qualifying examination. In the smaller towns and villages of the mountains, however, graduates of the teachers colleges are few. Here the qualifications of a teacher may vary from hardly more than the primary-school certificate to the *Baccalauréat,* Part II. The Commission found very few of the latter. There are a few teachers from Turkish days and a few teachers of Arabic who had their studies under *shaykhs.* The rest of the teachers were former students or graduates of private and foreign schools who had had one to six years of secondary or complementary education, but no professional training.

Teaching consisted almost entirely of imparting knowledge and skills to the pupils, the initiative being largely that of the teacher, pupils taking the passive, receptive role. Stress was laid on homework and the working-out of exercises. These were corrected by the teacher. The larger schools had special supervisors for maintaining discipline, keeping records of attendance, and watching that pupils went in and out of classes promptly and in an orderly manner. The pattern of teaching follows in general that of the French schools, though efficiency in its application varies with the schools. Usually the resemblance grows fainter as one moves farther out into the smaller villages.

The teachers' load in primary and higher primary schools varies from twenty-seven periods in the lower grades to twenty-four in the middle grades and twenty-one in the upper grades. A teacher is usually responsible for teaching all subjects to a primary class except when a school has one or more teachers who do not know French, in which case some adjustment is made in subject distribution. In the higher primary school the distribution of work is by subjects.

Government statistics showing the distribution of pupils in the grades were not available. The American Council Commission, however, was able to secure data on this point from 19 of the 23 schools visited, a summary of which follows.

Registration was progressively smaller in the upper grades. This is a phenomenon which was found in the public primary schools of all the six Arab countries studied. Pupils in the first grade constituted 30.4 percent of the total in the primary schools visited, while those in the sixth grade made up only 6.8 percent of the total. In the absence of adequate facts one can only speculate as to the factors bringing about such a situation. One reason is probably the incompleteness of some of the schools. Of the 19 schools studied, which it is believed constitute a fair sample, 7, which enrolled 565 pupils, were incomplete village primary schools having less than six grades. Another possible explanation is the removal of pupils to private and foreign schools which on the whole have a better

Grades	Enrollment
Primary Classes	
First	1,374
Second	909
Third	910
Fourth	593
Fifth	422
Sixth	307
Total	4,515
Higher Primary Classes	
Seventh	196
Eighth	127
Ninth	64
Total	387

reputation. A third reason is probably retardation, some examples of which the Commission was able to observe. In a check-up in a village boys school in northern Lebanon and in a girls school in Tripoli the average age of sixth-grade children was found to be 14.8 and 14.4 respectively, with a range from 12 to 17 years. Another check-up in 2 schools showed that children in the first grade were grouped into an advanced group and a retarded group. Most of the children in the retarded group usually had to spend another year in the first grade. In one school 30 out of 45 children in the first grade had been in that grade the year before. This tendency of many children to repeat the first grade is somewhat confirmed in the sharp decline in numbers between the first and second grade shown in the figures above.

The current view among the people seems to be that the government schools are surpassed in quality and efficiency by most foreign and private schools, though in the villages there may not be much to choose from. Here an occasional government school may be better than its private or foreign neighbor.

Public Primary-School Examinations

The Lebanese primary-certificate examination is given after the sixth grade at the present time but according to a new decree issued on the same day as the decree setting forth the new primary course of study, beginning with the year 1949 it is to take place at the end of the fifth

PUBLIC EDUCATION

year. The new examination system is summarized here, and reference to the current one is made only for the sake of comparison.

The public primary examination takes place once a year in June and is controlled by a committee headed by the Director General of Education, with members drawn from the public-school system. The Minister of National Education and Fine Arts, however, may appoint state officials of culture and experience to serve on the committee. The chairman makes the final selection of the questions and is responsible for their secrecy until the time of the examination and for keeping the identity of the pupils' examination papers unknown to the members of the committee.

The pupils taking the examinations are not only pupils of the public schools, but may come from private and foreign schools as well.

To be admitted to the examination, a pupil must be no less than ten years old and must present a certificate of identity and a certificate from the principal of his school that he had attended the fifth primary year in full.

Under the current system (up to 1949) the examination is written, but an oral examination also is held for both the Arabic and French language; examinations in Arabic language, history, and geography are conducted in Arabic; those of the French language and object lessons, in French; and the pupil is given the choice of answering arithmetic in Arabic or French. The new examination (beginning 1949) is to be entirely written, and all examinations are to be taken in Arabic except the foreign-language examination. Marking is on the basis of 10 for each subject. The subjects of the examination are shown in Table 77.

In Arabic composition the student writes a letter, a story, or a description. There must be three questions in history and geography, one of which involves the drawing of a map. In arithmetic at least one problem must show the method of its solution. The examination in object lessons

TABLE 77

Subjects for the Primary-Certificate Examination, Lebanon

Subject	Time Allotment	Weighting	Total Marks
Arabic composition	1 hour	3	30
Arithmetic	1 hour	2	20
Geography and history	45 minutes	2	20
Object lessons	30 minutes	1	10
Drawing for boys or sewing for girls	1 hour	1	10
Foreign-language dictation	1 hour	3	30
Total		12	120

consists of three questions to be answered briefly. In the foreign language, dictation must consist of at least ten lines and there must be three questions on the text, one of which involves comprehension and the other two grammar and vocabulary.

A pupil fails if he receives a zero in any subject or less than 2 in Arabic. In order to pass, a pupil must secure 60 out of the total of 120 possible marks. The following were the results of the public primary certificate examination in 1944–45:

	Entered	Passed	Percent Passing
Boys	2,077	999	48.1
Girls	1,046	704	67.3
Total	3,123	1,703	54.5

The Higher Primary Certificate examination is administered by a committee of public-school personnel under the chairmanship of the Director General and with competent government officials assisting when necessary. The pupil must be at least fourteen years of age, must hold the primary certificate, must pay a fee of £S3 ($1.38), and must present a certificate showing that he had attended the third and fourth years of a higher primary school.

The examination is both oral and written, and a pupil is admitted to the oral only after he has passed the written. The examination is held

TABLE 78

SUBJECTS FOR HIGHER PRIMARY CERTIFICATE EXAMINATION, LEBANON

WRITTEN EXAMINATION					ORAL EXAMINATION			
Subject	Hours	Weighting	Total Marks		Subject	Weighting	Total Marks
In the Arabic language:					*In the Arabic language:*		
Arabic composition	2	2	40		Arabic	2	40
History and geography	1	2	40		History and geography	1	20
					Civics	1	20
In the foreign language:					Physical education	1	20
French or English composition	2	2	40		Drawing or sewing	1	20
					In the foreign language:		
In Arabic or one of the two foreign languages:					French or English	2	40
Mathematics	2	3	60		*In Arabic or one of the two foreign languages:*		
Physics, chemistry, biology	2	3	60		Mathematics	2	40
					Science	2	40
Total marks			240		Total marks		240

twice a year, in June and October. The subjects of the examination and their time allotments and weighting are shown in Table 78. Papers are marked on a scale of zero to 20.

In order to pass the written examination, the pupil must receive a total of 120 marks. In both the written and oral examinations he fails if he receives a zero in any subject or less than 5 in Arabic composition and reading. In order to pass the whole examination he must receive a total of 240 marks.

Following is a tabulation of the results of the *brevet* examination for 1944–45:

	Entered	Passed	Percent
June session	360	135	37.5
October session	61	10	16.4
	421	145	34.4

The new decree prescribing the conditions of this examination, which was issued simultaneously with the new course of study on October 1, 1946, will come into effect beginning with the June session of 1953, that is, four years after the first application of the new primary-certificate examination system. In the meantime the old system for the *brevet* examination will be continued. The most important difference between the two is that of the language of the examination. While in the old system the examination in all subjects except Arabic could be taken in Arabic or French, in the new system all subjects except the foreign language, science, and mathematics, *must* be taken in Arabic, and in the latter two the student has the choice of using either Arabic, French, or English.

Secondary Education

Although the Lebanese government has no secondary schools, it acts as an examining authority and for that purpose has issued a detailed secondary course of study. The new secondary course was issued in October 1946 simultaneously with the primary course of study and is based on the latter. It is to be applied immediately after the pupils who follow the new primary course finish the fifth grade, that is, in 1949, and the first new-style secondary-school examination is to be held in 1955.

Secondary education is, as indicated in the preamble to the course, essentially different in aim and method from primary education. The aim is to train and select the youth of the country for the right orientation in matters of the mind, for carrying the major responsibilities of public life, and for enlightened specialization in the branches of higher education. Method is directed to the quality rather than the quantity of teaching, to theoretical proof more than to practical test, and to allowing time for the opening out of all man's gifts into a well-rounded personality that will assimilate the subject matter and transmute it into his own cultural existence. It has aptly been said that the ideal secondary culture is "what remains in man's make-up after he has forgotten what he learned."

In secondary education, therefore, the scientific-mathematical section will guide the select youth of Lebanon to deep insight, logical thinking, and right judgment, while the literary-philosophical section will guide them to a sensitiveness, disciplined imagination, good taste, holding in esteem the hierarchy of values and the universality of man.

THE SECONDARY PROGRAM OF STUDIES

The new secondary program of studies is given in Table 79. The distribution of periods in the first two years and the details of the syllabuses are exactly the same as those for the first two years of the higher primary school. In the third and fourth years, one-half hour is added to morals and civics and to history and geography, one hour to the foreign language, and two hours to Arabic. Correspondingly, one hour is taken from drawing and manual arts and from science, and two hours from mathematics.

As far as the details of the courses for the third and fourth years of the higher primary and the secondary schools are concerned, the difference is rather slight. In the secondary schools there is slightly more emphasis upon literature in fourth-year Arabic, and upon the reading of French authors in third- and fourth-year French. The course for French grammar is somewhat different, and grammar is reviewed in its entirety in the fourth year. In mathematics some topics are delayed to a later year and the details of solid geometry are omitted, while in science some topics in physics and chemistry are dropped. The program, uniform for all students in the first four years, is divided into literary and scientific sections in the fifth and sixth years, and into philosophy and mathematics sections in the seventh or last year.

Students may, however, select a classical-languages section in which they study Syriac, Hebrew, Latin, or Greek in addition to their regular program. Such study is planned to begin with the first year and last through the sixth year. This innovation, not yet in operation in 1946, is described hereafter.

TABLE 79
NEW PROGRAM OF STUDIES FOR SECONDARY SCHOOLS, LEBANON, 1946

FIRST TO FOURTH YEARS

Subject	1st and 2nd Years	3rd and 4th Years
In Arabic:		
Religion..................	1	1
Morals and civics.........	1½	2
Arabic...................	6	7
History and geography....	2½	3
Drawing and manual arts..	2	2
Music and singing........	1	1
Physical education........	2	2
Foreign language*........	6	6
*In Arabic or the foreign language:**		
Physics, chemistry, and biology	4	3
Mathematics..............	4	3
Total................	30	30

FIFTH AND SIXTH YEARS

Subject	Literary Section	Scientific Section
In Arabic:		
Religion and ethics............	2	2
Arabic language and literature.	8	5
History and geography.........	4	3
Drawing.......................	1	1
Music and singing.............	1	1
Physical education.............	2	2
Foreign language and literature*.........................	6	5
*In Arabic or the foreign language:**		
Physics and chemistry.........	3	6
Mathematics...................	3	5
Total.....................	30	30

SEVENTH YEAR

Subject	Philosophy Section	Mathematics Section
In Arabic:		
Religion and ethics............	2	2
Philosophy....................	7	3
History and geography.........	4	3
Physical education.............	2	2
*In the foreign language:**		
Philosophy....................	8	
*In Arabic or the foreign language:**		
Physics, chemistry, and biology	5	9
Mathematics...................	2	8
Total.....................	30	30

* French or English.

The Fifth and Sixth Years

Arabic literature.—Arabic is given in the fifth and sixth years and is entirely devoted to literature. After an introduction in general principles and a quick survey of the main periods in the history of Arabic literature, a somewhat full course is given. Literature is divided into two parts, prose and poetry, and each is taken in part in the two years. In prose are included the story and the novel, proverbs and maxims, scientific, historical, geographical writings, and travel, oratory, the *maqamat* (formalized stories in rhymed prose), moral and social "lessons," and literary criticism. Under poetry are included the categories familiar in Arabic poetry—lyric poetry, elegies, heroic poetry, philosophical and moralistic poetry, maxims, romantic poetry, Bacchic poetry, description, eulogies and diatribes, political and religious poetry. At least one selection from each of two to five poets from each of the periods is studied in each category. An extended study of three poets is made in the fifth year and of five in the sixth year. Composition involving moral, literary, and critical essays, translation, and the study of Lebanese literary figures in other languages completes the course.

Foreign languages.—French is given in the fifth and sixth years with emphasis on the evolution of the language and literature. The sixteenth and seventeenth centuries are well covered, with some attention given to the eighteenth and nineteenth. Special attention is paid to the works of Corneille, Racine, Molière, and La Fontaine among the poets, and to Voltaire, Rousseau, Bossuet, La Bruyère, and Pascal among the prose writers. Selections are studied from the nineteenth-century novelists and historians. The Orient in French literature as depicted in works by Volney, Chateaubriand, Lamartine, De Nervel, and Barrès, is discussed, and Romanticism, Realism, and Symbolism as schools of literature are defined. Essays on moral and literary topics and on literary analysis are written.

In English, a review of grammar and an outline history of English literature are studied. In the sixth year two prescribed texts, of which one is to be a Shakespeare play, are required. In both years, compositions on general topics and on literary subjects connected with the course are written.

History and geography.—The history course in the fifth year gives a general survey of the history of Lebanon from ancient times to the Mamluk period and in the sixth year extends to the middle of the nineteenth century. The European-history course includes the discovery of America, the Renaissance, the Reformation, the religious wars, the rise of Great Britain, France, the United States, the problem of Poland, and scientific discoveries and their influence on the social structure of the West.

PUBLIC EDUCATION

Fifth-year geography centers around the economic geography of the Americas. In the sixth year a detailed study is made of the economic geography of Lebanon, Syria, and Palestine, and a summary study of the economic geography of the countries of the Mediterranean basin including Iraq, Saʻudi Arabia, and Yaman.

Mathematics.—Fifth- and sixth-year mathematics includes a review of algebra, expanded study of the four fundamental operations, fractions, equations of the first and second degrees with graphic representation, and graphic solution of equations, rectangular coordinates, the parabola and the hyperbola, arithmetical and geometrical progression, compound interest, and definition and use of logarithms with 4 or 5 decimal places. A beginning of trigonometry is made in the sixth year. In geometry, the course in plane geometry begins in the fourth year and is completed in the sixth year. This is about the only important difference between the science and literary sections in the field of mathematics.

Science.—Science in the fifth and sixth years is confined to physics and chemistry. A rather extensive course in physics comprises mechanics, hydrostatics, heat, magnetism and static electricity in the fifth year, light and optics, and electricity in the sixth year. No mention is made of sound. The two-year course in chemistry comprises, aside from some general principles, the experimental study of air, oxygen and nitrogen, water and hydrogen, acids, bases and salts, sulphur and its compounds, phosphorus, carbon, silicon and their compounds, sodium, potassium, chlorine, calcium and their compounds, the three metals, iron, aluminum and copper, and their compounds. The difference between the science course for the literary and scientific sections of the sixth year is slight.

Physical education, music, drawing, and manual arts.—The courses in physical education, music, drawing, and manual arts are about the same as those for the higher primary course, with the exception that no courses in agriculture for boys and home economics for girls are given.

The Year of Philosophy and Mathematics

The syllabus for the philosophy and mathematics sections—the seventh year—lists the same subjects for both: religion and morals, philosophy, history and geography, science, mathematics, and physical education. The basic difference is that while the philosophy section takes fifteen hours of philosophy, five hours of science, and two hours of mathematics, the mathematics section takes six hours of philosophy, nine hours of science, and eight hours of mathematics. Certain of the courses are common, or almost so, including history and geography, biology, cosmography, Arabic philosophy, logic and ethics. The main difference is that the mathematics section takes a wider program of physics, chemistry, and mathematics, while only the philosophy section takes psychology and metaphysics.

Philosophy.—The course in Arabic philosophy starts with a brief survey of the intellectual development in Muslim countries, and is accompanied by a similar survey of Greek philosophy: Socrates, Plato, Aristotle, Plotinus, and Neoplatonism. This is followed by the study of the translation movement into Arabic and the role of the Christian Jacobites and Nestorians and of the Sabeans in this movement. A survey is made of the introduction and development among the Arabs of medicine, pharmacy, chemistry, mathematics, music, and logic. The interaction of culture in the 'Abbasid period is touched upon, together with its effects on Muslim thought in the growth of Muslim scholasticism, the new schools, especially the Mu'tazilite,[1] the reaction to the schools (Ash'ari[2] and Ghazzali[2]) and mysticism in Islam. Muslim philosophy in the East is then studied through Ikhwan al-Safa[3] and Ibn Sina[2] (Avicenna), and in Andalusia through Ibn Tufayl and Ibn Rushd[2] (Averroes). To these is added Ibn Khaldun and his sociology. Finally, the effects of Muslim philosophy on medieval Europe are studied including the translation of philosophic works into Hebrew and Latin by Maimonides and Albertus Magnus, and the effect of Muslim philosophy upon the theology of Saint Thomas Aquinas. This extensive program is accompanied by selected readings from eleven Arab philosophers. The whole is studied in Arabic.

Philosophy studied in the foreign language includes psychology, metaphysics, logic, and ethics. In psychology the treatment of the subject is typically French: After a discussion of preliminary topics, definitions, and methods, the course takes up (1) cognitive life including sensation, perception, the conscious and the unconscious, memory, association of ideas, imagination, conception, judgment, reasoning, symbols, and language; (2) affective life: pleasure and pain, tendencies, emotions, and passions; (3) active life: tropisms, irritability, instinct, the will, and liberty. An appendix to the course of study treats of spirituality and immortality of the soul. The whole is intertwined with the various theories of Descartes, Freud, Janet, Jean-Paul Sartre, Henri Bergson, H. Delacroix, and William James, as well as materialist and spiritualist theories.

[1] A school of comparatively liberal thinkers which grew up in Baghdad beginning with the ninth century A.D.
[2] Prominent Arab scholars and philosophers who lived between the seventh and fourteenth centuries.
[3] A group of thinkers during the 'Abbassid period, best known for their essays on philosophical subjects.

The study of metaphysics deals with (1) the problem of criticism, reason, and the origin and value of rational principles, the idea of truth; (2) rational cosmology: realism, idealism, space and time, matter, and life, with careful distinction drawn between the scientific and metaphysical points of view in the last three items; (3) theodicy, the origin of religion, the knowledge of God through experience as expounded in the theories of Hindu, Muslim, and Christian mystics, reasons for believing in the existence of God, the nature of God and His attributes, relation of the world to God: monism, pantheism, dualism, creationism, providence, liberty, and evil.

Logic deals with science and method. The distinction between science and the sciences is made, the scientific spirit, objectivity, the contributions of the Arabs to science, classification of the sciences, general mental processes (intuition, deduction, induction, analogy, analysis, and synthesis) are discussed. Under method are included the various types of sciences, their methods and their roles: mathematics, experimental sciences including history and sociology, and the theories of Tarde, Durkheim, and other contemporary writers in sociology.

Ethics is divided into theoretical and practical. Under theoretical are treated the various ethical doctrines, the rational bases of ethics (conscience, the good, duty, responsibility, social sanction, law, justice, charity, and equality). Under practical ethics are included: (1) duties of man to himself; (2) ethics of the family including theories on the origin and function of the family, children, and population and a critical treatment of the Malthusian theory, birth control, eugenics, racism, and the "crime of abortion"; (3) social ethics; property, capital, profit, work, division of labor, relation between capital and labor with liberal and socialist theories and directed economy; (4) civic and political ethics: political society, nation, country, state, government, the three powers of government, origin of political society and of power, civic and political rights and duties; (5) ethics and international relations: humanity.

History and geography.—In history, Lebanon from the middle of the nineteenth century to the present is studied in detail, together with the following topics in modern history: the unification of Germany and Italy, the American states, evolution of social ideas, and commerce and industry.

The economic geography of Great Britain, Germany, Russia, Iran, India, China, Indo-China, and Japan is studied.

Mathematics.—Mathematics for the philosophy section consists of a supplement to algebra in which a review is made of trigonometry already studied, with the addition of a study of the derivatives, speed as derived from space in its relation to time, and of cosmography which deals briefly with the Copernican system, the sun, the planets, the earth, the moon, comets and shooting stars, stars and nebulae, and the Milky Way.

The program in physics and chemistry is a shorter version of that given to the mathematics section which will be described later. However, the two sections take the same program in biology. This consists of a study of the anatomy and physiology of man, the anatomy and physiology of plants, and hygiene and prevention of disease. In this last, a brief study is made of infectious diseases, including malaria, smallpox, cerebral meningitis, pulmonary tuberculosis, typhoid and paratyphoid fevers, and amoebic dysentery. The topics of immunity, vaccines, and serums are touched upon.

Although no hours are specifically allotted to the teaching of a foreign language, a syllabus is set out for English précis work and for advanced composition on general, abstract, and literary topics. In literature, one play by Shakespeare, one prose work, and an anthology of poetry are studied. This program is identical for both sections.

Only a summary of the courses in physics, chemistry, and mathematics, therefore, which distinguish the mathematics section from that of philosophy, need be given here.

The course in physics comprises certain special topics in mechanics, sound, light and electricity, and ends with a study of the constitution of matter. In chemistry, elements of qualitative and quantitative (volumetric and gravimetric) analysis and of physical chemistry are given, but most of the course is devoted to a rather extensive treatment of organic chemistry.

The course in mathematics comprises arithmetic, algebra, trigonometry, geometry, mechanics, and cosmography (astronomy). In arithmetic some basic theories are taken and a more extended treatment is given to such topics as divisibility, highest common factor and lowest common multiple, ratio and proportion, common and decimal fractions, the metric system, the square of a whole or a fractional number, and relative and absolute error. The course in algebra begins with a treatment of whole, fractional, negative and positive indices, arithmetical and geometrical progression, and compound interest. The main part of the course, however, deals with analytical geometry. Trigonometry reviews what was taken in the sixth year, and completes plane trigonometry. Geometry comprises moderately detailed treatments of the transformation of figures (translation, rotation, similitude, inversion, projection), conics, and descriptive geometry. Mechanics takes up kinetics (rectilinear, curvilinear, and circular motions) and the simple motion of a solid body; to this is added a fairly extensive treatment of statics. The course in cosmography is the same as that given in the philosophy section.

PUBLIC EDUCATION

THE CLASSICAL-LANGUAGES SECTION

This is a novelty in the Lebanese course. As stated in the official course of study, this program is meant to "help bring up scholars in languages and archeology, for it is obvious that thorough study of the Arabic language requires a thorough study of ancient Semitic languages and especially Syriac and Hebrew, just as the science of archeology cannot be mastered except by him who prepares for it by studying Greek and Latin." Courses for these four languages are outlined, extending over the first six years of the secondary school.

The course for each of the classical languages is planned to start with the alphabet (except Latin) and the teaching of reading. Grammar and literature are to go side by side after that, with a study of masterpieces of poetry and prose.

The classical-languages section is still largely a project for the future. It is not indicated where the time will be found to include it in the studies of those who choose it. Nor is it known how much of a demand there will be for it. It is, however, an interesting experiment, unique in Lebanon and the Arab world.

Public Secondary-School or Baccalauréat Examinations

The *baccalauréat* examinations of the Lebanese government are held in parts: Part I, at the end of the sixth year of the secondary school; and Part II, at the end of the seventh year of the secondary school. Each is held in two sessions, in June and July, and in October of each year. The examinations are held in much the same way as the primary examinations previously described, except that the Minister of National Education himself is chairman of the examining committee which is made up of professors of higher institutions, with the help of competent government officials and teachers in public secondary schools, if necessary.

The student must be at least sixteen years of age and must present his school record for the fifth and sixth years in order to be allowed to sit for Part I, and for the seventh year in order to be allowed to sit for Part II. A fee of £L4 (about $1.80) is charged for Part I, and £L10 (about $4.55) for Part II.

The details of the examinations are given in Table 80. A study of the table shows that the difference between one section and another is a matter of emphasis rather than an important difference in subject matter, except for special papers in physics and chemistry for the scientific section (Part I), translation from a classical language for the classical-languages section (Part I), and a special paper in philosophy for the philosophy section (Part II). For example, the literary section of Part I has a weighting

TABLE 80
Subjects for Lebanese Baccalauréat Examinations: Part I

Subject	Literary Section Hours	Weighting	Total Marks	Scientific Section Hours	Weighting	Total Marks	Classical-Languages Section Hours	Weighting	Total Marks
Written examinations:									
Arabic composition	3	3	60	3	2	40	3	2	40
Mathematics	3	2	40	3	3	60	...	...	...
Arabic literary criticism, or translation, or translation from Latin	3	2	40	...	...	...	...	...	...
French or English composition	3	3	60	3	2	40	3	2	40
Translations from and to a classical language	...	...	...	...	...	...	3	3	60
Physics and chemistry	...	...	...	3	3	60	...	...	..
Oral examinations:									
Explanation of an Arabic text	...	3	60	...	2	40	...	2	40
History and geography	...	2	40	...	1	20	...	3	60
Mathematics	...	1	20	...	3	60	...	1	20
Physics and chemistry	...	1	20	...	3	60	...	...	...
Explanation of a French or English text	...	3	60	...	1	20	...	2	40
Explanation of a classical language text	...	...	...	...	...	...	...	3	60
Total	...	20	400	...	20	400	...	18	360

TABLE 80—Continued
Subjects for Lebanese Baccalauréat Examinations: Part II

Subject	Philosophy Section Hours	Weighting	Total Marks	Mathematics Section Hours	Weighting	Total Marks
Written examinations:						
Arabic composition in philosophy	4	3	60	3	2	40
Physics, chemistry, and biology	3	2	40	...	...	...
Physics and chemistry	...	...	...	4	3	60
Mathematics	...	...	...	4	3	60
French or English composition in philosophy	4	3	60	...	...	...
Oral examinations:						
Explanation of Arabic text in philosophy	...	2	40	...	1	20
History and geography	...	2	40	...	2	40
Physics and chemistry	...	1	20	...	3	60
Mathematics	...	1	20	...	3	60
Biology and hygiene	...	2	40	...	1	20
Philosophy in French or English	...	1	20	...	...	...
Explanation of French or English text in philosophy	...	2	40	...	1	20
Total	...	19	380	...	19	380

of 3 on Arabic and foreign language compositions, but a weighting of only 2 on mathematics. Inversely, the scientific section has a weighting of 3 on mathematics and science, but a weighting of only 2 on Arabic and foreign-language composition.

A candidate for the *baccalauréat* certificate is given a choice of an additional examination in modern foreign language, for which only the marks that are in excess of the passing mark of 50 percent are credited to his total marks.

In Arabic literature, Arabic philosophy, philosophy in the foreign language, mathematics, physics and chemistry, three questions in each are asked, out of which the student answers only one. In mathematics and science, however, an additional required question is set.

Papers or oral examinations are marked on the basis of zero to 20. In order to pass, a student must not receive a zero in any subject, and must get no less than 5 marks out of 20 in Arabic. The student must receive at least one-half of the possible marks in the written examination before he is allowed to enter the oral examination. He must aggregate at least 50 percent of the total marks in written and oral examinations before he finally passes and becomes eligible for the certificate. Students failing the oral examination in June may present themselves for oral examination in October. If they fail again, they must pass both the written and the oral examinations in subsequent years. A student gets a mention of "good" if he has received 14 out of 20 marks, and of "very good" if he has received 16 out of 20. A certificate signed by the Minister of National Education is given the student who passes the first part of the *baccalauréat* examination, while the diploma of the second part of the *baccalauréat* is signed by the President of the Republic.

The following are the results of the *baccalauréat* examinations in 1944–45 for the June and October sessions combined:

	Entered	Passed	Percent
Part I			
Literary section	329	188	57.1
Scientific section	437	249	57.0
Total	766	437	57.0
Part II			
Philosophy section	380	228	60.0
Mathematics section	96	60	62.5
Total	476	288	60.5

The Education of Primary Teachers

The education of primary-school teachers is undertaken in 2 rather small schools, 1 for men and 1 for women. The school for men is housed in a rented house, while that for women shares the same premises with a girls primary school which serves as its practice school. The 2 schools have essentially the same program of two years for which students are eligible after having secured their *brevet*. Students who have passed Part I

TABLE 81

Program of Studies for Preparation of Primary-School Teachers, Lebanon, 1946

Subject	Periods per Week — 1st Year	Periods per Week — 2nd Year
Psychology*	2	...
Ethics and civics*	2	...
Professional ethics and school administration*	...	1
Education*	...	1
Education†	...	1
Practice teaching*	1	3
Practice teaching†	1	3
Mathematics*	3	2
Science*	3	3
Arabic literature	5	2
French literature	5	2
History†	}3	1
Geography†		1
Sociology†	...	1
Manual arts	...	2
Drawing	2	2
Music	1	1
Physical education	1	1
Hygiene	...	1
Agriculture or home economics	1	2
Total	30	30

* Language of instruction is French.
† Language of instruction is Arabic.

or Part II of the *baccalauréat* examinations are also eligible. Admission is by a competitive examination. Holders of the *baccalauréat* certificate, Part II, are given an allowance of 20 marks, while those who have passed Part I are allowed 10 marks. No fees are charged. Allowances of £L90 (almost $41) a month are given to better students, and 44 out of a total of 85 students in both schools received such scholarships in 1945–46. It is hoped to grant scholarships to all out-of-town students in order to attract students from the villages.

The program of studies is shown in Table 81. Some of the courses are given in Arabic, others in French, while some, such as education and practice teaching, are conducted in both French and Arabic.

The course is designed to prepare teachers who could, if need be, teach some subjects in French. Practice teaching takes place in both the first and second years and is supervised by the teachers of education. A summer course of one month is held for practical work and some lectures in agriculture and physical education. After graduating, students may enter the second year of the agricultural course in the School of Arts and Crafts, and upon graduation be appointed as teachers with an addition of £L15 ($6.82) per month to their salary.

The final examination for each year of the normal school is laid down by the Ministry of Education. It is also the qualifying examination for noncertificated teachers. The examination is in two parts corresponding to each year of study. Part I consists of Arabic literature, French literature, history and geography, ethics and civics, mathematics, psychology, and science. The examinations in Arabic, history and geography, and ethics and civics are conducted in Arabic; the others, in French. Part II comprises examinations in education (in Arabic), education (in French), history and geography (in Arabic), professional ethics (in French), and Arabic literature, French literature, and science and hygiene (in French). Three practical examinations are also held in which a candidate teaches one lesson in Arabic, one in French and one in physical education. In addition to the normal-school students, 20 candidates took the qualifying examination, Part I, and 12 took Part II in 1944–45. A new appointee has to stay on probation for at least one year before he is confirmed as a full-fledged teacher.

In 1945–46 there were 33 students in the first year and 17 in the second year of the normal school for men, and 22 in the first year and 13 in the second year in the normal school for women. It is evident that in view of the large number of primary schools now being opened, not enough teachers are being prepared.

The School of Arts and Crafts

The School of Arts and Crafts at Beirut was founded during the Ottoman regime, and, as was usual at that time, started as an orphanage. It occupies a large building erected by the Turkish authorities and is well equipped with workshops, particularly in the mechanical section. Students who hold the primary-school certificate, the certificate of the first *bac-*

calauréat, or the *brevet,* are admitted on the basis of the results of a competitive examination which is both written and oral. The written examination comprises French, Arabic, arithmetic, handwriting, and drawing, while the oral examination comprises geometry, geography, history, biology, and object lessons. The School had a total of 317 students in 1945–46, of whom 265 were boarders. Instruction and board were free, and day students received free lunch.

The School has three main courses: a mechanical course of four years' duration, a weaving course of two years' duration, and an agricultural course which has been lengthened from two to three years. The mechanical and weaving sections admit holders of the primary-school certificate, and the agricultural section admits holders of the *brevet* or first *baccalauréat.*

The mechanical section gives instruction in the first two years in carpentry, blacksmithing, and fitting. Students get practical and theoretical instruction in these three specialties. Specialization begins in the third year, and the student may take one of the following seven specialties: auto mechanics, turning, blacksmithing, welding, foundry, woodcarving, and electricity. The latter includes radio, telegraph, and telephone. In addition, students receive throughout the course instruction in the following "theoretical" courses: arithmetic, geometry, algebra, physics, chemistry, general and applied mechanics, industrial drawing, technology as applied to machines, French, Arabic, history, geography, and industrial bookkeeping.

Instruction in the mechanical section is divided almost equally between theory and shopwork, except for the last year when shopwork is predominant. In each of the first two years approximately 600 hours of shopwork are divided among carpentry, blacksmithing, and fitting. In the third year each subject of specialization is allowed 800 hours, while in the fourth year the total shopwork for each specialization is 1,100 hours. Laboratory work is given in both physics and chemistry. The mechanical section is the most popular among the students, accounting for 246 out of a total of 317 students.

In the weaving section, the program is less theoretical and more practical. In the first year about 50 hours are given to theoretical work in weaving, while in the second year the total of theoretical work is 150 hours. Shopwork receives 1,100 hours in each of the two years. Only 38 students were registered in the course in 1945–46.

The agricultural section, giving a two-year course, was only two years old in 1946. At that time 33 students were registered, and the course was

Above: Some of the students in the preparatory department of the American University of Beirut, some in native costumes, some in Western clothes. These youths come from various parts of the Arabian peninsula
Below: Students approaching Rockefeller Hall of the American University of Beirut. This building, erected in 1910, was the gift of John D. Rockefeller, Sr.

Above: This view of the campus of the American University of Beirut shows the natural beauties of its location. At the left is the observatory, and at the right College Hall
Below: American School for Boys, Tripoli, Lebanon. Upper classmen in a tennis match. Outdoor sports are prominent in this school: all students participate in some sport

PUBLIC EDUCATION

being reorganized into a three-year course. Some teachers and graduates of the normal schools have been encouraged to enter the second year in order to become teachers in the rural schools. The school has no land for practical work.

Students of all three sections take an examination given by the School at the end of their study. Graduates of the School of Arts and Crafts are in demand, and are employed by the army, aviation workshops, the railroads, and electrical plants.

Chapter 26

FRENCH SCHOOLS

*A*MONG FOREIGN schools in Lebanon, French schools are the most numerous, in 1942–43 numbering 273 schools out of a total of 326. These had a total student registration of 39,513 out of 46,726 in all foreign institutions during that year.[1]

French missionary and educational activities have a long history in Lebanon. Late in the sixteenth and early in the seventeenth centuries Franciscan, Capucin, and Jesuit missionaries came to Syria and began to establish missionary posts in various parts of the country. The Jesuits were perhaps the most active. They established their first mission in Aleppo in 1628, which was followed by other missions in Damascus, Tripoli, Sidon, and 'Anturah. The latter, founded in 1636, still has a well-known college which will be described later. The fact that Lebanon had a large community of Maronites, who had centuries before acknowledged the authority of the Church of Rome, facilitated the entry of Catholic missions to Lebanon, and connection with the Maronite community is intimate up to the present day.

The early missionaries usually established a small school at each of their stations. They taught the rudiments of reading, writing, and arithmetic, catechism, and liturgy, occasionally teaching also French or Latin. At the same time some of the brighter pupils were sent to the Oriental Seminary in Rome where they took advanced studies in philosophy and theology, and sometimes became well-known scholars. At one time Louis XIV, upon the advice of his minister Colbert, brought at state expense oriental Christian children to Paris to study in the Collège Louis-le-Grand which was then under the direction of the Jesuits. It was these activities that eventually led to schisms among the oriental churches resulting in the establishment of a Catholic branch of each of the existing oriental churches.

The activities of Catholic missions were mainly missionary in the first

[1] See Table 74, p. 424.

two centuries, and it was not until the nineteenth century that educational work of an advanced sort began to be given. The college at 'Anturah was perhaps the first to be established along modern lines. It was founded in 1834 under the Lazarist order, which had taken over the station upon the closing of the Jesuit order in the middle of the eighteenth century. Not long afterward the Jesuits established a Catholic seminary (1846) and a secondary school (1855) at Ghazir to the northeast of Beirut in the same general region as 'Anturah. This seminary was later moved to Beirut and formed the nucleus of the present secondary school, the Oriental Seminary, and the Faculty of Theology at the French Jesuit Université Saint-Joseph. The University itself was founded in 1875. Other missionary orders also began to come in, and their activities increased particularly when the French mandate over Syria and Lebanon was established after World War I. Feeling that French missionary activity was giving a colored impression of France abroad and that it did not express the true spirit of modern France, some French laymen established a lay mission (Mission Laïque) which opened a school for boys, and a school for girls in Beirut in 1909. Other similar schools were later established in Damascus, Aleppo, and Tartus, all in Syria. The French mandatary government, anxious to spread the French language and culture and to bring up a generation which would sympathize with France and its position in Syria and Lebanon, encouraged French missionary activities to a large extent and gave subsidies to the large number of orders active in Syria and Lebanon. Among these may be cited the Jesuits, who have the largest number of schools, the Lazarists, the Capucins, the Franciscans, the Christian Brothers, and the Frères Maristes. Among the orders of nuns may be cited les Filles de la Charité, les Dames de Nazareth, les Sœurs de la Sainte Famille, les Sœurs de la Charité, les Sœurs de Besançon, and the Franciscan nuns of Mary. All these orders had schools, not only in the large cities such as Beirut and Tripoli, but some, especially the Jesuits, had (and still have) elementary schools even in remote villages. These schools did not come under the authority of the Lebanese government Department of Education (later Ministry of Education). They communicated directly with the Office of the French Adviser in the Haut Commissariat Français. Indeed, the Lebanese government had no authority over foreign schools in the days of the mandate. During World War II, financial resources from the mother country were cut off. French schools, therefore, had to rely very largely upon their income from tuition and upon some help from the Œuvres Françaises, a semiofficial organization which tried to keep up French cultural work abroad. This was still the situation at the time of the visit of the American Council Commission to Lebanon.

It was not possible for the Commission to visit even one example from each type of French schools in Lebanon. Aside from the schools of the Mission Laïque and the Collège Protestant Français, however, the pattern of the French missionary schools is substantially the same. The success of their work is shown by the large number of Lebanese men and women, especially Catholics, who speak French fluently, and some of whom think, speak, and write in French even more easily than they do in their native Arabic.

The large French schools usually have primary and secondary departments combined on the same premises so that the primary grades are actually preparatory to the secondary, or *lycée,* sections, in much the same way as is the general practice in France. They are usually fee-charging institutions, the fees ranging from £L100 ($45) to £L350 ($160) for tuition, on an ascending scale from the lowest primary to the highest secondary grade. Boarding fees may range between £L600 and £L750 ($275 to $344). Some of the orders, however, maintain special primary schools for poor children where instruction is free. This separation of the poor children from those who can pay seems to be a fairly prevalent practice.

The staffs of the schools are usually both French and Lebanese, the proportion varying. The number of Frenchmen may constitute as many as one-half and sometimes as low as one-third. A large part of the staff of missionary schools consists of monks or nuns who receive no pay for their services and cost only their maintenance. The rest are laymen, usually Lebanese. In spite of this, fees are usually higher than those charged in native schools. Some of the money seems to be spent on the schools for poor children, as well as on maintaining the work of the mission. Some missions have been known to save some money for future expansion of, and building programs for, the schools. At one time the Jesuits had their own normal school for the training of teachers for their village schools. This, however, has been discontinued.

The schools visited by the Commission were housed, on the whole, in good buildings, with spacious quarters, usually large classrooms, and more or less adequate yard-space for recreation periods, though not enough provision had been made for playgrounds for athletic activities. The better schools were usually well equipped with libraries, and some of them had laboratories and natural history museums. Boarding facilities were usually in large dormitories. Naturally, village schools were not so well equipped.

On the whole the schools enjoy great prestige, particularly among the Christians and those of higher economic status. This is especially true of the schools maintained by the nuns for the education of girls. About seven-eighths of the students in French schools are Christian. Out of a total of 39,513 students in French schools in 1942–43, 34,758 were Christian, 2,507 were Muslim, 1,544 were Jews, 631 were Druze, 73 were of other religions. Among the Christian students the majority were Catholic.

Program of Studies

The program of studies is primarily that used in France, preparing students for the French certificate of primary studies, the French *brevet*, or the French *baccalauréat*. As the schools must prepare a certain section of their students for the Lebanese examinations as well, certain modifications are introduced to adapt it for that purpose. The difference lies mainly in Arabic language, Lebanese and Arab history and geography, and in the introduction of a course in Arabic philosophy. For the rest the two programs are largely similar. Indeed, the comparison of the new secondary courses of study of the Lebanese government with the French program of secondary education shows great similarity, and some subjects, such as logic and ethics, are identical. In the days of the mandate, the Education Department of the Haut Commissariat issued a magazine, the *Bulletin de l'Enseignement*, in which it published regularly the decrees and *arrêtés* of the French Minister of National Education dealing with courses of study, examinations, and other school matters, so as to keep the French schools informed on developments in France. As educational practices were gradually modified in France, the French schools in Lebanon and Syria followed suit as a matter of course.

Some of the schools take children at the early age of four or five and put them in a *classe enfantine*. As they begin to learn the letters of the alphabet, they promote them to a prefirst grade (called the twelfth class —*douzième*). The formal first grade is the *onzième*. The primary school consists of five grades divided into three courses, the preparatory course in the first grade, the elementary in the second and third grades (*dixième* and *neuvième*), and the middle course (*cours moyen*) in the fourth and fifth grades (*huitième* and *septième*). After this, a student in good standing may pass to the secondary grades of his own school without having to pass a government examination. Pupils coming from other schools are examined by the school they are entering, for the purpose of placing them in the appropriate grade. The secondary course is of seven years, divided into a first cycle of grades one to four (*sixième* to *troisième*), and a second cycle, the first two years of which (*seconde* and *première*) lead to the *baccalauréat* examination, first part, and the third year (*classes de philosophie et de mathématique*) leads to the second part of the *baccalauréat* examination.

The French program followed is generally that of *Série B*, which is the program without classical languages and with some emphasis upon foreign languages and the sciences. The only exception to this is the pro-

TABLE 82

Distribution of Periods in Two Grades of the Lycée Français of the Mission Laïque, Beirut, 1946

Fifth Primary Grade		Fourth Secondary Year	
Subject	Hours per Week	Subject	Hours per Week
Arabic	8	Arabic	8
Moral and civic education	1½	Morals and civics	1
French language	6½	French	6
General history and geography	2	Foreign language	4
Arithmetic and the metric system	4	History and geography	3
Object lessons	2	Mathematics and drawing	4
Drawing and manual arts	2	Physiology and natural sciences	3
Physical education	1½	Physical education	1
Singing	1		
Total	28½	Total	30

gram of the Collège Secondaire of the Jesuit Université Saint-Joseph which follows *Série A*, including Latin and a foreign language, but no Greek. The same school, however, also gives the other courses of *Série B*. The foreign language taught is usually English and is begun in the first secondary grade (*sixième*), but it may also be German, Italian, or some other modern language. It is not necessary to give full details of the French program here. Adaptation to the local needs of Lebanon is well exemplified by the Lebanese program of studies. As far as the French schools themselves are concerned, however, this differs from school to school. Table 82 shows an example of the adaptation worked out in one primary and one secondary class.

It is interesting to note that the differences between complementary classes (the last two years of the higher primary school) and the lower secondary classes have been virtually obliterated, and the complementary classes are often referred to as secondary. More than one school refers to the first cycle of the secondary school as ending with the *brevet* examination, which originally was the examination ending the higher primary studies. This is in accord with the new tendencies in French education, but seems to have been easier to apply owing to the much less complicated situation in Lebanon, where class distinctions are not as marked and the tradition of classical studies has not developed.

A number of schools such as the schools of the Christian Brothers, in Beirut and Tripoli, and the Lycée Français and others maintain a commercial course beyond the fourth secondary year which extends from two to three years and leads to the higher diploma of commerce, and a certificate of bookkeeping. Table 83 gives the program given at the school of the Christian Brothers.

TABLE 83

PROGRAM OF STUDIES FOR THE COMMERCIAL SECTION, LYCÉE FRANÇAIS, TRIPOLI, LEBANON, 1946

Subject	Length of Period (Minutes)	1st Grade	2nd Grade	3rd Grade
French	45	6	6	6
Commerce and bookkeeping	75	6	6	6
Commercial and financial mathematics	60	6	6	6
Arabic	60	6	6	6
English	60	5	5	5
Economic geography and history of commerce	60	3	3	3
Merchandising	60	2	2	2
Stenography	30	6	(*)	(*)
Typewriting	30	(*)	(*)	(*)
Commercial law	20	1	1	1
Political economy	20	1	1	1

* Practice as much as possible out of class.

Students are supposed to practice outside school hours, especially on Thursday afternoons. Some of the better students do the work in two years. Others take an additional year in order to prepare for the *baccalauréat* examinations.

Methods

Methods of administration and teaching are the same as those prevailing in France. Beside the director of the school, there is usually a supervisor *(surveillant)* who has charge of the discipline, attendance of students, and the entrance and leaving of classes. The major subjects usually have directors of studies; this is particularly true of the two languages, French and Arabic. Their job is to see that teaching in their subjects is properly planned and executed. The teaching is essentially subject-matter teaching. Point by point, and topic by topic, the subject matter is systematically imparted to the students, reviewed and reviewed again, particularly in the teaching of languages and of arithmetic. Extensive use is made of exercises and homework. Much attention is given to penmanship and to the neatness of notebooks. Notebooks are collected almost daily, graded by the teacher (usually on the basis of 1 to 10), and returned to the children, after which the children take them home. Parents are constantly requested to take an interest in the marks the children receive and in the work they are doing, and are entreated to encourage diligence and to spur them on to better work. About once a month the average of the marks is taken and the students' standing in the class is worked out.

School examinations take place usually three or four times a year, and the results are made known to the parents through the student's report card. This is sent to the parents for their inspection, and they are sometimes asked to sign it in order to make sure that they have examined it. Irregular attendance, tardiness, and negligence result in lowering the marks and standing of the student. In some schools what is known as the *cahier d'honneur* is kept in each class. In this notebook the best achievement by any student in the class and in every topic studied is registered. By the end of the year this book would represent the ground covered by the class and the highest achievements attained.

Great attention is given to the teaching of French. The program is comparable to that given in France, and essentially the same standards of achievement are required. The fact that a large number of students pass the French primary and *baccalauréat* examinations is the best testimony that such a result is achieved. Instruction in French begins with the *classe enfantine*. Gradually the children build up a speaking vocabulary and learn to recognize the letters of the alphabet. Regular reading begins usually with the first grade *(onzième)*. Almost everything is taught in French except the lessons in Arabic and in local geography and history. Conversation in the classes and on the school grounds is in French. In some schools the speaking of French on the school grounds is obligatory and the speaking of Arabic is an offense. Thus, in both formal and informal ways, in work as in play, the students cannot help absorbing French from the very atmosphere of the schools. Before they are graduated from secondary school, students learn not only the basic structure of the language and acquire a good reading knowledge of it, but also speak it fluently and are able to write essays in French in a good style. Some of the outstanding students have been known to write French poetry and some artistic pieces of prose.

FRENCH SCHOOLS

The French schools are usually accused of giving less attention to Arabic, and their graduates are said to be less at home in the knowledge of Arabic literature and composition than in French. The accusation is made that the nature of the French examinations tends to encourage this weakness, for as long as a student receives the sum total of marks required for the examinations, he can pass, provided he does not receive a zero in any subject. Theoretically it is possible, therefore, for a pupil to get 1 mark out of 20 in Arabic and still pass. This criticism, however, is too general to apply to all schools. Some of the better schools maintain a high standard of Arabic and have produced a number of Arab poets and writers. Much the same criticism is made with regard to the history and geography of Lebanon and the Arab world. The students are said to know more about the history, geography, and literature of France than of their own country.

While the laboratories of some of the schools are fairly well equipped they do not seem to be adequately used. The Commission did not see a laboratory class in any of the French schools they visited, although this might have been an accident. The apparatus did not look as if it was regularly used. Better use is made of charts, especially for the study of zoology, botany, geology, and human anatomy and hygiene. The texts in use, except for the subjects taught in Arabic or for local subjects, are the same as those used in France. When the supply of books was cut off during the war, special editions were printed by the Œuvres Françaises in Cairo and Beirut and distributed to the schools.

In the French Catholic missionary schools, discipline is very strict. The students are constantly supervised, and boarders are allowed to go out only with their parent or guardians. Only their parents or persons authorized by the parents may visit them at school. The school may take an outing about once a week, usually on Sundays, under the supervision of the director and teachers. No student is allowed to bring into the school any book, magazine, pamphlet, or paper except the books directly in use at the school. In this way an attempt is made to shut out outside influences as much as possible. A long timetable keeps the day students at school from early morning until the late afternoon. The atmosphere of the Catholic schools is decidedly religious. Students are required to attend Mass every morning. Classes usually begin and end with prayers, and Sunday Mass and religious teaching are obligatory. Irreligion, insubordination, immorality, or even habitual laziness are reasons for expulsion.

The following daily timetable for boarding and day students at 'Anturah, although perhaps not universal, shows the type of daily disposition of work current in the Catholic missionary schools:

Hour	Activity — Boarding Students	Day Students
5:00 A.M.	Get up	...
5:30	Mass	...
6:00	Study period	...
7:00	Breakfast	Obligatory Mass
7:15	Recess	
7:30	Class	Class
9:00	Recess	Recess
9:15	Study period	Study period
9:45	Class	Class
10:45	Recess	Recess
11:00	Study period	Study period
11:55		Lunch period
12:00	Lunch	
12:30 P.M.	Recess	
1:20		Assembly in the court yard
1:30*	Study period	Study period
2:00	Class	Class
3:00	Recess	Recess
3:15	Study period	Study period
4:15	Recess and *goûter*	Recess and *goûter*
4:45	Study period, classes	
5:45		Middle and lower grade students go home
7:25	Evening prayer in chapel, dinner	Secondary students go home
8:00	Required study period for *baccalauréat* classes	

* Outings on Thursdays, 1:30 to 4:15, and on Sundays, 1:30 to 4:30.

Other French schools, such as those of the Christian Brothers, maintain a somewhat shorter day for the day pupils, starting at 7:15 or 7:30 and ending about 4:30 or 5:00. It is evident that the daily timetable is so long that the students are kept busy throughout the day and that supervision of their activities is constant and unwavering. Attendance on Thursdays and Sundays is in the morning only. On Sundays students attend Mass and also attend classes in religion and, in some schools, classes in drawing and singing.

A different disciplinary atmosphere prevails in the non-Catholic French schools, such as those of the Mission Laïque, and the French Protestant missions. In the words of the director of the French Lycée for boys in Beirut, "Our methods of discipline are inspired by a reasoned indulgence toward those faults which are due more to spontaneity than to premeditation. We repudiate brutal repression because it kindles the fire which has to be quenched, and we find ourselves satisfied with a frank and active supervision which finds nothing to note beyond a laziness proper to certain adolescents. Moreover we know, because we have experienced it for a long time, that it is clumsy and futile to wish to suppress temperament and character. The good method consists rather in foretelling their excessive manifestations, and trying to soften them by a persevering effort at persuasion."

Examinations

French schools prepare their students for at least two types of examinations: French and Lebanese. They also prepare for examinations of the French Delegation which has succeeded the old Haut Commissariat. The new Lebanese examinations have already been described.[2] The French examinations are the same as those given in France; they are those for the Certificate of Primary Studies, for the *Brevet Élémentaire,* and for the *Baccalauréat,* Parts I and II. The *baccalauréat* examination is usually based upon *Série B* which offers a choice of a foreign language—English, German, Italian, Spanish, Russian, Armenian, Turkish, Persian, modern Hebrew, or modern Greek. A modified program of examinations has been set down by the French Delegation which gives more attention to local needs. In this examination Arabic is required of all Arabic-speaking students. French Delegation examinations are given in various centers, not only in Lebanon and Syria, but also in Jerusalem, Haifa, Baghdad, and Larnaca in Cyprus. The Commission was not able to secure information on the latest results of these examinations.

Description of Some French Schools

Having given a generalized account of French education in Lebanon, it may be worthwhile to present short descriptions of some of the schools visited by the American Council Commission which would show how this education works in practice and some of the features peculiar to each school.

'Anturah College is perhaps the oldest existing French school in Lebanon. It occupies a beautiful site in the village of the same name in the heart of the Maronite district of Kasruwan to the northeast of Beirut. Occupied for the first time in 1656 by the Jesuits, the site was taken over by the Lazarists in 1775 after the abolition of the Jesuit order. The present school was founded in 1834 upon the request of the French consul, and later received the patronage of Guizot, the famous French Minister of Education, who gave the school some money for scholarships. It has been carrying on its work constantly for the last 114 years, except for temporary stoppages during the disturbances of 1860 in Lebanon and during World War I. During this long history it has produced many prominent men, some of whom play an important role in Lebanese life today.

The school admits pupils at the age of seven, starting with the equiva-

[2] See pp. 440–43, and 451–53.

lent of the second grade *(dixième)*, and continuing through the courses of philosophy and mathematics. It is essentially a boarding school and had 380 boarders in 1945–46. It has a large building which contains a theater seating 450 persons. The school year begins about October 1, and ends about the end of June. The classes attended by members of the Commission showed a high order of work in French, Arabic, and mathematics. The school is well equipped with laboratories for physics and chemistry, mainly for demonstration work. It has a large art room, and a music room in which individual lessons in piano and violin are offered at special rates. Music lessons, however, are said to be not too popular, mainly because they are not included in the official examinations. The teaching of English is started in the sixth grade and is continued until graduation. Students are given the average of their marks every month in the large theater in the presence of the whole school. They include marks in conduct and industry, and outstanding students have their names inscribed on the honor roll. The program of study is worked out in detail. The title of each composition for every class is indicated in the handbook which each student receives at the beginning of the year. These compositions fall into three categories: those in French have to do with philosophy, mathematics, geography, history, literature, physics, chemistry, biology, and religious instruction, and *explication de textes;* those in Arabic are mainly on the Arabic language, history and geography of Syria and Lebanon, and translation and literary criticism; a third set is in English covering the various phases of English work. A detailed calendar for every month is also included in the student's handbook and informs him about workdays and holidays, dates compositions are due, examinations, handing out of marks, religious retreats and communions, and various other activities of the school. The College is staffed with nine Lazarist brothers, two Maronite brothers, and twenty lay teachers. It has a Scout troop of about 100 scouts, and a dramatic society. A motion picture is shown to the students every Sunday evening. It has an active association of former students which publishes an attractive annual dealing with the school and its activities throughout the year. The annual is published largely in French, but it also has some Arabic articles and poems. Contributions are by professors, students, and alumni.

The Christian Brothers, popularly known as *"les Frères,"* have two large colleges, one in Tripoli founded in 1881, and one in Beirut founded in 1889. In addition they have six other schools in these two cities, and in Brummana, a Lebanese village and resort to the east of Beirut. These schools had approximately 4,000 boys in the year 1945–46. They are fee-charging schools except for one school in Tripoli and another in Beirut for poor children. The fee-charging schools pay for themselves. The free schools are paid for partly with money given by the French Delegation and partly with funds saved by the other schools. The Collège de-la-Sainte Famille in Tripoli, visited by the Commission, occupies a large site, and had 888 students ranging from the five-year-olds in the *classe enfantine* to the students in the classes of philosophy, mathematics, and commerce. There were 145 students who were boarders, drawn from Lebanon and Syria, and from some of the British and French colonies in Asia and Africa. The pupils in the Collège were distributed as follows: 507 in the primary school, 352 in the secondary school, and 29 in the commercial course. In addition an annex had 250 students, and another annex, 145. Both annexes were primary schools. The school year begins on October 11 and ends July 1. The school was staffed by thirteen Christian Brothers and thirty-three lay teachers. All the Brothers have French university degrees.

The large college of the Christian Brothers in Beirut, the Collège Français du Sacré Cœur, also ranges from the *classe enfantine* to the classes of philosophy, mathematics, and commerce. In 1945–46 it had 695 pupils in the primary school, 634 in the secondary school, and 49 in the commercial course, making a total of 1,378, of whom 110 were boarders. Three other schools exist in Beirut, the best known of which is the Collège La Salle. The school is staffed by twenty Brothers, all but seven of whom act as directors of studies, and by seventy-three lay teachers. It is housed in a large building which includes a spacious and beautiful chapel. In addition, it has an auditorium seating 360, laboratories of physics and chemistry, and a biology museum with an extensive herbarium. The school also has a good library of French, English, and Arabic books. It has a Scout troop affiliated with the Scouts of France, and a youth organization for its students known as Jeunesse Étudiante Chrétienne (Student Christian Youth). In addition, it has French and Arabic literary societies. The French society publishes an annual magazine with contributions by teachers and pupils. The Collège also has an alumni association that maintains a meeting place with provisions for games, reading rooms, and even a bar for soft drinks. The schools of the Christian Brothers pride themselves on the results in the public examinations, both French and Lebanese. The results are made public as part of the campaign to gain students. Discipline is strict, and the work day is quite long. Attendance is required even on Sunday mornings.

The schools of the Mission Laïque Française represent a different orientation from the usual French missionary school, and have a distinctly more liberal and free atmosphere. The Lycée Français de Garçons occupies a large modern building on the Damascus road in the southern part of Beirut. In 1946 it had a total enrollment of 950 students; the Lycée des Jeunes Filles, in another quarter of the city, had 630 students. The boys Lycée takes students from the age of four. It consists of a kindergarten of two years combined with a primary school of five years, a secondary school of seven years, and a commercial section. The girls Lycée has the same organization, but has no commercial classes or classes in philosophy or mathematics. Girls wishing to prepare for the second part of the *baccalauréat* come to the boys Lycée. There were 239 girls in attendance in the boys Lycée during the year. The Mission Laïque not only has schools in Syria, in Damascus, Aleppo, and Tartus (the latter coeducational), but it also has important schools in other parts of the Near East, in Cairo, Heliopolis near Cairo, Alexandria, Mansurah, and one *lycée* in Teheran.

The boys Lycée in Beirut had sixty teachers of whom thirty-three were French; of the remaining twenty-seven of Lebanese nationality, seventeen taught Arabic. The girls Lycée had thirty-six teachers of whom eighteen were French; and of the remaining eighteen of Lebanese nationality, ten taught Arabic.

These schools have a reputation for excellent teaching of Arabic, as well as of French. In order to achieve this purpose, students are classified according to their ability in Arabic and French. Considerably more freedom is also given to the students, and the Laïque schools pride themselves on the spirit of critical insight which they try to impart to their students. "Our methods of teaching," says the director of the boys school in a memorandum for the Commission, "are methods of thorough scrutiny. Far from wishing to anesthetize the critical sense of their pupils, our professors, themselves jealous for the independence of spirit so dear to the French university, search for it and sharpen it. Our teaching is not inspired by any system of intellectual conquest or by any mysticism. Our grown-up students can testify to the scruples which animate us in the exposition of all points of view and our frequent appeals to that control of thought which makes for intellectual honesty. . . ." The schools try to keep in touch with the parents, and invite their collaboration by visits to the school. The parents are kept in touch also through the homework given to their children (*cahiers de textes*) and by the marks and observations which are inscribed in their *carnets de notes*. Monthly examinations are held for the primary classes, and trimestrial examinations for the secondary classes. These are also reported to the parents, together with the remarks of the professors and of the disciplinary council with regard to the aptitudes, diligence, and progress of the student.

The Collège Protestant Français for girls in Beirut, founded in 1927, was the only French Protestant school visited by the Commission. It is situated in the heart of Beirut in a building that formerly belonged to German nuns, but was given to the Protestant French mission several years after World War I. Like the others, it consists of a primary and a secondary school, and has students from the age of three upward. In 1945–46 there was a total of 546 students. Among these the largest single group of students was the Muslim, followed by the Jewish, Greek Orthodox, Catholic, and Protestant. It had a staff of thirty-nine teachers of whom nineteen are French, four European, and sixteen Lebanese. The school is one of the more popular schools for girls in Beirut and is imbued with a progressive spirit. Considerable freedom is allowed the girls. In the primary school the work is organized on the basis of centers of interest, one for each month. The school accepts boys up to the age of ten.

The Jesuits are educationally the most active of the Catholic orders in Syria and Lebanon. Having re-established themselves in Lebanon in 1831, they opened a small school, and, as already mentioned, followed it with a seminary, and a secondary school at Ghazir. This was followed by the establishment of the Université Saint-Joseph, in 1875, and a large number of schools in various parts of Syria and Lebanon. It was not possible to secure recent data on the number of Jesuit schools in Syria and Lebanon, but it is known that in 1928 Jesuit schools numbered 145, with a total of 10,890 students. Of these 9,000 were in Lebanon, making up almost 10 percent of the total number of students in the schools of all kinds in that country. Of these schools, 48 were for girls.

The crowning work of the Jesuit mission in Syria is the Université Saint-Joseph which was founded partly to create leadership among the Christians of Lebanon, and partly to offset the influence and teaching of the Syrian Protestant College, which is now the American University of Beirut.

Starting with a Faculty of Theology and the secondary school, the Université added a Faculty of Medicine in 1883, and the School of Pharmacy in 1889. Later a School of Dentistry and a School for Midwives were opened. The Oriental Faculty for the teaching of oriental languages, history, and archeology was opened in 1902; it has since reduced its program and is today called the Institute of Oriental Letters. The Institute has a large library, the Bibliothèque Orientale. In 1913, the French

School of Law and the French School of Engineering were added. The Université also has under its administration the Catholic Press, first founded in 1847, and the observatory at Ksara on the Buqaʻ plain between the Lebanon and the Anti-Lebanon ranges.

The Université is administered by a rector who is a Jesuit priest. Each

TABLE 84

NUMBER OF STUDENTS AND OF FACULTY MEMBERS, UNIVERSITÉ SAINT-JOSEPH, LEBANON, 1945–46

School and Subject	Enrollment	Professors
Faculty of Theology		
Theology	48	
Philosophy	28	
Total	76	13
Institute of Oriental Letters	129*	11
Law School		
Law	570	
Political science	180	
Total	750	24
Engineering School		
Engineers	138	
Licence	49	
Total	187	31
Faculty of Medicine		
Medicine	344	
Pharmacy	57	
Dentistry	76	
Mechanical dentistry	6	
Applied chemistry	11	
Midwifery	24	
Visiting nurses	31	
P.C.B. preparatory	36	
Total	585	44
GRAND TOTAL	1,727	123

* Of the 129 students in the Institute of Oriental Letters, 49 were registered students and 80 were free auditors.

Faculty of the institution is also headed by a Jesuit priest. The teaching personnel is comprised of Jesuit priests, other religious men, and lay teachers. Some of the Jesuit Fathers in the past, as in the present, have been scholars of international standing, particularly in the field of oriental studies.

The Université maintains 3 primary schools in the city of Beirut which had a total registration of 741 pupils and twenty-nine teachers in 1945–46. Instruction is free for most of the students. The Collège Secondaire

FRENCH SCHOOLS

of the Université had a staff of ninety-nine and a student body of 1,131. This school was not visited by the Commission due to the fact that the classes were not open to inspection by visitors.

The number of teaching personnel and of students in the higher schools and Faculties of the Université are shown in Table 84.

The majority of the student body belong to the various Catholic oriental rites, as well as to the Latin church, but there are a large number belonging to the orthodox rites, Protestants, Jews, and the various Muslim sects.

With regard to nationality, eight of the Near Eastern countries are represented, thirteen countries of Europe, six of Central and South America, and two of Africa.

The Faculty of Medicine gives a course of six years exclusive of the preparatory year of P.C.B. The preparatory year consists of courses in physics, chemistry, geology, and animal, cellular, and plant biology. Each of these except geology is accompanied by laboratory work. The program of medicine naturally follows French lines.

The first and second years are given to elementary physiology, histology, embryology, biological chemistry, and biological physics with laboratory work in each subject. One difference from the American course is that the physics laboratory is limited to ten demonstrations each year. Clinical training in surgery and medicine begins with the first year and attains its full proportions in the second, third, and fourth years. In the fifth year it is divided among dermatology, pediatrics, obstetrics, and contagious diseases.

In the third year, medico-surgical anatomy, operative medicine, and pathological anatomy are given, together with bacteriology, experimental medicine, parasitology, radiology, and surgical and medical pathology.

The studies of the fourth year comprise more bacteriology, obstetrics, parasitology, surgical and medical pathology, as well as ophthalmology, otorhinolaryngology, pharmacology, and therapeutics.

The fifth year comprises medical ethics, dermatology, syphilology, hygiene, legal medicine, pediatrics, pharmacology, physiotherapy, stomatology, and therapeutics.

The sixth year is for internship.

Admission is granted to holders of secondary-school certificates after a competitive examination in physics, chemistry, and biology. Students from other countries of the Near East who hold a secondary-school certificate also are admitted to the examination, but are on a different priority list.

The course leads to the French state degree of Doctor of Medicine, after a final examination by an official French government jury. The students practice in the French hospital and, by agreement with the Lebanese health authorities, in the government hospitals and clinics. The Faculty is well supplied with laboratories. Connected with the Faculty of Medicine are four Institutes: the Physiotherapy Institute, Antirabic Institute, Institute of Bacteriological Research, and the Institute of Chemical Research.

The School of Pharmacy admits students after the same kind of competitive examination as for entrance to the School of Medicine, but requires a preliminary year of practical work in a pharmacy, after which a student must pass an examination known as the Examination for the Validation of the Practice Period (*stage*). The course in pharmacy is of four years, the first consisting of preparatory courses in general physics and chemistry, botany, and animal and plant biology, including laboratory work in chemistry and physics.

The second-year course consists of human anatomy and physiology, analytical chemistry, botany, hydrology, materia medica, micrography, pharmacy, and toxicology, with laboratory work in general and analytical chemistry, physics, and pharmacy.

Third-year work comprises human anatomy and physiology, biology, botany, analytical and biological chemistry, hydrology, materia medica, parasitology and toxicology, with laboratory work in biology, general biological and analytical chemistry, micrography, parasitology, and pharmacy.

The fourth-year course includes biological chemistry, professional ethics, hydrology, hygiene, materia medica, parsitology, pharmacy, and toxicology, with laboratory work in bacteriology, biology, chemistry, micrography, parasitology, and pharmacy.

The probationary examinations toward graduation are given by an official jury of the French government beginning with the end of the third year. Students passing these examinations are awarded the French State Diploma of Pharmacist.

Admission requirements for the School of Dentistry are the same as for the Faculty of Medicine. Two courses in dentistry are given: a two-year course for dental mechanics working under dentists, ending in a certificate; and a course of four years which, after examination by the School, leads to the degree of Doctor of Dental Surgery of the French Faculty of Medicine in Beirut.

The first-year course for the preparation of dentists comprises general

FRENCH SCHOOLS

anatomy, dental anatomy, embryology, dental histology, oral pathology, dental terminology, dental therapeutics, hygiene, and operative dentistry.

The second-year course includes physiochemistry, topographic anatomy, anesthesia, prosthetic dentistry, operative dentistry, dental surgery, oral pathology, stomatology, and physiology.

The third year includes bacteriology, histology, metallurgy, materia medica, dental bridges, dental pathology, general and internal pathology, oral pathology, and stomatology.

The fourth-year course comprises pathological anatomy, maxillo-facial surgery, prosthetics, dental equipment and clients, clinical courses and conferences, electrology, materia medica and therapeutics, orthodontia, dental pathology, and radiology.

Clinical work takes place regularly from 9:00 to 11:30 A.M., every day throughout the four years, and for the fourth year another period of special work takes place after five o'clock. There is also work in hospitals and prisons.

The course in midwifery admits only oriental women students and daughters of European families living in the Near East. They must be at least eighteen years of age and must pass an examination designed to test their knowledge of French. The course is of two years' duration, and comprises in the first year, anatomy, hygiene, and care of the sick.

The second year covers pathology, puericulture, obstetrics, and professional ethics. The course leads to a diploma of the School of Midwifery.

The course for visiting nurses admits students under the same conditions as the School of Midwifery. Students who have had that course may be admitted directly to the second year. The course is of two years' duration—eight months for the first year, and nine months for the second. It comprises courses in medicine, surgery, hygiene, prophylaxy, hygiene of the mother, and nursing of the child. Courses are also given in the battle against social scourges, sanitary organization, and professional, social, urban, and rural hygiene. Rudiments of sociology, political economy, labor legislation, pedagogy, history and functioning of the social services, professional ethics, domestic economy, and physical education are also given. Practice work in the wards takes place five afternoons a week. The course ends with a diploma of Visiting Nurse from the French Faculty of Medicine in Beirut.

The Faculty of Medicine has a special library with about 500 volumes for the use of students, and 10,000 volumes for the use of professors. Before the war it received about 75 periodicals.

CERTIFICATES OF HIGHER STUDIES

Recently the Université Saint-Joseph began to offer courses for preparing students for certificates of higher studies leading to the degree of *Licence ès Sciences*. Courses are offered in physical chemistry, biology, and geology. There is also an extensive course of two years in applied chemistry.

The School of Law comprises an undergraduate course of three years, an Institute of Lebanese Law, and the Center of Social Studies and of Preparation for Careers. Students admitted to the School must hold the *baccalauréat,* or an official secondary-school certificate in the case of countries other than Syria and Lebanon. Students are admitted by competitive examination which includes a written examination of three hours on a subject of general culture designed to show the ability of the student to think and write in French. Two oral examinations, one in philosophy, and one in history and geography, are also required from those who pass the written examination.

The undergraduate course includes in its first year civil law, Roman law, history of French law, political economy, constitutional law, and an introduction to juridical studies. In the second year are given civil law, administrative law, penal law and penal procedure, political economy, and Roman law. Studies of the third and final year are civil law, commercial law, civil procedure, private international law, public finance, and financial legislation, and one of the seven following courses: Muslim law, comparative law, social legislation, social science, public international law, maritime law, and ways and means of execution.

Examinations are held by a special jury at the end of each of the three years. Each examination is both written and oral. The degree of bachelor is given at the end of the second year. The *Licence ès Droit* is given at the end of the third year. Both are French state degrees. Examinations are held in June and October. Failure in the written examination eliminates the student from the oral.

In order to secure a doctorate, a student must acquire at least two diplomas and write a thesis. The diplomas may be secured in private law, public law, and political economy. The diplomas are granted after an oral examination of an hour's duration before a jury of four examiners. The time for study for each diploma usually takes a year or more. The thesis is written under the supervision of a *président de thèse* who approves it. The student has to defend it before a jury of three members for an hour and a half.

The Institute of Lebanese Law includes studies in public and administrative law and in financial law in the first year, on professional status, and on legal codes of obligations and procedures in the second year. These courses may be taken during the undergraduate studies for the *licence*. They lead to a diploma countersigned by the Lebanese Minister of National Education.

The Center of Social Studies and of Preparation for Careers is divided into two sections: The judicial section gives courses in judicial instruction, criminology, special penal law, and exercises in judicial technique; the administrative section gives courses in public law, social science and social legislation, Lebanese administrative law, public finance and Lebanese fiscal legislation, personal status, land laws, history of local public law, economics, and geography of the Levant states. The courses in each of these two sections are of one year's duration and lead to a special diploma after an oral examination. The School of Law is under the jurisdiction of the University of Lyons in France, which exercises control over the studies, appointing a director chosen from the law professors of that University.

The School of Engineering is also a subsidiary of the University of Lyons, which controls its studies by appointing a director from among its professors. Admission is based upon: (1) the Certificate of Higher Studies in Mathematics, Physics, and Chemistry (M.P.C.) or in General Mathematics, or (2) a competitive examination for holders of the French, Lebanese, or old Syrian *baccalauréat* in Philosophy or Mathematics, or equivalent official certificates from the neighboring countries. The course is of four years' duration. Specialization begins in the fourth year. Two choices are offered: civil engineering and industrial engineering. The course ends with a Diploma of the French School of Engineering in Beirut, on which are inscribed the words "Industrial Engineering," or "Civil Engineering," as the case may be.

Special courses for Certificate of Higher Studies based on the *baccalauréat* in preparation for the *Licence ès Sciences* were opened in 1942 for the duration of the war. The students could prepare for a certificate in mathematics, physics, and chemistry (M.P.C.) as well as certificates in each of the following: general mathematics, general physics, general chemistry, industrial physics, and applied mechanics. The first two certificates admit the student to the School of Engineering without examination.

The Institute of Oriental Letters gives courses to all those interested who hold the *baccalauréat*. Lectures are also open to the public without reference to certificates or diplomas. Courses change from year to year. The Institute offers courses in three departments: (1) Semitic Philology and Literature, including Arabic philology, history of Arabic literature, institutions of the Arab peoples, Islamic sociology, and history of Arabic philosophy. In some years, courses in the Aramaic languages (biblical Aramaic, ancient Aramaic epigraphy), and Syriac language and history are given; (2) archeology and history of Syria and Phoenicia; (3) Armenian language and culture. Completion of studies ends in an examination for certificates comparable to the certificates of the *Licence ès Lettres* in a French Faculty of Letters. The Université, however, is not entitled to grant this degree, and those students who receive four certificates are granted a Diploma of Oriental Studies of the Université.

The Institute publishes an Arabic review, *al-Mashriq,* first published in 1898, and a series of monographs known as *Les Mélanges de l'Université Saint-Joseph* which are studies in Semitics, archeology, history, and philology of the Near East.

French education and French culture have deep and long-established roots in Lebanon. They have exerted a tremendous influence on the thoughts, attitudes, and habits of the Lebanese, particularly the Catholics. When Lebanon attained its independence in 1943, the French government attempted to insure the ascendance of French cultural influence by proposing a cultural treaty which would have given it almost a monopoly on cultural and educational influence in Lebanon. This was, with slight modifications, the same treaty which was offered to Syria and rejected by it. It proved to be also unacceptable to the Lebanese government. The French, having lost Lebanon, are still exerting great efforts through the Œuvres Françaises and through their schools to maintain their cultural influence. There is no doubt that in this they have the support of a section of the Christian population which has been brought up along French lines and is loath to see that influence weaken. Already, however, a perceptible shift toward English and a demand for it are noticeable. Nevertheless, if what has happened in Egypt in the last century is any measure, French cultural influence will probably remain strong for a long time to come.

Chapter 27

AMERICAN AND BRITISH SCHOOLS

American Institutions

AMERICAN missionary connection with Syria began in 1822 with the arrival in Beirut of two American Protestant missionaries. By 1825 they had opened a small school for boys enrolling about 85 pupils. The American Press, which had been founded in Malta about the same time, was transferred to Beirut in 1831 and began publishing books in Arabic. A school for girls was started shortly before 1830 by the wife of one of the missionaries, Dr. Ely Smith, and a building for it, the first one of its kind in Syria, was erected on the grounds of the present mission. This school continued until the death of Mrs. Smith in 1843. Later another missionary school for girls was opened in the home of another missionary, and did not close until 1854 when that missionary family returned to America. In 1860 the foundations of the present American School for Girls were laid; it has been in operation ever since, continuing the work of its two predecessors.

In the meantime, another boys school was founded in 'Abay which acquired considerable fame as a school giving a modern type of secondary education and preparing Protestant ministers. In this school, books were prepared in Arabic by one of the greatest American missionaries who ever came to Syria, Dr. Cornelius V. A. Van Dyck. Having become a master of Arabic, he soon produced books in geography, algebra, geometry, logarithms, plane and spherical trigonometry, navigation, and biology. These books were printed at the American Press and remained standard works almost until the end of the century. It was Doctors Van Dyck and Ely Smith who worked for more than a decade on the translation of the Bible into Arabic. After the death of Ely Smith, Dr. Van Dyck brought the work to completion with the assistance of a great Syrian scholar of the time, Butrus Bustani.

It was not until after the troubles of 1860, however, that the firm foundations of American and British Protestant missionary work were laid and began to flourish and expand. After that, schools began to spring up, mainly in Lebanon, but also in Syria: in Sidon and the surrounding villages, in Tripoli and its outlying districts, in the Alawite Mountains, and in the northern and eastern part of Syria.[1] At one time in the late nineteenth century the number of schools was 123. Great stress was laid upon education of girls, and in a number of places, girls schools preceded those for boys. Many of the village schools were coeducational. Boarding schools were established in some of the larger localities. Among these can be counted the American schools for girls in Beirut, Tripoli, and Sidon, and the boys schools in Tripoli, Sidon, Suq al-Gharb, and Shuwayr,[2] and the preparatory school of the American University of Beirut, which took the place of the 'Abay seminary closed in 1878.

It was also after 1860 that the need was felt by the American Presbyterian Mission for a college to help prepare youth for leadership in the life of Syria and the Near East. The mission therefore entrusted to one of its prominent members, Dr. Daniel Bliss, the task of preparing the road for the foundation of an American college. After appeals were made in England, Scotland, and America, Dr. Bliss succeeded in opening the first college class in 1866, preparatory classes having been opened in 1863. The college was named the Syrian Protestant College.

The following year a medical course was started. From the very beginning it was decided to have the College outside the Mission with a separate board of trustees. The College operated under a charter granted by the legislature of the state of New York in 1863. The preparatory school was started in 1870, and fully organized in 1880. The School of Pharmacy was founded in 1872, the School of Commerce in 1900, the School of Nursing in 1905, and the School of Dentistry in 1910. The last mentioned was discontinued in 1939. In 1920 the charter of the College was amended, and the institution thereafter was named the American University of Beirut. In 1926 the French *Section Secondaire* was organized, and in 1929 an Institute of Music was established. In 1936 International College was transferred from Izmir in Turkey and became affiliated with the University. A year later a course in agriculture was begun, and within the last two years a complete course in engineering has been organized as part of the School of Arts and Sciences. The University became a coeducational institution in the year 1921–22. It is now a nondenominational institution.

[1] Syria is here used to include Lebanon which in the early nineteenth century had not yet had the clear-cut boundaries it acquired after 1860.
[2] This school was first started by the Scottish Mission and was later transferred to the American Presbyterian Mission.

AMERICAN AND BRITISH SCHOOLS

Finally the Syrian Mission of the Board of Foreign Missions of the Presbyterian Church of North America established the American Junior College for Women in 1924. Its buildings now stand not far from the site of the American University of Beirut on the promontory known as Ras-Beirut.

After World War I, with the growth of French schools, the establishment of many native schools, and the demand for French education which made easier entry to government jobs, American schools in the villages, though not in the larger cities, began to dwindle. In 1945–46 they numbered only 26, enrolling 1,902 pupils. Almost all the village schools have been transferred since 1939 from the Mission to the Evangelical Synod of Syria. The Mission contributes only a small sum toward their maintenance. Two of the well-known Mission secondary schools for boys, those at Suq al-Gharb and Shuwayr, have been closed. The village elementary schools are now under the control of the education committee of the Syrian Evangelical Synod, although the government permits for their direction are still in the name of the Presbyterian Mission. Education was formerly provided by them free of charge, but financial stringency has dictated that small fees be charged the students. In many places they are under the direction of the Protestant minister, and provide partial support for him. In other places they are conducted by one or more teachers. They are almost all coeducational. The two or three that were visited by the American Council Commission left much to be desired, although in one place the girls and boys seemed to be quite advanced in both Arabic and English.

The main educational work of the American Mission in Lebanon as distinct from the American University of Beirut is carried on in its boarding secondary schools which usually include elementary grades as well. These comprise girls schools in each of Beirut, Tripoli, and Sidon, and schools for boys in the last two cities. These occupy well-built and generally well-lighted buildings. They are usually well supplied with libraries as well as with other equipment. All 5 schools were visited by the Commission of the American Council on Education. At the time of the visit each of the schools had an American principal and a few American teachers while the rest of the staff were Syrian and Lebanese. For the higher classes they are generally, although not always, graduates of the American University of Beirut, while for the lower classes they are the products of the American high schools, or individuals who have not finished their college work at the University. Almost all the American members of the staff are college or university graduates.

Program of Studies

The program of studies is distributed over eleven grades, six in the elementary school and five in the high school. The program laid down in 1940 is in process of modification. At first these schools started English in the fourth or fifth grade but started French from the first grade. With the withdrawal of the French from Lebanon that arrangement is being gradually reversed. English starts in the first grade, and French begins in the fourth. The program of studies given in Table 85 shows this transition as witnessed by the fact that no French was given in the first grade in 1945–46, but was still being given in the second and third grades; and while English was begun in the first grade during that year, it was not given in the second grade.

TABLE 85

ELEMENTARY- AND HIGH-SCHOOL PROGRAMS OF STUDIES, AMERICAN PRESBYTERIAN MISSION SCHOOLS, LEBANON, 1945–46

Subject	1st Grade	2nd Grade	3rd Grade	4th Grade	5th Grade	6th Grade
Elementary program:						
Arabic	5	5	5	5	5	5
Arithmetic	5	5	5	4	4	4
English	2½	...	3	5	5	6
French	...	2½	4	5	4	4
Correlated studies: religion, social and nature studies, agriculture, hygiene, elementary science, history, geography, drawing, music, games, handwork	10	10	6	6	6	4
Study and games	...	...	...	...	2	2
Total	22½	22½	23	25	26	25

Subject	7th Grade	8th Grade	9th Grade	10th Grade	11th Grade
High-school program:					
Arabic	4	4	4	3	3
Mathematics: arithmetic, algebra, geometry	4	4	4	4	4
English	4	3	4	4	3
French	4	4	3	3	3
History and geography (in Arabic and English)	3	4	3	3	3
Religion (in Arabic and English)	2	2	2	2	2
Science (in French and English)	2	2	2	3	5
Music	...	...	1	1	...
Art	1	1	1	...	...
Athletics	...	...	...	1	1
Bookkeeping	...	...	1	1	1
Penmanship	1	1	...	...	...
Total	25	25	25	25	25

Most of the American schools receiving students from other schools where no English is taught have a special class for the teaching of English in which unclassified students are registered; and later they are distributed among the various classes if they make satisfactory progress in their study of English.

The program just outlined reflects clearly the difficulties under which American schools labored during the days of the French mandate. As Americans they naturally wanted to teach English well and to follow more or less American methods in education. On the other hand the presence of France in the country as a mandatary power, the importance of French types of examinations which led to government employment, and the demand of the parents that their children should learn French made it inevitable that the program of the American schools should be adapted to that situation. Moreover, the country being an Arab country, and Arabic being the mother-tongue of the children, it was desirable that, especially in the elementary schools, Arabic should be the medium of instruction and that due care should be taken in teaching it both in the elementary and secondary schools. The program of the American schools was, in actual fact, therefore, a compromise. In their attempt to satisfy these three demands, these schools went so far as to start the teaching of English three or four years after starting the teaching of the French language. Had they not done so, they might have found themselves handicapped and missed a great many of their clientele. They admittedly could not maintain the same standards in French as the French or Lebanese schools, but they—at least the good ones—managed to teach all three languages with a fair measure of proficiency. In their care for Arabic, American schools have largely escaped the criticism leveled against the French schools.

Considerable reliance is placed on the discretion of the teacher who in most cases is given a wide choice in the use of books and methods. The methods of discipline in American schools are also much freer than elsewhere. Not only is there a freer relationship between teacher and student, but students enjoy a great deal of freedom in their daily rounds in and out of school. Boarding students are allowed to leave the grounds at somewhat frequent specified times and on their own responsibility. They are not required to be accompanied by parents or guardians. Censorship of their correspondence, books, magazines, and papers is not even thought of. On the contrary students are encouraged to read their own books and magazines. Chapel attendance and religious teaching seem to be compulsory in most, if not all, mission schools.

Description of American Schools

The American School for Girls in Beirut is the oldest of the existing American institutions in the country, having been started about 1830 and with two interruptions continued to the present day.

The School consists of a kindergarten, elementary school, and a high school, plus a special class in English for unclassified students. In 1945–46 it had 373 pupils, of whom 60 were boarders. The boarding department has been in operation since 1862. Tuition fees range from £L60 to £L220 (approximately $27 to $100). Boarding fees are £L700 ($318). The School is self-supporting except for the salary of the principal. The Mission provides the building. The School has for a long time drawn students from various countries, and during 1945–46 had students from Lebanon, Syria, Iraq, Palestine, Iran, and Turkey. Instruction is in Arabic up to the eighth grade; thereafter most subjects are taught in English. Forty-five percent of the girls are Christian and an equal percentage Muslim. The remaining 10 percent are Jews. The School is of the academic college-preparatory type, and most of the graduates go to the American Junior College for Women. Indeed, the first classes of that College were started in the American School for Girls in 1924 so that the College may be considered as an outgrowth of the School. Extracurricular activities include a Girl Reserves, a choir, and a student society called the Loyal League. The School does not prepare directly for government examinations. Like the other American schools, it started the teaching of French from the kindergarten and first grade, but delayed the teaching of English until the fifth grade. This plan is now being gradually changed and informal work in English was begun in 1945 both in the kindergarten and first grade. It is planned to delay the teaching of French until the fifth grade.

The American School for Girls in Tripoli was founded in 1872 and for a long time was the only boarding school for girls serving northern Lebanon and Syria. It consists of a kindergarten, an elementary school, and a high school. In 1945–46 it had 356 pupils, of whom 60 were boys. The boys are admitted in the kindergarten and the first two grades, after which they are transferred to the Boys School. Tuition fees are £L70–£L220 (approximately $27–$100) and boarding fees are £L550 ($250).

The school is staffed with fifteen full-time and four part-time teachers. It had no principal, but was under the same direction as the other American school, the Tripoli Boys School. Instruction in the elementary and first secondary grades is in Arabic, shifts partially to English in the eighth and ninth grades, and is entirely in English in the last two grades. English is now begun informally in the kindergarten, and a visit to the first grade showed that most of the conversation in the class was being done in very simple English helped by some Arabic. Arabic reading is started in the advanced kindergarten group. Of the 17 graduates of the high school of the previous year, 6 entered the American Junior College for Women in Beirut, 2 entered the Nursing School of the American University of Beirut, 1 was married; there was no information about the other 8. The School occupies its own building, erected in 1928.

The Tripoli Boys School is under the same administration as that of the girls school. It occupies a fine site on the hill adjoining old Tripoli. The buildings were erected in 1912. The School had 343 students in 1945–46, of whom 116 were boarders. Fees are the same as those in the girls school. The School comprises an elementary school of six years, and a high school of five years, and accepts students not only from Tripoli, but from the surrounding districts of northern Lebanon and Syria. Fifty percent of the students are Greek Orthodox, 35 percent are Muslims, and 15 percent are Protestants or Catholics. It was staffed by fifteen full-time and two part-time teachers, of whom two were women. Four of the teachers had university degrees as compared with two in the girls school. The rest were men who had not finished their studies at the American University of Beirut or who were graduates of the Near East School of Theology in Beirut, holders of the French *baccalauréat,* and, the largest group, high-school graduates. The staff at the girls school had been similarly prepared, with the addition of graduates of the American Junior College for Women (eight), and graduates of the British-Syrian Training College in Beirut (two). The Boys School was founded in 1909, thirty-seven years after the girls school.

The American School for Girls in Sidon was founded in 1862 and now occupies a good site on the outskirts of that city. It is composed of a kindergarten, an elementary school, and a high school. In 1945–46 it had 238 students, of whom about 70 were boarders. Tuition fees ranged between £L80 to £L250 (approximately $36 to $114), and boarding fees were £L550 ($250). All girls in the last two years of the School must be boarders. The School is making a determined effort to teach home economics to all the girls. This is done by reducing the program of mathematics and replacing science with household chemistry and dietetics. Beginning with the seventh grade, about five to six periods each week are given to home economics. This program comprises sewing and cooking each year with the addition of family life, child care, dietetics, household chemistry, and similar subjects distributed over the various years. The

School has a small home-economics laboratory, sewing room, child-care room, a cooking laboratory, and a household-chemistry laboratory. It occupies a set of buildings so designed as to enable it to follow the "house" system. There are six houses, each occupying a floor. A "house" accommodates 12 girls of various ages under the supervision of a teacher who lives in the house. The girls do all the housework by dividing it among themselves and changing tasks every two weeks. While some would be in charge of cooking, others would take care of the cleaning. Each group is headed by an eleventh-grade girl. Light chores are given to the younger girls. Provisions are issued to each house for a period of one month, and the menu is planned in such a way to keep within the limits of the provisions supplied. At one time during the year the girls are given money for the purchase of provisions for a specified period, and they are required to budget it so as not to exceed the allowance.

The Gerard Institute for Boys in Sidon was founded in 1881 and for a time gave practical vocational training in the trades. When a site for the school was built on the hill outside Sidon, its distance from the city was too great a hardship for the students, and the school therefore moved back to its old premises in the city. The school comprises a kindergarten, an elementary school, and a high school. In 1945–46 the school had 422 pupils, of whom 160 were boarders. The student body was almost evenly divided between Christians and Muslims, the latter element almost evenly divided between Shi'ites, and Sunnites. The tuition fees are the same as those for the girls school. The staff included twenty teachers, of whom two were American and one British. Five of these had university degrees, the others were high-school graduates and holders of the *baccalauréat*. The school still emphasizes practical work, but this is no longer of a vocational, but rather of an educational, nature. The authorities of the school would like to include more practical work for the trades in their curriculum, but the desire of the parents to send their children to postsecondary schools counteracts that. Like the rest of the American schools, the school attempted to change its policy with regard to French, but the protests of the parents made it begin the teaching of French in the first grade. English is now also started in the first grade so that the teaching of all three languages—Arabic, English, and French—starts simultaneously. All students are required to study religion and to attend chapel.

Besides the schools described above and the village schools turned over to the Protestant synod, the American Mission operates a residential school for teen-age girls in a village near Tripoli, a school at Nabatiyah east of Sidon, and a small school in a village near Baalbak. These were not visited by the Commission.

AMERICAN AND BRITISH SCHOOLS

The American University of Beirut

The leading American institution in Lebanon, and, indeed, in the whole Arab world, is the American University of Beirut, founded in 1866 as the Syrian Protestant College. The name was changed in 1920. Though an outgrowth of the activities of the Presbyterian Mission, the University is a lay institution with a separate endowment and board of trustees. It draws its students not only from all the countries of the Near East, but also from Asia, Africa, Europe, and a few from North and South America. As a rule, some twenty-five or thirty nationalities are enrolled, representing most of the Christian, Muslim, and Jewish sects. Many of its graduates have occupied and now occupy leading positions in the political, economic, and cultural life of the Arab world.

Starting with 16 students in 1866, its enrollment in all its departments in 1945–46 was 2,399, as shown in Table 86. The total number of its graduates since its foundation was 6,167, of whom 4,348 hold university

TABLE 86
ENROLLMENT IN THE AMERICAN UNIVERSITY OF BEIRUT, 1945–46

School	Enrollment
School of Art and Sciences	
Final year, engineering	15
Graduate class	22
Junior and senior classes	301
Special students	79
Total	417
School of Medicine	
First, second, third, fourth, and fifth years	172
School of Pharmacy	
First, second, third, and fourth years	91
School of Nursing	
First, second, and third years	59
Total, University proper	739
Institute of Music	91
Intermediate Section	
Freshman and sophomore classes	367
First and second years, farm management	27
Special students	3
Special form	75
Total	472
Preparatory Section	409
Section Secondaire	446
Elementary School	242
Total, International College	1,569
Total Number of Students	2,399

degrees, the others, lower certificates or specialized certificates. Approximately four-fifths of its students are Arabic-speaking.

The University has a beautiful campus on the promontory of Ras-Beirut overlooking the Mediterranean Sea and the city of Beirut, with a view of a large part of the Lebanon Mountains. The campus comprises no less than thirty buildings of major size and a large number of smaller buildings, the whole interspersed with groves, wooded slopes, and playing fields. The University comprises a School of Arts and Sciences, a School of Medicine, a School of Pharmacy, a School of Nursing, and an Institute of Music; the lower division of the University is known as International College,[3] and is separately administered and financed. International College comprises: the intermediate section, covering the first two college years; the preparatory section, an American-type high school; the *Section Secondaire*, a French-type secondary school established in 1926; and an elementary school. Each section of International College has its own director and committee. International College admits boys only. Girls are admitted to all other departments of the University.

The elementary school has six grades and is under the administration of a professor of education in the University. Most of the children are day pupils, but boarding accommodations are available for twenty-five boys. Pupils must be six years of age, and each grade has an age range limit of about two years. Teaching is entirely in Arabic. English is begun in the fourth grade. French, however, is still begun in the first grade as was required under the French mandate. In the school year 1945–46 the elementary school had a total enrollment of 242 pupils. The school was staffed by fourteen teachers, of whom four were women; three teachers held the B.A. degree. Two of the women teachers were graduates of the British Syrian Training College, one was a graduate of the British school in Jerusalem, and one was a graduate of the Collège Protestant Français for girls. The other teachers were former students of the University of freshman or sophomore standing. The elementary school is used for practice teaching for students of education in the University.

The preparatory section, or American-type secondary school, is a counterpart of the American schools for boys in Tripoli and Sidon. It receives students not only from Lebanon and Syria but from other countries, including Palestine, Transjordan, Iraq, India, Bahrayn, Iran, and Ethiopia. In 1945–46 it had 405 students, of whom about 160 were boarders. Tuition fees range from $119 to $179, and boarding fees from $465 to $525 a year. It

---

[3] International College was formerly a high school at Izmir, Turkey. It moved to Beirut and became affiliated with the American University in 1936.

Above: A reading class in a village primary school, Bishmizzin, Lebanon
Below: A village primary school, Bishmizzin

Above: In this well-equipped laboratory at the American Junior College for Women, Beirut, students are engaged in chemistry experiments
Below: Undergraduates of the American Junior College for Women relax between classes in the rock garden in front of the dormitory

was staffed by twenty-five teachers, two of whom were American. Almost all of them had university degrees. The program of studies in both the elementary and secondary schools is similar to that of American mission schools. Instruction in the preparatory section is entirely in English except for the classes in Arabic and French languages. The preparatory section program extends over six years, called the seventh grade, eighth grade, first year, second year, third year, and fourth year. The best pupils of the sixth grade of the elementary school are often admitted directly to the eighth grade of the preparatory section. The seventh grade is treated as a flexible arrangement whereby the slower pupils are helped to catch up. Most of the graduates of the preparatory section enter the University classes. Students coming from other schools have to pass an entrance examination which is used in classifying them. Those weak in English may be asked to go to summer school in the mountains to make themselves more fluent in the language.

The *Section Secondaire* is the answer of the University to the imposition of French and French-designed Lebanese examinations during the period of the mandate. It is also an answer to the demands of those parents who wanted their sons to learn French well, but preferred some advantages of the American schools to other schools. In 1945–46 the school had 446 students distributed from the *classe de septième* to the *classe de philosophie et mathématique;* 30 were in the two-year commercial course, which starts after the *troisième* (ninth grade). The language of instruction is French, but special attention is given to Arabic and English. Students graduating from the school are admitted to the sophomore or junior year of the American University, and also to the French university, Université Saint-Joseph.

Table 87 gives the program of studies for the school and shows the type of adaptation of the French program which has been made.

With the passing of the French mandate the fate of the *Section Secondaire* was somewhat uncertain. When the new Lebanese program and the new law regulating private schools were issued, however, tentative ideas were being entertained of turning the *Section Secondaire* into a school following the new Lebanese program, and keeping the preparatory school with its present program. The first foreign language would then become English, and courses now taught in French would be taught in English. French would become simply the second foreign language. Under these circumstances the *Section Secondaire* would be attended almost entirely by Lebanese students, while the preparatory school would be attended largely by students coming from other countries.

TABLE 87

PROGRAM OF STUDIES FOR THE SECTION SECONDAIRE, REGULAR COURSE, AMERICAN UNIVERSITY OF BEIRUT, 1946

SUBJECT	Primary Instruction 7me	Classes of First Cycle					Classes of Second Cycle				
		6me	5me	4me	3me	2de L*	2de F*	1re L*	1re F*	Philosophie	Mathématique
Philosophy	...	...	...	...	...	...	...	...	...	10	3
French literature	...	...	...	...	...	...	...	...	6	...	...
French	9	7	7	7	7	...	...	...	...	...	...
Arabic philosophy	...	...	...	...	...	...	...	...	...	5	4
Arabic literature	...	...	...	...	...	5	5	6	...	...	...
Arabic and Arabic translation	6	6	6	6	5	...	...	2	5	2	2
English literature	...	...	...	...	...	4	4	3	3	...	...
English and English translation	...	6	5	5	5	1	1	2	2	2	...
History	2	2	2	1	2	2	2	2	2	1	2
Geography	1	1	1	1	1	1	1	1	...	1	1
Lebanese history	...	...	...	1	1	1	...	1	...	1	1
Lebanese geography	...	...	...	1	1	...	...	...	...	...	...
Mathematics	5	3	3	4	4	5	5	5	5	2	10
Physics	...	1	1	2	2	3	3	3	3	2	3
Chemistry	...	...	...	1	1	2	2	2	2	2	3
Biology	2	2	...	1	...	...	...	...	...	3	3
French writing	1	1	1	...	...	...	...	...	...	...	...
Arabic writing	1	1	1	...	...	...	...	...	...	...	...
Drawing and singing	1	1	1	...	...	...	...	...	...	...	...
Total	28	30	29	30	30	30	29	34	29	31	33

PERIODS PER WEEK

* F, for students preparing for French examinations; L, for students preparing for Lebanese examinations.

AMERICAN AND BRITISH SCHOOLS

The program of the commercial course, which starts after the *classe de troisième,* is shown in Table 88.

The intermediate section, for men, composed of freshman and sophomore classes, although administratively and financially a part of International College, is under the supervision of the School of Arts and Sciences of the University as to curriculum and academic standards. For admission to the intermediate section, a student must be at least sixteen years old, and have fifteen units of credit from an approved secondary school, or pass entrance examinations.

TABLE 88

Program of Studies for Section Secondaire, Commercial Course, American University of Beirut, 1946

Subjects	Periods per Week	
	1st Year	2nd Year
French	3	3
Arabic	3	3
English	5	4
History	1	1
Geography	2	1
Business mathematics	3	2
Correspondence	2	1
Commerce	2	2
Bookkeeping	5	5
Mathematics	...	2
Commercial law	...	3
Political economy	...	3
Stenography and typing	5	4
Total	31	34

The following certificates are accepted for admission to the freshman class: Certificate showing graduation from an approved secondary school, provided the candidate has spent at least two years in the school; the government secondary-school certificates of Egypt (general section), Palestine, Greece, Iraq, Transjordan, and the Iranian *Baccalauréat,* Part I, provided candidates pass an entrance examination in English; and the London Matriculation, and Oxford and Cambridge School certificates (without mathematics, history, and science).

Entrance examinations are held in four groups of subjects. Group I comprises English, Arabic, and French. English and either Arabic or the vernacular language of the student are required; French is required of Lebanese and Syrians only. Group II requires examination in geography, and one examination in history in one of the following fields: ancient history, medieval and modern history, modern history, general history. Group

III includes arithmetic, algebra, and plane geometry, all required. Group IV includes elementary science as a required subject, and either biology, chemistry, or physics.

Completion of the freshman year of the University or other officially recognized American institutions entitles students to admission to the sophomore class. Certain certificates are accepted for admission provided the student passes an examination in English: the Egyptian *baccalauréat;* French *Baccalauréat,* Part I; Iranian *Baccalauréat,* Part II; Lebanese *Baccalauréat,* Part I; Syrian *Baccalauréat,* Part I; the Iraq Government Secondary Certificate if the student has an average of 75 or more; the Palestine Matriculation Certificate; the Transjordan Matriculation Certificate if the student is in the upper half of the group taking the examination; the London Matriculation, and the Oxford and Cambridge School certificates if the candidates passed examinations in history, mathematics, and science. Those who hold the English certificates or the Palestine Matriculation Certificate are not required to take an entrance examination in English.

The freshman program is uniform, with Arabic or French (the former required of Arabic-speaking students), English, history of the Arabs, mathematics, science, sociology, and physical education required. A choice is given of engineering, music, or political science.

The sophomore class is divided into two sections: the arts section, which takes courses in Arabic or English, economics, history, philosophy, and political science; the science section, which takes required courses in chemistry, mathematics, physics, and philosophy, with a choice of biology, further mathematics, or engineering.

The intermediate section offers a special two-year course in farm management, consisting entirely of courses in agricultural subjects and taught in Arabic. There is also a "special form" for students who qualify for admission to the intermediate section, to the School of Arts and Sciences, and to the Schools of Medicine and Pharmacy *except for English*. The special form is divided into three divisions according to proficiency in English, and only courses in English are taught.

Regulations of the intermediate section with regard to examination and promotion are very much like those in American colleges. A certificate known as the Intermediate Certificate of the Arts (or Science) Program is given to those students who finish the regular course, while a Farm-Management Certificate is given to students pursuing the farm-management course. The certificates are given by International College.

The School of Arts and Sciences.—The School of Arts and Sciences covers the junior and senior college years. Two types of academic program are offered: (1) the general course, designed to provide a "liberal" education in which there is very little specialization, and which leads to a "Pass" degree granted on the basis of a passing mark of 60 in all courses, and an average of 65 or above; or (2) the honors course, which aims to train the student to do independent work in a specialized field, and which leads to an honors degree, which, among other things, requires a general average of 70 or above. The honors degree is awarded with first-, second-, or third-class honors. For first-class honors the student's average must be 85 or above in the senior year; for second-class honors, an average of 75 to 84.99 is required; for third-class honors, an average of 70 to 74.99. For first-class honors the student must also be recommended by his major department.

Both general and honors courses are given in the arts and sciences, and in commerce and economics. Engineering, however, is offered only in the honors program.

Work in the arts or sciences in the general course leads to the Bachelor of Arts Pass degree. Students completing the commercial course of the general course receive the degree of Bachelor of Business Administration —Pass. A two-year honors program in commerce and economics leads to the degree of Bachelor of Business Administration, with first-, second-, or third-class honors.

To be admitted to the honors course, students must hold the Intermediate Certificate, first- or second-class; graduates of Aleppo College or the American Junior College for Women must have an average of 70 and a minimum of 70 in at least two year-courses; other students must pass an examination in prerequisite subjects.

The course in engineering is a completely required curriculum, including surveying and practice courses during the summer. Graduates receive the Bachelor of Arts degree, with first-, second-, or third-class honors; an additional year of required courses leads to the Bachelor of Science in Engineering.

Students pursuing honors courses in arts and sciences have to take a major and a minor according to the following schedule:

Major	Minor
Arabic	Education—English—philosophy
Arabic Studies	Arabic—history
Biology	Chemistry—education—philosophy
Chemistry	Biology—education—physics
Economics	Commerce—philosophy—political science
Education	Arabic—biology—chemistry—English—Arabic history—mathematics—sociology

English	Arabic—education—history
Arabic history	Education—philosophy—political science
European history	Economics—philosophy—political science
Mathematics	Astronomy—education—physics
Philosophy	English—history—political science
Physics	Astronomy—chemistry—mathematics
Political Science	Economics—history—philosophy
Sociology	Economics—education—political science

Upon completion of the two-year course, the degree of Bachelor of Arts is awarded, with first-, second-, or third-class honors. Students who major in education—that is, complete a minimum of eight semester courses in education, with a minimum grade of 75 in each course—are awarded the Normal Certificate.

In addition to the regular course, described above, the School of Arts and Sciences offers three special courses: (1) the P.C.B. (physics, chemistry, biology) course, which is a preparatory year for entrance to the School of Medicine and is intended for holders of the Lebanese, Syrian, or French *Baccalauréat*, Part II; (2) the Bachelor of Science in Nursing course, open to graduates of the American Junior College for Women, or its equivalent, who are also graduates of the School of Nursing; (3) the combined course in theology and arts which may be taken either as a general course or as an honors course. This last-named program requires the completion of a minimum of twenty semester courses—fifteen in the Near East School of Theology and at least five in the University—and leads to the Bachelor of Arts Pass degree or honors degree, depending upon grades.

It would be impracticable to detail the courses offered in the various departments of the School of Arts and Sciences. Suffice it to say that the system followed is very similar to that in American universities and colleges. The following are the departments of the School: agriculture, Arabic, astronomy, biology, chemistry, commerce, economics, education, engineering, English, French, history, mathematics, music, philosophy, physical education (offering a freshman course only), physics, political science, psychology, religion (in the Near East School of Theology), science (offering courses in general science, world geography, and geology), and sociology. The number of courses in a single department ranges from one to twenty-nine.

An extensive study of the organization and curriculum of the School of Arts and Sciences has been made in recent years. While no final action had been taken up to the time of the American Council Commission's visit in 1946, the trends are toward establishing a three-year honors course after the sophomore year, leading to the degree of Master of Arts. The general course of the junior and senior years leading to a pass degree would remain.

Graduate Study.—Graduate work is offered in the School of Arts and Sciences leading to the degree of Master of Arts (for work in all departments *except* commerce), Master of Business Administration (for work in the department of commerce), and Master of Science (for students in the medical sciences preliminary to entering the School of Medicine). Graduation with first- or second-class honors is customarily required for admission to graduate classes, and the student must also pass a written comprehensive examination in his major field of study. Studies usually extend over an academic year except where students have a teaching fellowship, in which case two years may be required. A thesis and a final oral examination are required.

Division of Medicine.—The Division of Medicine is composed of the School of Medicine, School of Pharmacy, School of Nursing, and a course in midwifery.

To be admitted to the School of Medicine, the student must have satisfied the premedical-education requirements of his own country, and must have completed the junior year of the School of Arts and Sciences. Admission is selective and is restricted to 40 students a year. The five-year course meets the standards of schools rated "Class A" by the American Medical Association. Upon the successful completion of the course the degree of Doctor of Medicine and Surgery is awarded. The required hours range from 1,102 to 1,214 a year. The first two years are preclinical years. Beginning with the third year, students spend about two-thirds or more of their time in hospital or clinical work. The University hospital has a total of 214 beds, and a branch maternity and prenatal clinic is maintained in the city of Beirut. Students also get practice training in the Lebanon Hospital for Mental Diseases, which accommodates 365 patients; in two hospitals for tuberculosis, which accommodate 186 patients; and in the Kennedy Memorial Hospital in Tripoli, with accommodations for 52 patients. Plans were being drawn in 1946 for a big medical center near the present University hospital, which would add considerably to the bed space for patients as well as provide facilities for more laboratories and research.

The School of Pharmacy has a four-year course leading to the degree of Pharmaceutical Chemist. In addition, one year of practical work in an approved pharmacy is required, which is recommended to follow the first year of pharmacy study and in any event must be completed before the student enters the second year; occasionally a practice year spent immediately before entering the first year of the School is acceptable by special permission of the director of the School. Admission is selective and limited to 30 students a year. Candidates must have satisfied the official requirements of their own country regarding preliminary education and must have completed the freshman class of the intermediate section of the American University. Students who wish to practice pharmacy in Lebanon or Syria must have obtained the Lebanese *Baccalauréat,* Part II, or its equivalent, in addition to the degree of Pharmaceutical Chemist. The total hours required range from 794 to 880 a year. Graduates of the School of Pharmacy may take a one-year course (chiefly laboratory work in the analysis of foods, oils, waters, drugs, and industrial articles) leading to the Public Analyst Certificate.

The School of Nursing gives a course of three years comparable to the standards of the New York State requirements for registered schools of nursing. Admission is based on a high-school certificate or its equivalent, and students must be between the ages of eighteen and thirty. The first semester is devoted chiefly to class instruction in theoretical subjects; during the remainder of the two and one-half years, students are on hospital duty for eight hours daily in addition to class work. Students satisfactorily completing the course are granted the Nurses' Diploma. Graduates of the American Junior College for Women who subsequently graduate from the School of Nursing are eligible to enter the senior year of the School of Arts and Sciences for a special one-year course leading to the degree of Bachelor of Science in Nursing. A home for nurses is provided on the hospital grounds.

The course in midwifery extends over nine months for graduates of recognized schools of nursing. Students attend deliveries in the University maternity center, and after they have assisted in twenty-five cases they are allowed to assume responsibility alone. Most of the practice work is done in homes. Abnormal cases are observed in the delivery room of the University hospital. Upon completion of the course a Diploma of Midwifery is granted.

The Institute of Music.—The Institute, founded in 1928, is recognized by the École Normale de Musique de Paris through the courtesy of the director, M. Alfred Cortot, the well-known pianist. The program is divided into three main stages: lower, intermediate, and higher. There is also a one-year preparatory course for beginners preceding the regular

AMERICAN AND BRITISH SCHOOLS

course. Instruction is given in piano, violin, viola, cello, voice, ensemble, theory of music, solfeggio, harmony, history of music, and musical forms. Although the normal duration of the regular course covers six years (two years for each stage), advancement depends upon proficiency and may be more or less rapid. Graduates receive either a certificate or a diploma; the certificate is awarded for satisfactorily meeting the standard requirements of the curriculum, the diploma for satisfying the following requirements in addition: (1) giving an instrumental recital; (2) playing in ensemble; (3) completing specified required courses; and (4) giving a specific performance, the exact type depending upon the instrument used.

The Institute of Rural Life.—In addition to its regular schools and courses, the University maintains an Institute of Rural Life in conjunction with the Near East Foundation, an organization which succeeded the Near East Relief after 1928. The work includes teaching improved agricultural methods to school children and farmers in five villages in the Buqa', health work among the farmers, work with village girls, extension activities, and a program of scholarships. The Institute issues pamphlets on agricultural and health subjects, and a reader for illiterates written by a professor at the University has been in use for some time. Summer camps in the Buqa' region are held every year by volunteers from the faculty and students from the University. This provides experience for students in rural life and problems. The health service employs a full-time doctor and some nurses. The sociology and agricultural departments of the University have played an active role in conducting the Institute. Recently some scholarships have been offered to students from Iraq and Syria for study at the Sanitary Inspection Institute in Cyprus, and a nurse from Iraq was given a scholarship to study public health and home welfare in Jerusalem.

The University issues various series of research studies in archeology, Oriental studies, social science (including economics), the medical sciences, and natural sciences. It has a main library of about 50,000 volumes. There are branch libraries at the International College and the intermediate section. There are also the Nickoley Library in economics and political science, the extensive Islamic library, the philosophy seminar library, and the medical library, the latter comprising about 14,000 volumes, of which more than 9,000 are bound volumes of medical journals. The medical library subscribes to 218 different journals.

The University has a museum with sections of archeology, geology, botany (including an extensive herbarium), and zoology.

The American Junior College for Women

The American Junior College for Women was established by the Syria Mission of the Board of Foreign Missions of the Presbyterian Church in the United States. It began in 1924 as classes attached to the American School for Girls and later moved into temporary quarters in Ras-Beirut. It now occupies a campus comprising two fine buildings and the president's house. One of the buildings is a dormitory and the other an administration and classroom building. In 1945–46 it had 187 women students, of whom 88 were boarders. The students belonged to twelve nationalities and thirteen religious sects.

The purpose of the College is to provide general education for family life and for teaching positions and to prepare students for entry into the professional schools of the American University of Beirut. No women students are admitted to the University in the freshman and sophomore years so that in actual practice women desiring an American higher education must first pass through the American Junior College for Women. The College was staffed with twelve full-time and four part-time instructors besides the president. Of these, ten are holders of A.B. degrees from American universities or the American University of Beirut, four have the M.A. degree, one the Ph.D. degree, and one a Nurses' Diploma. Tuition fees are $225 a year, boarding fees $400, and room rent ranges from $50 to $125. In addition, some laboratory fees and fees for music, stenography, and examinations are charged. A limited number of students may earn money by doing some work at the College. Some full-tuition scholarships are offered.

Admission to the Junior College is on approximately the same conditions outlined for the American University of Beirut.

The two-year course consists, in the freshman year, of religion, sociology, Near East history, hygiene, English, and Arabic or French. These courses are all required. In addition, a student must take either mathematics or a basic course in the field of euthenics. In the sophomore year, four courses are required: euthenics, psychology, religion, and athletics, with the addition of another course each semester chosen by the student according to her interests. These courses are chosen from the following: English II, Arabic II, European history, political science, art appreciation, child psychology, social psychology, adolescent psychology, religion, home nursing, mathematics, educational methods, economics, family relations, philosophy, zoology, botany, chemistry, stenography, bookkeeping, typewriting, and music.

Students wishing to enter the American University of Beirut must include mathematics in the freshman year and must rank in the upper half of the students graduating. The College has affiliations with the Near East School of Theology whereby students who have completed their freshman year may receive their diploma in a combined course of the College and the School of Theology. The Institute of Music of the American University of Beirut provides instruction in music at the College for those interested.

The College is equipped with good laboratories for biology, chemistry, and hygiene. A special building houses the laboratories for the courses in euthenics and child psychology. Student activities include a student council, an Arabic club, an international relations club, a crafts club, and student-cooperative clubs. There are also class organizations. The construction of a special auditorium is planned.

British Schools

The British-Syrian Mission has had schools in Syria and Lebanon since 1860 when Mrs. J. Bowen Thompson opened her school in Beirut which is now the British-Syrian Training College. At one time these schools, scattered over many villages of southern Lebanon and in Damascus, reached the number of 40 schools, enrolling about 3,000 pupils. The Mission is nondenominational. Today British-Syrian Mission schools comprise schools in 'Ayn Zhalta, Damascus, Hasbayyah, Tyre, a Bible Training Institute at Shimlan, a boys school, a girls school, and a school for blind boys in Beirut, and the British-Syrian Training College in the same city. These are all elementary schools except for the Training College in Beirut, the school at Damascus which has two secondary classes, and the school at 'Ayn Zhalta, which has had the seventh and eighth grades added to it with a view to training rural teachers. Thus, the British-Syrian Mission by opening teachers training courses and a school for the blind is attempting to work along different lines from the other missions.

The most important institution is the British-Syrian Training College for girls located at Beirut in the heart of the city, not far from the headquarters of American Mission. This school now has a kindergarten of two years, an elementary and secondary course of ten years, and a teacher-training course of two years. In 1945–46 it had 352 students of whom 61 were boarders. Boys are admitted up to the age of nine. The school is primarily intended for Arabic-speaking students. Others may be accepted in the higher classes only, unless they are prepared to study Arabic. Teaching is in Arabic through the sixth grade, and in English after that. French is begun from the kindergarten; English begins in an informal way at the same time, but formal teaching of the language starts with the third grade. The school is staffed by a British principal and sixteen teachers, of whom four are British. Upon finishing their courses, students are granted a Secondary-School Leaving Certificate which entitles them to admission into the training department of the College, the American Junior College for Women, and the School of Nursing of the American University of Beirut. The subjects taught in the school are Arabic, French, English, mathematics, history, geography, science, needlework, drawing, singing, and physical drill.

The teacher-training department includes a one-year course for elementary and kindergarten teachers, a two-year course for either kinder-

TABLE 89

The Two-Year Course for Teachers at the British-Syrian Training College, Lebanon, 1945–46

Subjects	Periods per Week	
	1st Year	2nd Year
Scriptures	5	5
Teaching	3	15
Study	7	7
Method	2	5
Criticism	1	1
History of education	3	2
Kindergarten theory	4	...
School organization	...	2
Psychology	...	2
Singing	1	1
Hobbies (clubs)	2	2
Principles of education	4	...
Nature study	2	...
Child study	2	...
Class meeting	1	1
Sewing	2	...
Geography	2	...
Handwork	2	...
Drawing	1	...
Total	44	43

garten or elementary teachers, and a three-year course for a higher diploma. At the time of the visit of the American Council Commission the three-year course was not in operation. In actual practice there is little difference between the courses for elementary and kindergarten teachers. Table 89 gives the program of studies for the two training classes, which had 6 students in the first year and 5 in the second.

Practice teaching is carried on in the kindergarten and elementary grades of the school, and in the Mission girls school in Beirut as well. At the time of the visit of the Commission, students in attendance at the training classes came from Lebanon, Iraq, and Palestine. Most of the graduates of the training classes of the previous year have gone into teaching, 3 had come back for an additional year (second year); of the 20 graduates from the tenth grade, 11 had gone into the American Junior College for Women, 1 entered the teacher-training class, 3 were preparing for matriculation examinations in other schools, and 6 were not accounted for.

Another important British school belonging to a different mission is the Brummana High School conducted by the Committee of the Service Council of the London Yearly Meeting of the Society of Friends. This School has a long history, having been founded in 1876. It is situated in a large village to the east of Beirut, overlooking that city and its bay, at an altitude of about 2,700 feet. The School has a kindergarten and an elementary and secondary school of twelve grades. The School's High-School Certificate is accepted by the American University of Beirut and the American Junior College for Women. In 1945–46 the school had 361 students, of whom 139 were boarders. Ten of the students were girls admitted into the higher classes. Tuition fees range from £L55 to £L250 ($25 to $114), and boarding fees are £L650 ($296). Students came not only from Lebanon and Syria but also from Palestine, Transjordan, Iraq, Hijaz, and Iran. The teaching staff numbered twenty-seven, of whom six were British. French is begun in the first grade and English in the kindergarten. Instruction is in Arabic in the elementary school up to the sixth grade and in English beginning with the seventh grade. Students have to take their turn waiting tables in the dining-room and sweeping classrooms, and have to make up their own beds. It is a policy of the School as far as possible not to take new students above the age of fourteen. Boarders are accepted from the age of ten and above.

The Friends mission also has an orphanage with a school at Ras-al Matn across the valley from Brummana. This school was not visited by the Commission.

Other Foreign Schools

Aside from French, American, and British schools, there were one Greek and one Swiss school in Lebanon. These were not visited by the Commission. Before World War II, a few Italian schools existed, some of which seem to have gone in for Italian fascist propaganda, even to the point of taking some boys to Italy for a summer trip. When Italy entered the war, these schools were closed, never to open again. The remnants of one such school in Bsharri, northern Lebanon, now conducted by the Lebanese Carmelite sisters, was visited by the Commission. It had a kindergarten class and four elementary grades, and enrolled 60 pupils, of whom 24 were boys. It had a staff of four sisters and two lay women teachers. The school had a good building, evidently intended for a much larger school, and had some up-to-date furniture. The instruction in Arabic and French was indifferent.

Chapter 28

PRIVATE LEBANESE SCHOOLS

*M*ODERN EDUCATION in Lebanon goes back to the end of the eighteenth century when a Maronite patriarch, formerly a student in one of the oriental seminaries of Rome, opened a school at the monastery of 'Ayn Waraqah in 1789. This school therefore precedes by thirty-five years the elementary American school opened in 1824, and precedes 'Anturah College by forty-five years. Inspired in its plan by the seminaries in Rome, it gave instruction in Syriac, Arabic, Italian, Latin, philosophy, theology, and civil law, combining in its student body lay students as well as those destined for clerical life. It has often been called the mother of the national schools of Lebanon, and produced a number of learned Lebanese men of the nineteenth century. Among its distinguished alumni may be cited the linguist-lexicographer-journalist-encyclopedist, Butrus Bustani, already mentioned as one of the translators of the Bible into Arabic, Ahmad Faris al-Shidyaq, another linguist and journalist, and Monseigneur Yusuf al-Dibs, later Maronite Archbishop of Beirut and author of an eight-volume history of Syria, and founder of the well-known al-Hikmah College, which will be described later.[1] This school remained open well into the nineteenth century. Other schools were founded later by Maronites, Greek Catholics, Syrian Catholics, and Greek Orthodox (of the latter, the Syrian School at Dayr al-Shurfah and the Greek Orthodox School of Three Doctors are the best known), but they did not seem to have had the same influence as the school at 'Ayn Waraqah. Bustani founded the National School in Beirut, which prepared students for the American University of Beirut during its early years.

The Greek Catholics founded a school in Beirut known as the Patriarchal School, which is still in existence as one of the prominent schools of Lebanon. Later the Muslim Charitable Purposes Association founded a school in Beirut, in 1876. Down to the present day, private schools have been founded by sects, associations, and individuals in such numbers that it is impossible to enumerate them.

[1] See pp. 506-9.

In 1944–45 private Lebanese schools were the largest single group of schools in the country, numbering 963 schools and enrolling 71,524 pupils, or 60.3 percent of the schools and 49.4 percent of the enrollments. The period following the First World War was a period of great development in private schools. These grew up in the larger cities as well as in the smaller villages and may be divided from the standpoint of control into three categories: (1) sectarian schools; these are the largest group and are maintained by the various denominations in order to keep the education of their children under their wing; (2) schools controlled by committees and associations for national or purely educational purposes; (3) schools controlled by individuals—many of these are simply commercial ventures of private individuals for private gain.

TABLE 90
DISTRIBUTION OF PRIVATE SCHOOLS AND PUPILS ACCORDING TO DENOMINATION, LEBANON, 1941–42*

DENOMINATION	NUMBER OF SCHOOLS	Christian	Muslim	Druze	Jews	Miscellaneous	Total
Muslim	122	92	15,408	162	...	97	15,759
Druze	26	41	45	1,452	5	2	1,545
Jewish	1	...	...	...	236	...	236
Christian							
Maronite	406	20,600	523	175	2	15	21,315
Greek Catholic	148	7,856	500	231	...	6	8,593
Syrian Catholic	4	945	40	29	...	...	1,014
Armenian Catholic	9	1,586	...	...	...	...	1,586
Chaldean	1	141	1	1	...	...	143
Greek Orthodox	186	10,479	252	131	2	...	10,864
Syrian Orthodox	5	328	3	...	...	...	331
Armenian Orthodox	37	7,062	...	...	...	...	7,062
Armenian Protestant	13	1,151	...	...	...	...	1,151
Protestant	2	187	14	3	...	...	204
Miscellaneous private schools	26	2,806	211	615	17	156	3,805
Total	986	53,274	16,997	2,799	262	276	73,608

* Conseil Général des Intérêts Communs, *Recueil de Statistiques de la Syrie et du Liban, 1942–43* (Beirut: Imprimerie Catholique, 1945), p. 31.

From the standpoint of government statistics almost all the private schools are classified under the denominational affiliation of their controlling authorities as is shown in Table 90, which gives the distribution of private schools and pupils according to denomination in the year 1941–42.

The largest single group of schools and of pupils is the Maronite with 406 schools and 21,315 pupils. Next comes the Greek Orthodox with 186 schools and 10,864 pupils. The Greek Catholics come third with 148 schools and 8,593 pupils. The Muslims, though fourth in the number of schools, are second in the number of pupils; they had 122 schools with

15,759 students. Armenian schools, both Orthodox and Protestant, come next with 50 schools and 8,213 pupils. They are followed by the Druzes, with 26 schools and 1,545 pupils.

A careful study of Table 90 shows that each denomination is catering almost exclusively to children of its own religion, though not necessarily of its own sect. Only 715 pupils out of the more than 21,000 in Maronite schools are non-Christian. Similarly, 385 pupils out of 10,479 in Greek Orthodox schools are non-Christian. Only 92 Christians, 162 Druzes, and 97 pupils from various sects attend Muslim schools out of a total of 15,759. Thus, the sectarian differences already existing among the people of Lebanon are paralleled in the composition of the student bodies of the various private schools. It can perhaps be safely said that the schools help to perpetuate these cleavages, if not to make them more pronounced.

As a group the private schools represent no special philosophy of education or any attempt to experiment with new curriculums or methods. It is the rare school indeed which is trying to strike out in a new direction. Rather, the private schools follow the lead either of the French, American, or British types of education. Naturally, since the government conducts primary and secondary examinations, some schools also follow the program of studies set down by the government.

These statements must be qualified by two considerations. The first is the attempt of each sect to draw to its own schools the children of its own community, and annoyance lest these children may go to schools of a different sect. This is particularly true of the Greek Orthodox and Catholic sects. The same is true of some of the private Muslim schools which were established to prevent Muslim children entering Christian missionary schools where another religion might be taught to them, sometimes compulsorily, and where they would have no chance of studying their own religion. Some of the sectarian schools provide children for religious services in their churches, and the children are, therefore, taught the liturgy and hymns of their own church. In a large portion of the Catholic schools, the clergy is in full control, with nuns or priests as principals, directors of discipline and studies, and as teachers. The same is not true of the Greek Orthodox schools, though there is a close affiliation with the church.

The second consideration is the new outlook advocated by some of the Lebanese that their culture should follow the lines of the so-called "Mediterranean culture." The protagonists of this theory maintain that Lebanon has always been a bridge between the East and the West and has always been influenced by Eastern and Western cultures alike. Whether in Phoenician, Greco-Roman, or Crusading times, Lebanon was always in direct relationship with other parts of the Mediterranean world and was influenced by the cultures emanating from that world. At the same time since it was attached to the Eastern soil and populated by races of Semitic origin, it could not help being influenced by Eastern cultures as well. In this way "Mediterranean culture" seems to mean the present Arab culture of the East and its background of other Semitic cultures, as well as the present modern Western, particularly French-Catholic, culture and its background of Greco-Roman culture. It is further maintained by this group, made up largely of French Catholic sympathizers who have not taken easily to the participation of Lebanon in the Arab League, that Lebanon should not be swayed too far to the East, to the point of losing its identity in the Arab-Muslim majority and in the Arab-Muslim ideology. Rather, due care must be taken to keep in close touch with the West, the Christian Catholic West in particular, in order to have a balanced culture inside Lebanon.

Their antagonists, on the other hand, made up largely of sympathizers with the Arab cause who like to see the Arabic culture of Lebanon maintained, accuse them of not paying enough attention to Arabic and Eastern cultures, and assert that what is called "Mediterranean culture" is nothing more than a thin veil for the attempt to preserve French Catholic influence and education in Lebanon.

This controversy has come to the fore more specifically in the last several years with the end of the French mandate, the rise of the Arab League, and the declaration of Lebanon's independence. From the standpoint of the schools themselves, however, it has as yet made little difference either in the types of curriculum or methods followed. It is not necessary, therefore, to describe them further as a group. The descriptions which follow are of individual schools visited by the Commission.

Denominational Schools

Maronite schools

The outstanding Maronite school in Lebanon is the al-Hikmah College, a boys school founded in Beirut in 1876, by the Maronite Archbishop of Beirut, Monseigneur Yusuf al-Dibs, a learned man of his times. It is situated in the eastern part of the city in its own old building to which has been added a large new building constructed in 1938. It has a primary school, a secondary school, and a commercial course. It had an enrollment in 1945–46 of 1,565 students, of whom 350 were boarders. About 900 were in the secondary section. Students are drawn mainly from Lebanon, but about 100 boys came from Syria, a few from Palestine, while others were children of Lebanese emigrants to Africa. The school was staffed with a director, a prefect of discipline, two directors of studies of Arabic and French (all of them priests), and 70 men instructors, 12 women instructors, and some nuns. In addition there were 12 supervisors, all priests. The school is under the authority of the Maronite Archbishop of Beirut who appoints the principal and receives from him a written report on the school annually. It is self-supporting, the fees being sufficient normally to pay all expenses. Any additional expenses are paid, when need arises, out of endowments of the Diocese of Beirut. The buildings belong to the diocese.

The College is well known for the equal care given to the teaching of Arabic and French. It has produced a large number of the leading men of Lebanon, among whom are writers, poets, journalists, and clergymen. Originally both a seminary and a college, it is now only a college for lay instruction, the seminary having been moved elsewhere. The authorities of the College have been among the leaders in the movement for the accession of what has been called "Mediterranean culture" and have taken the lead in founding the Cultural League of Free Education. This is an association of private Lebanese secondary- and elementary-school principals and inspectors which has the following aims:

1. Intimate cooperation and participation with the government in propagating the spirit of independence and patriotism in the hearts of youth, and the unification of education inspired by the Lebanese spirit.
2. The maintenance of the separation between cultural and political orientation and respect for the national Lebanese ideal and its cultural superiority.
3. Maintenance of the freedom of educational method in private schools within the public programs.

Table 91 shows the program of studies of the school beginning with the fourth primary year (*huitième*) as an illustration of the attempt to give more or less equal emphasis to Arabic and French.

It should be added that though the hours given to French are somewhat less than those given to Arabic, a number of subjects are taught in French. The Commission in its visit to the school was impressed by the fact that the general atmosphere seemed to be decidedly French. The school authorities spoke French among themselves and kept some of the records in French. English is begun in the fifth primary grade (*septième*).

The school has a literary society, physical-education society, a Scout troup, and a choir of 150 voices which sings church and Lebanese music. Dramatic societies are also active, giving both Arabic and French plays.

The College seems to be attempting to foster the introduction of harmony into Arabic and church music.

An illustration of the efforts by the Maronite clergy to provide education for girls are the schools of les Sœurs de la Sainte Famille, known as the Nuns of 'Ibrin, named after the village where the mother convent is situated. These Maronite nuns maintain about 40 schools for girls, to which the government pays a small contribution. Some of these schools are in Syria, but the majority are in Lebanon. Their girls school in Beirut

TABLE 91
PROGRAM OF STUDIES OF AL-HIKMAH COLLEGE, LEBANON

SUBJECTS	PERIODS PER WEEK BY CLASSES*							
	8me	7me	6me	5me	4me	3me	2de	1re
Arabic	12	8	7	7	7	7	7	6
French	10	6	6	6	6	6	7	5
Mathematics	5	4	4	4	4	5	5	6
Science	...	1	1	2	2	2	4	4
English	...	3	3	4	4	4	4	4
History and geography	3	2	2	2	2	2	2	3
History of Lebanon	2	2	2	2	2	2	2	2
Translation	...	...	...	...	...	...	...	1
Religious instruction	2	2	2	2	2	1	1	1
Drawing	1	1	1	1	1	...	...	...
Writing	1	1	$\frac{1}{2}$	$\frac{1}{2}$	$\frac{1}{2}$	...	...	...
Total	36	30	$28\frac{1}{2}$	$30\frac{1}{2}$	$30\frac{1}{2}$	29	32	32

* The names of classes follow the French system of having the first class have the highest number; for example, the first class is called "*huitième*."

is perhaps the best illustration of the type of school for girls maintained by this order. It consists of the *classe enfantine,* a primary school, and a secondary school. In 1945–46 it had 450 pupils, of whom 110 were boarders. The students are mostly from Beirut and Lebanon though there are some from Damascus and Latakia. The student body, though largely Maronite, includes also other Catholics, Greek Orthodox, Druzes, Jews, and Muslims. In 1945–46 the school was staffed with forty teachers including fifteen nuns. Fifteen men and five women were part time. The school accepts boys up to the age of seven.

The program of studies shows no great differences from that of al-Hikmah College for boys. Home economics is taught on Saturday afternoon. On Sunday there is compulsory Mass and a lecture on ethics. School fees are £L50 to £L300 ($22.50 to $136) for day students and £L600 to £L800 ($273 to $354) including tuition for boarding students. Forty day students and 10 boarding students are exempted from paying fees.

Some of the boarding students come from immigrant families from Africa and America.

Greek orthodox schools

Two Greek Orthodox schools, one for boys and one for girls were visited by the Commission.

The School of Three Doctors, founded in 1835, was at one time one of the prominent schools of Beirut, but has had an uneven career. It is situated in the eastern part of the city, where it has its own building belonging to the Greek Orthodox community. It is controlled by a committee of the denominational council of the Greek Orthodox Church which is responsible to the Greek Orthodox Archbishop of Beirut. At the time of the visit of the Commission in 1945–46 the School consisted of an elementary and a secondary section. The school was in the process of being rebuilt educationally after some years of low standards. There were 303 pupils in attendance, of whom 120 were in the secondary section. The School had up to that year not presented students for the second *baccalauréat* examinations, but had started a class in philosophy with 4 students during the year. It was headed by a lay principal, staffed by twenty-three men and two women teachers, of whom seven were part time. Two of the teachers had the French university degrees of *Licence ès Lettres,* two had B.A. degrees from the American University of Beirut, one was an engineer, four were students at higher institutions, and the rest had second *baccalauréats*. The program of studies does not differ radically from the other schools with the exception that English is begun with the third grade of the primary school (*neuvième*).

The Greek Orthodox School for Girls in Tripoli was founded in 1921 by the present Greek Orthodox Patriarch who was then Archbishop of Tripoli. It was later taken over by the ladies committee. The grounds and the buildings had been supplied by the diocese. The School building was requisitioned by the British Air Forces between 1941–45, and consequently the School suffered, and has been building itself up again since its return to its old quarters. It consists of a kindergarten, a primary school, and the first three years of secondary school leading to the *brevet* certificate. In 1945–46 it had 350 pupils, of whom 50 were boarders. One hundred fifty of the pupils either received full or partial exemption from fees. The student body, largely Greek Orthodox, had about one-third Muslim students. The staff included sixteen teachers, of whom four were men. The principal of the school has for some time been the head of the Girl Scout movement in Lebanon.

Greek Catholic schools

The American Council Commission regrets that it was not able to visit the well-known Patriarchal College of the Greek Catholic denomination, founded in 1865, owing to a misunderstanding growing out of inaccurate reports of the purpose of the survey conducted by the Commission.

Muslim schools

Three well-known Muslim schools were visited by the American Council Commission, in Beirut, Sidon, and Tripoli. The best known of these is the College of the Muslim Charitable Purposes (al-Maqasid al-Khayriyah) at Beirut. This is conducted by an association made up of Muslim laymen headed by a prominent, wealthy resident of Beirut. The association not only maintains schools, but has other charitable activities. Its schools are under two educational committees, one for the schools in Beirut, and the other for village schools. It draws its income of about £L250,000 ($136,000) a year from endowments made up largely of property and from fees, which range from £L110 to £L300 ($50 to $136.50) a year. The association maintains a secondary school for boys and another for girls in Beirut together with four elementary schools for boys and two elementary schools for girls in the city. A number of schools in the villages around Beirut and in Buqa' are also maintained.

The College of Muslim Charitable Purposes, in Beirut, for boys, was founded in the last quarter of the nineteenth century under Ottoman government auspices, but had an uneven history until after World War I when the Muslim community, largely under the leadership of a public-spirited man, put the College on a sound foundation and developed it from a primary school into a full secondary school. It includes a kindergarten which accepts children of nursery age, two primary schools, and a full secondary school presenting students for the second *baccalauréat*. The College is situated in the southern part of Beirut adjoining the great pine grove. In 1945–46 it had 996 students almost all of whom were from Beirut. The secondary school and what is known as the old primary school constitute a unit which enrolls 728 pupils and is staffed by the head principal and forty-two men teachers. Another unit known as the new elementary primary school and kindergarten enrolls 248 pupils and is staffed by a principal and eleven women teachers. The nursery and kindergarten follow some of the most progressive methods witnessed in any of the countries visited by the Commission. The authorities of the school are planning to add primary grades to the kindergarten which would follow more progressive lines than the old school. At the time of the visit of the Commission only the first grade of the new primary school had been started, and the Commission was told that other grades would follow gradually in subsequent years.

The College follows the government program by giving first place to Arabic and French, both of which are started in the kindergarten. English is begun in the first secondary year. Like many other schools, however, the College authorities are thinking of giving the students a choice between French and English beginning with the kindergarten. Teaching was being conducted in Arabic in the primary school and in the first secondary year. It was hoped to turn all of the teaching into Arabic gradually, teaching the French language simply as a language. A commercial course of two years after the third secondary year is planned. The College presents students for all four Lebanese examinations, and its secondary-school certificate is recognized by the Egyptian government and by the American University of Beirut for entry into the freshman year. It is hoped that when the teaching of English is improved, graduates, or at least some of them, will be able to go into the sophomore year. The College receives help from the Egyptian government in the form of four teachers, three of whom were delegated by the Egyptian Ministry of Education and one by al-Azhar. This delegation of Egyptian teachers was first begun in the year 1936–37. In 1945–46, 22 graduates of the College were studying in Egyptian universities, where they were receiving free tuition and board.

The College of Muslim Charitable Purposes in Sidon represents another institution of the same kind as that of Beirut, though it belongs to an independent organization. The College is made up of a kindergarten department of three years and a secondary school of eleven years, including the classes of philosophy and mathematics. The College is 1 of 4 schools in Sidon supported by this same organization. One is a boys primary school, enrolling about 450 children; 2 are schools for girls, both of which are primary, with about 600 girls in one and 350 girls and small boys in the other. It is planned to expand the first girls school into a full secondary school, leading to the second *baccalauréat*.

The boys College visited by the Commission had in 1945–46, 584 students of whom 139 were boarders. Girls are admitted in the kindergarten. The students come not only from Sidon and the rural districts surrounding it, but also from Buqa', northern Lebanon, Beirut, and parts of Syria. About 35 boarders were children of Lebanese parents living in Africa.

The College is the only full public or private secondary school in southern Lebanon, and is, therefore, sought not only by Muslim children but by

Christians as well. Forty-five Christians were in the secondary section, which enrolled a total of 154 students. It is staffed by a principal, an assistant, and twenty-six teachers, not including nine women kindergarten teachers. Fees range from £L40 to £L325 ($18 to $148) with an addition of another £L500 ($228) for boarding students. The College is almost self-supporting and is said to charge the highest fees in Sidon. Children of teachers are accepted gratis in the primary school and on half-fees in the secondary school. Income from property is spent mostly on the other free schools.

The College has a library of about 2,000 books in Arabic and in French, a small chemical laboratory, and some maps in French and Arabic. It fosters a number of student activities including a literary and dramatic society, a lecture program, two library committees (one each for Arabic and for French books), a Boy Scout troop, and various athletic teams. A school magazine, edited largely by students, is published in Arabic.

The College is now preparing for first and second *baccalauréats*, as well as for the primary-school certificate and the *brevet*. Its diploma has been recognized by the universities in Egypt, and 4 students are already studying at Egyptian universities. At the time of the Commission's visit, English was started in the seventh grade, but it was planned to form a special English section by agreement with the American University of Beirut. In this section English would begin in the kindergarten and continue through the secondary school.

The leaders of the Muslim Charitable Purposes movement may be said to represent in their outlook the opposite pole of the ideology represented by the al-Hikmah College and the Cultural League of Free Education. To them there is nothing that can be called Lebanese culture, but there is an Arab culture, or rather a world culture. They believe that Arabic should be the language of instruction and of expression. They attack the idea of French as a language of expression for Lebanese and Arabs: foreign languages should be taught for purposes of opening the gateways for acquisition of Western thought, but the expression of thought, whether Western or Eastern, should be in Arabic.

They concede that the foreign-language situation in Lebanon is different from the rest of the Arab countries in that the Lebanese population is more urban, and a large part of the Lebanese villages are summer resorts frequented by people from abroad. The Lebanese, therefore, take more easily to the teaching of foreign languages because their environment fosters acquisition of languages. This, however, should not mean in any way the neglect of the Arabic language, and the use of a foreign language for purposes of teaching or of expression. The aim, therefore, should be to turn all teaching into Arabic while at the same time fostering the teaching of foreign languages.

A third Muslim institution is the National College of Education and Instruction in Tripoli. This includes a kindergarten of three years, a primary school of five years reaching the sixth-grade standard, a secondary school of five years, a religious school of four years above the primary school, a commercial section, and an English section is being planned. In 1945–46 the College had 616 students, of whom 213 were accepted gratis. Students come from Tripoli and vicinity, while boarding students come from Homs, Hama, Latakia, and Aleppo. Fees range from £L90 to £L300 ($41 to $136.50) to which is added £L550 to £L700 ($251 to $318) for boarding students. Exemption from fees is based on economic need. The boarding section includes 130 orphans free and ten religious students who pay no fees and 55 paying students. A student accepted gratis in the primary school is given the option of entering the religious section or the secondary section. If he chooses to go into the secondary section, he receives one-half exemption only, but full exemption is accorded him if he chooses the religious section.

The program of the College is that of the government program leading to the primary-school certificate, the *brevet,* and the *baccalauréats,* but with greater emphasis on English, religion, and Arabic history. English is started in the fourth grade. Prior to 1945 it was started in the first secondary grade. The idea now is to have a separate English section preparing students for entry into the American University of Beirut. The religious section, formerly of four years, has been reduced to three years. It endeavors to prepare students for entry into al-Azhar in Cairo. Applicants, however, were few in 1945–46, only 22 students being registered in all three classes.

The College has its own building, owned by a society maintaining it. It has a laboratory and a lecture hall. It fosters a number of student activities and has a Boy Scout troop and various athletic teams. In addition to the College, the society maintains a primary school for girls, and a primary school for boys in the old quarter of Tripoli. The College is typical of the attempt of Muslim communities to give a religious education to the younger generation, and also to impress upon the pupils the principles of Arab nationalism. Non-Muslims are accepted, but, in contrast with many Christian mission schools, no attempt is made to enforce compulsory Muhammadan religious instruction upon them.

Druze schools

These are maintained mainly by a Druze education committee under the leadership of a well-known Druze public figure. Fifteen schools are maintained, of which 4 are for girls. They enroll a total of 1,067 students. Four of these schools are complete primary schools. Another, the Daudiyah school in 'Abay, is a full primary and secondary school for boys; a girls primary school of six years is maintained in the same town. An orphanage in Beirut takes children up to the fourth grade after which the brighter pupils are transferred to 'Abay. The schools are supported mainly from fees, but also by income from property and endowment, and by a small government grant. Each village school charges its own fees and is administered by its own local committee. Any deficit is paid by the central committee, which has the academic and financial supervision of the schools.

The Daudiyah College for boys in 'Abay is undoubtedly the most important Druze educational institution. It was founded in 1862 by the Lebanese autonomous government and named for the first governor of Lebanon. It was for a long time the only public school maintained by the Lebanese government. Closed during World War I, it did not resume its activities until 1931, when it became a private denominational school. It consists of two sections: a French Lebanese section leading to the French and Lebanese examinations, and an English section preparing students for admission to the American University of Beirut. The French section comprises classes from the fourth grade to the class of philosophy; this section enrolled 124 students in 1945–46. There was no mathematics class at the time of the visit of the Commission. The English section, started only three years before, included classes from the fourth through the seventh grade, and it was planned gradually to develop it into a full high school. This section enrolled 62 students, making a total of 186 students, of whom 90 were boarders. Boys belonging to the first three grades were taught at the girls school in 'Abay, which had 120 pupils, of whom 30 were boarders; 40 pupils were boys. Students in the Daudiyah school were mainly from the villages of Lebanon as well as from Jabal Druze in Syria. The College is staffed by a principal and seventeen teachers, of whom three were contributed by the Egyptian government and one by the Œuvres Françaises.

The so-called French section follows the Lebanese government program while the English section is following the program of the preparatory school of the American University of Beirut. English is begun in the first secondary year in the French section, and, conversely, French is begun in the same year in the English section. Present plans call for the English section to be completed in three years. The girls school is substituting English for French.

The Daudiyah College occupies a new building built by special contributions and from Druze endowments. It has a library of about 1,000 books and is receiving contributions of books from Egypt. Student committees for Arabic, English, French, science, and student welfare exist. A number of athletic teams are organized, and a school magazine is published.

Nondenominational Schools

Nondenominational schools fall mainly into two types: those controlled by boards and societies and operated on a nonprofit basis, and those owned and controlled by individuals for profit. The number of the nondenominational schools is rather large both in the cities and in the villages of Lebanon. It was possible for the Commission to visit only a few of them. Four schools and institutions will here be mentioned.

The National (al-Ahliyah) School for Girls was founded in 1916 by a former teacher at the British-Syrian Training College partly, at least, for the purpose of filling the gap created by the closing of that College during World War I. It is controlled by a board of trustees composed of prominent people, most of whom are from Beirut. A boarding department was opened in 1926.

The School consists of a kindergarten, a primary school open to both boys and girls, a secondary school of five years, and a college freshman year which was opened for the first time in 1945–46. A matriculation class was also being conducted during the same year. The School had a total of 440 pupils, of whom 110 were boarders. Tuition fees range from £L100 to £L250 ($45 to $114), except for the freshman class for which they are £L400 ($182). Boarding fees are £L650 ($296). Some of the intelligent girls receive scholarships for work done at the School. The School is staffed by a principal, an assistant, and twenty-two teachers, of whom six are men. Most of the staff are American-trained.

The program of the School follows closely that of the American schools. Instruction is in Arabic through the seventh grade, partially so in the eighth grade, and entirely in English in the ninth grade and above. French is begun with the kindergarten, English in the third grade. French instruction reaches the standard of the *classe de deuxième* (tenth grade), and no attempt is made to prepare students for the government or French examinations. The authorities of the School have a firm belief in the teaching of foreign languages. Sectarian religion is not taught, and prayers are of a nonsectarian character. Study of the Bible in English is part of the teaching of literature in the upper grades. No rigid discipline is contemplated, and the authorities attempt to give the School a strong family atmosphere. Stress is laid on art and Western classical and sacred music. Some of the girl students are members of the choir of the Lebanese Academy of Fine Arts. The School receives no contribution from the government or any foreign source. It does, however, accept gifts of books.

As an example of a private school in a Lebanese village the school at Bishmizzin in northern Lebanon may be cited. This village has had private schools for a long time under various forms of control. For the last seven years, however, the school has been run by a committee of the citizens of Bishmizzin, most of whom are graduates of the American University of Beirut. The building occupied by the school was requisitioned during the war by the British military forces, and it was expected that it would be returned soon. At the time of the visit of the Commission the school occupied two rented houses. The school consists of an elementary school of six grades and a secondary school of four grades. It was planned to add an eleventh grade in 1946–47. By agreement with the American University of Beirut graduates recommended by the school would be accepted in the freshman class of the University provided at least two of the teachers have B.A. degrees and provided a laboratory is installed in the school.

In 1945–46 the school had 220 pupils, of whom 118 were boys and 102 were girls. Thus, the school is one of the outstanding examples of a coeducational primary and secondary school in Lebanon. It is staffed by a principal and eleven teachers, of whom six are women. The school follows the program of the government in the primary section, and that of the American University of Beirut in the secondary section. English is begun in the third grade and French in the sixth. The students come not only from Bishmizzin itself, but also from the various villages around it. The government gives an annual contribution of £L700 ($318). A deficit of £L1,500 ($682) in 1944–45 was paid by public-spirited citizens of the village.

The Lebanese Academy of Fine Arts was established in 1942–43 for the study of music. In the following year a course in architecture and another in art were added. These were scattered at first over three schools of the city. In 1944–45, however, the Academy rented its own building. It is maintained by a committee of Lebanese men and women and claims to be the only Lebanese institution of higher education.

Its course in architecture is of one preparatory year and four years of architectural training. Entrance is by a competitive examination based on the second *baccalauréat*. The preparatory year is for students who do not pass the examination or for holders of the first *baccalauréat*. Its program is identical with the *classe de mathématique* with the addition of drawing and design. In 1945–46 the architectural course consisted of only three years; the fourth year had not yet been started.

The course in music is divided into three stages: a first stage of three years, a middle stage of four years, and a final stage of two years consisting largely of repertoire selections. Every student must study at least one instrument. Instruction is given in piano, violin, cello, flute, clarinet, oboe, brass, and voice. All students take courses in theory of solfeggio, theory of music, harmony, counterpoint, composition, and instrumentation. The Academy has a choir composed of some of its men and women students and of girls from the National School. An amateur orchestra is made up of the Academy students, and for major performances some professional musicians are hired. The Academy has given programs in choral and instrumental music, including Beethoven's *Missa Solemnis,* Haydn's *The Creation,* Bach's *Christmas Oratorio,* Mendelssohn's *Elijah,* and Handel's *Messiah,* all under the direction of the president of the Academy.

The art section has no definite length of time for study. It gives instruction in painting, water colors, wood engraving, photography, and sculpture, together with theoretical studies in anatomy, shading, and history of art (the last named in conjunction with the School of Architecture).

In 1945–46 the Academy had 43 students in architecture, 130 in music, and 30 in art. It was staffed by about forty-five teachers, most of whom were part time. Fees were £L120 ($54.50) for art students, £L140 ($63.50) for music, and £L440 ($200) for architecture. Gifted poor students are exempted from payment of fees, as are students studying the rare musical instruments such as the oboe. The Lebanese government in 1945–46 granted £L8,000 ($3,636) toward the support of the Academy.

The movement for the foundation of private schools controlled by boards and societies seems to be spreading in Lebanon. For example, the League of Lebanese Women, which is perhaps the foremost association of women in Lebanon, established a progressive kindergarten in Beirut which quickly attained popularity. The Commission, however, was unable to visit it. In the summer of 1946 plans were being laid for the foundation of two boys schools of secondary level in the two well-known Lebanese villages of Suq al-Gharb and Shuwayr on premises formerly occupied by American and Scotch mission schools. The movement was led by graduates of the American University of Beirut. Still another school was being started in Marju'yun with money collected from emigrants from that region now living in England, Australia, and the United States.

Finally, as an example of the private school controlled by the individual initiative of one person, the Universal National College (al-Jami'ah al-Wataniyah) for boys at Aley may be cited. This school, founded in 1907, now has grown to large proportions. It has a French section leading to the first *baccalauréat,* an English section preparing for the American University of Beirut, a commercial section taught in English, and an agricultural section. There was a total of 625 students in 1946, of whom about 200 were boarders. A girls school of about 250 students is maintained in another part of town; it, too, has an English section of three secondary years, and a French section of two years in the secondary school. A summer school is maintained for those who fail in the examinations of the College or of other schools, and for students who wish to prepare for examinations. The student body is composed of students from Lebanon, Syria, Iraq, Palestine, Transjordan, Iran, Hijaz, and West Africa. Graduates of the English section recommended by the College are admitted into the freshman class of the American University of Beirut.

The College has a number of student societies and student teams. It has a library of about 1,200 volumes and occupies a building owned by its founder. Fees range from £L60 to £L230 ($27 to $104.50), and in addition a boarding fee of £L650 ($294) is charged.

Part Seven

INTERPRETATION

Chapter 29

EDUCATION AND CULTURAL CHANGE IN THE ARAB WORLD

*W*E HAVE NOW come to the end of our journey. Our account of Arab education has been mainly factual and descriptive. No attempt was made to evaluate the systems described or to present suggestions or recommendations. Problems and trends were depicted with hardly any indication as to their ultimate solution or outcome. The reader was left to decide for himself about the merits of each educational system and the problems confronting it. For that, only the most meager of background material was provided.

Yet education is essentially a social process, intimately connected with the stream of life around it, with the currents and crosscurrents of events, with the heritage of the past and the hopes of the future. It is only appropriate, therefore, that after this lengthy account of education in the six Arab states visited, an attempt should be made to gather up the threads of our inquiry; to summarize the problems and trends, and in general to throw the educational picture against the background of political, social, and economic life in the Arab East.

To do this properly would require a separate investigation in itself. Here only a comparatively brief attempt can be made. What in general is the present situation in the Arab world? What are the main characteristics of life in it? Which way is the Arab world heading, and what are the problems it is facing? And, finally, what are the educational measures which have been taken to cope with the major problems and needs and changes in Arab life today? How adequate are they, and what can be done to improve the educational endeavors of the various countries? To these question only a partial answer can be given at present. Our remarks will apply only to the Arab systems of education, and, unless specifically stated, they will not apply to the Hebrew system of education in Palestine.

Background of Arab and Near Eastern Life

The Near East, of which the Arab countries are a part, lies at one of the most strategic points in the world. It provides the connecting link between three continents—Asia, Europe, and Africa—and in this way lies at the crossroads of world communication, by land, sea, and air. This fact has affected Near Eastern history from very early times and has made it an area coveted by many nations and races. At least two other factors have tended in the same direction: the benign temperate climate which, at its hottest, is semitropical, and the potential wealth of the country. In its early days its agricultural wealth was of prime importance; more recently, mineral wealth in the form of oil has attracted international competition. It is not, therefore, an accident that the first civilizations known to history had their birthplace in this region, more particularly in the valleys of the Tigris, the Euphrates, and the Nile. Even the comparatively scanty supplies of such minerals as copper helped very early in history to transfer man from the stone age to an age in which he began to use metal tools in his peaceful, as well as warlike, pursuits.

It is this geographical position of the Arab East which made it the center of trade routes and of paths of invading armies from the very dawn of history. Routes converge upon it from the east through the Iranian plateau; from the north through the Caucasus, the Hellespont, and Asia Minor; from the west through the Mediterranean Sea; and from the south through the Arabian desert and Egypt, the Persian Gulf, and the Red Sea. Along these routes came invading armies and wholesale migrations of peoples, and from this center armies moved in all directions. This fact partly explains the racial composition of the Near East. As far as the Arab world is concerned—especially the Arab world in Asia—the races can be roughly divided into two groups: the Semitic groups coming from the south and including among them such peoples as the Babylonians, the Assyrians, the Aramæans, the Canaanites, the Hebrews, and finally the Arabs. They have given the region its predominant character and provided it with its main cultural heritage. The second group of races are the non-Semitic peoples, which include the early Sumerians, the Kassites, the Hittites, the Medo-Persians, the Philistines, the Greeks, the Romans, the Mongols, the Kurds, and the Turks. Between these two groups a battle seems to have gone on throughout history, with the Semites seeming to win out in the plains of Iraq, and in Syria and Palestine, and the non-Semites preponderant in Asia Minor and in the northern mountains of Iraq and the Persian mountains to the east of it. The Semites never seemed to be at home in the colder and the rougher mountainous regions, though they occasionally darted through them and controlled them for a while. The non-Semitic races, while getting a foothold every now and then in the plains, were usually driven out or assimilated.

Owing to this geographic determinism, the Near East has, in its long history, managed to be almost always in the center of the picture. The world does not seem able to leave it alone, nor can the Near East afford to remain isolated from world events. Events of the last century and a half and particularly of the immediate present seem amply to confirm this fact.

The welter of races invading the Near East, each leaving in it a stratum of racial deposit, has not only made of it a very ancient melting pot of races, but also a breeding ground of many cultures and the repository of foreign cultures introduced into it. With a clash of races there was also a clash of cultures, and as each race left its remnants in flesh and blood, so did it also leave its remnants in customs, moral standards, dress, religions, literature, art, architecture, languages, and many other aspects of life. Many of these are apparent even today, while many others exercise a more subtle influence. As the traveler or student goes through the Arab East, he cannot help realizing that many of the current practices and tools in use go back to very early times. The camel and the tent, the raft and the *gufa*[1] sliding down the Tigris and Euphrates, the *shaduf*[2] in Egypt or *chard*[2] in Iraq as methods of irrigation, the dress of the great majority of people, the religious beliefs, the superstitions, the customs of hospitality, the tribal and clannish feuds, the standards concerning women, and sundry other phases of life—these have their roots in the very remote past. To them are now being added, as has been done throughout the ages, new practices, new customs, new forms of dress, new tools, and new ideas and beliefs. The most superficial observer cannot fail to see that in any given spot in the Near East the old and the new stand side by side; the old never fully obliterated; the new not yet having its firm roots in the ground. The educator can only reflect that while education has to do with the present and the future, in the Arab Near East it cannot help being concerned with the past and the cultural heritage.

As far as the Arab world is concerned, for the last 1,300 years this racial and cultural heritage has been essentially a heritage from the Arab tribes that migrated into the Fertile Crescent, and established the Arabic language and the religion of Islam, with all the other components that go

---

[1] A round boat made of palm fronds and bitumen and propelled with paddles.
[2] Primitive device for lifting water from rivers and canals.

to make up culture. Yet, this Arab-Islamic culture is based on a firm foundation of the previous cultures that have nourished the Near East, Semitic or non-Semitic. A glance at the history of cultural migration shows that what is known today as Western or European civilization had its initial start in the Near East. Here it was born and through a few thousand years rose to a certain measure of maturity. Here were initiated so far as we know, advanced methods of agriculture and irrigation, of building and architecture, the wheel on land and the boat on the sea, the early geometrical and astronomical notions, the first phonetic alphabet, as well as the three important monotheistic religions of the world. This great cultural development was passed to the West, in the second and the first millenniums, B.C., largely through the travels and trading of the Phoenicians with the Greek and Italian shores, as well as through their colonies on the southern European shores, in Spain and in North Africa. The genius of the Greeks developed that culture to unheard-of heights, and gave the world its systematic philosophy, the systematizing of mathematics and astronomy, discoveries in medicine and some branches of science, and the great Greek literature, art, and architecture.

As the Greeks turned the tables on the Persians, and through Alexander the Great began to take the offensive, civilization began to go back to the East, which thereafter enjoyed the Hellenistic civilization reinforced later by the contributions of the Romans. For a thousand years the Near East was under the influence of Greek ideas, to which it added those of Christianity—an oriental contribution which spread far to the West. As the Arabs came into the scene in the seventh century, civilization had been for sometime on the decline. The Arabs in their turn, as representatives of the East, adopted certain phases of Greek civilization, merged them with some contributions of Persia and India, and with the religion of Islam, to constitute the great Arab-Islamic culture, which spread from India and Central Asia to Spain and the Atlantic. It was through Spain, southern Italy, and Sicily, through the Crusades and the traders of Venice and Genoa, that this civilization found its way into medieval Europe, and was a factor in bringing about the European Renaissance. As Europe took up the torch, the Near East fell a prey to a new wave of barbarian and semibarbarian invasions which obliterated its political and cultural life. Beginning with the nineteenth century, however, there has been a stream of cultural influence from the West back to the East, for the second time. And today the world is witnessing a new awakening in the Near East and the Arab world, owing to the impact of Western ideas.

Perhaps the best conclusion that can be drawn from this swift glance at

CULTURAL CHANGE IN THE ARAB WORLD

cultural migration is that the culture of the Near East and of the Arabs, while differing in some important respects from that of the West, falls essentially within the main cultural stream which has brought about the present Western civilization. In many fundamentals, therefore, the present Arab culture of the Near East is not entirely foreign to the culture or cultures of the West.

It is necessary to bear in mind these ideas about the racial and cultural heritage of the Arab East, and about the geographical location of the Arab countries, in thinking over the educational situation and problems in these countries. With this broad background it may be of use to survey briefly and pointedly the present situation in the Arab countries studied in this report and the main forces affecting their life and destiny.

Chief Aspects of Modern Arab Life

An agricultural economy

One of the most outstanding facts about Arab life is its fundamentally agricultural economy. The overwhelming majority of the people live on the land and subsist by agriculture. This is as true of Iraq as of Egypt, of Syria, of Arab Palestine, and Transjordan. Even Lebanon, which is proportionally the most largely urbanized because so many of its villages have been turned into summer resorts, is still largely rural. Built upon this agricultural economy is a system of trading and commerce whereby goods are exchanged within the country or exported and imported from and into the country. The farmer has to dispose of his produce in the towns and in return receives agricultural implements, clothing, tea, coffee, sugar, and a few other necessities and luxuries. The excess of the agricultural produce thus purchased in the towns is, naturally, shipped abroad, and in return goods are imported from abroad to meet the needs of the countries. A few industries exist which cater to the needs of the country districts. These industries, the remnants of a once-great past, have suffered a tremendous eclipse since the mass production of machine-made goods in the West. As a result most of the goods needed in the countryside are no longer produced locally but are imported from abroad, and the apparent balance of trade in almost all the countries surveyed shows an unfavorable balance of imports over exports. Thus, even the urban districts are to a great extent no more than marketing centers for the rural areas and live largely as mushroom growths on the countryside.

More recently, particularly after World War I, efforts have been made to revive industry and re-establish it on a modern machine basis. This movement is still in its infancy and has so far succeeded in introducing only lighter industries, such as the making of cotton goods, woolen cloth, soap, cement, sugar, leather products, and the like. In this movement Egypt is now undoubtedly the leader, partly because of the greater wealth of the country and partly because it has had an organized modern government and a modern economy for a longer time than the rest of the Arab world. World War II in some respects encouraged the growth of industry, especially in Egypt, owing to the difficult transport situation, which virtually cut off the inflow of manufactured goods from the West. How far the industrial movement can develop in the face of great competition of mass-produced goods is a difficult question to answer. There is no doubt that such a development is needed in order to raise the standard of living in the Arab countries and to improve the adverse balance of trade. It would also help utilize in a better way some of the agricultural produce of the countries, such as cotton and wool, which are now largely exported and are brought back in the form of manufactured goods from the West. So far as is known at present, the Near East has the power necessary to motivate the wheels of industry in the form of plentiful petroleum and water power, but does not have sufficient quantity of metal for the creation of heavy industry. Rich deposits of iron are reported in southern Egypt, but so far have remained unexploited.

The predominance of agricultural economy in the Arab East is perhaps the most important determinant of its low standard of living. More accurately it is the low level of efficiency in agricultural exploitation of the land and the prevailing methods of land ownership and tenancy which are the main causes of the low standard of living. On the whole the lands are fertile in Iraq, in Egypt, and in Syria, and less so in rocky Lebanon and Palestine. There is, therefore, a potentiality of high productivity in the soil if well exploited. At present, with the exception of Egypt, agriculture is more extensive than intensive, and the variety of produce is limited mainly to those grains more immediately necessary for the subsistence diet of the people. The growing of cotton in Egypt and of oranges in Palestine for purposes of export are almost the only exceptions. There is a great need for teaching the farmers more modern methods of agriculture, such as the use of fertilizers, the sound methods of irrigation, the improvement of strains of agricultural produce, the introduction of a greater variety of crops, the fighting of pests and parasites, the methods of grading the produce, and cooperative buying and selling of such produce. With these must be coupled more scientific methods of raising livestock, of improving the breeds, and of protecting them from diseases and scourges. In addition, there is need for the conservation of water resources and the better use of those resources, both for irrigation and for water power. Some of the lands of the Arab East today show many signs of better exploitation of water resources in the past than in the present. The remains of great canals in Iraq, of abandoned subterranean channels, and of wells in northern Iraq and Syria are the best testimony to that effect. At the same time the hillsides now largely denuded of trees, owing to centuries of cutting and little or no planting, are in crying need of reforestation. This will not only increase the timber wealth of the countries where timber is now largely imported, but will also help conserve the soil on the mountain slopes, and slow down the running of rain water in torrents, so that it could seep through the ground and be of more benefit to the vegetation. One might also add that in the great plains of Egypt, Syria, and Iraq there is an unlimited field for the use of agricultural machinery and improved farm tools.

The problem of land ownership

The systems of land ownership and land tenure are not such as encourage the development of agriculture and the improvement of the methods of farming. Indeed, they may perhaps be the greatest obstacle in the way of agricultural development. The prevailing system is either a situation where the government owns most of the land and leases it out to tribal chiefs and influential people, who in turn distribute it among individual farmers, or a system where large tracts of land are owned by wealthy landowners, usually living in the cities, who rent out the lands at comparatively high rentals to farmers, or exact from the farmers a more or less high share of the produce. Under such systems the individual farmer's annual income is very low and his interest in the improvement of the land is at a low level, with the result that in certain regions a deterioration of the land is manifest. As an added factor in Egypt, one must mention the fact that the amount of cultivable soil is limited as compared with the dense population of that country. While intensive farming is practiced, the exceedingly small plots exploited by each farmer, together with the payment of rent on them, make the income of the farmer sadly inadequate to take care of his usually large family. The net result is a very low standard of living and inability to support local institutions and social services, poor homes and clothing, the bare necessities of life, and barefootedness and disease. In some parts of the Arab world, notably in the Lebanon mountains, which form the original part of autonomous Lebanon, a system of individual land ownership prevails. Here one can readily see a more independent-minded farmer and at the same time a more prosperous one. Better and cleaner homes, better clothing for men, women, and children, and healthier bodies fostered also by the mountain climate are apparent.

Of late the Arab world has been showing signs of awareness of its land problem and of its injurious influence on its national interests and economic, political, and social development. The Iraq government is experimenting with a new method of distribution of state lands by fixing a limit on the number of acres that can be alienated to an individual. In Egypt an active movement of social service is spreading for the purpose of fighting illiteracy and disease, teaching better methods of farming and of social organization to the farmers. These are promising trends which, if pursued, may eventually lead to healthier farming communities.

This description of agricultural and rural life in the Arab world has its obvious bearing upon education. The low level of production and the meager wealth eked out of the land impede the development of education and sometimes make it impossible, but conversely there is also the fact that education, whether general or vocational, can be a tremendous force for the enlightenment of the people, for the improvement of agricultural technique, and for increasing the wealth of the farmer.

THE INFLUENCE OF ISLAM

Another outstanding fact about the Arab world is that it is predominantly Muslim. Islam is a religion preached by the Arab Prophet Muhammad and carried by Arabs and later their converts to the confines of the globe. It would be difficult here to do justice in describing Islam, as a system of faith, as a way of life, or as a world brotherhood. We are much more concerned here with the plain fact that Islam forms a predominant and substantial portion of the heritage of the Arab world. Not only has it influenced its beliefs and attitudes, its language, its expression and its mode of life to a very deep extent, but it has also literally brought the Arabs to a position of world dominion in the past and helped to preserve them as a nation, after the downfall of the Arab Empire. Largely though the Koran the classical Arabic language has been preserved as a living language centuries after Arab dominion disappeared. And as the Arab world reawakens, that same Arabic language regains a new vitality and a new force.

Muslim Arabs, whether they may be deeply religious or not, today are justly proud of their Muslim religion and heritage, and keep to it with an unshakable loyalty. This loyalty now manifests itself as an ally of Arab nationalism, and as a factor in the defensive struggle of the Arabs to maintain their identity in the face of Western imperialism. Often an attack from the West on the Arabs is pictured as a lurking danger, not only to the

Arabs, but to Islam, and forces are rallied for the defense of the cause of the Arabs, which is the cause of Islam as well. Thus today, as in the past, Islam is one of the forces that is helping to preserve the unity of the Arab peoples. In all of the countries studied, excepting Lebanon and Palestine, Islam is the official religion of the state, and its tenets are taught to Muslims in the public schools.

Today Islam, always a comparatively tolerant religion towards the adherents of other monotheistic religions, is becoming even more tolerant. There is a community of intercourse today between Christian and Muslim all over the Arab world, which is immeasurably greater than it was in previous centuries, in spite of the fact that religious lines still remain very distinct. In this movement the general enlightenment of the age, as well as the pressure of Western imperialism, have brought about a greater understanding among the adherents of the two religions engendered by a community of interests. This has been apparent in the national struggles of Egypt, of Palestine, of Syria, and of Iraq.

The rise of nationalism

A fourth aspect of life in the Arab world today is the resurgence of nationalism, which fills the air of the whole Near East and cannot be missed by even the most casual observer. Nationalism began in the Arab world in the latter half of the nineteenth century at the hands of literary men who rediscovered the beauties of Arabic literature and the glories of the old Arab Empire. Side by side with these were religious reformers who wanted to introduce reforms into the Ottoman government, which was then recognized as the successor of the Islamic Empire. As the two protagonists complained of the autocracy of the Ottoman sultans and the backwardness and corruption of their rule, the two voices tended to blend. Arab nationalism, however, did not begin to make rapid headway until the twentieth century when the overthrow of autocratic rule in 1908-9 brought to the fore the Young Turks as the ruling party in the Empire. The attempt of the Young Turks to pursue a pro-Turkish policy which did not give enough weight to the other national elements within the Empire brought a reaction amongst the Arabs, particularly their deputies in the Ottoman Parliament and their young students in the colleges of Istanbul. Open and secret societies began to be formed, some limiting themselves to internal reform, others asking for decentralized rule within the Empire, and still others calling for the independence of the Arabs. In its early aspects, therefore, Arab nationalism took the form of a struggle against the ruling Turkish element. In this it found encouragement from some of the foreign powers who entertained ambitions of partitioning the Empire for their benefit. World War I brought matters to a head when some of the Arab elements were dissatisfied with the entry of Turkey on the side of the Central Powers, and when the Young Turks took the opportunity to eliminate some of the leaders of the Arab national movement. The hanging of a large number of Arab leaders in Damascus and Beirut and the banishment of others gave the signal for plotting the Arab revolt. Sharif Husayn, of Hijaz, and his sons secured promises from Britain for the independence of the Arabs and declared a revolt against the Ottoman Sultan in 1916, joining the Allied campaign, which led finally to the overthrow of the Turkish armies. Thus, came to a close the first phase of the Arab national movement which was the struggle for the liberation from Turkish rule.

It was soon found out, however, that the Allies had, through secret treaties, partitioned the northern Arab countries into zones of influence and zones of outright occupation. At the same time the Balfour Declaration promised the Jews a National Home in Palestine. Strategic considerations, oil and other economic considerations brought final agreement between Britain and France which gave Britain the ascendancy over Iraq, Palestine, and Transjordan, and France control over Syria and Lebanon. As the League of Nations began to take shape, the idea of the mandate was invented as the form which British and French authority was to take over the Arab provinces of the former Ottoman Empire. The whole idea of spheres of influence and of mandates was opposed strenuously by the Arabs, who vainly sought for the application of the principle of self-determination to support their claim for independence. The demands remained unheeded, the mandates were granted to Britain and France, the principle of the National Home for the Jews was written into the mandate for Palestine, and the second phase of the Arab national struggle for liberation of the Arabs from British and French dominion and Zionist ambitions began.

The course of the national movement in Egypt has a different history. Muhammad 'Ali Pasha, the great founder of the present ruling dynasty of Egypt, had succeeded early in the nineteenth century in establishing himself as the ruler of Egypt owing allegiance to the Ottoman Crown. He had toyed with the idea of establishing an Arab Empire carved out of the Arab provinces of the Ottoman Empire. He had waged war against the Sultan and his armies, had threatened even the capital, Istanbul, but the interference of foreign powers finally led to the withdrawal of the Egyptian armies from Asia Minor and Syria, and Muhammad 'Ali had to be content with Egypt. His successors were given the title of Khedive or Viceroy, and for a long time Egypt pursued its own course within the nominal authority of the Sultan. The British occupation in 1882 gave an incentive to Egyptian nationalism which took definite form in the late nineteenth and earlier twentieth centuries by the establishment of the Egyptian Nationalist Party with the avowed aim of liberating the country from British rule. In their attempt to liberate Egypt from Britain, the Egyptian ruling class and the Nationalist party found a natural ally in the Ottoman Empire, a fact which created new ties with, and a new allegiance to, the Ottoman Sultan. It thus came about that Egyptian nationalism followed a different course from that of the rest of the Arab world which was trying to liberate itself from the Ottoman yoke. After World War I, however, the national struggle of both parts of the Arab world took the same direction, namely liberation from the two European powers dominating them, Great Britain and France.

The period between the two World Wars was largely occupied with the struggle for liberation which conditioned the attitudes and thought of the generation which went through it. A long series of demonstrations, boycotts, and revolts rose, now here, now there, in the countries under study. Slowly the nationalist movement made some headway. Egypt obtained some measure of independence and a constitution in 1922–23, and in 1937 secured the abolition of extraterritoriality and the promise of withdrawal of British forces to the Canal Zone. Iraq was finally declared independent and admitted into the League of Nations in 1932. Syria and Lebanon had a longer struggle, their independence being promised in 1941 by the de Gaullist regime, and put into effect in 1943. The withdrawal of French forces did not finally materialize until 1946. Transjordan was declared independent in 1946. In Palestine alone the struggle[3] of the Arabs against Britain and Zionism is still going on. A new nationalism, that of the Jewish Zionist immigrant, has sprung up. Though having conflicting interests, Arab and Jewish nationalism did not come into an open armed conflict except in isolated instances until 1948. Rather they have both, though at different times, directed their attacks at Great Britain, the author of the Balfour Declaration.

In the last few years Arab nationalism has taken a new direction, that of bringing together various Arab states into an Arab League which would try to bring some unity in their actions and policies and create a united front in the face of outside danger. The Arab League has also been trying to foster better communications among the countries of the Arab world, a more unified economic policy, bringing the various educational systems into

[3] The reader should keep in mind that this manuscript was completed in the summer of 1947.

closer relationships, encouraging Arab letters and science, and trying to bring about some sort of unified citizenship. All of these are still in their initial stages. Arab nationalism, however, seems to have the double task of bringing about internal reforms and of protecting the country from foreign intrusion. While Syria, Lebanon, Sa'udi Arabia, and Yaman are free from foreign armies, the other Arab states still have contingents of them.

Nationalism has not only been a potent force in the general life of the Arab world, but it has had an influence on its educational systems and practices. That influence is bound to continue for some time to come. The Arab educator usually thinks of schools as the main channel through which the Arab nationalist spirit can be spread and taught to the younger generation. Youth ought to be made proud of the nation's glorious past so as to be spurred to further action and to work for the revival of the Arab nation. They ought to be taught the geography of the Arab world and be made conscious of the possibilities of their land. There has gone into this phase of the struggle against Western imperialism an attitude of animosity toward any form of imperialism. This, naturally, has developed into some aversion toward some of the Western powers, though not against things Western in general. On the contrary, there is a general realization that acquisition of Western methods and techniques is in the national interest, although a dissenting voice may be heard here and there.

WESTERN IMPERIALISM

A discussion of nationalism among the Arabs brings up the topic of its antithesis—imperialism. Western imperialism has been responsible to a large extent for arousing the spirit of nationalism in the East. Western imperialism with regard to the Arab world had its roots in the nineteenth century when most of the known European powers had ambitions for the acquisition of land in Arab countries. Turkey being on the decline, there grew up in the nineteenth century what was known as the "Eastern Question," which in effect was little more than the problem of partitioning the Ottoman Empire among the ambitious powers. World War I provided the chance for it. While some of the contestants were out of the struggle—namely Russia, Germany, and Austria—the others, Britain and France, partitioned among themselves the Arab provinces in Syria, Palestine, and Iraq. Britain had already occupied Egypt, and Italy had wrested Libya. Britain besides had made treaties with a number of the Arab principalities around the coast of the Arabian peninsula which brought these definitely under her influence. For two generations in Egypt and for one generation in the rest of the Arab world, Western armies have been moving around in the Arab countries. There has naturally grown a desire for the withdrawal of these forces and for the realization of Arab independence in one state or in many states. This has created an attitude of defensiveness among the educated Arab class which is quite apparent in Arab youth and which has been nurtured by the press, the radio, the schools, and all other agencies.

It is difficult to predict the course of nationalism and imperialism in the Arab world. Most of the Arab states are now independent, but the conscious citizen of the Arab world has grown suspicious of any form of foreign influence, whether in the form of colonization, mandate, trusteeship, or economic developments. Even in cultural and educational activities Western efforts have now and then come under suspicion. The fact that the Arab world feels weak before the great force at the disposal of the Western powers aggravates this attitude. In some instances the attitude of aversion to imperialism has made students dislike the idea of learning a foreign language though the elders realize the benefits to be derived from that. In other instances, European powers have been accused of deliberately withholding facilities for education in the countries they occupied in an attempt to hold back the progress of those countries and keep them under their sway. In other cases they have been accused of intentionally spreading propaganda for their own countries through their own schools.

THE COMING OF DEMOCRACY

Political democracy came to the Arab world with the introduction of the constitutional reform in Turkey in 1908 and 1909.[4] Since then, with the rise of the new Arab states under the mandates of Great Britain and France and with the rise of independent Egypt in the twenties, all the Arab countries studied in this report except Palestine have developed their own democratic institutions which provide for elected representatives to meet in parliaments, either of one or two chambers. Cabinets are responsible to these parliaments, the king or president of a republic providing the final sanction for legislative and executive action. In theory therefore, the machinery exists for democratic rule by the majority.

In practice, however, this is limited by a number of considerations. In some of the countries, cabinets may be dismissed by the action of the chief of the state, without an adverse action by parliament, while in others the electoral system does not function as smoothly as is desirable. Elections may be by direct or indirect primary. At the same time, the fact that many of

[4] There had been an abortive attempt at constitutional government in the seventies.

the Arab states were under some form of foreign influence has meant, in some instances of conflict with the interest of the foreign powers, that democratic institutions have been maneuvered in order to sanction the interests of the outside powers.

Local and municipal councils also exist in most of the countries studied. These may be elected or appointed or both, so that the machinery for some measure of local government exists. However, it may be said that in a large number of cases, local councils are not strong enough to assert themselves in the face of the central government. Nor are their powers wide enough to respond fully to the wishes of the local population. The highly centralized forms of government naturally lead to policies being shaped more in the capitals than in the local communities. One justification for this is the widespread illiteracy and the lack of experience in handling local affairs with any degree of efficiency. Since the educated citizenry with its powers of progressive leadership is largely concentrated in the capitals, it naturally follows that progressive policies have to be formulated in the center and handed down to the provinces.

Thus, democratic institutions and ideas, though existing, have not yet taken firm root in the lives of the people. The average Arab is in his own way an inborn democrat. The old form of Arab tribal tradition, as well as the early Islamic tradition, is imbued with the ideals of equality among the members of the tribes or among Muslims, and matters are in the main decided not by individual autocratic methods but in council. The tradition of early Arab life, however, has throughout the ages been overshadowed by the autocratic rule of empires, so that the principles and ideals of modern democracies are not understood well enough at the present to insure the smooth running of democratic institutions. These are difficult enough to handle even in the most advanced countries. They will, therefore, need a long period of education before they take firm root. The Arab is an individualist by nature of his background, and democracy is in essence a cooperative method in which individuals act with due consideration to the will of the majority. Its essence is compromise between the conflicting points of view, a fact to which the extreme individualist does not take too easily.

SOCIALISM AND COMMUNISM

Yet, another, though more recent aspect, of the Arab scene is the appearance in the last decade or two of socialistic and communistic ideas and theories. These are not derived only from propaganda, more particularly Russian communistic propaganda. They have also come in through reading of French and English socialistic and communistic theories. Interest in these theories has also been developed by students studying in western Europe, particularly pre-Hitlerite Germany, France, and England. They represent a wide range of ideas from mild socialism to advanced forms of communism. The presence of widespread poverty among the masses of the people and the unequal distribution of land and of wealth provide a fertile field for socialistic and communistic propaganda, which can picture socialism as the natural and logical method of getting rid of all these evils. Another method used, especially by Communists, is to pose as an implacable enemy of imperialism and as a natural ally of the nationalist forces. The Western powers in Europe having been the aggressive powers occupying the Arab world, the net effect of communist propaganda would then be to discredit them and what they stand for in the eyes of the Arab public. It is in this way that the attitude taken by people sometimes takes the form of Communism *vs.* Democracy, Democracy being pictured as the ally of imperialism.

Socialism and communism are as yet too recent in the Arab world even to be considered as serious movements. The future spread of socialistic and communistic ideas will probably depend very largely on how the situation in the Near East is handled by the Western allies and how democratic the behavior of the so-called democratic powers is in the Arab world. It will probably also depend on whether the Western powers will be too busy looking after their interests and exploiting the resources of the country without giving due regard to the interests of the people themselves or whether they will ally themselves with the progressive forces in the countries working for reform and progress.

THE CHANGING SCENE

Finally, an atmosphere of change is one of the leading characteristics of modern life in the Near East and the Arab world. The habits, customs, attitudes of thousands of years are changing. The physical surroundings in the towns, as in the rural districts, are being gradually but surely changed by new forms of building and architecture, new methods of planting, of landscaping, and new ways of transportation. Along with these changes is coming a great change in ideas, values, and behavior, in art and literature, in character and moral affairs, and in political methods of organization. This change, which began in the early nineteenth century, has been gathering momentum with ever-increasing force. It is due almost entirely to the contact which modern communication has made possible between the East and the West. The invasion of things Western is not confined only to armies or to political predominance, but is also manifest in economic penetration whether by investment of foreign capital or the dumping of Western products of all sorts on the markets of the Arab world. It has also taken the shape of schools where Western ideas are expounded and taught to the new generations. Travel has played its part as has the study of Arab students abroad. More recently, the radio and the increasing supply of Western books and periodical literature have also played their role.

As a result, life in the Near East can be said to be in the melting pot. The old ideas and concepts are being gradually mollified and whittled down. There is, therefore, what could be called an increasingly liquid situation. Will it take any mold, and what type of mold will it be? Can this process of change be controlled or at least directed into certain channels? Or should it be left to the haphazard happenings of time? And if it is to be controlled and directed, then by what means? It would seem obvious that part of this direction at least can be exercised through education, though education alone is not strong enough to shape the things that are to come. The forces at play are too big and too varied to be confined in the schoolroom.

A number of anxious questions may be asked and are being asked about this cultural change. What will happen to the cultural heritage of the East? What of the religious concepts that have grown in the East? What of the customs, of the literature, and of the art can be saved under the driving force of Western civilization? Will most of these be swept away, or can they be adjusted to the new spirit and be so modified as to fit themselves into the new pattern of life? Will the Arab world be able to maintain not only its political independence but also its entity as a cultural unit? In the past the Near East succeeded in maintaining and assimilating within itself the cultural influences that bore upon it from outside. Will it be possible to repeat the process even in this dynamic age where things happen in a bewildering succession and where assimilation, therefore, becomes extremely difficult? Will the Near East, therefore, be culturally swept off its feet, or will the new culture so blend with the old as perhaps to provide a new message and a new contribution by the Near East to world civilization?

And what about Western civilization itself? Is it to be taken in its totality, or is it to be studied and scrutinized so that its virtues and weaknesses may be ascertained? Is the Near East to benefit from the mistakes made by the West in order to avoid some of them, or is it necessary that these mistakes be repeated? And how can the pitfalls be avoided? How shall Western civilization be understood? There is at present a pronounced tendency to be so dazzled by the achievements of Western civilization in the field of industry, of war and armament, and in the field of health and medicine that it is easy to overlook the other less apparent and more intangible forces that have made Western civilization, such as intellectual curiosity, freedom of thought and inquiry, the value of human life, the worth of the individual, his personality and ideas, the equality of woman with man, and many other ideals which have influenced the development of systems of government, economies, and social life. Will these more subtle aspects of Western civilization be appreciated well enough so that an intelligent attitude can be taken toward that civilization? And how is that going to be accomplished?

Moreover, Western civilization is coming to the East from many lands and national groups—from America, Great Britain, France, Germany, Russia, and many other sources. Naturally, the national rivalries of these countries tend to show themselves culturally also, and there is often a conscious or unconscious attempt by the protagonists to push themselves forward to the exclusion of the others. What shall the attitude of the Arabs be toward each of these particularized forms of Western civilization? With the many national rivalries shown in the various foreign schools in the Arab world and by persons studying in the various Western countries, there have grown advocates among the Arabs of this or that national culture, one discrediting the other. In this way there has developed culturally among the Arabs a house divided upon itself, and various schools of thought and even of behavior have shown themselves. How is it possible to make these groups with different cultural backgrounds cooperate with each other? Is there any way by which this difficulty can be obviated at its source? Is it possible or desirable for the Arabs to take an eclectic point of view and pick from each culture what appears to suit their needs? How can that be done without risking internal complications? In the face of international rivalries, can the channels of contact with the multitudinous cultural influences be kept open so that the new Arab culture will have the broadest bases for its development?

All these questions and a number more present themselves about the cultural situation and the future adjustment of the Arab world to this impact of Western civilization. But one more question is basic. Have the Arabs any choice in this matter of cultural adaptation, and how wide is this choice? Not only is the power of certain Western nations such as will force upon the Arabs certain courses of action and adaptation, but the forces at work in general are so varied and so great that the choice in many instances will be extremely difficult.

Finally, what does all this problem of cultural change in the Near East mean when translated into educational terms? What does it mean in terms of schools, curriculum, and methods? How can education be so shaped as to help modify that Arab tradition without losing its essence? How can it help introduce the best in Western civilization while avoiding some of the pitfalls? And how can it work for the integration of the two so as to create a new whole which shall operate in the lives of the Arabs in the future? The problem can only be posed here by stating the need for an educational philosophy that will guide Arab educators in the future. Things so far have not progressed much beyond the mere raising of these questions, but as the Arab world and Arab educators attain greater maturity, they are likely to receive greater attention.

SUMMARY

In summary the following points of significance to education in the Arab world are indicated.

The Arab world is now nationally conscious. This consciousness is increasing and in the past has taken the form of a struggle for the liberation of the Arabs from Turkish rule and later from Western domination. This objective, now largely achieved, is being directed toward establishing some unity of policy among Arab states, designed as a defense measure for the preservation of national independence. At the same time nationalism now has the constructive task of developing the resources of the countries and introducing widespread reform.

Democratic institutions have been established. They need to be strengthened by a more enlightened electorate which will be more conscious of its rights and responsibilities.

The Arab world can be said to have unlimited opportunities for economic development. Large tracts of cultivable land running into millions of acres remain unexploited and those parts that are now under cultivation can be exploited more efficiently by irrigation, the conservation and utilization of water resources, and the utilization of water power. There is a great opportunity for future development for generations to come. The same may be said of certain types of industrial development and of the development of oil resources. The small population, sparsely distributed (except in Egypt, Lebanon, and Palestine), may, for the time being, set limits to this development, but when health conditions are improved, a steady rise in the population is noticeable, which in the long run, may bring back to the Near East its concentration of human power. In the field of agriculture and industry, as in the field of health, education can play a great role.

Finally, the impact of Arab and Western cultures presents a problem of its own. This problem can be stated as: How to build up a new Arab culture which will have the broadest basis possible, one which will have its roots deep in Arab and Near Eastern culture, Western, and world cultures? In the present cultural change established standards are melting away, and there is a moral danger that youth may lose its balance; character education to help youth orient itself becomes, therefore, an imperative and crucial need.

It is against this background, however inadequately stated, that the problem of education must be projected; and in the light of this situation the achievements and potentialities of education must be gauged.

Educational Problems and Prospects in the Arab States

Educational progress between the two world wars

The student of education in the modern Arab world cannot help but be impressed by the great progress which has been achieved in the last quarter of a century. Judged by the absolute ideal of universal school attendance and literacy, this progress may, to the superficial observer, seem to fall short of the standard of the civilized world. Considered, however, from the standpoint of the starting point, about 1920, the advance, in spite of all the political struggles and economic hindrances, has been very great. In many instances school attendance has been trebled and quadrupled, and in some instances multiplied by ten and more times. This is true in all the countries surveyed, though in different degrees. Not only has there been a quantitative expansion of the educational systems, but also a rise in the standards, an establishment and advance of higher education, and some measure of qualitative change in the curriculum. One cannot ignore also the positive advance in the field of education of girls, a fact which holds great promise for the future. The sending of educational missions abroad has helped to educate a staff of specialists and leaders in the various fields, and all the countries are contemplating plans for increasing the number of missions. Coupled with all this is the rising demand for education among the people—a demand which cannot always be met with the resources at hand, resulting in a lag between demand and educational facilities provided. There has also been great improvement in textbooks, in equipment, and in school buildings. Before World War I governments were not fully conscious of their responsibilities in the educational field, and, therefore, education lagged far behind other activities of the state. Today all the governments in the countries visited are actively engaged in increasing educational facilities so that tax-supported schools form the bulk of the school system except in Lebanon.

A BREAK WITH THE PAST

In building up their educational systems, most of the Arab states have abandoned the old form of common, ungraded school, the *kuttab*, and established new forms of schools modeled after the Western graded types. The only exception to this is Egypt, where, along with the modern European type, the former *kuttab* has been developed, improved, and graded to include all the usual studies of elementary education except a foreign language, and with a greater emphasis on religion and Arabic. In a way, therefore, the new educational development in the Arab world represents a break with the past and an orientation in a new direction. The reasons for this break are largely historical. The gap between Western progress and life in the Arab world was so great that in their anxiety to catch up with the advance in science and to establish colleges for the training of medical men, engineers, army officers, and the like, the governments had to establish modern schools to prepare youths for entry into these colleges. The old school, limited to the Koran and the three R's, was hardly adequate for this purpose.

WESTERN INFLUENCE AND WESTERNIZED SCHOOLS

A contributing factor which brought about this trend was the influence of foreign individuals and groups operating in the Near East and the Arab world. The first educational council in Egypt, established in 1837, was made up almost entirely either of foreign persons in the employ of the Egyptian government, or of Egyptian students who had studied abroad, mainly in France. Later a foreign inspector was employed for almost twenty years, and after the occupation of Egypt by the British, British officials played a large role in the shaping of educational policies until 1922. In other parts of the Arab world—especially in Syria, Lebanon, and Palestine—foreign mission schools preceded any organized modern government schools established by the Turks and naturally served as models for both public and private schools established later. The public-school system of the Ottoman Empire, established in the latter half of the nineteenth century and improved in the early twentieth century, was largely influenced by Western models, notably the French. With the coming of the mandates of Syria, Lebanon, and Palestine, French and British educational authorities played a controlling influence in the shaping of education in the postwar period. In Iraq the new educational system was started in 1915 by the

British authorities and later was developed by Iraqi educators who had been influenced either by French or American types of education.

It is a source of no wonder, therefore, that education in the various countries studied shows many signs of imitation of Western models. Western curriculums and methods were borrowed. Western systems of examinations, mainly after the French model, were adopted, and today one of the main sources of pride in some of the countries is the fact that the standard of the baccalaureate is as high as the French, or that the standard of matriculation is higher or more difficult than that of the University of London. Things went so far even as to have the Arabic-speaking children in public schools taught in foreign languages. This was true in Egypt, for example, between 1885 and 1907, and of Lebanon during the French mandate. A high standard of proficiency in foreign language was required. The result was a high percentage of failures among those students who could not rise to the academic and linguistic standards set in elementary and secondary schools.

It was only natural that educators coming out of the West, or Easterners studying in the West, should fall to copying Western models, particularly at a time when educational research had not yet started in the Near East, and traditional forms of organization and of curriculums prevailed in the West. Transplanted from Europe and America to the East, methods and curriculums, however suitable they might have been to the needs of the Western countries because they had grown up within them, could not meet adequately the needs of Eastern countries. When large public-school systems began to be established, it became more and more a pressing problem to scrutinize critically these Western models and their suitability for the needs of the Arab countries. This has not been done to any marked degree. The reason is largely the fact that most of the educational systems are too recent to have had the long historical evolution which would make for their adaptation to their new environment.

NEED FOR PROFESSIONALLY TRAINED PERSONNEL

But there is yet a second reason. It is the lack of educationally trained personnel in the various departments and ministries of education in the Arab world. For the most part, educational policies are being shaped by people who have had some form of education, now usually higher education, but who have had little acquaintance with educational philosophy, with educational psychology, with modern techniques of educational methods and curriculum construction, and the various problems of educational administration and organization.

This seems to be one of the outstanding needs of the educational departments of the various countries. Some are completely lacking in professionally trained personnel, others have a very inadequate number of them. Yet the problems to be studied scientifically are legion. There is need for social and educational theorists who will be able to deal with the educational problems in relation to the general social, political, and economic background of the countries, who would translate into educational terms the various currents and changes in Arab life. There is need further for a study of the multitudinous needs of the environment in order to lay down curriculums that will meet these needs. The simplification of the teaching of Arabic is a problem faced by almost every Arab educator, and upon its proper solution depends to some extent the success of campaigns for combating illiteracy.

No standardized mental and achievement tests as yet exist in the Arab world, so that it is difficult to follow scientifically the progress of students, to diagnose their abilities or defects, and to make adequate provision for their needs. Educational administration is carried on in an amateurish fashion, which often is wasteful of time, effort, and funds. New buildings are sometimes constructed so poorly that they fall into ruin within a decade or two, and there is hardly any computation of a standard cost per unit of classroom or school. A professionally trained staff would help avoid many mistakes and pitfalls, and would help lay down sound and broad plans for the development of education in the future. Hundreds of such trained men and women are needed throughout the Arab world to occupy key positions in educational administration, in the teachers colleges, and in important strategic schools.

Along with the steps that need to be taken for the training of such personnel, there is need for establishing research centers in education and psychology which will study specific problems facing each country. Such research will make it possible to base educational policy on scientific studies and to adapt education to the needs of the countries.

Centralized Systems

The present study has clearly shown that education in the Arab states is almost completely centralized. Policies, curriculums, textbooks, plans for expansion, examinations, and certificates are all handed down from the central offices in the capital of each country. Under the central office there are usually regional offices which take their orders from it and which exercise a limited influence on the shaping of educational policies. Their job is to execute the orders of the central office and to see that those subordinate to them apply them properly. The local communities have little to say about courses of study, books, methods, the appointment of teachers, and in actual fact contribute little money or effort towards the maintenance of their own local schools. Throughout the various states (except possibly in Lebanon) there is a certain dependence on the central government which leaves almost everything in education to it. Education is financed almost entirely from the central budgets, and little local taxation exists. This does not make for local interest in the schools, or local concern about them, or local cooperation in their proper running. The school is not conceived of as a part of the community, but as a part of government which is something different from the people.

The reason for this state of affairs is in part the fact that all government and public institutions are centralized in the same fashion, and in every department of the government orders are received from the center and applied in the provinces or localities. Even local councils and the municipalities in which they exist do not have the strength that they have in Western countries. But there is still a deeper reason. The best talents are usually concentrated in the capitals, and the idea prevails that it is up to the intelligentsia to lead the way in the regeneration and development of the country. People in the smaller centers cannot be depended upon to lay down constructive, progressive policies. Since centralization prevails in all the departments of the government, it is naturally difficult to decentralize educational administration. Yet this is greatly needed at least to a degree. It is needed to arouse more interest by the people in the education of their own children. It is needed for levying local taxes and providing local funds for the better and wider development of schools. Today schools have to secure almost everything from the central government—buildings, desks, salaries, as well as library books. Local responsibility is also needed in order to establish a bond between the school and the community, so that the school can better influence the life of the community and the community provide a stimulus for the activity of the school. The development of local institutions is also needed for better democratic living as well as for better running of social and educational services.

Attempts have been made in some of the countries toward throwing some of the responsibility for education on the shoulders of local authorities. In Egypt provincial councils were asked to bear the cost of the compulsory schools, but not enough taxing power was granted these councils to enable them to support the schools, and the main burden, therefore, fell again on the central treasury. In Palestine the government has insisted that the Arab villagers provide the buildings for the schools, and councils have been empowered to levy taxes for the schools. In this way a large number of schools were built and even teachers employed by the local authorities. More interest in the schools by the people can be witnessed as a result, and while educational facilities are admitted to be inadequate by the government itself, throwing the responsibility on the local communities has had a beneficial effect in arousing in them a sense of responsibility for education. In Iraq the establishment of local councils has just been written into law, and it is not possible to predict how this scheme will operate. In Syria responsibility for village school buildings has also been laid upon the local authorities. These measures are still in their infancy and are far from being perfect. Why, for example, should villagers in some of the countries be required to provide the school buildings, while the government provides them in the cities—usually rich municipalities—is difficult to explain or justify.

LIQUIDATION OF ILLITERACY

Perhaps the most fundamental educational problem facing the Arab world today is the double problem of putting every child of elementary school age in school, and of liquidating illiteracy. The Arab states have arrived at various points along the road toward the solution of this problem. Table 92 gives a general idea of the relative educational progress in

TABLE 92
Proportion of Children in School in Six Arab Countries
(in the period, 1942-45)

Country	Estimated Population	Estimated Population of Elementary-School Age*	Number Attending Elementary Schools	Percentage of Appropriate Age-Group in School
Egypt	18,000,000	2,870,000	1,360,000	47.4
Iraq	4,500,000	675,000	135,000	20.0
Syria	3,000,000	375,000	148,000	39.4
Lebanon	1,100,000	165,000	120,000	72.7
Transjordan	400,000	50,000	14,000	28.0
Palestine (Arab)	1,250,000	207,000	107,000	51.6

* Estimates of the elementary-school-age population for all countries are based upon the age-distribution tables of the 1937 census for Egypt. Similar distribution figures were not available for the other countries. The estimates make allowance for a six-year range for Egypt, Iraq, and Lebanon, a five-year range in Syria and Transjordan, and a seven-year range in Palestine.

each country. The figures presented are only approximate, but they give some indication of the present situation and of the task ahead.

An examination of Table 92 shows that Lebanon has put in elementary school the largest percentage of its school-age population. Following in order are: Palestine, Egypt, Syria, Transjordan, and Iraq. It would seem that Lebanon has within its grasp the stamping out of illiteracy among the rising generation, provided an active policy is pursued by its Ministry of Education. Palestine would come next, where it is estimated by a responsible authority that the present education budget would have to be doubled if compulsory attendance in elementary schools was enforced. Palestine can, therefore, be considered to have within its grasp the possibility of compulsory attendance if the authorities are willing to pursue that aim actively.

In the other countries the position is somewhat more difficult because of the long road that still is to be traveled and the lack of funds; it was estimated in Egypt, for example, that the most modest compulsory attendance at an elementary school would cost approximately **twenty-four million Egyptian pounds ($96,000,000)**, or 25 percent of the present total budget of Egypt. Similar situations, though in different proportions, exist in the other Arab states. The main problem, therefore, is essentially financial, and its solution will depend on the rise of the standard of living of the common man in each country and the rise in his average income, so that he may be taxed sufficiently to support a complete educational system. This problem of educational expansion ties directly with economic development and reform in each of the countries. An agricultural economy running at a low level of productivity cannot support a system of universal education. Before that is possible, greater productivity and more extensive and intensive exploitation of the soil must be made, and perhaps more industrial development must take place in every country. It should be remembered that universal elementary education, long an aim in European and American countries, did not become a reality until the industrialization of these countries, or until an extremely efficient agricultural organization, such as that of Denmark, was achieved.

In some of the Arab countries universal education is hampered by other factors. The social organization of the large section of the population which is tribal and the sparcity of the population in many regions slow down the spread of education. The liquidation of illiteracy among adults is even a more difficult problem. In the preoccupation with the education of the young, not much effective work has been done for adults. In Iraq a vigorous movement for the liquidation of illiteracy started in 1922, had so slowed down by 1930 that it was taken over by the Ministry of Education as one of its routine activities in evening schools in towns and villages. Now some 10,000 students of all ages receive a small amount of instruction in these schools. In Egypt the Ministry of Social Affairs was launching a large program for fighting illiteracy in 1945–46. It is too early to judge its results. In other Arab states little was being done in this field.

What Type of Elementary School?

The problems of universal attendance and liquidation of illiteracy are not the only ones connected with elementary education in the Arab world. Indeed, some internationally known authorities on education have been shifting the emphasis from the liquidation of illiteracy to the whole question of raising the standard of living of the masses. This is undoubtedly the basic issue, but it cannot be dealt with purely by means of education. It requires a much wider program which is at once political, economic, hygienic, and social, sponsored by progressive governments. Education would then be one of the chief agencies for the realization of such a program.

It must, therefore, be asked: What type of elementary school and what types of curriculums are best calculated to improve the life of the masses, and indeed of all the people? At the present time elementary schools in each country have one common course of study prescribed by the central authorities.[5] This is to a large extent bookish and academic, borrowed from abroad, and designed to prepare for the passing of examinations. For the most part the only adaptation to local needs seems to be the teaching of Arabic and of the history and geography of the Arab lands, particularly the land in which the school happens to be. To this is added some instruction in health, again of a bookish type, and, in the village schools, some instruction in agriculture. For this there is little practical application except in Palestine and more recently in a few schools in Egypt and Transjordan. The best development along this line has undoubtedly been in the Arab system in Palestine where school gardens have been established in 238 schools and practical instruction in agriculture is given to the pupils of grades five through seven. The practical training varies with the locality. While fruit-raising may be emphasized in one environment, vegetables, cereals, or beekeeping or a combination of these may be emphasized in another. There is, however, even in Palestine little sign of any attempt to tie up the activities of the school with those of the community. As in the rest of the Arab states the elementary school moves in a world by itself, divorced from the world around it.

The new development in Egypt is too recent for any accurate evaluation. There is certainly a need in all of the Arab world to examine carefully the type or types of elementary schools that fit the rural environment of the large majority of the population, that would help raise the standard of

---

[5] Egypt has several, one for each type of elementary or primary school, all prescribed by the Ministry of Education.

agriculture, of health, of social consciousness, of citizenship, and of character. Even though such an ideal has been spoken of before by some Arab educators who have studied abroad, it has not yet been translated into action.

THE CURRICULUM AND THE ELIMINATION OF PUPILS

Another problem connected with elementary schools is an offshoot of the problem of compulsory attendance. In all the countries studied it was found that the number of pupils in the elementary schools eliminated in the successive grades was large. In some cases this elimination was so large that it raised a serious question about the effectiveness of the education given to the large majority of the children. In many places they did not average more than two or two and one-half years of school and, therefore, ran the danger of reverting to illiteracy after leaving school. In some cases, as in Egypt, while hundreds of thousands of pupils are registered in the first grade of the compulsory schools, only a few thousand were found in the fifth grade. In Iraq, Transjordan, and Syria, while the proportion was higher, no more than 5 to 10 percent of the total student body was in the upper grade. No figures are available for Lebanon, but, judging from some of the schools visited, a similar, but perhaps not as pronounced, situation seems to prevail. In Palestine elimination in the first four grades is comparatively limited, but registration begins to drop sharply after the fourth grade. Some of this is accomplished by design on the part of education authorities owing to lack of places in the schools. Some study of the phenomenon of elimination has been made in Iraq, but no thorough scientific investigation of it has been conducted with a view to analyzing its causes and prescribing some remedies. Such a study is needed in all the countries.

Elimination of pupils is due in part to social and economic forces, but it may also be due to the types of curriculums and methods followed. These are too dry and unattractive to the child and often to the parents. The courses of study are, as a rule, too filled with logically organized subject matter unrelated to the environment and too heavily loaded and difficult for the average student to be able to master them. This results in a large percentage of failure and retardation and tends to keep the lower grades overcrowded while depleting the number of pupils in the upper grades. The average age rises correspondingly in the upper grades so that pupils take an average of seven to eight years to complete an elementary school of six years. The problem of elimination and retardation, therefore, has its bearing not only on the measures to be taken to enforce attendance, but also on the type of curriculum to be followed. The large number of failures in the public examinations at the end of the elementary-school stage seems to confirm this point.

Too often it is assumed that a high standard must be maintained in elementary schools. Those pupils who cannot attain that standard are consciously or unconsciously thought of as unworthy and, therefore, are weeded out. The idea of fitting curriculums and standards to the capacity of pupils, though often admitted in theory, does not find much application in practice. It happens, therefore, that those who pass through the sieve of examinations are the minority that go on for further education and present the justification for the maintenance of the so-called high standards. In most of the Arab countries these students pursue their secondary or higher education only to gravitate for the most part toward government and "white collar" jobs. The other students can be said to fall into three groups: (1) those students who will keep on trying and who therefore pass from grade to grade taking a longer time at their work and providing the laggards and the misfits in the upper elementary classes and the secondary schools; (2) those who drop out in the upper elementary classes or in the secondary schools but who think of themselves as too well educated to work with their hands; (3) those who drop out early in their school life, often to revert to illiteracy, and become farmers, laborers, and artisans. Thus, a certain stratification results where skilled, as well as unskilled, labor becomes the province only of the dullards who cannot go through school and attain a higher academic standing.

It would seem evident that the pursuit by educational authorities of a high academic standard in the elementary school takes into account neither the abilities, interests, and needs of individual peoples, nor the economic needs of the countries concerned. It would seem evident that this outlook needs to be so modified as to make the course of study more in agreement with the needs of the environment on the one hand and of the individual pupils on the other. While certain basic minimum essentials might perhaps be required, there certainly exists a need for more gradation and variation in the courses of study. It must be said that the practice of dictating curriculums by the central authority and of examinations by the same authority does not leave much room for this variation.

The uniformity of the elementary course of study for all children is, however, defended on national grounds. It is argued that the country is in urgent need of a united citizenry and that it is the business of the school to give a unified course of study that would help to produce it. While this aim is a legitimate one and while there is certainly a need for greater unity among the citizens of the Arab world, it does not follow that this can be achieved by rigidly setting down courses. Some measure of uniformity may be legitimate in the so-called "national" studies, namely, Arabic, history and geography of the Arabs, and civics. But there is certainly room for variety in the other subjects of the curriculum which would facilitate fitting them to the needs of each locality and to the needs of individuals. Moreover, even in the national subjects there is possibility of variety of treatment, both in method and content. The insistence on uniformity may, in the long run, be injurious to educational advance in the Arab world because it stifles the possibility of experimentation and of trying to devise new curriculums and new methods.

SECONDARY EDUCATION

In the secondary schools the same tendencies prevail. All over the Arab world the only type of secondary school that exists is the academic secondary school. Division of the course into scientific and literary and sometimes mathematical and biological sections is almost the maximum of variety attempted. These schools are, therefore, of the college-preparatory type. The only exception is a commercial secondary school in Baghdad, the certificate of which is accepted for purposes of admission to some higher institutions. For the rest, any schools for the same age level which give a different course of study or give a vocational education are not accepted for purposes of university education. In Iraq and in some other countries, graduates of some of the vocational schools, thought of as equivalent to secondary schools, may continue their education in higher schools of the same type. But this is not usually the case, nor is the way open to the students to change over to another type of higher education without loss of time.

There is thus some preferential treatment in favor of academic secondary education which creates an attitude in all concerned—whether school authority, parent, or student—that this is a superior kind of education which it is the ambition of every parent to give to his child. As a rule, therefore, it is students with lower abilities who are squeezed out of academic schools and who take refuge in the vocational schools. Vocational education thus carries a stamp which does not attract students to it. This is one of the factors which has operated to make it largely unsuccessful in the various countries of the Arab world. In some of the Arab countries this problem has received some thought, notably in Iraq, where for some time the creation of a number of parallel secondary courses with a vocational bias has been advocated. The suggestion first came from the Monroe Commission in 1932. It has, however, met with strenuous opposition by the advocates of the unity of the courses of study. Recently this topic was again brought up, and it was thought that secondary courses with a commercial, agricultural, technical, and home-economics bias might be created. So far, this has not gone beyond the stage of preliminary thinking. Vocational education is given in separate schools. As yet the need has not been felt for vocational guidance of students after they graduate from elementary school. Since secondary education is of an academic type, it can readily be seen that hardly any grounds exist for raising the question.

Availability of secondary education.—Another aspect of secondary education—its availability to youth in general—needs some attention here. This problem has received some consideration in Iraq, Syria, and Egypt. In these countries a system of exemption from fees on the basis of economic need or academic achievement, or both, exists which may exempt wholly or partially from 25 to 40 percent of the student body. The annual fees at their highest are rather low: in Iraq,[6] $18, and in Syria, $27.30. They are considerably higher in Egypt, $80. In addition, Iraq has established for each of its fourteen provinces a system of complete scholarships with free board, lodging, and books for a number of brighter pupils. Thus secondary education may be said to be available to most of those who can graduate from elementary school, although the cost of maintenance away from home for village youth may be a barrier for many who are not at the top in the public examinations. Syria has recently established a system similar to that of Iraq. In Egypt, while a wider range of exemption has been allowed since 1943, it must be remembered that the division of the educational system into two ladders, primary and elementary, makes the secondary schools available only to the minority of the well-to-do who go through the primary schools, while the majority who graduate from elementary schools find the road to secondary education blocked before them. Not unless they can transfer to the primary schools and spend some additional time in study, can they hope to enter secondary schools.

In Palestine and Transjordan provision for public secondary education is extremely limited. Under a very stringent method of selection only the most capable of the students can finish their secondary education in the two or three public secondary schools that exist in Palestine. For the poorer of these students a system of scholarships exists, but the scope of secondary education is so limited as to make its availability to the youth of the country almost insignificant. In 1945–46 Transjordan maintained only one complete secondary school. Two others, however, were on the

Secondary school fees have since been abolished in Iraq.

point of being completed. In Lebanon, reliance has been laid on private and foreign secondary schools and the Ministry of Education maintains no complete secondary school. Any students, therefore, wanting to complete their secondary education must go to the private and foreign schools where high fees are charged with a minimum of exemptions. The poor boy or girl of Lebanon finds it exceedingly difficult to complete his secondary education. It is surprising how many sacrifices and privations Lebanese parents are willing to undergo in order to send their children through secondary school. A system of public secondary schools or at least of public scholarships for promising students is sorely needed.

Extension of the facilities for secondary education.—No clear-cut policy seems to have as yet emerged in any of the countries with regard to the expansion of secondary education. While Lebanon has thrown the responsibility for secondary education almost entirely on private and foreign schools, Palestine has followed the policy of restriction, apparently out of fear lest overproduction of secondary-school graduates would leave a large number of these graduates unemployed who would become a possible source of agitation. Students have, therefore, sought to enter private and foreign secondary schools in large numbers; and, as the demand grew, a larger number of private secondary schools were established to take care of it. It must be added that this restriction of facilities of public secondary education in Palestine is also attributed by the authorities to the lack of funds and to the preference to devote funds mostly to primary education. In the other countries expansion has been left to the pressure of circumstances. Ordinarily most of the graduates of primary schools in Egypt, Iraq, and Syria want to continue their education through secondary schools. Attempts by these countries to restrict entry into secondary schools have not been too successful. Iraq has wavered between what may be called the open-door policy and restriction with the former winning most of the time. The same may be said to be true of Egypt. As the provision for secondary education lagged behind the demand, there was a tendency for classes to become larger in Iraq and Egypt. Recently Iraq has been trying to base admission of pupils into public secondary schools on academic accomplishment in the public examinations. Students who fail more than once in any class are also eliminated. Exemption from fees has been linked with quality of achievement, so the beginnings of a policy seem to be emerging. However, if students fail to find a place in the public secondary schools, or if they are eliminated along the road, they have tended to enter the private schools, and a large number of these schools have been growing up in both Egypt and Iraq.

Up to the present the government authorities seem to take the attitude of being responsible only for the students capable of secondary education. What the governments can do to care for the education of those who are not so capable is a question that seems to have arisen very rarely, if at all. However, more recently under the influence of developments abroad, principally in England, Egypt has raised the question of other types of education parallel to secondary schools for the students of lesser ability. This attitude is still in its infancy.

Vocational education

Vocational education is perhaps the least successful aspect of education in the Arab world. On the whole it can be said that vocational schools are not popular, and in many instances there is difficulty getting recruits to fill the classes even moderately. The reasons for this are many, though no scientific study of them has been made. Perhaps the most fundamental among them is the fact that industry is still in its infancy in the Arab world. As the cottage hand trades have been waging a losing fight with modern Western industrial products, so has there been an industrial dislocation in the various Arab countries. The new industry based on machinery is beginning to make its appearance, but is still a struggling infant. Naturally the demand for skilled, industrial workers is not great, nor is the appreciation for the preparation of such workers. Rather, as small industries arise, the tendency has been to train skilled workers on the old apprenticeship basis, using illiterate boys as the principal source of supply. Workers so trained are willing to accept lower wages than are the graduates of trade or technical schools. As they have the more practical kind of training in the actual industry, they are usually more favored in finding jobs than the literate student who has combined theory with limited practice.

Among the reasons for the nonpopularity of vocational education is the fact that secondary-school graduates are reasonably sure of a steady income with no strenuous work to soil their hands. Since the government official in the past has enjoyed a great deal of prestige, government jobs are coveted. It follows that the academic studies leading their graduates to government jobs become the more popular. Even the educational authorities themselves have paid much less attention to vocational education, and have consciously or unconsciously held it in somewhat lower esteem, though often acknowledging the necessity for it.

Some other factors have impeded the progress of vocational education in some countries. In Iraq, a practice of discriminating against students in vocational schools in the form of nonexemption from military service has acted as a factor contributing to the small number of applicants for vocational schools. Students would rather enter the secondary schools, in which case their military service is postponed until after graduation. They then receive reserve-officers training for nine months. Vocational-school students are not so favored and have to serve for two years as privates. In Palestine vocational education has been hampered by the unsettled conditions of the country which necessitated the occupation by the military of the physical plants of the agricultural and trade schools almost continuously from 1936 to 1945.

With regard to agricultural and commercial schools, similar forces are in operation. Many businesses are content to conduct their accounts in a primitive way rather than employ the services of what they think is an expensive clerk. In this respect the various countries of the Arab world are not of the same level. In centers such as Beirut or Cairo one finds a greater trend toward accepting modern business methods than in Damascus, Aleppo, or Baghdad. Appreciation of agricultural education follows the agricultural development of the country. It is more advanced in Egypt because of the great agricultural development in that country for the last half-century. The prevailing systems of land ownership and distribution are a great hindrance to agricultural development and agricultural education. Farmers are at best conservative; but when a farmer does not own his land and lives on a subsistence level, he is not likely to want to improve his land nor is he capable of supporting a son through a vocational school. A further hindrance to the development of vocational education is the lack of experts. There is a great need for well-trained teachers and leaders in the various branches of vocational education. The problem of vocational education is crucial in the Arab world because upon it depends very largely the development of the resources of the countries, the efficient exploitation of the land, and the training of skilled workers for industries. Of late, efforts have been directed toward developing vocational education as a variety of secondary education. American experience and developments in England have been influential in creating this trend both in Iraq and Egypt. These plans, however, are still in the realm of ideas, and the leadership to put them through is lacking. Some progress has been achieved in Egypt, where fairly successful vocational schools of various levels—elementary, intermediate, and higher—exist.

PUBLIC EXAMINATIONS

All of the Arab systems studied emphasize examinations at the end of each period of study. The Government (Arab) system in Palestine holds only one public examination, the Palestine matriculation examination. No primary examinations exist, but a rigid system of selection of students on the basis of school records is practiced after the fifth grade. Transjordan has two public examinations—a primary and a secondary examination. Egypt, Syria, and Iraq have three—a primary, an intermediate (or general) examination, and a secondary (or special) examination. Lebanon has four examinations—a primary, a *brevet,* a *Baccalauréat,* Part I, and a *Baccalauréat,* Part II. Usually a pupil is not allowed to proceed to the next higher stage without first passing the examination at the end of the previous stage. Examinations thus serve the purpose of selecting students for the next step on the educational ladder and are often effective methods for eliminating pupils. Elimination may range in any examination from 25 to 50 percent, rarely less and rarely more. There is, therefore, a great fear of the examinations by students and teachers alike. Many schools have special classes outside regular school hours to help prepare students. The anxiety felt by the children, the cheating, and, rarely, a leaking of questions are part of the system.

Examinations also have an influence on the course of study. In government schools those who set the courses and the examinations are the central offices of the ministry of education. Students, whether in public or in private schools, are on the whole unwilling to pay much attention to studies that are not included in the public examinations, and school education becomes to a large extent a preparation for the examinations. Naturally education in its broad sense suffers. Private and public schools cannot venture very far in experimenting with new curriculums. Thus, examinations act as an obstacle to educational experimentation and progress. Public examinations are held under strict secrecy so that those who correct the papers cannot know the name of the pupil whose paper they are correcting. There is in the system, therefore, the element of mistrust of school authorities. Principals and teachers are not depended upon to judge the progress of their own pupils, and to base upon this judgment the recommendation for the granting of school certificates. It is said that teachers and principals if left to themselves become subject to pressures from parents and people in authority. The responsibility, therefore, is taken out of their hands and rests on the higher authorities. Naturally, this does not make for high morale or sense of responsibility among teachers, both badly needed in all the systems visited.

Examinations are further justified on two counts. It is said in the first place that they help raise the standards of teaching both in private and in public schools, but particularly in the commercialized private schools. Secondly, they are said to insure that private schools come under a certain measure of control by the government in the interest of national unity. Public-school curriculums require certain subjects of national importance, such as Arabic and local history and geography. Examinations are useful in insuring that these subjects shall be properly taught. It is hardly necessary to point out that school standards are being maintained in many countries, without the help of public examinations, by raising the standard of educating teachers, by better-equipped schools, by better libraries and laboratories, and by systems of supervision which help keep the teachers alert and create in them a sense of professional pride and responsibility. Subjects of national importance can be required from private and foreign schools as, indeed, they are now being required. The proper teaching of them can also be insured by proper supervision without the necessity of rigid examinations which create mistrust in all the teaching body, hinder experimentation, and are a constant source of neurotic worry besides being detrimental to character in the incentive they give to cheating. An easing up of the examination systems, especially in the lower stages of schooling, is greatly needed, and would be the first step toward liberalizing the courses of study and toward educational progress in general. This is, however, going to be difficult to achieve owing to the prevailing ideas about centralization which are difficult to eradicate.

EDUCATION OF TEACHERS

The problem of the expansion of the elementary schools in the six Arab countries naturally creates the problem of the preparation of teachers in adequate numbers and training for the system. Radical differences exist among the countries in the level of preparation and the number of trained teachers that they produce. Transjordan has no teacher-training institution. In Palestine and Lebanon the number of teachers graduated from normal schools and teachers colleges is extremely small. Accordingly, recourse has been had to appointing as teachers, graduates of secondary schools and individuals with much less education, sometimes even elementary-school graduates. Syria has recently recognized the problem and increased the capacity of its teacher-training institutions, though the existing facilities are still short of the need. Egypt and Iraq are the only two countries that are training elementary- and primary-school teachers in more or less adequate numbers.

The level at which elementary- and primary-school teachers are being prepared also differs radically. In the dual system of primary and elementary education in Egypt, primary-school teachers have for many years been prepared on a four-year college basis and in certain instances on the basis of two years of professional study beyond college work. More recently, a two-year course above the general secondary certificate has been instituted. This is now being lengthened to three years. On the other hand, elementary-school teachers receive an academic and professional training that is hardly equivalent to secondary education. In Palestine two years of academic and professional training beyond the secondary school are a standard practice for men teachers, while women teachers for city schools have thus far received a training of only one year beyond secondary school. Rural-school women teachers are of a much lower standard, and no school for the training of rural men teachers exists, except that those who have passed the matriculation examination could take a year at the Kadoorie Agricultural School at Tulkarm. The teacher-training course at this school, however, has not been in operation for some time.

In Lebanon, two years of training are given to both men and women students in a course that is hardly equivalent to Lebanese secondary education. In Syria, the new training scheme, which is likely to become general, is of three years above intermediate schools. In Iraq, rural teachers are trained in special institutions which are roughly equivalent to secondary schools, while city teachers receive a training equivalent to one or two years above secondary schools. Thus, the education of teachers in the Arab states ranges from a minimum of training that is less than a secondary-school certificate, to a maximum of two graduate years beyond college work.

The chief problems with regard to the education of teachers seem to be quantitative and qualitative. On the quantitative side it is the need for trained teachers in adequate numbers to meet the rising demand for elementary education. This has been met more or less well in Iraq and Egypt, although the rate of the education of teachers would prove inadequate once these countries embarked on a vigorous program of expanding their elementary education. In the other four countries supply is far short of the demand, and makeshift arrangements are resorted to which compel authorities to employ unqualified teachers in large numbers. A forward-looking policy is needed to prepare professionally trained teachers in numbers adequate to meet the demand for public elementary education. Private and foreign schools, however, are also finding some difficulty in recruiting professionally trained teachers. The teacher-training institutions are almost wholly public and prepare teachers for the public schools. The graduates of these institutions prefer to be in the public-school system because they are usually paid more adequate salaries, have more secure positions, and are usually protected by retirement plans. This leaves the private schools almost entirely without professionally trained teachers. The private schools are so heterogeneous that they cannot get together to establish teacher-training centers of their own.

The governments have not paid enough attention to this problem, being preoccupied with the problem of preparing their own teachers. Some measure of cooperation is needed between the government authorities and the private and foreign schools for the preparation of teachers for these schools. Such a cooperation will probably be hard to realize, partly because private schools will not have the resources, even with contributions from the governments, to maintain such an institution, and partly because the attitude of cooperation does not always exist between some of the government departments and some of the private and foreign schools, or among the private schools themselves. There is here certainly the opportunity for foreign institutions of higher education to render some real service in providing professional education for teachers of private schools. This has been done on a somewhat small scale in the field of high-school teaching. But there is a wide field in training for elementary-school teaching. So far, however, there has not been sufficient demand for such a course. The demand will probably not arise until a minimum of professional education is required by law from all elementary- (and secondary-) school teachers.

On the qualitative side, greater attention should be given to the preparation of rural-school teachers. The current practice of sending the poorest teachers to the countryside should be stopped. If it is true that the economy of all these countries depends largely on the development of their agricultural resources, then their rural life needs to be reconstructed. In this reconstruction a great role can be played by a special kind of rural school which pays adequate attention to the needs of its environment. Such a pioneering school needs well-prepared teachers. Teachers are needed for the rural districts who not only master the common subjects, but who also have an adequate acquaintance with agriculture and with the social and health problems of the countryside.

Iraq and Palestine are the only countries which have tried to grapple with this problem. Special rural-teachers colleges have been established in Iraq where agricultural and health training are given to the students along with academic subjects. Students are usually recruited from the countryside itself. The general plan seems to be correct, but it is feared that the way it is being handled, largely due to the lack of well-trained staffs in the teachers colleges, is not securing the quality of teachers that is wanted for the rural schools of Iraq.

The problem resolves itself into that of staffing the teachers colleges with capable men of vision and of adequate professional education. For the present, most of the staff of the teachers colleges are either former teachers of secondary schools or people who are academically but not professionally trained. Often principals of teachers colleges are men with no professional training and, therefore, have no conception of their task. Teachers-college instructors should be men and women who, in addition to experience in teaching in elementary schools, have had some graduate study in their field of specialization coupled with professional study in education. The teachers colleges need not only specialists in education, but also specialists in sociology who can conduct original research in the social problems of their country. In addition, there is a great need for teachers of the practical subjects such as agriculture, manual arts and crafts, physical education, and some of the fine arts, such as music, art, dance, and rhythm. Many of the teachers colleges are sadly lacking in this respect. The great potentialities of the people along these lines remain undeveloped.

One of the things for which rural-school teachers need to be specifically trained is the simultaneous teaching of more than one class. In the many rural schools visited in all of the six countries, the American Council Commission does not recall a single instance in which a teacher was able to conduct successfully the teaching of two groups, not to say three, at the same time. In almost all the instances one group remained idle while the other was being taught. Specific training in this technique is badly needed.

In the preparation of secondary-school teachers, Iraq has maintained a four- or five-year course above secondary school for men and women which combines academic training with the professional. Egypt followed the same system down to 1930 and later replaced it with the institutes of education which give two years of professional training beyond college work. For the rest, reliance in all the Arab world for recruiting secondary teachers has been on college or university graduates who are for the most part only academically trained. Graduates of the American University of Beirut and at Cairo have been a common source of recruiting, together with some graduates of French, British, and American universities. Many secondary-school teachers do not have a university training. Syria has just started a higher teachers college following roughly the lines of the Higher Teachers College in Iraq, while Egypt is re-establishing the higher teachers college for preparing teachers of science and mathematics.

Two schools of thought are current with respect to the professional education of secondary-school teachers. One is to postpone this training until after graduation from the university; this follows the Continental and the British method. The other is to combine in one course both academic and professional training. Arguments for both have been given. Iraq and Syria and the American Universities at Beirut and Cairo have generally followed the second scheme. Egypt, acting upon the advice of the late Professor Édouard Claparède of the University of Geneva, has for the last seventeen years followed the Continental scheme. Here, as in the case of elementary-school teachers, the problem is largely one of producing enough teachers and of staffing the teacher-training institutions with able professors. In addition, one must again mention the need for research centers in education connected with the teachers colleges—elementary, secondary, and higher.

Another angle of the problem of the preparation of teachers is their training in service. Little organized, regular, and constant effort is being exerted in this direction in any of the countries studied. Here and there a summer training course or evening classes are held. The teachers, therefore, tend to sink gradually in their professional competence, easily fall behind the times, and lose morale. School inspection is rarely directed toward improving the knowledge of the teacher. Nor are school principals usually much better trained than their fellow-teachers. Plans are needed in all the countries for regular summer and full-year courses for teachers and for the training of capable principals who can help their teachers improve themselves. Publications for the benefit of teachers are also needed. The Iraq Ministry of Education and the Education Department of the Haut Commissariat of the former French government in Syria and Lebanon have been the only public education departments that have published educational magazines for the benefit of teachers. Some governments have maintained qualifying examinations for teachers, but these are more for the purpose of raising the level of the unqualified teachers than for improving the level of those already qualified.

FOREIGN LANGUAGES

Foreign languages occupy an important place in the programs of modern schools of the Arab countries. The reason is not far to seek. The location of the Near Eastern countries on the world highways has forced upon them contacts with many peoples and cultures and, therefore, acquainted them with many foreign languages. It has made their people more sensitive to languages and more linguistically minded. Languages have been important for the relationships of the ruling and the ruled and for purposes of trade. Moreover, with the greater mobility afforded by modern communications, a large number of foreign tourists, travelers, and salesmen, as well as armies, have appeared on the Near Eastern scene. Illiterate boys coming in contact with British tommies picked up English on the streets of Baghdad in 1917, as do the dragomans on the streets of Cairo. The fact that the Near Eastern countries are learning Western science, Western technology, Western philosophy, and all other branches of Western knowledge has necessitated also their learning many Western languages, not only French and English, but also German, Italian, and Russian. The appearance of a large number of foreign schools in Egypt, Syria, and Palestine, each teaching in its foreign language, has enhanced this tendency. Some of these schools made the teaching of their own language one of their primary purposes and insisted as much on fluent speech as on a high standard of writing in it. In this, the French schools probably were the most successful. For a large number of students in foreign schools, it became easier to think, speak, and write in a foreign language than in their own Arabic.

As national systems of education grew, sometimes under the control of foreign powers, foreign languages naturally occupied a prominent place and sometimes were even made the medium of instruction. This was true for a certain period in Egypt, and in Lebanon and Palestine. This could not have failed to arouse an antagonistic reaction among the nationalistic elements in the various countries, and as the countries began to be liberated from foreign rule, the question of foreign languages began to come to the forefront. The controversy centers around four points: (1) What foreign languages? (2) How much foreign language, and when to begin to teach it? (3) Is it necessary to use the foreign language as a medium of instruction? (4) What is the effect of the emphasis on the teaching of a foreign language on the teaching of the national language?

With regard to the first question, there has been a transition over the whole of the Near East from French, which was predominant in the nineteenth century, to English. This is as true of Egypt as of Syria and Iraq. The shift from French to English has been very abrupt in Syria and has assumed the proportions of a boycott of the French language. French is still favored in Lebanon, but there is a perceptible shift to English. The question is being decided more by the growing political and economic prestige of the Anglo-Saxon world than by any educational considerations.

The amount and time of beginning foreign-language teaching are questions on which there is a wide difference of opinion. Lebanon lies at one extreme, for there the teaching of foreign languages in public, as well as in private, schools begins in the kindergarten. At the other extreme lies the new reaction in Syria which has led to the abolition of the teaching of foreign languages from all elementary schools. The middle position is taken in Iraq, Transjordan, Palestine, and Egypt, where a foreign language is generally begun with the equivalent of the fourth or fifth grade. A new movement in Egypt, however, advocates the postponement of the teaching of the foreign language to the first year of the secondary school. Two reasons are usually given for this stand. First, a student must be allowed to master the elements of his own language before being started on a different one, lest the teaching of the foreign language interfere with the mastery of the native language. The second is the difficulty of preparing enough teachers with a mastery of the foreign language to be able to give a good start to all children in the school system, that is, in remote rural districts as well as in urban communities. The advocates of the earlier teaching of foreign languages state that such early teaching insures learning the language with the least of trouble. It is said that starting a language at the age of eleven or twelve does not make for its mastery by most of the pupils. This point of view is taken in Lebanon, where it is pointed out with pride that foreign-language teaching, whether French or English, is most successful. There is general agreement, however, among all educational authorities that at least one foreign language is necessary in secondary education. All public-school systems give one foreign language in secondary schools, and some of them give two.

The national systems of Egypt, Palestine, Transjordan, Syria, and Iraq have decided against teaching through the medium of a foreign language in elementary and secondary schools, and all teaching in the public schools is done in Arabic. Most of the foreign schools, however, and some of the private schools, teach in a foreign language and not in Arabic, particularly in the secondary schools. We have seen that in Lebanon most of the teaching in elementary and secondary schools was formerly conducted in French, but that the new programs are giving greater place to teaching in Arabic, though allowing the teaching of some of the subjects in the foreign language. In higher education both practices are followed. Medical and technological schools, even the public ones, with the exception of the medical school of the Syrian University, teach in English or French while other schools usually teach in Arabic, but may give some courses in a foreign language.

This brings up the fourth point, namely the influence of teaching in a foreign language upon teaching the national language. The Arabs are anxious that their language shall be well taught to their children and shall become an adequate instrument for the expression of all kinds of ideas, whether social theory or scientific technology. They are, therefore, anxious that their children shall use Arabic as a medium of learning and instruction to the fullest extent possible. It is true that, after centuries of darkness, Arabic was outdistanced as a medium of expression by the modern European languages. There is, therefore, today the problem of coining scientific terminology in Arabic, and in general of expressing scientific ideas and abstruse theories in Arabic. Arab intellectual leaders contend that their language will rise to the occasion as it did in the past, but can only do so if it is used as such in the schools as the medium for expressing scientific ideas. They complain that the insistence of foreign schools on teaching in their own languages retards the development of Arabic, and accuse some of the foreign schools, particularly the French, of deliberately neglecting the teaching of Arabic.

The Commission was not, of course, able to go into this question thoroughly within the very limited time at its disposal. It did, however, make some attempt to explore it in the schools and to ask opinions of various authorities and teachers about it. As a result, the Commission has formed certain impressions and conclusions which it presents for what they are worth.

It is, indeed, unfortunate that the neglect by certain foreign schools of the Arabic language and the emphasis on their own language has led to the general impression that the teaching of a foreign language may be detrimental to the teaching of the national language. It has also created such resentment as to help confuse the issue and make it appear that it is the national language versus the foreign language. But this need not necessarily be so. In inquiring about this question, the Commission was told by a number of experienced teachers, particularly in Lebanon, that it was quite possible, given a healthy and sympathetic attitude on the part of school authorities, to teach the two languages to a high standard. Indeed, a number of such schools are found teaching English or French, as well as giving adequate attention to Arabic. There is no scientific evidence to support the theory that the teaching of a foreign language is necessarily detrimental to the teaching of the national language. The main trouble has been the wrong attitude taken by some schools which favored the foreign language over the national language. The Commission, therefore, would put a question mark over the whole theory and would suggest that here is a fertile field for experimentation, which can be conducted by public-, private-, and foreign-school authorities. It may very well be that in certain aspects, such as some topics in grammar or sentence construction, there may develop some interference between the two languages, but it may also be just as true that in certain other topics they might reinforce each other.

With regard to the time to begin foreign languages there is some evidence to show that an early start is better than a late one. Such seems to be the case in a bilingual country such as South Africa. The experience in Lebanon, where foreign languages are more successfully taught perhaps than in any other Arab country, would tend to point in the same direction. It is not, however, possible to dogmatize on this question. Lebanon has been so much in contact with foreigners and the teaching of foreign languages has been going on for such a long time that an interest and an atmosphere favorable for foreign languages have been created. Parents insist on their children learning a foreign language and may speak it at home themselves. Another factor also is the fact that in many of the schools foreign languages are not only taught as languages, but are a medium of instruction, and it is precisely in schools where these languages are used for instruction that they are best learned. Here, again, there is need of scientifically controlled experimentation. In the meantime most school systems are taking a compromise position.

In view of the need for foreign languages in the Arabic-speaking countries, the Commission is of the opinion that it would be unwise to postpone the teaching of a foreign language until the secondary school. The age of twelve is a late age to start a foreign language, and it must be remembered that the age at which the average pupil leaves elementary school is higher than twelve, so that a large number of children would begin their foreign language at the age of thirteen or fourteen. For all except the brighter pupils such a late start would preclude proficiency in the language, not to say mastery of it. One of the serious objections to starting foreign-language teaching in the elementary school is the administrative one of providing enough teachers of foreign languages for the outlying village schools. Another objection is the lack of need or interest in a foreign language in the villages. It must be admitted that it would be very difficult to train foreign-language teachers for all the present and future rural schools of the Arab world. The Commission is of the opinion, however, that teachers can be trained for a sufficiently wide selection of them. Again, the experience of Lebanon is illuminating where some of the farthest outlying schools have been able to secure teachers of French or English who have attained a fair degree of proficiency. It is not necessary that a foreign language shall be taught in all elementary schools, but that it should be taught in the more important ones where there is a sufficient demand for it and in schools so distributed that pupils desiring a foreign language in one village may obtain it in a nearby larger village school. Another possibility is to give additional hours of foreign-language teaching in secondary schools to those children who could not have it in their village elementary schools.

In considering the use of a foreign language as the medium of instruction, Arab educational leaders are undoubtedly right in wanting to develop Arabic as the medium of thought and expression for their own countrymen. They are, however, at the same time anxious to see their students master foreign languages well enough to be able to read foreign literature on all the subjects of specialization and on all aspects of life. The question of a new dynamic Arab culture is intimately connected with the problem of foreign languages, and it is necessary that the intellectual leaders of the Arab countries shall be masters of one, and perhaps more, foreign languages. This does not necessarily mean that content should be taught in a foreign language. Again, a compromise position may well be a solution. There is a good deal to be said for teaching certain subjects one year in the native language and another in a foreign language, and varying these subjects from year to year so as to give the student the experience of reading, thinking, and speaking about these subjects in the two languages. Some bold experimentation in this direction is needed.

FOREIGN SCHOOLS

Foreign schools have played an important part in the intellectual life of Syria, Lebanon, and Palestine in the last three-quarters of a century, and a somewhat lesser part in Egypt. Their influence in Iraq and Transjordan has been much less. Throughout this period, and particularly before the growth of the national systems of education, foreign schools did pioneering work in spreading education both in the cities and in rural areas. They spread the knowledge of foreign languages and acquainted the peoples of the countries with Western science and Western learning. They have been particularly strong in emphasizing character education. While their influence has been effective mainly among the minority groups of Christians and Jews, they nevertheless have influenced a considerable number of Muslims. Until 1920 almost the only worth-while higher education available in Syria, Palestine, and Iraq was at the American University of Beirut and at the French Université Saint-Joseph in the same city. Foreign missions have given special attention to the education of girls, often giving it precedence over the education of boys. This was clearly the case of the American schools for girls in both Beirut and Tripoli, which preceded the present American schools for boys. The French nuns also did, and still are doing, great and effective work in female education. Moreover, a number of the native leaders in the fields of politics, business, and medicine are graduates of foreign institutions. Even the national movement may be said to have been enhanced to a certain extent by some of the more liberal foreign schools. A number of outstanding leaders of the Arab national movement have been graduates of the American University at Beirut. For a long time foreign schools enjoyed a special prestige and a somewhat privileged position in the Arab countries.

However, certain aspects of foreign education and some types of foreign schools have come under sharp criticism. One of the important criticisms is found in some resentment among non-Christians at the attempt of most foreign-missionary schools to require attendance in Christian religious classes and in Christian devotional services, even of non-Christians. A similar resentment, though much milder, is often felt by a Christian parent belonging to one denomination who sends his child to a school of a different denomination. This is branded as an attempt at proselytizing and is resented particularly by Muhammadan parents. It does not prevent many parents, however, from sending their children to foreign schools although it is quite apparent that the enrollment of Muhammadan students in foreign schools would have been much larger had not the fear of Christianization deterred many a parent from sending his children. It is not without significance that in countries where the overwhelming majority of the people are Muhammadans, the majority of students in foreign schools are usually non-Muhammadan.

Another accusation leveled at some, though by no means all, of the schools, is that of creating sympathies for their countries of origin. This is often branded as active propaganda for these countries, and, with the growth of national feeling throughout the Arab world, this propaganda has come to be resented more and more strongly. Along with this goes the criticism of the neglect of the Arabic language and of the teaching of the geography and history of the Arab and Near Eastern countries, while at the same time great pains are taken to teach the foreign languages and the geography and history of the foreign countries. The net result of all this has been to alienate the sympathies of a large section of the younger generation from their own country and to make them look toward the particular foreign country of the school in which they were educated. In this way the national movement was handicapped. This criticism is particularly leveled at French and Italian schools. American schools, it is fair to say, have been rather free of this outlook. In no American school did the Commission find any special emphasis being put on the history or geography of America.

A third criticism has been that the foreign schools belonging to various nationalities have as a net result helped to divide the loyalties of the youth of the country among these nationalities. The different methods of education pursued in each have created different attitudes and different patterns of behavior which have tended to make cooperation among the graduates of the various institutions difficult. It is claimed, therefore, that this has been one of the principal obstacles in the way of the national movement. In catering largely to the minority groups, foreign schools have tended to sharpen the already wide cleavages between the various religious communities.

Finally, prior to the growth of the national systems, foreign schools were quite independent, and under the Ottoman rule were protected by the regime of the Capitulations. They were to a large extent a law unto themselves. During the autocratic rule of the Ottoman sultans, such a situation may have been helpful to more than one liberally minded teacher or student, but with the rise of national governments, the situation of the schools came to be more and more resented.

As a result there has been a gradual shift in the attitude toward foreign schools in the last twenty-five years. One factor in the new situation is the fact that the growth of the national school systems has made the various countries less dependent on foreign schools than they previously were. They are now subject to greater criticism than before, and some of them are under suspicion. The last two decades have witnessed the assertion by the various national governments of their authority in claiming and exercising the right of supervision of foreign schools. This right was first established by the mandate authorities in Iraq, Syria, Lebanon, Palestine, and Transjordan, but with the passing of the mandates it began to be exercised by the national governments. Along with the right of supervision, new laws have been passed in Egypt, Syria, Lebanon, and Iraq which set limits on the activities of foreign schools. Teachers and textbooks are to be approved by the governments, and in Iraq the right of elementary education for Iraqi children is given exclusively to the state and to the nationals of Iraq. In some of the countries the schools follow the same programs in the teaching of Arabic and Arabic history and geography and civics as those of the government schools, the government appointing the teachers. Foreign schools are in some countries definitely forbidden to spread foreign propaganda. Finally, the institution of public examinations has set definite limits on programs of studies which may be followed in private and foreign schools. Many of the parents are anxious that their children shall pass the government examinations. Entrance to government higher educational institutions as well as to government jobs and many other such privileges are dependent upon achievement of this goal. Foreign schools have been obliged by the pressure of circumstances to prepare their students or a large portion of them for the public examinations. Many of them have adopted the procedure of maintaining their own course of study on the one hand, and the government course of study on the other. In some instances the schools are required to follow the official government program.

It is clear that this whole trend of setting limitations on the foreign educational activities is due partly to the abuses committed by some foreign schools, and partly to the rise of national feeling in the Arab world. The trend is becoming increasingly pronounced and has been giving considerable food for thought to the authorities of foreign schools. In some cases doubts have arisen in the minds of certain of them about the worthwhileness of continuing in the face of such restrictions. It is undoubtedly true that some of the schools which have been free of the criticisms leveled at foreign schools are likely to suffer through no fault of their own. It is contended that rather than subject all schools of whatever kind to the same restrictions, based on suspicion, a system of supervision should be devised whereby schools violating the provisions of the law about propaganda and weakening the national sentiment should be severely punished. In applying the same standard to both the innocent and the violating schools, useful activity is likely to suffer.

It may be said that this whole trend may be a passing one, brought about by national feeling of the Arab world asserting itself. As the Arab countries begin to feel more secure and sure of their national existence, they may feel that they can afford to take a more liberal attitude toward foreign schools. Leading men interviewed by members of the Commission were almost unanimous in their desire to keep and expand the activities of foreign, especially American, schools. It is asserted that these schools have values which could not be secured through public education. Many, however, stated categorically that they expected foreign schools to produce loyal citizens of the countries to which they owed allegiance, rather than to any foreign power.

At this point it is appropriate to raise the question of how foreign schools may be of use to the Arab world in the changing atmosphere and setting which now prevail in it. It is clear that the situation has materially changed from what it was in the nineteenth and early twentieth centuries. The old autonomy of the foreign schools is gone, however that fact may be bemoaned by some foreign school authorities. It is also clear that while in the nineteenth century foreign schools performed a unique function in countries which were virtually deprived of even elementary education, the rise of the national educational systems in this century has now made foreign schools far outnumbered by both the public and the native private schools. In elementary and secondary education, and in some instances in higher education, the work of foreign schools is no longer unique. Some of the national systems may even claim to set higher academic standards. It may be said that foreign schools may supplement the educational provisions existing in each of the countries, which are admittedly inadequate at present to meet the needs of those countries. This is undoubtedly true, but it must be said that many a foreign school today, far from relying for financial support on its country of origin, is almost entirely self-supporting through the fees collected locally. In this respect, a foreign school may be no more than one more private school of the type increasingly being established by the natives of the country.

What, then, can be the place and function of foreign education in the Arab world today? What should be the attitude of foreign educators in the Arab world? What should be the attitude of Arab educational authorities toward foreign schools? There is certainly a need for rethinking this whole question. The following remarks are offered by way of suggestions:

1. If it is recognized that one of the main purposes justifying the existence of foreign schools is to help the people of the country to a better life, it follows that these schools shall have as their aim the education of useful and loyal citizens for the countries concerned. In this their aim should be the same as that of the national public schools. Schools undermining that aim and seeking to create a foreign allegiance should not be tolerated. This does not mean that foreign schools are called upon to create any chauvinism or extreme nationalism that finds itself at war with all other nations, but it does mean that a positive effort must be made to bring up an enlightened and loyal citizenry which is set to serve its homeland. If a certain sympathy toward the country of school origin should develop, this should be an unconscious by-product rather than a positive aim to be actively striven for. In return, and once confidence is established, foreign schools have a claim to a large measure of freedom in following their own curriculums and methods, once the government is assured that the national subjects—Arabic, national geography, history, and civics—as well as the national spirit are properly taken care of.

2. In view of the development of the national systems of education, foreign schools should, as far as possible, seek to break new ground and to do what the national public and private schools are not able to do. They should keep up their pioneering spirit either by supplementing the work of the public schools, or by showing the way for new and useful develop-

ments in education. In this they have a rich background of their own respective countries to draw upon. They can, therefore, serve as agencies for putting before the Arab countries the valuable experience gathered in their own home countries. They should try to study the needs of the field in which they are working and help meet those needs through their educational endeavors. The following are some of the fields in which particularly useful work can be done by foreign schools, aside from ordinary elementary and secondary education:

a) Vocational education. It has already been indicated that the public-school systems have not been particularly successful in their attempts at vocational education. Foreign schools coming from a background where considerable experience has accumulated in this field can be of particular help in passing it on to the Arabs.

b) Experimentation with newer methods of teaching and newer types of curriculums. This undoubtedly is going to be hindered by the present attitudes developing in the Arab world, but with greater confidence between the governments and the schools, it should be possible to make some developments along this line. The schools should, indeed, claim it as their right to break new educational ground and show the advantages that would accrue to the countries.

c) Along with experimentation foreign institutions have the opportunity of providing, especially in higher institutions, modern training and research in the field of education.

d) The pioneering work of foreign schools in the field of female education should be expanded. They also have a better knowledge of how to conduct coeducational institutions.

e) Foreign schools can do an outstanding job in character education, as they have done in the past. A real example can be set before the public schools in this field.

f) Along with character education can go education in citizenship and the working of democracy. American, British, and French schools, rising from democratic backgrounds, should be in a better position to teach the methods of cooperation and of democracy than the public or native private schools.

g) Foreign schools will always do useful and outstanding work in the teaching of foreign languages. While this should not be done in a way that would mean the weakening of Arabic, through the successful teaching of foreign languages foreign schools are outposts of contact between Eastern and Western cultures.

h) In spite of the development of native institutions of higher learning, there is still a great field for foreign higher education, both liberal and professional. It will help to provide the intellectual, social, economic, industrial, and agricultural leadership for the Arab world. Foreign higher education, if well endowed, should share in graduate training in pure and applied research which would help the Arab world in the long run to share in contributing to the advancement of knowledge and to develop its vast, largely unexploited, material resources. There is, however, a still greater opportunity for foreign higher institutions. They can become centers not only of training Arab specialists, but of Western specialists in fields connected with the Near East. This part of the world is largely an unstudied field, and Western and Eastern specialists on all phases of its life are not many. Yet the Near East is a paradise for the archeologist, the ethnologist, the anthropologist, the sociologist, the linguist, and the historian. A great deal of work needs to be done on its geology, flora, and fauna, its economic, industrial, and agricultural problems and possibilities, its politics, government, and jurisprudence, its art, handicrafts, music, folk-dancing, and folklore. Foreign higher institutions provide the opportunity for bringing together Western and Eastern scholars and students to work on common problems. Each of the two groups would be the finest interpreter of its culture to the other. Here is intellectual and cultural cooperation at its best. The same should also be true, though to a smaller extent, of foreign elementary and secondary schools. In this way foreign schools can contribute to bringing about a better understanding between East and West.

CONFLICT OF IDEOLOGIES

A frequent topic of comment in books and periodicals, as well as in private conversation, is the conflicting ideologies among the newly rising generation which is often ascribed to the influence of different foreign schools attended by students. The following, taken from a newspaper article in Beirut is typical:

One of the catastrophies which has hit the rising generation of this country is the divergence of outlook and tendency resulting from the divergence of teaching and education. We are stating nothing new if we say that a family of three brothers has no cultural unity within it when each brother has been educated at a different private school.[7]

Although this is ascribed to the influence of schools, particularly foreign schools, a close scrutiny of it shows that it goes much deeper than that. In

---

[7] Hanna Ghusn, "Submitting Private Schools to Supervision," *Al-Diyar*, Beirut, October 6, 1946.

the first place, it is not confined to the younger generation or to the literate individuals, but differences of outlook exist among the older generation and the illiterates as well. This can be ascribed to two main sources. First, the old religious and racial cleavages in the Near East, and, secondly, to the influence of modern private- and foreign-school education stemming from various sources—American, British, French, German, Italian, and Russian.

It is hardly necessary to go into any detail to describe the differences between Arabs and Kurds, Christians and Druzes; and among the Muslims themselves the differences between Shi'ites and Sunnites. In recent years the project of the Jewish National Home in Palestine has injected into Arab life a racial and religious problem which has reached international proportions. Naturally, one can point out also the differences existing between the multitudinous Christian sects. These differences, which have lasted for centuries, have created special attitudes within each sect or race, and sometimes have meant intersectarian or interracial animosity or cleavage. These differences, however, are now gradually melting away. The groups are learning to work together in conducting their governments and in friendly relation one with the other, with the exception of the tension existing between Arabs and Jews over Palestine. The conflict of attitudes and ideas will probably be worked out, given a sufficient period of time.

On top of these differences have come new differences brought to the fore by foreign education. This influence has been exercised in a number of ways. The most important has been the foreign schools, and indirectly the private schools fashioned after them. These have transmitted to the Arab world their own versions of Western life and culture, differing from nation to nation. The picture given is usually a purified picture of this life and culture set somewhat as a model and something superior to be followed. This naturally had its advantages. Another fact is that they directed attention to the better side of Western life which made for the education of character and generally created an incentive to do as well as the Westerners are doing. Yet, on the other hand, it had its disadvantages. Most of the schools, being missionary schools, gave a narrow conception of Western life, sometimes imbued with extreme sectarian attitudes. France, for example, though decidedly nonreligious in its state government and education, has been pictured as a Catholic country and a protector of Catholics. This was supported by French colonial policy. Catholics and Protestants have been living more or less in two separate worlds. Moreover, most of these schools give little or no indication of the more businesslike and sometimes sordid aims and ambitions of Western powers in the Near

East. In this way a somewhat warped view of Western civilization was given by this second-hand type of Western education.

More recently a broader acquaintance with the West has become possible partly by students going abroad by the hundreds and living among Westerners for a number of years. They have naturally brought back a broader conception of Western life, sometimes well understood and perhaps more often only partially understood. Western books and magazines in different languages have had their effect, as have Western radio broadcasts. Finally, there have been Western armies and Western secular government officials of varying abilities to carry out their responsibilities.

This diversity of influences naturally makes for diversity of outlook. Students studying in France do not mix too well with those studying in England or America. Graduates of British universities have a tendency to scoff at students of American universities and the type of education they receive. Students studying in Germany, though not numerous, have been influenced by the events and philosophies current in that country in the last two decades. There is, therefore, a problem involved in trying to make graduates of such schools and institutions work together for a common cause. The problem is the more important because the better-educated class of citizens is involved. The influence of missionary schools and private sectarian schools in catering to minorities and to sectarian differences has already been mentioned.

Against this centrifugal influence, one may set two unifying agencies. First, some of these foreign schools, particularly the higher institutions, have been bringing together students from various backgrounds and exposing them to the same type of education. Muslims, Christians, Druzes, Jews, Arabs, and Kurds may meet on the same campus and in the same classrooms, societies, and groups, at the American universities in Beirut and Cairo, and a community of outlook is thus developed. The same may perhaps be true of the French University in Beirut, or some of the *laïque* schools in Syria and Cairo. Between the two groups, however, there remains the difference between American and French education.

The second, and perhaps the more important, of these agencies is the public schools that have been founded and greatly expanded during this generation. Here students of all creeds come together and follow a program unified for each country and sometimes are taught by teachers of various religious backgrounds. The point of view taught in the public schools is national, and friendships are developed among the students which may last for a lifetime. It is this that makes educational authorities in some of the Arab countries anxious to have the new generation acquire a unified outlook. In the long run the public-school systems may be considered as the main agencies for the unification of the peoples of the Arab world and for the education of citizens who will have loyalties wider than those of the family, the tribe, the creed, or the race.

An Arab National System of Education?

To say that the public-school system is to be the main unifying factor among the various elements of the Arab world is to raise the question, "What kind of a public school system?" What constitutes a national system of education? And how does one national system differ from other national systems? How far have the Arab systems of education progressed toward being national systems? Is there to be one system for all Arabs, or many systems, one for each country? If the latter, how far can they be coordinated so as to approximate a single Arab system? These are difficult questions to answer. The following remarks are meant to be a contribution toward an answer.

What constitutes a national system of education?

1. A national system of education obviously must cover a whole geographical region over which a certain nation is spread out, and must maintain most or all the types of schools and education needed in that region.

2. A national system of education is one which has grown and evolved with the country, adapting itself to its needs by continuous adjustment throughout its history.

3. A national system of education has its own peculiar organization, legal provisions, and means of support. Whether loosely organized or highly centralized, and whether entirely public or partly public and partly private, these are simply features which are peculiar to any particular environment and are probably in accord with, or influenced by, the organization in other fields of national life.

4. A national system of education usually lays special emphasis on the national language and national history and geography and on the bringing-up of citizens who owe allegiance to the country and are willing to do service for it, who are capable of exercising their rights as citizens and sharing in the responsibilities of running the country in all phases of life.

5. Along with this and as part of it, a national system of education cultivates native arts and crafts, dances, folklore, and music, some useful and fine customs and traditions and all that goes to create a local atmosphere, a general background—in brief, a national spirit and character.

6. A national system of education studies the problems and needs of

the country, whether political, economic, social, hygienic, cultural, or otherwise, and tries to meet those needs as far as is possible in the school system.

To sum it all up, a national system is one which reflects the genius and peculiar character of a nation and forms part and parcel of its past achievement, its present preoccupation and problems, and its future hopes.

How far have the Arab countries studied in this report progressed toward the realization of a national system of education as envisaged in the criteria just set down?

If by a national school system is meant that each country has developed a public-school system for the education of its children, then each of the Arab countries studied has in varying degrees made some progress toward a national school system of its own. All of them have founded a fairly large number of elementary schools. Most of them have a variety of secondary, vocational, and teacher-training institutions. Some have established institutions of higher education. All of them stress the teaching of Arabic and of local, if not national, history, geography, and civics.

Yet the description of the school systems embodied in this report and the analysis of this chapter should have made it quite clear by now that the Arab school systems still have to travel a long way in order to measure up satisfactorily to the above criteria. No Arab educator would claim that these criteria have been met. Most of them are conscious of the long task ahead of them and of the problems confronting them. To put every child of school age in school, to provide him with a curriculum that fits his needs and those of the country, and to open for him the possibilities for further study from which he is capable of profiting, are still to a considerable extent matters of the future. Except for Egypt, the systems of education are so recent that they have not had time to evolve properly so as to meet the needs of their respective countries. All of them have been at one time under the domination of foreign powers. This foreign influence has naturally left its impress on the systems, so that they cannot as yet be called indigenous with their roots firmly established in the soil.

The Arab countries are still experimenting with various methods of educational organization. The present types of organization resemble each other in the fact that they are highly centralized, but the happy medium of cooperation between local and central authorities in educational matters is still unrealized. Nor can the schools be said to meet the needs and the problems of the countries adequately; nor have these problems been consciously studied and analyzed with a view to adjusting the school systems and curriculums and orienting them toward a solution. While the various school systems emphasize the teaching of Arabic and of national history and geography, not much has been done in the fields of native arts, crafts, music, dances, and folklore. Even in the national subjects, however, there is as yet little evidence of a clear conception of what the content and method of training for citizenship should be. In some countries, particularly Palestine, national history is treated merely as part of general history. In others, national history is little more than the teaching of the local history of the particular country, while in still others effort has been made to teach both local and general Arab history in conjunction with the history and the geography of the rest of the world. In some countries no more than a formal teaching of civics is offered, while in others, particularly in Iraq, an attempt is being made to deal in intermediate and secondary schools with current problems of the country. On the whole, however, a course dealing with current problems is looked at with suspicion, owing to the fact that it has to treat some burning and controversial issues of the day.

The fact that the Arab world has not yet arrived at an educational *modus vivendi* is hardly surprising. It is not only that in all the countries except Egypt any serious public educational effort is of rather recent date, nor is the educational leadership as yet adequate, but it must be conceded that the Arab world today is in a condition of profound change where the old is gradually being superseded by the new, with all the strains and stresses and confusion that such a change involves. The fact that the change is taking place more rapidly under the impact of world forces makes the problem even greater. The Arab world has not yet found itself and will not find itself for a long time to come. It is not surprising that its educational systems reflect the same unsettled and inadequate picture which its life in general presents to day. Not until a new level of cultural, political, and economic stability is brought about will Arab education find its rock bottom and will educators be able to build a system relatively adequate for Arab needs—a system which will express the genius and aspirations of the Arabs.

As regards the unity of Arab education some rather superficial discussions of it have been voiced occasionally in the press and in public pronouncements. It is glibly asserted that schools all over the Arab world should follow the same curriculum without realization of the stifling influence such a policy would have on the development of Arab education and Arab mentality. Already, however, there are signs that such a course would not prove satisfactory to the various educational and political leaders of the respective Arab countries. Each country has more or less struck out in its own direction, though often taking inspiration from the same source.

Certain patterns have been developed, and certain traditions, though recent, have begun to take shape. Moreover, there are local needs for each country which are bound to affect the education in that country and would, therefore, make for some measure of variety between the school systems.

In the opinion of the present writers, this variety will in the long run be a point of strength rather than weakness in Arab education because it will provide that freedom of experimentation and of striking out in new directions which is so vital to the growth of any educational system. The fact that French and American influences are so pronounced in Lebanon, British influence in Palestine, French and British in Egypt, and American and British in Iraq, however deplored by some, may provide one of the broad bases that are needed for developing in the future a well-rounded Arab national system. In the long run, it is the aspects of these foreign influences which meet the needs of the countries that are most likely to survive while the others will be discarded; and, in the long run, it is the steps that are taken by each country alone or in cooperation with the others to meet its problems as they arise that will finally result in a system that will be truly national.

Some measure of unity is undoubtedly essential, but care must be taken that the mold in which this unity is cast is not too rigid and will not fit Arab education into a strait jacket that will check its healthy growth. Unity should rather express itself in mutual recognition of diplomas, certificates, and degrees on the broadest possible basis, in exchange of views through publications and conferences, in exchange of teachers and professors, and in an anxious solicitude for the education of united citizens, conscious of the sense of kinship that ties them together. Unity should be that of spirit, of goals, and of basic principles rather than unity in all matters of detail. A unity with variety should be the motto of Arab education.

INDEX

INDEX

INDEX

'Abbas I, 90
Adult education
   in Egypt, 12 f., 25
   in Iraq, 125, 163
Agricultural School (Syria), 373, 377 f.
Agriculture, schools of
   in Egypt, 67 f., 83 f., 87 f.
   in Iraq, 178 f.
   in Arab Palestine, 230, 251 f.
   in Jewish Palestine, 286 ff., 292
   in Syria, 373, 377
   in Lebanon, 492
Aidi, Dr. Munif, 398
Aleppo College (Syria), 400, 402 ff.
Alliance Israelite Universelles, 211, 286, 389
American College for Girls (Egypt), 114 f.
American High School for Girls (Syria), 388
American Junior College (Syria), 388
American Junior College for Women (Lebanon), 420, 481, 498 f.
American Press (Lebanon), 479
American School for Boys (Iraq), 211 f.
American School for Girls (Iraq), 212
American Schools for Girls (Lebanon), 479, 484, 485
American University at Cairo (Egypt), 115 f.
American University of Beirut (Lebanon), 411, 416, 419, 487 ff.
Antiquities, Directorate of
   in Egypt, 12
   in Lebanon, 411
   in Syria, 332, 379
'Anturah College (Lebanon), 467 f.
Apprenticeship Training School (Jewish Palestine), 289
Arab Academy (Syria), 332, 379
Arab College (Arab Palestine), 219, 224, 230, 234, 246, 249
Arab League, 13, 531 f.
Arab nationalism, rise of, 529 ff.
Arab national system of education, 573 ff.
Arts, *see* Fine arts
Art Theater of the Kindergarten Teachers Society (Jewish Palestine), 296
Asyut College (Egypt), 113
Asyut Orphanage (Egypt), 118
'Ayn Waraqah monastery school (Lebanon), 503
Azhar, al-, University (Egypt), 3, 16 f., 36 f., 103 ff.

Baghdad College (Iraq), 212
Balfour Declaration, 257
Bayly, Mrs. S., 283
Beth HaKerem Training College (Jewish Palestine), 291
Bilu, 256
Bishmizzin school (Lebanon), 516
Bishop's School (Transjordan), 320 f.
Bliss, Daniel, 480
Brandeis Vocational Center (Jewish Palestine), 289
British Council, 213, 255, 305 f., 320, 373
British school for boys at Idlib (Syria), 400
British-Syrian Training College (Lebanon), 411 f., 499 ff.
Brummana High School (Lebanon), 501
Bustani, Butrus, 479, 503

Cairo Library Association, 118
Catholic Press (Lebanon), 472
Central Preparatory School (Iraq), 169
Central Turkey College (Syria), 402
Church of England Missionary Society School for Girls (Transjordan), 320
Collège de-la-Sainte Famille (Lebanon), 469
Collège Français du Sacré Cœur (Lebanon), 469
Collège La Salle (Lebanon), 469
College of Commerce (Iraq), 134 (footnote)
College of Engineering (Iraq), 205
College of the Muslim Charitable Purposes [al-Maqasid al-Khayriyah] (Lebanon), 510, 511
Collège Protestant Français (Lebanon), 416, 471
Commerce, School of, (Lebanon), 480
   See also Finance and commerce
Commercial School for Boys, Aleppo (Syria), 373, 376 f.
Commercial School for Boys, Damascus (Syria), 373
Commercial Secondary School (Iraq), 177
Commission of Enquiry (British), 263, 265
   See also McNair Commission
Cultural Committee of the Arab League, 13
Cultural Foundation (Egypt) 12
   See also People's University
Cultural League of Free Education, 507, 512

Damascus College (Syria), 400
Dar al-'Ulum (Egypt), 23, 72, 97 f.

579

580 EDUCATION IN ARAB COUNTRIES OF THE NEAR EAST

Daudiyah College (Lebanon), 407, 514 f.
Dawhat al-Adab school for girls (Syria), 398
Democracy, coming of, to the Arab world, 533 f.
Dentistry, schools of
  in Egypt, 81
  in Syria, 354, 381 f.
  in Lebanon, 471, 474 f., 480
Dibs, al-, Yusuf, Monseigneur, 503, 506
Dramatic art, school of (Egypt), 27

Educational missions
  in Egypt, 89
  in Iraq, 206 ff.
  in Syria, 384
Educational Museum (Egypt), 11
Egyptian Antiquities, Department of, 11
Egypt: background statistical data, 2
Egyptian Constitution of 1923, 21
Egyptian Education Bureau (Washington), 91, 94
Egyptian Library, 11
Elementary education
  in Egypt: description of schools, 41
    program of studies, 42 ff.
    rural elementary schools, 45
  in Arab Palestine, 239 f.
    rural elementary schools, 240 f.
    program of studies, 241 ff.
    description of schools, 245 f.
  in Jewish Palestine, 272, 279 f.
    program of studies, 280 ff.
  in Transjordan, 304 f., 310
    course of study, 310 ff.
  in Syria, 344 (*see also* Primary education, 356 ff.)
  in Lebanon: program of studies, 428, 482
    type of school needed, 546 ff.
  See also Primary education (Iraq), 146 ff.; Primary schools (Egypt), 49 ff.
Elementary Teachers College for Men (Syria), 385
Elementary Teachers College for Women (Iraq), 187
Engineering, schools of
  in Egypt, 27, 39, 68, 82, 87
  in Iraq, 133, 205
  in Jewish Palestine, 295
  in Lebanon, 472, 477
Evelina de Rothschild School for Girls (Palestine), 286

Fahmy, Madame Asma, 102 (footnote)
Faruq I University (Egypt), 6, 85 ff.
Feminine Culture Schools (Egypt), 69

Finance and commerce, schools of, (Egypt), 21, 71, 84, 89
Fine arts schools
  in Egypt, 11, 27, 89
  in Iraq, 179
  in Lebanon, 516 f.
Foreign languages in the curriculum, 559 ff.
Foreign schools, their role in the Arab world, 564 ff.
French School of Law (Egypt), 36, 117
Friends Schools (Arab Palestine), 253
Fuad I Academy of the Arabic Language (Egypt), 11
Fuad I University (Egypt), 6, 16, 71 ff.

General Party (Jewish Palestine), 258, 260 f., 278, 285, 290 f.
Gerard Institute for Boys (Lebanon), 486
Giligian primary schools (Syria), 397
Girls Colleges (Egypt), 63
Government Arab College (Arab Palestine), 219, 224, 230, 234, 246, 249
Greek Orthodox School for Girls in Tripoli (Lebanon), 509

Habimah Theater (Jewish Palestine), 296
Hadassah (Jewish Palestine), 283 f., 289
  See also Henrietta Szold Hadassah School of Nursing, 290
Hadassah Hospital (Jewish Palestine), 293
Haifa Technical School (Arab Palestine), 219, 230, 250 f.
Haifa Technion (Jewish Palestine), 256, 270, 290, 295
Half-day schools (Egypt), 24, 27 f., 40
Health Officials, School of (Iraq), 203
Hebrew Gymnasium (Jewish Palestine), 256
Hebrew Language Committee (Jewish Palestine), 296
Hebrew University (Jewish Palestine), 260, 270, 291 ff.
Henrietta Szold Hadassah School of Nursing (Jewish Palestine), 290
Hertzliah Gymnasium (Jewish Palestine), 256, 286 f.
Higher Committee of Studies and Curricula (Iraq), 183
Higher Institute for Men Teachers (Egypt), 27
Higher Institute for Women Teachers (Egypt), 27
Higher Institute of Agriculture (Egypt), 88
Higher School of Agriculture (Egypt), 27

INDEX

Higher School of Finance and Commerce (Egypt), 27
Higher School of Fine Arts (Egypt), 11, 27
Higher Teachers College (Iraq), 133, 172 ff., 188 ff.
Higher Teachers College, proposed, (Syria), 341 f., 379
Higher Training College (Egypt), 39
Hikmah, al-, College (Lebanon), 506 ff., 512
Histadruth (Jewish Palestine), 262, 288 f. See also Labor Party
Homemaking arts, schools of
 in Egypt, 69 f.
 in Iraq, 177
 in Syria, 375 f.
 in Lebanon, 485 f.
Hovevei Israel, 256
Husri, al-, Sati, 325, 337 f., 356

Idlib, British school for boys and girls at (Syria), 400
Illiteracy, 544 f.
Institute of Higher Studies (Arab Palestine), 255
Institute of Rural Life (Lebanon), 497
Intermediate schools (Iraq), 132
Intermediate schools of agriculture (Egypt), 67
Intermediate schools of commerce (Egypt), 67
International College (Lebanon), 480, 488
Iranian school in Basrah (Iraq), 211
Iraq: background statistical data, 120
Islamiyah College (Syria), 395
Isma'il Pasha 90, 105

Jewish Agency, 258, 260, 265 f., 295
Julian Mack School (Jewish Palestine), 289

Kadoorie, Sir Eli, 288
Kadoorie Agricultural School at Mount Tabor (Jewish Palestine), 288
Kadoorie Agricultural School at Tulkarm (Arab Palestine), 220, 230, 251, 305
Kindergartens
 in Egypt, 46 f.
 in Iraq, 147
 in Arab Palestine, 239
 in Jewish Palestine, 271 f., 279
 in Syria, 356
 in Lebanon, 418, 427
King Faysal College (Iraq), 133 f., 173 f.

Koran, schools for the memorization of the, (Egypt), 45
Kuttabs
 in Egypt, 24, 40
 in Iraq, 147
 in Transjordan, 310
 in Syria, 354, 357

Labor Party (Jewish Palestine), 258, 260 ff., 278, 285, 290 f.
Law Classes (Arab Palestine), 230, 252
Law College (Iraq), 204
"Law of the Officials Forgotten in Their Grades" (Egypt), 19
Law, schools of
 in Egypt, 82, 87
 in Iraq, 133 f., 204 f.
 in Arab Palestine, 230, 252
 in Syria, 354, 379, 383
 in Lebanon, 472, 476 f.
League of Lebanese Women, 517
Lebanon: background statistical data, 406
Lebanese Academy of Fine Arts (Lebanon), 516 f.
Lycée des Jeunes Filles (Lebanon), 470
Lycée Français de Garçons (Lebanon), 470
Lycée Français of the Mission Laïque (Lebanon), 462 f.

McNair Commission, 265, 268
 See also Commission of Enquiry, 263
McNair, Sir Arnold, 263
Matate theater (Jewish Palestine), 296
Maud Memorial Fund, 153
Max Pine Vocational School (Jewish Palestine), 288
Medicine, schools of
 in Egypt, 80
 in Iraq, 133 f., 199
 in Jewish Palestine, 293
 in Syria, 354, 379, 381 ff.
 in Lebanon, 420, 471, 473 f., 480, 495
Midwifery, courses in
 in Egypt, 81 f.
 in Iraq, 203
 in Arab Palestine, 250
 in Jewish Palestine, 290
 in Syria, 382 f.
 in Lebanon, 420, 475, 496
Mikveh-Israel Agricultural School (Palestine), 286 f.
Mishmar HaEmek (Jewish Palestine), 285
Mizrahi Party (Jewish Palestine), 258, 260 f., 278, 285, 290 f.
Monroe Commission, report of, (Iraq), 184

582 EDUCATION IN ARAB COUNTRIES OF THE NEAR EAST

Muhammad 'Ali, 4, 25, 89 ff., 530
Museum of Arab Antiquities (Egypt), 12
Museum of Biblical and Talmudic Botany and Jewish and Arab Plant Lore (Jewish Palestine), 293
Museum of Modern Art (Egypt), 12
"Music for the People" Association (Jewish Palestine), 296
Music, school of, (Lebanon), 411, 420, 496 f., 516 f.
Muslim Orphanage of Aleppo (Syria), 395

Najah College (Arab Palestine), 254
National (al-Ahliyah) School for Girls (Lebanon), 515 f.
National College of Education and Instruction (Lebanon), 513
National Conservatory of Music (Lebanon), 411
Nautical School (Jewish Palestine), 290
Near East School of Theology (Lebanon), 494
Normal School for Men (Lebanon), 411
Normal School for Women (Lebanon), 411
North Syria High School for Boys, 402
Nursery schools (Egypt), 46 f.
Nursing, schools of
 in Egypt, 81
 in Iraq, 202
 in Arab Palestine, 250
 in Jewish Palestine, 290
 in Syria, 354, 381 ff.
 in Lebanon, 420, 475, 480, 496

Ohel Theater (Jewish Palestine), 296
Oriental studies, schools of
 in Egypt, 115
 in Jewish Palestine, 292
 in Lebanon, 419, 471, 477 f.
Orman School (Egypt), 99

Palestine: background statistical data, 216
Palestine Folk Opera (Jewish Palestine), 296
Palestine Oratorio Society (Jewish Palestine), 296
Palestine Symphony Orchestra (Jewish Palestine), 296
Patriarchal School (Lebanon), 503, 510
Pensions for teachers
 in Egypt, 20
 in Iraq, 130
 in Arab Palestine, 226
 in Jewish Palestine, 270
 in Syria, 340
 in Lebanon, 411
People's University (Egypt), 12
Pharmacy, schools of
 in Egypt, 81
 in Iraq, 133 f., 201
 in Syria, 354, 381 f.
 in Lebanon, 420, 471, 474, 480, 494 f.
Physical Education Institute (Iraq), 198
Pressley Memorial Institute (Egypt), 114
Primary education: Law of Primary Education for Boys (Egypt), 21
 Estimated cost of by 1970 (Egypt), 30
 See also Elementary education
Primary schools
 in Egypt, 49
  program of studies, 50
 in Iraq, 131
  program of studies, 148 ff.
  description of schools, 152
 in Transjordan, 304 f., 310
  course of study, 310 ff.
 in Syria, 344
  program of studies, 358 ff.
  description of schools, 363 f.
 in Lebanon, 426 ff.
  program of studies, 428 ff.
  description of schools, 438
Primary Teachers College for Men (Syria), 385
Primary Teachers College for Men (Iraq), 133, 181 f.

Queen 'Aliyah Institute (Iraq), 133, 172 ff., 182, 196 f.

Rashidiyah School (Arab Palestine), 219, 230, 234, 246, 249
Rawdat al-Ma'arif, school, (Arab Palestine), 254
Review of the Arab Academy (Syria), 332
Rothschild, *see* Evelina de Rothschild School, 286
Royal College of Medicine (Iraq), 199 ff.
Rural elementary schools (Egypt), 45
Rural Training Center for Women (Arab Palestine), 220, 230, 246, 249
Rustumiyah rural teachers college, (Iraq), 185 f.

Sa'id Pasha, 4
Saint Marc School for Boys (Egypt), 116
Samuel, Edwin, 254

INDEX

Sanhuri, al-, Abd al-Razzaq, 379
Sargeant, Rev. Francis B., S.J., 212
Schapira, Hermann, 291
School of Agriculture (Iraq), 178
School of Applied Art (Egypt), 27
School of Applied Engineering (Egypt), 27
School of Arts and Crafts (Lebanon), 408, 411, 455 ff.
School of Dramatic Art (Egypt), 27
School of Social Service (Egypt), 27
School of Three Doctors (Lebanon), 503, 509
Schools for the memorization of the Koran (Egypt), 45
Schools of embroidery arts (Egypt), 69
Schools visited by American Council Commission: number and type in each country, vii
Scientific National College (Syria), 398
Secondary education, 549 ff.
   in Egypt, 57
      program of studies, 58 ff.
   in Iraq, 140 ff., 162
      program of studies, 166
   in Arab Palestine, 246
      program of studies, 247 ff.
   in Jewish Palestine, 284 ff.
   in Transjordan, 305
      program of studies, 315
   in Syria, 344 f., 353, 364 ff.
      course of study, 366 ff.
   in Lebanon, 443 f.
      program of studies, 445 ff., 484, 489 ff.
Shidyaq, al-, Ahmad Faris, 503
Simon, Sir Leon, 263
Smith, Ely, 479
Social Service, School of, (Egypt), 27
Social Welfare, Department of, (Arab Palestine), 255
Staudt, Dr. and Mrs. Calvin K., 212
Syria: background statistical data, 324
Syrian Orphanage (Arab Palestine), 253
Syrian Protestant College, 471, 480, 487
Syrian School at Dayr al-Shurfah (Lebanon), 503
Syrian University, 332, 341
Szold, Henrietta, 283
   See also Henrietta Szold Hadassah School of Nursing, 290

Tafayyud Society (Iraq), 210
Talmud Torahs (Jewish Palestine), 296
Tawfiq Pasha, 90
Teacher education, 555 ff.
   in Egypt, 95 ff.
   in Iraq, 181 ff.
   in Arab Palestine, 219 f.
   in Jewish Palestine, 274, 290 f.
   in Syria, 341 f., 354, 384 ff.
   in Lebanon, 454 f., 500 f.
Teachers Association (Iraq), 210
Teachers College for Men (Syria), 360
Teachers College for Women (Syria), 356, 385
Teachers Organization (Jewish Palestine), 270
Teachers Pension Fund (Jewish Palestine), 267 f., 270
Teachers' pensions, *see* Pensions
Teachers' salaries
   in Egypt, 19 f.
   in Iraq, 129, 158 f., 171 ff.
   in Arab Palestine, 223 ff.
   in Jewish Palestine, 269 f.
   in Transjordan, 301 f.
   in Syria, 335 ff.
   in Lebanon, 411
Teachers Training College for Women (Arab Palestine), 220, 224, 230, 246, 249, 305
Technical High School (Jewish Palestine), 289
Technical School (Transjordan), 305, 318 f.
Technical School for girls (Syria), 373, 375 f.
Technical Schools for boys (Syria), 373 ff.
Tel-Aviv Training College, 291
Terra Sancta College (Arab Palestine), 254
Thomas, Lowell, 212
Thompson, Mrs. J. Bowen, 499
Transjordan: background statistical data, 298
Trasher, Miss Lillian, 118
Tripoli Boys School (Lebanon), 484 f.

United States Information Service (Egypt), 118
Universal National College [al-Jami'ah al-Wataniyah] (Lebanon), 518
Université Saint-Joseph (Lebanon), 415, 419, 471 ff.

Vaad Hachinuch (Jewish Palestine), 256, 258, 260
Vaad Halashon (Jewish Palestine), 296
Vaad Leumi (Jewish Palestine), 217 f., 255, 257 ff.
Van Dyck, Cornelius V. A., 479

Van Ess, John, 211
Veterinary Medicine, School of, (Egypt), 84
Victoria College (Egypt), 117
Vocational education, 552 f.
 in Egypt, 66, 69 f.
 in Iraq, 132 ff., 140, 175 ff.
 in Arab Palestine, 250 ff.
 in Jewish Palestine, 286 ff., 295
 in Syria, 354, 373 ff.
 in Lebanon, 455 ff., 463, 469 f., 491

Vocational Guidance Center (Jewish Palestine), 289

Y.M.C.A.
 in Egypt, 117 f.
 in Arab Palestine, 254 f.
 in Transjordan, 321

Zionist Organization, 256, 258, 263, 265, 294
Zionist Organization of America, 258

THE AMERICAN COUNCIL ON EDUCATION

GEORGE F. ZOOK, *President*

A. J. BRUMBAUGH, *Vice President*

The American Council on Education is a *council* of national educational associations; organizations having related interests; approved universities, colleges, and technological schools; state departments of education; city school systems; selected private secondary schools; and selected educational departments of business and industrial companies. It is a center of cooperation and coordination whose influence has been apparent in the shaping of American educational policies as well as in the formulation of American educational practices during the past thirty-one years. Many leaders in American education and public life serve on the commissions and committees through which the Council operates.